Twentieth-Century Higher E

MARTIN TROW

Twentieth-Century Higher Education

Elite to Mass to Universal

Edited by

MICHAEL BURRAGE

The Johns Hopkins University Press
Baltimore

The Johns Hopkins University Press
2715 North Charles Street
Baltimore, Maryland 21218-4363
www.press.jhu.edu

Library of Congress Cataloging-in-Publication Data
Trow, Martin A., 1926–2007.
  Twentieth-century higher education : elite to mass to universal / Martin Trow ; edited by
Michael Burrage.
        p. cm.
  Includes bibliographical references and index.
  ISBN-13: 978-0-8018-9441-1 (hardcover : alk. paper)
  ISBN-10: 0-8018-9441-7 (hardcover : alk. paper)
  ISBN-13: 978-0-8018-9442-8 (pbk. : alk. paper)
  ISBN-10: 0-8018-9442-5 (pbk. : alk. paper)
  1. Education, Higher—United States.   2. Educational change—United States.
I. Burrage, Michael.   II. Title.
  LA227.4.T77 2010
  378.73—dc22   2009035573

A catalog record for this book is available from the British Library.

*Special discounts are available for bulk purchases of this book. For more information, please
contact Special Sales at 410-516-6936 or specialsales@press.jhu.edu.*

Contents

....

Twentieth-Century Higher Education

Introduction

Michael Burrage

....

There are few social scientists who single-handedly identify a social trend early in their careers; spend the best part of their working lives observing, analyzing, explaining, and debating its course and consequences; and then, at the end, find the trend not merely continuing, but still a live issue in public policy debates and still inviting further research. Martin Trow was able to do just that. The title of this volume identifies the trend that became the theme of most of his life's work, and the essays in this book are some landmarks of his remarkable intellectual marathon.

The essays have been selected and introduced by some of those who joined him at various times along the way, among them, his coauthors and editors, his former students and colleagues at the University of California, Berkeley, along with a former president of the University of California and his fellow researchers or teachers at various other universities around the world. The essays chosen fall well short of being a definitive collection of Trow's work on higher education. Chapter 1 was written in 1961 and refers to secondary education, though as his coauthor Oliver Fulton, who remembered and selected this essay, suggests, it might properly be seen as a preface to his work on higher education, the major theme of which he first enunciated some thirteen years later, in 1974, and which is reprinted as chapter 2. The other fifteen essays explore in varying ways that theme, the final one being a valedictory review written in 2006 shortly before his death. Whole swathes of his work on student culture and academic assessment, as well as numerous essays on English and Swedish higher education, have been omitted, but the essays that appear here are a reasonably representative sampling of his work, and should enable English-language readers to form an overall assessment of it, hitherto only possible for readers in China and Japan, where selections of his essays have already been published.[1]

One may say at the outset that these essays are not distinguished by their methodological rigor or sophistication, or by the reporting of fresh evidence about higher education in any country. Although Trow had collaborated in a number of surveys with some of the most notable researchers of the age, and had conducted a survey of his own during his short spell at Bennington College, he seems to have lost his enthusiasm for the familiar methodological apparatus of survey research in his middle years in favor of casual, or apparently casual, observation and conversation with fellow academics, university administrators, and higher education policy makers.[2] Combined with an assiduous study of both historical and contemporary documentary materials, these observations and conversations—as well as his own work as teacher, researcher, and member of the governing bodies of higher education institutions— formed the basis of more than 170 published analyses and commentaries. His "method," if we may call it that, is, however, worth a moment's consideration, since it evidently enabled him to see, and even to discover, many things that we, who had access to the same sources, didn't.

In reality, his conversations were not quite as casual as they appeared and frequently bordered on what researchers would call in-depth, open-ended interviews. No sooner had he arrived at a new institution than it became a field research site, where colleagues became research subjects and were not infrequently co-opted partners in some serendipitous ethnography. Trow was a ubiquitous and indefatigable ethnographer of the familiar and the taken-for-granted in the academic world. Indeed, for him, life itself sometimes seemed to be little more than an extended opportunity for field research. Events, exchanges, and routines that the rest of us define as normal and happily let slip into our subconscious remained for him worthy subjects of interest and analysis. How many other academics have considered the "post-lecture huddle" as a learning environment? Who, as Trow does in chapter 8, has thought much about the "informal ownership" and "appropriation" of waste space in academic institutions, or tried to explain why so many academic exchanges sink to the lowest common denominator of children's schooling and summer vacations?

In his company one often had the slightly guilty feeling that one simply hadn't been paying attention. After enjoying a convivial but routine evening supper with the director and faculty members at the London School of Economics, for instance, he left the room amazed that none of the assorted departmental conveners, research center directors seated around the director, saw their chance. "No one *wanted* anything!" he exclaimed, an observation that he no doubt filed away for his next comparative analysis of university leadership and governance. On being awarded an honorary degree at an English university ravaged by funding cuts, he was probably one of the few people in the hall who listened attentively to the vice chancellor's address and in particular he remembered, and quoted, his remarks about academic standards, which, the vice chancellor proudly claimed, had actually risen over the past year. To him, it was an example of the way victims and paymasters might collude when talking publicly about educational quality. Chapter 10, a hitherto unpublished study of the Princeton Institute of Advanced Studies during his year as a research fellow there, is a classic example of Trow the perpetual ethnographer. What other research fellow has bothered to analyze the social and intellectual setting in which he or she has been temporarily placed?

Being an ethnographer of ordinary academic routines was no doubt easier in semi-foreign England. In the introduction to a book about English higher education that Trow planned but never published, he reflected a little on his own way of working, which he never presumed to call a "method." He began by declaring that his English readers would know much more about his subject than he did, since "there is no way in which an outsider can know an institution better than participants who live in it every day, and know its unspoken assumptions and attitudes by sharing them." However, he then went on to suggest that, for a number of reasons, he might have "a marginal advantage over local observers." First, he said:

> I have been able to ask questions about the most ordinary matters
> in universities that participants cannot. For me, the questions re-
> flected my ignorance, real or assumed. For a British academic the
> same questions would have betrayed the questioner's stupidity. Aca-

demics in Britain as elsewhere have a high tolerance for ignorance; very little for stupidity. In addition, all of my studies of British arrangements were done with an explicit or implicit reference to American parallels—not to make judgments but to generate questions. So what struck a British observer as normal—as in the British context it was—often struck me as odd, leading me to ask why it was that way, or had developed that way, and not some other. Third, I could genuinely approach questions of British educational policy without a political bias—or at least a bias in the context of British politics. This was especially useful during the long Thatcher–Major governments. I could talk to people in those governments without their assuming my strong preference for alternative governments. And my often sharp questions could be seen as motivated not by parti pris but by scholarly curiosity. Not many British sociologists could approach Tory politicians in that way.

In a footnote he explained that he had another

minor advantage in my work in England—namely, that I was not a gentleman. This was not a quality that I acquired through close study and hard work—it was, so to speak, a natural quality of birth and rearing and education. I was an American, an engineer, and a sociologist. I don't know how many ways one can *not* be a gentleman— though I had other attributes to add to those that would have disqualified me. In any event, not being a gentleman helped in several ways. First, I had no compunctions about the close interrogation of my interview subjects, though I knew or learned that a gentleman does not press personal questions in the face of an evident reluctance to answer. Second, I was insensitive to the ways in which British academics, gentlemen all, defended their privacy; they put me down hard, though I didn't notice until much later while reading the transcripts. Third, I walked the minefields of British class relations fearlessly, transforming their potentially lethal explosions into something like a foot massage. I did not believe that it was a mark of personal virtue that an academic had working-class origins, nor was it a loss of virtue when he or she gained an Oxbridge fellowship. That was helpful in exploring the origins and trajectories of British academics, and their relations to their institutions and to other elites.

At the end of these comments, and still more so after reading his many essays on England, one is left in considerable doubt about his initial assertion that English readers would know much more about the subject than he did, and may even wonder whether they knew anything at all about their unspoken assumptions. Pat Hayashi, a former student of Trow's who went on to be associate president of the University of California, remembers him encouraging his students to identify their own unspoken assumptions by holding on to their first naïve response to any social phenomenon they were investigating. If the phenomenon seemed familiar, he asked them to try and recapture their first response by a kind of self-induced naivety, so that the familiar had the strangeness of the new, and the insider could look on his or her subject as an outsider. There are numerous instances of Trow doing the same thing in these essays.

Trow's working practices will not, however, cut much ice with teachers of research methods, unless by chance one of them wished to show how far their students might go without them. These teachers, however, might be advised to add—as long as they have a deep knowledge of the institutions they were studying; are extraordinarily keen and sympathetic observers of behavior within them; and have exceptional insight, imagination, rapier wit, and a gift for formulating their insights in mountain-clear English prose. As it happens, however, one of Trow's early papers has been regularly reprinted or cited in research methods texts.[3] Somewhat surprisingly, it contested the claim that participant observation was inherently superior to survey analysis and decided, reasonably enough, that "the problem under investigation properly dictates the methods of investigation." We can only conclude that Trow thought his "method" of conversation as an artless, naïve outsider with randomly encountered informants, supplemented by an ever-alert and sharp eye for revealing events, comments, and exchanges, was sufficient for the "problem" he had under investigation. These essays should enable us to decide whether he was right.

Social theorists (at least grand theorists or those who believe social theory can be discussed and taught with scant reference to any particular society) are also unlikely to be interested in Trow's work. In his essay on research methods just mentioned, he suggested that social science would progress through "systems of theoretically related propositions that are checked at more and more points against data collected by a variety of means." Social scientists often use the word *theory* rather loosely, but even so it would be a stretch to call his analyses of higher education "a system of theoretically related propositions." There is, to be sure, a system in his work, but it is a social system of relationships within higher education institutions and between them and other social institutions, and it remains embedded in his analyses of real-world institutions—hidden, one might say, and never isolated for separate discussion. Some of his arguments discussed below certainly have a law-like form, starting with the axiom that underpins much of his work: "No society, no matter how rich, can afford a system of higher education for 20 or 30 percent of the age grade at the cost levels of the elite higher education that it formerly provided for 5 percent of the population." But he never organized such propositions or presented them in a formal manner as a series of propositions or hypotheses that he intended to test. John Brennan had a shot at doing it for him, of which he did not disapprove, since he reproduced it in the valedictory essay that forms chapter 17.[4] He himself appears, however, to have been diverted from a formal hypothetico-deductive presentation of his analyses and arguments by his wish to inform and persuade public policy makers. Trow was a sociologist who became a professor of public policy, and more often discussed the "problems," "difficulties," "dilemmas," and "strains" of growth in higher education rather than formulating testable hypotheses about it. In describing his own work, he referred not to his theory but to his "analysis" or "perspective," which like all perspectives "omits and distorts even as it illuminates." Most accurately, perhaps, he sought to use "a conceptual system or framework" to raise questions, to identify critical variables, and to suggest probable outcomes.[5]

Since the merit and enduring interest of his work is not to be found in its methodological ingenuity or rigor, or in the collection of new evidence, or in a parsimonious and formally stated theory, we must look elsewhere. The first place we might look is the trend he identified, for it has proved an enduring one. Other trends, other waves of the future, identified by sociologists over these decades have come and gone, but we are still living with the one Trow identified and analyzed. It not only continues, but also evidently still has some way to run. If one were searching for other social analyses that similarly anchor their study of contemporary institutions within a long-term historical trend, the closest might be that of his friend David Riesman, another insightful observer of academic life, many of whose papers also remain unpublished. If one looks back for classical antecedents there is a marked resemblance to both Alexis de Tocqueville's notion of democratization and Max Weber's of rationalization. Trow's main theme might in fact be seen as a sub-trend of both, since he saw the transformation of higher education as a significant part of the democratization of society that entailed the rationalization of relationships previously governed by communal academic norms. Democratization was the propellant and rationalization its usual corollary.

Trow's work also merits our attention because, though the trend itself can be recognized easily enough by rising enrollments in higher educational institutions, he did not merely draw attention to it, but went on to identify precisely its probable ramifications for the "private" and "public" lives of higher education institutions, a distinction he introduced and used throughout his work. His first enunciation of these ramifications in 1974 reads like a table of contents or a shopping list. He mentioned almost every aspect of both the public and private lives of universities, their finance, governance, management, admission policies, curricula, teaching methods and examinations, as well as the relationships between research and teaching, between faculty and students, and beyond with secondary schools, adult education, and the labor market. In Trow's hands, however, it became more than a shopping list, since he explored the diverse—and often unexpected and subtle—systemic interconnections between many of the items mentioned, and enabled us to see them as integral and variable aspects of the process of growth rather than as discrete issues. He therefore provided a landscape or a context to analyze and understand the process of change in higher education. Moreover, since the growth of higher education was, in his view, an inevitable and universal process and an "essential precondition for survival in the modern world," this context was universal. One must immediately add, however, that his analyses had little in common with the literature on globalization, since he declined to make any precise predictions about when, where, why, or how rapidly this inevitable and universal trend would unfold. He was again rather like Tocqueville and Weber in that respect. Like them, he thought that a trend could only be properly under-stood by an intensive study of particular events and institutions in a particular society, alongside comparison with one or more others.

His comparisons did not venture far, indeed in any depth only to the United States and Britain. He puts me a little in mind of Jacques Domi-nique Cassini, cartographer to Louis XV, who, having completed the trigonometric survey of every part of France in 1787, explained to the king that he would have to make one final triangulation with the Royal Observatory in Greenwich to be quite sure where France itself was. Trow's first foreign triangulation point was Oxford, followed by a spell at Sussex, which left him pretty sure that he knew where American higher education was. Over subsequent decades he sought to confirm his conclusions about where British higher education might be, and also to understand why the trend he predicted had long stalled, sometimes de-toured, and why the British burdened themselves with so many unneces-sary costs, and inflicted so much damage on many of their own institu-tions, before finally approaching their declared destination. Unlike Cassini, and unlike his illustrious predecessor in the comparative analy-sis of universities Abraham Flexner, and his collaborator and friend Bur-ton Clark, Trow's attention was always firmly, even exclusively, fixed on the process of growth, on the debates that accompanied it, on the policies that sought to direct it, as well as on the obstacles that prevented it. Per-haps it was precisely because growth and change were his main subjects that this fluent and prolific author left only numerous brilliant shots of various stages of this prolonged process, while his book about higher education in Britain remained, like the process itself, unfinished.

One may therefore conclude by saying Trow's work deserves our at-tention because he chose an enduring theme of universal significance, identified its many subtly interrelated dimensions, and by comparative analyses showed how the process of growth would continue to affect diverse aspects of higher education in numerous ways, many of them unsuspected by other observers. And if his comparisons did not go very far, his ideas, concepts, arguments, and examples provide guidance for anyone wishing to take them further. Indeed, since he usually asks as many questions as he answers, his essays are an open invitation to do so.[6]

The United States figures largely in Trow's analyses of higher education, not just because he was formed by it and able to observe it firsthand on a daily basis, but also because critical political decisions had left the United States "normatively and structurally prepared for mass higher education" long before it actually emerged. These decisions are examined in chapter 4, "Federalism in American Higher Education," and frequently referred to elsewhere. Among the earliest were the exclusion of any reference to education in the federal Constitution, and the abandonment of the proposed University of the United States that might have dominated American higher education from the center. As a result, philanthropists, clergy, municipal leaders, state legislators, businesspersons, and assorted academic entrepreneurs were able to obtain state charters to establish degree-granting institutions according to their own predilections. Since none of these diverse institutions was ever established by guilds of scholars, like many European universities, American higher education institutions came to be governed by executive presidents responsible to governing boards drawn from the wider community, rather than collegially by academics. They were therefore always willing to respond to the needs and demands of the communities on which they depended, for their students as well as for financial, and sometimes electoral, support. Chapter 12 is, among other things, a case study of how UC Berkeley made use of that support to revive what it perceived at the time to be a failing discipline.

Neither the federal nor state governments were ever subsequently in a position to control the process of growth of higher education as a whole. The federal government later gave state governments the means of funding institutions of higher education, by passing the Land Grants Acts of 1862 and 1890, both of which looked forward to the emergence of mass higher education sometime in the future. But the federal government did not seek to control the institutions the states chose to create, nor did the states seek to control the independent institutions that they chartered. Hence "the size, shape, and rate of growth" of American higher education "was determined by ordinary families, not by the decisions of the political elite," and its institutions became spontaneously and spectacularly diverse as they individually responded to their own opportunities and circumstances without any national government imposing its vision of how they should properly be differentiated from one another.

In Trow's view these early political decisions meant that higher education was an integral part of the democratization of American society, and they gave America an "advantage," making it the world pioneer of mass higher education. Higher education institutions might, as he once put it, serve the "requirements of a postindustrial age that requires a wide distribution of knowledge and skills," but their function in this respect seems to have been a fortuitous side effect, and occasionally a retrospective justification for continuing along a path on which they were already set. Trow in fact spent little, if any, time analyzing the response of American higher education to "the requirements of the postindustrial age." In any case, these requirements were much the same in other industrial societies that lagged far behind in transforming their higher education institutions, so they can hardly take us far in explaining America's head start.

Nor can they take us far in explaining why colleges and universities should have assumed such a secure place in American life and popular culture and become "a central part of the nation's secular religion." They were backed, Trow once observed, by a "bipartisan consensus . . . around the notion that everyone should be involved in formal education for as long as possible," seen as "the grand road to social mobility," and their wide diversity provided numerous opportunities for those with different levels of ability or schooling, different aspirations, and different financial circumstances to find some point of entry or re-entry. In the contemporary world, they have become the threshold to the realization of the American Dream, a theme he explores in chapter 5, which includes a memorable rewrite of the final scene of the movie adaptation of John Steinbeck's *The Grapes of Wrath*, his version of the hero's American Dream being funnier than Steinbeck's and probably more typical. While American higher education performs many of the same functions as higher education elsewhere, it also performs, he observed, one function "that is perhaps unique." It is "the central institution that legitimates the social order, makes it seem broadly right and proper. It is at the heart of our promise to give all Americans a chance to fulfill their talents and to transform ambitions into achievements." Universities, he argued, were not only "the source of many of America's most important ideas, values, skills, and energies" but since they offer "a clear alternative to socialist principles and horizontal loyalty" they also explain why socialist or class movements have had little enduring appeal for Americans.[7]

European observers, among them Ulrich Teichler, who introduces chapter 2, and Trow's frequent coauthor, A. H. Halsey, who introduces chapter 7, have had, like others, certain reservations about Trow's argument that the United States enjoyed an advantage in making the transition to mass higher education, since it implied that Europe suffered from certain disadvantages, or, to use the word Trow preferred, *impediments*. One reason for European reservations was that Trow did not seem to spend much time criticizing the failings of American universities. None of the long line of domestic critics of the defects of American universities starting from Abraham Flexner, or still earlier Thorstein Veblen, or their many successors seemed to have had much impact on him. He was not much bothered by the decline of liberal education: the promiscuous multiplication of Basket Weaving 101 and kindred vocational courses hopelessly at odds with the high mission of universities, the corrupting impact of business donors and commercial contracts, the low standards of admission of some institutions, the appalling dropout rates, or the vast differences in the standards of elite institutions and the ordinary Slippery Rock State College. He was not bothered even by the commercialization and intermittent corruption of college sports. These and other failings had long allowed European observers to feel smugly superior and a little amused. Years ago, my own tutor suggested our discussion of Veblen might properly include not only *The Theory of the Leisure Class* but also his *The Higher Learning in America: A Memorandum on the Conduct of Universities by Business Men*, which even then I recognized as a dig.

European reservations about Trow's analyses only intensified when in successive essays he defined and reiterated what the disadvantages of European higher education systems were: they had too few private institutions, relied too heavily on state funding that brought with it the threat of state direction and control, and trusted too little in the invisible hand of the market. Europeans then began to feel that Trow's conceptual framework was normative as well as analytical, making judgments as well as generating questions, and that the ideal types he sometimes deployed embodied his own, distinctively American, ideals. As it turned out, they seemed to have the last word, since in the closing years of the twentieth century, for all their supposed disadvantages, some European societies surged ahead of the United States in the proportion of 20- to 24-year-olds enrolled in higher education institutions. This raised the question of whether America had somehow lost its advantage, or whether it had ever existed in the first place.

There can be no doubt at all that Trow said virtually nothing about the failings of American universities. He did not, however, ignore them because he was uninformed or complacent or chauvinistic, but because his primary aim was to identify the distinctive systemic properties of American higher education institutions, especially those that enabled them to provide access to large segments of the American population. Some of the things that shocked European observers, such as the wide variations in the academic standards between American universities, were not, to his mind, really problems at all since they had made mass enrollment possible, and that was the first requirement that any democratic system of higher education had to satisfy. "If our colleges and universities were to try to maintain a high and common standard for entry, as in the United Kingdom," he observed, "many of them would have no students at all."[8] Their high dropout rates were likewise, in his view, an inevitable accompaniment of mass higher education, and provided that re-entry was easy, were no particular reason for alarm. Only participants in an elite system, he once remarked, would think of describing time spent at college without graduating as "wastage." American universities' close relationships with private employers were an inevitable consequence of their early dependence on the local or regional communities they served, which had continued as they became regional, national, or international institutions. Hence the agreement between Swiss pharmaceutical company Novartis and UC Berkeley, which was widely thought to entail considerable risks to academic freedom, was significant to Trow as an instance of a public institution obtaining an alternative private source of income, and thereby obtaining a freedom to innovate denied to institutions wholly dependent on public funds.[9]

He approached college sports from the same angle. He regarded them with amusement and interest rather than concern, often taking visiting research fellows to Golden Bears football games. He was not at all disturbed by all the pregame razzmatazz: the perambulations of the two hundred-strong marching band that interrupted anyone working on the campus on Saturday mornings, or the ethnically diverse lines of sweating girls on the plaza in front of Zellerbach Auditorium hoping to make it as cheerleaders, or the alumni taking picnic lunches on the campus, or the chancellor's pre-match hospitality for likely donors. On one occasion, he adjourned a seminar discussion to the baseball diamond, where it continued though intermittently interrupted to point out some sociological aspect of the game such as members of a fraternity cheering their brother at the plate. He did not, as far as I recall, fret about the lectures the players or spectators might have been attending or their loss of valuable reading time. Organized sports was simply one of the ways in which American colleges reinforced their ties with their students, their students' parents, their alumni, their potential donors, as well as their surrounding communities. In his view, alumni resistance to faculty-led attempts to abolish college football in the early years of the twentieth century demonstrated the importance of sports to an institution, and explains why no college has felt able to abandon the game for long.

Late in his career, Trow became passionately involved in two controversial issues that were not systemic characteristics of American higher education, or if they were, this was certainly not the reason for his interest in them. One was the 1987–90 campaign to make colleges divest their endowment funds from South Africa and China. The second, more important, issue, which took a great deal of his attention from late 1996 until the end of his life, was affirmative action for ethnic minorities in college admissions. He strongly opposed both.[10] His interest in them appears, however, to have been a direct result of having assumed offices that required him to take sides and to become a participant rather than merely an observer. In 1980 he had become a trustee of Carleton College in Minnesota (and remained one for the next twenty-one years), and between 1990 and 1992 he served as vice chair and then chair of the Academic Council of the academic senate of the University of California, in which office he sat as a nonvoting member of the Board of Regents. Initially, he seemed to have welcomed both roles as peculiarly favorable opportunities to continue his fieldwork in new settings. Once accepted, however, they made it impossible for him to remain a naïve outsider who just interrogated and observed. He was asked to take sides and felt obliged to defend what he considered the cardinal principle of academic debate: a willingness to consider negative evidence and to resist the formation of organized factions that he thought would undermine academic communities. He did so energetically and courageously, both in person and in print—chapter 15, "California after Racial Preferences," is an example. He could hardly shed his scholarly and rhetorical skills in these debates, though he was participating as much, or more, as a trustee and a senate chair, than as a scholar.

His essays on endowments and affirmative action remain, perhaps regrettably, quite separate from the rest of his work. They do not refer to his conceptual framework, even though both were entirely consistent with his analysis of the effects of the growth of mass institutions. Nor did they involve any comparisons, and they were directed solely at American audiences. And they were also exceptional in one other respect, especially those on affirmative action, in that they included an extremely sharp critique of American universities for their cowardice in the face of real or imagined public opinion, leading many intellectually outstanding and otherwise independent minds to become tamely conformist, and even reluctant to engage in open debate when these issues were raised. For these reasons, his articles on these subjects can be clearly distinguished from his work's main focus, which was to understand the systemic characteristics that distinguish American higher education institutions from those elsewhere.

There can be little doubt that this "systemic" preoccupation was the reason why Trow spent so little time discussing the defects of American universities, since he spent equally little time assessing their virtues and achievements. Occasionally, he indicated that he thought that they compared favorably with universities elsewhere in the world. He once referred to "a widely held view that that the United States has the most successful system in the world," and observed that the contemporary American research university was "after the Constitution and the federal government, one of the most successful institutions Americans have ever created." But these were asides that he never bothered to document. His own experience and conversations during his frequent visits to English, Swedish, and other European universities may have persuaded him that there was not much reason to do so, since his European hosts were always inclined to look to the United States (and in particular to California) for inspiration or guidance about the shape of things to come in academic life rather than to any of their European neighbors. Had he wished to document the merits of American universities, however, he would not have found it difficult. The number of cross-national measures of academic excellence, or more precisely excellence in research, continues to increase, so it is now becoming still easier.

If, for instance, one takes Nobel and other international prizes as an index, one finds that while Germany dominated the first half of the twentieth century, it was eclipsed in the second by both the United States and the United Kingdom.[11] Taking the twentieth century as a whole, the United Kingdom seems to have had a slight edge per capita, but it seems unlikely to keep it in the twenty-first, at least if the sixty-one scientific Nobel prizewinners awarded thus far are any guide. Thirty-four of them have been awarded to Americans.[12] Such prizes are, however, a rarefied measure of excellence. Citations of academic research are more representative. One study of the years 1981–94 found that 49 percent of all citations in all the major scientific journals across the world were to American authors. To a large extent, one may fairly say, the rest of the world has come to depend on knowledge generated within American universities. Another annual, multidimensional measure of academic excellence, including cross-national citations and peer reviews, has been provided, since 2004, by the *Times Higher Education (THE)* of London. One set of its measures rates the world's top 50 universities in various disciplinary categories. In 2008, they showed that in the natural sciences 24 of the top 50 were American, in life sciences and biomedicine 22, in technology 19, in the social sciences 21, and in the humanities 18.[13] In the super-elite of the top 10 universities of the world in 2007 as chosen by peer reviews alone, 7 are American, number one by this measure being UC Berkeley. Overall, by this same measure, the *THE* survey editor concluded, "the US is the world centre of scholarly esteem." In the overall ratings for that year, 37 of the top 100, and 47 of the top 200 universities, were American.

Other cross-national measures point in the same direction.[14] It would be fair to say that over the twentieth century, while pioneering the development of mass higher education, American universities also came to occupy a position of intellectual pre-eminence. It was surely not unreasonable, therefore, for Trow to suggest that they may have enjoyed an "advantage," and to try and understand what that advantage might have been. Chapter 12 might well be seen as a case study of the American advantage in action at UC Berkeley—as it responded to market signals, took executive decisions, placed departments in receivership, lobbied the state legislature, and engaged in extensive fundraising from foundations and alumni. All the football razzamatazz, it seems, had a point.

Trow's perception of Europe's disadvantages relied heavily on his extended observation and detailed analyses of just one society—Britain—and more precisely England. In his discussion of its disadvantages, a critical fire usually lacking in his analysis of American institutions bursts into flame. It is directed not at the British universities themselves, of which he was generally an admirer, but at the settled assumptions of those who had the authority to decide the overall size of the higher education system, and to designate the relationship between its component parts: governments, policy makers, and administrators. Not only had they long limited access to higher education for the vast majority of the British youth, but when they finally decided to extend access, Trow felt that seriously threatened the freedom and innovativeness of many academic institutions, especially those that might be expected to make significant contributions to human knowledge. Academics shared the blame only in so far as by word, deed, or omission, they shared these assumptions.

Before examining them, we might notice the marked contrast between his running critique of British policy makers (and to a lesser degree of academics) and the neutral tone of most of his discussions of American higher education, since it throws into the sharpest possible light the two ideals that inspired his work. The first was a radical and passionate democratic aspiration that opportunities for higher education should be open to everyone who wants it at whatever age—an ideal most evident in this collection in his 1987 essay on British higher education (see chapter 6) and in his essay on the transition to universal access via the Internet (see chapter 16). The second ideal was an admiration for and backing of elite academic environments that support the very highest standards of learning for the minority who qualify for and seem likely to benefit from them. Chapter 3 conveys this sympathy for elite institutions, while chapter 11, though ostensibly an administrative report, describes the mission statement for the elite academic community he created at UC Berkeley.

These two ideals are usually thought to be at odds, if not diametrically opposed, but Trow was an equally resolute defender of both. Opinions of his politics therefore vary according to which part of his scattered oeuvre an observer happened to catch—the radical egalitarian or the conservative elitist. They also differ by which side of the Atlantic the reader happened to be, since these two ideals resonate differently in Europe and the United States, especially radical egalitarianism. In Europe, radical egalitarians are invariably committed to state intervention and see the market as their enemy and the main source of inequality they wish to eradicate. Not many European commentators have spent time wondering about the threat to elite institutions as Trow does in chapter 3. In the United States, it is not quite the other way around, but nearly so, and there are many radical egalitarians who, like Trow, think that markets may be agents of equality. His work prompts one to suggest that George Bernard Shaw got it wrong. The British and the Americans are not separated by the same language. Nothing Trow ever wrote supports that notion, but they are separated by their view of the legitimate spheres of action of states and markets.

In Trow's mind, Britain's main disadvantage was cultural, though he seldom used that term, and instead referred to "values which ordinarily are so widely and deeply accepted that hardly anybody talks about them, as being too obvious or too consensual to need articulation." As a result of not talking about them, they narrowly restricted debates about the available policy options with respect to the growth of higher education and intertwined silently in "a network of attitudes, values, and institutions that defined the British system of higher education." One might add, parenthetically, that since Trow's "problem under investigation" was the way these widely held, unexamined assumptions of British elites influenced policy debates and decisions, sustained institutions, and blocked growth, his own peculiar "method" of investigation was certainly more appropriate than a conventional opinion survey.

He singled out two of these guiding assumptions as especially powerful, the first being that all education leading to degrees should be funded by the state. At first glance, it is somewhat surprising that British policy makers and academics took this for granted since many English universities had been started by private and municipal initiatives, and until World War II some two-thirds of their income had come from these sources. After the war, however, they all came to share the view that universities should be state funded, and policy makers evidently agreed since the proportion of public funding steadily climbed to more than 90 percent. In 1993, the United Kingdom reported to the Organisation for Economic Co-operation and Development (OECD) that 100 percent of funding was from public sources.[15] The second key assumption was that the single-subject honors degree, the staple diet of a British university education, should be of a high and a common standard in every university, and earned only through full-time study over three years. "If one were to try," Trow once remarked, "to identify one aspect of British higher education that 'stands for' the complex of historical, institutional and normative factors preventing the adoption of an American pattern of higher education in Great Britain, it might be the nature of the bachelor's degree, of high and approximately uniform standard throughout the system of higher education."[16]

There were a number of other ancillary or derivative assumptions. Given universities' dependence on central government funding, it was generally accepted that there was no reason for them "to seek friends, provide services to the community at large to attract or hold their corner in politics of interest and power." The "court politics of 'the great and good' meeting with politicians and senior civil servants in the Athenaeum" would suffice. And since the universities were dependent on the state, it was also long taken as an article of faith that students admitted to their honors degrees should be wholly or largely supported by the state, so that they could devote themselves full-time to their demanding honors degree courses. All these assumptions were still deeply entrenched in 1987, when Trow wrote "Academic Standards and Mass Higher Education" (chapter 6), and it was still uncertain whether the British would or could take the plunge into mass higher education.

Trow did not spend much time exploring either the origins or the endurance of these assumptions. He noted that the commitment to central government funding was of a piece with the postwar extension of the welfare state, and that it then seemed like "a powerful democratizing force . . . in that it promised to make available to the whole society, at least its culturally gifted, without regard for class or social origins, that part of the cultural heritage that heretofore had been reserved for the privileged." He might, however, have said more about the promise of admission "without regard for class or social origins," for it helps to explain the universal commitment to central government funding. He once acutely observed that "cultures are defined in part by what they feel guilty about," adding that "Western European nations, on the whole, feel guilty about their working classes"—especially, he might have continued, the British. As it happened, however, the secondary schools from which British universities drew their students provided the most visible and widely cited examples of class distinctions. British academics and higher education policy makers therefore had a very negative reference forever at hand, continually reminding them of what they must at all costs avoid. Central state funding, along with student grants, were long seen as the means by which they might do so.[17] They were wrong in this respect, since class inequalities permeated higher education institutions by other routes, but they could at least console themselves with the thought that class differences were not as institutionalized and visible as they were in secondary schools.

The academic community's commitment to a common, high standard for their single honors degrees, their defense of the "gold standard" as Trow called it, may have been sustained, as he once suggested, by the fear that if each university were to find its own level "a kind of Gresham's Law of Higher Education" would begin to operate—with bad degrees driving out the good. British academics may also have felt the need for "some ordering, controlling, coordinating agencies so that institutions do not develop helter-skelter or destroy their integrity by bringing the manifold interests of the market into the heart of high cultural institutions." However, his references to the "relative weakness of the academic profession in the United States, as compared with its strength in the United Kingdom, especially in Oxbridge," seems nearer the mark if we hope to explain the tenacious commitment to the gold standard. It was, after all, British academics themselves, not the state, who organized the system of external examiners that upheld it. And in that respect they were little different from other well-organized professions. One way or another they all subscribe to the myth that their members uphold the same high and uniform standards. None of them readily admit to a diversity of standards and leave their clients to decide which might be best. Organized professions are united in the view, indeed around the view, that they alone should determine and distinguish the merits of their colleagues' work rather than accepting the verdict of their clients and of the marketplace.

Trow was, however, less interested in the origins or social supports of these assumptions than in their long-term impact on British public policy. Over four decades, in eighteen journal articles and numerous lectures, seminars, and conferences, he observed the reaffirmation of the two main ones in public debates and official reports as if they were self-evident truths. In his view, they were not self-evident, and as he repeatedly explained they had prevented the British from seeing or discussing the policy options open to them, and therefore long delayed the emergence of mass higher education. In 1989, reflecting on the Robbins Report of 1963 some twenty-five years after it had first boldly proclaimed the goal of mass higher education, he decided that it had "in fact set a trap," for while endorsing expansion, it had not questioned either of these two main assumptions. It had therefore made expansion over the intervening quarter century beyond a certain level, of about 15 percent of the age cohort, well nigh impossible.[18]

Eventually, mainly through the 1990s, the British made the transition to mass higher education. They did so, however, less as a deliberate strategy or an exhilarating mission to extend opportunities to the majority of young people as Robbins (and Trow) had hoped and no one hailed, or claimed credit, for the opening of "a grand road to social mobility."[19] Instead, universities were seen as one of the institutions responsible for the country's economic decline, and in urgent need of reform to help correct its crumbling public finances. Over the last quarter of the twentieth century, four main government policies toward higher education attracted Trow's attention. They were promoted most fervently by the Thatcher and Major governments (1979–97), but they had a few Old Labour precedents and New Labour under Blair and Brown were happy to continue them.

The first was to dismantle the self-imposed restraints meant to ensure the institutional autonomy of universities. Most notable among these restraints was the distribution of public funds as quinquennial block grants through an academic-dominated buffer agency, the University Grants Committee (UGC). In 1988, the UGC was replaced by a new funding agency that was unambiguously responsible to central government. University charters were then rewritten to eliminate academic tenure. Funding was earmarked and central government "started to make decisions not just about the broad character of the system, but about the internal academic and research life of individual institutions, as if they knew better than academics what should be taught, how and to whom, and what their research priorities should be." The second major policy was to cut, continuously and relentlessly, the government grant per student so that by 2000 it was, in real terms, about 50 percent of what it had been in 1976. The third was to try to simulate a marketplace in higher education, though since the state remained the only "customer" of the universities' services and universities were denied the usual resources and freedom of market actors, governments retained the power to control or "steer" the universities. The fourth was to impose various mechanisms to assess the quality of teaching and research in all university departments and to link these assessments directly to the funding they received from the government, so that success might be rewarded and failure punished.

Trow provided running commentaries on these policies and the universities' responses to them with all his customary insight, grace, and wit, but also, confirmed Anglophile that he was, with increasing sorrow and dismay. Chapter 7 is an example. Among the signs of change that caught his attention over the years was the tenacious and vociferous defense of student grants by "middle-class parents and their left-wing offspring," though at least he told himself grants had become a subject of public debate, and even part of the "rough and tumble of ordinary politics." Another was the way some universities were beginning to depend on supplementary private sources of income, such as fees from foreign, non-European Union (EU) students, and support from alumni and other potential donors, though he was mildly amused when one of the new breed of fundraisers told him that it was easier to get donations from their short-stay American alumni than from their British graduates, some of whom reacted to their requests as if they were being asked to donate to road building or refuse collection. In the early 1990s, he detected a significant change in the conduct of some vice chancellors who were now taking executive and entrepreneurial decisions rather than being merely the temporary spokespersons of their "academic guild" as they had been in the past.[20]

Trow followed with particular interest the behavior of universities in the rigged, quasi-markets in which they had been placed. When told they would have to bid a price annually for teaching so many students of a certain type and number, like other government contractors, he was pleased to see that they retaliated as a cartel, and all bid exactly the same price. When told their funding would henceforth depend on their measured research output, he was not surprised that a number responded "by buying some active researchers along with their bibliographies (or perhaps the other way around) to improve their standing in the next round of research assessments." And when he started an investigation with Oliver Fulton of the impact of quality assessment on the internal life of universities, he was struck by "how much of the creative imagination of the senior administrative staff has gone into trying to outwit HEFC (the Higher Education Funding Council) with one barely legal scam after another." Once again, one may note, Trow's own distinctive research method seems entirely appropriate for the problem he was investigating. It is difficult to believe that this research would have gone far with orthodox survey methods.

The low point of his long watch was undoubtedly the 1997 publication of the National Inquiry into Higher Education (the Dearing Committee) to which he had given evidence.[21] It was written, he thought, from outside the system looking in, and "did not include a single ordinary university teacher" whose experience might have informed its discussions. Despite the mass of evidence the committee gathered, "at point after point the report reveals a shocking ignorance about how universities actually work." It "simply does not know what is going on inside the colleges and universities, their classrooms and offices and laboratories, but still pronounces on what should be happening there with an air of great authority," oblivious to the fact that "if anything good is to happen in a university it must depend on the willing involvement, or at least the assent, of the teaching staff." It repeated "the recent history of British government policies for higher education: centrally organized and common responses to varying and particularized problems." Among the responses was the recommendation that two more bodies be added to the existing apparatus of assessment and control: one to formalize the external examination system with a selected cadre of examination experts, and another whose full-time staff were supposed to "possess the secrets of teaching and learning" and be prepared to examine and accredit "the teaching performance of every university teacher in every kind of institution against criteria that the national bodies themselves define and embody."[22]

The two main assumptions that Trow had identified thirty years earlier still guided most of the recommendations of this committee, though they qualified the first by approving the proposal that students should henceforth pay fees, which they hoped, though could not guarantee, "would remain with the institution in which the student was enrolled" to supplement state funding. However, the committee resolutely defended the second; hence their recommendation for a new agency to uphold the "gold standard" across all institutions and departments, a decision that reminded Trow of "King Canute's firm instructions to the incoming tide." The real challenge, he argued, "is to identify and accept the diversity of the system, and begin to develop policies that both reflect and encourage that diversity. And among those policies would be a major devolution of authority and power out of central government and its funding instruments, to individual institutions or groups of similar and associated institutions. Among those powers would be the power to set their own costs of tuition, their own salary schedules, their own standards for awarding their degrees and certificates." Academic life, Trow argued, "is continually bursting out of any predefined boundaries, never more than just now. That is what makes centralized efforts to manage and control intellectual life hopeless. But when those efforts are armed with the power of the state, they are also costly and destructive. British higher education has been paying those costs and suffering those injuries for some time now."

But were these centralized efforts really "costly and destructive"? Were the injuries lasting ones? Britain has now achieved a participation rate equal to that of the United States, and indeed may be overtaking it. In 2005, 29 percent of British 20- to 29-year-old students were enrolled full- or part-time versus only 23 percent of Americans of the same age. Britain has done this by spending, in 2004, a mere 1.1 percent of its GDP (gross domestic product) on higher education, which is significantly below both the OECD and EU means. It has therefore achieved, or seems to have achieved, exactly what the Thatcher and subsequent governments intended, and what taxpayers were always thought to want: value for money. The expansion of higher education has not been hailed, it seems fair to say, in quite the same spirit as the Americans. Trow noticed how British policy makers would commonly refer to the burdens, sacrifices, and difficulties that expansion would entail, rather than enthusiastically greeting the prospect of wider opportunities. Parents and media alike still seem likely to portray university education as something into which school leavers have been somehow dragooned, as an unnecessary extension of their compulsory education, giving them rather questionable qualifications, leaving them with little better job prospects and burdened with debt. This, however, may be mere mood music, or perhaps poor public relations. The important question is whether the transformation that Trow thought unnecessarily protracted and painful has had any of the long-term adverse effects on British higher education that he claimed. What visible and measurable signs are there of any such effects?

Not many it would seem. Those who lost out when the system failed to expand much in the 1970s and 1980s may wistfully regret their missed opportunities, but they are now in their forties or fifties or sixties, and have had many opportunities to re-enter education in some form if they had really wished to do so.[23] There is no sign that the policies of which Trow disapproved have affected the quality of university research. British universities compare rather well with American universities in all the cross-national ratings, such as the numbers in top 100 or 200, or the top 50 in specific disciplines; indeed, per capita sometimes surpass them. Britain is the only country other than the United States to have maintained a surplus in its intellectual balance of payments since this was first recorded by the OECD in 1983. There has been no recurrence of a brain drain to the United States, or at least none visible enough to be thought worth measuring. No one knows whether talented people are now avoiding the academic profession or leaving it, but even if they were, does it matter? British universities were previously thought to have kept too many of their most able students, and in any case, who is to say what their fair share might be? The morale of British academics may still be abysmally low, but the last time this was convincingly demonstrated by cross-national research was in 1993.[24] Even if it were repeated with similar results today, what significance should be attached to it? No one really knows what the impact of morale might be on creativity or teaching quality. Margaret Thatcher famously dismissed the morale of public servants as a nonissue. She thought that, like everyone else, they worked for an income, and the quality of their work depended on appropriate financial incentives and punishments, rather than on something as vague as their morale. There is one slim clue that British academics might be publishing less worthy pieces of research, and recycling it more than they once did to satisfy government measures of their productivity, which is that the citation scores of the top 20 British universities are now almost 20 points below those of the top 20 American universities, meaning that the authors of British articles are significantly less influential than their American counterparts. It would, however, require far more detailed research to demonstrate any deterioration over time in the quality of their publications that coincided with the policy measures of which Trow disapproved—research that no one is ever likely to conduct.

In Britain there are no reported cases where academic freedom has been suppressed. It may be that certain kinds of research are not supported because they do not conform to the priorities set by the state agencies distributing research funds, but any complaint on that score can plausibly be dismissed as sour grapes. Anyway, there are alternative private sources of funding. Academics might still be concocting the various scams that Trow observed, like preparing bogus departmental research plans to deceive government agencies or holding rehearsals for the flying visits of their reviewers. But these things are all hidden from view, their costs unknown. Academics might perhaps have spent their time more creatively or given more of it to their students, but how is that to be measured? There are no historical or comparative measures of the quality of teaching, and students are hardly likely to be able to make comparisons with their predecessors who benefited from one-to-one tutorials or had more time for discussions with their lecturers. About one-fifth of foreign students recently reported that they have received "poor or very poor value for money" at English universities, and England's share of the international market in university students is falling. However, the absolute number of foreign students, and the fees they are willing to pay, are still increasing, so the remarks of these disgruntled foreign students may be dismissed.[25]

In short, since there is no research to prove otherwise, it is entirely possible to portray Britain's transition to mass higher education over the past two decades as a success story. All the delays and uncertainties that Trow discussed, all the policy trials and errors, "the learning to drive by ear," as he once put it, might be seen simply as another example of Britain "muddling through" successfully. In time, we may expect the mood music to change, though that is unlikely to be soon, since "college" in Britain, unlike the United States, has to overcome the deep-rooted legitimacy of the practice-based and practitioner-controlled training in which the members of every organized occupation in the country, from the highest professions to the lowliest manual workers, had previously arranged for their new entrants without any kind of state intervention or funding. In time, however, the transition may come to be seen, as Trow saw it, as part of the evolution of British democracy, and even perhaps celebrated in mass media as a normal part of the British way of life.

One can only guess at Trow's response to this version of events. He would most certainly have lighted on the absolutely critical item of evidence that is missing—that referring to the quality of teaching. He simply did not believe that it could possibly remain the same while the resources devoted to it were halved—no matter how often he was assured that it had, or was presented with statistics on the number of first-class honors. He would not, I suspect, have been persuaded by the dismissal of the morale of academics as of no consequence since, as he once observed, "almost everything in a university depends on the inner motivations of teachers—their sense of pride, their intellectual involvement with their subjects, their professional commitments to the role of teacher, their love of students, or of learning—these and others are among the forces that lead teachers to bring their full resources to the teaching relationship." In the end his reply might have concentrated on the loss of institutional autonomy, and the "humbling of British academics," as the final chapter of his proposed book on British universities was to be called. In his view, it was inconceivable that state-appointed inspectors and assessors of various kinds could identify the defects of a university as well as its own administrators and faculty—or, given the appropriate form of governance, know better how to correct them. Institutional autonomy was "not an end in itself, but a prerequisite for intellectual distinction." But that was only his opinion, his hunch.[26] If British academics do not feel, or do not mind, the loss of their "freedom to define their own character and mission," and if they do not feel "humbled," then we might put his proposition down as another example of his American bias.

In the final analysis, it does not matter too much whether Trow's American advantage disguised an American bias, no more important, really, than knowing that Weber's ideal type of bureaucracy was excessively influenced by German or Prussian experience. In any event, it is unlikely that he would deny the charge, since so many of his essays were flagged as "an American perspective." The more important issue is whether the many questions he raised are still valid, either as matters of public policy or as significant research topics. Is there some other more powerful, more illuminating dynamic for understanding the process of change in higher education? Would some other country provide a better starting point? Would some other set of variables better capture changes in the private or public lives of universities? What did his American perspective omit or distort? What did he get wrong? To answer these questions, we need evidence, which is to say that the ultimate test of his work must be an empirical one. Answering all of them would take too much time, but we may glance briefly at a few of his arguments, along with some of the evidence that would be needed to evaluate them properly, beginning with one where he appears to have been overtaken by events.

Trow's primary indicator of the transformation of a system from elite to mass as a system change was the enrollment in higher education institutions as a proportion of the age cohort, which he took as a convenient quantitative index of a "fundamental qualitative difference in almost every aspect of the private and public lives of universities." By this measure, as already noted, the United States is no longer the world leader, and has been overtaken by a number of countries, in both Asia and Europe. Indeed, by 2005, the United States was slightly *below* the OECD average in the proportion of 18- to 24-year-olds graduating from tertiary institutions of one kind or another.[27] Since this has happened relatively recently, mainly through the late 1990s and the turn of the century, the United States still remains ahead of other OECD countries in cross-national measures of the educational attainment of older age groups or of the entire adult population, though not ahead of two OECD-affiliates, Russia and Israel.[28]

Having decided that Trow was wrong to assume that the first mover would remain ahead as higher education enrollments continued to grow, a number of questions immediately come to mind. Why did American growth stall and fall behind? How did European societies, for all their supposed disadvantages, manage to accelerate past the United States? Does this mean that America no longer has any advantage in the progression beyond mass higher education to universal access? An answer to the first question, about the stalling of American growth, would probably involve an analysis of the high school performance and dropout rates of African American and Latino students in the United States—especially Latinos, since the rate of college enrollment of American high school graduates alone would leave the United States still ahead of every other OECD country. The third question, about universal access, is discussed below, but the second, about the European societies that overtook the United States, deserves some brief comment.

Spain is one of these European societies. In 2004, a higher proportion of its 25- to 34-year-olds had been enrolled in higher or tertiary education than in the United States. Spain's achievement seems more impressive when one notices that the proportion of its GDP spent on higher education increased only moderately from 1.0 percent to 1.2 percent over the period when it overtook the United States, a proportion that was below the EU mean, and far below that of the United States, which spent proportionately more than twice as much: 2.9 percent. Italy is even more remarkable, having doubled the proportion of graduates in the same age group between 2000 and 2004, from 19.0 percent to 41 percent, while the proportion of its GDP spent on higher education remained constant, and was still lower than that of Spain, and indeed that of every other OECD country.[29] Spain and Italy have evidently been able to increase enrollments in higher education at a rapid pace, and at a modest or no cost. Russia, however, is perhaps the most remarkable of all, since it was far ahead of the United States in enrollments, while committing only 0.7 percent of GNP to higher education.

These comparisons lead one to wonder whether Trow's quantitative index was not quite the sure guide to qualitative changes that he supposed. Enrollments and attendance appear to mean qualitatively different things in different societies, and there seem to be economies of scale in higher education beyond anything he imagined. Comparisons of the expenditure per student—in constant purchasing power parity dollars—only reinforce these suspicions. In 2004, Spain spent $9,378 per student, Italy $7,723, and Russia only $2,562, while the United States spent $22,476.[30] If one wished to sustain Trow's argument about America's "advantage" or his view of its "secular religion," one would be advised to refer not to enrollments as a proportion of an age cohort, but to the resources it commits as a nation to higher education, as measured by a proportion of its GDP, or to the amount that it spends on each enrolled student.[31] In both of these respects, the United States remains distinctive, indeed, so far ahead of almost every other country that it will remain as distinctive as Trow supposed it to be for a considerable time to come.[32]

He always assumed, of course, that there were as many pathways to mass higher education as there were nations with universities, and suggested that comparisons between them should include the rate and sequence of growth as well as the level of enrollments.[33] However, it is fair to say that while he thoroughly explored differences in the rate, level, and sequence of growth in the two societies he knew best, he probably paid too little attention to one close similarity between them, namely, the character of the elite institutions that are the starting point of growth. There is still a family resemblance between Harvard College, the undergraduate part of Harvard, and the school of its founder in Cambridge, England, and the family resemblance extends to other elite institutions in the two countries, as well as, one might add, to their elite secondary schools. Yet some of the societies that have now overtaken the United States so effortlessly seem to have had radically different elite starting points.

It seems entirely possible for a society to have higher education institutions that once served only a small elite proportion of the population, but never provided an elite education in Trow's understanding of the term, which derived from his knowledge of elite institutions in the United States and the United Kingdom. In fact, their universities might have been giving what he considered a mass education to a small number of students; might have been elite in enrollment but mass in character; and might therefore have been able, given the political signal, to scale up effortlessly to become mass institutions in both respects. They would therefore have enjoyed an advantage in making the elite to mass transformation quite different from that enjoyed by the United States. If Trow had extended his comparisons to include Russia, he might well have been obliged to recognize that its universities had benefited from one of socialism's positive legacies—perhaps its only positive legacy—the commitment to the mass provision of higher education, without being encumbered by any of the cultural baggage of elite institutions in the United States or the United Kingdom—the tearful farewell from the parental home, the near-mandatory requirement to study at a university at the other end of the country, the socialization into a new residential community and into an entirely new way of learning by tutorials, seminars, and being able to choose from a superfluity of optional lectures and extracurricular events and societies. By contrast, Russia's tertiary education might have been little different, pedagogically, logistically, or culturally, from its secondary education, indeed merely a continuation of it, and hence it may have been supremely well prepared, both "normatively and structurally," for mass and even universal enrollments. Trow visited Leningrad University in the dying days of the Soviet Union, and searched briefly and vainly for signs of any corporate life, but the fate of the regime distracted him from further investigating the matter or drawing any conclusions about its apparent absence.

If the starting point of growth of mass higher education in a society was of this kind, and if, for instance, there were no elite universities to provide a normative benchmark or compelling reference group for the teachers in other universities, or for policy makers, as well as for students and parents, then we might expect it to have a rapid, and altogether less stressful rate of growth than societies enthralled by a certain "idea of a university." Clearly, we need comparative analyses of more elite institutions. In France, for instance, elite institutions do not seem to have been a starting point or relevant reference group for university growth at all. If these comparisons included societies where the rate of growth has been very rapid, we might also determine the long-term effects of different starting points, including the dislocating effects of asynchronous changes in the governance, faculty, curricula, and enrollments that Trow anticipated would accompany rapid growth. Korea would be an extreme test case in this respect, since the rate of growth has been so astonishingly rapid, creating intergenerational differences on an unprecedented scale. Only 10 percent of 55- to 64-year-olds in Korea have some experience of tertiary education, while 80 percent of 20-year-olds are at college. The intergenerational variations in Japan, Spain, and Ireland are not quite as large but nonetheless considerable. In such comparisons the United States might serve as a steady-state comparison, since there is little difference between 55- to 64-year-olds and 25- to 34-year-olds.[34]

Many of the empirical questions deriving from Trow's conceptual framework revolve around the relative merits and demerits of public and private nonprofit ownership, control, and funding, so it may be as well to recall that he saw this distinction as a matter of degree. On numerous occasions, and in many of the essays that follow, he readily acknowledges the contributions of state initiatives, of public institutions, and of public funding to the expansion of American higher education. His own university, UC Berkeley, was of course a public institution, though with around one-third of its operating expenses in recent times coming from the state of California. On one occasion he was tempted to refer to it as a "state-aided" rather than a state university. In his view, the most favorable environment for the growth, freedom, and creativity of higher educational institutions was a mixed economy in which the state performs certain minimal regulatory and referee functions, and state-created and -funded institutions participate in competition with private nonprofit ones. When the state occupies the "commanding heights" of higher education—or when it sought to supervise and manage all the institutions from the center and to determine the size and shape of the system as a whole—growth, freedom, and creativity were, in Trow's view, all threatened and still more so, of course, when it exercised a monopoly.

Whenever he made broad comparisons between the United States and the United Kingdom, differences of degree sometimes veered toward a dichotomous, almost cold war contrast between systems that accepted private institutions and benefited from competitive markets versus those that were public owned and funded and had no markets at all. Whenever he got down to cases and wrote on specific issues, he introduced finer distinctions and recognized that ownership, control, and funding might vary independently of one another. He observed, for instance, that private American institutions receive a significant proportion of their income from government sources of various kinds (an average of 17 percent during the early 1990s). And he noted that when British universities catered only to elite students, they acted as if they were private even though they were entirely state funded, and that without any change in their ownership or the source of funding, they had become more state controlled. And still more oddly perhaps, as they later "partially privatized" by charging fees, by encouraging income-earning spinoffs, by actively pursuing private donors, and by participating in various kinds of quasi- and state-managed "markets," they became still more closely state controlled.

One of Trow's key propositions was that in societies where universities are wholly or largely dependent on public funds, the state will eventually limit resources devoted to higher education. Enrollments and participation will therefore tend to be lower than in societies where universities can depend on private resources, and the ultimate size and shape of the higher education system is determined by ordinary families rather than by political decisions. He was not given to formulating laws, but this comes close to being one.

Japan and Korea provide the strongest support for his argument. In Japan, 60 percent of the funds of higher education institutions are from private sources, and they are third in OECD table of the proportion of 25- to 34-year-olds who had attained tertiary education in 2005. Korea, where 79 percent of higher education institutions are privately financed, is fourth in this same table. However, the first and second positions are occupied by Russia and Canada and therefore contradict Trow's argument. But neither does so in a wholly definitive manner. Although the figures for older age groups leave no doubt that Russia had a markedly higher participation rate than the United States when there were no private institutions at all, it is not possible to say whether Russia continues to lead, since there are no figures for public and private expenditures in post-socialist Russia. Canada is also not wholly convincing as a counterexample. Trow himself referred to Canada as an exceptional case since, contrary to his expectations, it spent a higher proportion of its GDP on tertiary education than the United States. He was, however, citing 1993 data, and Canada did not long remain an exceptional case.[35] By 1995, the proportion of its GDP devoted to higher education had fallen behind that of the United States, while the proportion of its expenditure from public sources had shrunk to 56.6 percent.[36] Oddly enough, like Russia,

Canada is frequently remiss or tardy in filing data with the OECD, and so we do not know whether or not this is still the case.

If one looks for more persuasive counter-examples, one may take the six OECD countries whose higher education institutions are most dependent on public funding, meaning 88 percent or more comes from public sources. Three of them—Austria, Greece, and Iceland—also devote low proportions of their GDP to higher education and all have lower enrollments than the United States, so they will not help to disprove Trow's argument, and on the contrary must be considered examples of it. At first glance, Sweden, Finland, and Denmark look as though they might refute it, since they all commit the same reasonably high proportion of their GDPs to higher education: 1.8 percent. On closer inspection, however, they are still less than wholly persuasive counter-examples. Compared to many other countries, 1.8 percent may be reasonably high, but it is still low compared to the 2.9 percent of the United States. Moreover, through 1995–2004, this proportion grew at a slow rate, leading one to suspect that they might all be reaching some kind of ceiling, while at the same time the private contribution to higher education was growing far more rapidly in all three countries, about twice as fast in Finland and Sweden, and more than five times as fast in Denmark. Hence they might best be considered as test cases to watch in the future rather than as clear refutations of Trow's argument.

Perhaps his argument about the leveling-down effect of public funding on universities is more marked in research than in enrollments, since research has lower political visibility than enrollments. Trow had noticed this leveling-down effect in the research expenditures of public universities in the United States, so that they usually compared unfavorably with private ones in American research ratings.[37] In 2008, the editor of the *THE* ratings underlined the point, observing that American "state universities, funded mainly by state taxes and comparatively modest student fees, are not well represented in this ranking (of the world's top 200 universities) or in national tables of US universities. With the anomalous exception of the University of California, most have fallen behind private institutions in both teaching and research."[38] The *THE* editor went on to note the importance of private funding for research in the United States, observing that the Bush administration's blocking of federal support for stem cell research had had little impact on American biomedical research since his evidence showed that "the US is where the top researchers in this field want to be."

Of course, no one in Europe or anywhere else would question the desirability of private donations for research. The key question is whether a leveling-down effect is identifiable elsewhere, making those universities most dependent on public funding less able to compete in research excellence and recognition with universities in a mixed and competitive economy of higher education. The modest to dismal ratings of some of the larger European countries where universities are most dependent on state funding—France, Italy, and Spain, as well as Germany, the original home of the research university—lend impressionistic support to this idea. If, however, one compares the R&D expenditures of universities in the six OECD countries that are most dependent on public funding with universities in the six countries that are least dependent, one finds the former group has a mean research expenditure about double that of the latter: $4,412 in purchasing power parity dollars versus $2,260, and therefore lends no support to the notion that publicly financed universities are being "leveled down" in their research funding. However, mean expenditures can be misleading. The variation around the mean might be, and probably is, far greater in those countries whose universities are most dependent on private funding, since as Trow often pointed out, states tend to prefer uniform and standardized funding formulas. Other comparisons convey a different picture. Universities in countries where private funding is highest not only appear more frequently in ratings of the world's best, such as the *THE*'s table of the world's top 200 universities, but more importantly, their performance, measured either by peer reviews or by citation scores, markedly exceeds that of universities in those countries where higher education is highly dependent on public funds.[39]

Clearly, these contrasts merit further investigation, both for reasons of research interest and for future public policy. For those who would like to refute Trow's arguments, the Netherlands is probably the best case. Although not among the top 6 countries most dependent on public funding, over three-quarters (77.6 percent) of its expenditure on higher education is from public sources, and while it has a few small private universities, private funding has been growing in recent years at a rate only marginally faster than public funding. At the same time its total expenditure as a proportion of GDP remains very low (1.3 percent), which is less than the OECD average. Yet the Netherlands not only has an enrollment rate as high as that of the United States, but from a population of only 16.5 million, has 11 universities in the world's top 200. It appears therefore to have achieved mass higher education at low cost, while depending largely on public funding without, it seems, compromising academic excellence.

Trow's defense of private institutions and private initiatives continued into his discussion of academic governance. He thought they promoted a benign competitive dynamics, for while they continuously compete among themselves to enhance their reputations, mainly by improving their research performance though also by raising their admission standards, public universities press for greater institutional autonomy from the state, so that they may respond nimbly to the innovations of their private rivals. Standards therefore rise, along with institutional autonomy, while state control declines. His experience within his own public university must have continually reassured him in this respect. Parking spaces marked "NL" are scattered around the UC Berkeley campus for the Nobel Laureates currently working there, and faculty and students seem almost as likely to know their current Nobel Laureate score versus that of their private near-neighbor Stanford as they are to know the score in last year's football game. Trow also had reason to refer to the familiar phenomenon of institutional or academic drift, another aspect of the benign dynamics to which he referred, whereby lower ranking, usually more vocationally oriented, institutions seek to emulate their betters by encouraging their faculty to conduct and publish research. California's Master Plan was intended to restrain such drift by California State University. He frequently observed similar drifting by British polytechnics, though in their case it was rewarded in 1992, when most of them were recognized overnight as universities.

For the moment we lack adequately researched comparative cases to say whether the benign dynamics of competition have worked elsewhere in the manner Trow suggested, or for that matter, if there are any negative dynamics at work, lowering both standards and fees. Japan and

Korea, with their substantial private sectors, are worth investigation from this point of view, though unlike the United States, it is the public universities that have made the running in terms of international research reputations. In Japan there are at least three private universities, Keio, Waseda, and Hitotsubashi, which have kept pace with them. In 2004, however, the Japanese government evidently came to accept the benign dynamics of competition and, declaring that it would no longer support its nine public, national universities "in the style of an armed convoy," turned each of them into "independent administrative corporations."[40] It is still too early to assess the impact of this legislation on the actual behavior of the national and private universities and whether the government's—and Trow's—faith in the benign dynamics of competition was justified.

In some respects, Korea might be said to take Trow's ideals to extremes, almost to the point of caricature, since the private sector is extremely large, diverse, and competitive. As Ki-Seok Kim explained, no "adequate functional differentiation" between types of institutions has been imposed by the state. As a result, "all universities" in this highly competitive environment are "aspiring to be flagship universities," even though some of them have "inadequate academic and institutional preparation and support." Kim does not say whether there is any sign of Gresham's Law of Higher Education among the lesser private institutions, with poor degrees driving out the good, though in his view the system is now "over-privatized." He thinks it unlikely that more of its universities will obtain international recognition until the government recognizes higher education as a public good, and assumes a greater responsibility for funding it, rather than relying almost entirely on parental zeal and ambition for their children's education.

In European countries, with only marginal private institutions, competition cannot take the form of competition between sectors, and if it is to emerge can only be between public institutions that are increasingly coming to rely on private support. This trend of increasing dependence on private funding is common to all OECD countries. They are all becoming "mixed economies" of higher education, albeit from very different starting points and at very different rates. The EU as a whole is the world laggard with just 16 percent of its higher education expenditure in 2004 coming from private sources, though in its two front-runners, Italy and the United Kingdom, the proportion was 31 percent. Elsewhere the trend has been more rapid. In 2004, more than half of the income (52.8 percent) of Australian universities came from private sources. In all probability, Canada has already crossed the line where the greater part of university income comes from private sources, and New Zealand will soon follow.[41]

As universities increasingly become public/private hybrids, like UC Berkeley itself, a critical question of public policy is whether and how far the state controls and public accountability imposed when they were mainly publicly funded will remain unchanged. There is no reason why there should be any reflex reaction. In most countries, state funding will remain both the largest and most predictable source of funds for the foreseeable future, and funding may even increase absolutely, even if it continues to decline as a proportion of overall income. Partial privatization and frequent use of market rhetoric did not prevent British governments from extending control over universities. Michael Shattock suggests that little has changed in this respect, and that British universities have, in effect, been converted into departments of state.[42] Nonetheless, one would expect that, if they continue to depend increasingly on private sources, universities would push more confidently and persistently for greater institutional autonomy, so that they are able to compete more vigorously with one another. In Europe they may well be assisted by another competitive dynamic, unlike that described by Trow, as universities in member states compare their autonomy with one another.[43] No member state, one imagines, will wish to have the most regulated universities in the Union.

Trow had only a rough ad hoc working typology of university governance. These included the academic guild (which, "at whatever level it appears, department, faculty, or board, is better at saying 'no' than 'yes'"), the state-controlled (into which the United Kingdom had fallen), the individual executive leader subject to a lay governing body (the only kind that he expected to be able to compete effectively, best exemplified in the United States and which he analyzes carefully in chapters 13 and 14), and universities that incorporated some form of democratic or representative governance (which "inevitably leads to a degradation of . . . intellectual quality, and over time, of . . . academic status"). These types were, however, never systematically defined and elaborated, and when he sought to describe a formal comparative framework, it focused not on the apparatus of governance within the university but on the way higher education institutions are linked to, and supported by, their surrounding societies, on the grounds that this would determine particular forms of governance. In his view, those links combined three elements: (1) trust, where an institution receives support without any specified services being demanded in return; (2) markets, where support is given in exchange for the provision of specified services; and (3) accountability, where support depends on an obligation to report to others. These three elements may be combined, he thought, "in complex ways, which will vary greatly, and in no predictable manner, by country, by institution," as well as over time.[44] Along with a number of sub-variations, he used them to conduct a few preliminary historical and cross-societal comparisons of higher education institutions.

In every society, he argued, higher education institutions are subject to some form of accountability, but the instruments by which American higher educations are held accountable, while varying greatly, were limited in scope and scale compared with those elsewhere. Hence their relationships with the surrounding society were, and are, distinguished by an emphasis on market relationships, but still more on trust. Trust, he argued, "is still a central element in the life and autonomy of our institutions," as indicated both by their dependence on donations, since "the donor has no guarantees that the university will spend funds wisely, or as he or she hoped," and by the "enormous amount of time, thought, and effort [that] goes into creating and sustaining the element of trust in support communities."[45] This reliance on trust was another advantage of the American system in his view, for even though it has sometimes been violated and exploited, it minimizes transaction costs. His first annual report as director of the Center for Studies in Higher Education (CSHE) at Berkeley in 1977–78 (chapter 11) is a stunning demonstration of trust in an American academic setting—in and by Trow at least, since he is blissfully indifferent to the kind of measures of output by which research units are normally held accountable.

In the 1990s, Trow detected rising levels of trust by governments in continental Europe, noting in particular the granting of greater autonomy to universities by the Swedish state and its endowment of two of them as private institutions. He also noticed a "similar very marked tendency toward the decentralization of authority to the institutions where we might least expect it, in France, where the old stereotype of a highly centralized Napoleonic university system is no longer tenable." Britain, however, attracted most of his attention, since it was moving in the opposite direction. Although its universities had been granted a high degree of trust when they catered only to an elite, the movement toward mass higher education had been accompanied by the sudden and complete withdrawal of trust, and an almost exclusive reliance on various highly intrusive instruments of accountability that resembled those that "might be expected of a civil service in a defeated country to an occupying power, or by state-owned industrial plants and farms to central government in a command economy."[46]

Trow was, it seems fair to say, simultaneously astonished, fascinated, and depressed by the result, which he analyzes in chapter 7. On one occasion, he watched in near-disbelief as a professor from the newly created University of Luton attended a nine-person seminar at the London School of Economics to determine whether it made adequate use of audiovisual aids, how often every member of the seminar during the inspection had spoken during it, whether the staff member had adequately recapitulated what he hoped had been learned the past hour, and various other items on a checklist—before announcing the grade he would award. His checklist did not include any assessment of the intellectual caliber of the paper delivered by the student, nor of its relevance either to what had preceded or was to follow it, nor whether the members might meet on other occasions—none of which, the inspector-professor freely admitted, he was capable of assessing.

Trow's first objection to the methods of assessing teaching and research adopted in Britain was that they were based on a spurious analogy with departments of commercial firms. Years earlier, in an article published in 1976 (chapter 9), he sought to analyze the complex social dynamics of academic departments and to show why they had nothing in common with those of industrial enterprises coordinated imperatively to perform a single designated function. Advised by their favored consultants of the day, the British government in the 1980s decided to treat them as if they were much the same, a policy premise that, in Trow's view, had certain unintended consequences, a phenomenon of which he was something of a connoisseur. Trow felt that the contribution of university departments to the creativity of their members had been in decline for decades and, in the United Kingdom as in the United States, they were commonly "an obstacle to innovation and reform." By making them the units of assessment and accountability, departments were encouraged to think they had "certain entitlements based on their nationally assessed grades," and the chances of vice chancellors exercising authority over them were thereby reduced.

Academic research, he pointed out, is not done by departments, but by individuals, or by interdisciplinary and interdepartmental teams. Attempts to find some standardized measure of departmental "output" or "productivity," or some academic equivalent of "a bottom line," were therefore in his view hopelessly misconceived, while linking them to funding was nothing less than a catastrophic Soviet-style error, since the incentive to obtain the rewards on offer was accompanied by an equally strong incentive to disguise the truth. "When information flowing up the line powerfully affects the reputation and resources flowing down from the center, then we know that those reports become less and less exercises in discovery or truth telling, and more and more public relations documents which are, shall we say, parsimonious with the truth, especially of awkward truths that reveal problems or shortcomings in the reporting institution. But accountability depends on truth-telling." By withdrawing their trust in academics, successive British governments had in fact made them decidedly less trustworthy. So "a central problem is how to create a system of accountability that does not punish truth-telling and reward the appearance of achievement."[47]

Trow believed that British universities had succumbed to an extreme form of state accountability for several reasons. The prime reason was the post–World War II assumption that higher education should rely exclusively on public funding. Over one or two generations all elite institutions had come to treat this as an article of faith, without caring about its probable consequences when circumstances changed, as they most certainly did when governments decided to embark on mass enrollments without increasing the overall cost to the exchequer. Although inspired by a market ideology, and mesmerized by bogus analogies with private industry, they could not bear to think of the consequences of a free market in higher education. Trow hoped that British universities might escape from the oppressive and high-cost apparatus of state control as they again slowly came to rely on private funding, but he made no predictions or suggestions about how they might do so. The chances are that the attempts of governments to restore public finances after the rescue of financial institutions in 2008–9 will exert irresistible pressure to reexamine the deep-rooted assumptions to which Trow referred, in a manner that policy makers would not otherwise have contemplated. No longer able to rely heavily on their financial services industry, governments might well realize that Britain's universities might better capitalize their significant comparative advantages when freed from the heavy costs and constraints of state control.

Trow did not live to see many such prospects of change. While drawing a little comfort from the newfound assertiveness of vice chancellors, he remained to the end deeply depressed about the future of higher education in Britain. There was little to choose, he thought, between the higher education policies of the three main political parties. He had little faith in the ability of faculty collectively to do much about anything, and even less in the lay governing councils of British universities. They were distinguished in his eyes by their timidity and passivity. He could not mention a single case, over four decades of closely observing British universities, where they had rallied to the defense of "their" university. A powerful electoral constituency of trustees, alumni, and grateful recipients of the university's many services, of the kind he observed in California, had yet to emerge in Britain. He could do little more than to suggest that, should British universities ever manage to escape, they create rigorous internal procedures of assessment and accountability "with real teeth and real consequences." His maxim was "without strong leadership within, there will be strong control from without." While university leaders should remain accountable to governing bodies and consult widely, both within their own institutions and elsewhere, they should also be left with sufficient discretion and resources to take innovative, entrepreneurial, and sometimes painful executive decisions. It was an ideal not so far removed from the form of governance that emerges from his account of reform at Berkeley (chapter 12), and from his analysis of UC more generally (chapters 13 and 14). He described it as "shared governance," and distinguished it sharply from academic self-government and from democracy. In Trow's view, shared governance and strong executive leadership were preconditions of freedom from oppressive forms of external accountability—and indeed of survival in the modern world.

Trow enthusiastically welcomed the final transition from mass to universal access in higher education. There was not much sign of the conservative elitist when he discussed it, though he readily acknowledged that he was peering though the mist when trying to discern its ultimate shape and character. He had originally envisaged the transition as more of the same: higher enrollments (albeit of diverse forms and duration) in more campuses, and perhaps increasing use of "teaching machines" and classroom television, which he had first written about as early as 1966.[48] When, however, a better "machine," the Internet, came along, he revised his image. The Internet represented "the fulfillment of an educator's dream," which "freed education from the constraints of time and space" and ended "the separation of learning from life." It did not, however, greatly clarify his picture of universal access. Institutions making most use of the Internet have, after all, no need for campuses, or resident faculty, or a student community centered around libraries and laboratories, since their students might hardly see or know one another, have only an intermittent commitment to their studies, and pursue them at home or at their workplace. Plainly it is somewhat difficult to count, document, and analyze such a form of education.

Nonetheless, in 1997–98, Trow set out to map distance learning in the western United States.[49] He described seven reasonably established e-learning enterprises, five public and two private, all of them fee-paying and one private for-profit. The diversified, competitive, and decentralized character of American higher education was evidently continuing, and the expansion toward universal access via the Internet would, he decided, "take the form of a continuing series of experiments." Trow was excited by them all and followed with pride and interest his own daughter's mid-career switch via the private for-profit institution. One incidental benefit of the present "organized anarchy" of these institutions in his view was that they would "be more difficult to assess and accredit or hold accountable to anyone" and therefore unlikely to fall under central state control. But there were also several costs and risks, as he explained in his 2000 discussion of e-learning (chapter 16).

If one had never read any of his essays, one might reasonably assume that public institutions would conduct most of the experiments in e-learning, lead the way out of the "organized anarchy," and pioneer the transition to universal access on the grounds that they would be more likely than private institutions to make their courses readily available on the Internet, at low cost or no cost, to the taxpayers who fund them or to their children. And if they did not spontaneously feel any such obligation, then we might expect their paymasters to remind them of it. By contrast, private institutions, one might reasonably suppose, would be more proprietary about their expertise, less likely to see education as "a public good," and therefore less inclined to share their knowledge with random, non-fee-paying members of the public.

Events disproved these reasonable assumptions, and tended to confirm Trow's view of both an American advantage and the benefits of a private sector. In 2002, MIT (Massachusetts Institute of Technology), a private institution, with the support of two foundations, began to provide lecture courses over the Internet, in video, audio, or written form, completely without charge, or even registration, to anyone who cared to visit their website.[50] Virtually all of MIT's regular faculty came to contribute, and some of their courses were then translated into other languages. Many other American universities, both public and private, subsequently joined in on the same basis, which led to the formation of the OpenCourseWare Consortium in 2005.[51] This consortium has since spread to universities in more than twenty countries. Both public and private universities in Japan and Korea are participants, as are more than two hundred universities in China. In 2007, the consortium offered 6,208 courses, about 15 percent of them in languages other than English, and it was then obtaining around 2 million visits per month for its English-language courses and about half a million for its non-English-language courses.[52] Although there is no reliable cross-national evidence about rates of participation, the OpenCourseWare Consortium seems to be the most innovative and imaginative e-learning initiative or "experiment" to date. Trow's essay on e-learning in chapter 16 is introduced by the consortium's present secretary.[53]

Trow saw the participation of American public universities as an example of their determination to win the trust of communities they serve and as an extension of the original land grant mission of "carrying the university to the people" beyond the borders of their own state, to the entire United States, and then to the entire world—or at least to individuals with access to the Internet. He could also have claimed that it demonstrates the benign competitive dynamics to which he referred, for though it was launched by the private sector, it was quickly taken up by many public institutions in the United States. These benign dynamics have not, however, spread evenly across the world along with the Internet. The largely taxpayer-funded universities of continental Europe have, for the most part, declined to participate. The notable exceptions are Spanish universities (perhaps because Spanish was one of the foreign languages into which courses were first translated) and French technical schools (perhaps eager to rate themselves against MIT). Public universities of the United Kingdom and Australia have been slow to participate. They each have just one participating university, as does North Korea.[54] Most European universities have still to make good on the declaration proclaimed by a convention of the heads of European universities at Lisbon in 2005, that they would make "lifelong learning a reality" and "strengthen the University-Society dialogue through optimum use of digital technology."[55] No doubt they will do so, but it is nonetheless curious that many of them have so far hesitated to participate in this relatively simple and low-cost method of making their courses freely available to the communities that support them.

This rapid review of a number of questions raised in Martin Trow's essays, and some of the evidence that might be used to answer them, has sought to show that they remain very much alive, both as issues of public policy debate (as the chapter introductions often indicate) and as significant research topics, which frequently invite one to extend his arguments beyond the societies he examined. No doubt if we were to do this in a thorough manner, we would have to count more than he did, and to find viable operational indices of some of his variables, such as institutional autonomy, diversity, executive leadership, trust, accountability and the like, which his two-country comparisons seldom obliged him to do. There would, however, be little point in accepting his invitation if we were to separate investigation and discussion from the theme of growth and transformation that guided his analyses or were to overlook the interdependent variables in the private and public lives of universities to which he drew our attention. They provide the context that gives meaning and significance to all his arguments and questions, both to the few I have considered, and to the many others raised in the essays that follow.

In his introduction to chapter 17, John Brennan observes that having set the agenda in higher education research for the past thirty years, Trow "will continue to inform debate and understanding about higher education's place and role in the world for the next thirty." This does not seem an excessively generous or controversial assessment. It might become so, I suppose, if we discover some other, more powerful dynamic moving higher education institutions, or when the transformation to universal access is complete, and we are all comfortably settled in "learning societies" and no longer care how we got there.

NOTES

....

1. Martin A. Trow, *Universities in Highly Educated Society: From Elite to Mass Higher Education*, trans. Ikuo Amano and Kazuyuki Kitamura (Tokyo: Tokyo University Press, 1976); idem, *Universities in Highly Educated Society: From Mass to Universal Higher Education*, trans. and ed. Kazuyuki Kitamura (Tamagawa University Press, 2000); idem, *Selected Essays on Martin Trow's Educational Thinking* (Xiamen, Fujian: Xiamen University Press, Xiamen, 2001). Professor Wanhua Ma of Beijing University is currently translating a further eighteen essays for a volume provisionally entitled *Diversity and Leadership: Martin Trow's Ideas on American Higher Education*.

2. His first annual report as director of the CSHE in 1977–78, reprinted as chapter 11, demonstrates this point since he explicitly rejected the survey research that the center had previously performed.

3. Martin Trow, "Comment on 'Participant Observation and Interviewing: A Comparison,'" *Human Organization* 16, no. 3 (Fall 1957): 33–35.

4. p. 558–59, above.

5. *Higher Education as a Stratification System: The Analysis of Status*, Center for Studies in Higher Education Occasional Paper, 29 (Berkeley: University of California, Berkeley, February 1983), p. 1.

6. Ki-Seok Kim is one scholar who recently accepted his invitation. His recent

analysis of the transformation of higher education in Korea is dedicated "To the Memory of the Late Martin Trow (1926–2007) Emeritus Professor of Public Policy at UC-Berkeley, especially of his seminal work on the transition from elite to mass to universal education." Ki-Seok Kim, "A Great Leap Forward to Excellence in Research at Seoul National University, 1994–2006," *Asia Pacific Education Review* 8, no. 1 (2007): 1–11; idem, "Isn't It a Pyrrhic Victory? A Historical Sociology of Tertiary Education for All in Korea," *Asia Pacific Education Review* (January 2009).

7. Some of these quotes are drawn from pp. 4, 30 of "American Higher Education: Past, Present, and Future," *Studies in Higher Education* 14, no. 1 (1988).

8. "American Higher Education: 'Exceptional' or Just Different?" in *Is America Different? A New Look at American Exceptionalism*, ed. Byron E. Shafer (Oxford: Clarendon Press, 1991), pp. 138–86.

9. Jennifer Washburn, *University Inc.: The Corporate Corruption of American Higher Education* (New York: Basic Books, 2005), pp. 3–23. His view on this issue was probably similar to that of the chancellor of UC Berkeley, quoted in Chapter 16, p. 548, n. 6.

10. There can be little doubt that his vehement opposition to the categorizing of applicants by their race, which is what affirmative action entails, was strongly reinforced by his Jewish parentage and faith. In no less than three of his unpublished papers on the same subject, he finds reason to mention the Nuremburg laws.

11. Robert M. May, "The Scientific Wealth of Nations," *Science* 275 (February 7, 1997). The eleven other prizes were all post–World War II, so Germany's pre-eminence was measured by Nobel prizes alone.

12. www.nobelprize.org.

13. The Times Higher Education *World University Rankings 2007: The Top 200 World Universities*, June 25, 2008, http://www.timeshighereducation.co.uk.

14. The United States has, for example, maintained a massive surplus in the balance of trade in intellectual goods since the OECD began to collect to cross-national data in 1983. It is virtually alone in this respect. OECD Dataset *Main Science and Technology Indicators*, OECD Stat. Beta version 2000–2006.

15. Chapter 16, pp. 531, 548, n. 27.

16. "Binary Dilemmas: An American View," *Higher Education Review* 1, no. 3 (Summer 1969): 27–43.

17. A similar, though more widespread, fear is observable in current debates in Britain that private funding might introduce class differences into the National Health Service.

18. "The Robbins Trap: British Attitudes and the Limits of Expansion," *Higher Education Quarterly* 43, no. 1 (Winter 1989): 55–75.

19. Which may have been just as well. In their careful reanalysis of earlier mobility data from nine societies, Müller et al. found that societies with "a lower degree

of credentialism," England being their foremost example, "also show signs of a lower degree of class inequalities of educational opportunities." There is a real possibility, therefore, that as England moved away from practice-based, practitioner-controlled training to school-based qualifications and "widened" educational opportunities, class inequalities in education will *increase*. Walter Müller et al., "Class and Education in Industrial Nations," in *Class Structure in Europe: New Findings from East-West Comparisons of Social Structure and Mobility,* ed. Max Haller (Armonk, N.Y.: Sharpe, 1990), pp. 61–89.

20. "Uncertainties in Britain's Transition From Elite to Mass Higher Education," in *Research and Higher Education: The UK and USA Scene,* ed. T. G. Whiston and R. Geiger (Maidenhead: The Open University Press, 1991).

21. "The Dearing Report: A Transatlantic View," *Higher Education Quarterly* 52, no. 1 (January 1998): 93–117.

22. The Quality Agency for Higher Education exists, though not performing quite the functions Dearing anticipated. www.qaa.ac.uk. The Institute for Teaching & Learning in Higher Education was merged into the Higher Education Academy, a state-funded but representative body, which aims "to help institutions, discipline groups and staff to provide the best possible learning experience for their students." www.heacademy.ac.uk. In 2004, they were joined by an Office for Fair Access requiring universities charging fees over the standard rate to submit an "access agreement" to ensure equality of access to those universities. www.offa.org.uk. Yet another representative but state-funded agency, the Leadership Foundation for Higher Education, provides "advice and guidance" on academic governance and management. www.lfhe.ac.uk.

23. Maybe they are doing so. In 2005, 7.8 percent of the U.K. population age 40 and over were enrolled full- or part-time in a tertiary educational institution, the highest proportion of this age group in the OECD. http://nces.ed.gov/programs/coe/2007/section.

24. The Carnegie Foundation Poll, *The International Academic Profession: Portraits of Fourteen Countries, 1991–1993* (New York: Carnegie Foundation, 1993).

25. Tom Sastry and Bahram Bekhradnia, *The Academic Experience of Students in English Universities* (Oxford: Higher Education Policy Institute, September 2007), para. 43, table 25.

26. His only attempt to demonstrate this point seems to be his brief comparison of the "two most distinguished public universities" in the United States, Michigan and California, with other less distinguished ones. Both Michigan and California, he pointed out, "can call on state constitutional provisions protecting their autonomy," and both depend on their state governments for only a minority part of their operating expenses (close to 20 percent in Michigan and 30 percent in California) whereas other state institutions often "suffer constant state interference in their

management and policies, interference facilitated by line-item budgeting, close state control over expenditures and limited discretionary funds." See chapter 4, p. 179.

27. *OECD Factbook 2008 Economic Environmental and Social Statistics* (Paris, 2008), http://ocde.p4.siteinternet.com; *Education at a Glance* (OECD, 2007), p. 289.

28. The educational attainments of the adult population of thirty-six countries in 2005 are given in *Education at a Glance* (OECD, 2007), Table A1.3a, p. 38.

29. *OECD Factbook, 2007*, p. 205.

30. *Education at a Glance* (OECD, 2007), p. 187.

31. He was moving in this direction. See chapter 16, p. 531.

32. Only Switzerland approaches it in total expenditure per student, though once R&D expenditures are separated, it too falls a long way behind.

33. For his extended comparison of the sequence of growth in the United States and the United Kingdom, see "American Higher Education Exceptional or Just Different?" pp. 21–43.

34. It is not alone in this respect. There is little age variation in university attendance in Russia, and some other ex-socialist countries like the Czech and Slovak Republics and Hungary—and we might also include Germany in this group, since it now contains a former socialist society. Germany is in fact quite exceptional, and deserves investigation in its own right. It is the only country where the older generations are *more* likely to have experienced tertiary education than the younger.

35. Chapter 16, p. 531, pp. 551–52 n. 26.

36. In 2000, Canada spent 2.3 percent of its GNP on tertiary education. *Education at a Glance*, OECD *indicators* (OECD, 2005), p. 205. No later figures are available.

37. He was not alone in doing so. Among many others, the present president of the University of California, when still president of the University of Minnesota, contributed to the debate. See Mark Yudoff, "Is the Public Research University Dead?" *The Chronicle of Higher Education* (January 11, 2002).

38. *Times Higher Education.*

39. The six societies most dependent on public funds have 22 universities in the *Times Higher Education* top 200 of 2007, while those most dependent on private funds have 116. However, apart from Germany, the former societies have small populations. Holding population constant, the differences are not great. The "more public dependent" have one university in this ranking of the world's best universities per 5.45 million population, and the "more private" one per 4.88 million. Their mean peer review scores are 64.6 percent and 75.6 percent, respectively, and their mean citation ratings are 69.6 percent and 76.6 percent. *Times Higher Education.* The calculations are mine.

40. There is an English outline of this legislation on the MEXT (Ministry of

Education, Culture and Sports, Science and Technology) website, www.mext.go.jp/english/news/2003.

41. The figures are from OECD reports cited. For an insightful global survey of private higher education, see Daniel C. Levy, "The Enlarged Expanse of Private Higher Education," *Die Hochschule. Journal für Wissenschaft und Bildung* 2 (2008): 19–35.

42. Michael Shattock, "The Change from Private to Public Governance of British Higher Education: Its Consequences for Higher Education Policy Making, 1980–2006," *Higher Education Quarterly* 62, no. 3 (July 2008): 181–203. Shattock concluded that "in moving from being self governed to state governed the policy drivers for higher education are no longer those of the system itself but are derived from a set of policies designed for the reform and modernisation of the public sector of the economy."

43. The European Commission has already conducted such an inquiry, though the results are questionable since each country self-reports against their own standards, and they may be inclined to flatter themselves. *The Extent and Impact of Higher Education Governance Reform across Europe: Final Report to the Directorate-General for Education and Culture of the European Commission* (Brussels: EU, 2006).

44. "Trust, Markets and Accountability in Higher Education: A Comparative Perspective," *Higher Education Policy* 9, no. 4 (1996): 309–24.

45. His evidence for these remarks was an investigation he conducted with Patricia Graham and Richard Lyman, published as *Accountability of Colleges and Universities* (New York: Columbia University, October 1995). It is further described in "On the Accountability of Higher Education in the United States," in *Universities and their Leadership,* ed. William G. Bowen and Harold K. Shapiro (Princeton: Princeton University Press, 1998), pp. 15–63.

46. "Thoughts on the White Paper of 1991," *Higher Education Quarterly* 46, no. 3 (Summer 1992): 213–26.

47. "Trust, Markets and Accountability." In his discussions of this policy, he frequently had in mind UC Berkeley's opposite response to the perceived failure of its biology departments in the late 1970s. Far from their failure being punished, they received massive additional funding and support, which enabled them raise their performance. This is the subject of his case study reprinted as chapter 12.

48. Though his focus was on their use in secondary schools, not colleges. "The New Media in the Evolution of American Education," in *The New Media and Education,* ed. Peter H. Rossi and Bruce J. Biddle (Chicago: Aldine, 1966), pp. 324–68.

49. "Notes on the Development of Informational Technology in Higher Education," in *Science, Technology and Society: University Leadership Today and for the*

Twenty-First Century, ed. Ingmar Grenthe et al. (Stockholm Papers in Library and Information Science, 1998), pp. 41–68; "Lifelong Learning through the New Information Technologies," in *Lifelong Learning Policy and Research,* ed. A. Tuijnman and T. Schuller (London: Portland, 1999), pp. 1297–1312.

50. ocw.mit.edu.

51. ocwconsortium.org.

52. Ibid. Member universities are committed to putting at least ten of their own courses online.

53. I. Elaine Allen and Jeff Seaman, *Online Nation: Five Years of Growth in Online Learning,* Sloan Consortium, 2007. www.sloan-c.org/publications. It did not eliminate successful private fee-paying institutions that also offer credits and credentials. Figures from a survey in 2007 found some 3.5 million students in the United States (that is, 20 percent of all those enrolled in higher education) were taking at least one course online in 2006. However, since these data were collected from institutions, it does not include the participation rates of any non-affiliated students. And they are not cross-national figures, so they do not allow us to say how far the United States is exceptional.

54. Though as I write Oxford and Cambridge joined the Open University and put some of their lectures on iTunes. *Daily Telegraph,* October 6, 2008. www.telegraph.co.uk.

55. www.eua.be. At many points, one might add, this declaration seems heavily indebted to Trow's work.

PART I

Emergence of
an Enduring Theme

1

I THINK THE RECORD OF MARTIN TROW'S WORK on higher education really should start here, in what I suspect may now be a largely forgotten article. I believe it represents the first time he laid out the elite-mass-universal distinction and began to unpack its implications for the "public" and "private" lives of educational institutions—though here, as so often in his work, these two categories are not just analytically linked but turn out to be themselves multidimensional.

The article, for those who don't know or recall it, takes off from "the past few years . . . [of] . . . a very large amount of public controversy over education in America," especially that "focus[ed] . . . on the public high school." It begins by using a basic range of statistics on school and college attendance and graduation rates, combined with labor force information, to put forward a three-phase analysis, in which the public high school first appeared as a minority (sc. elite) institution, then was "transformed" to a mass institution around 1910, and then "transformed" again during or just after World War II—the latter being accompanied by the "transformation" of higher education from elite to mass. Characteristically and satisfyingly, the transformations are demonstrated graphically as breaks in the trend lines. Remarkable as it may now seem, I suspect that no one else until then had actually documented these trends in this way.

I remember that in those days he was sometimes labeled a "technical-functionalist," and he certainly makes a strong link between education and economy-as-occupational-structure. However, there is already a nice mixture of economic "pull" (my term, not his) and social "push," with speculation on what makes the United States exceptional: "the role of public education in American thought and sentiment, and its perceived connection both with the national welfare and individual achievement." This dual approach, I think, was always very much part of his analytic toolbox.

But equally characteristic—and also, I believe, making its first appearance—was the way in which he unpacked the idea of "transformation" and the "dilemmas" that ensued as a consequence, the approach that he extended in the long series of theoretical and applied elite-mass-universal analyses of higher education that were to follow. Here it's applied to secondary education: there's a crisp account of the newfound applicability of Deweyan/progressive ideas to the middle, interwar mass phase (partly because of the occupational pull but mainly the push from the new clientele), and then the heart of the piece: the attribution of current "controversies" to the dilemmas caused by the "second transformation" into the third phase of secondary education, going hand in hand with the rise of mass higher education. The main dilemma is academic versus vocational, of course, but this is simultaneously reframed as preparatory versus terminal. And as with all of Trow's best analyses, it is multidimensional: the transition point has consequences for the curriculum and teaching methods, but also (and quite strongly emphasized here) for the recruitment, preparation, and careers/retention of school teachers; for the "changing public" (parents and their aspirations); and for students themselves. The possibilities and problems of diversity—and deliberate diversification—rear their heads at the end, which is probably the only part to have a dated feel in its specifics. But the issues haven't much changed.

Some of his lines bring his voice back to me with amazing clarity and remind me that his asides (as some of these are) were so often worth more than other people's big themes.

> The hopes of the earlier decade have become the expectations of today, and will probably be the enrollments of tomorrow.

> It is almost always easier to create new institutions to perform a new function than it is to transform existing institutions to meet new functions.

> . . . accounting for why the critics and defenders of the schools largely talk past one another.

Educators [i.e., teachers and those who train them and design the curriculum] paradoxically find that their professional expertise and judgment is increasingly challenged even while their professional standards and organizations are strengthened and as the body of knowledge on which their professional status rests is steadily enlarged . . . inevitably creat[ing] bewilderment and resentment . . . [despite] wistful and wholly misleading parallels with the enviable autonomy of doctors and lawyers.

— OLIVER FULTON

The Second Transformation of American Secondary Education

The past few years have seen a very large amount of public controversy over education in America. The controversy has touched on every aspect and level of education, from nursery school to graduate education, and the spokesmen have represented many different interests and points of view. But the focus of the controversy has been the public high school, its organization and curriculum, and the philosophy of education that governs it. On one side, with many individual exceptions and variations in views, stand the professional educators and their organizations. As the creators and administrators of the existing system, American educators not surprisingly by and large defend it, and while accepting and even initiating specific reforms, tend to justify existing practices, institutional arrangements, and dominant philosophies of education. On the other side, a more heterogeneous body of laymen, college and university professors, politicians and military men have attacked fundamental aspects of secondary education in America. The disputes

Originally published as Martin Trow, "The Second Transformation of American Secondary Education," *International Journal of Comparative Sociology* 2, no. 2 (1961): 144–66. Reprinted by permission of Koninklijke Brill N.V.

extend over a broad range of educational issues, but at the heart of the argument is the charge by the critics that the *quality* of American secondary education is poor, that the time and energies of teachers and students are scattered and dispersed over a great variety of activities and subjects, and that there ought to be far greater emphasis on intellectual training, academic subject matter, and the acquisition of traditional skills and knowledge.[1] Very often, the call for reform is coupled with attacks on the polices and philosophies of professional educators; the critics claim that a watered-down progressive education, doctrines of "life adjustment," the "child-centered school," and the "education of the whole person" have provided the rationale for an indifference to the acquisition of knowledge and the development of clarity of thought and expression that students gain when held to high standards of achievement in coursework centering on the traditional "solid" subject matters of English, history, mathematics, and the natural sciences.

The public debate has largely restricted itself to issues internal to education, to the curriculum, to teacher training and certification, and the like. But the forces that most heavily affect developments within education largely lie outside it, and are often not reflected in the debates about it. It may be useful to consider some of the historical forces that gave rise to the current controversies over secondary education.

The Transformation of America

The Civil War is the great watershed of American history. It stands midway between the Revolution and ourselves, and symbolically, but not just symbolically, separates the agrarian society of small farmers and small businessmen of the first half of the nineteenth century from the urbanized industrial society with its salaried employees that followed. And the mass public secondary school system as we know it has its roots in the transformation of the economy and society that took place after the Civil War.

In 1820, at least seven out of every ten Americans in the labor force were farmers or farm laborers. In 1870, farmers still comprised about half the labor force. By 1960, that figure was below 10 percent. At the same time, the proportion of salaried white-collar workers rose from less than

10 percent in 1870 to nearly 40 percent today.[2] The proportion of non-farm manual workers in the labor force rose until 1920, leveled off at about 40 percent since then, and has shown signs of falling over the past decade. Thus, there has been a large and rapid growth of a new salaried middle class, paralleled by a large and rapid decline in the proportion of the labor force in agriculture, with the proportions of manual workers rising until about 1920 but relatively constant over the past forty years.

These changes in the occupational structure have reflected tremendous changes in the economy and organization of work. Since the Civil War, and especially in the past fifty years, an economy based on thousands of small farms and businesses has been transformed into one based on large bureaucratized organizations characterized by centralized decision making and administration carried out through coordinated managerial and clerical staffs.

When small organizations grow large, papers replace verbal orders, papers replace rule of thumb calculations of price and profit, papers carry records of work flow and inventory that in a small operation can be seen at a glance on the shop floor and materials shed. And as organizations grew, people had to be trained to handle those papers—to prepare them, to type them, to file them, to process them, to assess and use them. The growth of the secondary school system after 1870 was in large part a response to the pull of the economy for a mass of white-collar employees with more than an elementary school education.

The First Transformation of American Secondary Education

In 1870, there were roughly 80,000 students enrolled in high schools of all kinds in this country, and the bulk of these were in tuition academies. Public high schools were just beginning to grow in numbers—there were perhaps no more than 500 in the whole country, concentrated in the Northeast, and still greatly outnumbered by the tuition academies.[3] The 16,000 high school graduates in that year comprised only about 2 percent of the 17-year-olds in the country.[4] Moreover, a very large proportion of those who went to secondary school went on to college.[5]

The American secondary school system of 1870 offered a classical liberal education to a small number of middle- and upper-middle-class boys.[6] Very few students went to secondary school, most who went graduated, and many who graduated went on to college. By 1910, there were more than 1,100,000 high school students, nearly 90 percent of them enrolled in the more than 10,000 public high schools, and they comprised about 15 percent of the 14–17 year age group.[7] But for the bulk of these students, high school was as far as they were going. By 1957, 90 percent of the 14–17 year age group were in school, while 62 percent of the 17-year-old cohort were gaining high school diplomas. Before 1870, the small secondary school system offered a curriculum and maintained standards of scholarship geared to the admissions requirements of the colleges.[8] After 1870, the growing mass secondary system was largely terminal, providing a useful and increasingly vocational education for the new body of white-collar workers.

The evidence for the connection between education and occupation that developed after the Civil War is embedded in the census reports. In 1950, at the end of the fifty-year period that might be called "the age of the terminal high school" the median years of schooling completed by men and women 25 years and older in various occupational groups were as follows:[9]

professionals	16+
managers, officials, and proprietors	11.3
clerical and kindred	11.4
sales workers	11.2
craftsmen, foremen, and kindred	8.3
operatives and kindred	7.7
laborers, except mine and farm	7.0
service workers	7.8

Of course, changes in the occupational structure do not provide the whole explanation of the extraordinary growth of secondary and higher education in the United States. The changes in the occupational structure have raised the educational aspirations of large parts of the American population, and the educational system has been responsive to these higher aspirations. The role of public education in American thought and popular sentiment, and its perceived connection with the national welfare and individual achievement, have, at least until recently, been greater in America than in any other country. Other countries, Great Britain to name one, have had comparable revolutions in their economic structure without comparable educational transformation. The commitment of America to equality of opportunity, the immense importance attached to education throughout American history, the very great role of education as an avenue of mobility in a society where status ascribed at birth is felt to be an illegitimate barrier to advancement—all of these historical and social psychological forces are involved in the extraordinary American commitment to mass secondary and higher education. Moreover, there were forces involved in the growth of the high school—such as large-scale immigration and urbanization, and the movement to abolish child labor[10]—which are not present in the growth of mass higher education, whereas transformations of the occupational structure are common to both educational movements.

Now, the creation of a system of mass secondary education that accompanied the growth of mass organizations after 1870 could not be simply the extension of the old elite secondary system; it would be different in function (terminal rather than preparatory) and in organization (public locally controlled rather than private tuition and endowed schools). Moreover, it needed its own curriculum and its own teacher-training programs and institutions. It needed its own teacher-training programs first because the sheer number of secondary teachers required by mass secondary education was far beyond the capacities of the traditional colleges to supply, as they had supplied the older tuition academies.[11] In the old academies, the principals and masters were products of the colleges, and often went on to teach in the colleges; there was no sharp break between the academies and the colleges since they taught roughly the same subjects to the same kinds of students.[12] This was no longer possible with the new terminal public high school; the students were different, the curriculum was not preparation for college, by and large, and new departments of education and state teachers colleges were created at least in part to train the staffs of these new high schools.[13] These centers of professional education were not identified with the older, elite traditions of higher education, but created their own traditions of education for life, for citizenship, for useful tasks, the traditions, that is, of the mass democratic terminal secondary system that came to full flower between 1910 and 1940.[14]

By 1935, an observer sympathetic to these developments could write:

> The twentieth century so far has witnessed a steady shifting of . . . control [over secondary education] by college presidents and faculties to people more immediately concerned with the operation or professional study of secondary education . . . Not only are national committees dealing with the general aspects of secondary education becoming exclusively manned by secondary school leaders and specialists, but the whole process of curriculum making for high schools within states and within local school systems is rapidly becoming assumed by these professional categories. High school courses of study are less and less often handed down by college authorities even in the old academic fields. Secondary textbooks are more and more written by public school superintendents, high school principals, supervisors, teachers, and students of educational methods.
>
> A further evidence of this general trend is the continuing introduction of new subjects and courses. Whereas in the past most new subjects appeared in the secondary school as reflections of the growing differentiation of the academic disciplines, most of the new subjects now appearing represent hitherto neglected aspects of social existence. As illustrations may be cited innumerable vocational courses, health courses, citizenship courses, and character courses.[15]

In the fifty years between 1880 and 1930, the numbers of students in public high schools in the United States roughly doubled every decade, rising from 110,000 to nearly four and a half million. And the new secondary education was shaped both by the enormous increase in numbers of students and by their social characteristics. Many of the new students were in school unwillingly, in obedience to the new or more stringent state compulsory education laws; many came from poor, culturally impoverished homes and had modest vocational goals; many of these were the sons and daughters of recent immigrants, and seemed to observers very much in need of "Americanization."[16] These new students posed new problems for secondary education, and these problems, and the answers that they engendered, transformed public secondary education, its philosophy and its curriculum. Commenting on the influential National Education Association Report of 1918 entitled *Cardinal Principles of Secondary Education*, a report strongly influenced by the writings of John Dewey, and responsive to the new demands of mass secondary education, James Conant observes:

> Confronted with a "heterogeneous high school population destined to enter all sorts of occupations," high school teachers and administrators and professors of education needed some justification for a complete overhauling of a high school curriculum originally designed for a homogeneous student body. The progressives with their emphasis on the child, "on learning by doing," on democracy and citizenship, and with their attack on the arguments used to support a classical curriculum were bringing up just the sort of *new* ideas that were sorely needed. After closing John Dewey's volume, *Democracy and Education*, I had the feeling that, like the Austro-Hungarian Empire of the nineteenth century, if John Dewey hadn't existed he would have had to be invented. In a sense perhaps he was, or at least his doctrines were shaped by school people with whom he talked and worked.[17]

The creation of a mass terminal system, with functions and orientations quite different from that of the traditional college preparatory system it succeeded, forced not merely certain changes in the curriculum, but a drastic shift in the basic assumptions underlying secondary education. Speaking of the writings of G. Stanley Hall in support of the "child-centers school," Lawrence Cremin notes that they

> paved the way for a fundamental shift in the meaning of equal opportunity at the secondary level. Formerly, when the content and purpose of the secondary school had been fairly well defined, equal opportunity meant the right of all who might profit from secondary education as so defined to enjoy its benefits. Now, the "given" of the equation was no longer the school with its content and purposes, but the children with their background and needs. Equal opportunity now meant simply the right of all who came to be offered something of value, and it was the school's obligation to offer it. The magnitude of this shift cannot be overestimated; it was truly Copernican

in character. And tied as it was to the fortunes of the child-study movement, it gained vast popularity during the first decade of the twentieth century.[18]

The popularity of these new ideas and assumptions, and their impact on secondary education in the succeeding decades, suggests how educational doctrines are influenced by social trends.[19] With schools full of children for whom the traditional content and purpose of the secondary school curriculum were irrelevant, educators needed some rationale and justification for what they were doing. And what they were doing was trying to teach something that promised to be of some use for these terminal students, in ways that would hold, at least fleetingly, the interest of indifferent students whose basic interests lay outside the classroom. It was precisely the interest and motivation that one could no longer assume in the student, but had to engender in the school, that lay at the heart of W. H. Kilpatrick's influential *The Project Method*,[20] and before that, underlay the importance of motivation in Dewey's writings.

The Growth of Mass Higher Education in America

During the decades when the institutions, the curriculum, and the philosophies of mass terminal education were being created, the college population was rising very slowly.[21] As recently as 1940, the total number of students enrolled in college comprised only 15 percent of the college age group (the 18- to 21-year-olds). By 1954, that proportion was up to 30 percent, and by 1960 it was around 37.5 percent. Over both the longer 20-year period between 1940 and 1960 and the recent 6-year period, 1954–60, the rate of increase in college enrollments as a proportion of the college age group has been about 1.3 percent a year. If that rate of increase is maintained, and that is a conservative forecast, then by 1970 college enrollments will comprise about half of the college age group.[22] The rapid rate of increase since 1940 is in marked contrast with the average rate of increase of only 0.35 percent per annum between 1920, when college enrollments comprised 8 percent of the college age group, and 1940, when that figure had risen to 15 percent.

Figure 1.1 shows the phases in the parallel development of American

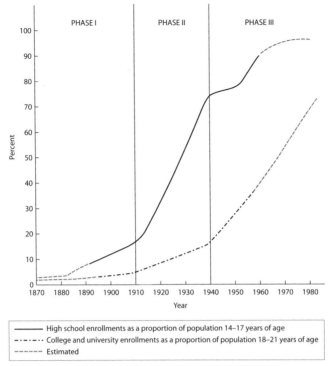

PHASE I   PHASE II   PHASE III

FIGURE 1.1. Enrollment rates in secondary higher education, United States, 1870–1980.

Sources: Progress of Public Education in the United States, 1959–1960; Historical Statistics; Fact Book; Bogue, *The Population of the United States.*

Note: These curves are based on the figures at ten-year intervals, and do not show the enrollment rates during World War II and the Korean War.

secondary and higher education graphically. If we take, somewhat arbitrarily, an enrollment of 15 percent of the age grade as the beginning of the mass phase of an educational system, then secondary education passed this line around 1910, and higher education in 1940. The period 1870–80 with which we are dealing falls naturally then into three phases. In Phase I secondary and higher education were by and large offering an academic education to an elite minority. Phase II, between roughly 1910 and 1940, saw the rapid growth of mass terminal education, with higher education still offered to a small but slowly growing minority.[23] Since 1940, or more precisely, since World War II, we are (in Phase III) seeing the rapid growth of mass higher education. With enrollments in higher education continuing to grow, and with secondary school enrollments (as a proportion of the 14–17-year-old population) near saturation, the transformation of the terminal secondary system into a mass preparatory system is well under way.

It is interesting to compare rates of increase in college attendance during the first two decades of Phase III with the rate of increase in high school enrollments during the decades 1909–39 (Phase II), the years of growth of the mass secondary system. In the last twenty years of Phase I, 1889–1909, the high school population (as a proportion of the 14–17-year-olds) rose from 6.7 percent to 15.4 percent, an annual rate of increase of about 0.44 percent. Over the next three decades (Phase II), the rate increased from 15.4 percent to 73.3 percent, an annual rate of increase of about 1.9 percent. While this is somewhat higher than the rate of increase of about 1.3 percent annually in college attendance (as a proportion of the 18–21-year-olds) thus far in Phase III, there is in both cases a marked increase in the rate of growth over the previous period. In the case of both secondary and higher education, the rate of increase has been about four times as great in the period of rapid growth as compared with the immediately preceding periods of slow growth. In both cases we see the rapid transformation of an education for a relatively small elite into a system of mass education. This process is about completed for the secondary education (in 1958, the high school population comprised nearly 90 percent of the high school age group), while we are in the middle of the expansion of opportunities for higher education. And as with secondary education, there is no reason to believe that the United States will stop short of providing opportunities and facilities for nearly universal experience of some kind in higher education.

The immediate force behind these trends in both secondary and higher education are changes in public sentiment—in people's ideas of what they want and expect for their children in the way of formal education. Whereas most Americans have come to see a high school education as the ordinary, expected thing for their children, they are now coming to think of at least some time in college in the same way.[24] Behind these changes in sentiment are other social forces, not least among which is another change in our occupational structure, parallel to the massive growth in the white-collar population that underlay the growth of the public secondary school system. The current change is the immense growth of demand for more highly trained and educated people of all kinds. Between 1940 and 1950, the number of engineers in the country doubled, the number of research workers increased by 50 percent. Even more striking, between 1950 and 1960, the total labor force increased by only 8 percent, but the number of professional, technical, and kindred workers grew by 68 percent[25]—and these, of course, are the occupations that call for at least some part of a college education. Moreover, it is estimated that the period 1957–70 will see an increase of a further 60 percent in this category of highly educated workers.[26] Whereas in the decades 1900–1930, clerical and kindred workers were the fastest-growing occupational classification and by far, in the period 1950–70 it has been and will be the professional and technical occupations.[27]

The Second Transformation of American Secondary Education

There are two major points to be made in summary here. First, much the same forces that made for the development of the mass secondary system in this country are now at work creating a system of mass higher education. And second, this development is rapidly changing the function of the secondary system. Secondary education in the United States began as an elite preparatory system, during its great years of growth it became a mass terminal system, and it is now having to make a second painful transition on its way to becoming a mass preparatory system. But this transition is a good deal more difficult than the first, because while the first involved the *creation* of the necessary institutions, the second is requiring the *transformation* of a huge existing institutional complex. It is almost always easier to create new institutions to perform a new function than it is to transform existing institutions to meet new functions. And as a further complication, during these long decades of transition, the secondary schools are going to have to continue to perform the old terminal education functions for very large if decreasing proportions of students who are not equipped, motivated, or oriented toward college. In the earlier transition, the old college preparatory schools continued to exist and to perform their preparatory functions, with much the same curriculum and kinds of personnel, thus permitting a rough division of function between the older and the newer schools. And where this was not possible, the number of preparatory students was shortly so small as compared with the terminal students that the schools did not have quite the same sense of equal but conflicting functions that secondary people are now coming to feel.[28]

By contrast, now and for the foreseeable future, both the preparatory and terminal functions will have to be performed by the same institutions and the same personnel. Of course, that has always been true to some extent—there have always been college-oriented students in our high schools, and provisions have been made for them. But by and large, they have been a minority in an institution created for the great mass of terminal students. The dominant philosophies and structure of the high school could be determined by its central function of providing a terminal secondary education for the mass of American youth. As preparatory students become an increasingly large proportion of all high school youth, and in more and more places a majority, they provide by their existence not just a demand for special provision, but a challenge to the basic structure and philosophy of the school. And this is the challenge that underlies the criticism of secondary education that flows from many sources.

The rough equality of the terminal and preparatory functions today may account for why the critics and the defenders of the schools largely talk past one another. The critics, who are often university professors, say, in effect, "We need not merely better provision for the preparatory student, but rather, a different guiding educational philosophy for a preparatory secondary system."[29] And the defenders, who are often professional educators, since it is they who created the educational system now under attack, reply, "We cannot ignore the needs and requirements of the great numbers of students who are not going on to college."[30] And when the numbers going on and the numbers not going on are approximately equal, as they are now in many places, neither side can point to numbers as simple justification for its argument.

The High School and Its Changing Public

In the coming decades the high schools will be dealing not only with a different kind of student, but also with a different kind of parent. During the formative years of the mass terminal secondary system in the United States, the teachers and educators who were building the system were dealing by and large with parents who themselves had gone no further than grade school. These people, many of them immigrants or of rural origins, whose children were going no further than high school, had neither the competence nor the motivation to be greatly concerned with the high school curriculum. And the debates about secondary education were carried on largely over the heads of these parents, among the professionals themselves, and between the educators and sections of the academic community. But increasingly, secondary school people are dealing with educated parents of preparatory students, who possess both the competence and the direct motivation to be concerned with the character of their children's secondary education. As recently as 1940, three American adults in five had never been to high school, and only one in four had completed high school.[31] By 1960 three in five had been to high school, and over 40 percent were high school graduates.[32] By 1970 over 50 percent will be high school graduates, and by 1980 it is estimated that figure will reach 60 percent.[33] Parents who themselves have been through high school, and many of them through some years of college as well, feel themselves more competent to pass judgment on the secondary education of their children, and are less likely to accept passively and on faith the professional recommendations of school administrators, educators, and counselors. It is this rapidly growing group of educated parents whose children are going on to college that provides both the audience and the support for the "academic" critics of the secondary school and its curriculum. There is every reason to believe that their interest will grow as their numbers increase, and as competition among their children for the better college places becomes sharper.

This development places a strain on the professional autonomy of educators, who paradoxically find that their professional expertise and judgment is increasingly challenged even while their professional standards and organizations are strengthened, and as the body of knowledge and theory on which their professional status rests is steadily enlarged. This paradox inevitably creates bewilderment and resentment among the professional educators. But it may be that as educators recognize that the very success of their efforts to extend educational opportunities through high school and beyond creates a large body of parents who take a detailed and active interest in the education of their children, they may find some solace in what is probably a permanent condition of external scrutiny and criticism. Moreover, wistful and wholly misleading parallels with the enviable autonomy of doctors and lawyers only sharpen their bewilderment and resentment; they will neither reduce the volume of lay criticism nor account for its existence.[34] Professional educators in America will have to resign themselves to the fact that mass public education, especially at the secondary level, involves conflicts of values and interests that are independent of professional skills and knowledge, and which are increasingly less likely to be left solely to professional decision. And foremost among these is the relative weight and importance placed in each school and district on college preparation as over against a terminal "education for life."

Teachers for Mass Preparatory Secondary Education

The difficulties of strengthening secondary education for college preparatory students in public high schools are complicated by what is clearly a pattern of negative selection to teaching below the college level. And this pattern is especially marked for the recruitment of men, who comprise about half of all high school teachers.[35] Moreover, a recent nationwide study of beginning teachers conducted by the U.S. Office of Education shows that 70 percent of the men and more than 80 percent of the women did not expect to continue teaching until retirement.[36] The bulk of the women said, as might be expected, that they hoped to leave teaching for homemaking. More significant for the college preparatory programs in high schools, more than half of the men in the sample expected to leave teaching for some other job in education, chiefly administration, while fully 20 percent were already planning to leave education entirely. And the evidence suggests that the men who remain in the classroom are by and large less able than those who move on to administration or out of educational altogether.[37]

The much lower incomes of teachers, as compared with school administrators, with men who leave education, and with most other occupations requiring a comparable amount of education, account for much of this unfortunate pattern of recruitment and retention of male teacher.[38]

Moreover, the relatively low status of teaching below the college level, which is both a cause and a consequence of the low salaries, also helps to explain why teaching attracts and holds too few of the most able men.[39] And while teachers' salaries are rising, it is unlikely that the gross differentials in pay and prestige between high school teaching and other occupations requiring a college education are likely to be significantly narrowed in the near future. On the contrary, there is reason to fear they may be widened. The continued extension of opportunities for higher education to able students—through public and private scholarships, the expansion of public higher education, and the like—is offering to able young college men a wider range of occupational alternatives, many of which carry greater prestige and higher incomes than does secondary teaching. In the past a career in teaching was often the only intellectual occupation (aside from the ministry) open to serious young boys from farms and small towns, and the local normal schools or state teachers colleges were often the only educational avenues of mobility open to such boys. There are proportionately fewer boys from farms and small towns today, and wider opportunities for them, as for the great mass of urban youth, in higher education. This, together with the continued growth of the "intellectual occupations" is almost certain to make the competition for able men sharper in the years to come. Our society's demands for scientists, engineers, technically trained people of all kinds appears insatiable, and the rewards for work in these fields are usually considerably more generous than for high school teaching. Of even greater importance, the very rapid expansion of higher education currently under way in this country, and the enormous demands for college teachers that it creates, constitutes perhaps the strongest set of competitive opportunities open to young men who want to teach.[40]

Substantial increases in pay for public school teachers may ameliorate, but are not likely to reverse, the pattern of recruitment of academically less able men to high school teaching.[41] And men comprise roughly half the population of American high school teachers.[42] Thus, no matter how teacher education, secondary school curricula, and school organization are reformed to strengthen the college preparatory function of high schools, a substantial part of the actual teaching itself will be carried on by relatively poorly paid, low-status, and often academically less able people. These things may not have mattered so much when secondary education was largely terminal; at least it can be argued that qualities other than academic ability—for example, a deep interest in young people and skills in working with them—are more important for teachers of students whose interests are not academic or intellectual. But that can hardly be claimed for teachers of college-bound youngsters, whose success in college will rest very heavily on the knowledge and intellectual habits they acquire in secondary school.

Pressures for Reform of the Curriculum

The character and quality of high school teachers are especially important in view of the recent efforts to strengthen the preparatory aspects of the high school curriculum, which are predicated on the existence of large numbers of teachers in the schools able to put the new curriculum into effect. The pressures for reform of the curriculum have been strongest in the areas of science and mathematics. The enormous expansion during and since World War II of scientific research and development, in both government and industry, has created a continuing demand for large numbers of highly trained technicians, and at the same time has generated very strong pressures for the reform of what was a manifestly inadequate curriculum in high school science and mathematics. And this in turn has revolved many more academic scientists in efforts to reform the secondary school curriculum.[43] Largely on the initiative of the university scientists, a number of studies and programs have been initiated expressly to develop new secondary school courses in the sciences and mathematics, and to prepare textbooks and other materials for use in them. The first of these was the Physical Science Study Committee, begun at the Massachusetts Institute of Technology in 1956, followed closely by the School Mathematics Study Group (1958), the Biological Sciences Curriculum Study (1958), the Chemical Education Material Study (1959), and many others. There are movements afoot to extend these programs and studies aiming at the reform of the secondary school curriculum to the social studies and the humanities. Moreover, the Advanced Placement Program has introduced college-level work directly into the high school by allowing students who have taken college-level work in high school and who pass standard achievement tests in those fields to be admitted to a

large number of colleges with advanced standing. This program is growing rapidly, as more and more able students, most with graduate and professional schools in mind, try for advanced placement to improve their
chances for admission to the better colleges and also as a way of saving
time in the early stages of a lengthy higher education.[44]

All of these efforts to reform and strengthen the preparatory work
offered by the high schools require teachers with both academic ability
and training. The lack of preparation of many teachers in academic fields
is real though reparable.[45] Extensive program of summer training sessions and workshops, supported in large part by federal funds, are now
organized on a continuing basis to strengthen the high school teachers'
own skills in the subjects they teach and to introduce them to more recent developments in their subject.[46] A more serious question raised by
the evidence cited earlier is that of the academic aptitudes and abilities of
high school teachers; this question conditions every proposal for the reform of the curriculum. Of course, efforts can and should be made to
recruit and retain highly competent teachers. Meanwhile, the reform of
the curriculum calls for new ways to make the best use of the most able
teachers already in the schools.

It may be that the matching of academically oriented and able teachers and students that already takes place informally will be encouraged
and even formalized. But it is precisely such invidious distinctions that
American public schools try hard to avoid. It is in the schools that the
American value of equality is most deeply rooted, and it is in the doctrines of democratic education that we find the most determined equa-
tion and encouragement of all kinds of talents and abilities, with academic abilities only one kind among many. When college preparatory
students were only a small minority of all students in high schools, they
could be dealt with as "exceptions" without challenging the basic equalitarian ethos of the school that equated all students and all activities and
interest.[47] But the transformation of the secondary schools into predominantly preparatory institutions profoundly challenges this ethos; the criteria of academic ability and achievement that are so much more important in higher education are increasingly relevant to and applied within
the walls of the high school.[48]

Under pressures such as these, it is likely that both the philosophy
and organization of American secondary education will change in the

decades ahead. And the nature of these changes will in turn affect the kinds of people drawn to high school teaching, how they are trained, [49] and how they are used in the schools The more emphasis placed on academic subject matter in the high school curriculum, and in the training and employment of teachers, the more likely people with academic interests will be attracted to teaching. This is certainly the direction of change in public secondary education's Phase III. But where does this leave the high school's remaining responsibility for terminal education?

The Impact of the Transformation on Terminal Education

The expansion of the college-going population fills the high schools with college preparatory students, and generates the pressures for a strengthening of the preparatory function that we have spoken of. But this development also affects the character of the terminal students, and of terminal education in high school, as well. When few students went on to college, there was no disgrace in not doing so; moreover, except for the professions, it was not so clear that occupational success was closely linked to academic achievement. The Horatio Alger myth, and the American folklore celebrating the successes of the self-made (and self-educated) man, served to define school achievement as only one among several legitimate avenues to success. But the rationalization of industry, and the increased importance of higher education for advancement beyond the lowest levels of the occupational structure, make educational achievement objectively more important for later success; the increased numbers of college-going students make this importance visible to high school students. The consequence of all this is to change the character of the students who do not go on to college when increasing majorities of students do so. Already in some localities, and increasingly in coming decades, the students not going on to college are being reduced to a hard core composed of two group: children from ethnic and racial groups that do not place strong emphasis on high educational and occupational aspirations—for example, Negroes and Mexicans, and children of low intelligence who simply cannot handle college preparatory work.

The transformation of "not going to college" into "failure" has both social and psychological consequences. Among those who want to succeed in school but cannot, the effects of failure may be a loss of self-respect, with widespread if not highly visible and dramatic consequences for the social behaviors of those so affected. One English observer suggests that

> As a result of the close relationship between education and occupation a situation may soon be reached when the educational institutions legitimize social inequality by individualizing failure. Democratization of the means of education together with the internalizing of the achievement ethic by members of the working-class strata may lead to an individualizing of their failure, to a loss of self-respect which in turn modifies an individual's attitude both to his group and to the demands made upon him by his society.[50]

This problem of the motivated student of low ability may be more severe in England, and in other Western countries in earlier stages of the democratization of education, than in the United States, where among our nearly two thousand institutions of higher education there is a college somewhere for everybody.[51] Moreover, the elaborate student counseling programs in our mass public institutions are designed explicitly to help students of low academic ability accept their limitations, and direct their energies toward attainable educational and occupational goals without a sense of personal failure and resentment toward society.[52]

But while the emerging American educational system promises to make some provision for all those who accept its values, regardless of their academic ability, it is not so clear what it can do for those who deeply reject its values and purposes, along with many of the values and purposes of the larger society. The increasing extent and violence of juvenile delinquency in the United States may be closely linked to the extension of educational opportunities to the conforming majority. Where educational achievement (in terms at least of years completed) becomes more widespread and thus more visible, and more important to even modest success in the occupational world, then educational failure *pari passu* becomes more devastating to one's hopes of achieving the advertised "good life" through legitimate channels. Failure in school for many is part of a familiar vicious cycle. Absence of encouragement or concern with school performance in the home (especially marked in certain ethnic and racial groups) leads to failure to acquire basic skills, such as reading, in the early grades, which ensures academic failure in higher grades. These repeated failures make school seem a punishing prison, from which the boy escapes as early as the law allows. But lacking education or training, it is unlikely that he can get any but the poorest jobs. And the habits and resentments generated at home, on the street, and in school make it unlikely that such a boy can move into better jobs. After repeated failures in school and a succession of poorly paid odd jobs, the rewards of membership in a gang and of participation in its delinquent subculture are considerable. And the more the high school is organized around the college preparatory programs, the more it stresses academic achievement, the more punishing it will be for the non-achievers.[53] The delinquent subculture is a way of dealing with deprivations of status, very largely experienced in the schools, and as a response to these deprivations, "the gang offers an heroic rather than an economic [or intellectual] basis of self-respect."[54]

Special school programs may help meet the complex problems of low aspirations and juvenile delinquency, though children growing up in disorganized families, or in cultures cut off from the dominant American value systems, or exposed to the corrosive effects of racial prejudice, present problems that cannot be wholly dealt with in and by the schools. The point here is that the growth of educational opportunity threatens to make the greater part of terminal education in high schools coincidental with the social problems of juvenile delinquency. This is not to say that every classroom full of non-college-going students is or will be a "blackboard jungle." It does mean that the hostility toward the school characteristic of the juvenile gangs, but much more widespread than their membership, will be an increasing part of the educational problem faced by schools and teachers dealing with terminal students. The cluster of values that characterize juvenile delinquency—"the search for kicks, the disdain of work . . . and the acceptance of aggressive toughness as proof of masculinity"[55]—is incompatible with disciplined schoolwork, either academic *or* vocational. Moreover, much of the serious vocational training the high schools have offered in the past is being increasingly shifted to higher education, especially to the junior colleges.[56]

The terminal education of the future will not simply be the terminal education of the past offered to a decreasing proportion of students. The growth of the college-going population changes the character of the remaining terminal students, it changes the meaning of their terminal work, and it will force changes in the organization and curriculum of terminal secondary education. It may also call for teachers with special skills and training in dealing with the problems of the minority or "hard core" of terminal students. But if the increasingly important preparatory programs claim the best resources of secondary education and command the most able teachers, then terminal education will indeed be a second-class program for second-class students. And they will know it, and that knowledge will feed their bitterness and resentment. Neither the old terminal education for life nor the strengthened academic programs will meet their needs. If the terminal education of the future is not to be an educational slum, it will demand large resources and much intelligence. But these are always in short supply, and terminal education will be competing for both with the more attractive programs of preparatory education.

Conclusion

Universal secondary education in the United States was achieved through a system of comprehensive high schools, devoted primarily to the education of the great mass of its students for work and life, and secondarily to the preparation of a small minority for higher education. The present concern with the reform of the high school curriculum and teacher training reflects the rapid growth of the college-going population and the increased importance of the preparatory function.

Nevertheless, it may have been possible to combine terminal education for a majority and preparatory education for a minority more successfully than it will be to combine preparatory education for a majority and terminal education for a minority under one roof. Moreover, the shortage of highly qualified and motivated teachers of academic subjects may require that they be used where their talents and interests are most productive—that is, in teaching the academically most talented fraction of the student body. Secondary education in America may have to accept a higher measure of division of labor and differentiation of function than it has in the past. As a terminal system, it could in its comprehensiveness and emphasis on "education for life" simply carry further the basic education of the elementary school of which it was an outgrowth. As it becomes increasingly a preparatory system, it may be forced to take on some of the characteristics of higher education for which it is preparing, and place greater emphasis on differences among both teachers and students in academic ability and intellectual and occupational interests.

American higher education deals with the diversity of student abilities and talents largely through the great diversity of institutions that compose it, institutions that vary greatly in their selectivity, and in the academic abilities of their students.[57] American comprehensive high schools contain all this diversity within themselves, providing different streams or tracks for students with different educational or vocational intentions, or, as Conant has urged, grouping by ability, subject by subject.[58] But these arrangements ignore the effects of the students on one another, and of the student "mix" on the intellectual climate of the school. In a school where the academically motivated students are in a minority, they cannot help but be affected by the predominantly anti-intellectual values (and behaviors) of the majority;[59] similarly, where the low-achieving terminal students are in the minority, it is hard for them not to be defined as second-class students by other students and teachers, with the effects on them discussed earlier. It may be that the period we are entering will call for a critical evaluation of the comprehensive high school, the institution created by and for mass terminal secondary education.[60]

The current controversies in and about secondary education in America are a natural and healthy response to the transformation of the secondary education in this country. It can be expected that the discussion will grow in volume and scope as this transformation proceeds in the decades ahead. It can also be expected that the discussion ahead will be carried on largely between critics located outside the schools and professional educators inside them. On one side there is a detached perspective but without firsthand knowledge of the schools, on the other, defensiveness, but also intimate experience with the problems under discussion. If the critics and the professional educators can sharpen and clarify the issues in the course of their discussion, and go on to learn from one another about the inconvenient facts that their respective positions do not adequately take into account, then the controversy may become a dialogue, and perhaps a fruitful one for American secondary education.

NOTES
....

1. For discussion and analysis of the controversy, and references to representative books and articles about the issues, see Paul Woodring, *A Fourth of a Nation* (New York: McGraw Hill, 1957), chapters 1–3. For a very different view of the controversy and the issues, see Myron Lieberman, *The Future of Public Education* (Chicago: University of Chicago Press, 1960), chapters 1 and 2.

2. *Sources*: U.S. Bureau of the Census, *Statistical Abstract of the United States: 1960* (Eighty-first edition, Washington, D.C., 1960), Table 279, p. 216; Donald J. Bogue, *The Population of the United States* (Glencoe, Ill: The Free Press, 1959); Kurt Mayer, "Recent Changes in the Class Structure of the United States," *Transactions of the Third World Congress of Sociology* (Amsterdam, 1956), vol. 3, 66–80.

3. Ellwood P. Cubberly, *Public Education in the United States* (New York: Houghton-Mifflen) Co., 1934), pp. 255, 627.

4. U.S. Bureau of the Census, *Historical Statistics of the United States, Colonial Times to 1957* Washington, D.C., 1960), p. 207.

5. Compare the annual output of the secondary schools in 1870 (16,000 graduates) with the total college enrollment of 52,000 in that year. Ibid.

6. On the academies in the nineteenth century, see E. E. Brown, *The Making of Our Middle Schools* (New York: Longmans, Green and Co., 1903). While the early academies were not intended as preparatory schools, "the idea of liberal culture [was] the dominant note of both academy and college education in the nineteenth century" ibid., p. 229).

7. U.S. Department of Health, Education, and Welfare, *Progress of Public Education in the United States, 1959–60* (Washington, D.C., 1960), Table 2, p. 11; *Historical Statistics of the United States, Colonial Times to 1957*, p. 207.

8. Brown, *The Making of Our Middle Schools*, p. 231.

9. Bogue, *The Population of the United States*, Table 17–11, p. 510. For more than sixty years, the dominant stereotype of social class in America, based on solid reality but enshrined in folklore and mass fiction, has been that white-collar people have been to high school, while manual workers by and large have not. These educational and class cleavages in America have also roughly coincided with religious and ethnic cleavages—between the older Protestant immigration from Northern and Western Europe and the later Catholic immigration from Southern and Eastern Europe. But the educational dimension of this cleavage is now changing See note 23.

10. Although "the raising of the school-leaving age in many states followed the change in the pattern of school attendance of a majority of the youth." James Conant, *The Child, The Parent and The State* (Cambridge, Mass.: Harvard University Press, 1959), p. 95. Intern Journal of Comp Sociology II

11. The number of public high school teachers increased from about 20,000 in 1900 to more than 200,000 in 1930. U.S. Office of Education, *Biennial Survey of Education, 1928–1930, Bulletin,* no. 20, vol. 2 (1931), pp. 8, 222.

12. "In 1872, 70 per cent of the students entering the eastern colleges were graduates of the academies." Cubberley, *Publication Education in the United States,* p. 260, footnote 1.

13. On the upgrading of normal schools to the status of four-year state teachers colleges, and the establishment of departments of education in other colleges and universities in the decades before 1920, see Benjamin W. Frazier, "History of the Professional Education of Teachers in the United States," and E. S. Evenden et al., "Summary and Interpretations," U.S. Office of Education, *National Survey of Education Bulletin, 1933,* no. 10, vols. 5 and 6 (1935).

14. "During the first half of the present century, while many liberal arts colleges turned their backs on the problems of teacher education, legal requirements for certification were established in nearly all states . . . [W]hile the liberal arts colleges were preoccupied with other things, while they ignored the problems of teacher education, a like-minded group of school administrators and other professional educators came to agreement among themselves on the necessity for professional preparation for teachers and transmitted their convictions into law. It was during this same period that the educators became imbued with a new philosophy of education, one far removed from the academic traditions of the liberal arts colleges." Paul Woodring, *New Directions in Teacher Education* (New York: The Fund for the Advancement of Education, 1957), p. 23. See also Merle L. Borrowman. *The Liberal and Technical in Teacher Education* (New York: Teachers College, Columbia University, 1956).

15. Matthew H. Willing, "Recent Trends in American Secondary Education," in *The Academic and Professional Preparation of Secondary-School Teachers,* ed. William S. Gray (Chicago: University of Chicago Press, 1935), pp. 8–9, 12. See also Alfred L. Hall-Quest, *Professional Secondary Education in the Teachers Colleges,* "Contributions to Education," no. 169 (New York: Teachers College, Columbia University, 1925), pp. 20–27.

16. During the twelve years immediately preceding World War I, an average of almost one million new immigrants a year arrived in America; they were predominantly from Southern and Eastern Europe, and settled chiefly in the big cities of the Midwest and the Eastern Seaboard.

17. Conant, *The Child,* pp. 93–94.

18. Lawrence A. Cremin, "The Revolution in American Secondary Education, 1893–1918," *Teachers College Record* 56, no. 6, (1955): 303.

19. For a detailed account of the transformation of secondary education in Muncie, Indiana, during the 1920s and early 1930s, see Robert S. and Helen Merrell Lynd, *Middletown* (New York: Harcourt, Brace and Co., 1929), and *Middletown in Transition* (New York: Harcourt Brace and Co., 1937). The Lynds make clear that in the mid-1920s the Muncie high school offered a terminal, primarily vocational education, although the formal curriculum was still predominantly composed of the traditional academic courses. As the president of the school board of Muncie said to them, "For a long time all boys were trained to be President. Then for a while we trained them all to be professional men. Now we are training boys to get jobs" (*Middletown*, p. 194). The hollowness of the traditional coursework under those circumstances is reflected in the remark of one high school English teacher: "Thank goodness, we've finished Chaucer's *Prologue!* I am thankful and the children are, too. They think of it almost as if it were in a foreign language, and they *hate* it" (ibid., p. 193). These sentiments, shared by both teachers and students in Muncie were reflected in the quality of the academic preparation given those students who did go on to college; as the Lynds report, most of them dropped out or did poorly (ibid., p. 195).

By 1930, the new "scientific" educational philosophy had found expression in Muncie in a new curriculum "devoted to the principle that the schools should fit the needs of the individual pupil instead of forcing the child to fit himself to the standard curriculum, as has been the practice in the past" (*Middletown in Transition*, p. 221). "With the high school and even the college no longer serving as a screen sifting out the 'scholars' from the 'non-scholars' even as roughly as they did before the World War, and with secondary education becoming a mass experience, the feeling has grown that education must not only be good but must be good for something—to the individual and to society" (ibid., p. 222).

20. *Teachers College Record*, 19, no. 4 (1918). Kilpatrick describes the "project" as "the hearty purposeful act" wherein the student pursues his own purposes wholeheartedly and with enthusiasm. And as "the purposeful act is . . . the typical unit of the worthy life in a democratic society, so also should it be made the typical unit of school procedure" (p. 323). The aim of this education would be "the man who is master of his fate, who with deliberate regard for a total situation forms clear and far-reaching purposes, who plans and executes with nice care the purposes so formed" (ibid., p. 322). This is, of course, the ideal citizen of liberal democratic theory, a kind of man American had produced in larger numbers during the eighteenth and nineteenth centuries than any other society in history, and without benefit of the "project method." It was the decline of this liberal society, under the impact of industrialization and large organization, that led Kilpatrick and others to seek to

achieve in and through education what one could no longer assume could be achieved through the economic and political life of the society.

The new philosophy of education was a response not merely to a new kind of student but also to a new kind of society. An emphasis on the new students in the schools lead to a new curriculum keyed to their vocational interests, an emphasis on the new society led to calls for the radical reconstruction of society through education. It was the first emphasis that found a response in Muncie and had by far the greater impact on the schools there and elsewhere.

21. Data on enrollments in both high school and college drawn from *Historical Statistics of the United States, Colonial Times to 1957, Progress of Public Education in the United States, 1959–60;* Bogue, *The Population of the United States*; American Council on Education, *Fact Book on Higher Education* (Washington, D.C., n.d.)

22. Indeed, protections of the college age population of the United States reported in the *Fact Book* coupled with U.S. Bureau of the Census estimates of college enrollments in 1970 (reported in Bogue, *The Population of the United States*, Table 26–10, p. 778), give a figure of 55 percent of the 18–21 age group and a recent Roper study of parental expectations regarding their children's education suggests that even this figure may be considerably low (see "Why College Enrollments May Triple by 1970," *College Board Review*, no. 40 [Winter 1960]: 18–19).

23. But the social composition of this minority was changing during this phase. Already in 1920, when college enrollments comprised only 8 percent of the 18–21-year-old population, some 40 percent of the college population, by one estimate, came from lower-middle and working-class backgrounds By 1940, at the end of Phase II, 60 percent of college students came out of those classes (R. J. Havighurst, *American Higher Education in the 1960s* [Columbus: Ohio State University Press, 1960]), Table 7, p. 34).

24. Compare the recent Roper study done in 1959 (*Parents' College Plans Study*, The Ford Foundation, New York, mimeographed, n.d.), which shows that nearly 70 percent of children under 12 are expected by their parents to go to college, with the Roper study of a decade earlier (*Higher Education*, a supplement to *Fortune*, September 1949). The hopes of the earlier decade have become the expectations of today, and will probably be the enrollments of tomorrow. Of the latest Roper study, one observer noted that "it demonstrated that a college education has come to be widely regarded as the *sine qua non* of personal success, just as the high school diploma did earlier" (Philip Coombs, *College Board Review*, no. 40 [1960]: 18).

25. *Statistical Abstract of the United States, 1960*, p. 216.

26. Bureau of Labor Statistics estimates, reported in Newell Brown, "The Manpower Outlook for the 1960's: Its Implications for Higher Education," Office of Education, U.S. Department of Education, *Higher Education* (December, 1959), pp. 3–6. It is also estimated that the number of engineers will double during this period.

27. Bogue, *The Population of the United States*, Table 17-2, p. 475, and *Fact Book*, p. 146.

28. For example, of those students entering high school in 1928, only 1 in 5 went on to college years later, and only 2 in 5 of the high school graduates of 1932 went on to college. But in the coming decades the numbers of terminal and preparatory students in the high schools will be nearly equal. One-third of the students entering high school in 1954 went on to college, and by 1958 half of the high school graduates in the United States were going on to some kind of higher education. (computed from data in *Progress of Public Education*, Figure 1, p. 13). And in some parts of the country that proportion is very much higher.

These transformations can be shown in another way. In 1880, there were roughly the same number of students in American colleges and universities as in our public high schools. By 1940, there were nearly five times as many students in the public high schools as in institutions of higher education. But by 1960, the ratio of high school to college students had fallen to about three to one (*Historical Statistics*, pp. 207 and 209, and for 1960, *Fact Book*, pp. 10 and 237).

29. See, for example, the *Report of the San Francisco Curriculum Survey Committee* (April 1960), prepared for the board of education, San Francisco Unified School District, by a committee of faculty members from various academic departments of the University of California, Berkeley, and Stanford University.

30. See *Judging and Improving the Schools: Current Issues*, California Teachers Association, 1960, prepared in answer to the San Francisco Curriculum Survey Committee Report cited above.

31. Bogue, *The Population of the United States*, Table 13–8, p. 343.

32. Between 1940 and 1959, the average educational level of the whole adult population rose from 8.4 to 11.0 years of schooling complemented (U.S. Bureau of the Census, *Current Population Reports*, series P-20, no. 99 [1959], p. 5). Moreover, recent increases in educational opportunity are closing the historic gap in education between white-collar people and manual workers In 1940, at the end of Phase II, the broad white-collar categories had on the average completed high school, while manual workers had on the average no more than an elementary schooling (Mayer, "Recent Changes," Table 5, p. 76). By 1950, young men between 25 and 29 who were skilled workers and foremen already had an average of nearly 12 years of schooling—less than a year of schooling separated them as a group from young white-collar people Even the semi-skilled and service workers among these young men had completed two or three years of high school on the average (ibid.). By 1959, semi-skilled and service workers of all ages had completed an average of two years of high school.

33. Bogue, *The Population of the United States*, Table 26–11, p. 779.

34. The relation of professional educators to their public resembles that of the

organized medical profession, whose position on medical insurance is under wide-spread public criticism, more than it does that of the individual physician or hospital staff.

35. The extensive studies done with national samples by the Educational Testing Service and others show that students who major in education score lowest, on comprehensive tests of verbal and mathematical competence, as compared with majors in almost every other field (Henry Chauncey, "The Use of the Selective Service College Qualification Test of the Deferment of College Students," *Science*. 116, no. 3301 [July 4, 1952]: 75). See also Dael Wolfle and Toby Oxtoby, "Distribution of Ability of Students Specializing in Different Fields," *Science* (September 26, 1952), pp. 311–14, and Dael Wolfle, Director, *America's Resources of Specialized Talent*, The Report of the Commission on Human Resources and Advanced Training (New York: Harper and Brothers, 1934), pp. 189–208. This finding is supported by a recent study on the campus of the University of California, Berkeley, which shows that the men who took the education courses had, on the average, poorer grades and less knowledge about public affairs than did men in other majors. They were also, as a group, both less informed and more illiberal on matters of political tolerance and academic freedom than men on the same campus in others areas of specialization (H. C. Selvin and Warren O. Hagstrom, "Determinants of Support for Civil Liberties," *The British Journal of Sociology* 11 [March, 1960]: 51–73).

36. W. S. Mason, R. J. Dressel, and R. K. Bain, "Sex Role and Career Orientations of Beginning Teachers," *Harvard Educational Review*, 29, no. 4 (Fall, 1959): 370–84. A study done of men who entered education below the college level after World War II showed that by 1955 fewer than half of them (48 percent) were still in the classroom, 23 percent had become educational administrators, and 29 percent had left education entirely. R. L. Thorndike and Elizabeth Hagen, *Characteristics of Men Who Remained in and Left Teaching* (Teachers College, Columbia University, n.d.), Table 3, p. 19.

37. The study of Thorndike and Hagen of a group of men who were aviation cadet candidates in World War II shows that of all those who went into public school teaching after the war, "those who were academically more capable and talented tended to drop out of teaching and that those who remained as classroom teachers in the elementary and secondary schools were the less intellectually able members of the original group" (ibid., 10). Both the men who remained in education as administrators, and those who had left education completely, showed more academic ability on the air force tests than did those who stayed in the classrooms.

38. In the study by Thorndike and Hagen fewer than one in ten of the men still in classroom teaching were earning more than $600 a month, while more than half of both the school administrators and the men who had left education were earning

more than that. The median earnings of the administrators and the ex-teachers exceeded that of the teachers by more than 25 percent. Two-thirds of the ex-teachers in this study mentioned "low pay" as one of the major reasons for their having left teachings.

39. In addition, teaching in primary and secondary schools, by contrast both with school administration and with college teaching, is widely perceived as a woman's occupation And "female occupations" are generally less well paid and give less status to the men in them than do comparable "male occupations."

40. See M. A. Trow, "Reflections on Recruitment to College Teaching," in *Education, Economy and Society*, ed. A. H. Halsey Jean Floud, and C. Arnold Anderson (Glencoe, Ill.: The Free Press, 1961). Junior colleges, in particular, draw a substantial proportion of their faculties directly from the high schools, and in all likelihood the more academically oriented teachers at that. The continued expansion of the junior colleges cannot help but impoverish the teaching staffs of the high schools.

41. Over the four years between 1955–56 and 1959–60, the average salaries of all public school teachers, principals, and supervisors rose by nearly one-quarter. But during the same period, the salaries of college teachers in all ranks rose by about as much, and in most categories of institutions by more. From data in *Fact Book*, pp. 105, 106, 239.

42. Women who enter high school teaching probably compare more favorably with women in other occupations requiring equivalent amounts of education; among other things, the alternative opportunities are not as broad or attractive for them as for the men. But women are almost as eager to leave the classroom as are men, though for different reasons. Nor, in light of their interests and preparation, can we count on women to carry the burden of teaching the advanced courses in the college preparatory subjects.

43. See Bentley Glass, "The Academic Scientist, 1940–1960," *AAUP Bulletin*, June 1960, p. 153.

44. See Richard Pearson, "Advanced Placement Programs: Opportunities Ahead," *College Board Review*, no. 39 (Fall 1959): 24–27.

45. For example, a recent study by the U.S. Office of Education shows that 39 percent of the teachers in the study who were teaching one or more courses in high school mathematics had not had the calculus or a more advanced course in mathematics, while 7 percent had had no college mathematics at all (K. E. Brown and E. S. Obourn, *Qualifications and Teaching Loads of Mathematics and Science Teachers in Maryland, New Jersey, and Virginia*, U.S. Department of Health, Education, and Welfare, Office of Education, Circular 575 [1959], Tables 20 and 22, p. 46). Similarly, a recent report of the National Council of Teachers of English observes that half of the nation's high school English teachers do not have a college major in

English, and that because of deficiencies in preparation, 70 percent of American colleges and universities must offer remedial work in English (reported in *Phi Delta Kappan* 42, no. 6 [March 1961]: 271).

46. For example, the National Science Foundation through its Summer Institute Program during 1961 supported the attendance of about 20,000 high school and college teachers of science, mathematics, and engineering at some 400 Institutes around the country.

47. See I. L. Kandel, *The Dilemma of Democracy* (Cambridge, Mass.: Harvard University Press, 1934).

48. But this will almost certainly continue to be the comprehensive high school. The resistance of most American educators to selective schools that segregate students of academic ability and interest is very great, despite the reputation and accomplishments of such academically segregaged high schools as New York's High School of Music and Art, the Bronx High School of Science, and the late Townsend Harris High School. See I. L. Kandel, "Current Issues in Expanding Secondary Education," *International Review of Education* 2 (1959): 155–65.

49. We cannot here discuss the controversies over teacher training, certification, and the like except to suggest that they also reflect the deep cleavage between the terminal and preparatory functions of secondary education. In most other advanced countries, which have rather distinct terminal and preparatory school systems, the patterns of social recruitment and training of teachers for these systems also differs. Teachers in the terminal systems usually get their training in teacher training institutes, while teachers in the preparatory systems are educated in the universities for which they are preparing the best of their students. It is probably neither possible nor desirable to reintroduce this pattern into American education. Yet pressures for a reform in teacher education rise in response to the changing function of the schools. For example, a bill introduced in the California legislature in 1961 would eliminate the education major in college by requiring all teachers to have a degree in some academic discipline.

50. Basil Bernstein, "Some Sociological Determinants of Perception: An Enquiry Into Sub-cultural Differences," *The British Journal of Sociology* 1, no. 2 (June 1958): 173.

51. See T. R. McConnell and Paul Heist, "The Diverse College Student Population," in *The American College*, ed. N. Sanford (New York: John Wiley and Sons, 1962).

52. See Burton R. Clark, "The Cooling-Out Function in Higher Education," *American Journal of Sociology*, 45, no. 6 (May 1960).

53. Speaking of this group "for whom adaptation to educational expectations at *any* level is difficult," Parsons notes: "As the acceptable minimum of educational qualifications rises, persons near and below the margin will tend to be pushed into

an attitude of repudiation of these expectations. Truancy and delinquency are ways of expressing this repudiation Thus the very *improvement* of educational standards in the society at large may well be a major factor in the failure of the educational process for a growing number at the lower end of the status and ability distribution" (Talcott Parsons, "The Social Class as a Social System: Some of its Functions in American Society," *Harvard Educational Review* 4, no. 4 [Fall 1959]: 313).

54. Jackson Toby, "Hoodlum or Business Man An American Dilemma," in *The Jews*, ed. Marshall Sklare (Glencoe, Ill.: The Free Press, 1958), p. 546. See also R. K. Merton, *Social Theory and Social Structure*, (rev. ed. (Glencoe, Ill.: The Free Press, 1957), chapter iv, "Social Structure and Anomie"; and Albert K. Cohen, *Delinquent Boys: The Culture of the Gang* (Glencoe: The Free Press, 1955), especially chapter 5, "A Delinquent Solution."

55. David Matza and Gresham Sykes, "Juvenile Delinquency and Subterranean Values," *American Sociological Review* 26, no. 5 (October 1961): 712–19.

56. See Burton R. Clark, *The Open Door College* (New York: McGraw-Hill Book Co., 1960).

57. McConnell and Heist, "The Diverse College Student Population."

58. See his remarks on ability grouping in *The American High School Today* (New York: McGraw-Hill Book Co., 1959), pp. 49–50.

59. See James S. Coleman, "Academic Achievement and the Structure of Competition," *Harvard Educational Review* 29, no. 4 (Fall 1959): 330–52. See also Alan B. Wilson "Residential Segregation of Social Classes and Aspirations of High School Boys," *American Sociological Review* 24, no. 6 (December 1959): 836–45.

60. One possibility, in the best experimental tradition of American education, would be to organize one or two academically selective high schools in each major city, where some of the gains and losses of institutional differentiation can be observed, and where experimental programs can be developed for later application in the comprehensive schools. The "hard-core" terminal students present a more difficult problem.

2

NO OTHER HIGHER EDUCATION RESEARCHER was as successful as Martin Trow in characterizing a phenomenon, or a trend, in higher education so aptly that both researchers and actors thereafter accepted it as a relevant and appropriate notion. *Elite education* and *mass education* became such commonly used terms that younger scholars repeated them without remembering who had coined them, or what the prevailing assumption had been when Trow began to present his developmental theory of higher education. Even before he presented his conceptual framework to the OECD (Organisation for Economic Co-operation and Development) in 1974 and reached a worldwide audience, he had added *universal higher education* though he did not elaborate in much detail how this sector, emerging when half of the corresponding age group has been absorbed by the elite and the mass sectors, differs from the latter.

Although he obviously did not wish to base his "functionally oriented model," as he called it in 1978, on any single national higher education system, he was convinced that the United States came closest to it. The pressures for expansion of enrollment began earlier there, he pointed out, because no powerful actors restricted universities' response to market pressures, and substantial differences in the quality of higher education institutions were more readily accepted than in other countries, thereby "protecting" elite higher education. As a consequence, American reality came close to his "ideal type."

Although he thought the actual development in each country reflects its "unique historical, social, economic, cultural, and political characteristics," he seems to have remained confident over more than thirty years that his notion of elite and mass higher education applied to every modern society. In 1978, however, he may have had some doubts. After noting that expansion in European countries had remained slower than expected, he wondered whether he himself might have believed too strongly in a common trend. About a decade later, he blamed irrational policies for preventing higher education in Europe from developing according to his ideal type model. In his speech at the 600th anniversary of the University of Heidelberg in 1987 he argued: "I underestimated the conservative forces."

What were the "constraints" and who "resisted" expansion in Europe in Trow's view? Initially, he saw governments and other social forces disliking substantial expansion, and even strongly opposing a high degree of diversity, while market forces contributed to expansion and diversification and institutional autonomy was the major driving force of diversity. In 1987, he said, "Most of the reforms I have mentioned require a measure of institutional autonomy and the capacity to take initiatives that are likely over time to create a measure of diversity among the universities, to lift the quality and reputation of some over the others."

Without saying it in so many words Trow seems to have had university leaders in mind when he talked about resistance to expansion. In later years, when expansion was occurring in many European countries, he pointed at academics in the elite universities as opponents of a voluminous sector of mass higher education and as resisting diversity. In 2005, he put it bluntly: "beyond all these forms of resistance lies the deep self-confidence—perhaps we can call it the self-satisfaction, even the arrogance—of the university academic community itself."

Martin Trow presented his views in many European countries. Those who had the privilege of knowing him remember how much he enjoyed absorbing detailed information from other countries when communicating with colleagues at home and abroad. The success of the Center for the Study of Higher Education at the University of California, Berkeley, was clearly built on his efforts to stimulate communication among higher education experts all over the world. Nevertheless, he had preferences. He spent most of his time abroad in the United Kingdom and Sweden, and only discussed British higher education in detail in his writings, while remaining cautious about other European countries—apart from occasional critiques of singular phenomena in particular countries.

Some observers argue that he underestimated the variations

between the individual European countries. When many European countries had reached higher enrollment rates than those of the United States, and when diversification of higher education was most clearly visible at the beginning of the twenty-first century, he continued to point to the constraints and resistances in Europe. He did not interpret the Bologna Process as a breakthrough of expansionist models, but as just another unwise governmental intervention. He had little sympathy for the European combination of a more positive appreciation of the "visible hand" of governments, and a higher mistrust of strong university leadership, and remained suspicious of the elitist views of academics in the elite sector. For Europeans, Martin Trow was strongly shaped by normative views prevailing in the United States, but paradoxically we admire him as the scholar who most successfully underscored a universalistic dynamic force in modern higher education systems.

—ULRICH TEICHLER

Problems in the Transition from Elite to Mass Higher Education

In every advanced society the problems of higher education are problems associated with growth. Growth poses a variety of problems for the educational systems that experience it and for the societies that support them. These problems arise in every part of higher education—in its finance; in its government and administration; in its recruitment and selection of students; in its curriculum and forms of instruction; in its recruitment, training, and socialization of staff; in the setting and maintenance of standards; in the forms of examinations and the nature

---

Originally published as Martin Trow, "Problems in the Transition from Elite to Mass Higher Education," in General Report on the Conference on Future Structures of Post-Secondary Education, 55–101. Paris: OECD, 1974.

of qualifications awarded; in student housing and job placement; in motivation and morale; in the relation of research to teaching; and in the relation of higher education to the secondary school system on one hand, and to adult education on the other—growth has its impact on every form of activity and manifestation of higher education.

In most of the writing on higher education in recent years, these problems are treated in isolation. Curriculum reform and finance and administration are commonly discussed by different people, with different methods and assumptions and often with different values; they are reported in different conferences and published in different journals for different audiences. Similarly, discussions of student unrest and disruptions in the universities more often make reference to student politics and ideology than to the changing relation of higher education to the occupational structures of advanced industrial societies. This essay will argue that these problems can be understood better as different manifestations of a related cluster of problems, and that they arise out of the transition from one phase to another in a broad pattern of development of higher education, a transition—underway in every advanced society—from elite to mass higher education and subsequently to universal access.[1] Underlying this pattern of development lies growth and expansion.

Aspects of Growth

The growth of higher education manifests itself in at least three quite different ways, and these in turn give rise to different sets of problems. There is first the rate of growth: in many countries of Western Europe the numbers of students in higher education doubled within five-year periods during the decade of the 1960s and are doubling again in seven, eight, or ten years by the middle of the 1970s. Second, growth obviously affects the absolute size of both systems and individual institutions. And third, growth is reflected in changes in the proportion of the relevant age grade enrolled in institutions of higher education.

Each of these manifestations of growth carries its own peculiar problems in its train. For example, a high growth rate places great strains on the existing structures of governance, of administration, and, above all, of socialization. When a very large proportion of all the members of an institution are new recruits, they threaten to overwhelm the processes whereby recruits to a more slowly growing system are inducted into its value system and learn its norms and forms. When a faculty or department grows from, say, five to twenty members within three or four years, and when the new staff are predominantly young men and women fresh from postgraduate study, then they largely define the norms of academic life in that faculty and its standards. And if the postgraduate student population also grows rapidly and there is loss of a close apprenticeship relationship between faculty members and students, then the student culture becomes the chief socializing force for new postgraduate students, with consequences for the intellectual and academic life of the institution that we have seen in America as well as in France, Italy, West Germany, and Japan. High growth rates increase the chances for academic innovation; they also weaken the forms and processes by which teachers and students are inducted into a community of scholars during periods of stability or slow growth.

Absolute size has a variety of consequences for academic life. Growth may take the form of very large institutions, or of a very large system, or of both. When growth results in large institutions it has effects on the nature of the milieus in which teaching and learning and research go on. Large size affects the norms as well as the structures of higher education. For example, there is an academic norm, quite appropriate to the relatively small institutions of elite higher education, which prescribes that an academic man has an obligation to be of help with his time, advice, and so forth to anyone in any discipline in his own university, and to anyone in his own discipline anywhere in the world. During the past two decades in every advanced country in the world the numbers in almost every discipline have grown very substantially, while many institutions have doubled, tripled, or quadrupled their size. The norms of academic life have not significantly changed over this time. And that gives rise to what might be called a pattern of "institutionalized distraction." Academic men of middle and senior rank find that the number of requests for demands on their time and attention increase at least in proportion with the growth in the numbers of relevant colleagues and probably much faster, given the patterns of communication in scholarly life. The whole level of pace and activity increases: men are invited to consult on other people's projects, to go to increasing numbers of conferences, to referee more papers for more journals, and to carry the much more complex burdens of administration that are associated with large institutions and systems. It becomes increasingly difficult for academic men to protect the uninterrupted time that they need for fresh thinking about their subjects or for carrying on their scholarly work and research. This is a price paid for growth that is rarely taken into account by students of the costs and benefits of higher education. In response to increased demands on people's time academic men begin to devise patterns of evasion: men spend less time in their offices and more at home; they are more likely to take research leave away from their institutions; they rely more on their research institutes and centers. These centrifugal forces in turn tend to weaken the academic communities that have sustained the norms of academic life, with very marked consequences both for the governance of universities and for the training and socialization of students undergraduate and graduate.

Growth affects the size of the national system as well as its component units, and here the effects are primarily economic and political. As a system grows it emerges from the obscurity of the relatively small elite system with its relatively modest demands on national resources, and becomes an increasingly substantial competitor for public expenditures along with housing, welfare, and defense. And as it does, higher education comes increasingly to the attention of larger numbers of people, both in government and in the general public, who have other, often quite legitimate, ideas about where public funds should be spent, and, if given to higher education, how they should be spent. The relation of higher education to the state becomes increasingly critical the bigger the system of higher education is; this is especially true in most European countries, where the state and local governments are almost the sole source of funds for higher education. Under these conditions the questions of academic freedom and institutional autonomy become central political questions, and not something to be arranged, as formerly, by a few old friends in the universities and in the ministries of education and finance who share very similar views of the world and who may well have been to the elite universities together. Growth raises the question of the relation of the state to higher education in new and disturbing ways.

Growth also manifests itself in the growing proportions of the age grade in any society enrolled in institutions of higher education. In many European countries, that proportion, just after World War II, was about 4 or 5 percent; it is now, only twenty-five years later, between 10 and 20 percent. A few countries exceed the upper figure. Growth in the proportions of the population that have access to higher education raises a number of questions central to the issue of mass higher education. For example, the proportions entering higher education in every country vary sharply in different regional groups, religious and ethnic groups, and socioeconomic classes. Everywhere the proportions from the upper and middle classes are significantly higher than from the working classes or farmers. When the proportions of an age grade going into higher education were very small, the political issue of equality of educational opportunity was centered much more on higher primary and secondary education. But the higher the proportion of the age grade going on to higher education, the more the democratic and egalitarian concerns for equality of opportunity come to center on the increasingly important sector of tertiary education. These differences in access to higher education, which are not reduced but rather increased during the early stages of expansion, become a sharp political issue in the context of the democratic and egalitarian values that are increasingly strong in Western European countries, and these values create strong pressures for reducing these differences in group rates of enrollment. The more important access to higher education is for the life chances of large number of students, the stronger these pressures become. The persistent tendency of intellectually elite institutions such as the universities to be also the home of the social and economic elite, is a major source of tension between the institutions of higher education and the increasingly strong egalitarian values of Western society.

The rising rate of enrollment of an age grade has another important significance, one not so directly political. As more students from an age cohort go to college or university each year, the meaning of college attendance changes—first from being a privilege to being a right, and then, as is increasingly true in the United States, to being something close to an obligation. This shift in the meaning and significance of attendance in the tertiary sector has enormous consequences for student motivation, and thus also for the curriculum and for the intellectual climate of these institutions. I will return to this question later in this essay.

Phases in the Development of Higher Education

On the extent and speed of expansion of European higher education there is no question; indeed, that story has been documented in great detail in recent OECD [Organisation for Economic Co-operation and Development] publications. For example, Sweden had 14,000 university students in 1947. By 1960, the number had more than doubled to 35,000; by 1965, it had doubled again to about 70,000 with another doubling by 1971, when university students comprised about 24 percent of the relevant age group. France saw a growth in its university population between 1960 and 1965 of from 200,000 to more than 400,000, with another doubling projected by the mid-1970s, to an enrollment of about 17 percent of the age group. Denmark doubled its university student population between 1960 and 1966 from 19,000 to 34,000; by the mid-1970s, it will double again to 70,000, about 13 percent of the age group. In the United Kingdom the Robbins Report anticipated university enrollments growing from about 130,000 in 1962 to 220,000 by 1973 and to nearly 350,000 by 1980. These projections have already been substantially revised upward toward 400,000 (about 13 percent of the age group) in all forms of full-time higher education by 1973, and somewhere between 800,000 and 1,000,000 by 1981, with roughly half in universities.

What these numbers conceal are two fundamentally different processes. One of these is the expansion of the elite universities—the growth of traditional university functions in traditional, if somewhat modified, forms of universities. The other is the transformation of elite university systems into systems of mass higher education performing a great variety of new functions (at least new to universities) for a much larger proportion of the university age group. In Britain, as on the Continent, growth, up to the present, has mainly been achieved by expanding the elite university system. But, I have argued, the old institutions cannot expand indefinitely; they are limited by their traditions, organizations, functions, and finance. In European countries, it is likely that an increased enrollment in higher education beyond about 15 percent of the age grade requires not merely the further expansion of the elite university systems, but the rapid development of mass higher education through the growth of popular non-elite institutions. Mass higher education differs from elite higher education not just quantitatively but qualitatively. They differ obviously in the proportions of the age grade that they enroll, but also in the ways in which students and teachers view attendance in university or college; in the functions of gaining entry for the student; in the functions of the system for the society; in the curriculum; in the typical student's career; in the degree of student homogeneity; in the character of academic standards; in the size of institutions; in the forms of instruction; in the relationships between students and faculty; in the nature of institutional boundaries; in the patterns of institutional administration and governance; and in the principles and procedures for selecting both students and staff. In other words, the differences between these phases are quite fundamental and go through every aspect of higher education. Let us look at each of these aspects of higher education in its several phases a little more closely.

Aspects of Transition

Size of the system. Countries that develop a system of elite higher education in modern times seem able to expand it without changing its character in fundamental ways until it is providing places for about 15 percent of the age grade. At that point or thereabouts the system begins to change its character; if the transition is made successfully, the system is then able to develop institutions that can grow without being transformed until they reach about 50 percent of the age grade. Beyond that, and thus far only in the United States, large sections of the population are sending nearly all their sons and daughters to some kind of higher education, and the system must again create new forms of higher education as it begins to move rapidly toward universal access.

Attitudes toward access. The ease of access to higher education is closely linked to conceptions that people—students and their parents, and increasingly college and university teachers and administrators—have of college and university attendance. When access is highly limited, it is generally seen as a privilege, of either birth or talent or both. Above about 15 percent of the age grade, people increasingly begin to see entry to higher education as a right for those who have certain formal qualifications. And when the proportion of the whole population comes to be about 50 percent, and in certain sectors of the society it is then of course much higher, attendance in higher education is increasingly seen as an obligation: for children from the middle and upper middle classes, in European countries as well as in the United States, failure to go on to higher education from secondary school is increasingly a mark of some defect of mind or character that has to be explained or justified or apologized for. Moreover, as more people go on to higher education, the best jobs and opportunities and the economic rewards in life come to be reserved for people who have completed a university degree, and this greatly contributes to the sense of obligation that is felt by many students on entry.

Functions of higher education. The different phases are also associated with different functions of higher education both for students and for society at large. Elite higher education is concerned primarily with shaping the mind and character of the ruling class, as it prepares students for broad elite roles in government and the learned professions. In mass higher education, the institutions are still preparing elites, but a much broader range of elites that includes the leading strata of all the technical and economic organizations of the society. And the emphasis shifts from the shaping of character to the transmission of skills for more specific technical elite roles. In institutions marked by universal access there is concern for the first time with the preparation of large numbers for life in an advanced industrial society; they are training not primarily elites, either broad or narrow, but the whole population, and their chief concern is to maximize the adaptability of that population to a society whose chief characteristic is rapid social and technological change.

The curriculum and forms of instruction. The curriculum and forms of instruction naturally reflect changes in the definition of the meaning of being a student and of the functions that higher education plays for students and for the society at large. The curriculum in elite institutions has tended to be highly structured, reflecting academic conceptions of the degree course or professional conceptions of professional requirements. The courses of study, shaped largely by the character of the final examination, were on the whole highly specialized and governed by the professors' notions of what constituted an educated man or a qualified professional. In institutions of mass higher education, education becomes more modular, marked by semi-structured sequences of courses, increasingly earning unit credits (the unit of exchange in modular courses) allowing more flexible combinations of courses and easier access and movement between major fields and indeed among institutions.[2] In universal higher education, as it emerges, there is a survival of the modular course, but increasingly instruction is relatively unstructured; the boundaries of the course itself begin to break down as do required sequences of courses. It is very difficult to justify course requirements where no single conception of higher education obtains, and the rejection of academic forms, structures, and standards also extends to examinations and assessment, as distinctions between learning and life become attenuated. Attendance at the emerging institutions of higher education designed for universal access is merely another kind of experience not qualitatively different from any other experiences in modern society that give one resources for coping with the problems of contemporary life. And, in universal access, since coursework does not clearly qualify people for specific jobs it is less clear why assessment of performances is necessary.

There are parallel differences in the typical forms of instruction and thus in the relationships between student and teacher. In elite systems, the characteristic form of instruction is the tutorial or seminar, marked, on the whole, by a personal relationship between student and teacher.[3] This is compatible with the central function of the shaping of character and the preparation of a broad or general elite whose specific adult roles and activities would vary widely so that one could hardly train for them in the course of the university career. And the defense of these forms of instruction in the "higher schools" of France during the period of rapid expansion that filled the lecture rooms of the universities to overflowing made it clear where the elite functions in France are meant to survive. Under the conditions of mass higher education the emphasis is on the transmission of skill and knowledge, and increasingly formal instruction is carried on through large lectures supplemented by seminars often taught by teaching assistants. In universal higher education the direct personal relationship of the student and teacher is subordinated to a broad exposure of the student to new or more sophisticated perspectives. There is heavier reliance on correspondence, on use of videocassettes and TVs, and on computer and other technological aids to instruction.

The student "career." The academic career of the student differs also. In elite institutions the student ordinarily enters directly after completion of secondary schooling; the student is in residence and continues his work uninterruptedly (except for holidays) until he gains a degree. He is in this sense sponsored and in competition only for academic honors. In the mass institution, students also, for the most part, attend immediately after finishing secondary school, although increasing numbers delay entry until after a period of work or travel. Easier access and a more heterogeneous student population lead to higher "wastage" rates. But the students are now a mixed residential commuting population as vocational training becomes a larger component of higher education. In institutions of universal access there is much postponement of entry, "stopping out" (i.e., periods when the student is not in attendance), and large numbers of students with experience in adult occupations. The emphasis on lifelong learning is compatible with the softening of the boundaries between formal education and other forms of life experience.

Moreover, as student numbers grow, with increasing numbers from poor homes, a growing proportion are also working for pay at nonacademic jobs—first during vacations and then during term time. This trend has implications for the meaning of being a student, for the curriculum (less outside reading and study can be assigned or assumed), for student motivations, and for the relationships of students with their teachers. And it is hard to discourage this practice, especially when it is done out of necessity by needy students. It can be ignored when it is the occasional poor but able student who has to work for his fees and maintenance. But it is a different institution when the proportion of working students is 30, 40, or 50 percent. The provision of state stipends for university students (as in Britain) is designed precisely to permit the maintenance of elite forms of higher education with a more democratic student intake. But the high and growing costs of stipends ironically act as a brake on expansion—only one of the ways in which the principle of equality in higher education is at odds with expansion. The growing interest in student loans in several countries is a part of the effort to solve this dilemma in ways that will protect the university against part-time work by students. The "sandwich course" for technical and vocational students is another solution that makes a virtue of necessity by incorporating paid work into the regular curriculum.

Institutional diversity, characteristics, and boundaries. Systems at different phases of their development differ also in their diversity. Elite systems tend to be highly homogeneous, the component institutions very much like one another. They tend to be universities with high and common standards, though they may include highly specialized technical schools with special access to parts of the civil service. Mass systems begin to be more comprehensive, with more diverse standards, though with some linkages among the several segments of the system that allow mobility of students and staff. In systems of universal access there is very great diversity in the character of component institutions, with no common standards among them. Indeed, the very notion of standards is itself challenged and problematical.

The typical institutions in the three systems differ in size and character as well. Elite institutions are commonly "communities" that range up to two or three thousand students in residence. If larger than three thousand they are sub-structured so that their component units, such as the Oxford and Cambridge colleges, tend to be relatively small. The comprehensive institutions that characterize mass higher education are less "communities" than they are "cities of intellect" with up to thirty or forty thousand students and staff making up a mixed residential and commuting population. Institutions of universal access are unlimited in size; they may be simply aggregates of people enrolled for instruction, most of whom are rarely or never on the central campus; they may share little in common and do not in any sense comprise a community rooted in frequent association, shared norms and values, and a sense of common identification.

As we might guess from the foregoing elite institutions are marked off from the surrounding society very sharply by clear and relatively impermeable boundaries, in the extreme case by physical walls. In mass institutions there are still boundaries, but they are more fuzzy and more permeable; there is relatively easy movement in and out of mass institutions, and a much less clear concept of membership, though there are still formal definitions of membership that are relevant for a variety of academic and nonacademic purposes. In institutions of universal access, boundaries are very weak, shading off to none at all. At some point anyone who may switch on a televised broadcast of a lecture may be thought of for that moment as being part of an extended university, and the question of whether he is submitting work regularly or has matriculated is of only marginal significance.[4]

The locus of power and decision making. The three types of systems differ in their source of ultimate authority; in the nature of their academic standards; and in their principles of recruitment and selection. With respect to both ultimate power and effective decisions, elite institutions are dominated by relatively small elite groups: leaders in significant institutions—political, economic, and academic—who know one another, share basic values and assumptions, and make decisions through informal face-to-face contact. An example of this would be the small number of leading civil servants, government ministers, university vice chancellors, and members of the University Grants Commission who shaped the face of the British university system for many years in small committee rooms or around tables at the Athenaeum Club. Mass higher education continues to be influenced by these elite groups, but is increasingly shaped by more democratic political processes and influenced by attentive audiences. These are parts of the general public who have special interests and qualifications, and develop a common view about higher education in general or some special aspect, such as the forms and content of technical education. Higher education policies increasingly become subject to the ordinary political processes of interest groups and party programs. One kind of attentive audience is the employers of the products of mass higher education, who are interested in the nature of their skills and qualifications. Another attentive audience is the body of old graduates who retain an interest in the character and fortunes of their old university. These groups often develop political instrumentalities of their own, such as associations with an elected leadership, and develop lines of communication to the smaller groups in government, legislatures, and the universities themselves who make the actual decisions, both day to day and over the long range. When the system moves toward universal access, increasingly large portions of the population begin to be affected by it, through either their own past or present attendance, or that of some friend or relative. In addition, the universities and colleges—what is taught there, and the activities of their staff and students—come to be of general interest, leave the pages of the serious press and magazines, and are reported in the popular journals and on television. They thus attract the interest of mass publics that increasingly come to see themselves as having a legitimate interest in what goes on in the institutions of higher education, if for no other reason than their enormous cost and obvious impact on society. And these mass publics begin to make their sentiments known, either through letters to public officials or through their votes in special or general elections. The change in the size and character of the publics who have an interest in higher education and exert an influence on higher educational policy greatly influences the nature and content of the discussions about higher education, who takes part in them, and the decisions that flow out of them. The claims of academic men to a special expertise, and of their institutions to special privileges and immunities, are increasingly questioned; much of what academic men understand by academic freedom, and the significance of the security of academic tenure for the protection of their pursuit of truth regardless of political interests or popular sentiment, all are challenged by the growing intervention of popular sentiments into these formerly elite arenas.

Academic standards. The implications for academic standards are equally clear: in elite systems and institutions, at least in their meritocratic phase, these are likely to be broadly shared and relatively high. In the systems and institutions of mass higher education standards become variable, differing in severity and character in different parts of the system or institution, appropriately so since both system and institution have become holding companies for quite different kinds of academic enterprises. In institutions of universal access there tends to be a different criterion of achievement: not so much the achievement of some academic standard, as whether there has been any "value added" by virtue of the educational experience. That is the justification of universal higher education, as it is of the nonacademic forms of primary and secondary school; obviously this changes in a fundamental way the basis for judging individual or institutional activities. (For example, if the criterion of success is "value added," it may be better to admit students who are academically very weak, rather than those with a strong record, since presumably it will be easier to raise the performance of those who start low than of those who are already performing well. That argument is in fact made for the principle of "open access." Whatever substance it has, it does suggest how fundamental is the shift to "universal access.")

Access and selection. The principles of student selection also differ in the different phases. In elite systems the criterion of ascribed status gave way more or less rapidly over the past century to meritocratic achievement measured by secondary school performance or grades on special examinations. In institutions of mass higher education there is a general acceptance of meritocratic criteria where access is limited, but this is qualified by a commitment to equality of educational opportunity, leading to compensatory programs and the introduction of additional nonacademic criteria designed to reduce inequities in the opportunities for admission of deprived social groups and categories. In the institutions of universal higher education, which by definition are wholly open either to anyone who wishes to join or to those who have certain minimal educational qualifications, the criterion is whether an individual has chosen to associate himself with the institution voluntarily. The aim of universal access is toward the equality of group achievement rather than an equality of individual opportunity, and efforts are made to achieve a social, class, ethnic, and racial distribution in higher education reflecting that of the population at large. And of course the more nearly the system enrolls the whole of an age grade, the more closely it reflects the distribution of subgroups in the population at large. At the limiting case, of course, it is democratic in the same sense that compulsory forms of primary and secondary education are, with surviving variations in the character and quality of the education offered in different places and different kinds of institutions. We can already see hints of this philosophy of admissions and of these criteria for access even in the present transitional period between mass and elite higher education in European countries.

Forms of academic administration. The characteristic institutions in the three systems differ also in their forms of institutional administration. The typical elite university is governed by part-time academics who are essentially amateurs at administration. In some countries they may have the help of a full-time civil servant or registrar to deal with routine matters of financial problems. But the head of the administrative staff is commonly an academic elected or appointed to the office for a limited period of time. As institutions become larger and their functions more varied in the phase of mass higher education, their administrative staff becomes larger; there is now more commonly a top leadership of men who were formerly academics but who now are clearly full-time university administrators. And below them there is a large and growing bureaucratic staff. As the system grows even further toward universal access the enormous costs generate pressures for greater financial accountability and more sophisticated forms of program management. Universities employ increasingly large numbers of full-time professionals, such as systems analysts and economists knowledgeable in program budgeting. The rationalization of university administration generates problems in that phase, since the functions of the institution itself have become increasingly more diverse, and its outputs more difficult to quantify, as the management procedures have become more dependent on quantified data for the assessment of costs and benefits.

The rationalization of university administration based on the systematic collection and analysis of quantitative data on the costs of discrete activities, and on measures of the outputs or benefits of these activities, is a response to the growth of the size and cost of higher education, and to growing demands for public accountability regarding its efficiency. In their heavy reliance on quantified data, however, these managerial techniques become a powerful independent force working against the survival of elite institutions, functions, and activities that cannot be easily justified by reference to quantitative measures of either their costs or benefits.[5]

But the development of mass higher education does not necessarily involve the destruction of elite institutions or parts of institutions, or their transformation into mass institutions. Indeed, elite forms of higher education continue to perform functions that cannot be performed as well by mass higher education—among them, the education, training, and socialization of very highly selected students for intellectual work at the highest standards of performance and creativity. And as we observe the system of mass higher education in the United States and the patterns of growth toward mass higher education elsewhere, we see that it involves the creation and extension of functions and activities and institutions rather than the disappearance of the old.

But while elite institutions and centers tend to survive and defend their unique characteristics in the face of the growth and transformation of the system around them, they are not always successful. Their special characteristics and integrity are threatened by those egalitarian values that define all differences as inequities; by the standardizing force of central governmental control; and by the powerful leveling influence of the new forms of rationalized management and administration. The rationalization of academic administration is a reflection and a product of the movement toward mass higher education, but it is not neutral toward other forms of higher education. In this respect it works against the diversity of the system that is also a characteristic—indeed, a central defining characteristic—of mass higher education. And this creates a dilemma to which I will return later in this essay.

Internal governance. The forms and processes of internal governance of institutions of higher education vary enormously, from country to country and between institutions. But on the whole, elite institutions everywhere tend to be governed by their senior professors;[6] those who do not hold chairs ordinarily play little or no part in major institutional decisions. As institutions, and especially their non-professorial staff, grow, the latter increasingly challenge the monopolistic power of what comes to be seen as a professorial oligarchy. And in mass higher education, internal power comes to be shared to varying degrees with junior staff. Moreover, students increasingly claim a right to influence institutional decisions, and the forms and extent of student participation become a major issue during the transition from elite to mass higher education.

Problems of institutional governance are greatly sharpened by the breakdown of the academic consensus that occurs with growth and the transition from elite to mass higher education. Elite universities, with their narrow traditional range of functions and homogeneous bodies of students and teachers, could assume the broad acceptance by their participants of the basic character and values of the institution. But the movement toward mass higher education, with its wider range of functions, means the recruitment of new kinds of students and teachers, from more diverse backgrounds and with more varied views and conceptions of what higher education and their own institutions ought to be. At the same time, junior staff, whose interests and attitudes often differ sharply from those of the senior professors, are gaining in power and influence. And students, drawn from more diverse backgrounds and affected by radical political currents, challenge many of the traditional values and assumptions of the university. In many institutions, the old consensus on which elite universities were based has broken down, both within the faculty and among the students.[7] Relations among colleagues and between teachers and students no longer can be built on a broad set of shared assumptions, but are increasingly uncertain and a source of continual strain and conflict. The move toward participatory forms of governance often presupposes the survival of the old consensus, or the possibility of its recreation. But if that is an illusion, as I believe, then participatory forms of democracy may introduce into the institutions of mass higher education the conflicts of interest and ideology that are more familiar (and more easily managed) in the political institutions of society.[8]

The politicization of the university is a familiar problem in almost all advanced societies, and the theme of much current literature. Its solution may be linked to the larger problem of devising structures that sustain educational diversity within an emerging system of mass higher education while allowing its component institutions and units to preserve their own unique identities, a narrower range of functions, and staff and students who share attitudes and values appropriate to their own institution. Consensus within units is wholly compatible with variety and diversity of forms and conceptions of higher education between units and within the larger system. But if the diversity of the whole system is reflected in each of its component units, the problems of institutional governance may become almost insoluble, and in that event, as we see in some countries already, effective power and decision making inevitably flow out of the colleges and universities into the hands of political authorities whose authority is based not on their roles in higher education but on the political processes of the larger society. The breakdown of institutional governance arising out of value dissensus and fiercely politicized conflicts of values and interests tends to weaken the autonomy of an institution: someone has to make decisions and account for public funds in ways broadly acceptable to the society at large; if this cannot be done inside the institution, then it will be done by outsiders or their appointees.

Caveats

There are several important caveats to be made before I develop this perspective further.

1. The three phases—elite, mass, and universal education—are, in Max Weber's sense, ideal types. They are abstracted from empirical reality, and emphasize the functional relationships among the several components of an institutional system common to all advanced industrial societies rather than the unique characteristics of any one. Therefore, the description of any phase cannot be taken as a full or adequate description of any single national system.

2. These ideal types are designed to define and illuminate the problems of higher education common to a number of countries. These problems are of three broad kinds:

   a. The functional relationships among the various components or aspects of given systems; for example, the degree of compatibility or strain between a given pattern of student admissions and the dominant forms of university curriculum.

   b. The problems arising during the transition from one phase to the next when existing, more or less functional, relationships are progressively disrupted by uneven and differently timed changes in the patterns and characteristics of the system. An example might be the survival of the professorial oligarchy as a mode of institutional, faculty, or departmental governance as the growth in the numbers and functions of junior staff increases their responsibilities, importance, and self-confidence.

   c. The problems arising in the relations between institutions of higher education and the larger society and its economic and political institutions, as higher education moves from one phase to another. An example here might be the greater concern for public accountability of funds spent on higher education, and the greater interference in the autonomy of higher educational institutions in the allocation and use of these funds, as costs rise and the higher educational system becomes more consequential and more significant to a wider range of social, political, and economic activities.

3. It must be emphasized that the movement of a system from elite to mass higher education or from mass to universal higher education does not necessarily mean that the forms and patterns of the prior

phase or phases disappear or are transformed. On the contrary, the evidence suggests that each phase survives in some institutions and in parts of others while the system as a whole evolves to carry the larger numbers of students and the broader, more diverse functions of the next phase. Its newest, and gradually its most important, institutions have the characteristics of the next phase. So, in a mass system elite institutions may not only survive but flourish, and elite functions continue to be performed within mass institutions. (Similarly, both elite and mass institutions survive as the United States moves toward universal access to higher education.) But this observation points to a characteristic problem of all mixed-phase systems: the problem arising from the strains inherent in the continuing existence of forms of higher education based on fundamentally different principles and oriented to quite different kinds of functions. The question follows: how successfully, through what institutions and mechanisms, does a system continue to perform elite functions when the emphasis of the system has shifted to the forms and functions of mass higher education? How successfully can a system perform diverse functions that require quite different structures, values, and relationships—especially when central governing agencies are pressed, both by bureaucratic rules and egalitarian politics, to treat institutions and individuals equally and in standard ways?

4. The analysis of the phases of development of higher education should not be taken to imply that the elements and components of a system of higher education change at equal rates, and that a system moves evenly toward the characteristic forms of the next phase. In fact, development is very uneven: numerical expansion may produce a more diversified student body before the curriculum has been similarly diversified; the curriculum may become more diversified before the recruitment and training of staff has changed to meet the new requirements of the changed curriculum; the staff may have become more diverse before the forms of institutional governance reflect the changes in the character of university and college teachers and begin to distribute institutional authority to reflect more closely academic responsibility. A close analysis of developments in any given system must attend (a) to the sequence of

change of its several parts and patterns; (b) to the strains and problems arising therefrom; and (c) to the extent to which the changes in different countries show common sequential patterns among the various parts and elements of their systems.

In short, the analysis of the phases of higher education in advanced industrial societies, of the developments of parts of the system during these phases, and of the problems that arise at the transition points between phases and among elements changing at different rates within a phase is designed to illuminate problems and patterns common to different societies and systems.

Variations in the Patterns of Change

There are several questions we may ask about the patterns of change in the course of the growth and transformation of higher education in advanced industrial societies.

1. Is there a characteristic pattern in the sequence of change of systems of higher education? If there is, what is that pattern?

2. Which elements of higher education change more or less easily and which are highly resistant to change in the course of growth?

3. What are the consequences of variations in the rate of change among the several elements of a system of higher education?

I cannot do any more here than suggest tentative and provisional answers to these questions.

The expansion of student numbers seems to precede other institutional change in almost all cases. Systems of higher education do not characteristically modify their arrangements in anticipation of growth. (Indeed, the rate and amount of expansion, at least in the earlier phases of growth spurts, is commonly underestimated.) The one major exception to this was the land grant state universities in America after the Civil War. These institutions, already democratic and comprehensive in conception, and devoted to scholarship, vocational studies, and public service equally, were far ahead of their time; they were, in fact, institutions dedicated to mass higher education long before college and university enrollments reached anything like the proportions that characterize mass higher education. This important development, arising out of egalitarian values of the United States and the role of education in its political philosophy, greatly eased the transition from elite to mass higher education in that country. Thus it is only experiencing now, in its move toward universal higher education, the problems that European countries are experiencing in their move from elite to mass higher education.

The growth of numbers, in itself, begins to change the conception that students have of their attendance in college or university. When enrollment rates are 4 or 5 percent of the age grade, students naturally see themselves as part of a highly privileged minority; although this does not mean that they are necessarily passive or deferential, it does make them feel, along with their professors and lecturers, part of a small privileged institution with a very clear set of common interests embodied in common values, symbols, and ceremonies, modes of speech, and lifestyle. All that affirmed the communal identity of the academic institution over against the rest of society. Students might indeed be highly rebellious, but their actions and demonstrations were typically directed against state or political institutions rather than against members of their own institution.

Growth toward 15 or 20 percent of the age grade, and, in the larger European countries, toward student numbers of half a million rather than fifty thousand, inevitably changed that. Students have come to see their entry into a university as a right earned by fulfilling certain requirements. And for some, an increasing proportion, attendance is in part obligatory: larger numbers in all countries attend university at least partly because people in their parents' social strata send their children to university as a matter of course. Such students feel less like members of a chosen elite on arrival, and they enter universities that are larger (and in some cases very much larger) than their counterparts of twenty years ago. These big institutions are marked in many cases by impersonality, turbulence, and continuing political activity. There is little question that the communal aspects of universities have declined along with the sense on the part of the students and teachers of their being members of a special estate.

The growth of numbers and the shift in the conception of attendance from privilege to right is accompanied by changes in the principles and processes of selection. As the gates gradually open, the older almost exclusive links between a handful of elite preparatory schools (whether private or state-supported) and the universities become attenuated, and new avenues of access to higher education begin to open up. Logically, if the move toward mass education were state policy and carefully planned, the development of a broad system of comprehensive secondary schools, carrying larger and larger numbers from every social strata to the point of university entry, would precede the growth of mass higher education itself. In practice, however, the explosive expansion of higher education over the past two decades has almost everywhere preceded the move toward comprehensive secondary education. (The exceptions here again are the United States, where universal comprehensive education had been achieved by World War II when enrollments in higher education were only about 15 percent, and Sweden, where the establishment of a fully comprehensive secondary school system and the rapid move toward mass higher education have proceeded by plan together over the past decade.) It is more true to say that mass higher education is forcing the growth of a popular system of comprehensive secondary education, rather than that the creation of the latter has made possible the expansion of higher education. (It is true, however, that the continued growth of higher education beyond, perhaps, 15 percent of the age grade, will depend on the continued democratization of the secondary school system and the transformation of more and more terminal secondary schools into schools that qualify students for university entry.)

But the change in the principles underlying the preparation and selection of university entrants has itself proceeded through a series of phases:

1. First there was the simple principle of admitting those qualified for entry according to more or less strict meritocratic principles. This process, however, rested heavily on very marked social inequalities in the opportunities to gain those qualifications—opportunities almost exclusively offered by a small set of elite academic preparatory schools. The demand for the abolition of inequality was in the first instance met solely by an emphasis on meritocratic procedures and criteria, without much regard for the role of social inequality in affecting the chances of meeting those criteria. Qualifications took such forms as Britain's passes in its "A" level examinations or, in other countries, the successful completion of the preparatory secondary school program and the earning of a "Bac" or "abitur."

2. The set of complementary forces—increasing democratic pressures, needs of the economy, and the growth of higher education itself—lead to an expansion of those secondary schools and streams that qualify for university entry. This phase is marked by a growing concern for an increase in educational opportunities that would enable able students from lower social strata to enter university. However, during this phase, the growth in student members at university was very largely made up of an increase in the proportion of middle-class students, who almost everywhere are the first to take advantage of increases in educational opportunities of every kind and at every level.

3. In the third phase, partly as a result of the work of sociologists and partly under political pressures, there emerges a clear and more widespread recognition of the effect of social inequalities on educational achievement. And this in turn leads to special efforts to reduce the effects of those social inequalities. These take the form of proposals to modify the structure of secondary education, especially toward the comprehensive principle, or at least the extension of the educational channels through which access to higher education may be gained. In addition, there is a call for efforts to compensate for the disadvantaging effects of lower-class origins. Increasingly, schools and streams that formerly led to vocational schools or simply to early termination of formal education are modified to allow for university entry for at least some of their students, at least in principle.

4. In the fourth stage (and in part because social inequalities show everywhere a stubbornly persistent effect on educational achievement, despite the best efforts of reformers), the egalitarians attack the selective principle of higher education in principle, and demand open access to the universities (as at Vincennes) or a greater expansion of non-university institutions of higher education that do not require the same formal academic qualifications for entry as do the universities. This phase (clearly visible in the United States though less so in European countries) marks a very significant shift from the principle of equality of opportunity for educational achievement, to more radical principles of equality of educational achievement for all definable social groups and strata. The principle of equality of individual opportunity is compatible with the maintenance of meritocratic criteria for entry: the effort is to enable more students from lower social strata to meet those qualifications. The latter

principle, the equality of group achievement, affirms that social justice requires that students from all social strata be equally represented among all elite groups in society, and this, at least in the short run, is incompatible with the maintenance of most meritocratic criteria for admission. Needless to say, even where put into practice, the principle of equality of group achievement is usually introduced in a highly qualified or compromised way, and immediately introduces very substantial problems, among them the relation of students in open institutions to those in institutions still governed by meritocratic principles, and also the significance of the qualifications earned in institutions where meritocratic criteria have been subordinated to other values (at Vincennes, for example, the French government simply ceased to recognize its diplomas).

The question of the principles and processes of selection and admission to higher education is the crucial point where higher education touches most closely on the social structure. What expansion does initially is to increase the opportunities for the children of the middle classes to gain an education that still promises to provide (though to a larger number of people) the dignified and rewarding professional occupations and traditional social status formerly reserved for a much smaller elite. While a detached observer might suggest that tripling or quadrupling the number of university graduates must reduce the special status and privileges accorded to the graduate, it does not appear so at the time to participants in the process—for example, to the parents of the would-be university entrant. And resistance to expansion—say from 5 to 15 percent of the age grade—has almost everywhere been remarkably weak in the face of democratic values and presumed economic needs. But already the overproduction of university graduates for the traditional graduate occupations is causing misgivings among conservatives, who are beginning to see more and more clearly that mass higher education is a corrosive solvent of traditional social relations, status, hierarchies, and privileged access to elite careers. As a larger number of working-class youth begin to enter university, the impact of university expansion on the life chances of upper-middle-class youth will become even more visible and threatening. It is hard to imagine a successful move to end the expansion of higher education, although that is certainly talked about in conservative circles in all Western countries. But the establishment of different sectors of higher education, reflecting the status hierarchies in the larger society, is a more effective way of using higher education to buttress rather than undermine the class structure. It would be useful to examine and compare the history and development of modes of access to higher education in different advanced industrial societies, to see just how they have moved through the phases I have sketched, and where they are now.

I have suggested that after expansion itself, the earliest and most rapid changes in the system occur in the meaning of university student status, and in the principles of admission. But other components of the system are more resistant and slower to change. And that is because while the decision to expand, the definition of attendance, and the rules for admission are governed largely by forces outside the university, the curriculum, the forms of administration and internal governance, the structure of the academic career, modes of instruction, and academic standards themselves are all largely shaped (though again with exceptions) more within the academy than by outside forces. And these internal processes are, for better or worse, highly conservative. This is in part because of how universities are governed, in part because of the characteristics and orientations of academic men. Let us look briefly at the latter.

Academic Orientations

How do academic men—the rectors and professors and associate professors, the docents and lecturers, who staff the old and the new institutions of higher education in every advanced society—view the rapid developments occurring all around them? We do not have a detailed study of the academic professions in most countries that would allow us to say with precision just how these men and women view their own institutions, students, and subjects, and the great changes underway or just over the horizon. But if we cannot know the distribution of academic attitudes—the relative size and strength of the several most important positions that university teachers take toward growth and change in their institutions—we can identify the major dimensions along which those attitudes divide.

The great changes in recent decades in the size and functions of higher education have generated a diversity of orientations within the academic profession in every advanced society. Until after World War II, the small university system in most countries was staffed by professors and their assistants, men who had made or were making their careers through a life of scholarship or scientific research. The bulk of their students went into a small number of professions traditionally linked to the university degree: into higher secondary school teaching, the civil service, law, medicine, and the church, and in some countries into certain sectors of finance and industry. A small number of students stayed on for higher degrees as apprentices to the professors in their fields. The expansion and diversification, and partial democratization, of higher education over the past two decades has created different functions for higher education, and in so doing has brought different kinds of students to the universities. And, as I have suggested earlier, within the university the old consensus about the nature and proper functions of the university has broken down; in every country academic men differ among themselves in their attitudes toward changes in the university that are already under way or are likely to accompany further growth.

At first glance, it may seem that the major division among academic men is between those who give their approval and support to the transformation of their institutions and systems as they move from elite to mass higher education, with all the implications for selection, curriculum, and the like, that we've discussed earlier, as opposed to those who tenaciously defend the forms and functions of elite higher education. But in fact many academic men (like politicians, civil servants, and ordinary people) do not draw the full implications of growth or see its logical consequences, and many support the continued expansion of higher education while opposing its transformation into mass higher education. Others are wary of growth, while accepting and even supporting important changes in the character of their institutions. Thus we see that support among academics for substantial expansion, beyond 15 to 20 percent of the age grade in higher education, is to some degree independent of their attitudes toward the fundamental changes in governance, curriculum, and the like, that we associate with the movement toward mass higher education.

I am suggesting that a useful analysis of the variations in perspective and orientation among university teachers has to combine their attitudes toward the expansion of higher education with their views about its proper character and functions. Basic differences in academic orientations are best represented not along a single traditionalist-expansionist continuum, but more accurately by a typology, one dimension of which is defined by their opposition to or support for continued rapid expansion; the other by a commitment to traditional university forms and functions versus an acceptance of the transformation of the basic functions and characteristics of the system as it moves from being an elite to being a mass system. This typology is shown graphically in Figure 2.1.

Attitudes regarding the proper forms and functions of higher education	Attitudes toward the growth of higher education	
	ELITISTS	EXPANSIONISTS
TRADITIONALISTS	I	II
REFORMERS	III	IV

FIGURE 2.1

These stark polarities, of course, do not do justice to the complex views and attitudes held by individual university teachers. Nor do they capture the nuances of thought and feeling by which men manage to maintain conceptions of the universities and of their academic roles that reflect both expansionist and elitist values, or that accept some changes but not others in the character of their institutions. Nevertheless, men do differ in the emphasis they place on these values, the priorities they put on their embodiment in university organizations, and the allocation of both national and personal resources. And it is the relative emphasis in their values and orientations that is crucial during a period of expansion and change, when men can oppose, or attempt to delay, or welcome, or even try to accelerate the changes that are associated with the expansion and democratization of higher education.

1. Traditionalist Elitist

This complex of values and attitudes was the dominant orientation of European academic men (and, indeed, of nearly everyone who had views about universities) before World War II. And they are still held by many university teachers, especially the senior professors, in many countries. In their purest forms they rarely are articulated or defended any longer in speech or print, but their power lies in the extent to which they continue to guide action. They are reflected most clearly in the work of senior academic men in their senates and committees, defending deeply held and cherished values that for some represent the very essence of the university, values that give meaning and substance to civilized society. In this view, the function of higher education is to prepare small numbers of very able and ambitious students who have been rigorously educated in highly selective elite secondary schools—lycees or gymnasiums—for the professions traditionally requiring a university degree, and to prepare an even smaller number for a life of scholarship and scientific research. This university is defined by its traditional curriculum and governed as an autonomous corporate body by senior professors. Graduates of the university, whether they remain there as scholars or go into the world in the learned professions, should hold a distinctive status in society, and indeed comprise a special estate, marked by a way of life and thought as well as by the dignities and privileges of their status. This conception of the university has its roots in the classical and humane studies of the medieval and post-medieval universities, as modified and extended by the inclusion of natural science in departments and research institutes during the nineteenth century. But this orientation is compatible with the democratic view that entry to the university should be governed by strictly meritocratic criteria rather than by social origins, and thus in principle should be open to students from every social stratum, though in practice the nature of selection and preparation for entry effectively restricts membership almost wholly to the children of the professional and upper middle classes.

In an egalitarian age, men who hold these views are often attacked as reactionary defenders of their own special privileges. But in their own minds they are defending an important bulwark of civilization against the new barbarism of mass society as they defend the values of scholarship, learning, and disinterested inquiry against the enormous pressures to subordinate the university to the needs of vocational training, economic growth, social leveling, and contemporary politics. It is an important question for societies and educators whether these views and these men will merely be defeated and "swept into the dustbin of history," or whether their views will inform and fructify the developments now occurring, and will survive in at least certain segments of the diverse systems of higher education now emerging. The fate of those values will be determined in part by the unique social and political histories of the several societies whose educational systems are now undergoing change, and in part by the ways in which these changes are accomplished. It may be that the central questions for educators in the near future will be not how to dislodge elitist traditionalists from their positions of power in academic senates, institutes, and departments, but how to preserve and defend the best of the values that they represent under conditions of mass higher education.

2. Traditionalist Expansionist

Academic men holding this position have welcomed or at least accepted the rapid growth of their institutions and systems, while defending the traditional university values discussed above. In a word, these are men who have believed it possible to expand very considerably the elite university systems without transforming them in fundamental ways or adding to them quite different kinds of institutions—it is a belief in the expansion rather than the transformation of higher education. These views are perhaps the most widely held of the four basic orientations we are describing. Everywhere the pressures for expansion that followed World War II met with surprisingly little resistance among academics, in part because they recognized the changed economic and social circumstances of the postwar world, in part because, in the short run, expansion greatly increased their resources and their capacities to do many things they had wanted to do, and in part because their institutions showed a surprising capacity to carry larger numbers of students and employ more staff without a fundamental change in their character. But as I suggest elsewhere, growth alone begins to create strains in the traditional forms and functions of higher education, and this orientation, inherently unstable, has no answers to the solution of the problems engendered by growth, except more growth or the cessation of growth.

3. Elitist Reformers

This is a small but significant body of academic men who wish to preserve the unique role of universities as elite centers for scholarship and research at its highest level, but who recognize the need for certain internal reforms that would reflect the changed map of learning and the changing relationships between higher education and the larger society. Among the reforms these men have urged have been a modification of the professorial oligarchy that has governed most European universities and an improvement in the status of junior staff—in their conditions of work, their tenure, and their role in departmental and university government. In addition, such men have also pressed for more support for research and a movement away from the traditional faculty toward a departmental organization that more closely reflected the actual organization of intellectual and scientific work; in this they were undoubtedly influenced by the American model in which the department is the arm of the discipline in the university. In a sense, this perspective aimed to modernize the university in its organizational structure without changing its basic character as the center for intellectual work at the highest standards, access to which is limited by meritocratic criteria to a relatively small number of able and highly motivated students. Many of these men have learned in the past few decades how much easier it is simply to increase the numbers of students and staff than to carry out the serious structural reforms that they have recommended. But in their view, a slowing down or even a cessation in the rate of growth of higher education or the shifting of growth wholly to the non-university sectors may provide the breathing space and opportunity to reform the conditions of teaching and learning in the universities, and thus afford an opportunity for reestablishing and reinforcing those high standards threatened by the indiscriminate growth of unreformed structures.

4. Expansionist Reformers

Expansionist reformers, concentrated very much on the political left, and among younger faculty in the social sciences and some of the arts subjects, see many of the traditional forms and functions of the university as the greatest obstacle to the democratization and expansion of higher education. The problem appears to many of them as much political as educational: to change the distribution of power within universities so as to break the capacity for resistance of the more conservative professorial elite. In this they often have the cooperation of political parties and movements, and sometimes of higher civil servants in the relevant ministries of education. The views of this body of thought are marked by a conviction that there must be a substantial transformation of higher education; it must be extended vertically in the class structure—fundamentally democratized in its patterns of recruitment—and also horizontally into a broad range of social, economic, and political activities of the society. For example, they want to provide useful training for a much wider range of occupations and professions than the traditional learned professions of the old university. Also, it is not uncommon for people with these views to link the transformation of the university to broader ideas of social transformation or revolution. Moreover, the proponents of this position do not ordinarily recommend the creation of institutions to carry these additional functions alongside the elite universities, but rather urge the transformation of those elite universities into larger, more heterogeneous, more democratic and socially responsive institutions of mass higher education. And in many countries young faculty have found support for their views in the student body; the main weight of student demands for changes in the university falls into this category.

The attitudes and orientations of university teachers and administrators toward the future of higher education in their countries, summarized in this typology, both reflect and influence its growth and development. The rapid growth of higher education after World War II brought large numbers of new men into the system. In the climate of Europe after World War II many of these did not accept the old assumptions of European elite education, especially its narrow class base for recruitment and the undemocratic rule of the professoriate.

In addition, rapid growth, both in rate and absolute numbers, weakened the close personal ties of junior and senior men that had softened and legitimated the traditional arrangements. The powerlessness and insecurity of the junior staff has become more visible and more resented.

The broad-based demand for expansion set off a train of consequences, most of which undermined the old assumptions and arrangements and led to calls for further democratization and reform. For example, higher education during the 1950s and 1960s was increasingly justified by reference to its presumed contribution to economic growth, and there was a strong emphasis on the links between university training and industrial development. At the same time that tendency created pressures for an expansion of technological and business studies and for more directly applied research in the universities. On the other hand, the growing welfare state created a continuing demand for people with skills in the applied social sciences—in public administration, in social work, in penology—indeed, for the whole range of social problems to which the state was giving increased and systematic attention. Both of these broad developments strengthened certain sections of the university and imbued them with a spirit inevitably at variance with that of the traditional elite university. Many of the problems of European higher education have centered on the accommodation of these new functions and activities, and the new kinds of people drawn to them and thus into the university, with the older functions and traditional conceptions of university life.

The typology of academic orientations sketched above, although not meant to be descriptive of the full range of views held by individual teachers and administrators, is designed to be helpful in addressing such questions as these:

- How diverse are the conceptions of academic life; are they captured in this kind of typology, or are there better ways of describing the main currents of thought among academic men about their own institutions? And do we find the same types of attitudes among politicians and civil servants—or are differences among them along different lines of cleavage?

- What is the distribution of these types within a university, or a national system, and how has that distribution been changing over time?

- What is the organizational structure of this normative diversity? Do we find representatives of all of these types within every faculty, every department, in ways that are making it increasingly difficult to govern these units and carry on the ordinary business of education? Or do we find a continued consensus on the conceptions of education within faculties and departments, with the dissensus reflecting the new departments and faculties and research institutes within the expanded universities—and thus somewhat insulated from one another in the ordinary running of the institution?

- Where are the concentrations of views held in terms of subject areas, age, kind of institution, and the like? New experimental institutions tend to recruit men interested in reform and expansion initially. Do the new institutions have much higher concentrations of expansionist reformers, or do they increasingly become "more royalist than the king," with strongly conservative positions as a result of the insecurity of their status within their national systems of higher education?

- What are the patterns of coalition and conflict within the universities? On what kinds of issues do men and groups holding one or another of these different views join with others on such issues as curriculum reform, and to what extent are lines of conflict and cleavage drawn along these lines of academic orientations?

Briefly, we are asking whether this typology of academic orientations helps to illuminate and clarify the dynamics of conflict and change in the systems and institutions of higher education now, and whether it aids us to study and understand the evolution of these systems in the future. At the very least, if this typology shows a certain congruence with the realities of institutional life, it suggests that we need solid empirical data on the distributions of these views in different systems and parts of systems. Broad comparative survey research centering on a typology something like this may allow us to get a better sense of the role of academic attitudes and values in institutional change in European higher education. For, whatever may be the best way to discuss and analyze them, the distribution of attitudes and orientations of university teachers and administrators about their own institutions is a major force in determining whether a society moves toward mass higher education, how it deals with the strains that inevitably arise as it grows before it transforms its institutions, what forms the new mass institutions take, and whether the older functions and institutions survive and continue to perform their traditional university functions.

Dilemmas of Growth in the Transition toward
Mass Higher Education

The expansion of higher education and the transition of elite to mass systems generate a set of dilemmas that are not easily solved, but that persist as continuing problems for teachers, students, and administrators. The forms these dilemmas take and their relative importance vary from country to country, but in some form they are visible in every advanced society whose systems of higher education are growing.

Quality, Equality, and Expansion

The steady expansion of higher education appears to some observers to constitute a serious threat to academic standards. The question of standards is nominally a question of the quality of an academic program, how rigorous and demanding on the one hand, how rich and stimulating on the other. At one extreme we think of a group of learned and imaginative scholars teaching highly selected and motivated students in a situation of rich intellectual resources, cultural, scientific, and academic. At the other extreme are institutions staffed by less well-educated and less accomplished teachers, teaching less able and less well-motivated students under less favorable conditions—marked by lower salaries, a poorer staff-student ratio, a smaller library, fewer laboratory places, and all in a less stimulating and lively intellectual environment. Many countries are committed to the expansion of their systems of higher education, but to an expansion that does not lower the quality and standards of the higher education already offered. This involves the achievement of education at a high and common standard of quality throughout the system, whatever the varied functions of the different institutions may be. And this dual commitment—to continued growth and also to high quality in all parts of the system—poses the dilemma.

The dilemma has three components. First, there is the strong egalitarian sentiment that all provision in higher education ought to be substantially of equal quality (and thus of cost). (In the absence of good or reliable measures of the effects of higher education on the adult careers of graduates, we tend to assess the quality of education by reference to its internal processes, and this leads us to equate quality with cost.) The second is that the criteria against which new forms of mass higher education are assessed are typically those of the older, costlier forms of elite higher education. And third, a rapid and potentially almost unlimited growth of higher education, at the per capita cost levels of the former small elite systems, places intolerable burdens on national and state budgets that are also having to cope with growing demands from other public agencies, such as social welfare, preschool education and child care, primary and secondary school systems, housing, transportation, and defense.

When applied to higher education, the egalitarian position, which cuts across class lines and party preferences, is highly critical of any tendency to institutionalize differences between one sector and another of higher education. Egalitarians in many countries are committed to closing the gulf between the several parts of their higher educational systems, and to reducing the differentials in the status, quality, costs, and amenities of its different segments and institutions. Men with these sentiments, who might be called "unitarians" in their commitment to a single system of institutions, governed by common standards of education throughout, are often also committed to reforming universities and making them serve more of the functions of the non-elite forms of higher education, while at the same time raising the quality of the non-elite forms of higher education, especially of higher technical education, to that of the university standard. (These are the people I have described earlier as "expansionist reformers.") This position, liberal, humane, and generous, argues that the formal differentiations between the different forms and sectors of higher education almost always lead to invidious distinctions between them, and ultimately to very marked differences in the quality of their staff and students, and in other respects as well. Men holding these views also observe that the weaker or low-status segments of the system are those characteristically associated with and used by students from working- and lower-middle-class origins, so that the status differentiation in higher education is closely linked to that of the class structure as a whole. They argue that any sectors of education outside the system that include the universities must necessarily be made up of second-class institutions for second-class (and most commonly working-class) citizens, as historically they have been. Essentially their slogan is "nothing if not the best"—especially for youngsters from those strata of the society that have often gotten less or, if anything, second best.

But while this position is humane and generous in its concern for the equality of educational opportunities for working-class people, it is, in its insistence on a leveling upward, in cost as well as quality, inevitably in conflict with a continued and rapid expansion of the provision for higher education. No society, no matter how rich, can afford a system of higher education for 20 or 30 percent of the age grade at the cost levels of the elite higher education that it formerly provided for 5 percent of the population. Insofar as egalitarians insist that there be no major differentials in per capita costs among various sectors of the system of higher education, and also insist on expansion, then they force a leveling downward in costs, and perhaps in quality as well. Insofar as they are committed to a high and common set of standards throughout the system, they are also necessarily urging a restraint on expansion, though they themselves may not recognize this. The crucial question in this unitarian position is whether it is a commitment only to a common set of standards throughout the system, or to a common high set of standards as well.

The unitarian position, I suggest, is basically incompatible with very marked differences between institutions in their status, staff-student ratios, and other aspects of cost and quality. While it is possible in principle to argue that some institutions would be more expensive because they carry a larger research responsibility, it is very difficult in practice to argue for a genuine unitarian system while forbidding certain parts of that system or institutions within it to engage in research. And research is inherently highly expensive. Moreover, there is a tendency everywhere to identify research with the highest standards of higher education, an identification that has a strong component of reality in it. It is research that attracts the most able and creative academic minds, and it is the institutions that recruit these men that gain higher status in any system of higher education. Therefore, a genuinely egalitarian policy must allow every institution to attract people who are innovative intellectually, and that means supporting their research and giving them the high degree of autonomy they need to create new knowledge, new fields of study, and new combinations of disciplines. These activities are very hard to rationalize and program closely despite the new forms of systems management being introduced everywhere. For this and other reasons, a unitarian position that wants to raise standards in all institutions to that of the leading universities tends to constrain the growth of the system; if every new place, every new institution is potentially as expensive as the most costly of the old, then growth must be very carefully planned and sharply restricted. However, where the egalitarian spirit overrides that of a commitment to high standards, as in much of the United States, the slogan is not "nothing if not the best" but rather the expansionist slogan "something is better than nothing." Under those circumstances there tends to be a leveling downward coupled with expansion, rather than a leveling upward with its inherent tendencies toward a constraint on growth.

The key question in this dilemma is whether new forms of higher education can fulfill their functions at a standard that earns high status and satisfies egalitarians, while reducing per capita costs in ways that will allow genuine expansion toward mass higher education. The Open University in Great Britain is certainly one effort in that direction. Alternatively, a society may reject the arguments of the unitarians and egalitarians and develop a system that sustains internal diversity in costs and quality as well as in forms and functions, on the American model. (As I suggest later, this is much more difficult in systems that are financed, and thus ultimately governed, from a central government agency.) But in either case, the more ambitious and energetic the new institutions are, the more they will demand the libraries and research facilities, the salary schedules and the other amenities, of the old institutions, and the more likely they are to drive their per capita costs up. It may be worth exploring how the forms of this dilemma differ in different societies.

The effect of expansion on standards and quality is a complex and uncertain issue. In the early stages of the current phase of growth, in the 1950s, there was widespread concern among academic men and others that the pool of talented youth able to profit from higher education was small and limited, and that expansion beyond the numbers provided by this pool would necessarily mean a decline in student quality. But this fear has declined and in some cases disappeared as numbers have grown without a demonstrable decline in overall student quality.[9] Nevertheless, some observers suggest the new students are, if not less able, then less highly motivated, or less well prepared in their secondary schools, for serious academic work. This feeling is widespread, even if there is no good evidence to support the hypothesis, and some reason to suspect that real students in the present are being compared with idealized students in some mythical Golden Age located variously in the past, depending on the age of the speaker.

There is a somewhat more persistent and plausible concern held by many that the rapid expansion of higher education has lowered the average quality or the adequacy of preparation of college and university teachers, especially among the new recruits. Still others fear that growth has affected the relations between teachers and students adversely, making them more remote and impersonal (where they were not so already). And others suggest that mass higher education must affect the intellectual climate of colleges and universities, introducing into them the vulgarities of the marketplace, of vocational training, of mass politics and popular culture.

Whatever the validity of these fears, and they are not wholly without substance, it seems likely that the impact of expansion on the quality of higher education would be greatly influenced in every society by how it deals with the dilemmas discussed above, and particularly whether it strives to achieve a common level of quality throughout or finds ways of creating and sustaining diversity within its system in all the characteristics that mark higher educational institutions, including their quality and costs. It may be that in the interaction of quality, equality, and expansion, educators must accept the inequalities inherent in genuine diversity if they are to defend the highest standards of scholarly and academic life in some parts of an expanding system. But that solution, of course, has its own costs—moral and intellectual as well as financial and political—and some societies may well opt for equality at high standards at the cost of continued rapid expansion. But I suspect that only in rhetoric can all of these desirable characteristics of higher education be maximized within the same system.

Patterns of Planning under Conditions of Uncertainty and Rapid Change

An analysis of the phases of development of higher education of the kind we are undertaking in this essay involves some effort to see ahead into the future. And that, of course, raises the question of the extent to which some kind of planning, either for systems or for single institutions, can help to ease the transitions and solve the problems during the transition phases uncovered by this analysis. That, in turn, involves some consideration of the nature of forecasting and the role that it may play in educational planning. Let me start by making a distinction between secular trends and unforeseen developments.

Secular Trends

Secular trends, the broad movements of social institutions of the kind that we have been discussing in this essay, can reasonably be expected to continue short of a catastrophe over a period of decades. Among the secular trends in higher education that we can reasonably expect to continue for the rest of the century the most important are growth, democratization, and diversification.

Growth

Despite the problems that the growth of higher education brings in its train and despite the arguments one hears from various quarters that the growth should be slowed or stopped, it seems to me very unlikely that any advanced industrial society can or will be able to stabilize the numbers going on to some form of higher education any time in the near future. And this is true for a number of reasons that I think will be compelling for any government or ministry.

1. There is almost certainly going to be a continued popular demand for an increase in the number of places in colleges and universities. Despite much loose talk about graduate unemployment or of an oversupply of educated men, it is still clear that people who have gone on to higher education thereby increase their chances for having more secure, more interesting, and better-paid work throughout their lives. The concern of young men and women and of their parents for access to the best and most highly rewarding jobs in the society (rewarding in every sense) will ensure that the demand for places continues high.

2. These rational calculations and anticipations initially affect those people (and their sons and daughters) who are, so to speak, at the margin of higher education, who would a few years earlier have ended their for-

mal education on the completion of secondary schooling. But growth and the movement from elite to mass higher education itself creates a set of social and psychological forces that tend to sustain it. As more and more people go to college or university, and as an even larger number become aware of it as a possible and reasonable aspiration for themselves and their children, higher education enters into the standard of living of growing sectors of the population. Sending one's sons and daughters to college or university increasingly becomes one of the decencies of life rather than an extraordinary privilege reserved for people of high status or extraordinary ability. Giving one's children a higher education begins to resemble the acquisition of an automobile or washing machine, one of the symbols of increasing affluence—and there can be little doubt that the populations of advanced industrial societies have the settled expectation of a rising standard of living. But in addition, sending one's sons and daughters to college or university is already, and will increasingly be, a symbol of rising social status. Not only does it give evidence of status mobility in the adult generation—in this respect resembling the purchase of a home in the country or an automobile—but it also lays the necessary foundation for the social mobility of a family across generations. Everywhere the numbers of people who have completed secondary education grows, and as more people complete secondary education, it will be more necessary for their sons and daughters to go on to higher education if they are to qualify for still higher-status occupations. And this is increasingly the case as more and more occupations require a degree or other higher educational qualification for entry.

3. But, of course, the wishes of parents and youngsters to go on to higher education would be inhibited if there were no growth in the jobs that require postsecondary education. And on this score, there is presently much talk of an oversupply of graduates and of a decline in the market for people who have had further education. But I think there is little evidence for that oversupply, certainly over the next three or four decades. For closely related to the growth of demand for places, which might be called the "push" from the general population, there is the "pull" of the economy, marked particularly by the continued growth of the tertiary or service sector of the society. And this takes two forms. One is the growth of those occupations that traditionally or presently require higher educational qualifications. The growth of every advanced

economy is marked by a much more rapid growth in the numbers of managerial and technical personnel than of manual or skilled workers. The rationalization of production and the growth of industrial and commercial organizations generate enormous bureaucratic structures that in their middle and higher reaches clearly call for the skills and attitudes and orientations that are provided by postsecondary education. Moreover, there is a whole range of new professions and semi-professions, particularly those linked to the welfare functions of government—the social workers, penologists, experts in the environment, transport, housing, and urban problems—that call for advanced training.

But in addition, and equally important, is the educational inflation of occupations. As the supply of educated people grows, job requirements are redefined so that occupations that formerly were filled by secondary school graduates are increasingly restricted to people with postsecondary education. But in fact, people with more formal education compete with growing success for those jobs with people who have less formal qualifications. And once in those jobs, they tend to reshape them, by exercising responsibility, taking initiative, applying skill and imagination, in ways that the job may not have required when it was being filled by people with lower qualifications. This is an aspect of the impact of the extension of higher education on the occupational structure that manpower analysts almost never take into account, partly because until recently graduates have been going into traditional graduate occupations rather than redefining and reshaping jobs formerly filled by people who had not been to college or university. But one of the most important aspects of the movement from elite to mass higher education lies precisely in this transformation of jobs by people of greater education than formerly were employed in those jobs.

What mass higher education does is to break the old rigid connection between education and the occupational structure under which a degree not only qualified men for a certain range of occupations and professions, but also disqualified them for all the jobs that formerly did not employ graduates. Thus graduate unemployment has never meant that graduates could not get jobs competitively with non-graduates, but that they could not get the kind of jobs that they thought appropriate to their status and dignity. The growth of mass higher education breaks this connection, and allows people who have gained a higher education to seek employment without loss of dignity wherever the jobs may exist. By entering the job market without prior conceptions of "inappropriate" jobs, graduates can upgrade the jobs that they do take, both in status and in the scope they give for the application of skill and initiative. At the same time, by competing with those who have not been through college or university they increase the pressures on the latter to gain formal qualifications so that they too can compete successfully for the same range of white-collar occupations. And that process (like the rising standards of living as applied to formal education) is one of the processes that inexorably increases the demand for higher education both from the populations of industrial societies and from their occupational structures.

4. Alongside these social, psychological, and economic forces are the institutional changes in secondary education that bring more and more students to the point of college or university entry. The raising of the school-leaving age, the broad extension of university preparatory studies, the spread of comprehensive schooling, are all institutional encouragements to students to stay on longer and to qualify for entry to college or university. The extension of educational opportunities in secondary education reflects both the fundamental democratization of modern society and changes in the economy that I have spoken of. But it works independently of these other forces to increase the pool of young men and women at the margin of higher education, and thus inevitably the absolute numbers and the proportion of the age grade who are able to go on in response to a variety of other economic and social motivations.

It is widely recognized that the rate of social, economic, and technological change in modern societies is very high and increasing. Inventions such as the computer, changes in the supply of energy implicit in nuclear fission and fusion, changes in forms of transportation and entertainment and communication all create new industries almost overnight while sentencing others to rapid decay and obsolescence. The more highly developed the economy, the more rapid these transformations of the economy and its underlying technological base, and all of this in turn forces changes throughout life on people in the labor force. One student of social and technological change has estimated that a man who is presently entering the labor market in the United States will change not just his job but the industry in which he works nine or ten times in the course of his working life.

The rapidity of social change, largely though not exclusively due to rapid technological change, puts a very great premium on the ability to learn over the mastery of specific skills. This in turn greatly increases the functional importance of formal schooling over apprenticeship or on-the-job training. Formal education provides a base of broad understanding of managerial and technical principles, and above all a training in the capacity to acquire new knowledge, while apprenticeship and on-the-job training more often transmit skills that are likely to become obsolete very shortly. Rapid technological and organizational changes loosen the links between formal education and specific parts of the occupational structure; but they increase the role of formal schooling in underpinning the whole structure of a rapidly changing technological system. This fact argues against the widespread assumption that non-technical studies have no vocational component. On the contrary, it is likely that the most important skill acquired in higher education is the capacity to respond sensitively and successfully to rapid social and technological change. Above any specific skill acquired, this adaptability gives students in colleges and universities significant advantage over those who have not received any higher education. Indeed, it may well be that formal education is the major determinant of whether men and women are the beneficiaries or the victims of social and economic changes. It is clear that these changes benefit some sections of the population while hurting others, and those hurt most are those with inflexible skills who have not the capacity to adapt readily to new requirements or opportunities. It is not only the ability to adapt to new jobs but the capacity to learn where new opportunities are arising that is the mark of the educated man, and this is a very great advantage that he has over less well-educated people in contemporary societies.

Democratization

One secular trend in modern times—a movement that in Western countries is unbroken for at least two centuries and shows no signs of weakening—is the fundamental democratization of society. In its earliest forms this involved the extension of the franchise and other aspects of political power to larger and larger sections of the society. In addition, there has been a continued weakening of traditional social distinctions and the extension of various social and economic rights (which were once privileges) to ever broader sections of the community. Traditional social hierarchies still survive, and patterns of deference are deeply embedded in the social structures of many societies. Nevertheless, everywhere in the West they are weakening under the impact of World Wars, the growth of the consuming society, and the leveling forces of democratic politics, the mass media, and mass education. The movement toward mass higher education will contribute to this fundamental democratization of society, but also the democratization of society will feed back upon and contribute to the extension of educational opportunities. But the expansion and democratization of educational opportunity, the opening of doors, so to speak, is only part of this process. Sooner or later the argument is made that the ultimate results of a policy of equality of opportunity must be visible in the equality of achievement of social groups and strata. If intelligence is randomly distributed in a population—an empirical question that has come to be a political affirmation—then any differences in the proportions of youth from different social groups or strata who enter higher education and gain its degrees and certificates must be due to patterns of social discrimination and not to variations in individual ability. These differences in an egalitarian age are increasingly defined as inequities and the product of injustice, and very strong social and political forces are at work to reduce or obliterate them. The net result of these forces must be the expansion of places, if the proportions from every social class are to be equalized. This is clearly more a long-range goal than any immediate achievable outcome of public policy; and moreover there are many arguments in principle against these policies. But whatever one may think of those arguments, it is difficult to imagine that they will be decisive, and that the fundamental democratization of the society will not also extend to the provision of places in higher education as it has for primary school and is in the process of doing at the secondary levels.

Diversification

Another broad trend in higher education that we might reasonably expect to continue is the diversification of the forms and functions of higher education. As I have suggested several times in this essay, the growth of numbers has also meant an increasing diversity of students in respect to their social origins and other characteristics, in their motivations, aspirations, interests, and adult careers. All of this places great pressures on the system to reflect the diversity of students in a similar diversity of educational provision—in the curriculum, in forms of instruction, and the like. A central issue, as I have suggested, is the continuing struggle on the part of more traditionally oriented educations against the threat, as they see it, to standards, values, and indeed the very essence of the traditional university, posed by the pressures for diversification arising out of the growing and changing student population.

But in addition to the familiar changes within the regular colleges and universities, there is also a movement to diversify higher education upward and outward: upward to provide adult education or lifelong learning for a very large part of the adult population; outward, to bring it to people in their own homes or workplaces. The pressures behind this are many. There is obviously the force of rapid social and technological change, which alone creates a need for the provision of new skills or renewed formal training for people who are changing their occupations, or whose jobs and professions are changing more rapidly than their capacity to keep up through on-the-job experience. For example, engineers and doctors are increasingly out of touch with the latest developments in their professions unless they are able to get formal refresher training during their professional careers. But in addition many educators are noting that substantial sections of the old university student body, entering directly from secondary school, are for various reasons somewhat resentful of their prolonged formal education and rather weakly motivated. By contrast, the motivation of adults already in the occupational structure for further formal education is often very high. They are much more rewarding to teach and indeed bring a new and stimulating element back into the classroom by way of their own job experience. Also, they tend to be less highly politicized and have a more exclusively academic or vocational interest, and this appeals to many educators as well as to politicians. Add to this the fact that adult education, offered part-time or in the evenings for people already in the occupational structure, often turns out to be less expensive than traditional forms of higher education. The students do not have to be expensively maintained in halls of residence; moreover, there is not the hidden cost of their forgone earnings if they are actually at work while attending college or university courses. A great deal has been written on the subject of permanent education; I share the view of many that this may well be the most rapidly growing sector of higher education over the next three or four decades. And if adults are brought directly into the central college and university facilities and are taught alongside of young men and women directly out of secondary school, it may be enormously beneficial for both sides, and in important respects change the character of higher education for the older and younger groups alike.

But adult education, already liberated from the traditional forms associated with the education of young men and women, is likely to break with all sorts of traditional assumptions about how higher education is accomplished. It is likely to be more dispersed and brought much closer to where people live and work. Already the Open University in Britain has demonstrated that higher education at the high standard of British universities can be offered to men and women in their own homes, and this is a lesson that is being learned by similar forms of off-campus and extended education in the United States and other countries. The imaginative use of television, videocassettes, and remote computer consoles will greatly facilitate the provision of higher education outside the traditional boundaries of the university or college buildings. Although these developments are likely to occur first in connection with adult education, they may very well be adapted to the education of postsecondary youth in the near future.

Growth, democratization, diversification—these are the secular trends in higher education that we can anticipate continuing, though at different rates and in different forms in different places, over the next three or four decades. And if the future were the product of the secular trends alone we could plan for it with some assurance, some sense of our capacity to master the future, first intellectually and then institutionally. But the future is not just the aggregate of secular trends. It is also full of unforeseen events and developments that sharply limit our power to anticipate the nature of the world for which we plan, or our capacity to make our plans achieve the results that we intend.

Unforeseen Developments

Unforeseen developments take a number of different forms. They take the form of new techniques and technologies in industries; they take the form of broad changes in the values of sections of the society and most especially of youth. Who could have forecast only two or three decades ago the development of the computer industry, or of electronics more generally? These industries have affected the economies and occupational structures of advanced industrial societies very considerably. And in a narrower perspective, they have greatly changed the resources available to education. Videocassettes, television, computers, and the like make it possible at least to imagine extended forms of higher education very different from the correspondence courses of the "external degree" before World War II.

Specific historical events also affect our power to forecast the developments of institutions. The assassinations of John and Robert Kennedy profoundly changed the politics (and the colleges and universities) of the United States, not least through their effect on the extent and duration of American military involvement in Indo-China. The balance of payments crisis in Britain and its effect on the British National Plan in the late 1960s very substantially modified the development of higher education in that country. Or to take a more speculative example, a substantial easing of tensions between East and West, and very sharp control of the arms race, may in the future release substantial resources in Western countries for higher education that are now spent on defense.

There are also broad changes in values, in whole societies or in major segments, that affect higher education. For example, the quite unanticipated growth of concern for the environment in all industrial societies will affect higher education in various ways—on one hand, increasing the demand for people with broad combinations of advanced learning in social and technical areas; on the other hand, providing important additional competition for resources that might otherwise go to higher education. Another example is the growth of the counterculture in every Western society, and what is clearly a retreat from reason among sections of middle-class youth toward neo-romanticism and unconventional forms of religiosity. Closely related to this there is, among certain sections of youth, what might be called a crisis of ambition, marked by the primacy of moral considerations and a quest for community as over against the striving for individual achievement and a personal career. These changes in values, whose significance it is hard now to assess over the long run, may have very large consequences for institutions such as universities based so substantially on the rule of reason and on the preparation for adult careers based on knowledge and expertise. The heightened political concerns of university students in the late 1960s, and the readiness to carry political activism into the university itself, has posed another set of problems for institutions of higher education, and it is difficult to know how that pattern will develop in the decades ahead. In addition, there are changes in the relations between the generations, in the strength and basis of authority, and in a whole variety of fundamental beliefs and values that make problematic the traditional forms of relationships in colleges and universities.

Forms of Planning

In the face of so much that is so problematic and fortuitous in historical development, as against what is reasonably anticipatable as the outcome of foreseeable secular change, it is useful to make a distinction between what might be called "prescriptive planning" and "systems planning."

Prescriptive planning, the kind that is most commonly practiced by the governing agencies and ministries of advanced societies, aims to spell out in detail the size and shape of the system of higher education over the next several decades, and the content and forms of instruction: in brief, what will be taught, to whom, to how many, and in what kind of institutions at what expense. Prescriptive planning necessarily rests on an analysis of secular trends (and only some of those). Typically, it bases itself on estimates and projections of the demand for higher education, both by the population at large and by the economy, and the resources available to higher education over a period of years. Systems planning, by contrast, would have as its aim the evolution of a system of higher education marked by diversity and flexibility. It would not aim to specify in detail what those institutions of higher education will look like, or how and what they will teach to whom. The difference in these modes of planning is between planning the specific size, shape, and content of an educational system, and planning the structure or form of a system of higher education that is best able to respond to the combination of secular trends and unforeseen developments.

The forces for prescriptive planning are everywhere dominant, despite the fact that they are probably inappropriate for a future that inevitably involves unforeseen developments. They are dominant, first, because of the very existence of agencies of central control. The existence of a central state administrative apparatus with the power to plan prescriptively is the first guarantee that will be the form that planning will take. There is, in addition, the illusion that higher education constitutes a closed system relatively impervious to unforeseen developments. This is a hangover from the period when almost the whole of education consisted of compulsory schooling plus a very small system of elite higher education; the bulk of planning for that kind of system was largely a planning for space and for the number of teachers necessary for a known population of youngsters. The forms and patterns of broad, nationwide prescriptive planning for primary and secondary education are now being adapted to higher education. Yet it is easy to see how much more vulnerable higher education is to unforeseen developments in technology, historical events, and broad changes in values than is the system of primary and secondary education. And third, growth itself stimulates prescriptive planning: the more higher education grows, the more money is needed for it, the more interest there is in it among larger parts of the population, the greater demand there is for tight control over its shape and costs. The growing demand for accountability of higher education, for its ability to demonstrate its efficiency in the achievement of mandated and budgeted goals, inevitably translates itself into tighter controls and prescriptive planning. But this control can only be exercised rationally in terms of available knowledge, based on foreseeable trends and projections. The growth of higher education, given a prescriptive control system, places ever greater demands on that system to maintain and increase its control over numbers and costs, structures and standards.

But prescriptive planning involving that kind of close control has very little flexibility to respond to the unforeseen and a very slow response rate to new developments. In addition, it politicizes many educational issues by locating the key decisions in central political agencies.

But perhaps most important, prescriptive planning by central planning agencies does not and perhaps cannot create genuine diversity in the forms and structures of higher education, although diversity itself constitutes the major resource that higher education has for responding to the unforeseen as well as to the anticipated developments and secular trends of modern society.

Central governing bodies tend to exert pressures toward uniformity among the institutions under their control. And these tendencies are only slowed rather than reversed by the formal allocation of different functions to different sectors, as they are, for example, in Britain's binary system. The pressures for uniformity or convergence associated with central governmental control over higher education, are several:

- The uniform application of administrative forms and principles, as in formulas linking support to enrollments; formulas governing building standards and the provision and allocation of space; formulas governing research support, and the like;

- Broad norms of equity, which prescribe equal treatment for equivalent units under a single governing body;

- Increasingly strong egalitarian values, which define all differences among public institutions in their functions, standards, and support—as inequitable.

Add to these the tendency for institutions to converge toward the forms and practices of the most prestigious models of higher education, a tendency that operates independently of government control, and we see that the forces working against diversity in higher education are very strong at a time when expansion increases the needs for diversification of forms and functions beyond what presently exists.

In many countries the struggle to contain diversity takes the form of an effort to maintain tight controls over standards, costs, functions, forms, and so forth, all in the service of the traditional values of higher education. Diversity is seen not only as a threat to the power of the state over a major claimant on public resources, as a threat to orderly governmental and bureaucratic process, as a challenge to the norms of equity and equality; diversity is also seen as academic anarchy and a threat to the traditional values of higher education itself. In part, there is in this a hostility to the market that is seen, correctly, as subversive of prescriptive controls, embodying the mastery of the unqualified over what ought to be a protected sphere of cultural life. Add to this the relation of growth to high costs and public accountability, and the consequent rationalization of administration in the service of efficiency, and we see how strong are the forces making for prescriptive planning. Everywhere one sees the distaste of central governmental agencies for the messiness and unpredictability of genuine and evolving diversity, and their continued efforts to bring their systems back under control and along desired lines of development. One may ask whether that tendency, which emerges more strongly during the confusions and uncertainties of transition from elite to mass higher education, is in fact likely to produce the kind of diverse system appropriate to mass higher education.

There are counter-forces that help to sustain and even increase diversity in higher education (and these, of course, vary in strength in different countries). In some places there is a multiplicity of governmental bodies involved in higher education: the United States is an extreme case in this respect. More generally, there are variations in the degree of diversity of sources of support, of both public and private funds. Third, there is, among some politicians and educators, a growing recognition of the desirability of diversity of forms and functions in higher education, and this leads to efforts to create and defend these institutional differences, through legislative and budgetary means.[10] In addition there is a growing sense of the inadequacy of the existing educational forms and a growing readiness to provide support for educational innovations on every level of higher education. Perhaps most important, rapid growth and large size make it more difficult for governing agencies to impose uniform patterns in systems already very large and diverse. The growth of institutions and systems toward mass higher education puts a strain on administrative structures designed for a smaller, simpler, elite system, and activities begin to elude the controls of an overburdened and understaffed administration. And finally, whether or not it is desirable, it is difficult to rationalize the multiplicity of functions and activities that go on within higher education. Much of what is done in higher education is esoteric and hard to understand for anyone outside a narrow academic or professional specialty. This near monopoly within the academic world of specialized knowledge about the nature of the academic fields and their needs and requirements is the ultimate basis of academic autonomy, and slows (though it may not prevent) rationalization and the application of standardized formulas governing admissions, academic standards, support, workloads, and the like. (This is, of course, the more true where the knowledge base is greater and the intellectual authority of the academics concerned is higher—which is why academic autonomy is defended more successfully in elite institutions.)

The multiplicity of academic activities, and the specialized knowledge required to assess or evaluate them, interferes also with the flow of accurate and standardized information about what is going on in an institution to its top management, and even more to higher governmental agencies and authorities. The resulting areas of ignorance and obscurity make it more difficult to develop standardized procedures and formulas, and thus sustain diversities.

Systems planning, by contrast, would aim to strengthen the forces making for diversity in higher education. It would, for example, increase the range and diversity of governing agencies and sources of support; it would encourage an increase in the range of functions performed and constituencies served by the system (though not necessarily by an individual institution); it would create forms of budgetary control in the service of accountability that did not impose the same formulas, standards, or criteria of efficient performance on all parts of the system. It would, in the terms of this essay, defend elite institutions in an emerging system of mass higher education without allowing the old elite institutions to impose their forms, standards, and costs on the new institutions or on the system as a whole.

But planning for a system marked by diversity runs against the habits and structures of educational planning in most European countries. Planning for diversity clearly involves risks, whereas prescriptive planning gives the illusion of meeting a contingent future more effectively (though I suspect the reverse is true). Prescriptive planning, and the central administrative and control structures that make it possible, are, I have suggested, the enemies of diversity, because diversity makes prescriptive planning and control more difficult and because it violates the principles of equitable treatment by government agencies and equality of status of public institutions. For these and other reasons, it seems unlikely that those governmental agencies that have the responsibility for higher education can or will surrender their control.

Thus, on balance, I believe that the forces working against genuine diversity in higher education in most European countries are rather stronger than those working to sustain or increase it. This may be debatable, in which case it is an issue that deserves further comparative study. But if that assumption is true, then several questions deserve close attention.

1. Is increasing control over the forms and functions of higher education by central public agencies or authorities an inevitable concomitant of expansion and increased costs?

2. Is the (increasing) role of public authorities presently a force working against diversity in higher education, in their functions and standards, their modes of governance, their forms of instruction, their sources of support, and their relation to other institutions of society?

3. If so, are these standardizing tendencies inherent in central governmental control, or is it possible for central governing and financing agencies to function in ways that sustain and increase the diversity in higher education? If so, what governing and funding structures would have that effect, and what principles of operation would govern their activities? How can efforts to support diversity be sustained against the political pressures in almost all advanced industrial societies arising out of (a) the norms that prescribe equitable treatment of all comparable units and (b) growing egalitarian sentiments and policies?

Conclusion

It is, needless to say, impossible to say anything very specific that is broadly true of all the emerging forms of higher education in fifteen or twenty complex industrial societies. Therefore, to say anything that might be useful, or at least interesting, it is necessary to carry on the discussion at a somewhat higher level of abstraction. But this means, as I have suggested earlier, that my remarks cannot be true in detail for any institution or even any single national system.

Moreover, this essay is not intended to increase or disseminate knowledge, in the way, for example, that a statistical report or a comparative survey of some emerging educational patterns does. It is rather an effort to suggest a way of thinking about the development of higher education in advanced societies, and to provide a way of framing a set of interrelated questions about this development. Many of my apparently confident assertions will be challenged, and some may in fact be empirically wrong, at least in some places. But that is less important than whether the questions thus raised, the problems and issues thus identified, are in fact the problems, issues, and dilemmas of higher education that educators and politicians, students and citizens, face in societies whose systems of higher education are moving from elite to mass forms. My aim was to help identify and clarify those questions, not to answer them. In keeping with my evident bias in favor of diversity, I can only hope that even if the questions that higher education in advanced societies face are similar, their answers will be different.

NOTES
....

1. This essay develops and extends ideas I first sketched out in two earlier essays, "Reflections on the Transition from Mass to Universal Higher Education," *Daedalus* (Winter 1970), and "The Expansion and Transformation of Higher Education," *The International Review of Education* (February 1972).

2. Unit credits and a modular curriculum are much more common in higher technical colleges than in European universities.

3. While the distance between the senior professor and the ordinary undergraduate may be very great, his research students are likely to be working with him in a close apprentice relationship.

4. It should not be thought that the Open University in England, despite its name, is a typical institution of universal access. On the contrary, it is a characteristically ingenious way of increasing access to an elite institution by substituting motivation for formal qualifications, and by allowing people to combine university work with full-time employment. Some of the characteristics of an elite university have been discarded, but the university maintains the high standards of elite British universities and its very clear boundaries. The Open University is an interesting transitional institution between the elite and mass phases of British higher education.

5. There is a certain danger in the argument that the development of these managerial techniques, as also of the increasing centralization of control, are inevitable, given the growth in the size and cost of higher education. An emphasis on the

inevitability of these trends and forces may preclude our asking the critical questions: how are these new techniques of administration being applied, what are their consequences, and what are the limits of centralization in relation to institutional autonomy? We should at least be aware of how these techniques may undermine those activities and functions of higher education that cannot be justified by reference to visible and easily measurable outputs.

6. Oxford and Cambridge, with their aristocratic egalitarianism among the whole body of teachers (dons), are an exception to this general rule. See A. H. Halsey and Martin Trow, *The British Academics* (London: Faber & Faber, 1971), especially chapter 6.

7. The United States, as it moves toward universal access, is experiencing strains in the somewhat different kind of consensus on which its multiversities are based.

8. This reference to student participation illustrates a general principle that emerges from this analysis: that the same phenomenon may have very different meaning and consequences in different phases of higher education. Thus student participation in the governance of a small elite institution marked by high value consensus, may in fact be merely the participation of the most junior members of a corporate body. By contrast, student participation in a large mass institution marked by value dissensus may heighten the kind of interest and ideological conflicts that academic institutions, whatever their size or character, have great difficulty in containing or resolving. This is not always recognized; and the arguments for student participation drawn from experience in elite universities is often applied indiscriminately to mass institutions. (This is true of other aspects of governance and forms of administration as well.)

9. Though it appears that with larger numbers the range of student abilities is wider.

10. This effort to achieve diversity through prescriptive planning runs against the political forces of equality, the bureaucratic preferences for standardization, and the academic tendency of institutions to model themselves on the most prestigious. This is an intent of the binary policy in Britain. For a discussion of its recent problems, see the comments of its author, Anthony Crosland, in the *Times Higher Educational Supplement*, June 6, 1972.

3

THROUGHOUT HIS CAREER, Martin Trow worried about the
fate of elite higher education as mass higher education inspired by
egalitarianism, democracy, and functionalism advanced. He was a
keen observer of its beauty and its warts. Above all, he anxiously
watched efforts in Europe to level the playing field among old and
new universities, among mass and vocational institutions and those
that created a community of scholars, as governments, sustained by
popular sentiment, sought to smash the sources of class privilege.

To make higher education a central part of a social and economic restructuring of society, many European governments rapidly increased the number of institutions, treating them as largely
equal, with the same purpose, with the same aspirations, and with
similar claims of public resources. When Trow published this essay
in 1976, this drive to equality was incomplete. He felt it was ill-
conceived, and should be checked. In the United States, there were
also strong elements of equalitarian thought, but in sharp contrast
with Europe, institution building and mass higher education had
occurred over a long period of time and resulted in a great array of
public and private institutions.

Many of the constructs of Trow's thinking on higher education
and society are to be found in this essay. He wishes to show the value
of elite higher education, to stake a claim that it should be preserved,
even nurtured, as part of a larger higher education system; governments should avoid interventions into the academic sphere and give
institutions, particularly elite ones, significant autonomy. He was
always wary of government's socioeconomic engineering of higher
education—a worldview that later informs his opposition to affirmative action—and detested the bureaucratic mindset of government
and university officials.

Trow the sociologist almost always adhered to a skillful analytical style that helps the reader see the various political and social camps and decipher a knowable cause of conflict and a rational conclusion. In this essay he identifies two enemies of elite institutions, "Those who dislike them for what they are or are purported to be— we might call these opponents on grounds of principle—and those who support policies which threaten elite higher education, whether or not they intend to." The first group saw elite institutions as incompatible with democracy and equality, as depriving newer and more egalitarian institutions of resources and reinforcing socioeconomic class biases.

But for Trow, the child of a family of moderate means, who traveled a long path to an elite graduate education and an elite professional career at Berkeley, this was a hopelessly historical view of elite institutions. Elite institutions, or elite programs within large universities, need not be bastions of the privileged. When writing this piece for *Minerva* in the mid-1970s, the privileged still had a strong hold on the American private elite institutions, but less so on public ones. Trow saw, and I think accurately, the many benefits of elite education as exceptional environments for educating broadly minded and creative individuals, as places that mere mass higher education institutions could not hope to replicate and that needed nurturing and were, in the end, value for money. Critics of elite higher education did not understand the rapid changes within these institutions, and they did not comprehend the profound expansion in the nature of knowledge or the fragile social environment of academic communities.

Over time, Trow's contrarian view became the accepted norm. The need for high-quality research-oriented institutions and "centers of excellence" within larger mass systems has recently been recognized by most European leaders and ministers of education and embraced by some of the higher education community. Governments are now deeply in love with the concept of the *knowledge economy*, which requires research-intensive universities. They are now creating incentives and space for high-quality research and selecting teaching programs within their mass higher education systems via national and, in the case of the European Union (EU), supranational policies. They are coming to terms with the inoperable dogma that, as Trow states, the "only values worth cultivating and pursuing are organizational efficiency and social equality"—although with top-down policy frameworks Trow thought misguided.

Our views are shaped by our own personal journeys. Trow the New Yorker, the descendant of Jewish immigrants, the longtime faculty member at Berkeley, experienced and observed the model he wished to promote and maintain—highly differentiated networks of higher education institutions that give room to the elite function, including the large research university where mass and elite forms coexist; where a student with talent, and of low or moderate means, could navigate a path to an elite academic community of thinkers and innovators and to the life of the mind. For Trow, mass higher education was a profound, enlightened, and evolving component in the modern world, as long as it also allowed for the "survival of elite higher education in modern society."

—JOHN AUBREY DOUGLASS

Elite Higher Education

An Endangered Species?

The term *elite higher education* can be used in quite different ways. It has been used, almost always pejoratively, to refer to education for the offspring of wealthy and powerful families, but not available to those from families of lower status and less power, wealth, or income.

Elite higher education has also been used to refer to a traditional humanistic education centering on the study of the classics, which included ancient philosophy and history and mathematics. That traditional humanistic education has been broadened in the course of several centuries to include modern languages and literatures, the sciences and social

Originally published as Martin Trow, "Elite Higher Education: An Endangered Species?" *Minerva* 14, no. 3 (Autumn 1976): 355–76. With kind permission of Springer Science and Business Media.

sciences, which together provide a broad cultural rather than a narrowly practical vocational training.

There is another way of viewing elite higher education, not in terms of the social origins of the student body or of the substance of what is studied and taught, but rather by reference to the mode of education and the level of intensity and complexity at which the subject is pursued. In this last sense it stands in contrast with the mass higher education that has emerged in every advanced industrial society over the past twenty-five years. This is the type of elite higher education that will be dealt with in this essay.

The relatively small university systems that provided this kind of education and that most industrial societies fostered in the nineteenth and early twentieth centuries enrolled between 2 and 5 percent of the group of appropriate age for attendance at university. These systems were able to expand after World War II, without changing in fundamental ways, to the point where they could deal with about 15 percent of that cohort. But as these systems admitted a larger proportion of the age group, they increasingly offered a rather different kind of higher education, in part within the old universities, in part in new institutions of mass higher education.

The essential characteristics of universities that offered elite higher education before World War II were their relatively small size and their function in the selection and preparation of the political elites and the elites of the learned professions. By contrast, forms of mass higher education were created to prepare young persons for careers in a great variety of new or expanding technical, semi-professional, and managerial occupations.[1]

The two types of higher education differ obviously in the proportions of the age group that they enroll; they also differ in the ways in which students and teachers engaged in them view higher education; in the typical student's career; in the homogeneity of the student body; in their forms of university administration and government; and in their principles and procedures for selecting students and appointing teachers. For example, attitudes toward admission are shaped by the relative ease of admission. Where admission is very restricted—as it is in those institutions offering elite higher education—it is generally seen as a privilege, accorded by virtue of birth or of talent or of both. By contrast, admission to institutions of mass higher education is seen as a right, subject only to certain formal qualifications. Students typically entered institutions of the former type directly from the secondary schools that were intended to prepare them for that kind of education, and they remained "in residence" uninterruptedly to their first degree. The rate of "wastage" from these institutions was and is low. By contrast, institutions of mass higher education have increasingly accepted students from comprehensive secondary schools, and increasing numbers enter after a period of employment or travel between secondary school and university. The student body of the institutions of mass higher education has been more heterogeneous, and rates of attrition have been higher. Moreover, as student numbers have increased, with larger proportions from families with low incomes, growing proportions tend also to be employed in fields not related to their studies—first during vacations and then during term. This has been increasingly acknowledged through the provision of part-time study and "sandwich courses." Syllabuses have been accordingly altered in recognition of the likelihood that the students would be able to read less, that they would be less interested in their studies, and that they would have less close relationships with their teachers. In contrast with this, those institutions that saw themselves as providing for an elite tended, on average, to be smaller, they were socially and physically more set off from their environment, the role of being a student was more exclusive, their teaching staffs enjoyed more self-government, and their academic standards were both higher and more consensual.

Can Elite Higher Education Survive?

The modes of elite higher education have shown a capacity for change and adaptation to new educational and social circumstances. It can now be found in other than its older forms and indeed in forms that are quite new to it. But it is important to make clear the common and essential features of the older and newer forms of elite higher education. First, its aim is to shape mind and character and not merely to transmit information and theories or to form skills. It is concerned as much with the acquisition of ways of thinking and feeling, not least about oneself in relation to the world, as it is about the knowledge acquired. Dr. A. H. Halsey has described higher education of an elite in its ideal collegiate form at Oxford and Cambridge where it still survives recognizably.

> the collegiate ideal associated with traditional Oxford and Cambridge is one of a community of established older and aspiring younger scholars . . . transmitting a cultivated way of life. This collegiate system is not conceived as narrowly intellectual in its scope, and far less as a tradition of occupational training. It is intended to pass on to each new generation of scholars a total culture or style of life, including carefully nurtured elements of mind and aesthetic taste and character in due measure. Relations of teachers and taught within this system are particularistic, affective, and attended by diffuse obligations.[2]

Dr. Halsey then goes on to contrast this conception of higher education as a cultivated way of life with a technical or vocational education:

> By contrast, in the kind of college that trains the student for a lucrative, specialised technical position in business or the professions, the typical organisation is bureaucratic. The institution assumes no responsibility for the values or social character of the novitiate; teacher and taught meet only in the context of formal instruction. The relationship is segmental rather than comprehensive and the obligation is specific rather than diffuse.[3]

The higher education of an elite was defined both by its cultural content and by the character of the relationships through which it was carried on. In much of traditional elite higher education, as at Oxford and Cambridge, the two were very closely linked, as they are in Dr. Halsey's comments: a certain kind of relation between teacher and student within a community of scholars was designed to teach gentlemen how to live a certain way of life; it was not meant to train young persons for specific occupations. Indeed, it rather looked down on that. Elite higher education conceived as the education of a gentleman for a style of life appropriate to a certain status in society was contrasted sharply with the training of experts for specific occupations. Max Weber regarded this distinction between the education of the cultivated man and of the expert as the source of the main conflict emerging in higher education.[4] The rise of mass higher education since World War II has been widely viewed as the ascendancy of technical and vocational education over liberal and general education.

But the growth of mass higher education has led to changes in the character of both liberal and vocational studies, and not merely to the expansion of the latter. The pronounced distinction between them—with elite higher education always taken to be a variety of liberal education, and mass higher education a form of vocational education—no longer obtains.

Both undergraduate and graduate studies at such leading technological universities as the Massachusetts Institute of Technology are in fact forms of elite higher education. There are many graduate professional schools that are very much oriented toward specialized training for careers in government or industry, and yet are carried on through a pattern of relations between students and teachers that is not much different from that which characterized the collegiate arrangements at Oxford or Cambridge. In these professional schools and graduate departments, relationships are broad rather than narrow; the teachers are concerned with the values and character of the students; teachers and taught often meet outside the setting of formal instruction; their concerns when they meet are not confined to what is contained in syllabus and lectures.

The emphasis on the transmission of a general culture and a style of life was a characteristic feature of the traditional forms of elite higher education. However, this may mislead us in our search for its descendants today. I think that we will find forms of elite higher education in the *grandes écoles*, in the advanced research seminars of the German universities, in the graduate departments and some of the professional schools of American universities, in the undergraduate courses of study at the Massachusetts Institute of Technology as well as in the undergraduate colleges of Harvard and Chicago universities, in the leading American liberal art colleges, and in much of both graduate and undergraduate studies at British universities.

The Distinctive Features of Elite Higher Education

What do these quite varied kinds of higher education have in common? Surely not a commitment to the cultivation of the particular qualities of mind and bearing that marked the traditional collegiate ideal at Oxford and Cambridge. The higher education of elites over the hundred years between 1850 and 1950 rested on a broad consensus among educated persons about what knowledge was of most worth, and what qualities of mind and character, should be possessed by the educated person. Notions about what characterized an educated person changed over time, and varied to some extent from one Western society to another, and even to some extent between parts of the same society. Nevertheless, there was some agreement on the question. Today there is no agreement on what is the irreducible and essential content of higher education for an elite, and we are required to describe it more by reference to its forms than to its content.

Under present-day circumstances, then, elite forms of higher education are marked by attempts to infuse a general moral and cultural outlook, by efforts to shape qualities of mind and feeling, attitudes and character, and not merely train or inform students. It may also try to transmit skills and knowledge, but that is not what makes it elite higher education in our third sense. This kind of education is carried on through a relatively close and prolonged relationship between student and teacher, and depends on the creation and maintenance of settings within which such a relationship can exist. Whatever the specific content of the course of study and syllabus—and that indeed varies very widely—this form of higher education conveys, and intends to convey, to students that they can accomplish large and important things in the world, that they can make important discoveries, lead great institutions, influence their country's laws and government, and add substantially to knowledge. In this sense, institutions of elite higher education are arrangements for raising ambition and for providing social support and intellectual resources for the achievement of ambition. By contrast, mass higher education is centered on the transmission of skills and knowledge through relations between teachers and students that are briefer and more impersonal, and is designed to prepare students for relatively modest roles in society, even in such occupations of high status as the learned professions, the civil service, and business management. (Of course, these two types of higher education often overlap or merge imperceptibly into one another.)

Elite higher education makes large demands on students. These demands are implicit in its intention to infuse a moral and cultural outlook, in contrast with the provision of training. It is in severe competition with other formations and institutions in society that also make large demands on the young person—for example, the family, careers, groups of peers, and radical political movements. Elite higher education thus places students in conflicting roles and generates forms of tension in ways that mass higher education does not. It also tries to provide greater social and psychological support for students who are exposed to these normative demands and emotional strains. Thus, to perform its tasks, elite higher education is more likely to be residential than is mass higher education, and for the same reasons it is an activity to which the student must give all his time, at least during term.

The encouragement of ambition is a central distinguishing characteristic of elite higher education. The institutions that offer this kind of education recruit students who are ambitious, they nurture and focus that ambition, and their products are disproportionately successful in the competition for positions of leadership in the larger society. In the United States, this is the feature that distinguishes forms of elite higher education from the myriad small, often denominational, liberal arts colleges, institutions that also try to shape character through personal relations between students and teachers. Similarly, British training colleges, which are also often quite small, are not part of British elite higher education, because while their traditions and ratios of staff to students encourage a collegiate atmosphere to an even greater degree than in many universities, they do not award degrees, they do not encourage ambition, nor, with some exceptions, do they aim to supply leaders for other social institutions outside the state system of education—and not even always there.

Ambition and its encouragement are only one of the cluster of features that links elite higher education to the status and function of elites in society. We see here a process through which advantage engenders advantage and through which elite institutions tend to become centers of academic distinction. In the United States, the relatively small numbers of scholars and scientists who later make significant contributions to their disciplines are disproportionately the graduates of a small number of graduate schools and departments of elite universities. The elements involved are very many, and very hard to disentangle. In general, the leading departments of leading universities are known and favored by able and ambitious students, and departments can be highly selective in their policy of admission. In part by virtue of their attractiveness to leading scholars and scientists, these departments are able to give their students a superior education in their respective disciplines. They are then able to place their better graduates on the teaching staffs of their own and other leading departments in their disciplines, and this in turn gives those graduates access to better students, more stimulating colleagues, better resources such as libraries and laboratories, and more congenial arrangements for learning. The prestige of a degree from a leading department and of teaching in another such department gives an individual scientist or scholar access to opportunities for research which in turn help him—or her—to make important contributions to the discipline. A young person gains a heightened self-confidence from association with and approval by leading figures in the field, and this self-confidence is important in forming the individual's level of intellectual aspiration and heightening his capacity.

While there is surely a relationship between elite higher education and intellectual distinction, they are not identical. Higher education for an elite is not necessarily and always intellectually distinguished, nor is academic excellence found only in the institutions that provide an education of the type I have described.

The Enemies of Elite Higher Education

Institutions and modes of elite higher education may have two kinds of enemies: those who dislike them for what they are or are purported to be—we might call these opponents on grounds of principle—and those who support policies that threaten elite higher education, whether or not they so intend. The main opponents on principle of elite higher education are those committed to egalitarian values and policies. Elite higher education is disliked in large part because of its historical associations, that is, its connections with privilege. To support it is said to be incompatible with democracy and equality. It is charged with being inegalitarian in at least three respects: universities that educate young persons in ways that foster their entry into positions in the elites of their society tend almost invariably to recruit disproportionately from higher social strata, and to a greater extent than do the institutions of mass higher education. Second, it is charged with being inegalitarian in its emphasis on the personal qualities and values, styles of thought and fields of knowledge that were associated with the hereditary upper classes in an hierarchical society. Thus, even when it draws to itself students who have originated in families with lower incomes and in occupations of lower status, it prompts them to adopt a style of life like that of the strata which they will enter.[5] Third, higher educational institutions that offer the sort of education that leads to entry into positions in the elite reinforce social hierarchies by giving their graduates a marked advantage in the competition for higher positions in society. They do this not only by helping them to acquire the skills and modes of conduct of leadership, but also by conferring a status on them independently of their substantive knowledge or skills. The status thus conferred, so it is argued, is a large and illegitimate advantage to those fortunate enough to have access to the institutions that aid entry into the future elites of their society.

Egalitarian Criticisms of Elite Higher Education

There are two quite distinct strands in egalitarian thought. One, stemming from the liberal tradition, presses for greater equality of opportunity for all to compete for the highest position in society; as part of this belief, it is committed to more equal access to higher education. The other, more radical type of egalitarianism demands greater equality of result or rewards; it presses for a greater substantive equality among all the members of the society.

The liberal and the radical types of egalitarianism criticize elite higher education on different grounds. The liberal critics do not in principle object to the existence of this kind of higher education if in fact there is or could be greater equality of opportunity to acquire it. This seems to have been the attitude of parts of the British Labour Party in supporting the selective state grammar schools in the Education Act of 1944. But liberal egalitarians are sometimes also uneasy at the marked competitive advantages that these educational institutions confer on those who are educated in them. If they come to believe—as many have—that no amount of legislation can really cancel the enormous influence of familial wealth and environment on access to elite institutions, then liberal egalitarians move closer to the radicals, who are hostile to the very existence of the institutions that educate for entry into elites, on the grounds that they are by their very nature generators of social inequality.

Threats to Elite Higher Education: Economy and Reform

While a belief in the rightness of social equality, either of opportunity or of reward, is the source of the main attacks on elite higher education, it is vulnerable to other powerful attacks that are not derived from principle or ideology. One of these is that it is too expensive. This attitude, which is held by many who are not particularly egalitarian in principle, is a serious one, especially when the elite institutions are both large and publicly supported. Whenever it is thought necessary to reduce public expenditures, politicians who are not conspicuously egalitarian become enemies of elite higher education since their policies, aimed at reducing budgets and costs, threaten the conditions that enable elite higher education to be carried on. Foremost among these conditions is a relatively high ratio of staff to students. Elite higher education is also injured by reductions in grants and stipends for students, since this makes it necessary for more students to take employment at the expense of their studies and academic life; it is also harmed by the reduction of expenditures on housing for students and increased charges for residence in university since both require more of them to live at home, and this dilutes the intense academic relationships through which elite higher education is conducted.

No one kind of reduction in resources will necessarily destroy an institution of elite higher education; it usually has the capacity for survival even under conditions of financial stringency. But higher education is relatively expensive, and sums of money that will support mass higher education quite adequately are not adequate for the requirements of elite higher education.

Among the most vigorous spokesmen for radical egalitarianism are persons who seek to expiate the sins of their own privileged birth and education. Many students, teachers, and administrators attack their own elite institutions from within; of particular importance are the presidents of elite institutions of higher education who are hostile to the distinctive qualities of their own institutions. The romantic radicalism of the beneficiaries and custodians of elite higher education leads to proposals for immediate and comprehensive rather than incremental reforms. Elite higher education is threatened, both by this kind of doctrinaire commitment to reform and by a technocratic rationalism that also espouses comprehensive reform and planning.

The comprehensive reformers of universities tend to see education as a set of specifiable activities that employ determinate resources to produce certain specific outcomes. Reforms introduce changes in the employment of these resources—for example, in the ways teachers and students use their time and energy, in the structure and content of courses of study, or the use of space. The outcome of such reforms may be a reduction in the costs of instruction per student, a shorter period of study for a degree, certain measurable gains in skills and knowledge, or even changes in attitudes. Common to this kind of program of academic reform is a conception of higher education as an instrument for the achievement of certain ends. It is often indifferent to the historical circumstances that gave rise to a set of educational patterns and relationships and to the social, organizational, and intellectual circumstances that surround and sustain them; it may even regard these circumstances as part of the problem to be resolved by "educational change."

But to many, academic change under the name of "reform" is desirable for its own sake, and resistance to change, whatever the nature of the change and whatever the circumstance, is inherently illegitimate and calls for stronger efforts to override resistance rather than to understand its sources and nature. Perhaps there has not been enough concern with the costs of this kind of academic reform, and especially with the possibility that among these costs are the conditions that sustain elite higher education.

Egalitarians claim that elite higher education is conservative and resistant to change. This charge, ironically, is made during a time of rapid growth in scholarly and scientific knowledge. In every academic area and subject there have been enormous changes in the map of knowledge since the end of World War II, and these changes have often been accompanied by equally large changes in the forms and content of teaching. New disciplines and sub-disciplines have emerged, sometimes giving rise to new academic departments. There is constant ferment and change in the private internal life of higher education, but these are changes which, by their internal character, have been given little publicity.

Elite higher education is conservative about the set of conditions that enables its kind of teaching and learning to go on; it is not conservative about the organization and content of knowledge. In a recent address to the United States National Academy of Sciences, its president, Dr. Philip Handler, reviewed the difficult and indeed somewhat threatening state of relations between the scientific community and the federal government. He spoke with particular alarm about the direct intervention of the federal government into university affairs, coupled with the great threat held over the universities by the power to suspend their federal grants and contracts. And then with a sudden change of tone, he said:

> Meanwhile, back in the nation's laboratories, American science seems to hurtle along with enormous vigor and success. I have just returned from the annual meeting of the Federation of American Societies for Experimental Biology, where I found myself caught up by that excitement I first knew as a graduate student. The scope, the sweep, the sophistication of detail, the newly-revealed, profound insights in such areas of enzymology, control of metabolism, mechanism of hormone action, molecular genetic mechanism, organisation and function of sub-cellular organelles, particularly membranes, immunochemistry, and the functioning of the nervous system was breathtaking. And the light these offer on the pathogenesis of diverse diseases offers ever greater promise of the understanding required if these disorders are, one day, to be brought under some measure of control.[6]

And he went on to offer similar summaries of new developments in elementary particle physics, in geology, in astrophysics, in the social sciences, and in advanced engineering. Nor has there been any slackening in humanistic scholarship. This important current of life and energy, this quest for new knowledge of the workings of nature and a deeper understanding of the works of man, is carried on in the United States and in many other countries to a very large extent within the institutions of higher education, and there almost completely within those of elite higher education. Where research is carried on for the most part within the universities, then the strength of science and scholarship are the strongest arguments for the survival of elite higher education.

The communities of science and scholarship put a premium on new contributions to knowledge and on fresh perspectives on perennial issues. Their activities are marked by a boldness, energy, and curiosity about what is unknown, which seems to be at marked variance with their conservatism in their administrative arrangements. But the connection between these two features is not accidental.

There are many innovative, experimental educational arrangements that offer a trivial and conventionally fashionable kind of education. Those academics who defend the institutions and practices of elite higher education might well resist academic reforms in order to preserve an environment favorable to the pursuit of knowledge. Intellectual courage and creativity require a relatively stable and orderly institutional environment. The enormous expenditure of time and energy devoted to creating new forms of academic government in French, West German, and Dutch universities have drained off the time and talents of many teachers and students as well as destroying the delicate personal relationships that teaching and research of higher quality require. I suggest that those who succeed in carrying on research and teaching of the highest quality under these circumstances will be those who have managed to insulate themselves from the noise and turmoil of latter-day university politics and academic reform.

Programs of comprehensive reform threaten elite higher education directly by reducing the resources and breaking the structures within which it goes on. But such efforts also affect it indirectly by inviting the cost-benefit analysis of educational institutions. Proposals for comprehensive academic reform nowadays usually include systematic evaluation as an integral part of it. Those who want sweeping reforms of higher education and those who want to evaluate the efficiency of its performance agree, for the most part, that higher education is an instrument for the achievement of ends. They believe that for any given department or discipline, its ends must be specified, measured, and compared with others in order to assess the relative efficiency with which these ends are achieved. The evaluation of the performance of higher educational institutions has become a thriving industry that proceeds on assumptions that, in practice, discriminate against elite higher education. It assumes that the effects of a period of experience of a specific form of higher education can be distinguished from the effects of other social forces in an individual's life; that these effects manifest themselves immediately on the conclusion of the course of study; and that they are measurable in the short term. These assumptions are congruent with the notion that higher education is an instrument for the conversion of educational resources into desired, measurable, and short-term outputs, which become the criteria by which its success and efficiency are appraised.

Elite higher education is not, or at least is not only, a form of education for achieving stipulated and readily measurable ends but is also a form that embodies values; it is a set of activities that possesses intrinsic worth. Moreover, its effects on individuals and on the larger society are inextricably intertwined with effects on the rest of the experience of the individuals concerned. These effects show themselves, if at all, only in the course of the lifetime of the individual and the history of the society. If elite forms of higher education are assessed by the analysis of cost and benefit over a short term, they are likely to come off poorly in that assessment in the light of those criteria; they are unable to justify themselves persuasively, and appear to be in need of rationalization and reform.

The movement to rationalize academic administration is a product and a reflection of the movement toward mass higher education; but it is not neutral with regard to other forms of higher education, and to elite higher education in particular. As a result, it works against the diversity of the system, the very diversity that is also characteristic—indeed, a central characteristic—of mass higher education.

Access to Elite Higher Education

Much of the hostility to elite higher education has arisen from the tendency to recruit its student body from the more prosperous and influential strata of society. The links between elite institutions and the higher and professional classes have been very strong in all Western societies. This association has been a result of the direct costs of attendance and of income forgone through prolonged full-time study. It has also resulted from simple discrimination on grounds of class status, from differences in access to and success in elite secondary education, differences in access to the high culture and its values and language in the home, and differences in patterns of aspiration among social classes. Even where governmental policy has tried to reduce the effects of some of these factors, for example, by the abolition of fees, the provision of student grants and stipends, and the partial democratization of the secondary school system, there remain other very powerful influences that are for the most part quite outside the educational system, for example, cultural differences among classes, regions, and ethnic groups, which affect access to elite institutions very much in favor of the sons and daughters of the better-educated and more prosperous strata.

There are a number of different but not necessarily incompatible policies that democratic and egalitarian societies have followed in the face of the problem of differences in access to elite higher education arising from the disadvantages of having been born in the lower classes. One has been the effort to create or to increase access to superior secondary schools for children from the working and lower middle classes. The British grammar schools and the German *Oberrealschulen* were intended to achieve this end. Another has been to make the whole secondary system more democratic by doing away with the elite educational system as a separate path; Sweden, for example, has in effect done that. Most Western societies in recent decades have tried to bring a larger proportion of the appropriate age cohorts to the point of selection for elite higher education by raising the school-leaving age. Other efforts, beginning earlier in the lifecycle, have been made to reform primary education and have moved down into the nursery schools, and thus into family patterns of child-rearing through compensatory education and programs of enriched preschool education for both children and parents. Another approach has been to modify the size and shape of systems of higher education through the expansion of the institution and the range of courses in elite higher education; this approach has in fact improved the educational opportunities of offspring of the upper and middle classes more than it has those of the lower and working classes. And finally, there has been in many Western countries a very great expansion of other than elite forms of higher education, and, in some, notably the United States, this provides access to elite institutions through transfer at the undergraduate level, or through entry to graduate or professional schools.

It is tempting to argue that the historical connection between privileged social origins and access to elite higher educational institutions is merely a technical problem, which can be ameliorated and eventually obliterated by wise and democratic public policies. The dream, or perhaps the illusion, here is that we can achieve equality of educational opportunity, and then through a God-given random distribution of talents and interests this in turn will lead to a rough equality of group achievements. It is, however, now clear that the links between class origins and academic achievement are enormously tenacious and that the class and ethnic cultures that shape academic talents, interests, and achievements are extremely resilient.

Elite higher educational institutions, in part as a result of their intrinsic merits and also because of the substantial advantages they confer in the competition for high status in adult life, are almost everywhere the most desired forms of higher education. Democratization in this century has meant the replacement of familial qualifications by the qualifications of intelligence and achievement as the only legitimate basis for admission to these scarce and desirable opportunities. But elite higher education has an inherently ambiguous relation to reward for intellectual achievement. In so far as elite institutions are centers of academic distinction, that is, of high academic standards and high quality of achievement in science and scholarship, then they are sustained and legitimated by their reliance on intellectual criteria of academic achievement. In so far as we emphasize the functions of elite higher education in transmitting certain social and cultural values, and in shaping character and imagination, then the competition for pre-eminent achievement may not provide good conditions for the kind of moral and cultural education that depends on the quality of personal relations. Assessment in terms of intellectual criteria focuses the attention of teacher and pupils on the latter's achievement and performance and it relegates moral and cultural qualities to a secondary position. Institutions that try to combine the functions of cultural and moral education and assessment of intellectual performance sometimes sharply separate the two roles of teacher and examiner, as in the British universities. Where this does not occur, teachers in disciplines that deal with values frequently try to confine their role as assessors; for example, they often confine assessment to the marking of a paper or an examination at the end of term. Or they may welcome the substitution of pass-fail marks for more discriminating grades. Another compromise in some institutions, notably in Japan, has been to make entry to elite institutions dependent on prior intellectual attainment, and then to make the student's career within the institution less dependent on success in competition. This solution is less effective if performance within the institution itself is a condition for access to higher status at the next step in the student's career, either admission to graduate departments that are very selective or to competitive posts in government, universities, or research institutions. In any event, it may be useful to distinguish the severity of competition for access to elite higher educational institutions and the severity of competition for academic honors within them. These vary somewhat independently of each other.

The stronger the link between elite higher educational institutions and status in the adult world, the more that elite institutions monopolize entry to elite careers, the severer the competition for entry into them. Those institutions of elite higher education that truly dominate the channels of mobility to high status in the adult world, as do the two or three leading Japanese universities, run the risk of becoming prizes to be gained through competition rather than places where serious learning takes place. Where higher education that qualifies for entrance into elite positions is wholly concentrated in a particular class of institutions, and where there is intense competition for entry to them, these institutions are driven toward becoming the academic equivalents of high-compression chambers in which there is little room for the moral and cultural education or the personal relations that are integral parts of elite higher education. For that reason, those who are concerned with the survival of elite higher education should welcome the expansion of other paths of social ascent, and these include the institutions of mass higher education. This would reduce the pressures on the elite institutions and allow interest and personal motivation a larger role in determining who attends them.

But while the most intense competition may be unfavorable to the effectiveness of elite higher education in transmitting and adapting high cultural values, questions of academic ability cannot simply be set aside by the new romanticism that says that all talents and preferences are equal. At the level of higher education, a general inability to meet the requirements of studies—an unpleasant and often painful experience—is likely to lead students to leave college or university or to do the minimum. On the other hand, strong motivation in students with normal intelligence leads to academic success and even to a discovery of the intrinsic rewards of learning. This brings us back to the question of the social correlates of the motivation and the ability to do academic work at a high standard of proficiency. I do not think we can avoid confronting the awkward issue raised by the persistence of a social bias in the recruitment of students of elite higher education. The question is whether this bias is a sufficient ground for suppressing or destroying elite higher educational institutions, however much provision they make for social mobility, however much they nurture what Lord Ashby has called "the clear streams of excellence." Despite all our efforts at widening the availability of higher education, elite higher education continues to translate the higher social origins of children into their higher social status as adults. This is a political and moral issue, and the position we take depends in part on our readiness to use state power to intervene powerfully and actively in the educational system where it touches on the distribution of social status. In our reflections on that issue, we must count not only the gains but also the costs to individuals and society that such intervention carries with it. Egalitarians may well ask: what are the human and social costs of not intervening for the purpose of wider access? But here one must ask in reply: what are the specific forms of social intervention that are proposed, and what are their actual consequences? We run the risk of having the worst of both worlds: massive reforms that have great costs yet do not achieve the desired social benefits. In the United States the abolition of selective high schools and compulsory busing to attain racial balance are examples that come to mind.

Varieties of Elite Higher Education

Elite higher education can be the only higher education available in a society; this is most closely approximated in Great Britain, even now. Alternatively, elite forms of higher education can be only one part of the entire system of higher education that includes other forms as well; the French *grandes écoles* and universities make up such a system. A third alternative is the existence of individual elite institutions that are not planned and coordinated by a central authority: the leading American private colleges and universities are in this category. A fourth alternative is the existence of elite higher education within mass higher educational institutions as particular departments and as informally constituted arrangements, hidden, unnoticed, and yet protected within large institutions of mass higher education; the advanced research seminars in the larger German universities and some parts of large American state universities represent this type. These alternatives are not incompatible. The survival of elite higher education in modern society is not dependent on its survival in any one of these particular forms.

The huge American state universities, which Dr. Clark Kerr has called "multiversities," are comprehensive in almost every respect, both in the diversity of their students and in the very wide range of social functions they perform. Their large undergraduate colleges admit students of modest academic capacities and interests and also of modest ambitions. Rates of "wastage" are very high; many of the undergraduates moreover enter in their third year after having been for two years at a community or state college. The average period of continuous enrollment for the students in the huge state universities of the United States is much shorter than four years; it is closer to a year and a half. These institutions offer a large number of courses of lectures coupled with a high degree of freedom of choice among them, and it is quite rare for any given student to have any single teacher for longer than ten or twelve weeks. The ratio of students to teachers is very high, and much of the teaching, especially in the first two years, is done by graduate students employed as teaching assistants.

This is certainly not elite higher education; it lacks the quality in the relations between students and teachers, the duration and intensity of that relationship, and its emphasis on the shaping of mind, character, and aspiration of the students, which are characteristic of elite higher education. Nevertheless, the large American state universities provide a quite significant amount of elite higher education within their boundaries. The relationship of elite to mass higher education within these institutions is partly symbiotic and partly parasitic. Elite higher education in mass higher educational institutions is available in part in an explicit and acknowledged form and in part in an informal and wholly unofficial way. The best example of the first kind is the bulk of graduate education, especially that part associated with work that students and teachers do on doctoral dissertations.

The departments of leading American universities are relatively autonomous bodies; their autonomy, at least in academic matters, rests on their claim to a monopoly in a recognized discipline. The graduate students in such departments are, in effect, not members of a university of 30,000 or 40,000, with 1,500 or 2,000 teachers, but of a department of 10 to 80 teachers. In their advanced work, they have a close and prolonged relationship with one or two of these—the supervisor of the dissertation or members of a dissertation committee; often there is a genuine relationship of master and apprentice. The department has a relationship with its graduate students quite different from what the university has with its thousands of undergraduates. It does not merely provide services and instruction; it undertakes a much broader responsibility for the education of the student. It inducts the student into an academic discipline; it not only trains in skills and transmits knowledge, but shapes and creates values and attitudes—it inculcates an ethos—which prizes knowledge and prescribes the ways of pursuing it. It teaches students how to look upon their subjects, and themselves in relation to their subjects. The assimilation by graduate students of a pattern of values, attitudes, and ways of thought and appreciation is the most important single function that a university department performs. It often has a powerful and lasting effect on students, providing them with perspectives and orientations that guide them through a lifetime of academic teaching and research.

This, of course, is the very paradigm of elite higher education; it is much the same in "multiversities"—like the University of California, Berkeley, and the University of Wisconsin—as it is, for example, in the University of Chicago or at Princeton University, which offer elite education to their undergraduates as well. At the graduate level, the standards and the quality of accomplishment of the great private universities and the great state universities are about the same. It is only a slight distortion to say that the graduate schools of the great state universities such as the University of California, Berkeley, and the Universities of Michigan or Wisconsin are like the graduate departments of the University of Chicago, Princeton, and Harvard superimposed on very large undergraduate state colleges devoted to mass undergraduate education.

In the American "multiversity" mass and elite types of higher education exist side by side within the same institution. This of course does not happen without tension, both intellectual and financial. Elite higher education is more costly than mass higher education, and graduate studies in the "multiversity" are in a sense subsidized by the undergraduate colleges in the same institution. At the same time, graduate departments, thanks to the employment of their graduate students as teaching assistants, perform a good deal of undergraduate instruction in these same institutions. Undergraduate education in the large state universities could hardly be carried on without them.

It should also be pointed out that elite higher education also goes on informally and in a scattered but important way in the mass higher education of undergraduates. It exists on a small scale within the interstices of a system that does not provide for it. It is of course difficult to maintain under conditions that are not meant to be congenial to it. Its mode of existence may be illustrated by a large required course for undergraduate majors in sociology in the methods of social research.

This course was to meet twice weekly; it was attended by 150 students and was conducted partly through a weekly lecture and partly through a weekly discussion. After two weeks, the teacher announced that he was prepared to meet regularly with any members of the class who wished to come on a certain afternoon each week for the rest of the quarter for discussion of a research project just about to begin. The class as a whole, it was announced, would not be held responsible in the final examination for work done in these extra sessions. Twenty students attended the first extra session and roughly fifteen the weekly sessions thereafter. These undergraduates became intimately involved in the design of a large investigation that the teacher was just beginning; they received close personal attention from him in the course of their work. Some members of the group continued their association with the investigation after the course was concluded. The same point may be illustrated by another even larger undergraduate lecture course on the history of the Reformation; five hundred students attended this course. The teacher, a distinguished authority on the subject, announced at the first meeting that she would be having lunch after class each week at a local café and invited those who wished to join her there for informal discussion. Ten to fifteen students accepted the invitation on that and subsequent weeks for the rest of the term. These meetings developed into a small, informal seminar on the subject. In both instances, the personal contact between teacher and students was salvaged from a situation that was not designed to permit it.

This appearance of elite higher education within institutions of mass higher education requires that an effort be made to separate interested from uninterested students by offering them the opportunity for close association with teachers around work for which the rewards are more intrinsic than extrinsic. Such extra work does not advance the student further toward the degree nor does it promise higher marks in the final examination. Under these conditions, there is a pronounced self-selection of students who are prepared to work harder in order to learn more. They might, quite incidentally, receive higher marks but that is by no means assured since the material covered is not necessarily a part of the syllabus on which they will be examined. There must also be a certain proportion of these students who want to take advantage of such opportunities in large mass institutions, but the proportion must indeed be relatively small. If it were large, it would prevent the emergence of those features that are to be found in elite higher education. Given the extremely high ratios of students to teachers in the large state universities, the additional work could then be little more than an extension of the mass educational courses being offered. Furthermore, the teachers who create these situations must themselves be ready to undertake the additional teaching; like the students they must do it for the intrinsic value of the intellectual relationship itself. What is more, the teachers and students both must have the time and energy for such work. And finally, there must be a place for such unauthorized and unofficial teaching and study to go on. All these conditions are probably not met very often. Teachers who offer this kind of education often do so without mentioning it to anyone else, including their colleagues.

However much of this kind of education is created within a mass institution, it is at best only an approximation of elite higher education. While it offers a bit of an education based on voluntary association between students and teachers around a shared set of intellectual interests, it is rarely prolonged past the end of the term in which it begins. It must be said, however, that such experiences have a very great importance in the education and intellectual development of those students who take advantage of these informal opportunities. For short periods they break the impersonality and anonymity of the institution by introducing a living, personal relationship with a teacher. Students acquire a sense of what a serious education of this kind is like.

The workings of these institutions do not encourage such activities. For one thing, the teacher who takes part in them reduces thereby the time and energy that he could devote to research, and in these institutions achievement in research is the primary and almost the only criterion on which the junior teacher is assessed for reappointment and promotion. The administrators who allocate rooms know nothing of these informal arrangements, and when space is scarce there may simply be no place to meet other than a teacher's own small and often quite inadequate room. In a "multiversity," this kind of teaching might have to take place at the end of a corridor in a hall of residence, in a temporary building left over from World War II, at the back of a laboratory, or in an unused room in a research institute—-most commonly in the most inconvenient buildings or in space which the university has forgotten or regards as useless.

This kind of unofficial elite education is possible only if both teachers and students are genuinely interested: they must have strong motives to overcome the many difficulties in the way of such unauthorized and unofficial education. Yet it happens, and often enough so that many— but certainly not all—serious and interested students can gain an education at a large state university, which in its cumulative effect approximates what he might have received at a small elite college. Indeed, one of the major and almost wholly unrecognized functions of the large state universities is that they provide for some really interested students an approximation of an elite higher education. These are often students who did not attempt or who failed to gain admission to a private elite university or college because of poor performance in secondary school, insufficient funds, or modest aspirations. Such students are sometimes rallied and deeply aroused intellectually by the improvised elite higher education that emerges in large universities.

This kind of education often requires quite remarkable ingenuity on the part of teachers and students within mass institutions, who draw off and concentrate the resources necessary for these pockets of elite education, and then defend and preserve them. They must, for example, create milieus marked by effective ratios of students and teachers of five to one, as compared with the ratios of twenty or thirty to one that are characteristic of the undergraduate college of the university as a whole.

This kind of education, however, presupposes the existence of uncommitted space, time, and energy. University administrators who are zealous to eliminate waste are inimical to such enclaves of elite higher education. The increase in the ratio of students to teacher at many large American universities over the past five years has apparently reduced the amount and variety of this unauthorized elite undergraduate education. (The loss has been made up by rhetoric about the importance of undergraduate teaching.)

The Vulnerability of Elite Higher Education

The fortunes of elite higher education are affected by the size of the total system and the proportion in it of elite higher education. The larger the proportion of elite higher education, the more vulnerable it will be. It is also affected by whether it occurs in institutions that are wholly or primarily devoted to it; by whether its products, students, and intellectual works are regarded as beneficial to society; by whether the political and administrative elites themselves have had an elite higher education; and finally by whether the elite higher educational institutions are maintained by the state or whether they are private institutions.

In France, for example, the *grandes écoles* are the only parts of the French system that would qualify as elite higher education. Their endurance in that country is owed to a combination of their relatively small size, the vital importance of their graduates to state and society, and the fact that high government officials and civil servants have had such an education. Thanks to these factors, the *grandes écoles* were successfully protected from the effects of the *loi d'orientation* enacted after the events of 1968. In the United States, elite forms of undergraduate education develop covertly and transiently within large state universities. Public authorities in the United States, whether federal, state, or local, are not prepared to support undergraduate education that rests on stringent criteria of admission and that requires an expensive ratio of students to teachers.[7] Hence elite undergraduate education in the United States depends on the well-being of the leading private colleges and universities, and on the peculiar problems of the economics of private education in that country.

Private institutions in the United States are hard pressed by inflation, recession, the labor-intensive nature of teaching and research, and the increased costs of custodial and secretarial services. The only possibility for significant savings lies in higher ratios of students to teachers. But colleges like Swarthmore, Bryn Mawr, and Dartmouth and universities like Chicago have been able to preserve their stringent standards of selection and show a remarkable resourcefulness in defending their unique educational procedures despite the pressing need for economy.

In this respect, they resemble the British universities, which have, more successfully than American state universities, been able to act like private universities although supported by the state. British opinion and the British government, unlike those in the United States, have been willing to support elite undergraduate education within institutions dependent on the state. The British idea of the university has been strong enough, especially among politicians and civil servants who are graduates of these universities, so that they have not until recently had to reduce the ratio of teachers to students. These ratios, however, are now declining in Britain. The elite tradition is very strong, so strong that it still dominates higher education. It is almost impossible for the British to imagine higher education that is not elite, and when it emerges, at the technical-vocational fringes or in continuing education, there is a tendency for it to be absorbed into the elite tradition as fast as possible. It was that way with the provincial universities of the nineteenth century, and it is that way with the colleges of advanced technology and the polytechnics now. The British system has done for sectors of higher education of humble origins what every elite university tries to do for individual students of humble origins.

The smaller the elite sector is, both absolutely and relative to the mass sector, the less vulnerable to the egalitarians and economists it will be. When the elite part of the higher educational system is very large and thus a major competitor for public funds, it becomes vulnerable.

In Britain, the elite universities have retained their traditional role as the dominant type of higher education—it is not only large but keeps on growing. It is being forced to grow. This growth is accompanied by further pressure to take on some of the forms of mass higher education, both economically and in its functions. Of course, these pressures have by no means gone as far as they have in the United States, but they are likely to become more severe with further growth. This is inherent in the commitment of British universities to uniform and high standards of admission and ratios of students to teachers—together with a commitment to raising all higher educational institutions to the level of the best.[8] It has recently been said regarding British universities that "a decision to stay smaller and to concentrate on their traditional activities of scholarship, research and teaching will entitle them to make the special claim on the national purse that such activities deserve."[9] But the prospect of continued growth of elite higher education has definite advantages. It makes possible entry into new lines of study and research without the necessity to discontinue or reduce existing fields. And it seems to make possible the provision of the best higher education for the sons and daughters of classes excluded from higher education in the past. It concentrates the bulk of scarce funds in outstanding institutions rather than diluting its effects. Moreover, while the British universities are relatively expensive, they are paradoxically and in the short term also the least expensive way of expanding provision of higher education in Great Britain. The cost at the margin is relatively low, especially if expansion is accompanied by a moderate decrease in the ratios of teachers to students.

As elite universities are forced to compete with other objects of public expenditure, a reduction in expenditure per student seems inevitable. New and broader social and educational functions are likely to be imposed on them. Governments scrutinize more carefully the internal allocation of available funds and they insist on more efficient operation; as a result the autonomy of the universities declines. The combination of growth with closer scrutiny by government requires larger administrative staffs and the introduction of bureaucratic methods of management. This pushes elite universities toward standards and practices that are associated with mass higher education.

Britain is unique among modern societies in the proportion of its higher education given over to elite higher education. About 10 percent of the nine million students in American four-year colleges and universities are studying in elite institutions, or in elite parts of mass institutions. The enrollment in the *grandes écoles* is about 10 percent of the enrollment in the French universities and *grandes écoles* taken together. The numbers studying in elite parts of mass institutions are harder to estimate, but probably do not exceed 10 percent of the total enrollment in universities and other institutions of higher education. A much higher proportion of students in British higher education is enrolled in elite institutions. This must have some bearing on their vulnerability in the future.

Conclusion

I do not believe that elite higher education is in most places an endangered species. But neither is it entirely safe. It does not survive precariously on the slowly eroding sentiments and values, privileges, and prestige that came to be associated with it in its traditional forms. Rather, it is sustained by powerful and continuing functions for society, for government, industry, science, and culture, and for the growth and satisfaction of individuals. Governments do, however, follow policies that are inimical to their own interests, especially when they are possessed by the passionate conviction that the only values worth cultivating and pursuing are organizational efficiency and social equality.

While elite higher education has enemies, some of whom cannot be placated, it should not strengthen their arguments. The proponents of elite higher education must accept that mass higher education, universal access, and continuing education are not the enemies of elite higher education. In modern societies these democratic forms of postsecondary education must flourish if elite higher education is to survive. Our societies must provide very generously for opportunities to obtain postsecondary education. This is necessary for political, economic, and cultural reasons, as well as for greater social justice. But the bulk of that provision need not and cannot be in elite forms of higher education. Elite higher education is too costly, and only a fraction of the students and teachers have the interest, desire, and ability to take part in the intense intellectual collaboration that marks elite higher education.

Modern systems of higher education must take into account the broad diversity of student interests and social functions. This requires a parallel diversity in the forms of higher education. Elite higher education is a part of that diversity—an important and necessary part, but only a part. In the broad range of postsecondary education, elite higher education must find its ecological niche, relatively modest in size and cost, though of transcendent importance to society and to those who experience it.

NOTES

1. See Martin Trow, "Problems in the Transition from Elite to Mass Higher Education," in *Policies for Higher Education: General Report on the Conference on Future Structures of Post-Secondary Education* (Paris: OECD, 1974), pp. 51–101. Reprinted as chapter 2 in this volume.

2. A. H. Halsey, "Educational Organisation," in *International Encyclopedia of the Social Science* (New York: Macmillan and The Free Press, 1968), vol. 4, p. 530.

3. Ibid., p. 503.

4. Max Weber, *Essays on Sociology*, ed. and trans. Hans Gerth and C. W. Mills (London: Routledge and Kegan Paul, 1946), pp. 240–44.

5. There has been a significant shift in many elite institutions in the United States in the location of the models of conduct, with some upper-class students trying to acquire what they think are the personal styles and qualities of poor black or white ethnic groups. These styles and values are largely at variance with those which elite institutions have traditionally taught, and the conflict between these systems of values is the source of considerable tension in such institutions. If this conflict is less intense in institutions of mass higher education, it is because they are not much concerned with the acquisition of modes of conduct and care less what values their students hold, so long as they learn the prescribed skills and bodies of knowledge.

6. Philip Handler, *Annual Report of the President* (Washington, D.C.: National Academy of Sciences, April 22, 1975).

7. Efforts have been made in American state higher educational systems to establish small undergraduate units that resemble the best liberal arts colleges. These succeed for a few years when they can concentrate special resources around small numbers of teachers and students. In time, the enthusiasm that carried such experiments and the special resources allocated to them tend to run down, and they are then reabsorbed into the mass institution.

8. See my essay in *Policies for Higher Education*.

9. *Times Higher Education Supplement*, no. 287 (May 23, 1975).

PART II

Causes and Consequences of America's Advantage

4

ONE OF THE MORE PUZZLING, and frankly weak-kneed, characteristics of contemporary policy analysis in higher education is the often heard lament that the days of "the big narrative" are long past. This is especially puzzling at a time when higher education policy debates repeatedly refer to global outreach and to international relations, and are beset with attempts to insert the development of systems against the backdrop of globalization. Perhaps this timidity is due to the comparative perspective itself, since it invites one either to trip lightly over large numbers of systems in the act of comparing, or to go into considerable detail and concentrate on a few. Maybe it is because higher education policy increasingly concerns itself with the immediate, with the present, and with future options, rather than being concerned with how the current situation came to pass.

It is not a matter of concern that it is taken up with the immediate, but it is deeply disturbing that it often justifies its focus on contemporary ephemera on the grounds that the current state of the world in general, and higher education in particular, has no historical precedent. And, it is more devastating by far when it assumes that a long-term perspective is simply not relevant to the pressing issues of the hour. This is an extreme form of ahistorical determinism. It fails to acknowledge that the past may constrain the range of options that may realistically be contemplated. There is a world of difference between shaping higher education and seeing it as locked in by the past.

One of Martin Trow's outstanding strengths as a scholar was his refusal to separate the contemporary from its long-term roots and causes. This essay is a splendid illustration of the erudition, analytical power, and leaps of insight he brought to the study of higher education, and to the depth, sweep, and history he brought to policy analysis. That, however, is not all: for this tour de force also shows a special gift of empathy with the political and university cultures of two nations other than his own, the United Kingdom and Sweden. This was grounded on towering knowledge, regularly updated by his descents, usually invited, to give insight and to open up new ways of viewing the problems each faced.

As the Scottish bard Robert Burns, pointed out in his poem "To a Mouse" 'to see ourse'ls as others see us' is not just a gift all too seldom granted. It also endows comparison of countries and their systems of higher education with its central message and significance. It can be achieved only if the scholar fully grasps not just the takens-for-granted in the system he dissects, but also has no less a firm grasp over the takens-for-granted his readers entertain about their own system or academic culture. A bold narrative then takes on meaning, insight, and audacity.

This essay, to my mind, is a quintessential example of these two rare qualities. It can be read with profit as much by Trow's fellow scholars in the United States as by his numberless followers and students in England, Sweden, and the rest of Europe. His account is not limited by the time it was written—in 1992. Still less is it constrained by focusing on American higher education. True, from a European standpoint, it is a portrayal of an institution as dynamic as it was anarchic, and one where, as he shows, sheer weakness was an evolutionary virtue, but his analysis is enormously significant when placed against current developments in the European Union.

The rise of the federal model in America and its consequences, direct and indirect, happens to be a superb account of the rise of a continental multisystem construct. This is precisely the task to which the European Union is, with varying degrees of boldness and blundering, committed. Whether the looming shape of a European system of higher education will be grounded on a federal or a confederal arrangement is anyone's guess. But the issues Trow tracked across two and a half centuries and in another land remind us of questions that in the European setting have still to be fully debated: What are to be the limits to the powers of the federal layer of government? What is the exact configuration of power that every institution should have to meet the expectations of its community?

Trow's bold narrative, and his perceptive interpretation of feder-

alism in American higher education, reveal those basic questions
that Europe would do well to give its most earnest attention.

—GUY NEAVE

Federalism in American Higher Education

Introduction

L ike Canada, but unlike most other countries in the world, the
United States places the primary responsibility for education (including higher education) on the states rather than on the federal
government. In the United States this reflects the deep suspicion of central government reflected in the separation of powers in the Constitution.
Moreover, the Tenth Amendment of the Bill of Rights says simply: "The
powers not delegated to the United States by the Constitution, nor prohibited by it to the States, are reserved to the States respectively or to the
people." Provision of education at any level is not among the powers
delegated to the federal government by the Constitution. In Canada education at all levels is also the constitutional responsibility of the provinces. There are, however, significant differences between the American
and the Canadian arrangements for higher education: for one thing,
Canada has a much smaller private sector; for another, Canadian higher
education, while the responsibility of the provinces, is largely funded by
federal government money passed through the provinces. Both of these
differences bear on the wider diversity of sources of support for American higher education.

The issue of federalism in the United States must thus be seen as one

Adapted from Martin Trow, "Federalism in American Higher Education," in *Higher
Learning in America, 1980–2000*, edited by Arthur Levine, 39–66. Baltimore: Johns
Hopkins University Press, 1983. It was revised from a paper prepared for the Interna-
tional Colloquium on Higher Education in Federal Systems, Queen's College, Ontario,
May 8–10, 1991.

aspect of the broader issue of the governance and finance of its system of higher education. American colleges and universities get support not only from federal, state, and local governments, but from many private sources such as churches, business firms, foundations, alumni, and other individuals, from students in the form of tuition and fees for room, board, and health services, and from many other clients of its services, for example, patients in its hospitals. The concept of federalism focuses our attention on the role of regional governments; in the case of the American higher education these are usually the states, though sometimes counties and cities are also relevant. And federalism also is concerned with the relation of central authorities to regional or local authorities. But in the case of American higher education, the role of private, nongovernmental sources of support is extremely important, especially for many of the leading institutions, both public and private. Thus, federalism in American higher education cannot be separated from the broader issue of how American higher education developed in the curious and unique ways that is has—so large, untidy, uncoordinated from the center, without national (or even state) standards for the admissions of students, the appointment of academic staff, or the awarding of degrees. For that reason, if no other, a discussion of federalism must be rooted in reflections on the nature and emergence of American higher education as a whole.

Aspects of Federalism in Contemporary American Higher Education

The radical decentralization of control of American higher education (of which federalism is one aspect) is both required by and contributes to its size and diversity. Total enrollments in 1990 were just short of 14 million in some 3,500 colleges and universities. Of these some 12.1 million were undergraduates, and 1.9 million were graduate and professional students. Some 78 percent were enrolled in public institutions, though it is important to stress that many public institutions receive funds from private sources, and all private institutions are aided by public funds, through research support, student aid, or both. Of the total enrollment of 14 million, some 5.4 million, or over one-third, were enrolled in two-year colleges, almost all of them public institutions. More than 7.9 million, or 56 percent, were classified as "full-time students," that is, they met the requirements for full-time status as reported by the institutions, though many of these were also working part-time, while 6 million students were formally studying part-time.[1]

Indeed, the proportions of part-time students has been growing in recent years, as has the numbers and proportions of older students and students from historically under-represented minorities, largely blacks and Hispanics. Students of nontraditional age—that is, 25 years and older—accounted for well over two-fifths of American college students, and racial and ethnic minorities nearly 20 percent. Women comprised 54 percent of the total enrollment.[2]

The size and diversity of the student body in American colleges and universities reflects the numbers and diversity of the institutions in which they are enrolled.[3] No central law or authority governs or coordinates American higher education. The nearly 2,000 private institutions are governed by lay boards that appoint their own members; the 1,560 public institutions (including nearly 1,000 public community colleges) are accountable in varying degrees to state or local authorities, but usually have a lay board of trustees as a buffer against direct state management, preserving a high if variable measure of institutional autonomy. Differences in the forms of governance and finance among the public institutions are very large, both between and within states. For example, the universities of Michigan and California are able to call on state constitutional provisions protecting their autonomy against political intrusion; it is perhaps not coincidental that they are also the two most distinguished public universities in the country. Moreover, over the years both have used their freedom to diversify their sources of support; currently only 30 percent of the operating expenses of the University of California comes from state government, and the proportion in the University of Michigan is even smaller—closer to 20 percent. (They are perhaps more accurately "state-aided" than "state" universities.) Other state institutions by contrast suffer constant state interference in their management and policies, interference facilitated by line-item budgeting, close state control over expenditures, and limited discretionary funds.

But while an observer can see contrasting patterns in the legal and formal organizational arrangements from state to state, actual relationships between public institutions and state authorities vary also by historical tradition, the strength and character of institutional leaders, and the values and sentiments of governors and key legislators. Variations in the autonomy of public institutions can be seen not only between states, but between sectors of higher education within states, and even between institutions within the same state sector. Examples of the latter are the differences between the University of California (UC), on its nine campuses, and the twenty-campus system of the California State University (CSU), defined as primarily undergraduate institutions, though also offering master's degrees, but without the power to award the doctoral degree (except rarely in conjunction with a campus of the University of California), and therefore doing little funded research. CSU also does not have UC's constitutional protection, and is funded on a line-item basis. Nevertheless, at least one of its campuses, CSU San Diego, has encouraged its faculty to do research and to write proposals for outside funding; in these respects, and in its success in gaining such support, it begins to resemble a campus of the University of California rather than other institutions in its own sector.

The diversity of funding is at the heart of the diversity of character and function of American higher education. In 1988–89 expenditures of all kinds on American colleges and universities were estimated to be more than $131 billion, an increase in current dollars of 70 percent, and in constant dollars of 31 percent, over 1981–82, and represented roughly 2.7 percent of the gross national product.[4] Government at all levels together provides less than half of all current revenues for American higher education, currently about 42 percent. The federal government itself provides only about 13 percent of the support for higher education, chiefly in the form of grants and contracts for research and development in the universities. That figure includes grants to students but excludes the federal government's loans and loan subsidies. (If it included those, the federal contribution would be closer to 20 percent, and the students' contribution reduced by the same amount.) State and local governments (mostly state) provide one-third of all support for higher education. Students themselves (and their families) provide about one-quarter of the funds for higher education, and the institutions themselves about 27 percent from their own endowments and from other enterprises they operate and services they provide, such as hospitals. Another 6 percent is provided by gifts, grants, and contracts from private individuals, foundations, and business firms. So in brief, students provide about one-quarter of the revenues for higher education (perhaps half of which comes from student aid from various sources); the institutions provide about one-third from their own endowments, gifts, and enterprises; and the rest comes from government—that is, cities and counties, the fifty state governments, and the many federal sources and agencies whose expenditures are not coordinated by any policy or office.[5]

These proportions, of course, differ between American public and private colleges and universities, though it must be stressed that all American colleges and universities are supported by a mixture of public and private funds. For example, while public colleges and universities currently get about half their operating budgets from their state governments, private institutions get less than 2 percent from state sources. But the private colleges get a slightly larger proportion of their support funds from the federal government than do public institutions, 17 percent as compared with 11 percent. The other big difference lies in the importance of student tuition payments that go directly to the institution: these account for less than 15 percent of the revenues of public institutions, but nearly 40 percent of the support for private institutions.[6] And those proportions differ sharply among finer categories of colleges and universities: for example, as between research universities and four-year colleges in both public and private categories. For example, the University of California last year got roughly $1 billion in research grants and contracts from agencies of the federal government, most of it directly to individual researchers and faculty members on UC's nine campuses. (About one-third of that money, incidentally, took the form of overhead, which is split half and half between the state government, where it goes into the general fund and the university, for whom it is a discretionary fund.)

In 1989–90, total student aid from all sources was running at more than $27 billion a year, 62 percent higher in current dollars, and 10 percent higher in real terms, than in 1980–81. Of this sum, nearly $2 billion came from state grant programs, and about $6 billion from the resources of the institutions themselves, such as gifts and endowment funds. The remainder, more than $20 billion, came from federal sources in a complex combination of student grants, loans, and subsidized work-study programs. Of that large sum nearly two-thirds, or $12.6 billion, was distributed through various loan programs (which are not included in the estimates of federal support cited above). As the total amount of federal aid has grown, the proportion taking the form of loans has grown: in 1975–76 three-quarters of federal student aid was awarded in the form of grants, but by 1989–90 the share of federal student aid in the form of grants had fallen to about one-third.[7]

In 1986–87, nearly half (46 percent) of all undergraduates received some form of financial aid; more than one-third (35 percent) were receiving federal aid.[8] In real terms, student support from all sources increased by about 10 percent over 1980–81, a little less than the increase in total enrollments (up about 12 percent over that period), but probably close to the increase in full-time equivalent enrollments. Aid from federally supported programs decreased by about 3 percent from 1980–81 when adjusted for inflation. But large increases in student aid at the state and institutional levels (which now comprise more than one-quarter of the total student aid from all sources) have more than offset the drop in federal funds for student aid. State student grant programs grew by 52 percent, and aid awarded directly by the institutions grew by 90 percent, both in real terms, in the decade of the 1980s.[9] In this area, as in others, the states and the institutions (and their constituencies) are providing more of the support for higher education, though the shift is slow and is not reflected in absolute declines in the federal commitment.

Looking at patterns of state support over the past decade, we see that many states cut their support for public colleges and universities during the severe recession of 1980–82, but that thereafter the levels of state support tended to rise about as fast as the economic recovery and rising revenues permitted. State tax funds for the operation of higher education (this does not include capital costs) were nearly $31 billion for 1984–85, up 19 percent over 1983–84.[10] By 1990, the states were spending nearly $41 billion on operating expenses for higher education, up 23 percent (adjusted for inflation) over 1980–81. The current recession is causing a decline, not in state spending on higher education, but in the rate of growth of state spending. Spending on higher education by the states in 1990–91 was 11.6 percent higher than two years earlier, but this was the lowest rate of increase in state support for higher education in thirty years.[11]

This brief overview is intended to put into perspective the federal role in American higher education, one that is substantial in overall size, but much smaller in its direct influence or power over the system than is the role of the several states. How the states have used their primacy in this area of public policy varies enormously from one state and region to another. For example, in the New England and North Central states, private colleges and universities developed early in our history, and have tended to resist the competition of big publicly supported institutions. While public institutions have grown there as elsewhere in recent decades, the effects of that heritage can still be seen, for example, in Massachusetts and New York, where great universities like Harvard, MIT [Massachusetts Institute of Technology], Columbia, and Cornell, and a host of other vigorous private institutions overshadow and overpower the public colleges and universities in those states. By contrast, in some western states there is little private higher education at all; public institutions, such as land grant universities and public community colleges, have a virtual monopoly on the provision of postsecondary education within the state's borders.

Differences among the states in support for higher education are quite large as compared with regional differences in other OECD [Organisation for Economic Co-operation and Development] countries, and take many different forms. For example, in 1990 per capita appropriations by the fifty states for higher education in their borders ranged from $312 in Alaska to $67 in New Hampshire, a difference of nearly five to one. If we drop out the two extreme states, a comparison of the second with the forty-ninth, Hawaii and Vermont, gives a ratio of two and a half to one. (The average, incidentally, was $159.) A slightly different index, state appropriations per $1,000 of state income (which attempts to control for state wealth, giving thus a measure of "effort"), shows similar results: again a ratio of five to one, though the extreme states on this measure are Wyoming ($18/$1,000) and New Hampshire ($3.50/$1,000).[12] The United States is evidently prepared to sustain differences (or inequalities) in support for higher education among the several states of this order of magnitude. This is perhaps one of the most significant and least remarked differences between American and European systems, and is inherent in our system of educational federalism. The effort to achieve or approximate equality in the provision of public services between and among states or regions would require considerable direct intervention by central government. The federal government is prepared to intervene strongly to defend the civil rights of citizens, mostly notably in connection with the potential for discrimination on the basis of race or gender. The federal government can also modestly reduce inequalities among states by providing federal funds directly to students and to researchers. But with a few exceptions, the federal government does not try to stimulate state spending on higher education, compensate for differences in state wealth or effort, or give the states unrestricted funds for support of higher education. One important historical exception was the contribution of the federal government to the states through the first Morrill Act, which clearly aimed at stimulating state spending for agricultural and technical education, and the introduction of the principle of requiring the states to provide matching dollars (to some ratio) for specific purposes, most notably in the second Morrill Act.[13] After World War II President [Harry S.] Truman's Commission on Higher Education recommended that the federal government undertake a massive program of "general support of institutions of higher education," precisely by channeling federal funds to the states "on an equalization basis," and limiting the recipients to public colleges and universities.[14] The defeat of this effort to equalize higher education across the states, and the further defeat (in the Education Amendments of 1972) of efforts to channel federal funding directly to the institutions through unrestricted grants (see below), has established federal policy for the present and foreseeable future. The current reluctance (or constitutional inability) of the federal government to intervene directly to affect state policy toward higher education (outside the realm of the protection of civil rights and liberties) underlies the considerable power of the states to organize and fund their systems of higher education relatively free of the leveling hand of the federal government. The rather stronger egalitarian instincts of Europeans and Canadians lead them to view that freedom with some skepticism and on the whole critically.

The states also differ markedly among themselves in the way they organize, govern, or coordinate their systems of higher education. In some states, such as Massachusetts and Utah, coordinating councils are very powerful, serving as consolidated boards that govern the whole of the public sector of postsecondary education in the state. In California, the Postsecondary Education Commission has relatively little formal power, serving chiefly as a fact-gathering advisory body to state government, and is itself largely governed by representatives of the public institutions it is coordinating. In still other states, like Vermont and Delaware, there are no statutory coordinating bodies at all.[15]

Since its founding the federal government has come to play a role, and often a dominant role, in many areas of social and economic life in ways its founders never anticipated. Nevertheless, the role of the federal government in American higher education, while significant, is still felt primarily through its support for research and student aid. That broad assessment must be qualified by reference to developments in the past two decades, especially in connection with the role of all branches of the federal government, not least the judiciary, in relation to racial and other forms of discrimination. I will return to those issues below.

In the following section I want to explore the roots of the unique character of American higher education in the colonial experience, and the impact of the American Revolution on the attitudes and arrangements for higher education that came out of the colonial period. In brief, the colonies gave us diversity, while the Revolution gave us freedom from central state power and, for most of our colleges, from governmental control or influence of any kind.

In the section following I will explore what I take to be the emergence after the Revolution of a national policy toward higher education, a policy nowhere articulated as such, but defined by the actions of federal officials and agencies toward the institutions of higher education. I will discuss briefly five salient events that helped to define that policy, at least in retrospect. The broad purpose of federal policy as defined by those events was to encourage the provision of higher education, to broaden access to college and university to ever wider sectors of the population, to encourage the contribution of higher education to the practical work of society as well as to learning and scholarship, and to do all this without directly impinging on the autonomy of the institutions or on the constitutional responsibility for higher education reposing in the states. This meant a policy that paradoxically was active yet had the effect of driving power in higher education progressively farther away from Washington, D.C., down toward the individual states, the institutions, and their individual members, students, and faculty. One can see this as a kind of continuing self-denying ordinance by which the federal government acted to facilitate decisions made by others, rather than forcing its own decisions on the states, institutions, or members.

In the final section I will point briefly to a number of areas in which federal influence is now being felt more directly by the institutions of higher education in America, and will raise the question of whether these developments and tendencies mark a sharp change in the character and direction of federal policy in the realm of higher education, associated with the federal government's increased role as protector of civil rights (whose definition has been broadened by federal courts in recent decades), and also with the sheer growth in the size, cost, and national importance of the education, training, and research done in American universities and colleges. Alternatively, one can see these developments as dramatic but limited changes in policy, leaving issues of basic character and mission of American colleges and universities to their own governing boards and state authorities.

The Roots of American Federalism in the Colonial Experience[16]

Despite all the changes and transformations of state, society, and economy in modern times, the American system of higher education has its roots in the colonial period, when it developed characteristics distinguishable from all other systems of higher education in the world, notably in its governance patterns, marked by a strong president and lay governing board, its extraordinary diversity of forms and functions, and its marked responsiveness to forces in society as well as in state and church. In one other respect the colonial colleges are familiar to us, and that is in the importance attached to them by the societies and governments of the colonies. At a time when most European universities were not really central to the vitality of their societies, and were more or less preoccupied with the preparation of theologians and divines serving an established church, or with defining the virtues and polishing the accomplishments of a ruling elite, seventeenth- and eighteenth-century colonial colleges in America were regarded by their founders and supporters as forces for survival in a hostile environment. They were seen as crucial, indeed indispensable instruments for staving off the threat of reversion to barbarism, the threatened decline into the savagery of the surrounding forest and its Indian inhabitants.[17] The colleges also played a familiar role for these early Calvinists of maintaining a learned ministry and a literate laity. Moreover, in the young colonies as on the later frontier, civilization and its institutions could never be assumed to be inherited. They had always to be created and re-created, and for this purpose, learning and learned persons and the institutions that engendered them were needed.

The colonial colleges were founded as public bodies. They were established and then chartered by a public authority and were supported in part by public funds, in part by private gifts and endowments, in part by student fees. The mixing of public and private support, functions, and authority has persisted as a central characteristic of American higher education to this day, blurring the distinction between public and private colleges and universities. Americans have tended to regard all their higher education institutions as having a public dimension, and they also allowed for a private dimension in their public institutions. As Jurgen Herbst argues, one cannot see the colonial colleges as either "public" or "private" institutions, but as "provincial," stressing their function of service to their sponsoring and chartering colony, rather than to their source of support or authority.[18] While the distinction between "public" and "private" emerged with a certain clarity in the nineteenth century, and especially after the Civil War, it is still more appropriate to see the broad spectrum of American colleges and universities as lying along a continuum from fully public to nearly purely private.

Both the geography of the Eastern Seaboard and the accidents of settlement created a series of distinct and largely self-governing colonies, each tied to metropolitan London through a charter and governor, yet separate from one another in character, social structure, and forms of governance. That, in turn, meant that when colonial colleges were established they differed from one another in their origins, links to colonial government, and denominational ties.[19] Until the Revolution there was no central government on the American continent with broad jurisdiction over them all, and thus no governmental body that would accept responsibility for ordering and governing an emerging class of institutions in similar ways, in response to a common law or governmental policy. Indeed, even after a federal government emerged, it explicitly renounced its authority over education, including higher education, delegating that power to the constituent states. That self-denying ordinance was reinforced during the early years of the Republic when an attempt to create a national university in the capital was defeated, thus preventing what might well have introduced formal and informal constraints on the promiscuous creation of new colleges and universities after the Revolution.[20] So the colonies had the experience, before the Revolution, of having created a multiplicity of colleges or "university colleges" similar in certain respects but differing in others. They also had the experience of having created these institutions of higher education at the initiative or with the encouragement of public authorities and powerful private constituencies. Such support stands in marked contrast to the conspicuous lack of such encouragement, and indeed the stubborn resistance, or deeply divided responses, by political and ecclesiastical authorities in England to the creation of new institutions of higher education, especially and particularly those originating outside the Establishment, in the decades before 1830. The many dissenting academies created in England in the second half of the eighteenth century never had the encouragement of central or local government, and their failure to be fully acknowledged or gain a charter and the right to grant degrees were among the factors leading them to short lives and a dead end, of no real use or inspiration to those who created the new English colleges and universities in the next century. By contrast, for Americans the colonial experience provided a training in the arts of establishing institutions of higher education. And the skills and attitudes necessary for the creation of new colleges that were gained in the colonial period, along with the models of governance provided by the older institutions, led (in a more favorable environment than England provided) directly to the proliferation of colleges and universities after the Revolution: sixteen more between 1776 and 1800,[21] and literally hundreds over the next half century.

The eight colonial colleges differed widely among themselves. In a sense, these early and most prestigious American colleges, the nurseries of so many of the Revolutionary leaders, legitimated diversity. But similarities also existed. The colonial colleges had to be created in the absence of a body of learned men. In the New World no guild of scholars existed, no body of learned men who could take the governance of a college into its own hands. The very survival of the new institutions in the absence of buildings, an assured income, or a guild of scholars required a higher and more continuous level of governmental interest and involvement in institutions that had become much too important for the colonies to be allowed to wither or die. Moreover, a concern for doctrinal orthodoxy, especially in the seventeenth century, provided further grounds for public authorities to create governance machinery in which its own representatives were visible, or held a final veto and continuing visitorial and supervisory powers. The medieval idea of a university as an autonomous corporation composed of masters and scholars was certainly present in the minds of the founders of colonial colleges, but the actual circumstances of colonial life forced a drastic modification in the application of this inheritance. At Harvard, for example, the charter of 1650 "exemplified a carefully wrought compromise between a medieval tradition of corporate autonomy and a modern concern for territorial authorities over all matters of state and religion. The former was preserved, even though weakly, in the Corporation; the latter was institutionalized in the Board of Overseers."[22]

Other colonies as well, for reasons similar to those of Massachusetts, carefully circumscribed the powers of the corporate universities, each making sure that its governors and legislatures retained ultimate power over the college through the composition of its external board, or through the reserve powers of the colonial government as visitor. Even in Connecticut, where Yale's trustees were all Congregational ministers, the charter that incorporated the trustees as the president and fellows of Yale College preserved to the colonial court the right "'as often as required' to inspect the college's laws, rules, and ordinances, and to repeal or disallow them 'when they shall think proper.'"[23] The charter, Herbst notes, "thus upheld the ultimate authority of the Court over the college, but also guaranteed the school's autonomy within specific limits."[24]

Indeed, only Harvard and William and Mary College (in Massachusetts and Virginia), the only two seventeenth-century foundations, were established with a two-board government, one representing the institution or corporation, the other the external trustees. And in both of these "the governmental practice . . . soon lost its distinctiveness and came to resemble that of the one-board colleges. American colleges were to be ruled by powerful and respected citizens, who would govern them for their own and their children's benefit."[25] Ironically, the nearest American colleges and universities ever came to re-creating the first, or corporate board, was when they finally were able to gather together a guild of learned men who could command respect and gain a measure of professional authority. It was not until after the turn of the twentieth century that academic senates became significant parts of the governance machinery of American colleges and universities, and then only in the most prestigious institutions employing scholars who were able to use the academic marketplace to compel respect and attention from presidents and boards concerned with the status and distinction of their institutions. The relative weakness of the academic profession in the United States, as compared with its strength in the United Kingdom, especially in Oxbridge, has had large consequences for the diverging development of the two systems.[26]

With the exception of New Jersey which, because of religious diversity occurring at the end of the colonial period, chartered two colleges, each colony granted a monopoly position to its college. In this respect, each colony behaved toward its college as England behaved toward Oxford and Cambridge, and Scotland toward its universities, granting their colleges the power to award degrees within their respective province. American colonial governments were attempting to prevent or inhibit the appearance of rival and competitive institutions, in much the same way that the government in England had prevented the dissenting academies from widening the educational market in the eighteenth century. Consequently (and other factors were doubtless involved), in England the dissenting academies never emerged as serious competitive degree-granting institutions, and were destined to failure and, with one or two exceptions, to eventual extinction.[27] But their existence—and relevance—was noted in the colonies, and reference was made to them, during a dispute over sectarian issues at Yale in the 1750s, as better models than the ancient universities.[28] As models they were even more relevant to the proliferation of American colleges on the frontier between the Revolution and the Civil War, with the significant difference that the American colleges were encouraged and sometimes even modestly supported by public authorities.

Charters expressly reserved for colonial governments a continuing role in the governance of colleges, placing colonial officers directly on boards of trustees, or assigning to the courts and legislatures the power of review. For example, the 1766 charter of Queen's College (later to become Rutgers) included among its lay trustees the governor, council president, chief justice, and attorney general of the province of New Jersey.[29] By its charter of 1748, the College of New Jersey (later Princeton) placed the governor of the colony on the board as its presiding officer.[30] And in the turbulent sectarian climate of eighteenth-century America, those reserve powers were in fact employed from time to time.

All the colonial colleges were provided with public funds of various kinds, though in varying amounts and degrees of consistency. Some received a flat sum or subsidy to make up an annual shortfall in operating expenses or salaries, others assistance in the construction and maintenance of buildings. The assembly of Virginia provided the College of William and Mary with a percentage of the duties collected on furs, skins, and imported liquor.[31] These subventions reflected an organic connection between the colony and "its" college, and the colonies were not reluctant to use the power of the purse as a constraint on colleges when they were alleged to have carried their autonomy too far. The Connecticut legislature in 1755 refused its annual grant of £100 to Yale because of a sectarian dispute with the college's president.[32]

The power of colonial governments over their colleges, then, derived from three fundamental sources: the power to give or withhold a charter; the continuing powers reserved for government within the charter; and the power of the public purse. As Bernard Bailyn has stated the situation, "The autonomy that comes from an independent, reliable, self-perpetuating income was everywhere lacking. The economic basis of self-direction in education failed to develop."[33]

Effects of the American Revolution

Before 1776, the colonies displayed a stronger or at least as strong a connection between state and college as was apparent in the mother country, but the relationship changed drastically after the Declaration of Independence. In a formal sense, the Revolution transformed colonial governments into state governments and superimposed a national confederacy and then a federal government on top of them. However, at the same time the Revolution weakened all agencies of government by stressing the roots of the new nation in popular sovereignty, the subordination of the government to "the people," and the primacy of individual and group freedom and initiative. "The individual replaced the state as the unit of politics," writes one historian, "and the Constitution and Bill of Rights confirmed this Copernican revolution in authority." And "unlike the eighteenth-century venture in building a society from the top down," American society after the Revolution "originated in a multitude of everyday needs that responded to the long lines of settlement and enterprise, not the imperatives of union."[34]

But at least as important as the new conception of the relation of the citizen to the state that emerged from independence was the opening of the frontier beyond the Alleghenies, which gave many Americans a chance to walk away from the settled and "European" states that succeeded the old colonies, requiring them to create, indeed invent, new forms of self-government on the frontier.[35] Among the institutions of the frontier were new colleges, resembling the colonial colleges in some ways but differing in others, and linking the recently opened territories to the original culture of the Atlantic. In the twenty-five years after the Declaration of Independence, sixteen colleges were established (and have survived), thus tripling the total number in existence.[36] Of these, no less than fourteen were created on the frontier. After 1800, the floodgates of education opened, and hundreds of institutions were established in both old states and new territories. Most of them were small and malnourished, and many collapsed within a few years of their founding. The reason for this explosion of educational activity was a change in the three conditions that had hitherto characterized government-college relations in the colonial period: restrictive chartering, direct interest by government in the administration of colleges, and public support of higher education.

The new states, both those that succeeded the old colonies and those carved out of the new lands in the West, did not give a monopoly to any single state college or university, reflecting the quite different relationship of state and societal institutions that emerged from the Revolution. The states granted charters much more readily than had colonies before the Revolution, and on decidedly different terms. Herbst tells of efforts in 1762 by Congregationalists dissatisfied with the liberal Unitarian tendencies of Harvard to create a Queen's College in western Massachusetts. The nation's oldest college and its overseers opposed the proposal and prevailed, using the argument that Harvard "was a provincial monopoly, funded and supported by the General Court for reasons of state" and "properly the College of the Government."[37] The principle that reserved a monopoly to the "College of the Government," with its attendant rights and privileges, had to be overthrown for American higher education to break out of the restrictive chartering of higher education that had been historical practice. What is astonishing is not that it was subsequently overthrown, but that it was done with such ease as to scarcely occasion comment.

The ease with which new colleges were granted charters after the Revolution, and especially after the turn of the century, was both symbol and instrument of the triumph of society over the state that the Revolution had achieved.[38] Despite the efforts of the Federalists, central government itself over time came not to be a dominant institution (alongside the churches), but merely one player in social life, and not a very important one at that. By the fifth decade of the nineteenth century, the national government was scarcely visible in American life: no national bank, no military worth mentioning, no taxes that a growing majority of citizens could remember paying its officials.[39] And even state governments, closer to the people and with constitutional responsibility for education, confined their role to serving as the instruments of groups and interests in the society at large, including groups that wanted to create colleges for a whole variety of motives, cultural, religious, and mercenary, in all weights and combinations.

Long-term Federal Policy toward Higher Education after the Revolution

The colonial period taught Americans how to create colleges, and gave us diversity among them. The Revolution, as I have suggested, gave us freedom from central state power, especially from the power of government, both federal and state, to prevent the creation of independent colleges and universities. But these new freedoms were reinforced and given substance through a further set of decisions by federal actors and agencies after the Revolution. These together define federal policy toward higher education over the two hundred years from the founding of the Republic to the present. I will discuss five of them, with brief reference to others:

1. The failure of George Washington and his immediate presidential successors to establish a national university in the District of Columbia. The defeat of a proposal is a policy decision too, and in the case of the failure of the University of the United States, perhaps the most momentous in the history of American higher education.

2. The Supreme Court's decision of 1819 in the Dartmouth College case.

3. The Morrill, or Land Grant, Acts of 1862 and 1890, and the Hatch Act of 1887.

4. The Servicemen's Readjustment Act of 1944, better known as the GI Bill.

5. The Higher Education Amendments of 1972, which created the broad-spectrum programs of student aid that we have inherited, much amended and expanded.

How did these decisions, taken together, constitute a policy, and why, in retrospect, might one think of them as successful? I suggest that in each case the decision contributed to the diversity of American higher education, a diversity of type, of educational character and mission, of academic standard, and of access. In each case public policy tended to strengthen the competitive market in higher education by weakening any central authority that could substitute regulations and standards for competition. It accomplished this by driving decisions downward and outward, by giving more resources and discretion to the consumers of education and the institutions most responsive to them: they strengthened the states in relation to the federal government, as in the defeat of the University of the United States and the passage of the Morrill Acts; the institutions in relation to state governments, as in the Dartmouth College case and the Hatch Act; and the students in relation to the institutions, as in the GI Bill and the Higher Education Amendments of 1972.

The University of the United States

Consider first the failure to establish a national university. A multiplicity of forces and motives lay behind the establishment of colleges and universities throughout our history. Among these have been a variety of religious motives, a fear of relapse into barbarism at the frontier, the need for various kinds of professionals, state pride and local boosterism, philanthropy, idealism, educational reform, and speculation in land, among others and in all combinations. But the number and diversity of institutions, competing with one another for students, resources, teachers, bringing market considerations and market mechanisms right into the heart of this ancient cultural institution—all that also required the absence of any central force of authority that could restrain it, that could limit or control the proliferation of institutions of higher education. The states could not be that restraining force: under the pressures of competition and emulation, they have tended throughout our history to create institutions and programs in the numbers and to the standards of their neighbors. Crucially important has been the absence of a federal ministry of education with the power to charter (or to refuse to charter) new institutions, or of a single pre-eminent university that could influence them in other ways.

The closest we have come as a nation to establishing such a central force was the attempt first by George Washington, and then, though with less enthusiasm, by the next five presidents, to found a University of the United States at the seat of government in Washington, D.C.[40] Washington, in fact, made provision for such a university in his will. His strongest plea for it came in his last message to Congress, where he argued that a national university would promote national unity, a matter of deep concern at a time when the primary loyalties of many Americans were to their sovereign states rather than to the infant nation.

In addition, Washington saw the possibility of creating one really first-class university by concentrating money and other resources in it. As Washington noted in his last message to Congress: "Our Country, much to its honor, contains many Seminaries of learning highly respectable and useful; but the funds upon which they rest are too narrow to command the ablest Professors, in the different departments of liberal knowledge, for the Institution contemplated, though they would be excellent auxiliaries."[41] Here, indeed, Washington was right in his diagnosis. The many institutions that sprang up between the Revolution and the Civil War all competed for very scarce resources and all suffered to some degree from malnutrition. Malnutrition at the margin is still a characteristic of a system of institutions influenced so heavily by market forces.

Defeat of the national university meant that American higher education would develop, to this day, without a single capstone institution. Had we instead concentrated resources in one university of high standard early in our national life, it might have been the equal of the great and ancient universities of Europe, or the distinguished new universities then being established in Germany and elsewhere. As it was, whatever the United States called its institutions of higher learning, the nation simply did not have a single genuine university—no institution of really first-class standing that could bring its students as far or as deep into the various branches of learning as could the institutions of the Old World—until after the Civil War.

A national university would have profoundly affected American higher education. As the pre-eminent university, it would have had an enormous influence, direct and indirect, on every other college in the country, and through them, on the secondary schools as well. Its standards of entry, its curricula, its educational philosophies, even its forms of instruction, would have been models for every institution that hoped to send some of its graduates to the university in Washington. A federal system of high standard would surely have inhibited the emergence of the hundreds of small, half-starved state and denominational colleges that sprang up over the next century. They simply could not have offered work to the standard that the University of the United States would have set for the baccalaureate degree, and demanded of applicants to its own postgraduate studies. In the United States, after the defeat of the University of the United States, no one has challenged the principle of high academic standards across the whole system because no one has proposed it: there have been no common standards, high or otherwise. And in that spirit, we have created a multitude of institutions of every sort, offering academic work of every description and at every level of seriousness and standard.

Dartmouth College Case

Another major event in the early history of the Republic had powerful effects on the shape and character of American higher education as we know it today. This was the 1819 decision of the Supreme Court in the Dartmouth College case. It was a landmark decision in that it affirmed the principle of the sanctity of contracts between governments and private institutions. In so doing, it gave expression to the Federalist belief that the government should not interfere with private property even for the purpose of benefiting the public welfare. John Marshall, then chief justice of the Supreme Court, had written earlier: "I consider the interference of the legislature in the management of our private affairs, whether those affairs are committed to a company or remain under individual direction as equally dangerous and unwise." That anti-statist position today sounds deeply conservative; but from another perspective it is radically libertarian and had broad and liberalizing effects on higher education. Marshall and his colleagues on the Court decided in the Dartmouth College case that a charter of a private college or university was a contract that a state could not retroactively abridge. And that had important repercussions both for the growth of capitalist enterprises and for the future development of higher education in the United States.

The rationale for the proposed changes in Dartmouth's charter was the plausible argument that, as the college had been established (though as a private corporation) to benefit the people of New Hampshire, this could best be accomplished by giving the public, through the state legislature, a voice in the operation of the institution. The state wanted to improve the college as a place of learning by modernizing its administration, creating the framework for a university, and encouraging a freer, nonsectarian atmosphere conducive to republicanism.

These goals were very much in the Jeffersonian tradition that encouraged the creation of republican institutions—by the states—to meet the needs of a new nation. In this spirit, in 1816 the New Hampshire legislature had passed a bill giving the state government broad powers to reform Dartmouth. Chief Justice Marshall, ruling in favor of the college trustees, declared that state legislatures were forbidden by the Constitution to pass any law "impairing the obligation of contracts," and that the charter originally granted the college was a contract.[42] In many ways

Marshall's opinion followed the traditional view of the role of educational institutions in English society.

The Dartmouth College decision, preventing the state of New Hampshire from taking over the college, sustained the older, more modest role of the state in educational affairs against those who looked to the government to take a greater role in the working of society and its institutions. Marshall's decision had the practical effect of safeguarding the founding and proliferation of privately controlled colleges, even poor ones. Thereafter, promoters of private colleges knew that once they had obtained a state charter they were secure in the future control of the institution. After this decision, state control over the whole of higher education, including the private sector, was no longer possible.

The failure of the University of the United States and the success of Dartmouth College in its appeal to the Supreme Court were both victories for local initiative and for private entrepreneurship. The first of these set limits on the role of the federal government in shaping the character of the whole of American higher education; the second set even sharper limits on the power of the state over private colleges. Together, these two events constituted a kind of charter for unrestrained individual and group initiative in the creation of colleges of all sizes, shapes, and creeds. Almost any motive or combination of motives and interests could bring a college into being between the Revolution and the Civil War, and thereafter its survival depended largely on its being able to secure support from a church, from wealthy benefactors, from student fees, and even perhaps from the state. The colleges thus created were established relatively easily, but without guarantees of survival. And as a result, there arose a situation resembling the behavior of living organisms in an ecological system—competitive for resources, highly sensitive to the demands of the environment, and inclined, over time, through the ruthless process of natural selection, to be adaptive to those aspects of their environment that permitted their survival. Their environment also has included other colleges, and later, universities. So we see in this frog pond a set of mechanisms that we usually associate with the behavior of small entrepreneurs in a market: the anxious concern for what the market wants, the readiness to adapt to its apparent preferences, the effort to find a special place in that market through the marginal differentiation of the product, a readiness to enter into symbiotic or parasitic relationships with other producers for a portion of that market. That is, to this day, the world of American higher education.

The Morrill Act

The Morrill Act, which created the land grant colleges and universities, is indeed a landmark in American higher education. It was very far from being the first provision of support for higher education by central government through grants of government-owned land; indeed, under the Articles of Confederation the Northwest Ordinance provided for tracts of land to be set aside for the support of institutions of higher education in the Western Reserve. Ohio University among others was a beneficiary of such an early grant. But the Morrill Act provided support on an altogether different scale; in 1862, the federal government gave land to the states for the support of colleges and universities of an area equal to the whole of Switzerland or the Netherlands, about 11,000 square miles. And it did this in the most extraordinarily permissive way. The Act made no fixed requirements as to type of institution or, beyond broad designations of fields of study, as to content of instruction. The only positive obligations were to dispose of the land or scrip, in manner or on terms left to state discretion; maintain the fund as a perpetual endowment invested at 5 percent; devote the income to one or more institutions which, while including the traditional college subjects, must provide instruction in agriculture, mechanic arts, and military tactics; and make an annual report on the results.[43]

The beneficiaries of the Act were whomever the states decided they should be—among them, Cornell in New York, MIT in Massachusetts, and Yale's Sheffield School in Connecticut. In some states the money went to an existing state-supported institution; in California, the university was created through a merger of an existing private liberal arts college with the land grant endowment. In Oregon and Kentucky it went to a denominational college that remained under church control.[44] In many states, especially in the South and West, a new "A. and M." college was created to be the beneficiary of the land grant fund.

But basically, the federal government put the money—or at least the scrip—on the stump and walked away, partly because there was no consensus about what these institutions should look like, or should be doing,[45] and partly because there was no federal educational bureaucracy to provide for federal direction and control of state policy.

The result, needless to say, was various and messy, marked by ineptitude and corruption in places, confusion almost everywhere, but also by great imagination, creativity, and even genius—one thinks of the role of Ezra Cornell in New York. Some states got 50 cents an acre for their land, others ten times that much, and the variation in educational practice and academic standard was of the same order of magnitude.

We might ask what the costs would have been of trying to create a tidier system, more rationally coordinated, marked by a clearer common sense of academic direction, higher academic standards, more highly qualified and better-paid staff, better-prepared students, and more adequate initial funding for buildings and equipment. We are, of course, describing the creation of the modern European university systems—and they have been trying to break out of the straitjacket of those constricting commitments and structures since the end of World War II, with great difficulties and only partial success.

The GI Bill and the Higher Education Amendments of 1972

We now think of the GI Bill, and rightly so, as one of the best things that ever happened to American higher education. It broadened the idea of college-going enormously, and moved the enrollment rate from 15 percent of the age grade in 1939 toward 50 percent or more currently. And it brought a seriousness and maturity to undergraduate classrooms that were not accustomed to it, and that they have never quite lost.

But no one at the time it was debated expected it to be quite as successful as it was. Most estimates during the debates were that perhaps 800,000 veterans would take advantage of the program. By 1956, when the last veteran had received his last check, 2.25 million veterans had attended college under the GI Bill.[46] Just for comparison, the United Kingdom had a comparable program, the "Further Education and Training Scheme," which raised university enrollments from about 50,000 before World War II to 80,000 shortly after the war, causing great concern in the ministry of education regarding a possible decline in standards.[47] In the United Kingdom that problem was met by raising standards for entry to the universities steadily after the war. As a result, the proportion enrolled in British higher education in 1987 (14 percent of the age grade) was roughly the same as the proportion enrolled in American colleges and universities fifty years earlier.

There are two points to be made about the GI Bill: first, veterans could take their tuition payments and stipends anywhere they wished, certainly to any accredited college or university that would accept them, and to many other non-accredited postsecondary education institutions, too. Again there were irregularities at the edges: some corruption, some institutions that took tuition money without doing much teaching, whose students enrolled for the modest stipends provided. But again, we must consider the costs of closing those loopholes: the proliferation of forms and surveillance, the steady pressure to rationalize and standardize in order to make assessment, management, and credentialing easier. The federal government accepted the probability of abuse of the legislation, perhaps recognizing that rationalization in higher education as elsewhere is the enemy of diversity. And, as we have seen, federal policies on the whole have consistently favored diversity.

Second, one crucial provision of the GI Bill stipulated that "no department, agency, or officer of the United States, in carrying out the provisions [of this Act] shall exercise any supervision or control, whatsoever, over any State, educational agency . . . or any educational or training institution."[48] Of course, that is in the tradition of our constitutional reservation of responsibility for education to the states. But beyond that, we see here the same self-denying ordinance—the sharp separation of financial support from academic influence—that marked earlier federal policy, and that became the model and precedent for the Education Amendments of 1972 and thereafter provides substantial non-categorical need-based federal aid to students by way of grants and loans.[49]

Current Expansion of Federal Interventions

From the early land grants to speculators encouraging settlement in the Northwest Territories to the latest Pell grants to needy students, the federal government's central policy has been to expand and extend access to higher education more and more widely throughout the society. And since World War II, the federal government, with an expressed interest in the economic and military strength of the nation, has been the major source of support of both basic and applied research in the universities. These commitments of funds, directly to researchers and students, are still the largest and most visible forms of federal involvement in American higher education, the extent of which is sketched above. There is also the substantial but largely hidden subsidy provided by the federal government (and most state governments as well) through provision in the tax code for full deduction for income tax purposes of contributions to institutions of higher education (along with most other kinds of nonprofit charitable institutions). A further subsidy in the tax code gives parents a dependent's exemption for children who are full-time college or university students for whom they provide more than half the support.

In the past three decades the federal government has extended its interest in higher education in ways that reflect the central role that this institution now plays in American society and the economy. Some of these further interventions reflect the hugely increased size of the federal role in support for research since the end of World War II. The federal government's decisions about how to allocate its research support funds now affect the whole shape and direction of American science. One set of issues centers around the competitive claims of "big science"—such enormous and expensive enterprises as the superconductor-supercollider, the plan to map the human genome, the launching of the Hubble telescope, and the exploration of space—and the ordinary claims of university-based researchers doing studies on their own initiative individually or in small teams. Big science is necessarily competitive with small science for funds, but its decisions are each so expensive and consequential that they inevitably bring political considerations (and pressures) into the heart of the scientific decision-making process. Efforts continue to be made to insulate these decisions from the most crass political forces, and to make them "on their merits," but these mechanisms are strained by the traditions of state competition for federal funds in Congress and the White House, the traditions of political deals, and pork barrel legislation in a populist society.

Until recently, the nature and administration of research overhead funds, paid by the federal government as part of their grants and contracts with university researchers, would have nicely illustrated my theme of the federal government's self-denying principle with respect to American higher education. These overheads, intended to reimburse the universities for the costs of maintaining the research facilities in which the federally funded scientific work was done, were negotiated with the individual universities, public and private, and then very loosely monitored, in ways that suggested that government funders of research were primarily interested in supporting the infrastructures of research without trying to manage them. The recent embarrassing revelations of inappropriate and (in part) illegal charges for overhead costs at Stanford threaten to change this older, looser relationship between the universities and their federal funding agencies, not just for Stanford but for the whole universe of research universities.[50] The case has also brought committees of Congress (and their staff members) directly into the overhead picture. To a considerable degree, the freedom of American colleges and universities from the kind of close governmental oversight familiar in other societies has been based on a relatively high degree of trust on the part of American society (and its governmental institutions) in higher education. If that trust is eroded through such scandals as at Stanford, the autonomy of the universities may be similarly eroded. It is too early to tell the effects of this event on the larger question of the relations of higher education with agencies of the federal government.

Some observers of federally funded research believe that we may already have reached the point of no return. In an editorial in *Science*, Philip Abelson observes that

a particularly dismaying feature of the government-university interface is that relationships continue on a long-term course of evolving deterioration. In the early days after World War II, there was a high degree of mutual trust and an absence of bureaucratic requirement. Scientists had freedom to formulate and conduct their programs of research. Later the bureaucrats took over and placed emphasis on project research with highly detailed budgets and detailed research proposals. That, of course, is the road to pedestrian research.[51]

And Abelson cites the proliferation of administrative requirements and regulations as a serious drag on the freedom and quality of scientific work in the universities.

In recent decades the federal government—indeed all three branches—

has become increasingly active in connection with its interest in the protection of the civil rights of citizens, most notably in relation to possible forms of discrimination against racial and ethnic minorities, women, and other vulnerable groups in American colleges and universities. These activities, affecting such issues as the confidentiality of academic personnel files, the monitoring of student admissions and faculty appointment and promotion practices, the protection of human subjects in scientific research, and many rules and regulations governing federally funded research, have bypassed state agencies and brought the federal government directly into the daily life of the colleges and universities.

These developments are at odds with the pattern of federal support without the exercise of substantial directive power that I have suggested has been the historical relation of the federal government to American higher education. It remains to be seen whether a decline in public trust in the institutions of higher education, or government's legitimate interest in the defense of equal rights for all citizens, will lead to fundamental changes in what has been a unique and fruitful three-cornered relationship between American colleges and universities and their state and federal governments.

NOTES

1. *Chronicle of Higher Education,* February 27, 1991, p. 1.
2. *Chronicle of Higher Education,* September 1, 1988.
3. "Almanac," *Chronicle of Higher Education*, September 5, 1990, p. 3.
4. *Digest of Education Statistics* (Washington, D.C.: U.S. Department of Education, 1989), Tables 126 and 133, pp. 30 and 36.
5. *Digest,* 1989, Table 269, p. 292; "Almanac," p. 25.
6. *Digest,* 1989, Tables 270 and 271, pp. 293–94.
7. *Chronicle of Higher Education*, September 6, 1989, p. A31; "Almanac," p. 13.
8. "Almanac," pp. 13 and 20.
9. *Chronicle of Higher Education*, September 6, 1989, p. A31.
10. J. Evangelauf, "States' Spending on Colleges Rises 19 pct. in 2 Years, Nears $31–billion for '85–86," *Chronicle of Higher Education*, October 30, 1985, p. 1.
11. *Chronicle of Higher Education*, October 24, 1990, p. 1.
12. Daniel T. Layzell and Jan W. Lyddon, *Budgeting for Higher Education at*

the State Level: Enigma, Paradox, and Ritual (Washington, D.C.: The George Washington University, 1990), Table 2, pp. 23–24.

13. John S. Brubacher and Willis Rudy, *Higher Education in Transition* (New York: Harper and Bros., 1958), p. 227.

14. Chester E. Finn, Jr., *Scholars, Dollars, and Bureaucrats* (Washington, D.C.: The Brookings Institution, 1978), p. 122.

15. Clark Kerr and Marion L. Gade, *The Guardians: Boards of Trustees of American Colleges and Universities* (Washington, D.C., Association of Governing Boards of Universities and Colleges, 1989), p. 129.

16. This section draws on my unpublished paper (with Sheldon Rothblatt), "Government Policies and Higher Education: A Comparison of Britain and the United States, 1630–1860," in *The Sociology of Social Reform*, ed. Colin Crouch and Anthony Heath (Oxford: Oxford University Press, 1992).

17. "From the very beginnings, the expressed purpose of colonial education had been to preserve society against barbarism, and, so far as possible, against sin." Henry May, *The Enlightenment in America* (New York, 1978), pp. 32–33.

18. John S. Whitehead and Jurgen Herbst, "How to Think about the Dartmouth College Case," *History of Education Quarterly* 26 (Fall 1986): 344.

19. Jurgen Herbst, *From Crisis to Crisis: American College Government, 1636–1819* (Cambridge, Mass.: Harvard University Press, 1982).

20. Martin Trow, "Aspects of Diversity in American Higher Education," in *On the Making of Americans*, ed. Herbert Gans et al. (Philadelphia: University of Pennsylvania Press, 1979), pp. 271–90.

21. David W. Robson, "College Founding in the New Republic, 1776–1800," *History of Education Quarterly* (Fall 1983): 323–41.

22. Herbst, *Crisis*, p. 16.

23. Ibid., p. 47.

24. Ibid.

25. Ibid., p. 61.

26. Martin Trow, "Comparative Reflections on Leadership in Higher Education," *European Journal of Education* 20 (1985): 143–59. Reprinted as chapter 13 in this volume.

27. W. H. G. Armytage, *Civic Universities: Aspects of a British Tradition* (London, 1955), pp. 128–40, 153–56, and Irene Parker, *Dissenting Academies in England* (Cambridge: The University Press, 1914), pp. 124–36.

28. Herbst, *Crisis*, p. 77. Another historian observes that "The founders [of the mid-eighteenth century colonial colleges] . . . . transplanted the essentials of the educational system of the English dissenting academies and saw the system take root." Beverly McAnear, "College Founding in the American Colonies, 1745–75," *The Mississippi Valley Historical Review* 42 (June 1955): 44.

29. Herbst, *Crisis*, p. 111.

30. Ibid., pp. 86–87.

31. David W. Robson, *Educating Republicans: The College in the Era of the American Revolution, 1750–1800* (Westport, Conn.: Greenwood, 1985), p. 19.

32. Herbst, *Crisis*, p. 76.

33. For remarks on funding in relation to institutional independence, see Bernard Bailyn, *Education in the Forming of American Society* (New York, 1960), p. 44.

34. Robert H. Wiebe, *The Opening of American Society* (New York: Vintage, 1984), p. 353.

35. Stanley Elkins and Eric McKitrick, "A Meaning for Turner's Frontier: Democracy in the Old Northwest," in *Turner and the Sociology of the Frontier*, ed. Richard Hofstadter and Seymour Martin Lipset (New York: Basic, 1968), pp. 120–51.

36. Robson, "College Founding," p. 323.

37. Herbst, *Crisis*, p. 136.

38. Charters were granted rather promiscuously to any group that seemed prepared to accept responsibility for raising funds for a building and hiring a president. On the founding of Allegheny College in western Pennsylvania in 1815, see Rothblatt and Trow, "Government Policies and Higher Education," pp. 14–17.

39. Wiebe, *The Opening of American Society*, p. 353.

40. Trow, "Aspects of Diversity in American Higher Education," pp. 271–90.

41. Richard Hofstadter and Wilson Smith, eds., *American Higher Education: A Documentary History*, 2 vols. (Chicago: University of Chicago Press, 1961), p. 158.

42. Ibid., p. 218.

43. Earle D. Ross, *Democracy's College: The Land-Grant Movement in the Formative Stage* (Ames: The Iowa State College Press, 1942), p. 68.

44. Ibid., p. 75.

45. There were very sharp differences in Congress and outside it about the relative emphasis to be placed in these new institutions on pure or applied science, on practical experience and manual work, or on the old classical curriculum. The federal government's solution was to allow these contending forces to fight it out in each state, where indeed the results added to an already high level of diversity in American higher education.

46. Keith W. Olson, *The G.I. Bill, The Veterans and the Colleges* (Lexington: University of Kentucky Press, 1974), p. 43.

47. H. Peston and H. M. Peston, "The Further Education and Training Scheme," in *Recurrent Education*, ed. Selma J. Mushken (Washington, D.C.: National Institute of Education, U.S. Department of Education, 1974).

48. Olson, *The G.I. Bill,* pp. 17–18.

49. For a discussion of the debate in Congress and elsewhere leading up to the passage of this law, see Finn, *Scholars, Dollars, and Bureaucrats,* esp. pp. 121–28.

50. *Science,* March 22, 1991, p. 1420.

51. Philip Abelson, *Science,* February 8, 1991, p. 605.

5

....

THIS ESSAY WAS FIRST DELIVERED as a presentation to a seminar dealing with higher education in Sweden in 1990, and then published in a number of places, including a volume in honor of Seymour
Martin Lipset. Lipset had been the principal author and organizer
of the major study *Union Democracy*, in 1956, on which Trow and
James Coleman collaborated and of which they became coauthors.
In both their cases, it became the first book publication in distinguished careers. I mention this early connection with the work of
Lipset because one sees in this essay a concern that activated the
research that led to *Union Democracy* and the effort to understand
the distinctiveness of American labor unions, and that is the significance of the absence of a tradition of a major socialist party in the
United States. This was a topic with which Lipset dealt all his life
but which Trow raised only on occasion, this presentation being one
of them. And I mention the place of the first presentation of this paper, in Sweden, because I believe its original formulation for a non-
American audience influenced its content and tone and emphases.

In particular, the presentation to a non-American audience led
Trow to emphasize sharply the role of the hope and expectation of
individual advancement in the United States, and how that hope and
expectation affects American institutions and beliefs. This he presents in contrast with the greater role in European societies of socialist parties and movements working to advance the working class as
a class. In America, in contrast, the ideal role of colleges and universities is to give opportunity to talented and ambitious individuals.
The issue of the rise of the working class as result of educational opportunity simply is not on the agenda. Trow notes that "a culture is
defined, in part, by what it feels guilty about. Western European nations, on the whole, feel guilty about their working classes . . . We as

a nation still feel intensely guilty about our history of race relations, and especially about our history of black slavery,"

The essay makes a particular effort to explain why American colleges and universities are so much more concerned, as they have become more democratic in their ambitions, with the role they may play in the advancement of blacks, and similarly disadvantaged ethnic and racial groups, than in the advancement of the working class. Sociologists may be concerned with the latter, and why they are so poorly represented in more selective American universities, but college presidents and administrators rarely are. Thus Trow points to the striking fact that while the Organisation for Economic Co-operation and Development (OECD) in its research has explored the representation of working-class origin students in European universities, and could track the record of the increase in their numbers, it could find no similar statistics at the University of California: there, as in other American universities, the emphasis is overwhelmingly on the percentage of black students, of Hispanic or Latino students, of American Indian students (often dubbed today "Native Americans"), or of Asian American students. This view of America through glasses emphasizing racial or ethnic affiliation, rather than class affiliation, was also evident in the past; but then blacks were excluded from many institutions, and, as we know from a series of major and remarkably detailed studies of the practices of leading American universities, there was equal concern with the numbers of Jewish students. This was not for purposes of extending the universities' role in overcoming disadvantage, as is true of the present obsession with racial and ethnic statistics, but for the purpose of trying to control the numbers of an overachieving minority that presidents and administrators feared would swamp their institutions and make them less attractive to potential students from older and more established ethnic groups, Americans of English and related heritage.

That is all now in the past. But the obsession with racial and ethnic statistics persists. As I write this headnote, during commencement week at Harvard, the first thing we are told about the graduating class, as the first thing we are told about each entering class, is what percentage of black and Hispanic students has been reached.

Trow tries to explain the remarkable absence of statistics, whether public and official or institutional, on students of working-class background with two factors. The first, already noted, is the American emphasis on individual advancement, the lack of major interest even among those concerned with the disadvantages of the working class to expand their numbers in colleges and universities, the absence of any major efforts, aside from some specific periods (such as the Depression), to build up independent working-class traditions and institutions. The emphasis, in a word, is on rising out of your class, rather than with your class, and as a consequence of this aspect of American exceptionalism, we note the absence of a major socialist party, and traditions or institutions associated with it.

But another reason for this ignoring of working-class advancement, as against the individual advancement that higher education makes possible, is that the great wound and fault in American society is not its treatment of the working classes, but its treatment of the black population, descended from slaves (though in recent decades immigrants have made up an ever larger part of the black population). Even with the abolition of slavery, blacks were kept in a condition of near subjection as a result of a century of discrimination and segregation. This is the problem that higher education has tried steadily to address as it becomes more democratic and inclusive and extends its efforts to deal with the problem of inequality in society.

Many efforts of different kinds have been addressed to this problem but the most controversial has been affirmative action, which in the case of higher education has not been governmentally imposed (as it has been in the case of employment) but has been a voluntary effort on the part of individual institutions of higher education to expand the number of blacks that are admitted and graduated. Since the major path taken to advance this effort has been to reduce the academic requirements for admission for black applicants, this policy, which is in effect in almost all highly selective institutions, to one degree or another, has been much disputed, much analyzed, and has been the cause of significant litigation, reaching to the Supreme Court. Trow describes this policy and the reasons for it in this essay. His approach here is almost neutral: he adverts to some of the problems with this policy but he is no advocate, for or against. Indeed in his treatment explaining the reasons for this policy he appears more as a supporter than a critic. I believe this is because Trow was presenting the story outside the United States, to foreigners, and wanted to emphasize its character as a benign and progressive effort, part of the great civil rights movement to ameliorate the condition of blacks. It is indeed that, from one perspective. But it also opposes some of the central values of the university, the emphasis on merit and achievement. Trow was presenting in a way the best case to be made for this large-scale effort of the universities to advance the condition of blacks. Had the essay been written for an audience at the University of California, and indeed for any American audience, these policies would have been subjected to much closer critical analysis, as it indeed they were in other papers (see chapter 13 in this volume).

—NATHAN GLAZER

Class, Race, and Higher Education in America

Social Class and Higher Education

Mass higher education in the United States, with universal access in many places, has many functions that it shares with similar institutions around the world. However, it has one function that is perhaps unique to us: it is the central instrument for the legitimation of a society around the principle of broad (and in principle, equal), opportunities open to all individuals, opportunities to improve

Originally published as Martin Trow, "Class, Race, and Higher Education in the United States," in *Reexamining Democracy: Essays in Honor of Seymour Martin Lipset*, 138–56. Thousand Oaks, Calif.: Sage, 1992. It was revised from a paper prepared for a seminar on the report of a Review of Higher Education Policy in California, delivered to the Organization for Economic Cooperation and Development, by a committee chaired by A. H. Halsey, 1989. The seminar was sponsored by the Center for Studies in Higher Education, UC Berkeley, June 1990. Reprinted by permission of Sage Publications, Inc.

themselves and to make their careers and lives through their own efforts and talents. Our 3,500 accredited colleges and universities, offering coursework at every level of standard and difficulty to an enormously diverse student body, serve a wide variety of functions for the students and for the society at large. While most of them offer some liberal and general studies, they serve as the chief avenue of entry to middle-class occupations—even to quite modest lower-middle-class occupations, which in most countries would not require or reward exposure to postsecondary education. These institutions, without the kinds of educational ceilings common in European non-university forms of postsecondary schooling, encourage students to raise their aspirations through further study, full- or part-time, and provide the possibility of transfer to advanced studies elsewhere if they do not have such provisions themselves. They thus reflect and reinforce the radical individualism of American values, a set of values deeply opposed to socialist principles that center on cooperative efforts at group advancement, and on the common effort to create a society whose members all profit (more or less equally) from the common effort. American higher education, as a system, both serves and celebrates the American Dream of individual careers open to talents, a dream given much of its institutional reality in the contemporary world precisely by America's system of mass higher education offering a clear alternative to socialist principles of class identification and horizontal loyalty. The contrast between these competitive visions is captured in the stirring appeal of Eugene Debs, the last socialist leader in the United States with any significant following (he gained nearly a million votes for president on the socialist ticket in 1920), when he called on his followers, most of them in the working class, to "Rise with your class, not out of it."

Mass higher education in the United States (and to some extent elsewhere as well)[1] is deeply opposed to this vision of society, to which it offers the alternative exhortation, "Rise out of your class, not with it." That unexpressed call (unexpressed precisely because it is understood beyond need for explication by all Americans) touches a fundamental chord in American society, and not least among its workers and immigrants. It is a long-standing cliché of American life that parents say with fervor of their children: "I want them to have a better life than I have had," a better life seen as achievable not through collective or political action, but through more and better education, and in recent decades, through college education. George Ticknor, then a professor at Harvard, expressed an American truism in 1825 when he observed: "There is, at this moment, hardly a father in our country, who does not count among his chief anxieties, and most earnest hopes, the desire to give his children a better education than he has been able to obtain for himself" (Rudolph, p. 216). In the same year, the president of the University of Nashville, then near the frontier, declared that "every individual, who wishes to rise above the level of a mere labourer at task-work, ought to endeavor to obtain a liberal education" (Rudolph, p. 214). Already 160 years ago, "every individual," not just gentlemen, as in most of Europe, was being exhorted to rise out of the ranks of the "mere day labourer" through education. And while higher education in the United States would not be providing the means of social mobility for large numbers for a century or more, and not for the whole society until after World War II, the sense of the possibilities for achievement through education are there very early indeed. And these are the expressions not of radical leaders, but of members of the solid professional middle class who believe that they are voicing perfectly ordinary middle-class sentiments, not those of political radicalism.

The idea of higher education as an instrument of mobility for poor young men "making their way" was present in America throughout the eighteenth century. But it required the enormous growth in the numbers of colleges after 1800, the fierce competition among them, and the effect this competition had on the costs of college attendance, to bring large numbers of penurious students to college.

Allmendinger, an historian of this period, notes that

> poor young men, sometimes described as "needy" or "indigent" or even "paupers" gathered in large numbers in the colleges of New England during the years between 1800 and 1860. They came down from the hill towns, where opportunities were few, to the small colleges at Hanover or Williamstown or Brunswick. Even before New York State and Ohio drew many of their kind to the West, they began to infiltrate—almost imperceptibly at first—the student population. They did not want new farm lands, nor would they try to find

places at home as hired workers in an agricultural proletariat; they joined, instead, a rural intelligentsia of students and teachers aspiring to the middle class professions. (p. 8)[2]

The proliferation of colleges in the United States in the first half of the nineteenth century resulted chiefly from the weakening of political constraints on their establishment. In the colonies, as in most countries to this day, governments (in America the colonial governments) controlled the establishment of colleges and universities through their control over the awarding of charters to institutions that allow them to award degrees. Governments almost everywhere have had political and religious reason for limiting the numbers of institutions of higher education; moreover, new universities have been subsidized by the state or been given guarantees of their continued survival. The Revolution in America greatly weakened central state power over higher education as over almost everything else. The Constitution took education (including higher education) completely out of the authority of the federal government; it took both federal and state governments out of the direct administration of the new independent colleges springing up everywhere after the Revolution, and it also removed any firm commitment by government of public funds for their support. The hundreds of new colleges that sprang up between the Revolution and the Civil War, many sponsored by the competitive Protestant denominations, had few academic or social pretensions, and in their need they were open and available to poor students. It did not take the democratic revolutions of the post–World War II era to create the possibility of a college education for poor youth; America had its democratic revolution in the first half of the nineteenth century. The nineteenth century, and especially the freeing of higher education from the control of the state, created the potential for the expansion of access, for mass higher education in the United States, but that potential was only fulfilled after World War II (Rothblatt and Trow, 1992; Trow, 1991).

This spirit of individual aspiration, opportunity, and achievement, present throughout our history but taking special force during and after the Revolution, is at marked variance with socialist principles of collective aspiration, opportunity, and achievement. It is at odds also with the instruments of that collective spirit, notably trade unions and the European socialist (or social democratic) parties of the past century, along with the cultural institutions that were created in many European nations around those institutions. Those institutions—schools, newspapers, sports clubs, cooperatives, and others—together contributed not just a political/economic movement, but an alternative subculture, the achievement of socialism in everyday life even before the triumph of socialism nationally.[3] But this subculture tied the individual worker firmly to his class; it did not encourage mobility out of it. And even the adult education it provided was aimed at raising the moral and cultural level of workers, not at providing them an avenue of mobility into the middle class: they characteristically offered humanistic studies designed to raise the cultural level of the working-class members of the subculture, not vocational courses designed to equip its members for mobility up and out of their class. For example, the studies provided the British working man in his leisure hours by the Mechanics' Institutes, and later by the Worker's Education Association, pivoted around literature and pure science, not professional engineering.[4]

Mass higher education is the enemy of a class-oriented society, and of class-oriented institutions such as trade unions. In the United States it has always been so, but dramatically so since enrollments have broadened and grown to include large numbers who would formerly have joined the labor force directly from high school. The turning point was World War II, when the wartime effort created a quasi-socialist society for a few years without affecting the underlying individualistic ethos of the society (with the partial exception of its academic and intellectual elites). At the end of World War II, American trade unions enrolled nearly 40 percent of the nonagricultural labor force, the highest level it ever achieved. It reached this level largely on the strength of wartime governmental requirements that firms having contracts with the government allow trade union organization of their labor force, a policy that in part reflected the close connections between organized labor and the northern wing of the Democratic Party, and in part because of the usefulness of the unions in organizing a wartime labor force and supporting the war. When the wartime rules were rescinded, along with the direct role of the government in the economy, and a little later the decline of the industries in which unions were heavily represented (e.g., steel and mining), the proportion of the labor force in unions declined precipitously. During the forty-five years since World War II, while enrollments in higher education have grown from 1.5 million to more than 14 million, and the proportion of the age grade enrolled in colleges and universities increased from 15 percent to about 50 percent, the proportion of the non-farm labor force in trade unions fell from roughly 40 percent just after World War II to about 19 percent in 1988, and in the private sector to 14 percent.[5]

I am not suggesting a simple direct causal relationship between these figures—for example, that all those who didn't join the unions were going to college instead. Both sets of figures point to and reflect even more fundamental changes in the economy and society, changes that also occurred in other societies, but that in the United States took on characteristically individualistic forms. As traditional heavy industry and the big manual occupations such as mining and cargo handling, which everywhere have been the heart of the trade union movement, declined, other occupations that required (or came to be seen as requiring) a postsecondary education grew. In the United States this meant a massive growth of enrollment in the same institutions that had educated the older social and professional elite groups, and in the reinforcement of the individualistic ethos of opportunity and social mobility. All horizontal bondings that might inhibit or discourage individual mobility were avoided or weakened—not only trade union membership, but also church membership, and neighborhood and friendship ties. At the very least, they were modified and made instruments of this individual mobility, as, for example, family ties. The family, for most people (outside of a small social elite that could pass on substantial wealth across generations), became not the source of an individual's inherited social status, but a launching pad for an individual career, with the advantages of money and higher social status translated into opportunities for more and better formal education, and thus of better life chances for individual achievement and mobility. Indeed, the very idea of a "career," the planned sequence of upward steps in a chosen occupation, as against a series of jobs gained and changed in the course of working life, is in the United States now largely a function of some experience of higher education; it is hard to have a career without having been to college. And a career is inherently the property of the individual, and not that of an organization or class.

Institutions have survived in America by adapting to the conditions of a society marked by easy social and geographical mobility. Already in the eighteenth and nineteenth centuries, as George Homans shows, New England farmers (not peasants) were alert to the main chance; only one farm in five was passed on from father to son, and thus only one farm in twenty-five stayed in the same family over three generations. New England farmers' sons left for better land in the West or for better opportunities in other callings, as Americans have always done. Those who remained farmers showed little attachment to the land, but rather to the idea of individual betterment: a betterment that in many cases also included attendance at a state land grant university, with its school of agriculture, and use of the university's agricultural research and demonstration units.

After World War II, the trade union movement survived least well because it could not adapt to social mobility; unions are intrinsically instruments of horizontal bonding, and are the enemy of individual achievement and mobility except for the tiny number who could make the unions a career. (Many of its leaders were and are college educated, and came to the unions out of ideological commitment rather than as a reflection of common class membership.) The absence in America of a solidly based socialist party and its related institutions narrowed further the possible reconciliation of class-linked organizations with some possibilities for individual mobility and achievement within the labor movement, as, for example, has been possible in Sweden and the United Kingdom, until recently.

The radically individualistic spirit of America is also opposed to a more conservative concept of social organizations that envisions society as organized around status groups and strata or corporate guilds, the careers (or, echoing [Max] Weber, the life fates) of whose members are closely tied to those larger social entities. That spirit is embedded in most Western European societies, whether governed by social democratic or more conservative parties. And while market forces (the economic reflections of an individualistic ethos) has been gaining ascendancy everywhere over more corporativist modes of economic organization, it is still resisted by most European systems of higher education, or is adapted within close constraints on access. Such constraints, tying access to universities to highly selective upper secondary schools, minimize the power of the consumer and thus limit (or at least postpone) the emergence of a system of higher education at the service of the society rather than of the state, or of specific elite strata that will serve the state.

American society, throughout its history has, for many reasons, provided an unfriendly environment for socialist ideas and institutions. The absence of a feudal past, our early extension of the vote to all white men, the frontier, our relative affluence, our ethnic heterogeneity, religious roots, and social mobility have all been cited as explanations of why the United States has been and continues to be the only industrialized society in the world without a significant socialist movement or party.[6] Mass higher education has been an important element in this "unfriendly environment," especially over the past half century. And it works in a variety of ways. For example, mass higher education, especially since the great expansion following World War II, has drained off from the working and lower middle classes many of their brightest and ablest young men and women—not only the most intelligent, but also those with the most energy and initiative—making for a kind of brain drain out of the working class and weakening its organizations.

Ironically, the strong cultural emphasis on social mobility, on "getting ahead" in life, may have accounted equally for the leaders who governed and ran the unions, the businessmen they bargained with, and the mob bosses with whom they all too often were allied. Strong aspirations for personal achievement, for getting ahead, drive Americans of all kinds to seek avenues of mobility of all kinds, both legitimate and illegitimate. The chief legitimate avenues have been through speculation in land, entrepreneurship, and education. The latter two have historically been alternative routes up, for different groups in different generations. The chief illegitimate channel of mobility, of course, is crime, both blue and white collar, of which we have a fair amount. And white-collar crime increasingly requires an MBA, or at least the opportunities and access gained through higher education, both its skills and its connections. These channels have all been in competition with one another throughout American history, a competition that has provided the story for much of our literature, and even more of our movies. Since World War II, they have become complementary. One can still start a small grocery store in an ethnic neighborhood without a college degree, but you need a college education to be a consultant about anything, or to provide the sophisticated services of modern urban life.

But all of this—the multiple channels of mobility open to ordinary people, and the ambitions behind them—are strongly corrosive of all institutions that depend on horizontal solidarity and collective improvement, not least the labor unions.[7] The brain drain through education out of the unions of their best and brightest young members is part, but only part, of that corrosion; it is one of the mechanisms of that corrosion.

We can see this also when we look at the last great period of union growth in the United States—the creation of the big industrial unions— the steel workers, the automobile workers, the electrical workers, and then the CIO [Congress of Industrial Organizations]—during the Great Depression of the 1930s. This period preceded the great expansion of American higher education; while our system in the 1930s was large by European standards, it was still exceptional then for poor or working-class youth to go to a college or university.[8] For the ordinary industrial worker, something closer to the classic conditions of class struggle between labor and capital seemed to prevail. The new industrial unions— led to some considerable extent by socialists such as Walter Reuther and his brother in the Auto Workers—had broader dreams and hopes for what a labor movement could do to reshape the politics, the economics, and indeed the basic character of American society. Such unions could evoke the deep loyalties of their members, and could also be a real alternative to "getting ahead" as the guiding principle of life. It was perhaps not a fair test for the unions, since during most of that decade there was not much chance for anybody to get ahead in the United States. Still, perhaps for the first and last time in the United States, large numbers of people could envision building a working-class movement, one with real weight and influence on one of the two major political parties. The Roosevelt Democratic coalition provided an opening, with the more radical or visionary union leaders seeing perhaps a labor party of their own in the future.

Indeed, there seemed to be some historical warrant for such hopes. Had not the democratic socialist and labor parties of Western Europe emerged out of just such coalitions with liberal bourgeois parties thirty to fifty years earlier? Could the United States replicate that history? Some, in any event, believed so.

Yet another element contributed to the building of working-class institutions during those Depression years, and that is the production, really for the first time, of a sizeable group of unemployed college and university graduates, many of whom had themselves come from working- or lower-middle-class backgrounds. Many had grown up in homes with socialist ties or sympathies, "red diaper babies," as they were called, and had early taken advantage of relatively open access to higher education, particularly to free urban public universities such as New York's City College and Temple University in Philadelphia. Moreover, many of these young men were themselves socialists—of both the democratic and communist varieties. For these young men, job prospects in the 1930s were poor. Some, trained as economists or sociologists, could find work in the expanding welfare agencies of the New Deal, and could believe themselves contributing in that way to a nascent socialism in America. Others threw in their lot with the new unions, sometimes serving an apprenticeship on the shop floor and then getting elected to union office. Some went directly into union management by appointment to a staff position, as aides and advisors to the new, more politically minded, socialist-minded leaders. Sometimes the young men who went from college into the unions were members of the Communist Party, and occasionally they were members of the Socialist Party of America. But for a short while, union leadership offered the prospect of a real ideologically oriented career for a small number of college-educated youth.[9]

But the dream of a politically relevant mass labor movement, one that would evolve into an independent Labor Party embodying socialist principles, died with World War II.[10] It more obviously collapsed with the election of [Harry S.] Truman in 1948, because that kept the labor movement inside the Democratic Party. The pent-up wartime demand fueled an immediate boom; moreover, the government economists had learned something from the New Deal and the war about how central government interventions could avoid deep depressions as well as shorten and mitigate recessions. The growing economy, together with the GI Bill, encouraged and supported literally millions of veterans to go back to college, and the subtle permeation of democratic sentiments and higher aspirations throughout the society created a burst of demand for access to postsecondary education. The educational system thus grew to meet the demand. There were similar tendencies in all Western European countries; the difference is that in the United States demand for education at every level drives supply; at the level of higher education, it is not constrained by either resources or academic standards. In 1950, a comprehensive secondary system was already bringing 50 percent of the young to high school graduation; that figure by 1990 was about 75 percent. During those postwar decades, the United States built and opened hundreds and hundreds of colleges of every kind, in some years nearly one every day, under the implicit, sometimes explicit doctrine that "Something is better than nothing; let the future worry about standards. Right now, let us provide as good an education as possible for as many as possible."

And so between 1940 and 1970, nationwide enrollments rose from about 1.5 million to about 8.5 million. By 1991, enrollment in all American colleges and universities was about 14 million. Roughly two-thirds of high school graduates get some exposure to postsecondary education in the seven years directly after high school graduation, meaning roughly half of the age cohort. And some 44 percent of the whole labor force, including of course older people, have now had some exposure to postsecondary education.

The enormous expansion of the postwar years changed the perceptions of higher education among broad strata who had never before seen it as a realistic possibility for people like themselves. Higher education thus became for many the vehicle for social mobility that high school graduation had been for the half century between 1890 and 1940. Those fifty years had seen the growth of a broad system of state-supported secondary education all over the country. While higher education had actually served as a vehicle of mobility for many before 1945, especially for youth from farms preparing themselves for teaching, and for such educationally precocious ethnic groups as Jews and Armenians, it had not been seen as available for career making and mobility by broad segments of the population, as it came to be seen after World War II.

The significance of World War II as a watershed of values and attitudes ushering in the mass higher education that followed is suggested by the novel *The Grapes of Wrath*. John Steinbeck's powerful novel, which was published in 1939, is about the mid-1930s in America, the Great Depression, and the migration of thousands of impoverished farmers from Oklahoma and Arkansas (the "Okies" of American history) to California. This great internal migration can best be compared to the post–World War II mass immigrations to California from other countries: Mexicans, Chinese from Hong Kong and Singapore, Vietnamese, Koreans and Filipinos. Like the Okies, these more recent immigrants from around the Pacific Rim are predominantly poor people, and they in turn resemble the earlier European migrations of the decades from 1860 to 1925. But the extent to which (and the ways in which) these different groups have used education in their strategies of acculturation have differed. *The Grapes of Wrath*, like so much of Depression-era literature, is a story infused with socialist values, marked by anger at the exploitation of workers by employers and the condemnation of injustice and inequality. It is a story of the class struggle, even if in the non-ideological form in which that struggle was experienced and expressed by the migratory workers created by the Depression and fleeing to California from the Dust Bowl.

At the end of that novel, Casey, the itinerant preacher turned union organizer, is clubbed to death by some goons, thugs hired by the big farm company (or agro-business), to break a strike of migratory workers. In the melee, Tom Joad is injured, but in turn kills the company thug, thus becoming a fugitive. He hides out in a field for a few days near his family, whose members are picking cotton for starvation wages. Ma Joad comes out to him to give him some food, and to tell him he must go away to avoid arrest. He agrees, and in a final stirring speech tells her that he is going to take up Casey's work, become a union organizer allied with poor people like himself against the rich and the exploitative. Ma asks where she will be able to find him, and his answer to her moves us over half a century later.

> Well, maybe like Casey says, a fella ain't got a soul of his own, but only a piece of a big one . . . And then it don't matter—then I'll be all around in the dark. I'll be everywhere—wherever you look. Wherever you look. Wherever there's a fight so hungry people can eat, I'll be there. Wherever there's a cop beatin' up a guy, I'll be there . . . I'll be in the way guys yell when they're mad . . . And when our folks

eat the stuff they raise, an' live in the houses they build—why, I'll
be there.

Tom goes out to fight for his people, the ordinary poor people pushed
around by big corporations and their cops and thugs—a man committing his life to the struggle to rise with his class, not out of it. "Like Casey
says, a fella ain't got a soul of his own, but on'y a piece of a big one."

What Tom Joad does not say to his Ma, in that hole in the ground
where he's hiding near the box cars in which she and the rest of his family
are living and starving along with the other cotton-pickers in pre-war
California—is:

> Ma, I've got to go and make it on my own. This is my chance to find
> out who I am, and what I'm made of. So, Ma, I'm going to Fresno
> State College down the road. If they don't take me in I'll go to one
> of these community colleges springin' up all over the place, and I'll
> work my way through school, and get my bachelor's degree, and
> then get my state license, and mebbe an MBA, and buy and sell real
> estate. Maybe I'll start up my own little consulting firm, and make
> a pile of money, and build a big house for you and Pa and Rose
> a'Sharon and the kids, with four bathrooms and a swimming pool.

Tom doesn't say that, but he might have done so, in a different novel,
out of a different but equally authentic American tradition. What Tom
didn't say is essentially what migrants both to and within America have
said since our beginning, and certainly what most of Tom's successors
have said in the great migrations to California since World War II. These
new immigrants, and the children and grandchildren of the Okies too—
the descendants of the Joads and their friends from Oklahoma—have
flooded into California's colleges and universities, which have expanded
enormously in number and size to meet that demand. Since World War II,
very little has been heard in California of "rising with your class," and
a great deal about the need to create more truly equal opportunities for
individual advancement for all, rich and poor, black, brown and white,
through education—and especially through higher education.

There is in American history and popular culture a heroic saga to
compete with the socialist saga, the heroic story of the self-made man
rising through his own talents and industry. The saga is also often about

the loneliness of that climb, and the pain that accompanies the breaking of strong ties to family, class, ethnic group, and even of friendship—a different kind of sacrifice in a different kind of struggle. We hear it first in the stories of the frontiersman, and in the saga of Swedish emigration to America in Moberg's great epic. It is a sacrifice not for social ties, ties of class and ethnicity, but of ties, and that can be an equally wrenching sacrifice. We see and hear it endlessly, in the films and stories of men and women rising out of the urban slums and neighborhoods of the big Eastern melting pot cities, and it often has a bitter and sardonic twist of failed ambition and thwarted aspiration. But after World War II, that saga usually includes attendance at college or university, as that becomes the alternative to failure or crime.

Today, we are not hearing many heroic sagas about young men and women struggling out of the barrios (the Mexican American slums of Los Angeles) up to UCLA and law school, and on to a partnership in a big law firm or elected office. We are not hearing many black sagas of the rise out of the "projects"—the public housing units that have become black slums, up to UC Berkeley and beyond. These sagas are waiting to be told; it may be that we haven't heard many yet because they don't seem heroic to those who experience them. Or maybe the tellers are too busy just now making it up the ladder to write about it.

Race, Ethnicity, and Higher Education

A culture is defined, in part, by what it feels guilty about. Western European nations, on the whole, feel guilty about their working classes, about the sacrifices they made during the rapid industrialization of the nineteenth and early twentieth centuries, about their substantial exclusion from opportunities to get good health care, recreation and leisure, good education, economic security and security in old age, and to share in the high culture of their society. Much of public policy in European countries over the past hundred years, and more rapidly over the past fifty years, has been aimed at ameliorating and reducing those disadvantages linked to class.

Americans, in contrast, are remarkably free of guilt toward working-class people, individually or collectively. There is, of course, an enormous body of legislation on the books that aims at helping people who are, as we used to put it, "down on their luck," or as we would say now say, "disadvantaged." Some of it is federal law, much is state law.

The United States has more social legislation on the books than Europeans give us credit for, and less, probably, than we need. But it has not been put there, for the most part, out of a sense of class guilt. If we have any national policy regarding social or economic class, it is an educational policy designed not to strengthen the working class, or ameliorate its conditions, but to abolish it. The American Dream, I believe, is that eventually everyone will be either self-employed, or a salaried professional, and higher education is the instrument for the achievement of both.

If Americans do not feel especially guilty about the working class—even if they accept that there is such a thing—we as a nation still feel intensely guilty about our history of race relations, and especially about our history of black slavery, and the elaborate social and legal machinery (much of it at the state level) for the subordination of blacks from the end of Reconstruction after the Civil War, all the way to the burst of Supreme Court decisions and legislation that marked the racial revolution of the 1950s and 1960s. There is, of course, still plenty of racist sentiment in the society, though the polls show less all the time. But at the level of public policy, policies that are put in place by legislatures that are elected for the most part by white voters, the commitment to what only can be called a pro-minority policy is strong and persistent. The general term for pro-minority policies, policies aimed at benefiting particular racial or ethnic groups, is affirmative action. Affirmative action is pervasive throughout American society—in the hiring policies of private business, in public housing, in federal employment and its policies for contracting in the private sector for goods and services, in the military—throughout the society we see the influence of affirmative action programs. Nowhere can the presence of affirmative action be seen more clearly than in the policies of higher education. It is apparent not only in the public institutions, in response to legislative or government pressure, but also in private institutions, in response chiefly to the powerful dictates of a collective conscience—a force that also operates in publicly supported institutions, where its effects are mixed up with those of expediency and institutional responsiveness to external pressures from government and interest groups.

Affirmative action as a concept and a set of institutional policies is the subject of intense debate and controversy, chiefly centering on whether governmental intervention in favor of racial or ethnic groups should be aimed at equalizing the opportunities for achievement and advancement of members of that group, or whether those efforts should continue in ways that will ensure instead the equality of achievement itself for that group, as compared with the more advantaged groups in the society. The differences between these conceptions—of equality of opportunity, or of achievement—are large, and the issue is still in doubt; all such issues in America end up in the Supreme Court, which determines what the constitutional rights of the groups and individuals involved are.

While sharp differences exist about the proper scope of affirmative action in American higher education, and the appropriate degree of governmental or institutional intervention against the free play of competitive meritocracy, there is a near unanimity in our colleges and universities that some kind and degree of affirmative action is appropriate and necessary.

Affirmative action makes the contrast sharp between our policies regarding class and our policies regarding race. Perhaps I can capture the difference in the realm of higher education by observing that I cannot remember ever hearing a California legislator demand that the university increase access to it for the sons and daughters of working-class families. Moreover, a recent report of the Organization for Educational and Cultural Development (OECD) in California higher education could not say what proportion of the students at Berkeley are of working-class origins; our statistics are simply not collected that way. Chapter 2 of that OECD report, "Planning and Market in Higher Education," treats "education and stratification," and "education and social selection," familiar categories when analyzing European education systems. But its authors are unable to discuss specifically Californian issues within these categories; the necessary statistics are not available, and the discussions carried on in California are rarely couched in these terms. It is the only chapter that rests completely on European perspectives and theories; its distance from Californian realities is apparent by contrast with the rest of the report.

The failure of traditional models of social stratification and social mobility to illuminate California's society helps clarify American exceptionalism. Elsewhere in advanced societies, education is seen as a vehicle or instrument for social mobility, both between generations and within a single lifetime. Social class is ordinarily defined by the physical nature of one's job or occupation, by the income it commands, or the status it enjoys, or the sense of horizontal identity it engenders, or by some combination of these dimensions of class position. In California at the end of the twentieth century, education is not so much a vehicle or channel to higher social status as it is itself the defining feature of one's social status. To place a person in the social world, one ordinarily asks where one went to school (i.e., college or university), and perhaps whether one finished and took a degree, and what one studied. (In 1987, fewer than 20 percent of Californians 25 years and older had not graduated from high school; nearly half had attended college, and the proportions are much higher among the younger cohorts.) It is less important what one happens to be working at at any given moment, since people change jobs and occupations frequently, and what they do, or appear to do, correlates poorly with their education. And education predicts their lifestyles, attitudes, and loyalties much better than does whether they are manual workers, or self-employed, or in one of the other ordinary categories of social stratification.

Ethnicity is the other great defining feature of Californians; if one knows a person's ethnicity and formal education, one knows a great deal about them. In contrast to the paucity of data on the class positions of Californians, the official statistics are rich in ethnic and racial data. The legislature is constantly affirming the importance of special efforts to recruit, retain, graduate, and sponsor members of disadvantaged minority groups. (In California, this includes blacks and Hispanics, but now excludes almost all those of Asian origin. They are too successful to qualify for the special benefits and attention of affirmative action policies.) Many university policies pivot around racial issues, enormous amounts of statistics are collected within racial and ethnic categories, and discussions of affirmative action (mostly how to strengthen it, and make it more effective in the university) are central themes in academia, from the departmental level on up.

In California, as elsewhere in the United States, student admissions are heavily influenced by affirmative action policies. As just one example of these policies, the proportion of blacks and Hispanics in the entering freshman class at UC Berkeley rose from about 11 percent in 1983 to about 29 percent in 1990, more than doubling their proportions. The percentages of Asians in entering classes remained roughly constant at 29 percent, while the proportion of white enrollees fell from 58 percent to about 37 percent.[11] This was accomplished by applying quite different criteria for admissions to students in these different racial and ethnic groups. Similar policies are in place in almost every American college and university; the numbers in many are not as dramatic as at Berkeley only because they have fewer minority applicants.

Two questions might be asked: (1) How can we explain these quite dramatic policies, and (2) Why has there not been a vigorous backlash by the now discriminated-against white students, and their parents?

Part of the answer to both questions is surely the sense of guilt among white Americans toward certain minority groups, especially blacks and Native Americans, that I spoke of earlier. But the other, related reason arises out of a national commitment to achieving a genuinely multiracial society, one in which blacks and other minorities are represented in numbers roughly similar to their proportion within the population at large, and are represented proportionally in the leadership of all the institutions of the society—in its political, economic, military, and educational institutions. To attain leadership in almost all of these social institutions, experience of, if not a degree from, an institution of higher education is a necessity. And that, in a word, is the driving force behind these affirmative action policies in higher education—policies keyed to the mobility of individuals through competitive performance.

Blacks and Hispanics in America have made conspicuous progress in some areas of national life, but less in others. I'll be speaking here mainly of blacks; the situation of recent immigrants from Mexico is similar in some respects, but different in others.

Blacks are very well represented in all ranks of our armed forces; General Colin Powell, chairman of the Joint Chiefs of Staff, our highest-ranking military officer during the war with Iraq, is only the most prominent. Blacks have also done well in politics; thousands have been elected to local and municipal office, many are in Congress, the mayor of almost every big city in the country is black, and a black man has recently been elected governor of Virginia.

Blacks as a whole have done much less well economically, or in the leadership of economic institutions, or in academic life. A few figures can stand for all: in 1988, 625 Americans nationwide received PhDs in mathematics or computer science. Of those, only 2 were black. Of the roughly 500 doctorates in marine, atmospheric, and earth sciences, only another 2 were black. The problems are not confined to the physical or natural sciences: in that same year of 1988, only 5 American-born blacks gained PhDs in anthropology; 11 were granted doctorates in economics, 7 in political science, and 14 in sociology.[12] This is the situation in a country with 3,500 colleges and universities, most of which require a PhD for a regular tenure-track appointment.

The indicators of educational handicaps for blacks in the United States are many and striking, and go all the way back to performance in grade school, on up to scores on national tests of scholastic aptitude. Blacks do not enter colleges or universities in proportions that reflect their proportions in the general population. A university like Berkeley can attract and admit blacks at higher rates than their proportion in the California population, but nationally, despite many academic and financial support efforts on the part of these colleges, only about 7 percent of college and university enrollments are black, as compared to their 12 percent proportion of the population. This represents a huge improvement over the terribly low numbers before the racial revolution of the 1960s, but it's sad to say that that figure of 7 percent has not changed much in the past fifteen years, and indeed has declined somewhat for young black males.

Moreover, blacks are far more likely to drop out of college before graduation, and those who do graduate are much less likely to go on to graduate school than their white counterparts.

All of this may help explain something of the near-desperate efforts American colleges and research universities have been making to enroll black undergraduates, hoping that some will do well, gain entry to graduate studies, and that perhaps some growing fraction of those will opt for a career in science or scholarship, while still others will enter both old and new professions, thus providing leadership not only to these institutions but to the black community at large.

American universities, and not least those in California, have been making great efforts to identify talented minority youngsters at the secondary and even primary levels, and have encouraged and sponsored those individuals for university entry. In these and related ways, American higher education has become a part, indeed a central part, of a national effort to transform American blacks from a racial caste into a "normal" American ethnic group. A caste, of course, is a social category in which membership defines an individual's life fate permanently, even more rigidly than that of class, while membership in an ethnic group in the American context says something about an individual's origins, but in principle does not define or limit present or future prospects. The nature and strength of an individual's connections with an ethnic group are, in principle, voluntary; one may use them as an aid to individual advancement, but those ties need not be a hindrance to personal achievement. The reality behind these norms, of course, varies. It is great for most "old" ethnic groups, more problematical for, say, recent Mexican immigrants, and most for blacks. Since World War II, to be treated as an ethnic rather than a racial group has become an increasing reality for most people of Asian origins, both recent immigrants and the children of earlier immigrants. There is remarkably little racial prejudice today against Asian Americans of any kind. Racial identity is still a handicap for blacks—although less so for middle-class, well-educated blacks than for the less well-educated. Thus, education is still the quickest road to ethnic status for blacks.

The nation's preference for ethnic rather than racial identities and relations is clear historically. The United States, on the whole, has not had an enviable record in race relations. On the other hand, it has had a comparatively good record on ethnic relations, starting with the assimilation and integration of peoples from all over the world to a common, overriding identity as Americans. Scholars still argue whether the metaphor of the "melting pot" is the best way to describe this process, or whether some other term is necessary to describe the nature and mechanisms of this process. Whatever they decide, in the United States, Protestants and Catholics of Irish origins live peacefully side by side, as do Jews and Arabs and Maronite Christians; Turks and Armenians, and so on. A multiethnic society is our model of a good society; it encompasses the possibility of continuing strong voluntary cultural ties to one's ethnic origins. And the historical images of the mobility of whole ethnic groups reflect the parallel mobility of their individual members. We have watched these mobility patterns over two, three, four, and more generations, with the first poor immigrants from an ethnic group coming in at the bottom of the social and economic ladder, living usually in ethnic enclaves (sometimes miscalled ghettos), speaking the mother tongue, and striving to advance their children's opportunities. This next generation tends to get more education, and then to move out of those neighborhoods into whatever suburbia of American life the individual's ambition, talent, and achievement will allow. The ethnic ties may remain strong into the third and even fourth generations, but usually only when these ties aid rather than hinder individual mobility.

This is of course a greatly oversimplified model of reality, but not too far from popular image and sentiment. In some sense, for Americans, this is the way things are supposed to be. To some important extent, the racial revolution of the 1960s, the enormous changes in law, and the parallel changes in sentiment and institutional behavior have brought American blacks into this model. The 1960s also gave to blacks the political and social freedom (and to some extent the economic affluence) of a rising ethnic group, rather than that of a low and despised caste, while permitting up to half or two-thirds to move into the mainstream of American life. Perhaps one-third live middle-class lives (i.e., have careers as opposed to jobs), and perhaps half are in reasonably stable working-class occupations. But somewhere between 15 percent and 25 percent of blacks (2 percent–3 percent of the whole American population), comprise an underclass, living mostly in the central cities, caught in a morass of problems: crime, alcoholism, drugs, the collapse of family ties and responsibility, child and spousal abuse, and welfare dependency. These are the things that constitute the greatest problem facing American society; thus far we have been conspicuously unsuccessful in our approaches to it and to them.

For the rest of the black population, movement is visible and appreciable, if too slow. It may be reasonably fast by the standards, say, of the Irish in America in the 1860s or the Italians in the 1920s. But that rate of change is not acceptable by or for blacks in 1990, both because of our special guilt regarding blacks in the United States and because of our heightened standards regarding the rights and opportunities due all citizens. Moreover, blacks also point out that they are not new immigrants, but have been in America as a group longer than most white ethnic groups and all Asians, though some proportion of the black population seems always to fill the niche left by the most recent immigrant group, at the bottom of the social and economic ladder.

Nevertheless, affirmative action throughout American life, but most especially in higher education, is a conscious effort to accelerate the transformation of blacks as a whole from a racial into an ethnic group, and this accelerates their mobility as a group by accelerating their mobility as individuals, upward through American society. Looked at another way, it is an effort to accomplish for blacks in one generation what may have taken two generations for Irish or Swedish Americans, and perhaps three for Italian and Polish Americans. It is, in short, a set of policies designed to improve the opportunities for individual members of certain racial and ethnic groups toward whom we as a society feel especially guilty. These efforts are made by many social institutions, and not just the government, to improve life chances, to enable blacks to rise in the society, with a common goal being for some significant proportion of blacks to take their places in leadership positions in all the social institutions.

The final irony is that policies designed to improve and thus equalize life chances for disadvantaged individuals may, by the very character of the enormous advantages they carry for designated ethnic and racial groups, be creating status groups whose members, and especially whose leaders, have more to gain through emphasizing their group memberships than by asserting their independence of group ties. These patterns, and their associated ideological claims and assertions, point to a new kind of permanent, racially based group identity, which differs from the old in being voluntary and privileged, rather than involuntary and disadvantaged.

These new claims to racial identity and cultural autonomy involve stronger horizontal bondings than do most class-based institutions, such as trade unions or socialist parties. Unlike working-class identification, "race consciousness" does not inhibit or discourage college attendance, but is brought onto the campuses by the next generation of minority groups themselves. It is clear that the assertion of the primacy of racial identity for most blacks and Hispanics arises out of a shared life experience; not so clear that it anticipates a shared life fate. That poses a special challenge to minority group leadership, which has to struggle against the corrosive effect on the primacy of racial identity posed by an institution that in principle is indifferent to it, and that prepares people for life in a competitive world that is also, and increasingly, indifferent to racial identity. The intense efforts currently being made to rationalize and reinforce the primacy of racial identity in the colleges and universities where the future leadership of racial groups is being educated and prepared—by "multiculturalism" in the curriculum, and social segregation outside the classroom—attests to the sharp tensions created by these new forms of horizontal bonding in institutions that have led society in throwing them off. The danger is that the new conceptions of permanent and self-conscious racial groups may be no more assimilable to the classic models of an ethnically diverse society of individual careers and achievement than the old caste groups. This raises many more questions for higher education, but at the least suggests that public policies often have perverse and unintended effects. Sometimes they generate new problems as great as the ones they overcome. But higher education in America has already had some experience with those ironies of history and public policy.

NOTES

....

1. In Western European countries, fewer youth of modest social origins have taken advantage of the call to mobility inherent in mass higher education, in part because of tight restraints on access to higher education, restraints chiefly through a class-linked stratification of the secondary school system, and of related requirements and standards for entry to higher education. But institutions of higher education everywhere serve to weaken working-class ties and affiliations.

2. Allmendinger did his research on poor students in the emerging colleges of New England, but I believe that the patterns he describes were also to be found in the much larger number of small, modest, largely denominational colleges springing up along the western frontier. Indeed, then as now "one clear sign of the presence of the poor was the increasing maturity of the student population . . . Men in their middle twenties now enrolled in large numbers, along with boys in their early teens . . . Many had started trades, and then having changed their minds, had continued in their work to get money for education. This brought about a mixing of the

social classes, as well as ages" (p. 9). It was crucial that these new, mostly "private" colleges were cheap, not too far away, provided charity (i.e., student aid), and were not too particular about their students' academic preparation. The students' education was also substantially subsidized—indeed, made possible—by the tiny salaries paid to the teaching staff who themselves did not have the dignity of the guilds of learned men in the old countries.

3. On the concept of an "occupational community" in the American context facilitating the development of class-based institutions, see Lipset, Trow, and Coleman (1956).

4. Writing in the 1920s, Lillian Herstein observed that "the differentiation between adult and workers' education . . . has been stated and can be accepted. The responsibility of providing schooling for those who are seeking a way out of industry by means of education can be placed on the public schools. Workers' education should concern itself, let us grant, with those who are willing to be the apostles of a new order." "Labor education," says Mr. Horace Kallen . . . "should become conversant with control rather than escape." "From "Realities in Workers' Education," in Hardman, *American Labor Dynamics*, pp. 378–79.

5. See Bureau of the Census, Table 689, p. 419. Calculated from data in the *Handbook of Labor Statistics*, U.S. Department of Labor, Bulletin 2340, August 1989, Table 68, p. 290, and Historical Statistics of the U.S.: Colonial Times to 1970, Series D927–939, pp. 176–77. The figures for California show the same pattern, the proportion of union members as a percentage of non-farm wage and salary workers in 1951 was 41 percent; in 1987 it was 19 percent (Fay and Fay, eds., *California Almanac*, p. 235).

6. The literature on the problem is very large. See, for example, Laslett and Lipset, eds., *Failure of a Dream?*

7. This applies also to research universities, which try (with only partial success) to harness the individual ambitions of scholars and scientists to the welfare of the institution.

8. M. Trow, "The Second Transformation of American Secondary Education," *International Journal of Comparative Sociology* (1961). Reprinted as chapter 1 in this volume.

9. At the end of World War II, when C. Wright Mills did the study reported in his *New Men of Power*, (1948), his sample of American labor leaders was distinctly better educated than the American adult population. Already one-quarter of AFL [American Federation of Labor] and one-third of the CIO [Congress of Industrial Organizations] leaders had been to college, as compared with only 10 percent of adult Americans.

10. I remember going to a meeting of a democratic socialist group in 1946. It

was addressed by a young Irving Howe, later to become the distinguished literary critic, professor, and editor of a small socialist journal. He gave a gloomy speech, anticipating a major economic collapse in America, an event which, in his view, would give socialists an opportunity to create a mass party. (It was perhaps always a handicap for socialists in America that they had to seem to hope for, and not just predict, depression and misery, before they came to the cheerier part.) I was a bit skeptical of the imminence of a depression in America, and afterward asked the speaker how the socialist movement would respond if there were no depression. His answer, with its hard realism, surprised and impressed me. "If capitalism can buy the workers off with low unemployment and good wages," he said, "it deserves to win." Howe was betting his life that it couldn't meet those tests. It could, and it did.

11. Figures provided by the Office of Student Research, University of California, Berkeley.

12. National Science Foundation, 1990, Table 47, p. 151.

REFERENCES

Allmendinger, D. F., Jr. *Paupers and Scholars: The Transformation of Student Life in Nineteenth-Century New England.* New York: St. Martin's, 1975.

Fay, J. S., and S. W. Fay, eds. *California Almanac.* 4th ed. Santa Barbara: Pacific Data Resources, 1990.

Hardman, J. B. S. *American Labor Dynamics in the Light of Post-War Developments.* New York: Harcourt, Brace and Co., 1928.

Laslett, J. H. M., and S. M. Lipset, eds. *Failure of a Dream? Essays in the History of American Socialism.* Garden City: Anchor Press/Doubleday, 1974.

Lipset, S. M., M. A. Trow, and J. S. Coleman. *Union Democracy.* Glencoe, Ill.: The Free Press, 1956.

Mills, C. W. *The New Men of Power.* New York: Harcourt, Brace and Co., 1948.

National Science Foundation. *Women and Minorities in Science and Engineering.* Author, 1990. Table 47, p. 151.

Organization for Economic Cooperation and Development. *Review of Higher Education Policy In California.* Paris: Author, 1989.

Rothblatt, S., and M. Trow. "Government Policies and Higher Education, A Comparison of Britain and the United States, 1630–1860." In *The Sociology of Social Reform,* edited by C. Crouch and A. Heath. Oxford: Oxford University Press, 1992.

Rudolph, F. *The American College and University.* New York: Alfred A. Knopf, 1962.

Trow, M. "American Higher Education: Exceptional or Just Different?" in *Is America Different? A New Look at American Exceptionalism*, edited by B. Shafer. Oxford: Clarendon, 1991.

U.S. Bureau of the Census. *Statistical Abstracts of the United States: Historical Statistics of the U.S.: Colonial Times to 1970*, Series D927-939. Washington, D.C.: Government Printing Office, 1990.

PART III

Britain as
a Contrasting Case

6

IN AN INFLUENTIAL SERIES OF ESSAYS published during the 1980s, Martin Trow cast a transatlantic eye on the problems and dilemmas of British higher education during the transition between elite and mass higher education. That fundamental shift was inhibited if not precluded in the United Kingdom, he argued, by an absolute unyielding commitment to high and uniform standards across the whole of higher education. His essays were, however, much more than a test of predictive elements in his original model or a way of raising questions in a comparative context. They offered observations, insights, and judgments that challenged conventional thinking about British arrangements and that caught the attention of politicians as well as scholars. Most of all—perhaps best of all—they provoked and irritated, and not just intellectually.

This 1987 essay is a prime example of the style and force of Trow's reflections on the British and their attitudes to expansion in higher education. Here was a binary pattern of publicly funded universities, polytechnics, and higher education colleges that stood on the threshold of a mass phase but where participation rates for young people had remained more or less stable for more than a decade. This lack of growth and the deep problems it created for British society were attributed by Trow to its reluctance or refusal to come to terms with diversity: a diversity of mission, costs, and standards.

His was not a criticism directed at the high standards of the system itself—far from it. Rather, it was the way in which a defense of elite standards served to deny or delay the emergence of other segments of higher education with lower costs and lesser standards. The British had "a positive horror" of "education on the cheap," and getting them to think differently about access, quality, and growth was the whole point of his interventions. In this, he took full advantage of perspectives that came from outside the shared values of British academic community, while arguing for the survival of British institutions, which he much admired, and for the maintenance of their elite standards within a mass system.

Underpinning this argument were three claims, each counter to current and conventional thinking. First was the contention that universities and polytechnics were much more alike than either cared to admit, and part of a common system of elite higher education, irrespective of binary arrangements. Trow's second claim was that the Open University, a pioneering open-access institution, was rather less of an alternative or radical organization than it seemed. Functioning as a kind of safety valve for the highly selective British system, it was "the enemy of a genuine system of mass higher education."

There was, however, another set of institutions in this society that might be the instrument for the provision of mass higher education to large sections of the population—further education colleges. They were not part of higher education: "of course not, since they did not award the degree." More than that, further and higher education were "simply not part of a common system of postsecondary education," and their teachers rarely saw themselves engaged in a common enterprise, differentiated or otherwise. While there were more connections between further and higher education than Trow appreciated, this third and most important line of argument about the emergence of mass forms of higher education from further education touched many nerves. Polytechnics had no wish to be reminded of their further education origins and universities had still to come to terms with the rise of the polytechnics.

At the end of this article, Trow presented the British with two scenarios. Either future expansion was taken by its elite academic institutions or by institutions that already performed mass functions. The latter was preferable but the former was probable. Shortly after publication of this paper, British higher education underwent a spectacular phase of expansion, with the polytechnics followed by universities taking the bulk of the new growth and leading to removal of the binary divide. The next phase of expansion, to near-universal levels of access will, however, see a larger role for further education colleges. Significantly, a broad comparability of standards is still deemed essential, albeit now at a minimum or threshold level.

The directions taken since 1987 show why the essay is still a point of reference in contemporary debates, especially in England. For someone like me, working in further education during the 1980s and searching for an analysis of English preoccupations, the essay was a turning-point. An essay that puzzled over "the manifest inequalities in the relationship of higher and further education" and the "envy and resentment" generated on one side and the "guilty defensiveness and snobberies" on the other was not obviously the product of an English mind. It spoke to a democratization of higher education that, under English conditions, was otherwise muted or missing.

—GARETH PARRY

Academic Standards and Mass Higher Education

I

In this essay* I want to reflect on standards in academic life, and the somewhat different question of the maintenance of high and roughly uniform academic standards across the whole range of degree-granting institutions in the United Kingdom. The first question—the issue of academic standards in a particular college or university—is one of the most important issues that an institution has to confront. Every college or university has to concern itself continually to maintain the highest levels of teaching, and in some, of research, that it can achieve. But the

---

* Paper prepared for the Plenary Session of the conference on "Quality Assurance in First Degree Courses," sponsored by Higher Education International, Birmingham, England, September 6, 1986.

Originally published as Martin Trow, "Academic Standards and Mass Higher Education," *Higher Education Quarterly* 41, no. 3 (1987): 268–92. Reprinted by permission of Wiley-Blackwell.

second issue—of the maintenance of those standards across a whole range or category of institutions—is a quite different question, as much an issue of public policy as of academic vigilance, and like most issues of public policy, any solution has its costs as well as its benefits. A central problem for modern societies is how to reconcile the survival and provision of elite education, at high levels of both cost and excellence, with the emergence of mass education, the provision of postsecondary education to large sections of the whole population.

I use the term *elite higher education* neutrally, not as a term of abuse, as is common these days, nor in reference to the social origins of students, but as a way of pointing to a form of higher education marked by high selectivity, and staff-student ratios that allow close student-teacher relations centering around studies at high levels of intensity and complexity, leading to degrees of high and recognized standards. In English and Welsh universities (and to a lesser extent in Scotland) elite higher education, at least for the past two centuries, has been associated with the idea of "liberal" studies, sharply distinguished from "vocational" studies (Rothblatt, 1976). And to the extent that the polytechnics provide education keyed to preparation for specific jobs and careers, they are not considered part of elite higher education in Britain. But this conception would also include the Massachusetts Institute of Technology (MIT) and Imperial College. Moreover, the distinction between liberal and vocational studies is increasingly difficult to make as undergraduate education, even in liberal fields, becomes increasingly specialized and professionalized. It is, therefore, more useful to distinguish elite from mass higher education not by reference to the content of the curriculum but to the character of the students and the nature of instruction. Thus, mass, by contrast to elite, higher education is marked by its relatively open access to a more heterogeneous student body, many of whom are older, work part-time, are less well prepared, are less highly motivated, with higher rates of attrition (wastage), taught less intensively, and to lower standards of achievement (Trow, 1974).

To British academics, that may seem to describe the polytechnics. And from a certain perspective, the creation of the polytechnics, across the binary line, was a move toward mass higher education. But, as Guy Neave has observed,

The British move toward mass higher education extended elite criteria to the nonelite sector of polytechnics and colleges of education, thus giving rise to a far greater degree of homogeneity in patterns of access between the different sectors—university and nonuniversity—than had ever existed. In short, mass higher education in Britain was elite higher education written a little larger. (Neave, 1985)

From American perspectives, British universities and polys are more alike than either will admit. In respect to access, cost, staff-student ratios, forms of instruction, wastage, the education of teaching staff, above all in their approach to knowledge, universities and polys are *both* part of a common system of elite higher education. Of course, the old status distinctions between "noble" and "less noble," "liberal" and "vocational" studies, survive and continue to affect the recruitment, both of staff and of students, to universities and polys, and to some extent their governance and funding as well. But those differences, which seem so large in England, seem much smaller from a transatlantic perspective, and from American universities that embody both liberal and vocational (or Professional) studies. From that perspective, the unity of British higher education is a result of the transformation of both liberal and vocational education over the past century.

[While] the trend towards greater specialisation in university education remains basically uncontested, and liberal education continues to narrow in subject concentration, there has been an opposite tread in vocational education. There the instruction has broadened . . . The result has been that what were once regarded as servile occupations have been elevated into the ranks of professions, where they have then been brought into the world of university education. Because of this reformation in the teaching of vocational subjects, it has become nearly impossible today to distinguish between various kinds of institutions offering advanced instruction, whether or not they are actually called universities. All of them, whether Oxford and Cambridge, London, Redbrick, Plateglass, and Scottish and Welsh universities, and the colleges of advanced technology, incorporate similar ranges of educational methods and ideals, and offer similar mixtures of liberal and professional forms of education. It can be said that the balance of subjects varies from institution to institution, as does the technical or liberal emphasis, and certainly the quality and appeal of institutions differ enormously. But this does not alter the conclusion that all institutions of advanced education share more educational values than at first they might be inclined to believe. (Rothblatt, 1976)

In some societies the two forms of education—elite and mass—can be found within the same university, as in France and Germany, and in the big American state universities. In other societies, notably the United Kingdom, the division of labor is between sectors, between "higher" and "further" education, and only the sector that maintains high academic standards is given the status of "higher education" and permitted to award the degree. In this essay, and taking advantage of perspectives that come from outside the shared values and assumptions of British academics, I would like to reflect on some implications of that separation, and on the costs and consequences of systemwide academic standards, the standards that characterize the British system of elite higher education.

II

When I speak of a high and uniform standard of quality in British higher education, I am, of course, referring to the standard for the honors degree. British academics and their supporting institutions make a determined effort to maintain that standard of the honors degree, as high and as uniform as possible throughout the system of higher education. While it is understood (though not much discussed) that some subjects are more difficult than others, or attract students of higher academic ability, nevertheless within subjects there is an effort to maintain a roughly equally high standard for the degree among the several universities. Indeed, it is recognized that since some universities tend to attract more able students than others, on average, they will award more first- and upper second-degrees. That in itself is taken as evidence for the uniformity of standards throughout the university system.

But there are variety of other institutional arrangements that work to maintain this parity of standards. Perhaps the most powerful is the institution of the external examiner, a mechanism recently reaffirmed and reinforced by the Reynolds report to the Committee of Vice Chancellors and Principals (CVCP) (Reynolds, 1986). The external examiner— which British academics all take as a matter of course—appears to Americans to be an admirable device for maintaining standards of performance, effectively preventing what we would call "grade Inflation," that tendency for teachers to give higher marks to students than they deserve because they are diligent, or amiable, or perhaps because a better mark will get them a better job or a place in graduate or professional school at no (apparent) cost to anyone. External examiners do indeed keep internal examiners honest, in this regard at least. The external examiner, of course, is an instrument of quality control. But even more important, the external examiner is there to maintain comparability. As Reynolds puts it: "It is of first importance . . . that degree classifications from different institutions approach as nearly as possible to common standards within the limits on comparability" (Reynolds, 1986). In the United States we do not, with one or two exceptions, employ external examiners for the first degree. In our universities (and here we betray where it is that we take the maintenance of standards of performance to be most important, that is, in our graduate and professional schools), the examining committees for advancement to candidacy for the doctorate, and for the oral examination on presentation of the dissertation itself almost always include members from outside the awarding department and discipline. But this latter arrangement, in the United States, is for the most part internal to a given university and is very often *pro forma*; we have no arrangements comparable to Britain's for maintaining a standard of degree among colleges and universities, broadly recognized as representing a common standard of excellence or achievement wherever earned.

In support of the external examiner, the British have a number of other arrangements to help guarantee the common high standard of degree. One is the protection of a common "unit of resource" across universities. Some British universities, in response to cuts and threats of cuts in their annual support grants, have offered, indeed petitioned, to be allowed to enroll more students, even with fewer staff and less funds. The University Grants Committee (UGC) until now at least has adamantly refused such permission. The defense of the unit of resource—that is, essentially, the staff-student ratio—has been in its eyes and in the eyes of many British academics the first defense of academic standards that even the individual universities, under stress and pain, would not be allowed to endanger. While student-staff ratios have drifted upward in the British universities over the past few decades, it has not been offered as an option to an individual university to dilute its own unit of resource in the service of some other ideas about access, or the survival of a threatened small department, or whatever. Indeed, in relation to the idea of a common high standard, the emphasis has been equally on the words *common* and *high*.

A variety of structural features of the British system ensure that the standard is common to all degree-granting institutions, as well as high. There is, for example, the common level of minimum achievement, two "A" level passes, required for admission to universities and polytechnics, though here there is considerable variation in the requirement beyond this minimum among different subject and universities. Nevertheless the requirement of two "A" level passes itself is a very considerable barrier to entry to higher education. Fewer than one-quarter (22 percent) of the age grade currently take these examinations, and only 15 percent pass in the two or more subjects that is the minimum qualification for entry to a degree course. If this is not selective enough, those who pass with "D"s or "E"s on these tests are commonly regarded by the universities as "poor caliber," with three passes and higher grades increasingly necessary for entry to the more popular universities and subjects.

There is, in addition, the roughly common salary schedule for academic staff, and the common formulas for the proportion of staff in different ranks, both of which reduce the incentives available to any particular university that might want to concentrate abler or more productive scholars in some particular favored department. That happens, of course—there are other incentives besides salary and rank to attract staff to more prestigious departments, and we hardly need the latest UGC league table to tell us that. But the national pay scales, common appointment procedures, external referees, and fixed ratios among the several ranks and grades all tend to damp down the differences between universities in respect to the quality of their staffs.

At the other end, the absence of tuition costs to the students, and the provision of grants to most students, coupled with the similarity of costs and amenities among universities—Oxbridge aside—is another set of forces for the leveling of average student abilities across institutions. What the students get is much the same everywhere, and they might as well go anywhere. Perhaps the most powerful leveling force of all is the formula by which the UGC distributes the Treasury grant to universities. A great deal of attention has naturally been directed to the recent (1986) exercise by the UGC in ranking university departments, and for the role of those rankings in the allocation of the annual grants to the universities. Since that exercise, most of the discussion has been directed to the fraction of the grant that is intended to be distributed unequally, by reference to the supposed research quality of departments in universities. (And how that was ascertained in quite another story.) But little attention is paid to the fact that the bulk of the UGC's grant is still distributed as a grant in support of teaching, and very much on the basis of a standard per capita formula. It may be that the UGC will discover ways of measuring the quality of instruction, and introduce inequalities in its rewards and incentives in that portion of the university grants as well. But up until now the UGC has tried through its grants to universities to maintain the unit of resource for instructional purposes roughly constant over time, and remarkably equal across institutions. British academics, I suspect, are sensitive to the variations in those allocations; to an outsider, it is the similarity of those allocations that is most impressive. All of these mechanisms and arrangements that I have been describing, taken together, allow us to think of the British universities as the separate campuses of "the University of the United Kingdom" (Caston, 1979).

I have been speaking chiefly of the universities, but what I have said applies for the most part to the polytechnics and other degree-granting institutions. The concern for the maintenance of the standard of the degree in British higher education—that is, the university standard—could nowhere be more strongly symbolized than in the institution of the Council for National Academic Awards (CNAA), under whose tutelage and supervision, through committees staffed largely by university academics, the standard of degree offered by the polytechnics was initially ensured. In recent years the responsibility for the maintenance of the degree standard has been increasingly shifted over to the polytechnics themselves, as particular departments and institutions have emerged from their trial period and demonstrated their capacity to maintain their standards without close external supervision. There is here a direct parallel to the great tradition of the London external degree, and its tutelary relationship to the then university colleges, from Owens to Leicester. For many years, beginning with the establishment of Owens College in Manchester, as new university colleges were created they were not permitted to award their own degrees, but were allowed to prepare students to take the London examinations. It was only as they emerged from their period of trial and tutelage, and gained the strength, size, and staff necessary to be granted a university charter, that they were authorized to award their own degrees. The polytechnics are currently undergoing the same transition.

I have described, or at least pointed to, a network of institutions and arrangements that together helps sustain the value attached to the first or bachelor's degree, as awarded chiefly by the universities and polytechnics, but also by such other institutions as the Open University and the colleges of higher education. Underlying all these are norms, beliefs, and sentiments, broadly held among British academics but also by civil servants and politicians, to the effect that this degree, wherever offered and awarded, should be of high and roughly common value. In this respect the British first degree is, so to speak, still on the gold standard. This is something in which most educated Britons take pride; and indeed, there is, it seems, a constant anxiety that perhaps the value of the degree is not what it was or what it should be, and that the quality of teaching, or the nature of the curriculum, or the abilities of students or of staff, or of the resources available to the universities have changed in ways that threaten the quality and value of that degree.

This fear, that standards are slipping, that "more means worse," or will mean worse, has been a strong element in British higher education at least since World War II, and has been a major constraint on growth, even during periods of expansion. After World War II, British university enrollments grew to some 80,000, up from 50,000 just before the war, in response to an imaginative "Further Education and Training Scheme" (FETS), embodying grants to all ex-servicemen and women. (This was the origin of Britain's present program of student grants.) But postwar enrollments probably would have grown even further if the universities had not used this opportunity to raise their marginal entry qualifications so as to eliminate "a large number of the extremely weak students who used to gain entry before the war" (H. and H. M. Peston, 1974). But *despite* this rise in entry qualifications, "the UGC was also worried that the number of very bright students was not rising at the same rate as the total student body" (ibid.). This fear grew stronger in the early 1950s, when the FETS was coming to an end and when it was felt that maintaining universities at their new scale, let alone moving to a larger one, would mean a decline in the relative numbers of those getting first- or second-class honors degrees. The ministry of education itself was worried about all this. "It remains also to be seen how large a number of students can attend universities and other higher institutions without depressing the general intellectual standard" (ibid.).

I happen not to share that anxiety, not only because I am not British, but because I believe that, within broad limits, "more" does not mean "worse," and also because I believe that British universities and leading polytechnics are still among the finest in the world, making important contributions to knowledge in every subject and discipline out of proportion to their size and the number of their scholars and scientists, with ·patterns of teaching and learning, teacher-student relationships, and levels of efficiency that are models for the world.

I find it perfectly reasonable that those in Britain should continue to look seriously and critically at how the high standards of teaching and research in their universities can be maintained. But the question that I want to address is not the one that has been raised so imperiously by Sir Keith Joseph and the chairman of the UGC: are standards falling, and how can they be sustained and raised? In the remainder of this essay I want to raise the quite different question: what price is paid by British higher education, by its members both junior and senior, and by the society at large, for the effort to sustain this high standard of degree throughout the system, by the effort, that is, to maintain the British first degree on an academic gold standard? I do this not to try to suggest that Britain should go off that gold standard—indeed, I think the forces in support of that principle are too strong for any such suggestion. I hope rather to shed light on the system from another quarter, and to point to some consequences of those arrangements that may not be noticed otherwise, since they largely take the form of things that do not happen rather than things that occur. Such negative consequences are surely as real as things that do occur, but obviously a good deal less visible, or maybe only visible in comparative perspective. Moreover, being nonevents, it is harder to make the causal connections strongly and persuasively between the forms of higher education and what does not happen in the surrounding society as a result.

III

The question might be posed in this way: what developments in higher education or elsewhere are precluded, or at least inhibited, by the British commitment to an elite higher education system, marked by high and uniform standards throughout its member institutions, at levels of cost that press against current and prospective resource constraints?

One thing that such a commitment precludes is wide diversity in the system, diversity within and among institutions in their function, level of standards, and per capita cost. This is almost inherent in a commitment to high national standards, which as I have said is at the heart both of the academic excellence of the British university and of its lack of flexibility in the face of new challenges. It is, for example, hard to add new schools or departments of business administration, or electrical engineering, or social welfare, or policy analysis, to existing institutions, not only because their budgets are already fully committed (and, indeed, in recent years overcommitted), but also because creating new subjects and departments cannot be accomplished unless the UGC and the institution itself can be sure that the provision of instruction in that subject will almost from the very beginning be of a high enough quality to qualify as of genuine university standard. Two questions are asked of every proposal to expand the range of subjects taught: first, is the subject itself worthy of inclusion in the university curriculum? And second, even if the subject qualifies, is it possible to offer work in that subject at a high enough standard in a particular university? The first question is really a question for the national system, since graduates in that subject from any university will have a university degree, which is backed by a national reputation and stands for a certain level of achievement. It is not enough for University "X" to believe that subject "Y" is an important or regionally useful subject to offer for study and research: it must also have national recognition as an appropriate university subject. That does not mean, of course, that it has to be offered in every university, but only that the subject and its degree has been attested as worthy of support by central government. This is another form, one might say, of quality control.

New subjects typically find their way into the curriculum under the wing of old ones, as sub-disciplines, so to speak. Thus did molecular biology creep into established departments of biology or botany; thus did psychology and politics and a host of other subjects come into the university under the wing of philosophy, gradually gaining a foothold, creating their own bodies of literature and special ways of looking at the world and studying it, and training increasing numbers of scholars and scientists to look at the world or study it in that way. That is the way in which a subject gives solid evidence of its academic credentials, of being worthy of being accepted as an equal, worthy indeed of being taught and examined as an independent subject in its own right, with people appointed to teach it as their major responsibility and not their private hobby or special interest.

That is, of course, a slow process, but the only way you can expand the curriculum without the danger of watering it down with what appear to be the latest academic fads and fly-by-night enthusiasms. Nothing, you might say, could be more ludicrous than to offer instruction in any subject to any person (Ashby, 1971); nothing could lead more quickly to a decline in academic standards, to the loss of the meaning and value of the degree itself. And you would be quite right; while any individual university might defend its degree standards, the national standards of the system as a whole, and the meaning and value of the degree, would have to be sacrificed to achieve that kind of diversity of curriculum and function. But when the protection of a national degree standard is the first and highest value in a system, diversity of curriculum and function are among the costs.

Perhaps the greatest constraint imposed by a national standard is on expansion. No country in the world could operate a system of mass higher education at the per capita cost levels of the British universities and polytechnics. These cost levels are not inappropriate for elite higher education—the higher education of full-time, highly selected, and able students, taught at the most demanding levels of intellectual intensity and complexity. That is what British universities and colleges do, for the most part, extremely efficiently and extremely well. But genuine diversity would mean institutions operating at different levels of cost as well as of standard, and the possibility of lower-cost higher education would allow academics and officials to at least think about the expansion of higher education. But there is, I believe, a positive horror among the British, academics and politicians alike, at the very thought of the provision of "education on the cheap"; the chief objection, of course, is that such education would threaten standards. Yes it would, but that, of course, is just my point: the absolute unyielding commitment to high academic standards throughout the system is also a defense of the relatively high costs associated with elite forms of higher education, and that in turn puts an effective brake on expansion.

This horror of "education on the cheap" helps explain why the polytechnics need to operate at cost levels very close to those of the universities. If we make the adjustments for the most expensive research carried on in universities, and for the peculiarly expensive subjects, especially medicine, taught only in universities, the unit of resource in the polys was close to that in the universities. Only in recent years as polytechnic enrolments increased by some 25 percent, partly in response to UGC cutbacks, has a gap appeared, and of course the evidence of this gap has resulted in concerns being expressed about the effect on the quality of polytechnic higher education. I do not know if equality of per capita cost was in Anthony Crosland's mind when, as minister of education in 1965, he called for the creation of a binary system marked by "equality of esteem," to accompany a modest differentiation of function between the two sectors. But the stress on equality of esteem, and the firm determination that the polytechnics would maintain standards equal to or only slightly different from those of the universities, ensure that their costs must be similar—if they were not, what better evidence that they were designed to provide education "on the cheap"? And the careful monitoring by the CNAA subject committees, largely staffed at least initially by university academics, has ensured that degrees from the polys would be roughly at university standard—and cost.

And, of course, as the polys were drawn into the university orbit they sloughed off much of their non-degree work, which fell from 70 percent to 30 percent of their enrollments between 1969 and 1982, along with most of their part-time students, from 60 percent of the total in 1969 to under one-third in 1981 (Cantor and Roberts, 1983). At the same time, and for the same reasons, they have increased their research activities, and will continue to do so "if only for reasons of prestige" (ibid.). This development, which some have called "drift" as function follows cost, quality and esteem, also was encouraged, I believe, by the bad conscience among British middle-class and professional people toward the British working class. Where Americans feel guilt toward our racial minorities for past ill-treatment, and our policies reflect it, the United Kingdom shows a parallel guilt-driven policy toward its working class. Or at least they have done so until recently. As a result many Britons of all political persuasions are sensitive to the fact that new, low-cost, and low-status segments of a system of higher education are commonly first associated with and used by students from working- and lower-middle-class origins: status differentiation in higher education is closely linked to the social origins of students. So many who make this connection are hostile to the whole idea of a binary system, with its non-U sector especially oriented toward technical and practical subjects, which in the English context have lower status in themselves (Weiner, 1981; Rothblatt, 1968). These "unitarians," as we may call them, are committed to the slogan "nothing if not the best" in higher education, and especially so for youngsters from those strata of society that have historically gotten less, or second best (Trow, 1974). But even those academics who support the binary system are not inclined to want per capita costs in the polys to be markedly lower than they are in the universities—both for the political reasons that I mentioned, (i.e., the ideological egalitarianism of a class-haunted society) as well as for the role of common costs in maintaining common standards for the degree. If the polytechnics are allowed to offer a degree, so this argument goes, then they must be supported as if they were universities or something very near to them, and their students likewise.

If diversity of function is constrained by a national standard of degree, and the size of the system is constrained by its costs, so are the size and diversity of the student body. The requirement that entrants to degree courses have two "A" level passes immediately disqualifies more than 80 percent of its youth from entering English universities polys. There are now some experiments, especially in the public sector (Fulton, 1986), to admit students without these qualifications, but the numbers of these "nonstandard" entrants are not very large, and probably are not intended to rise very high. Indeed, even in the Open University, widely advertised as an "open access" institution, more than 60 percent of the entrants are people who already have earned two "A" level passes or their equivalent, and that proportion has been constant almost since its creation (Cerych and Sabatier, 1986; Williams, 1985). Those "A" level examinations may or may not screen effectively for future academic achievement, but they are certainly intended to do so. The new "AS" exam is not likely to modify that statement very much; it is, I believe, designed to somewhat broaden the academic preparation of students, and thus avoid what many believe to be a prematurely high level of specialisation in sixth form, rather than to dilute the quality of their academic preparation.

So the "A" level as the requirement for entry to higher education effectively constrains demand, whatever the capacity of the system of higher education, whatever its budgets. More resources from central government—much to be desired by all—would, I think, not mean more students: it would mean better student support grants, better pay for staff, improved staff-student ratios, better instruments and equipment for research, more secretaries and support staff—all good and desirable, even necessary things, but not more students, or at least not many more.

And yet there is every reason to believe that modern societies, as they develop into societies that depend on the creation and distribution of information—what have been called "information societies"—need more and more highly trained and educated people. In the United States, with more than 12 million students enrolled in postsecondary education of one kind or another, "graduate unemployment is less than half that of the general labour force, less than one-third that of all 24-year-olds" (Williams, 1985). And, as Shirley Williams observes, "The ability of the education system to match the needs of the information society for highly educated people has now become the main determinant of a country's employment prospects" (ibid.).

I am not here talking about the production of electrical engineers, or experts in the design and maintenance of computer systems, though current shortages in those categories are not unimportant for Britain's future. I am talking about people who have had some experience of education beyond secondary school—almost regardless of its content, and not necessarily to the completion of the first degree. In Britain those who leave college or university before taking their degree are commonly referred to as "wastage"; no value is assigned to a year or two of experience in higher education beyond secondary school if it does not lead to a degree. That makes sense when the highest value in a system is the academic integrity of the first degree; it makes less sense if we ask what effect, what influence that experience may have on the students and on their subsequent lives and careers. I do not know of any research in the United Kingdom that follows the dropouts to see what happens to them—their rates of employment or unemployment, of occupational or professional success, however measured. In the United States, there is a clear inverse relationship between the number of years that people have had of postsecondary education and their rates of unemployment, and a positive relationship to their income.

I stress the importance of some experience of higher education, even short of the degree, because I suggest that the latent functions, the by-products so to speak, of postsecondary education are for many people more important in the long run than the technical skills or knowledge that they may acquire there. The Victorians and their successors in this country knew that when they spoke of the cultivation of character, of sensibility, of the qualities of mind and spirit that the university was primarily aimed at creating or enhancing. I am suggesting that that transformation can happen even outside of Oxbridge, even in the absence of the individual tutor, even in nonresidential institutions, and for older part-time students who have not earned two "A" level passes. Of course, the positive effects of exposure to higher education, short of the degree, can be effectively precluded by labeling people who drop out as "failures." But in a world of lifelong learning, every dropout is merely a "stop-out."

The central difference between schooling and higher education, as we all know, is that, on the whole, schools teach the conventional wisdom—the skills and knowledge that are broadly thought necessary if one is to hold most of the middle-range occupations of life, and for a special few, as a necessary foundation for a higher education. But with some exceptions, schools are places where students learn to show a decent deference to their teachers and their texts, and to the knowledge and wisdom that they can impart. But in higher education, by contrast, students are encouraged, indeed even required to question the conventional wisdom, and are rewarded for it. Of course, in colleges and universities there continues to be a large and continuing emphasis on higher skills and more complex knowledge. But in a genuine college or university even this advanced level of skill transmission is carried on in an educational environment quite different from that of secondary schools: "facts" are more likely to be presented as elements of problems to be solved or interpreted, and indeed the "facts" themselves are sometimes subject to question. At its best, students in higher education learn, often in a sudden flash, that they can have ideas of their own, even ideas at variance with the conventional wisdom, at variance with those of their teachers, even, possibly, ideas that no one else has had before.

Of course, this is not a description of every college or university in either the United States or the United Kingdom. But there is a *tendency* for higher education to broaden students' horizons, strengthen their confidence in their ability to have ideas and to act on them, and merely follow work routines. Nor is this as romantic or idealized a view as it may appear. Students can be *tested* on their knowledge of the standard views (or arguments) of a field, and yet be judged informally by their ability to develop critical and original views of the material. And I submit that higher education in most Western societies is indeed a critical education, marked by the steady undermining of deference for the conventional wisdom and the encouragement of the belief that one can actually have ideas of one's own. That perspective, I believe, is going to be increasingly important, both for individuals and for the society, as the effects of the new technological revolutions of information systems and bioengineering transform our economies over the next decades, as they have already begun to do. I believe that higher education of *some kind*, not necessarily in elite institutions, and not necessarily to the honors degree, will determine for individuals whether they are to be beneficiaries or victims of the rapid social and economic changes already underway. And for modern societies, the number and proportion of people who feel at home in society, who are not captive to a skill or perspective that is obsolescent almost before it is acquired, will be the main determinant of a country's employment prospects and, more generally, of its economic health and social stability. I do not believe that 14 percent of the age grade in higher education is adequate to this challenge.

Higher education, I am suggesting, is for society a functional substitute for deference. As deference to traditional political authority erodes or collapses, we had better substitute a great deal of education. Your Victorian ancestors knew it, and we all need to be reminded of it. Social deference in the United Kingdom is based on traditional claims to authority of the upper classes; the authority of the modern workplace is increasingly based on claims to technical competence, linked to education. So education is also a substitute for deference in the workplace, and for the customary routines of production and distribution of goods and services. Those routines are being challenged by new ideas, by new technologies, by other societies. We need many people, not just at the top of enterprises but all through them, who are not captive to those routines, who do not defend them as the only (even if illusory) points of security in a rapidly changing world. The mass production of people who have been to college or university—whether at age 19 or 29 or 39—places people in the middle levels of enterprise who can adapt to change, and even sometimes initiate it, who can accept and use the larger amounts of discretion and initiative that modern industrial enterprises find so important for success in rapidly changing markets. And these same people are more likely to take the risks of entrepreneurship, to start the small enterprises (beyond the family-owned shops) where, as we know, the majority of new jobs are being created.

Alongside the cultivation of critical capacities and personal initiative, higher education teaches people to learn how to learn. All the evidence, from Sweden to California to Britain's Open University, shows that the people who continue their education as adults are, on the whole, people who have had a good deal of it when they were young (OECD, 1977a and 1977b). This tendency of education to generate a thirst for more of it is hardly even taken into account in estimates of the cost-benefit ratios of higher education, in the United Kingdom or anywhere else. But in the contemporary world, hardly any characteristic of a working population is more valuable than its propensity and capacity for continuing education throughout life.

Some may protest that all that is precisely the mission of the Open University, the function for which it was created. I yield to no one in my admiration for the Open University, which I have watched closely and with the deepest respect and appreciation since its earliest days. But in a sense, it is the enemy of a genuine system of mass higher education in Britain, because it contains those qualities, or some of them, in one institution, with one budget, and its own boundaries and limits. The Open University, I suggest, is a kind of safety valve, a token institution by which a highly selective elite system defends itself by accepting in principle the existence of a different kind of university, not quite elite but not a mass university either, which reconciles "open access" with a commitment to the university standard for the first degree. While the Open University is nominally open, we know that more than half of its entrants could qualify for entry to the universities or polytechnics. And what makes the Open University acceptable finally is that its degree is a genuine degree, up to national standard, attested so by the external examiners from other universities.

The extraordinary consensus around that gold standard is illustrated by a remark of Shirley Williams. In the course of praising the role of the Open University in British life, she too notes with pride that "the standards of its degrees have been vigorously maintained, examination papers and course work being regularly assessed by examiners from outside universities" (Williams, 1985). But what might the Open University be like if it were not so constrained? Perhaps it had to be if it were to have been permitted to exist at all, and been allowed to survive its early and vulnerable years (Cerych and Sabatier, 1986). But that cultural-political requirement has surely limited its impact on British society, and has given the United Kingdom another kind of elite university, and not the alternative network of institutions for mass higher education that arguably it needs. Indeed, it can be argued that the existence of the Open University has helped to justify the lack of expansion of the university system itself—one can always point to the Open University as the safety valve that would take increased demand for university entrance by those who did not have the full qualification for entry. It is the kind of institutional gesture that accommodates strains and pressures for broader access without endangering the elite institutions themselves, and without threatening a radical change in the system as a whole. It is not irrelevant that the budget of the Open University is less than 5 percent of the total recurrent expenditure of British universities—and in this respect remains quite marginal (Cerych and Sabatier, 1986). Moreover, the Open University is not competitive with the traditional universities—it does not accept university-age students. And it is not competitive for UGC grants, but gets its money directly from the DES. The Open University has many virtues—and the pioneering role it has played in distance learning, and as a model for similar institutions all over the world, not least in the United States, can hardly be praised too highly. But that is very different from seeing it as an institution that might provide broader access of much larger numbers to a system of mass higher education, unconstrained by the standards of the elite universities and polytechnics.

The provision of mass higher education that I have been pointing to is incompatible with the defense of elite standards for the *whole* of higher education, and, of course, with the national standard for the first degree. Mass higher education would involve enrolling, somewhere in a system of postsecondary education, people who do not have the academic credentials that are now required, people who are older, or working, people with families, people who cannot fit into the framework of the British university or even the degree work of most polys. I am not suggesting that British universities and polytechnics transform themselves into American state universities. That is not possible or desirable for a host of reasons, some of which Britons may be too polite to mention. But the greatest price that the United Kingdom pays for its elite system of higher education, for its jealously guarded standards of academic achievement and performance, may be that it does not address one of the most important requirements of this age, the creation of a broadly educated society that continues to learn. A "learning society," I believe, is central to— indeed, implicit in—the great social and economic transformation that Britain, along with all the other advanced industrial societies, is currently undergoing.

One cannot stress too often that a criticism of a system of elite higher education need not be directed at the high standards of that system itself, but rather at the way in which that elite system inhibits the emergence of other systems of higher education with lesser, more modest standards. And comments on the costs of elite higher education are not meant to imply that the universities and polys can be maintained on less money, but rather to point out what their costs do to the possibilities of the emergence of a more diverse system of mass higher education. I have said that no country in the world is rich enough to support a system of mass higher education at the per capita costs of elite higher education, either as Britain provides it or as we do in the United States. As rich as it is, comparatively, the United States could never make provision in colleges and universities for 12.5 million students at the per capita costs of students in Yale or Stanford or Swarthmore or MIT.

And, of course, the costs of Britain's elite system are not only those represented by the unit of resource. We must also add the student grants for all but the children of the affluent, stipends that are intended to make it possible for students to study continuously and intensively for the relatively short period of three years within which they earn the degree. And that grant is supported by very strong sentiments among its recipients. In the winter of 1984–85 Sir Keith Joseph's effort to introduce student loans, thereby shifting some funds away from student support grants into the research budgets, was defeated by a coalition of backbench Tories, representing parents of children in the universities and polys, and a delegation from the National Union of Students, representing those parents' left-wing children. The student grant system in Britain almost certainly involves a significant transfer of money from the poor to the middle class. But another way of looking at its defenders is as a coalition of the "ins" against the "outs." And indeed that is one way to look at the defense of an elite system based on high and uniform standards throughout. Student grants are a part of the elite system, part of that network of costs and sentiments that constrain the expansion of higher education. Student loans would have a very different significance if they were a means of expanding access rather than merely of cutting costs. It will be interesting to see what political coalitions develop to oppose or support loans, if and when they are proposed, and on what grounds.

Many British academic are bitterly hostile to the Thatcher government for its policy toward higher education, a policy that combined savage cuts with a steady pattern of increased intervention into the autonomy of the institutions and a growing institutional structure of direct management from the center. The irony, of course, is that the government has gone only a little further than most academics in its passionate defense of high academic standards. The government simply sees too many students and teachers, whereas most academics would like to see a few more. But the appeal of higher standards to the government is that it can be achieved, in their view, by weeding out some dim students and staff, and the creation of a smaller, leaner, and still more efficient system, which happily will cost somewhat less money.

IV

The postwar democratization of society in all our countries has not taken the form of an extension of the franchise—that went as far as it could many years earlier. Rather, it has taken the form of a growing tendency to call on the intelligence and initiative of larger and larger proportions of the society in the direction and management of more and more complex and rapidly changing social, political, and economic organizations. The demands for intelligence and initiative from technology and the economy we know. What is less visible is the need for more highly educated people to manage the transition to a multiracial society; to assess competing political conceptions of the right balance of freedom and authority, of public and private initiative, of foreign relations and military commitments. The erosion of traditional class and party loyalties in Britain and the transformation of the two-party into a three- and perhaps four-party system, all make greater demands on the citizens of a democracy of a kind that your Victorian ancestors understood and responded to appropriately for their time. What is the appropriate response of British society to these new forms of democratization, and what contribution can the members of an elite system of higher education make to that response?

The answer to that question neither can nor should be the transformation of British universities into institutions of mass higher education, comprehensive universities where "any student can study any subject" (Ashby, 1971). There cannot be American solutions to British problems. And the powerful structural and normative forces that I have been sketching—not least the institutional commitment to high academic standards in all degree-granting institutions—surely preclude that. But there is another set of institutions in this society, very little spoken of by educators and almost never by academics, which might be the instrument for the provision of postsecondary education to really large proportions of the adult population. I refer, of course, to the colleges of further education, or regional colleges, under whatever name they may bear. They are, one may hastily point out, not part of higher education: of course not, since they do not award the degree, and do not come under the various rules and mechanisms designed to defend the standard of that degree. I know, of course, that a part of their work is at what in Britain is called "secondary level," and much else is "narrowly vocational," keyed to particular skills, trades, and occupations that do not require a "higher education." They are, one might say, institutions for the noncommissioned officers of the society, the technicians and foremen who manage the small units of economic life under the broad direction of their better-educated superiors.

Whatever they do, whatever service they perform, it must be admitted that the colleges of further education do serve substantial parts of the total society, and not just its leadership. In 1980, approximately 500 colleges of further education under various names, and some 5,300 evening institutes, enrolled some 3.5 million "non-advanced" students, the great majority part-time (Cantor and Roberts, 1983). In 1978 more than a million students were taking non-advanced courses leading to specified qualifications in further education establishments (DES, 1979). What strikes an outsider—perhaps an American especially—is the enormous gulf that exists between further and higher education in Britain. Further and higher education are simply not part of a common system of post-secondary education, marked by diversity and a broad division of labor. My impression is that a university or poly teacher in the United Kingdom does not feel himself to be engaged in a common enterprise with teachers in colleges of further education, any more than he might with a secondary school teacher or a master chef who teaches the culinary arts.

And yet, to American eyes, your colleges of non-advanced further education are remarkably like our community colleges in many ways— they are relatively inexpensive, open access, full of mostly part-time, older students who have full- or part-time jobs; they are heavily vocational, and yet offer academic courses at both the advanced secondary and postsecondary levels. Neither system offers the bachelor's degree. And yet, in the United States community colleges are very much part of higher education: they are included in its statistics of enrollment, and in its calculations of cost and expenditure. And they are linked in everyone's mind as part of a common if differentiated enterprise, and, most important, are so linked in the minds of politicians, civil servants, and laymen when broad plans for the reform or expansion of higher education are being discussed. They are linked with the degree-granting institutions in most states through coordinating councils, and thus naturally become part of national and statewide planning for higher education. But they are linked with the degree-granting institutions in at least two other ways: first, their teaching staffs all have earned degrees in four-year colleges and universities, and for the most part have higher degrees, and they have that experience on which to model their own teaching. Second, there are regular paths by which students can transfer from community colleges to four-year institutions, and be accorded credit for at least part of the work that they did in the community college, if that work was of high enough quality and in courses roughly comparable to those offered in the four-year colleges.

Now it cannot be said that many community college students in America do transfer to elite colleges and universities, such as, say, Amherst or Princeton or Stanford. But many transfer to big comprehensive state universities, a movement that is warmly encouraged on both sides. And many more transfer to less distinguished four-year state colleges and universities all over the country.

My point is that the connection does in fact bring that whole very large sector of postsecondary education into the realm of higher education, and infuses its forms of instruction, its curriculum, its teaching staffs with the kind of critical independence that I spoke of earlier as a distinguishing mark of higher education. Community colleges thus are genuinely part of higher education, with all its subtle effects on their students' level of ambition, initiative, self-confidence, and the like, without their being especially distinguished academically, as given their open access and their almost total absence of research they could not be. Moreover, in many places the teachers in community colleges have a remarkably high level of morale and sense of mission—many of them take pride in being part of genuinely open access institutions, and of reaching students who would otherwise never have gone beyond high school. Above all, community colleges do not see themselves as failed degree-granting institutions.

One aspect of the apotheosis of academic excellence in higher education in Britain is that institutions that cannot claim academic distinction are often thought to be failed in some sense. That message came through very clearly in the UGC allocation of the deep cuts of 1981 and 1982, and in its 1986 exercise in department rankings. But just as a regional college of technology (or Salford) is not a failed Imperial College or MIT, but a different kind of institution, so an American community college is not a failed Yale or Swarthmore.

One can understand why university and poly academics would not want to bring further education into the charmed circle of British higher education: in their conception, these colleges are simply not institutions of higher education, by definition. But rather than absorb further education into higher education, it might he easier for university and polytechnic people to conceive of themselves as parts of a large and diverse system of British postsecondary education. This does not mean a false claim to equality of further education and higher education—a claim that would be patently false in the circumstances. But to make that connection, for universities and polys to accept a role as the elite sectors of a broad and differentiated system of postsecondary education, might have very large consequences, and I think good ones, for higher education, for further education, and for the society at large. Without in any way surrendering their own jealously defended standards of excellence, institutions of higher education might well find themselves able to redefine the political and financial issues that have recently been formulated by British governments so much to their disadvantage. To become part of a system of postsecondary education, with broad service functions among the several parts and to the larger society, is a way of reformulating a public policy issue that currently focuses on whether the universities and polytechnics are performing well enough, or efficiently enough, or at high enough standards. I cannot help but think that the problems of higher education as they are currently defined by government and its agencies must continually generate answers to the disadvantage of the universities and polytechnics. In 1986, the party political debate in England over higher education centers on whether to discard the binary line, and bring the polys and universities into a single system (*THES*, 1986). However, important that question may be to the polys and universities, I cannot believe it has great significance for Britain, except by making further structural differentiation more difficult.

Let me put the matter more sharply, I submit that pressures for the expansion of postsecondary education are inherent in the development of modern societies. But the more this expansion is taken by the elite selective system, the more it tends to become a system of mass higher education, with less money per capita, less autonomy, more central intervention and control; and lower standards. The only way a system of higher education marked by very high academic standards throughout can survive is if there stands alongside it—and related to it—a truly mass system of institutions marked by lower per capita costs and lower standards—one that accepts those democratizing pressures, demands, and functions, willingly. In this country that system, I suspect, will emerge, if at all, from further education. For universities and polys to welcome that development would be an act not of benevolence or sacrifice, but of survival.

The alternative, which one can see already on the horizon, is the abolition of the binary division, and the welding of the 45 universities to the roughly 30 polytechnics, making some 75 degree-graining institutions, with perhaps another 20 or 30 institutions added to this expanded sector out of the existing colleges and institutions of higher education. Both Labour and the Alliance have called for something like that—though the Social Democratic Party (SDP) does not want to "abolish" the binary line but "believe it may well wither away over the next decade" (THES, October 3, 1986; SDP, 1986). But this large new system of degree-granting higher education would also expand student numbers, especially of part-timers. It will, in other words, begin to resemble a system of mass higher education. I cannot help but believe that this system will over time become increasingly differentiated in character, function, and cost and standard. Is that not what the UGC's current efforts are aimed at? I think we will see a genuine stratification of institutions emerge, though with unclear boundaries and disputed functions— and as a result, the emergence of a reluctant and resentful sector of mass higher education. One might ask whether it might not be preferable to upgrade further education to the status of mass higher education than to downgrade some universities and polys to perform the same functions for part-time, older students, for less money and at lower standards. One can see the problems in the latter scenario, which I myself believe to be the more probable one.

It may be that the manifest inequalities in the relationship of higher and further education in this country doom any closer links between them to envy and resentment on one side, guilty defensiveness and snobberies on the other. Those feelings have not been unknown in the relationship of the universities and the polytechnics, and that has been a factor in the pressure for the equalization of their standards and costs. That equalization would not be possible in the case of further education, but that very fact might ease the relationship. Where there is no possibility of competition, there may be greater possibilities for cooperation.

As I have said, I am not particularly optimistic about this particular scenario coming to pass in the United Kingdom. Yet, faced with what I take to be a manifest need for a substantial expansion of higher education in Britain, and the deep impediments to that expansion built into the costs, structures, and values of elite higher education in this country, an outside observer must look elsewhere. And there, not very far away, is an educational system that might serve such purposes well. A closer association of further and higher education in the British context is fraught with problems and difficulties. There is no way in which those problems and difficulties can be resolved until the possibility of such an association is put on the agenda for discussion. But who is to do that, in the absence of strong popular demand? Not, I think, the institutions of higher education, or the political parties, or industry, for different reasons. And that is why I do not think it will happen.

I do appreciate that some steps have been taken to forge these links between further and higher education: the Education Counselling and Credit Transfer System, developed by the Open University; the Credit Accumulation Transfer Scheme created by the CNAA; the moves to organize higher education into modules; connections such as those made by Warwick University and many polytechnics with their nearby further education colleges, are all examples of a growing flexibility in this area. But these are all small-scale, rather experimental steps, many under attack and on the defensive. What is lacking still is the broad recognition that all degree-granting higher education is only a part—of course, a central part—of a system of postsecondary and continuing education, marked by a diversity of standard, mission, and cost, which has as its mission the advanced education of a whole society, and not just of its leadership. British universities and polytechnics can help create that new relationship between learning and society, or they can resist it. History will be making its own judgment of the part that the institutions of higher education will play in the postsecondary education of British society, and it will be an unforgiving one.

REFERENCES

Ashby, Eric. *Any Person, Any Study: An Essay on Higher Education in the United States.* New York: McGraw-Hill, 1971.

Cantor, Leonard M., and I. F. Roberts. *Further Education Today: A Critical Review.* 2nd ed. London: Routledge & Kegan Paul, 1983.

Caston, Geoffrey. "Planning, Governments, and Administration in Two University Systems: California and the United Kingdom." *Oxford Review of Education* 5, no. 2 (1979).

Cerych, Ladislav, and Paul Sabatier. *Great Expectations and Mixed Performance: The Implementation of Higher Education Reform in Europe.* Stoke-on-Trent: Trentham, 1986.

DES. *Education Statistics for the United Kingdom.* London: HMSO, 1979.

Fulton, Oliver. "Entry Standards." Paper prepared for a SRHE conference, London, October 1986.

Neave, Guy. "Elite and Mass Higher Education in Britain: A Regressive Model?" *Comparative Education Review* 29, no. 3 (1985).

OECD. *Learning Opportunities for Adults,* vol. 1, *General Report.* Paris: OECD, 1977a.

———. *Learning Opportunities for Adults,* vol. 4, *Participation in Adult Education.* Paris: OECD, 1977b.

Peston, H., and H. M. Peston. "The Further Education and Training Scheme." In *Recurrent Education,* edited by Selma J. Mushken. Washington, D.C.: National Institute of Education, U.S. Department of Health, Education, and Welfare.

Reynolds, P. A. *Academic Standards in Universities.* London: CVCP, 1986.

Rothblatt, Sheldon. *The Revolution of the Dons: Cambridge and Society in Victorian England.* Cambridge: Cambridge University Press, 1968.

———. *Tradition and Change in English Liberal Education.* London: Faber and Faber, 1976.

SDP. *More Means Better.* London: SDP, 1986.

THES. "Defiant Labour to Erase Binary Line." October 3, 1986.

Trow, Martin. "Problems in the Transition from Elite to Mass Higher Education."

In *Policies for Higher Education,* from the General Report on the Conference on Further Structures of Post-Secondary Education. Paris: OECD, 1974. Reprinted as chapter 2 in this volume.

Weiner, Martin J. *English Culture and the Decline of the Industrial Spirit, 1850–1980.* Cambridge: Cambridge University Press, 1981.

Williams, Shirley. *A Job to Live.* Harmondsworth: Penguin, 1985.

7

MARTIN TROW WAS ONE OF MY CLOSEST FRIENDS. We first met in the 1950s, when he was still in the Department of Sociology at UC Berkeley and working alongside Burton Clark on the sociology of education. We immediately started a lifetime conversation on the comparative study of educational systems, I from an English and he from an American point of view. Trow and Clark subsequently built up an impressive international knowledge, Trow from his many essays and his directorship of the Center for the Study of Higher Education at Berkeley and Clark from his widely read books on the universities in United States and Italy.

Trow was fascinated by the English universities, then designed for a minute elite of the high born and the highly gifted: they took in 2 percent of the relevant age group who were the most successful secondary school leavers and were destined to enter the higher echelons of the home and colonial civil service or the major professions of medicine, law, and education.

Trow's next step toward international knowledge and fame was to come to Oxford and to carry out with me a survey of British university teachers using the sample kindly provided by the Robbins Committee from its study in 1962. We also shared the intriguing and enlightening task of preliminary interviews with a rough cross section of our university colleagues to decide what questions should go into our questionnaire. Our discussions in Oxford demonstrated Trow's extraordinary capacity for insight into the lives and outlook of British university teachers. In the process and without formal intention, he taught me a lot about American academia but also a great deal about the British system that had previously escaped my notice. We eventually wrote a substantial book under the title *The British Academics,* which was published in 1971 by Faber and later by Harvard University Press.

Meanwhile a Conservative government had accepted the Robbins recommendation that the tertiary system be expanded. Thus our pivotal question in the book was, How would academics in Britain adapt themselves and their institutions to a period of expansion and redefinition of higher education? A central conclusion was that "the continuing expansion of the university system . . . is not the first stage of the development of mass higher education . . . No society can yet afford to educate 30 percent of its youth at the cost of education at Harvard, Oxford or Sussex" (p. 464).

That was in the 1970s and Trow went on to formulate an historical generalization describing the evolution of higher education in three stages from elite to mass to universal modeled on his experience of California and his "visiting" anthropology in the United Kingdom, Sweden, and the OECD (Organisation for Economic Development and Co-operation) countries generally.

His account of British higher education since 1980, including the colossal and unforeseen expansion of 1992, is summarized in the following essay. The reader may notice that in the meantime Trow has learned from his further studies that, quite apart from its economics, higher education in any country can be assessed in terms of its diversity, its autonomy, and its trust (by government). All three, he argues, have declined since 1980. I agree about autonomy but am much less sure about diversity and trust.

In the preceding elite system all these features could be taken for granted. Oxbridge graduates met on trustful and collegial terms in their London clubs and Whitehall committees; both had shared autonomy and the social solidarity of a common classical education. Diversity was socially provided in the vast system of apprenticeship, job placement, and cultural localism of the great majority of compatriots. Moreover it could be argued that internal diversity depends on plurality in the social origins of financial support. The United Kingdom in American eyes relies too much on the state. But the European ethical socialist still regards the state, with R. H. Tawney, as a "reliable drudge." As to governmental trust, the present discontent among academics is with bureaucratic impediments to both teaching and research. But would the market remove these impediments and set the academics free?

—A. H. HALSEY

Managerialism and the Academic Profession

The Case of England

Introduction

S ince World War II the central problem for higher education in most Western industrial societies has been how to transform the small elite university systems of the nineteenth and first half of the twentieth centuries into the systems of mass higher education required to meet the growing demands both for wider access from segments of their societies and for more highly trained and educated workers from their labor markets. The pressures for expansion have varied in intensity among the major European countries, as have the responses to that demand by European governments. (The United States for various historical reasons is a marked exception here.) But on the whole, it is fair to say that the United Kingdom has moved more slowly than most modern societies toward mass higher education; it is only in the past few years that it has started firmly down that path. Moreover, it has done so not by allowing its universities to grow greatly in size, or by creating permanent parallel non-university systems, but by promoting to full university status first the university colleges, then the regional colleges (some first to CATs [Colleges of Advanced Technology] and then to universities); still other regional colleges have recently (1991) become universities after a delay of a quarter of a century as polytechnics. That pattern of expansion poses special problems for the research universities in the emerging system of mass higher education, as we will see.

Over the past ten or twelve years British higher education has undergone a more profound reorientation than any other system in industrial

Originally published as Martin Trow, "Managerialism and the Academic Profession: The Case of England," *Higher Education Policy* 7, no. 2 (1994): 11–18. It was revised from a paper presented to a conference on "The Quality Debate," sponsored by the *Times Higher Education Supplement*, Milton Keynes, September 24, 1993. Reproduced with permission of Palgrave Macmillan.

societies. One aspect of that revolution has been the emergence of managerialism in the governance and direction of British universities. I suggest that managerialism as understood by central government in Britain is a substitute for a relationship of trust between government and universities, trust in the ability of the institutions of higher education to broadly govern themselves. The chosen managerial mechanisms in the United Kingdom currently are assessments of the quality of the teaching and research done in universities, carried out by committees and individuals appointed by the central funding agency, and linked directly to funding. It is not difficult to see that the character and criteria of these assessments will have great influence on the direction and work of the universities and departments being assessed. I want to raise the question of how effective this policy is and is likely to be, and what consequences for the life of British higher education seem to follow from it. It may be that other countries, and not least my own, have something to learn from the British experience.

The Concept of Managerialism

What do we mean by "managerialism"? It is not just a concern for the effective management of specific institutions in specific situations. The "ism" points to an ideology, to a faith or belief in the truth of a set of ideas that are independent of specific situations. Managerialism as applied to the institutions of British higher education takes two distinct forms, a soft and a hard concept. The soft concept sees managerial effectiveness as an important element in the provision of higher education of high quality at lowest cost; it is focused around the idea of improving the efficiency of the existing institutions. The hard conception elevates institutional and system management to a dominant position in higher education; its advocates argue that higher education must be reshaped and reformed by the introduction of management systems that then become a continuing force ensuring the steady improvement in the provision of higher education. In this conception management would provide this continuing improvement in quality and efficiency (i.e., cost) through the establishment of criteria and mechanisms for the continual assessment of the outcomes of educational activities, and the consequent reward and punishment of institutions and primary units of education through formulas linking these assessments to funding.[1]

Those who hold the soft conception of managerialism—on the whole senior administrators and some academics in the universities themselves—are critical of at least some of the norms and attitudes that have marked British universities and academics in the past: their complacency and conservatism, their administrative inefficiency, their indifference to establishing links with industry and commerce or to broadening access to larger sectors of the population. Nevertheless, the soft managerialists still see higher education as an autonomous activity, governed by its own norms and traditions, with a more effective and rationalized management still serving functions defined by the academic community itself. By contrast, those holding the hard conception of managerialism, people on the whole in government and business rather than in the universities themselves, have no such trust in the wisdom of the academic community, and are resolved to reshape and redirect the activities of that community through funding formulas and other mechanisms of accountability imposed from outside the academic community, management mechanisms created and largely shaped for application to large commercial enterprises. Business models are central to the hard conception of managerialism; when applied to higher education, as the current government does, the commitment is to transform universities into organizations similar enough to ordinary commercial firms so that they can be assessed and managed in roughly similar ways.

This hard concept of managerialism is currently the dominant force reshaping British higher education day by day and week by week. Its two characteristics of greatest interest to the present analysis are: (1) the withdrawal of trust by government in the academic community, and in its capacity to critically assess its own activities and improve them; and (2) its need to find or create a bottom line that performs the function of a profit and loss sheet for commercial business. This bottom line, if it could be found or created, would allow top managers in government departments and funding agencies to identify and assess the strengths and weaknesses of an enterprise (a university), its strong and weak units, and serve as an analytical tool for the continual improvement of the product and the lowering of unit costs.[2]

In brief, then, the withdrawal of trust in its universities by the British government has forced it to create bureaucratic machinery and formulas to steer and manage the universities from outside the system. In the absence of an effective competitive market, effectively precluded by government policies, bureaucratic institutions and their mechanisms are the alternative to a relationship of trust between state and universities. The bureaucratic agencies then create criteria of performance and rules for reporting and accountability necessary for the assessment of the system and its primary units (i.e., academic departments) and for the application of the formulas linking assessed quality and funding. These links of assessment to funding are intended to ensure the automatic improvement of the efficiency and effectiveness of the higher education industry. In British higher education policy, external assessment linked to funding is thus a substitute not only for trust but also for the effective competitive market, which is the chief control of both quality and cost in commercial enterprises.

Here I want to raise three questions:

1. Why was it that the government led by Margaret Thatcher that came to power in 1979, and its successor that is still in power in the United Kingdom, have withdrawn trust from the universities, and undertaken the radical reforms in organization and funding that we have seen over the past decade?

2. What are some of the consequences of this withdrawal of trust for the universities?

3. What are some of the assumptions underlying current central government policy in the United Kingdom, and how do those assumptions accord with the realities of academic life, particularly the realities of teaching and research?

These are broad questions and I could not possibly answer them adequately here. I can only point in the directions in which answers might be found.

British Higher Education before the Thatcher Government

With the election of the government headed by Margaret Thatcher in 1979, the attitudes and policies of the British government toward the country's institutions of higher education changed dramatically and profoundly as compared with the policies of previous governments. Before World War II, British universities, taken all in all, received about one-third of their operating expenses from central government, raising the rest from tuition payments, local governmental subsidies, and, especially important for Oxford and Cambridge, from endowments old and new. After World War II, the spirit of democratization, the expansion of the welfare state under both Labour and Conservative governments, and growing belief that national strength and prosperity depended in part on its educated manpower led the state to take a more active role in the expansion and support of the universities and of other institutions of higher education, some of which became universities in the 1960s and others of which became polytechnics in the 1970s and universities in the 1990s. By 1951–52, the state was providing roughly three-quarters of the universities' income, and had assumed the bulk of student fees and student support grants. By 1970, that proportion had grown to nearly 90 percent.

During this period, that is, from 1945 to 1981, the central institution for funding the universities was the University Grants Committee (UGC), created in 1919 precisely to serve as the buffer between the universities, autonomous in intellectual matters under the royal charters, and the state, which provided a substantial part of their support. And the UGC continued to serve this function during a period of substantial growth in British higher education. While the overall size and shape of the system was determined by central government—as for example, the decision to elevate the Colleges of Advanced Technology to university status in 1963, and the parallel decision to create a group of new universities during the period 1958–63—still central government did not intervene in the internal life of the universities it helped to create and pay for. In both parties and all governments it was accepted that British universities were among the finest in the world, and as a unique system of elite institutions of higher education perhaps pre-eminent. Knowledgeable foreign observers of the British universities before the Thatcher era broadly agreed on three major points: (1) they were unexcelled as teaching institutions at the first degree level; (2) they were distinguished research institutions, whose provisions for systematic graduate instruction varied among disciplines, but were gradually improving; but (3) the society had not found a fully satisfactory way to provide mass higher education with broad access alongside the highly selective elite universities, though the creation and encouragement of the polytechnics was a major step in that direction if their tendencies toward institutional drift could be constrained through the binary system.

The years leading up to the Thatcher victory saw British governments struggling with the mounting costs of the university system while dealing with an economy that had never fully recovered from the war— or perhaps from the two wars. Nevertheless, while previous governments had asked, rather politely, whether the universities could not find ways of providing more education for less money, the universities continued to submit budgets through the UGC that reflected per capita cost levels matched only by the most affluent private liberal arts colleges and universities in the United States—cost levels that were reflected in average student-staff ratios of about 8:1 across the board.

The Thatcher Revolution

The government led by Margaret Thatcher that came to power in 1979 broke in fundamental ways with its predecessors in its relations with the universities as in other areas of public life—though it took some time for the universities to understand the depth of the change. Mrs. Thatcher and her ministers of education had a fundamentally different view of the nature of the universities than their own leaders, and a quite different conception of their future. Their views, as they evolved over the next decade, can be summarized thus:

a. British universities are backward, conservative, self-serving institutions, and are in part responsible for Britain's poor performance in the international competition for markets. In brief, they, along with the trades unions, the state-owned industries, and the professions generally, are among the established institutions that impede Britain's economic progress.

b. British universities, like other established institutions, are incapable of reform from within, but must be forced to reshape their roles, missions, and functions. This conception of the failings of British universities still guides central government policy.

c. Initially, the transformation of British higher education was to be accomplished by radically cutting their budgets, forcing them to seek new funds from sources outside of government. That in turn would require them to become more efficient administratively, and require a measure of rationalization of their internal operations to be achieved by pressure from the (then) Department of Education and Science, with the help and advice of lay and business groups. These views, largely an expression of the soft or weak version of managerialism mentioned above, were captured in the Jarratt Report of 1985.[3]

d. Progressively declining support from central government would also make the universities more responsive to the real requirements of the market, and most especially of business and industry who employ their graduates.

e. While in the long run one could hope that better internal management and the sharp disciplines of the market and its climate of competition would force the universities to become both more efficient and more relevant, in the short and medium terms central government would still be supplying a substantial part of both operating and capital costs of the universities. That insulation from market forces—required by the traditions of British higher education and the practical impossibilities of cutting them loose overnight—meant that central government would have to administer its support grants in ways that encouraged the continuing reform of the universities and did not provide subsidies for a return to the bad old ways.

f. Therefore (and here emerges the hard version of managerialism), continuing support by central government of the universities would have to be accompanied by policies and regulations that would prod the universities to greater efficiency and relevance. Among the policies laid down by government were:

1. the abolition of the UGC and its replacement by funding councils, initially separate for the universities and the polytechnics, and then combined when the polytechnics were granted university status in 1992. The new Higher Education Funding Councils (HEFCs)[4] are not intended to serve, like the UGC, as a buffer between government and the universities, to protect the autonomy and independence of the universities from govern-

ment and political pressure. On the contrary, and quite explicitly, they are an arm of government, an instrument for the implementation of government policy on universities which, in government's view, are by their nature and traditions recalcitrant, and tend to defend their own parochial interests against the national interest as defined by the government of the day.

2. the separation of funding for teaching and research, and the institution of separate assessments by committees of academics appointed by the Higher Education Funding Council for England (HEFCE) of each set of activities at the departmental level.

3. these separate assessments, of teaching and research, linked to funding, are intended to introduce a measure of competitiveness into university life and thought that had been absent during the UGC regime of assured block grants. They would thus function, especially in the context of level or reduced funding, as a kind of quasi-market, with the inherent disciplines of market processes on the economy and efficiency of the producing units. But it is a peculiar market, a firmly rigged market. It leaves central government and its officials (rather than the student "consumers") to decide both on the quality of university activities and on the criteria by which those judgments are made. Moreover, government sets the prices of places, subject by subject, for fully funded students, and also decides on that year's fees, and allows universities to bid for places at or below those prices. The elevation of the polytechnics more than doubled the number of suppliers, but reduced the number of buyers in the market effectively to one—very convenient for the buyer. What we have is the rhetoric of the market, coupled with a substantial increase in the power of the external assessing and funding agencies, marking a real shift in power in the world of British higher education.

Other changes introduced by the present government—for example, the abolition of tenure in academic appointments—are aspects of the new relation between government and the universities, part of the effort to transform the universities into something more like commercial enterprises. But they lie outside the scope of this essay.

The Assessment of Research

British universities currently get their support grants from central government through what is called a "dual system" of funding research and teaching separately, as if they were distinct activities. That is a system that could only have been invented by non-academics. People who actually teach and do research in universities know how deeply research interests, and even more, research perspectives, are brought into teaching, and how much of the teaching of postgraduate students and increasingly of undergraduates is done through participating in their research and drawing them into one's own. The sharp separation of funding for teaching and research in the provision of general support for departments and universities is simply at odds with the realities of academic life. And the further that policy retreats from the realities for which it is designed, the more distorted must be its effects.

But setting this important issue aside, there remain the policies themselves: the separate assessments of the research and teaching activities of academics in English universities, in ways designed to determine how much money their departments and, in the aggregate, their universities will be given annually by central government. It is important to stress that what is being assessed are not individuals or universities, but departments. The allocations resulting from these assessments are made known to the departments that have been assessed, which of course strengthens their claim on those allocations to the detriment of the authority of the vice chancellor and the integrity of the university. The effects, of course, are variable among the universities.

We are accustomed to assessing specific research projects and outcomes along a single yardstick of excellence—an amalgam of elegance, predictive power, scholarly scope, effect on a field of study, imaginative grasp of large bodies of information. But whatever the possibilities for assessing particular research proposals and projects, the assessment of the research performance of whole departments in the British universities has peculiar unintended consequences. Among them, we find, is a tendency for department heads to encourage their colleagues to teach less and write more, and in some fields, to encourage research with short-term outcomes rather than long-range studies. The conversion of the polytechnics into full-fledged universities also seems to be bringing into the research community numbers of academics who have never done research, and are not adequately prepared to do it.[5] Moreover, the assessments center on the aggregate output of the members of a department who are actually doing research, which leads to subtle judgments by department heads about whether to count as members of their research staff members of the department whose research productivity is (at least at the moment) low in their reports to the funding council. (Two identical departments will be differently funded, depending on how they report their staff.) The pressures on longtime members of a department who are not thus counted can be imagined. Moreover, the assessment procedures cannot tell (or differentially respond to) whether a department is, in research terms, becoming stronger or weaker, or whether its research output and reputation rests on the work of a few "stars" or is more widely distributed among its members. In short, the assessments cannot tell much about the actual life of the department as a center and context for research.

There are even more fundamental questions about the research assessment exercise in the United Kingdom as a basis for funding departments and universities, not least its unexamined assumption that research strength should be rewarded with more support, research weakness with less. At the University of California, Berkeley, the discovery of serious deficiencies in the research quality of some of its departments of biology in the early 1980s led to a major study and reform of the organization of biology at the university, a reform involving major investments in both buildings and people.[6] The question of whether to respond to research weakness with more support or less is properly a decision to be taken in light of a close study of the particular department, faculty, or institute and its problems, not by the mechanical operation of a funding formula driven by a research ranking of a department on a scale from 1 to 5. The energies spent by British administrators and academics in manipulating the formula to generate the greatest sum locally—some of which involve what might be called "creative accounting," or colloquially "scams"— might better be spent on more productive activity. The withdrawal of trust by government from the universities has led to the parallel withdrawal of trust by universities in government, and from a cooperative to an adversarial relationship, and inevitably, the manipulation of information and data going up the line. That in turn may call forth more audits and site visits, calling forth more ingenious defensive behavior in the universities, and so forth.

The managerialists in central government appear to have little understanding of the actual processes of university administration. The enormous burden of the forms and reports that flow down to the universities, of dubious value to any conceivable policy, suggests that they do not know or much care about the administrative costs they impose on the universities, or the hidden effects of the opportunity costs to academics of doing anything that is subject to the increasingly elaborate processes of accountability established by the funding councils.[7]

I do not get the sense that this government has ever taken as a problem the implementation of their policies in and by the universities; they have more or less taken for granted that the policies and procedures they promulgate will be obeyed and implemented by university administrators, as in other areas of public life. (It made a similar mistake about implementation in 1993 with respect to its policies mandating a range of central examinations for students in primary and secondary education.) But universities differ from most other areas of the social services (though not all, e.g., the health service) in that much power is inherently exercised by the academics at the bottom of the chain of authority. Moreover, the services provided in and by higher education are enormously diverse and resist conformity to any broad and general rules. If government policy has provided the motives for institutional resistance, the nature of the institutions and of academic life itself provides the opportunities and resources.

The Assessment of Teaching

But if the assessment of the research qualities of whole departments rather than individual scholars or proposals raises a host of difficulties and unanticipated outcomes, the external assessment of the quality of a department's teaching probably rests on a basic misconception of what teaching is about. The assumptions of managerialism have come to dominate discussions about teaching. Some English academics remark that they need to be reminded about the actual nature of what they do, even if that is at odds with the assumptions of the assessments. The fundamental problem of trying to assess teaching lies in the assumption that it is one kind of activity, and excellence in it one kind of excellence. But teaching involves at least two parties, teachers and the taught. The quality of teaching is not a quality of a teacher but of a relationship, aspects of which are defined by the character, talents, and motivations of the learners. Teaching is not an action but a transaction; not an outcome but a process; not a performance, but an emotional and intellectual connection between teacher and learner. Therefore, it cannot be assessed as an attribute or skill of a teacher or a department, independent of the learners who have their own characteristics that affect whether and how much they learn (about what) from a particular teacher, and indeed, how much he learns from them. That also means, among other things, that teaching cannot be assessed along any single dimension of quality, nor can it be assessed at all without deep knowledge of its setting, of the styles and orientations of the teachers, of the character and diversity of students, and of its long-term effects, effects that may be very different from what students report about teaching as they experience it.

In fact, the quality of teaching, which surely means an assessment of its effects on students, can hardly be assessed at all in the short term. What can be assessed is not teaching but the absence of teaching, as when people do not meet their classes, or substitute such things as political or religious views and doctrines for teaching. We can and should pay attention to how much teaching people do, both formally and informally, whether they actually get to their meetings with students sober and on time, read and respond to their written work, and the like. We can also expect and require that teachers in their formal relationships with students confine their teaching to their areas of professional competence—and need not approve teachers who exploit their privileged positions and the vulnerability of their students in the service of some sectarian positions or political or social doctrine. Moreover, we can be responsive to students' complaints about teachers who verbally abuse them, express racial or gender prejudice, or simply treat them disrespectfully. We can demand of university lecturers professional responsibility toward their jobs and a humane non-exploitative relationship with their students. But beyond that, we must depend on our appointment procedures to ensure that teachers know their subjects and are competent to transmit knowledge, or broaden perspectives, or stimulate curiosity, or raise ambitions, or prepare students to be able to learn throughout their lifetimes, or achieve some of the many other things that teachers accomplish through their relationships with students. And we need strong clear internal procedures of review of the crucial processes and relationships to ensure that the standards that the university sets for itself are being met—and if not, why not.

All this means that almost everything in a university depends on the inner motivations of teachers—their sense of pride, their intellectual involvement with their subjects, their professional commitments to the role of teacher, their love of students or of learning—these and others are among the forces that lead teachers to bring their full resources to the teaching relationships. And these motivations of academics are usually quite independent of unpredictable external assessments, and the remote incentives and punishments that can be attached to them.

But the withdrawal of trust by government in the universities means that it is not prepared to accept the inner motivations of teachers as an adequate basis for motivating and directing their behavior. That is precisely the basis on which all professions, not least the academic profession, have claimed a measure of autonomy over their spheres of competence. But if, as I believe, this government is (and for a decade or more has been) deeply dissatisfied with the performance of its universities, then justifications of the autonomy and self-direction of academics and their institutions by reference to the primacy of inner professional norms and motivations are seen as merely expressions of a familiar academic rhetoric that has defended and justified the self-serving and unsatisfactory performance of its institutions in the past.

But if it cannot trust the inner motivations of scholars, scientists, and professionals (and they are not all exactly the same, though similar in springing from inner values), how can government shape the behaviors of academics and thus of their institutions?

One way, and the first employed, was simply to cut the budgets for the universities drastically. That certainly got the attention of the academics, and has affected their behavior even without directly influencing their inner motivations. As student-staff ratios have roughly doubled over the decade, activities and relationships that were possible a decade ago become less easy or impossible now; class sizes grow, tutorials are phased out, and behaviors of academics and institutions are affected in other ways that are less obvious. No one, to my knowledge, has assessed the impact of the changing ratio of students to staff in British universities over this past decade, nor is the question even asked. The only aspect of university life that seems to be immune to assessment is the quality and wisdom of central government policy toward higher education.

But it is not enough to cut budgets. So long as academics have substantial control over their own time, they may or may not actually work harder, more efficiently, and more effectively, as government thinks they should. In the government's view, the way to get more efficient and effective behavior out of employees is to generate a competitive environment for the academics, and then begin to tie rewards to more effective performance on the job. Or put differently, it is to replace what it sees as inadequate and self-serving inner motivations with a system of externally provided incentives and penalties keyed to approved performance. This linkage of performance to external rewards cannot exist side by side with the older structure of internal motivations, which to the government was indifferent to (the government's conception of) the public interest, but was keyed rather to the special interests of the academic guild and its institutions and prejudices. So the problem presented itself: how to replace one structure of motivations—rooted in the traditional patterns of academic life—by a different structure of motivations whose source and model was the competitive world of private enterprise. This problem, articulated the more clearly the longer the government remained in office, led to the emergence of the two forms of managerialism to which I referred earlier. The soft and hard forms of managerialism correspond roughly to two phases of the managerial revolution in British higher education; the first that developed within the universities under the pressures of coping with the huge budget cuts of the early 1980s, and the second, which developed, after the demise of the UGC, around the central government funding agency, now the HEFC(E), aiming at introducing businesslike attitudes toward work and performance into the universities, changing their functions as it changes the motivations of their employees, not merely introducing more efficient rationalized structures of management as in the first phase.

The new philosophers of higher education in and around government were faced with a number of problems: one, obviously, was the deeply entrenched attitudes and arrangements within universities that were based on quite different norms and values, and indeed held the norms and values of business in some contempt, as least as they were applied to the universities. These traditional academic norms and values were much more deeply embedded in the "older" universities; indeed, there is a clear if not perfect relationship between how deeply embedded those traditional notions of institutional governance are and how old a particular university is. But those traditional values of autonomy were on the whole less firmly embedded in the polytechnics, which had always had less autonomy, and were, so to speak, used to substantial influence from local authorities, local industry, and later on, from the Council for National Academic Awards (CNAA). Putting the polys on a businesslike basis would have seemed to politicians and civil servants an easier and more realistic mission than accomplishing the same transformation in the universities. And the notion of keeping the polys a separate sector, more responsive to political and external direction, must have seemed attractive to some observers in and around government.

Despite these and other advantages, the political costs of maintaining the binary system would have been high. First, there was the steady pressure from poly directors and councils themselves: having phased out the CNAA oversight, the polys were giving degrees and even doing research. How then could they be withheld the title and status of "university"? But if "universities," then how could they be distinguished from all other universities; would that not be precisely the invidious distinction on status (ultimately class-linked) grounds to which British education has been subjected since its origins? Not only would abolishing the binary line appeal to the polys, and even to many university academics, guilty about their status and privileges in relation to the polys. For the government it would have had another substantial effect to recommend it: ending the binary system would permit the application of many of the governing structures and mechanisms developed in connection with the polys to the old universities as well, and thus, so to speak, help bring them to heel. Our study suggests that is what is happening now. There is a strange irony here: as the polytechnics emerged from the tutelage of the CNAA they enjoyed a brief period of academic autonomy, only to lose it as they became universities and again found their work being assessed by agencies of central government.

The Search for a Bottom Line

Where does assessment come into this? One problem in patterning universities on the model of private business and industry is that the latter have a fairly simple bottom line of productivity and profitability, a bottom line that allows all observers to see how a concern is meeting its competitive environment. But British universities in the past have not had to compete for resources, nor do they have any very clear or obvious bottom line that government can use in assessing the institutions' performance. The extraordinary focus in government policy on quality in higher education—in a system in which it has not in this century been problematic, and where no responsible observer saw major problems—is part of the government's search for a bottom line, a way of assessing individual and group performance in the absence of the ability to assess a university's success or profitability.

If market mechanisms and indicators in higher education are weak, or were made to be weak, that has made it all the more necessary to find some way of developing indicators of desired performance. Of these there were only two the government could imagine: one was the amount (and quality) of research academics and their departments and institutions would produce; the other is the amount and quality of their teaching. The assessment of research has been going on for a few years, and it is having a variety of effects on the behaviors of academics in both the old and the new universities, as we have suggested above.

But the government is currently also introducing a bottom line into the teaching work of academics, and will try to assess and reward it as it does research. As I have suggested, I do not believe teaching can be assessed and rewarded by external agencies in any way that actually links rewards to excellence in teaching. Of course, a system linking assessments of teaching to rewards can be invented and put into operation. But it requires efforts to shift British academics from the internal motivations associated with professional work—intrinsic work norms and the desire for a good reputation among one's peers—to the external motivations that these managers believe are characteristic of private business and industry: the rewards of departmental and institutional grants for superior teaching that are deployed by the funding agency. While the assessment of teaching in the universities by the funding agency is just getting under way, it is perhaps not too soon to see this as the next step of a systematic effort to make universities into "knowledge shops" run in business-like ways, without all the traditional norms and values that (in the view of government) have crippled British higher education, and reduced its contribution to national economic development.

This effort by central government requires—indeed, it assumes—the subordination of inner motivations to external incentives linked to these assessments. It can also be seen as requiring the deprofessionalization of the academic workforce, their transformation into middle managers or skilled craftsmen, interested in promotion and better pay as rewards for better performance as determined by external assessors against yardsticks supplied by government agencies. It also means that these skilled workmen are producing and delivering a more or less standardized product subject, as in other industries, to control by management of costs and quality. That process of deprofessionalization is already under way as a natural and inevitable consequence of the withdrawal of trust by government in the universities and their guilds of academics.

For example, in the assessment of teaching by the funding councils, a central criterion, as one senior official in a funding council recently put it, is whether the teacher "delivers the course the customer (i.e., the student) expected to get." In this conception of the academic's role, the teacher produces a product that the customer buys, and expects to get what he paid for. And that is a reasonably accurate (if partial) description of some parts of higher education: the straightforward transmission of skills and knowledge, where students and teachers share a notion of what skills and knowledge are involved in the transaction. Even there, a good deal more happens in those relationships than is described by that transaction, much of it not part of the students' expectations when they enter the course. But more strikingly, there is no provision in this conception of "teaching to expectations" for the possibility that the teacher does not want to meet the students' expectations, but wants rather to modify those expectations, and more broadly, to modify (and enlarge) the student's mind, character, and sensibility. That is what many British academics think they are doing, or are trying to do; and there is much evidence to suggest that they are remarkably successful, certainly as successful as any group of academics in the world. Nor will they easily surrender those conceptions of teaching, embedded as they are in the norms of the university and the habits of academics, in response to the quite different assumptions of the external assessment exercises.

If British academics do not easily surrender their own notions of what teaching is about, how will they cope with the pressures of these assessments and their ambiguous criteria? We already have heard of various coping mechanisms by the university officers under conditions of high uncertainty: these are variously referred to as "games" and "scams," and involve the creative reporting of numbers and events, all wrapped in what is hoped is persuasive rhetoric that bears a somewhat loose relation to reality. But however successful these coping mechanisms, aimed primarily at gaining a workable grant, or at least reducing threatened cuts, one should not imagine that the assessments have little effect. Perhaps their effects are achieved most powerfully through their criteria which, however resented, come over time to be internalized, and through the values implicit in the language in which discussions of teaching and learning are carried on in official papers.

Diversity and a Typology of Orientations to Teaching

Let us look briefly at the nature of teaching in universities, to see whether it is reasonable to expect committees of the funding council to be able to assess the teaching performance of academic staff and departments in ways that will allow government to rationally link institutional funding to the quality of teaching.

We can see some of the difficulties more clearly if we consider just one way of characterizing teachers by reference to their relationships with students, that is, by looking at four familiar but distinguishable patterns of teaching styles. Let us look at the four styles generated by the cross tabulation of two simple dimensions of teachers' orientations toward teaching. One dimension distinguishes the orientation of teachers primarily toward their students or toward their subjects. The other dimension distinguishes between teachers who are oriented more toward the transmission of knowledge, or toward the creation of knowledge. These two dimensions then define four familiar types of orientations of academics toward teaching.

TYPOLOGY OF ORIENTATIONS TOWARD TEACHING

Orientation toward:	subject	student
transmitting knowledge	I	II
creating knowledge	III	IV

Type I reflects a traditional teacher-student relationship: "I know my subject, and I will teach you about it." The subject, an academic discipline or the explicit aspects of a profession, is what competent scholars and scientists have said and learned about the substance of the field, about its theories and its methodologies. The assumption is that the student is motivated to learn, and the teacher's task is to provide expert guidance about what is of greatest importance in the literature, and to help the student to learn how to read it.

Type II is a more modern or progressive orientation toward teaching, since it no longer assumes a high measure of motivation on the part of the student, and accepts that a considerable part of the teacher's job is to motivate the student to learn. This may require nontraditional forms of instruction, most commonly finding a way to involve the students' own experiences in the subject so as to make them see the relevance of it for their own lives and future. This orientation is a natural concomitant of the growth of broader access and mass higher education. It emerged earlier among teachers in the primary and secondary schools (and even earlier in the schools and departments of education) with the lengthening of the school-leaving age and the growth in the population of reluctant and resistant students. This perspective lies at the heart of the Copernican revolution in education[8] that transformed American pedagogy in the schools as far back as the turn of the century. Its late arrival in British higher education reflects that society's long resistance to the incorporation of institutions of mass higher education into full university status. That has now happened, and we will be seeing the characteristics of Type II teaching gradually emerge as the criteria of quality in teaching employed by the new teaching assessment bodies.

Types III and IV, which center teaching around the creation of knowledge, are the natural orientations of research scholars and scientists who specialize in teaching postgraduate students: they are the orientations of people who see existing knowledge primarily as a way of gaining knowledge—the knowledge one needs to have in order to advance it. For such teachers the transmission of knowledge is, so to speak, a byproduct of learning how to create it. But the lines are not clear. In the great research universities in both the United Kingdom and the United States, research scholars and scientists also teach undergraduates. Such research-oriented academics often cannot change their perspectives on their subjects just because their students are undergraduates, and teach the latter as if they were graduate students, though with lower expectations about the undergraduates' performance or their contributions to knowledge. Such teachers assume a measure of motivation to learn whether it is there or not; "if they aren't motivated they shouldn't be here." That perspective is assailed as elitist by supporters of mass higher education who know that whatever its other virtues, it brings larger numbers of more weakly motivated students into higher education.

These two different orientations (Types III and IV) are typically assumed by research scholars, depending on how far advanced their research students are in their preparation for research. Research scholars and scientists teaching students in the first year or so of their graduate studies may well stress the nature of knowledge in their subject, assuming, as they might well do with respect to postgraduate students, that they are motivated to learn (Type III). The other orientation (Type IV) is assumed by teachers (usually graduate advisors and mentors) who may try to learn the unique qualities of an advanced research student's mind and talents, and shape their relationship increasingly more in response to each student's interests and qualities than merely to the subject alone.

Matters are a little different when these orientations are held by teachers of undergraduates. In the United States teaching undergraduates through direct exposure to research is sometimes decried as at variance with the nature of liberal education and the gaining of a broad sense of the map of knowledge. Education oriented around research is inherently specialized, since academic research and the advance of knowledge is specialized. And research scholars are sometimes unable to drop their intense orientation toward creating knowledge as they face a classroom of undergraduates. But there is evidence that involving students directly in the research activities of their teachers has great potential for motivating them to want to learn, as they see at first hand the intrinsic rewards of the pursuit of knowledge, as well as some of the disciplines associated with it. The broad success of the Undergraduate Research Opportunities

Program at MIT, which involves a very large proportion of MIT undergraduates in live, ongoing research under the direction of a research scientist at some point during their studies, attests to that. But MIT students can be assumed to be highly motivated; similar programs at the University of California and Stanford have had marked success with minority students from educationally weak backgrounds that required that their motivation be engendered rather than assumed before their real education could begin.

There are several points to be made about this typology of orientations toward teaching. First, it is a typology of orientations and not of people; individuals may have different orientations when facing different kinds of students—as, for example, graduates and undergraduates. Second, teachers may combine some of these kinds of orientations in their teaching—for example, a teacher intensely interested in creating knowledge may do it in part through a focus on where the frontiers of knowledge are and how the specific student can be brought there (Types III and IV). Or a bookish teacher, focused on his subject and rather insensitive or uninterested in variations among his students, may discuss the field in his lectures and seminars both in terms of how the knowledge in the field is understood and organized by the discipline, and also how that area of knowledge is currently being advanced through research (Types I and III).

Third, teachers change over time; their orientations toward their fields and toward their students may also change and move from type to type.

Fourth, and important for my argument, all of these orientations can be found in our lecture halls and seminar rooms currently. Moreover, the diversity of orientations reflects the growing diversity of student interests, talents, and ambitions. All this means that there is no single dimension along which teaching can be assessed as "unsatisfactory" to "excellent." Put differently, a university will have, and indeed will want to have, people with all these kinds of orientations to teaching—teachers more concerned with their subject than with their students, teachers more concerned with creating knowledge than in transmitting it, and the other kinds too. And they are present, though not in the same distributions everywhere, in almost every kind of college and university. In the old polytechnics there are more transmitters than creators; in some fields teachers are more likely to be focused on the student than on the subject.

But all these kinds of teachers are there in their variety, resisting all efforts to assess them as if teaching were a performance, the performance of a skill that can be assessed and graded. As we who have taught and done research know, teaching and learning are not like that, not like that at all.

On the Long Delay of Effects

There are other forces besides the diversity of teacher-learner relationships that defeat efforts at assessment. One of these is the difficulty of knowing what the effects of teaching will be on the student over his or her lifetime. All of us have had the experience of reassessing our experience in college or university during the course of our lives, reflecting on how empty or ephemeral were some courses of study, how enduring in their influence on our thinking and feeling were others. And how different those later assessments are in many cases from the feelings we had about those teachers and their courses or seminars when we experienced them, in most cases before we were 25 years old.

Evidence for this beyond the anecdotal is provided in a study by Katherine Trow, who has recently interviewed a group of forty graduates who had gone through a particular course of study at UC Berkeley twenty to twenty-five years earlier.[9] Almost uniformly these people in their forties reported that they had been influenced during their lives after they left the university by their experience of that particular course of study and reading. But while the experience had this continuing influence, it also underwent a reassessment by the students—one that is not yet finished.

One former student, now a businessman, describes the effects for him of that particular program of study as "an intellectual net that has stretched over time." Another graduate, now a lawyer, observed that "As I've grown older, the impact sort of accumulated . . . I remember somebody saying in 1967 or 1968 that 'you won't know about the truth of what we're saying, you're just children now.' And of course we were. But what's happened for me is that the longer I've lived with these books . . . the more I see [their relevance] in my life, and also in terms of my overview of history and culture and the present." And he goes on to say what we all know, but cannot measure: "As you get older, you just know more, and you live more, and you have suffered more losses, and you have more sense of the complexity of the world and then you start to see . . . You read a poem of Yeats when you are 15 or 16 or 17, and you read a poem of Yeats now and . . . you can have it now; you couldn't have it then." We cannot disentangle the impact of what that man read at Berkeley twenty-five years ago, or of the peculiar talents of his teachers, from what he has become since, or from all his life experience. But he has come to "have more sense of the complexity of the world," and grapples with it as his teachers twenty-five years ago hoped he would. What he read was at least in part what they put in his way—and they put those readings and ideas in his way in such a fashion that he did not discard them, but is still living and struggling with them a quarter of a century later. My point is not to praise a liberal education, however much it needs praising. My point is that whatever is happening in a relationship between a student and his teachers (and other students and the broader academic environment), assessment teams cannot measure those effects while the students are still, in a sense, children, and not even very precisely later on, when the effects of education are mixed with all the experiences of life. The measurement of the effects of education in the short term may be crucial to the bottom line, but it is an illusion.

Conclusion

In my critical discussion of trends in central government policy toward higher education in the United Kingdom, it should be clear that I believe that a university should be continually engaged in critical reviews of its own activities and departments. I have pointed to the great danger that the criteria of success or quality adopted in external quality assessments or reviews tend be chosen with an eye to the possibilities of the quantitative measurement of quality, since those measures seem to be more objective, are more easily accepted outside the institution, and are part of the ethos of managerialism. The paradoxical result may well be that vigorous efforts by agencies of central government to assess the quality of university work lead to its decline, as more and more energy is spent on bureaucratic reports, and as university activities themselves begin to adapt to the simplifying tendencies of the quantification of outputs. Our research suggests that departments and individuals shape their activities to what counts in the assessments, to the impoverishment of the life of the university, which is always more complex and varied than assessments of outputs can capture.

The only effective defense by the university against this tendency is to create procedures for review and maintenance of the quality of teaching and research that are firmly rooted in the intellectual life of the institution and its academic departments and members. And that in turn calls for a process of continual assessment through procedures and committees that work with departments and not against them, that try to understand the university and its departments qualitatively as well as quantitatively, and that coordinate its internal assessments in ways that are in the service of its intellectual life. The members of such committees, most of whom should be drawn from units outside the departments under review, must learn enough about those departments and programs to be able to recommend directions of development and corrective action, not merely give them scores. And those recommendations to senior academic officers should have consequences for the internal allocation of the university's resources.

In the United Kingdom, the greatly strengthened administrative leadership of universities that has grown out of the movement I have called "soft managerialism" is the best defense of university autonomy, and in current circumstances nearly its only defense. Our study shows us how effectively administrators, especially the professional managerial staff, defend their universities in a game whose rules are invented by others and are constantly changing. But the continuing decline of the unit of resource widens the gulf between administration and the academic staff. There are under the best of circumstances inevitable tensions between administrators and academics, arising out of their different values and interests. In most universities that is a healthy tension—between spontaneity and predictability, creativity and accountability, centrifugal and centripetal forces. But it makes all the difference to the life of the institution whether the administrators who manage the university and take responsibility for the whole of it are inside or outside it.

In criticizing the current trend toward the external assessments of educational quality, and in seeing them as more the product of an ideology of managerialism than as a way of improving the quality of education, I do not mean to suggest that the quality of higher education cannot or should not be improved. Indeed, a strong case can be made that higher education, in both teaching and research, is facing a grave crisis, for some aspects of which we academics must be held responsible. And teachers can be helped to be more effective, whatever their orientations toward teaching, whatever their talents and temperaments, as many successful programs of staff development attest.

But some of the fundamental problems facing the academic world currently are only partly of our making and not wholly in our power to correct. I need only refer to the collapse of consensus about the nature of the cultural disciplines and the loss of confidence that any scholarship affords any authority to assert anything. The deconstructionists continue to threaten to saw off the limb on which they are sitting. Even in fields not so devastated, the extreme specialization of studies arising out of the explosion of knowledge atomizes the curriculum and undermines any coherence in higher education. The incoherence of undergraduate studies in the United States results also from the modularization of courses, and the freedom students have to elect among these modules in their accumulation of credits toward their degree, where again we were pioneers. And British universities move rapidly (if variably) toward modularization. Modularization gives students the freedom to drop in and out of universities, move from subject to subject and from institution to institution over their whole lives, banking their unit credits in academic transcripts. How admirable (and indeed necessary) are these mechanisms of mass higher education, how wonderfully responsive to the diversity of student talents and preferences and to societal needs. And yet, with what consequences for the character of higher education?

Beyond this, what is happening to our students, and to their inclination and capacity to study what we present to them as worthy of study? We slowly begin to recognize the effects of thousands of hours of TV and computer games on young minds, not just on the minds of school dropouts but also on the minds of our students. A recent commentator suggests that "The problem here is the emergence of widespread aliteracy— a growth in the number of people who, although they can read, do not see reading as a pleasurable activity." And he notes that "In 1976 in Britain, 83 percent of those between the age of 15 and 24 regularly read a daily paper, but by 1992 this had fallen to 59 percent."[10] And this was happening as the proportion of the age grade staying on through upper secondary school and entering universities was growing rapidly.

These great problems facing academic, indeed intellectual, life—profound failures of nerve in some fields of inquiry, the explosive growth, transformation, and atomization of knowledge in others, the impact of mass culture on mass higher education—these and similar problems fall quite outside the assessment of teaching as the Higher Education Funding Council (England) imagines it. Managerialism, at least in its hard version, may allow governments to imagine that they control the uncontrollable. But for academics it is at best an irrelevance and a distraction from the daily business of teaching and learning, and at worst a serious threat to already vulnerable institutions. Once again, it may be that the major task facing British higher education is to educate its masters.

NOTES

1. The government's White Paper, *Higher Education: A New Framework* (1991), is a document of hard managerialism: a brief collection of assertions and instructions to the academic community, wholly without argument or evidence for the policies it sets forth. (Indeed, on first reading I took it to be the Executive Summary of a longer paper that provided the evidence, argument, and context for the policies, but found none.) Its character can be suggested by the fact that this authoritative document speaks of a 50 percent growth in enrollments in British universities by the year 2000, and devotes no fewer than twenty-eight numbered paragraphs to the issue of "quality assurance," while saying nothing about capital investment in laboratories, libraries, classrooms, or equipment during this anticipated growth. (See Trow, "Thoughts on the White Paper of 1991," *Higher Education Quarterly* 46, no. 3 [Summer 1992]: 213–26.)

If the White Paper of 1991 is a statement of hard managerialism, the Jarratt Report (CVCP, 1985) was for British higher education the defining document of soft managerialism, a reaction by academic and professional administrators to the deep cuts in university funding of the early 1980s. It called for the strengthening and rationalizing of university administration, a goal that has been substantially achieved since its publication.

2. Another illustration of "hard managerialism," as well as an indication of the government's lack of trust in the academic community, can be seen in the chief consultative document commissioned by the HEFCE on "possible ways for institutions to account for the use of research funds allocated to them by the Funding Council." The report was prepared by a firm of accountants and business consultants, and written by men none of whom was an academic. Moreover, the study was "overseen" by a "Steering Group" of sixteen persons, all of them civil servants or university administrators, no single one of whom was currently engaged in either research or teaching. A more dramatic statement of attitudes toward the academic community that actually does the research the document is discussing could hardly be imagined. This lack of trust is visible also in the document's recommendations, one of which is that a detailed record of time spent on each of six types of activities be kept and reported by each academic researcher and linked to funding (*Research Accountability*, Coopers and Lybrand, for the Higher Education Funding Council for England, n.d., but 1992).

3. Committee of Vice Chancellors and Principals, "Report of the Steering Committee for Efficiency Studies in Universities," March 1985.

4. There are separate funding councils for England, Scotland, and Wales. They follow broadly similar policies, but with some differences in implementation. In this essay I am speaking chiefly of the funding council for England, which governs the bulk of British higher education.

5. The provision of workshops and start-up funds to encourage research in the former polytechnics may be welcomed by some in the former polytechnics, but it encourages institutional drift (a perennial problem for British higher education), and also could seem to be at odds with the government's announced intention to concentrate research funds in a small number of "centers of excellence."

6. Martin Trow, "Leadership and Organization: The Case of Biology at Berkeley," in *Higher Education Organization: Conditions for Policy Implementation*, ed. Rune Premfors (Stockholm: Almqvist and Wiksell International, 1984), pp. 148–78. Reprinted as chapter 12 in this volume.

7. Similarly, "The existence of trust economizes on transaction costs." Janet T. Landa, "Culture and Entrepreneurship in Less-Developed Countries: Ethnic Trading Networks as Economic Organizations," in *The Culture of Entrepreneurship*, ed. Brigitte Berger (San Francisco: ICS, 1991), pp. 53–72. Conversely, the withdrawal or absence of trust greatly increases transaction costs. But these transaction and opportunity costs, in time, money, or other things not done, are mostly hidden, and not included in government's estimations of institutional efficiency or effectiveness.

8. This refers to the replacement of the subject by the student at the center of the universe of teaching. The metaphor is found in the seminal writings of Lawrence

Cremin, the distinguished historian of American education. See Cremin, "The Revolution in American Secondary Education, 1893–1918," *Teachers College Record* 46, no. 6 (1955): 303.

9. Katherine Trow, "The Experimental College Program at Berkeley: Some of its Long Term Effects and Implications for Educational Practice," Council for the Renewal of Undergraduate Education, Stockholm, Sweden, 1992.

10. Richard Woods, "No Quick Cure for Newspapers Suffering from Poor Circulation," *The Independent*," August 4, 1993, p. 17.

PART IV

The Private Lives
of American Universities

8

I GOT TO KNOW MARTIN TROW in the late 1960s at Berkeley, where I was a young architecture professor and he a distinguished social scientist. I was the chair of the Campus Housing and Environment Committee that advised the university administration on issues related to the design of campus facilities. Trow was also a member, and I suspect he was responsible for my appointment to that position.

Reading his essay "Notes on Education and Architecture" exactly forty years later, I am struck by how well he understood the relationship between the two. In those years when the construction of facilities of higher education was in full swing due to the growing demand for mass higher education, he identified the problems that mass institutions would face by eliminating the human face in design and going for bureaucratic solutions far removed from the actual conditions of use or the needs of a building's users.

Trow also discusses the lack of good information on how buildings are used, of what works and what doesn't. He suggests, "Perhaps the most fruitful form of investigation could be simply looking at how people use space, successfully or unsuccessfully, through a kind of participant observation. This is very rare, in part because it does not look like work or science."

Several years before Trow wrote these words, I had undertaken just such a study of a highly acclaimed pinwheel of four high-rise dormitories a block from Berkeley's architecture school with my graduate seminar in environmental analysis. The monograph resulting from our work was published as *Dorms at Berkeley: An Environmental Analysis* (UC Center for Planning and Development Research, 1967). Our focus was on the actual behaviors and preferences of the silent partner in any design process—the user who has to live with untested design assumptions.

We were concerned with developing an approach to architectural programming that went beyond a specification of square footage requirements for various building uses. What we documented through deep participatory observation and interviews with dorm inhabitants was that the long-held assumptions of administrators and architects were inconsistent with the actual preferences and activities of student dorm living. Out of this first study and Trow's insights and advice, a new field was created, post-occupancy evaluation, and with it a new professional organization that is still active, the Environmental Design Research Association (www.edra.org), which includes both designers and social scientists. I consider Martin Trow one of its patron saints.

Ten years after his essay was first presented, I found myself appointed California state architect responsible for managing the state's design and construction program. My boss was Governor Jerry Brown, whose brilliant improvement to government by insiders was to appoint outsiders to run every major state agency. In my role as California state architect, I tried to include post-occupancy evaluation of each project we completed as part of the process. But it was not to be. My client agencies—the departments of corrections, general services, motor vehicles, parks—were afraid that if we found that facilities didn't work as they had intended, it would reflect negatively on the bureaucracy. At the same time, important post-evaluation studies of public housing by Professor Clare Cooper-Marcus at Berkeley and Oscar Newman's study of high-rise public housing projects, "Defensible Space," resulted in a major policy shift in federal housing and the dramatic dynamiting of the Pruitt-Igoe project in St. Louis and others.

Martin Trow was a sensitive observer of how spatial design and organization affected the quality and tone of education. Architects and administrators obsessed with the metrics of dollars and square feet seldom acknowledge that buildings and campuses are complex ecologies that are created with little or no scientific understanding of how humans and built environments interact. Indeed, the problem has grown worse over the decades as modernism—once a socially progressive movement in architecture—was replaced by new ideologies that focus on buildings as objects and artistic statements seemingly independent from their use.

Just as we have ignored our impact on the natural environment, we have ignored design's impact on humankind. Martin Trow was an early observer of both conditions and in celebrating his life and work, we can only hope that reason and humanism will re-enter the halls of academia and the hearts and minds of designers and their institutional clients.

—SIM VAN DER RYN

The Campus as a Context for Learning
Notes on Education and Architecture

When we look at the relationship between the character of learning that goes on within an institution and the nature of the physical forms in which it is housed, the questions arise: by what criteria can we assess the forms that we build and inhabit; how can we determine what is successful and what is unsuccessful; by what criteria should we condemn; by what criteria should we praise? The initial inclination is to say we must do this by reference to the ultimate ends of the institution, that we want to see whether the physical forms really are reflected in the outcomes that the institutions hope to effect. I think that this is not a useful line of inquiry, in part because the qualities of mind, the qualities of sensibility, the modes of thought and character, which are the ultimate ends of liberal education, are extremely difficult to measure. Moreover, they are deeply confounded with the results of the whole of the individual's life experience, and they are very long delayed in their appearance. Many of the things that happen in higher education

Adapted from a speech given at a Colloquium on Education and Architecture, Sarah Lawrence College, spring 1968.

create potentials within students that are not initially visible, but that make themselves visible when those people have certain kinds of experiences later in life and face certain challenges in their lives, and it is only then that those potentials are realized. This creates a considerable degree of uncertainty about the specific connection between the physical circumstances in which higher education is conducted and the ultimate outcomes with which it is concerned. If we cannot address ourselves to those outcomes, by what criteria can we begin to assess our environment and what criteria can we use to evaluate the circumstances in which we teach and learn? I think we have to turn to more proximate ends, to the kinds of activities and relationships which, while they bear some problematic relations to the ultimate outcomes of higher education, nevertheless have intrinsic worth and value in themselves. We have to look for kinds of relationships and activities in a college that we believe are desirable and whose development we hope its physical forms and spaces will enhance. Among these, I think, are what we might call micro-climates, milieus, stable configurations of people, of space, and of activities, which provide the conditions for the elaboration of values and interests, for the developer of a more intense consciousness on the part of the participants, a higher degree of self-awareness, as well as the acquisition of specific kinds of skills and knowledge. We want to create the conditions under which ideas and sensibilities are created, refined, and elaborated. This, it seems to me, is one of the central things we ought to look for. If the physical and social conditions in an institution do not permit the kinds of activities in which those processes are going forward, then I think we can say there's something very much amiss.

Let us look at some of these more specific, proximate ends in the institution. For example, we can see whether the institution provides possibilities for the spontaneous use of space, for people with interests that have not been preprogrammed, which are not routine or simply the elaboration of some pre-existing set of activities, but which have suddenly been created and which need a home. We want some space for spontaneous use. We want also to provide conditions under which students and teachers are able to make a connection between their study and their leisure, their work and their leisure. We have an intuitive feeling, and I think rightly, that a very sharp separation of these aspects of our lives is an impoverishment of both, and we're concerned whether space indeed insulates what is nominally called work from what is leisure. We want to provide space in which students and faculty can engage one another in other than the formal prescribed classroom situations. We want space that will be adaptable to a variety of student subcultures, to the variations among the students that are more obvious as the system of higher education grows and as its student body becomes more varied. We want all of those things and more, and we also want an environment that delights the eye.

Let me speak first about some of the pathologies of the planning and organization of space, particularly in large institutions. What I have to say I think is true for smaller institutions, but gross examples allow us to identify these pathologies more easily. In the big institutions, and not just the public ones, there is a very considerable division of labor in the organization of the physical development of the campus, a very considerable degree of remoteness of the decision-making process that goes on, for the most part, very far from the users. Indeed, it is not only that the process is very far from the users but it is enveloped in unbelievable clouds of obscurity; it is extremely difficult at the University of California, and at some other places I know, to discover how indeed decisions are made about where buildings should be, what functions they should nominally perform, what shapes and sizes they should have; a great many things about them are very difficult to discover. There's a sort of vague "offstage" that establishes certain conditions, understandings, and assumptions, the sources of which are very obscure, but which are very consequential. The consequence of this is that the planning of space and the use of space are separated geographically and socially by quite a lot of distance.

Also visible in these institutions is the enormous attractiveness of standardization. There are great rewards for planners of a certain kind to be able to set down certain formal regulations governing space use and to make these quite standard over very broad stretches of the institution— indeed, the whole of the institution that falls under some central governing body. The rewards of standardization are not only the relatively fewer people who have to be involved, but also the mechanical adaptability of these standardized forms to a wide range of circumstances, so that the whole thing can be done more "economically." Also, and I think at least as important, it solves the problems of legitimacy, it reduces the extent to which different parts of the institution can complain about preferential treatment of other parts of the institution. If all of the students in the university have the same number of square feet of bedroom space, the same number of square feet of lounge space, within very limits, then it is very easy to deal with the always dangerous charge of unfairness. And here the connection with the scope of the planning agency and the varieties of participants who have a legitimate claim to fair treatment is the central issue. The wider that scope the more attractive is a high measure of standardization.

There is also (I think somewhat greater in the public institutions) the pressure of some kind of logic of efficient space use, the necessity of planners to justify to public funding agencies the ways in which space is used, to meet some widely shared notions of what is right and proper. These are not academic notions, not even the planners' notions or the public institutions', but rather are the common wisdom of what is right, how much space a student should have in a dormitory. It is right for them to have a lounge, so students have to have a lounge. But do they need one on every floor, do they need libraries in their dormitories when thay have a big one in the central university block? And many such notions and assumptions, none of them very carefully thought out, are in large part based on legislators' own dim recollections of what it was like when they went to the university or their impressions of the institutions that their children go to. It is not altogether clear how these notions develop, but they are very important as a kind of coercive normative force on the planners who are very sensitive to the charge of wasting of public funds. So there is here an enormous pressure not to waste space, which is after all very, very expensive. This has a lot of consequences. I will take a not so trivial example: when you do not waste space, then you use it efficiently. Take a lecture room: you make sure that lecture room is used quite a lot of time during the day and increasingly during the summer. After a lecture is over, students often want to come up and ask the instructor something about the lecture and begin some discussion. But since another class is scheduled in that room for the next hour, they have to get out of the room. They cannot just stay there and chat for another fifteen or twenty minutes and scribble on the blackboard; they have to clear out. So they are cleared out into a corridor. There is not any obvious place for them to go; the corridors are full of people, streams move along and sweep away this little knot of students who have clustered around the faculty member. In a kind of graphic way they have disrupted a momentarily unique milieu in which some learning was going on, effectively broken it up in a very direct consequence of some conception of efficient space use.

There is also, as a consequence of the power of the canon of efficient space use, the notion that it is better to design space for multiple uses than for a special or unique use. We can see some of the consequences if I choose as an illustration a combination of what the British would call junior (or student) and senior (or faculty) common rooms. In many of the universities I know there are lounges in departmental areas but they are very rarely defined as exclusively for the use of the faculty. They are thrown open to faculty and students. Now if we look at that, it partly reflects the canon of efficient space use, and partly a specifically American cultural value, of togetherness, the uneasiness about excluding anybody from anything, particularily our uneasiness about status-linked privileges. Thus, we are uneasy about having rooms from which students are excluded in general and not just during a faculty meeting. There is, in addition, and related to this, a peculiarly American distrust of impermeable boundaries. There is a general feeling that there should be easy access to common, public places most of the time, unless there is a very strong justification for excluding people for a special purpose.

Now what are the consequences of a mixed student-faculty lounge? One consequence is that there is nowhere that faculty members can meet informally without prearrangement for the discussion of their mutual concerns, such as, for example, the discussion of individual students, or the recruitment and promotion of faculty members, or course requirements, and so forth. The absence of this kind of space means that faculty discussion tends to be confined to formal meetings or visits to one another's offices, kinds of connections that require motives or justification. The absence of a departmental faculty lounge simply means that the corporate business of the department gets far less discussion, consideration, and attention than it does where such a common room exists. In the absence of a customary forum for the informal and casual discussion of departmental business there is an attenuation of common concerns, which diminish toward the irreducible core of absolutely necessary collective decisions that can be reached in formal meetings.

The group of men and women who make up the department do not, under these circumstances, make up a continuing intellectual community; rather there is a marked privatization of intellectual life that then centers on the individual interests of each professor rather than on the common intellectual or administrative concerns. The chief common concern of the department is the curriculum and the students. The private individual interests of the academic men are commonly their own scholarship and their research, and exert a centrifugal force on a department. An interest in students and the curriculum is a centripetal force. The provision of a departmental faculty lounge is not the only factor that affects the communal life of a department, or the amount and quality of attention it devotes to the curriculum as over against research interests (there are other factors involved—the size of the department, the nature of faculty recruitment, the reward structure of the institution, faculty-student ratios, and other things). But the provision of space for casual, customary, recurrent meetings among faculty without prearrangement has a large independent effect on the vitality and strength of the common interest in students and teaching.

I have drawn this illustration from the life of an academic department, but the general principle holds throughout academic life. The question is: that provision is there for the housing of special intellectual interests, and for the protection of those interests against dilution and distraction? An intellectual milieu is created by a group of people who share specific intellectual interests, and who pursue or discuss them together recurrently in special places. It is in these milieus I believe that some of the most important work of a college or university goes on. It is there, through the common cultivation of shared interests, that occurs the heightening of sensibility and intensifying of consciousness, the emergence of new questions and perspectives, that underlie most contributions to knowledge and understanding. It is in such milieus, among people who do not have to define their terms or create a working vocabulary, who have come over time to share a body of assumptions and knowledge and skills, that ideas are created, developed, and elaborated. What is involved in an intellectual milieu is recurrent interaction around shared differentiated interests.

At the other extreme is the fleeting or non-recurrent interaction of people who do not share unique intellectual interests. Under these circumstances the content of interaction—what people actually say to one another—moves inexorably down toward the lowest common denominator of the popular culture or institutional gossip, or some other aspect of the world in which some broadly shared knowledge or interest can be assumed. In our society, this tends to mean sports or, in some groups, politics; or automobiles or pop music or movies; among middle-aged academics, their children's schooling or vacations past and future. A very large amount of that conversation is really what the anthropologists would call "phatic communion"—friendly noises that affirm a common humanity or a common membership in an instituion or an age grade. Now this is a very important function of communication, and social life would be a great deal grittier, perhaps downright impossible, without it. But it is not the *special* task of a college or a university to provide for that kind of interaction—nor does any special provision have to be made for it. Like a weed, it flourishes in the rockiest soil, in every uncultivated spot, in barbershops and in buses as well as in dormitories and in faculty clubs. The problem of physical planning in an academic setting is to provide places where interaction based on the lowest common denominator of interests doesn't overwhelm and disrupt conversation on the highest possible denominators of differentiated shared interests and knowledge. We have to plan so that the popular culture, whatever form it takes, is not the only basis for our interaction with one another.

That is not easy to do, for a number of reasons. On the whole, there is more generous provision for general purpose space—for instance, centrally located coffee shops and dining halls to which all are welcome—as compared with special purpose space—for example, a small lunch room or coffee shop for biochemists. But we know how differently those spaces are used, and what different relations they have to the intellectual life of the campus. Other things being equal, the more heterogeneous the purposes and interests of users of space, the lower will be the common denominator of the subjects of their conversations; the less differentiated, the more common.

How can a space on a campus be adapted for serious and sustained conversation, and protected against dilution and distraction? In a number of ways: first, through the formal assignment of space to people who share highly differentiated interests. Second, through their ability to achieve privacy in public places. Third, through their appropriation of waste space. Fourth, through the transformation of common space into private space, what we might call the informal ownership of turf. Let me try to suggest some examples of these.

Let us first turn to the space formally assigned to a group sharing special and differentiated interests. I have already pointed to one such example in the departmental faculty lounge. Another example is a seminar room assigned to the exclusive use of students and staff enrolled in an honors seminar in which are stored books and papers used by the seminar. Here we have an example of space that is not merely in the formal possession of a small defined body of people, at least temporarily, but is also assigned to them in connection with a specific intellectual function. But there is a tendency for people to elaborate the content of their interactions beyond the formal and assigned function; unless prevented, they do not confine their interactions to the content of the seminar. There are some things that encourage that elaboration: for example, the presence of a coffee pot, which immediately signals a relaxation or broadening of formal definitions of roles. The pot says that individuals legitimately using this space may relate to one another as persons or as students and not merely as members of a specific seminar. Unless prevented, people tend to broaden and elaborate their relations beyond the narrowest role definitions; pretty soon we begin to find in such spaces books and magazines that have no direct relation to the work of the seminar. Members of the seminar will be seen hanging around the place, and not only when they are working on seminar problems and materials. And all that can be encouraged, for example, by the provision of coffee and newspapers and magazines and easy chairs. And now it begins to look like a lounge—not a general purpose lounge, but rather one used almost exclusively by staff and students of the seminar who have some differentiated interest in common, and whose diffuse interaction is therefore likely to be serious, creative, differentiated, rather than on some lower common denominator. And when that happens, some very important kinds of liberal education are likely to be occurring in that space.

But if that kind of space, whose use is neither confined to the narrowest range of formal interaction nor given over to the broadest, most promiscuous relationships—space where interactions are at once differentiated and diffuse—if that kind of space use is so often and so clearly successful, in terms of liberal education, as I think it is, why is there not more of it? I think there are several reasons. First, it is an expensive use of space. Or at least it appears to be expensive, and it can rarely pass the criteria of efficient space use as applied by the offices that govern space allocation in most institutions. Second, it smacks of special privilege; apart from its cost, it seems just wrong, illegitimate, unfair for a small number of students to have private possession of a seminar room and a small library, especially if they begin to make it into a lounge. Students can and do take possession of space for such purposes, but in our society it is felt to be wrong to assign it to them formally, especially when everybody else cannot have the same privileges and amenities. Now some institutions are more relentlessly egalitarian than others; in some places, the combination of being seniors and being honors students is just enough distinction to justify the assignment of such a room in such a way. But even that is a luxury that cannot stand against a shortage of space— which is the chronic condition in growing institutions, and that means most American, and just about all public, colleges and universities.

Conceptions of efficiency and equality are usually adequate to ensure that that kind of space allocation is rare. In addition, it is just not common for the educational functions of that kind of space to be recognized by college authorities. It is recognized by the *users*, which accounts for why, when it happens, it is more often by expropriation than by formal assignment. But formal assignment of space is done by others elsewhere, usually by people who are neither students nor teachers, and for whom these functions have no reality in their own experience, and thus go unrecognized.

Moreover, space use of that fruitful and creative kind is highly vulnerable to disruption. The boundaries around the space and its functions are fragile. The function can be destroyed by dilution or by overload. A seminar room, for example, assigned to more than one class is no longer in any group's possession, and its use tends then to be confined to the formal interactions at the scheduled times; paradoxically, that same space tends to remain empty between the formally assigned class hours, since nobody has legitimate possession of it all the time.

I have been speaking of the formal assignment of space use on a round-the-clock basis to people with shared interests. The honors seminar room is an example; more commonly it is some extracurricular group that qualifies—the student or community newspaper or magazine, political groups or parties, and so forth. Anyone who has been a part of such a group knows how the group elaborates its use of its space—it is not confined to the nominal purposes of the group, but spills over into bull sessions or card games or a study hall. A good deal of living gets done in such spaces, and it is a question in each case, partly of fact and partly of one's own values, what contribution such living makes to the education of its members.

But what is done occasionally or rarely by formal assignment happens much more commonly by expropriation of what is nominally common space for exclusive use by one group. The members of the drama society somehow establish squatters' rights on the theater and backstage or rehearsal areas—and not just during production time. A group of senior chemistry majors appropriates part of a lab; they always seem to be there, cooking up coffee on the bunsen burners. A sociology class is doing a joint field project; they have a thin excuse for using the calculating machines and somehow the room that holds the desk calculators becomes a headquarters, but not just for the fieldwork. And so on. Nobody in the administration building knows about these things, nor do they care very much. In fact, nobody but the janitors really care, and the educational issue of who owns that space often comes down to the question of who is going to police the cigarette butts and coke bottles that suddenly begin to sprout at all hours, and when is that room or building going to be locked at night, and who has the key. Now all of this is very familiar and very innocent, except that the attention paid to it bears no relation to its importance for education. My impression is that these milieus, these tiny subcultures in which values and interests can develop in protective settings are more consequential for the intellectual and aesthetic life of a college than many of the formal curricula decisions, for example, about major requirements and pass-fail courses, on which so much faculty and administrative time is spent.

It is true that the kind of space-activity combinations I'm describing involve a measure of spontaneity and informality: they evolve around genuinely shared interests, and those interests cannot be called into being by authoritative decision. You cannot require drama majors to work on their papers in English Lit in the wings of the theater at 11:30 at night on Wednesdays and Fridays. But if the authorities cannot order up those occasions—in the way they can schedule classes, for example—they *can* make it easier or more difficult for space to be appropriated and used that way. It is clear, for example, that this kind of space use is easiest for groups that use labs or studios of some sort, and that means painters and sculptors and architects, as well as people in drama and dance, some natural scientists, some of the social scientists when they need room for experiments or headquarters for fieldwork. The essence of a studio or lab, as opposed to a classroom, is that its use tends to burst the academic timetable, the ordinary scheduling of different classes. People need* to work on their projects in those places not just during regularly scheduled hours, but at other times as well. Thus, work outside of class hours tends to be done in the same space rather than elsewhere, for example, in the dorm or library. And thus these people have a legitimate reason for being in their labs or studios at all hours of the day and night. One can always claim an extraordinary interest in a piece of work as the most legitimate reason for being anywhere in a college or university. Now this tendency for a project to be centered in the workplace provides the basis for an around-the-clock claim on some space. That interferes with the scheduling of other groups in the same space. And the moment that happens the people with a special interest in that kind of work start to make proprietary claims to part of that space as their turf. Ordinarily, these labs and studios also have to be used by other students and classes; they are, after all, common space, and the freshmen taking design I or introductory organic chemistry have to go somewhere. The compromise is usually a division of the lab or studio—part for the tourists who come and go, who take their courses but have their lives elsewhere, and part for the natives, the art majors or drama majors, the people whose college lives are beginning to center on one or another of these activities. And it is the intellectual and aesthetic life of the natives, of course, that I am really talking about; they are the people who are making the commitments to modes of thought and work, acquiring new kinds of seeing and feeling, who are entering apprenticeships, developing skills and perspectives through intense personal involvement, which I think is what liberal education is mostly about. The tourists in the introductory or survey courses are being shown, in a variety of ways, that things like that can happen, but it is not often happening to them.

*Or can make a plausible claim to need to be in those places, which comes to the same thing.

Now a central question is whether there is any space for the natives, or whether all the lab and studio space is in demand for the hordes of tourists. Really efficient space use will have classes scheduled for every lab and studio much of the time, and overload can destroy the possibilities for private turf. Natives have ways of protecting their turf against casual intrusion by tourists; people can be made to feel acutely uncomfortable in other people's places in ways that we all know very well, and those people tend not to come back. But the norms of informal space ownership cannot resist formally scheduled classes or sightseeing required of the tourists after hours. It is easy to prevent the creation of private turf, a good deal easier than it is to create the conditions for its coming into being.

But where it does come into being, its educational effects are dramatic. San Francisco State College has nearly 20,000 students, almost all of whom commute. The great majority come to campus only to attend class; many hold jobs off campus. The turnover rate is high; students drop in and out of college rather casually, accumulating credits toward a college degree over a period of six or seven, or eight or ten years, rather than the customary Eastern four. For most students the college is a facility, a useful one, for gaining skills and earning a degree, but not much more than that. One notable exception are the students in the visual arts, painting, and sculpture. They and their teachers comprise a genuine community of artists, based on their own building and in their own studios. The life of those departments elaborates itself beyond the confines of courses and credits into all sorts of communal activities, and into a lively connection with groups and movements in the surrounding area. Similarly, at Berkeley, students in the school of architecture have a relationship with their school, with their teachers, and with one another that is totally lacking in the huge, amorphous departments of the central liberal arts college of Letters and Science, whose people have no place. The life of such departments is in part a reflection of intensely shared interests, rarer among majors in the academic departments. But it also is bound up with *their* buildings, *their* space.

I have been speaking about space taken out of the common or public domain and appropriated by groups, centering on special interests and shared activities, but then becoming the locus for a more diffuse communal life that serves as a milieu for growth and differentiation. A special case of this kind of space is "waste" space, space that nobody much wants, that therefore is available for spontaneous activity, and that may or may not become informal turf. Swarthmore College, for example, abolished its sororities sometime in the late 1920s; the buildings that housed them, on campus and convenient to everything, somehow were never fully assigned a special function. They are just there, a series of small and medium-sized rooms, furnished rather shabbily, but comfortably, with big easy chairs and couches and writing tables, one with a big old grand piano, very much like a series of attached private houses, but all joined on the ground floor. Needless to say, those spaces are put to considerable use. A guest speaker can meet with twenty or twenty-five students who want to hear him; study dates meet in the next room; while a boy plays the piano and disturbs no one (with the doors closed) in the third. So far as I could see, no one owned that space; everyone used it. But there was no sense of overload; on my visit there were actually empty rooms where one could get away from people and just read or do nothing. This may strike you all as too commonplace to mention, except that for thousands of students in the residence halls at Berkeley there is simply no equivalent. They "own" part of their two-person bedrooms; and below are the huge and forbidding lounges with all the character of the main lounges in a Hilton Hotel; and below that in the basement a bare rec room which, in its brutal bareness, resembles nothing so much as a waiting room in a bus station.

The contrast in these resources of space is very great, and involves a number of elements that are cumulative in their effect. First, let us consider how very often people prefer old buildings to new ones; how often older, shabby, seedy rooms and buildings are successful in enhancing the activities that go on in them, as compared with the shiny new buildings that replace them. I raised this question with a friend of mine at Berkeley, an architect*; we asked ourselves what spaces we knew on campus seemed most successful in terms of the way people use them, or were most liked by their occupants. What we came up with were several kinds of old, small wooden structures. There was an old wooden Maybeck building that had housed the school of architecture or rather into which it had fitted like an old shoe; the set of old "temporary" wooden build-

*Sim van der Ryn

ings erected during World War II for the cadets and since used for a host of special purposes, buildings of no architectural distinction, but very useful indeed. And then there is the row of substantial former fraternity houses since taken over by a variety of research institutes and centers. The acid test was that every activity and function we knew of that had moved from a little old building to shiny quarters in a big new one had suffered or lost by the change. This I believe is not an expression of sentimental antiquarian prejudice, but a fairly objective assessment of real consequences. Take one example: for a while I was a member of a research center that was housed in a little old building. The center had to be taken down for a new big building and the research unit was moved to quarters in another new building. Immediately the character of the research unit changed: the boundaries surrounding the small community were breached, and its shared life broken and diluted. In the new building our offices housed not only our research work but *also* teaching, advising, and a lot of other things. There were many more people with whom we interacted about many more things, and the chronic fragmentation of life, the constant distractions that are the fate of students and faculty alike in these big universities, here had its inevitable effect on the research work of the center.

By some criteria, the new building into which we moved used space more efficiently. Our multipurpose offices and conference rooms could indeed contain the activities assigned to them, but what they could not do was effectively protect the delicate structure of privacies and consultations by which the research group carried on its work.

Continual distraction is a major and growing intellectual problem for faculty and students in large universities. I was talking with a professor of engineering at MIT in his office, and as he looked out the window toward where a big new university building was going up, he observed: "You see that . . . you know, that's going to be finished in a few months and it's going to be seventeen stories, and there are going to be a great many engineers and scientists on each floor . . . [and he paused for a second] . . . and they are all going to want to talk to *me*." He said this with something near to despair, because it wasn't at all a joke; indeed, most of the people in that new building would have some legitimate claim on his attention, and he had begun to anticipate what would happen to his life as a consequence of the sudden intrusion into it of a great many more relevant people. Now I do not know that any-body raised the question of how they could protect him and his work and his intellectual life when they began to build that building. I think the problem of academic distraction has a number of sources, including the persistence of certain older intellectual and academic norms—among them, that you do not say "no" to people who have a legitimate claim on your attention—into a period when the number of relevant people has increased by several orders of magnitude. But it makes the protection of privacy, for individuals and small groups, even more important in our big universities.

I want to close with this observation about the virtues of old build-ings. Old space is cheap space, and not ordinarily subjected to the same rigorous criteria of efficient space use as is new space. (Jane Jacobs made a very similar point about old buildings in the housing of artists in big cities.) Since old space is cheap, or seems to be, more of it can be assigned to a given activity, it is easier to gain full possession of it—it is less likely to be required to serve multiple uses. Thus the activities that go on in it are less likely to be diluted. Moreover, since the space is seen as worthless anyway, old buildings can be fairly cheaply remodeled—partitions can be moved and thus space can be more flexibly adapted to the activities it houses.

If we can identify the virtues of old space, why cannot those virtues in some way be designed into new space? I am not sure what the answer is, except that it does not happen very often.

In what ways can more knowledge be brought to bear on the ques-tions we are not talking about? It seems to me that there are two rel-atively common ways in which space planners attempt to collect infor-mation; in part, they consult with users and ask them to what use they are going to put the space. The users, so far as the design is concerned, are usually laymen; they have very narrow conceptions of what the pos-sibilities are, they have perhaps never really thought through what they do, they have misconceptions of themselves and stereotypes of how they spend their time. In the consultations that I have witnessed, in depart-ments that are so consulted, the members of the faculty are more con-cerned with making claims for a lot of space than for anything else. If they can just get more offices so they are not cramped for space, very often they are happy. But that is not an adequate basis of knowledge on which to plan such an environment. In addition, some planners are now beginning to send surveys around, particularly to students, asking them if they are happy. But the students have an even narrower range of alternatives that they are aware of; they suffer from what Karl Marx called the "damned wantlessness of the poor." In this case, the poor in experience are very rarely able to tell anybody what might be done. (They are often reasonably happy under circumstances in which they ought not to be happy, or at least they become more or less inured to conditions, and as reasonably flexible and adaptive people, they often can do no more than say, "Well, I am not really very happy.")

Perhaps the most fruitful form of investigation could be simply looking at how people use space, successfully or unsuccessfully, through a kind of participant observation. This is very rare, in part because it does not look like work or science. It requires that a grown person hang around a lounge, not doing useful things like collecting surveys and processing them, but just hanging around. And very few social scientists are secure enough to be able to do that. Nevertheless, I think that is the basis on which more insight or better knowledge about the relation of space and its use to learning might be gained.

To return to my initial theme, the fundamental significance of this topic is for the quality of life in our institutions. I think the central problem for American higher education is the preservation of certain elite qualities of life and experience under the conditions and provisions of mass higher education. There are very powerful forces that can depress the forms and conditions of mass higher education down to the bare bones that allow for the transmission of certain kinds of skill and knowledge. Such institutions need not have any regard for the kinds of milieus I have been talking about, but can concern themselves narrowly with whether people can be sheltered and whether spaces can be provided for them to be talked at under formal conditions. The question I have been raising is whether and how, through its use of its spaces and physical forms, a college or university can help create and protect milieus in which a humane, liberal education can be carried on. It is just possible that the slowup of the growth of higher education may free some energy, attention, and evaluation for that question.

9

HIGH ON THE LIST OF SUBJECTS so familiar to social scientists that they do not define them as research topics is the environment in which most of them spend their working lives—the academic department. In this slim essay, written to open a symposium in Gothenburg in 1975, Martin Trow starts by observing that this "central building block" of every university is both an administrative unit, performing functions with the resources assigned to it, and "an arm" of a specialized discipline, "an international fraternity of scholars who carry on a tradition of work in a defined area of inquiry." Departments emerged in the United States in the late nineteenth century, along with the expansion of both universities and disciplines, and their mixed parenthood creates "cross-pressures." Academic careers are made within an administrative unit, but they depend on reputation within a discipline.

The demands of their disciplines ensure departments almost complete autonomy from the university administration in what is "probably the most important single function" they perform: namely, the selection and socialization of their graduate students, "shaping and creating values and attitudes regarding what knowledge is and how best to pursue it." In Trow's view, this is also one of departments' "very few collective acts," since their members must together define "what constitutes 'competence' in the field, and how to train for it," though they may not always agree or perform these functions in the same way.

The slightly surprising turn in his analysis is that, despite their critical role in the transmission of disciplinary knowledge, he does not think departments are particularly "significant for the furtherance of its members' own research," nor even to the advance of knowledge in their discipline, since "any one department is unlikely to have more than one or two colleagues (and often none at all) who have any interest or expertise in a member's special area of research." Hence disciplinary communities are more likely to be found in ill-defined and self-created invisible colleges of "the handful of people around the world working in some sub-discipline or line of inquiry," or in interdisciplinary research centers.

By comparison with their graduate program, departments' undergraduate teaching must inevitably be, Trow suggests, a secondary function, and also one in which administrators are far more interested and involved. At the time he was writing many universities had created various structures and ad hoc interdisciplinary courses to provide the liberal education that they thought their departments were failing to provide. Trow judges most of them to be "short-lived failures." Students resisted their constraints, and professors had few incentives to participate and often failed to agree on their content. Moreover, their rigor was questionable, partly because "disciplinary courtesy" prompted teachers to move on "to another part of the intellectual forest," rather than press demanding questions about the assumptions or theories of another discipline.

Since Trow was writing from a research university, and moved within it from a department to a research center and on to a graduate school, he not surprisingly displays a greater sympathy for the disciplinary community than for the administrative unit. It recurs throughout his work. "Only the disciplines care," he says, "whether an assertion is empirically or logically true . . . Other approaches to issues, outside the constraints of a discipline, are more concerned whether a statement is plausible, interesting, or morally and politically virtuous (e.g., progressive)." Moreover, the natural process of change within disciplines, has, he thinks, been "very rapid and produced enormous changes in the map of the knowledge, often accompanied by equally large changes in the forms and contents of instruction." By contrast, externally induced, widely publicized innovations are often intended merely "to catch the eye of the public and politicians." He even raises the question whether the disciplinary communities might not themselves provide a satisfactory liberal education, since they invariably instill one cardinal moral imperative: the obligation to confront negative evidence.

We do not know how anyone at the symposium responded to

Trow's observations or to the other questions he raises: why, for instance, the members of relatively few departments make a disproportionate contribution to knowledge; how educational research can or should contribute to curricula innovations, especially in departments that have a strong claim to expertise and therefore to exclusive authority within own field; or to his closing remarks about the spontaneous and informal division of labor he thought emerged within departments. The only later study known to me to address some of the issues raised in this paper (Charles L. Bosk, *Forgive and Remember: Managing Medical Failure* [Chicago, 1979]) resoundingly corroborated Trow's view of the collective conscience surrounding the teaching of graduate students, combined with idiosyncratic interpretations of how it might best be transmitted. However, it says much for an essay intended to start a discussion in 1975, that it could serve equally well more than three decades later.

— MICHAEL BURRAGE

The American Academic Department as a Context for Learning

My subject is the American academic department as a context for teaching and learning. I will, for the most part, be describing the department in the basic arts, letters, and science disciplines in the large research universities, both public and private. The department has somewhat different characteristics in professional schools and four-year colleges, though the university academic department is a powerful model for both.

Adapted from Martin Trow, "The American Academic Department as a Context for Learning," *Studies in Higher Education* 1, no. 1 (1976): 11–22. Reprinted by permission of Taylor & Francis Group.

I

The department is the central building block—the molecule—of the American university. Indeed, it is not far wrong to think of the university as a kind of administrative arrangement for coordinating the activities and providing basic support services for fifty to one hundred relatively autonomous departments. That description was never wholly true, and is perhaps less so today than it was ten or twenty years ago: under the impact of zero or slow growth rates and tighter budgets, more authority is being drawn toward central university administration as it in turn is held more closely responsible to the public and private authorities that provide its basic support. Nevertheless, the university as a loosely coordinated aggregate of semiautonomous departments is one way of understanding that peculiar institution, far closer to the realities of academic life than the bureaucratic, hierarchical, quasi-industrial models held by so many politicians and servants in state and federal government.

The academic department is the central link between the university and the discipline, that is to say, between an organized body of learning—a body of knowledge and characteristic ways of extending knowledge—and the institution in which teaching and learning is carried on. It thus links an international fraternity of scholars who carry on a tradition of work in a defined area of inquiry to an institution that supports and houses the people who are actually engaged in transmitting and extending knowledge. In the United States, not quite all basic scientific and scholarly work is carried on in universities, but the map of learning would not be significantly different if the institutions outside of universities that support basic research did not exist.[1]

II

Departments are a relatively late development in American academic life. Their emergence in roughly their present form took place for the most part between 1890 and 1910. While there were units referred to as "departments" in some American "universities" in the early nineteenth century, the academic department as we know it arose with the emergence of graduate education and the research-oriented university in the latter three decades of the nineteenth century. Indeed, the link between the department and the university in American is very close: as one observer has observe, "During the 19th century, departmentalism was indeed a product of the same general movement toward academic reform that produced the university itself" (Storr, 1966).

> Although Cornell University and Johns Hopkins succeeded in establishing autonomous departments in the 1880's, the real solidification of the structure and the academic ranking system came in the 1890's. Harvard moved decidedly toward further departmentalization around 1891–92; Columbia was thoroughly departmentalized by the late 1890's, with Yale and Princeton close behind . . . the University of Chicago, in 1892–93, the first year of instruction, listed 26 [autonomous] departments . . . By the first decade of the twentieth century, the department, with all of its inherent strengths and weaknesses was firmly entrenched in the American university. (Dressel and Reichard, 1970)

The forces that gave rise to the academic department are in large part the same as those that sustain it today, in the face of great changes in the size and scope of higher education over the past seventy-five years and also of continuous and steadily growing criticism from academic theorists and reformers. The purely historical factor was the influence of the German university to which Americans had been going for advanced studies since the early decades of the nineteenth century. By 1914, some 10,000 Americans had studied for varying periods at German universities, and many on their return brought with them the ideas and ideals of the research-oriented university. What they helped create was a research-oriented American university and not a copy of the German university. Whereas in Germany the discipline was represented by the chair-holding professor and his Institute, in the United States a more democratic ethos, a wider variety of functions, and growing size led rather quickly to the appointment of more than one professor in the same field in the same university, and a regular graded set of salaried academic ranks that together comprised the academic career. Moreover, in the United States a full professorship became the normal expectation of every academic man or woman, as the terminal grade of the career. While not every instructor became a full professor, it was a sign of relative failure not to, rather than, as in England or on the Continent, a mark of singular success to gain that rank before retirement. For this and other cultural reasons the "professor" has never commanded the towering status of his European counterpart, either in the society at large or in the university itself. This has been a matter of considerable significance in the development of the department as well as in the professor's relations with his colleagues and his students.

But while the German model and its enormous success on the Continent provided the ideal, it was the development of knowledge on the one hand, and of American universities, on the other, that shaped the realities of the academic department. The growth of knowledge in the last half of the nineteenth century broke out of the boundaries of the old classical curriculum and led to a specialization in scholarship that disrupted the intellectual unity reflected in the broad "schools" (corresponding roughly to the "faculties" of European universities) of the first half of the nineteenth century. But specialization and the emergence of disciplinary boundaries reflected not only the growth of knowledge, but also the emergence of the research spirit, the belief in systematic and cumulative studies as the central method for extending knowledge.

The emergence of specialized disciplines coincided with the growth in the size of American universities. The two together changed the role of the university president: he could no longer define the curriculum in detail and hire all the staff. The department, then, was as much an organizational as an intellectual necessity, an efficient unit for making decisions about the curriculum, student careers, and the appointments and promotion of staff that could no longer be made effectively or credibly by university presidents.

Today, as in its origins, the department is an arm of a specialized discipline in a university, as well as the administrative unit that legitimately applies the resources given to it by the university to the variety of functions assigned to it, centrally those of teaching and research.

III

The Functions of the Department

Graduate education. The departments in most universities have almost complete autonomy over graduate education in their disciplines. The university may set limits, after discussion and negotiation, on the numbers of graduate students admitted, and also require that examining committees for the "orals" or qualifying examinations and the committee supervising the doctoral thesis include members of neighboring departments. But on the whole, the department determines the graduate curriculum, and recruits and admits students. It then inducts them into the discipline, transmitting skills and knowledge, and shaping and creating values and attitudes regarding what knowledge is and how best to pursue it. This component of graduate education, the socialization of graduate students into a structure of values, attitudes, and ways of thinking and feeling, is perhaps the most important single function that departments perform. The effects on students are often very strong, providing an individual with the perspective and orientations that guide a lifetime of academic teaching and research.

In the course of graduate education, departments also screen and assess students, first at the point of entry, and then periodically throughout the student's career, through grades in coursework, performance on various qualifying examinations, and finally and most important, through an assessment of the doctoral dissertation. Some students withdraw during the first year of their graduate work, others leave after gaining the master's degree, which is often awarded as a consolation prize for those unable for whatever reason to continue on to the doctorate. The MA may qualify students for teaching in secondary schools or community (two-year) colleges; in the sciences and social sciences, it may also equip students for applied research work outside the university. But for most university academic departments[2]; the focus of the graduate training is on the doctoral degree. The time it takes for a student to gain a degree varies greatly both between fields and among individuals in the same department. But the chief work of the university department is in the preparation of new recruits to the discipline, that is to say, the next generation of scholars and scientists, some of whom will be doing the research and scholarship that will advance knowledge in the field.

But while the basic forms and functions of graduate education are similar across a wide range of disciplines in the various universities, the actual processes of that education are enormously varied, between disciplines, between different departments in the same discipline, and even between sub-disciplines and individual teachers and students in the same department. The training of an historian, an anthropologist, and a chemist obviously involves quite different relations to the existing body of knowledge, to their fellow students, and between students and teachers. In the same subject, some departments (often the large departments in public universities) maintain a competitive environment for students, admitting more than will gain the degree, and accepting, even ensuring, high rates of attrition on the way to the doctorate. Other departments (usually smaller and in private universities) are more severely selective at entry and then sponsor students so that the most who are admitted are brought along to eventually gain the doctorate. While there are advantages and disadvantages to each of these departmental policies, they constitute very different contexts for learning. Similarly, some professors who supervise doctoral theses give their students close and detailed supervision, helping them to avoid serious errors in the course of their work; others are more distant and permissive, and allow students to make (and learn from) their errors, even at the cost of some of them failing to complete their dissertations. But the enormous variety in the actual processes of doctoral education is very little known or understood, even by academics themselves outside their own disciplines, and often not at all by the administrators, politicians, and civil servants who make policies affecting academic life. This deep knowledge of the intellectual, social, and psychological processes and relationships of graduate teaching and learning is not well known both because it is highly valuable and also because it is so highly esoteric. We each know something about our own variable relationships with our students; something less about how our colleagues relate to their students; much less about what goes on in neighboring disciplines; and little or nothing about practices in more distant subjects about which we have no technical or professional expertise. If that is true for practicing academics, it is even more so for people further removed from the actual processes of graduate education.

Graduate education involves two quite different components: the acquisition by students of competence in their subjects—the qualification to engage in high-level teaching and applied research; and the development of their capacity to do creative and original work on their own.

The cultivation of originality and creativity is quite obviously not susceptible to routine or standard procedures. It is only in part a function of the student's own talents and quality of mind. Beyond that, it seems to be elicited by both personal and working relationships with a creative and gifted teacher, who serves in part as a model. But in addition, the crucial factor in the creativity of students is their belief that they can in fact do significant and original work, that they can actually have ideas and not merely rearrange and apply the ideas of others. The encouragement and approval of a distinguished professor seems to be of great importance to the emergence of this kind of confidence and intellectual boldness.

It has been observed that the relatively small number of academics who make large and significant contributions to their disciplines are products disproportionately of a very small number of leading graduate departments. This may be the result of a number of factors that are very hard to disentangle empirically: it may be that the best minds apply to and are accepted by the leading departments; that those departments give their students a superior training and education in their disciplines; that those departments are able to place their better students on the teaching staffs of their own and other leading departments in their disciplines, and that this in turn gives them access to better students, more stimulating colleagues, larger resources (libraries, laboratories, lighter teaching loads, etc.); and that the prestige associated with gaining a degree at a leading department and then teaching in one together gives an individual access to research opportunities that in turn allow him or her to make important contributions to the discipline. Part of this network of mutually reinforcing and favorable conditions is the heightened self-confidence that comes to the student from association with and approbation of leading figures in the field. Merely listing the conditions that affect the emergence of creativity in academic scholars and scientists suggests the complex interweaving of intellectual, emotional, and institutional functions performed by graduate departments. They select, train, socialize students; certify them to others and confer state on them; and thus affect their intellectual and academic life chances in a multitude of ways.

The education of graduate students for creative and original work is very closely linked to the student's own embryonic scholarship and research, often through an apprenticeship to the scholarship and research of his thesis advisor or some other faculty member with whom he works closely. The training for competence in the discipline is more commonly the collective work of the department as a whole, or of a significant sub-discipline within it. Indeed, the definition of what constitutes competence in the field, and how to train for it, is one of the very few collective acts of the department. Normally, the department collectively[3] arrives at a rough consensus regarding what constitutes competence in their discipline, and shapes a graduate curriculum of courses and examinations designed to ensure that such competence is acquired and demonstrated. But as disciplines develop and change, and generate sub-disciplines and new problems and links to other fields, even this concept of competence may not be shared consensually. Where dissensus among the departmental staff on the nature of competence in the field is wide and deep, it may no longer be possible to create a common curriculum for the first year or two of graduate work, and different students may move through the same department with quite different kinds of education, both in the skills acquired and in their basic perspectives about the nature of the discipline. This situation, which seems to be increasingly common in recent years—more in the social than in the natural sciences, more in sociology than in economics, for example—creates a special problem for the individual student and for the discipline. Among other things, it threatens the department's claim to a monopoly of expertise in the subject that is the ultimate basis of both its authority and its claim on the resources of the university and the society.

Recruitment and promotion of academic staff. The department is the locus of the academic career. In the leading universities it is the department that initiates the appointment of new members to the staff and that then recommends them for promotion to higher rank. The department may have to gain the approval of its recommendations from academics in other departments and from academic administrators. But without the recommendation of his departmental colleagues, and especially of his senior colleagues, an individual will not be given the initial appointment or subsequent promotion. Nevertheless, the department is not as decisive for the career of a scholar or scientist who has the doctorate as it is for the career of a graduate student, since appointments and promotions are, in the best universities, in large part merely reflecting and ratifying the status that the scholar or scientist has achieved in the broader discipline through his or her published work. This implies that promotions are based largely on an individual's reputation or standing in the field, that is, based almost exclusively on published work, and so it is. While teaching performance is, or at least is supposed to be, "taken into account" in recommending individuals for promotion, in fact the departments are judged within their disciplines largely on the national and international reputations of their members. The university, and those academic administrators who represent its broader interests, are under cross-pressures: on the one hand, they have a responsibility to the undergraduates to maintain standards of teaching as well as of scholarship; on the other hand, they are sensitive to the status and reputation of the university in the broader academic community, and *that* in turn is largely determined by the aggregate standing of its academic department—that is, the quality and quantity of their published research.

The university department selects for and rewards research productivity in its staff members, and thereby strongly influences how academic men and women spend their time and energies. This serves the collective status of the department, which is roughly the aggregate of the academic statuses of its members, and it serves the academic status of the university, which is roughly the aggregate of the academic statuses of its departments. But at the same time, it is educating and socializing its members, and especially its junior members, completing and reinforcing the socialization to the discipline that had begun in their graduate training or earlier. This function, of developing the appropriate habits of mind and work in what are now fully independent scholars and scientists (as they are even as junior members of the departments), is only visible when it is performed badly, as it has been in recent years in some rather demoralizing departments whose members no longer share a common sense of the nature of their discipline or of the scholar's craft and calling.

Research. Graduate university departments are commonly seen as existing largely to further the creation of knowledge through scholarship and research. And so in a way they do. But ironically, the department *qua* department is less significant for the furtherance of its members' research than it is as a center of graduate training and the academic career. And that is because science and scholarship are so highly specialized that an individual is unlikely to have more than one or two colleagues in his own department (and often none at all) who have any interest in or expert knowledge about his or her special area of research. The true research communities are the "invisible colleges"—the handful of people around the world working in some sub-discipline or line of inquiry. Moreover, the physical home and source of research support within the university (at least for natural and social scientists, though less so for humanistic scholars) is likely to be an interdisciplinary research center or institute. These institutes, unlike the institute in the traditional German university, are not the lengthened shadow of a single chairholder, but rather are administrative units that exist to further the research work of a group of scientists, both senior and junior, drawn usually from a number of related academic departments. (Examples, though they will have different names in different universities, would be an institute for international studies, a center for the study of law and society, a center for research in higher education, a high-energy radiation laboratory, an institute for the study of personality, and so forth.) Full membership in such institutes ordinarily requires that the person have full membership in an academic department, though these centers also usually have other full-time professional research staff, who may also play a role in the teaching and graduate programs of the academic departments. But the *department's* direct contribution to the research work of its members is, except in the humanities, likely to be less significant than the external support that an individual can gain from government agencies or private foundations, research that is then administered and housed in the university's research institutes and centers. The department is not insignificant in that it provides the scholar/scientist with a basic salary, time for research, and perhaps modest research funds allocated to the department by the university itself.

The growth of federal funds for research after World War II, and the way those funds were granted and administered, greatly strengthened the autonomy of the department vis à vis the university, and of the individual scientist vis à vis his department. In addition, the rapid growth of enrollments in higher education, and the resulting sharp competition for able or even competent scholars and scientists, also greatly strengthened the individual professor in relation to his department. External research support has leveled off, but remains an important factor in the autonomy of departments and scientists, especially in the natural sciences. But the slowing of growth has sharply reduced the demand for academics, and thus their bargaining power within their own institutions. This in turn strengthens the hand of both the institution and the department in relation to the individual scholar or scientist. With few exceptions, he can no longer threaten so credibly to leave the institution if his demands for salary, teaching load, research support, and the like are not met.

Parenthetically, the reduced demand for academics reduces the mobility of academics between institutions. Less mobility between institutions encourages the development of more stable relationships within departments, both among colleagues and between teachers and students. That, in turn may, on the whole, be very good for the department as context for learning.

Undergraduate education. Up to this point, little has been said about the role of the department in undergraduate education. And that of course is the major charge that its critics lay against the department: that because of its emphasis on specialized research and the doctoral degree, the department is not able to develop or usefully contribute to a nonspecialized liberal education. Liberal education, as some perceive it, aims to free students from the narrow prejudices and assumptions of region, class, and ethnic group, by extending their understanding of the human condition and their range of sympathies through an exposure to literature, poetry, philosophy, mathematics, the sciences, and social sciences. Such an education aims to refine sensibilities and strengthen the capacities for making independent and informed judgments in art, in science, and in life. But, so this argument goes, this kind of education requires that teachers seek and communicate the underlying connections among the various facets of life with which the separate disciplines deal. It is not advanced, so the argument goes, by undergraduate courses that are narrowly constrained within the boundaries of a discipline, and focus on a watered-down elementary treatment of a discipline's own stock of certified and current research problems. It is perfectly clear that many problems do not present themselves in the convenient categories of the academic disciplines, that many of the most important questions about man and society transcend the disciplinary boundaries. The natural response to this is to argue against the department as the unit of organization of undergraduate education, and to make attempts to organize interdisciplinary studies that are more appropriate in their range of perspectives and intellectual resources to the questions that students and society ask of them.

There is considerable substance to these charges. The university department may well not be the best unit for providing a liberal and unspecialized education. It recruits research-oriented specialists and rewards their specialized research. Much of the energies of its members go into research and into their graduate program; a very large part of the actual instruction of undergraduates, especially in the big public universities, is carried by graduate teaching assistants who teach the small lab and lecture sections. Insofar as the department has an interest in undergraduate education, much of that goes into its program of courses for its undergraduate majors who are specializing in the subject in their latter two undergraduate years. And since the number of undergraduate majors often has a bearing on the size of the department's budget, departments commonly have an interest in retaining their own majors: interdisciplinary majors may be seen as competitive for students and for related resources.

At their very best, a carefully thought-out program of interdisciplinary studies, involving senior professors possessing great breadth of learning across disciplinary lines, is arguably the best introduction to higher learning that able and motivated undergraduates can experience. Certainly the programs of general and interdisciplinary studies that were developed, in their several ways, at Harvard, Chicago, and Columbia after World War II, were models of what undergraduate education in great research universities might be. But it is wrong and misleading to compare the rare best forms of interdisciplinary studies with the average coursework offered by departments. And even those exemplary models at Harvard, Columbia, and Chicago no longer exist, at least in their early forms. Such broad programs, as over against ad hoc interdisciplinary courses involving instructors from two or three neighboring departments, involve a measure of contraint on the student's freedom to study what he likes. Students increasingly resist such constraints. This resistance has led to the dismantling of the far less coherent or integrated "breadth and depth" requirements, which were an effort by the university to require students to be exposed to a variety of subjects, and to find the links and connections among them themselves. These requirements were thus a kind of "half-way house" between coherent interdisciplinary programs and the system, now most common, which consists of little or no structure of studies in the first two years, and a departmental major in the last two undergraduate years.

Moreover, interdisciplinary programs require a large measure of consensus regarding what knowledge is of most worth, and such consensus is increasingly hard—in most cases, I believe, quite impossible—for a university academic staff to achieve.[4] In addition, such a program makes very large demands on the time and energies of its staff, time and energy necessarily taken from their own research, their work with graduate students and their more advanced undergraduate majors. Moreover, the academic reward system is still keyed to a professor's published work; for a variety of reasons, it is difficult for a university to assess and reward teaching ability, though it may generate much rhetoric in that direction. Perhaps most important, the qualities of mind and breadth of learning and perspective that make a really strong interdisciplinary program are very rare. Very few academics, even those who have achieved high distinction in their own field, have the intellectual qualities that make for first-rate interdisciplinary teachers. When courses and programs are created in the face of these difficulties, they are very often short-lived failures; a genuine integration of perspective and knowledge around a problem or issue is rarely achieved, and such courses often descend to a lowest common denominator of relatively uninformed discussion among teachers and students, none of whom has a solid mastery of the topic or its problems. As one scholar with experience has observed: "Interdisciplinary programs are devices for bringing creative people together and arranging for them to be less creative," at least in the short run. There is a measure of truth in that gloomy observation.

Moreover, there may be a considerable price that we pay for interdisciplinary studies, to the extent that we substitute a richer but less systematic discussion of issues for a narrower but more systematic one. I mean by "systematic" here the impersonal pressures that a discipline exerts on those who work within its boundaries, pressures to formulate problems in ways that can be addressed by evidence. Disciplines embody a variety of controls over the influence of personal bias, and not least among these are the procedures that force a confrontation with negative evidence. Interdisciplinary studies may bring a rich variety of perspectives to bear on an issue, but my impression is that when difficult problems arise, the tendency of such courses is to look at the matter from yet another perspective rather than confront the difficulty head on. There is also at work the well-known but little documented phenomenon of "disciplinary courtesy": we are not inclined to challenge the professional judgment or competence of colleagues in other disciplines. We are disinclined both by the norm of professional courtesy and by our own lack of specialized expertise in other fields to go behind the assertions of other disciplines to the structure of concepts and data on which they are, sometimes precariously, based.

It is perhaps not widely enough recognized that academic disciplines, and the departments that embody them in universities, constitute a kind of moral community, centering on the powerful norms implicit in the canons of verification, and in our scholarly and scientific methods and procedures. This is perhaps most clear in our commitment to the search for negative evidence. For Max Weber this is the central moral role of education. In his great essay "Science as Vocation," he asserts that

> The primary task of the useful teacher is to teach his students to recognize "inconvenient" facts—I mean facts that are inconvenient for their party opinions. And for every party opinion there are facts that are extremely inconvenient, for my own opinion no less than for others. I believe the teacher accomplishes more than a mere intellectual task if he compels his audience to accustom itself to the existence of such facts. I would be so immodest as even to apply the expression "moral achievement," though perhaps this may sound too grandiose for something that should go without saying.

The academic disciplines embody, in their methods of work, procedures designed to force their practioners to confront inconvenient facts. Indeed, it may be said that only the disciplines care whether an assertion is empirically or logically true, and are concerned with the evidence on which it is based. Other approaches to issues, outside the constraints of a discipline, are more concerned whether a statement is plausible or interesting or morally or politically virtuous (e.g., "progressive"). It might be argued that universities, perhaps alone among social institutions, should ground their central functions of teaching and learning in the issues of truth, falsity, and the quality of evidence. (Of course, the nature of truth and its relation to evidence will differ in different disciplines, but it is a central issue in each.) It is not an accident that in those courses furthest removed from the restraints of the academic disciplines, we are most likely to see academic work highly politicized. And indeed, those who wish to politicize higher education are very often most hostile to the autonomous norms and values of the academic disciplines, and for good reason.

To what extent are undergraduate students drawn into the "moral communities" of science and scholarship, to what extent do they acquire the norms and values of the disciplines as well as their knowledge and perspectives? That is, of course, highly variable. It has, traditionally, been a central concern of graduate education—and if graduate students in the department are not, for some reason, being socialized into the moral community—if, for example, they pursue graduate studies as a continuation of their liberal education, or use their graduate study for political or other ends of their own without accepting the special research norms of science and scholarship—then departments, and perhaps the disciplines, are in some difficulty. The acquisition of these scholarly and scientific norms—in other words, the values of the discipline as a research enterprise—has not been stressed for undergraduates; it has been seen often as a symptom of premature professionalization or specialization. But increasingly colleges and universities are beginning to offer freshmen research seminars to introduce beginning students to the discipline as a community of seekers for knowledge. And that, inevitably, must bring them at least to the borders of the discipline as a moral community. How successfully that is accomplished with undergraduates, is, as I have said, variable and uncertain.

We should also ask whether early introduction to the norms and values of research in a discipline need be at the expense of a liberal education, a broad exposure to a variety of ways of looking at the worlds of man and nature, each with its own, somewhat different, moral lessons to teach. In the design of an undergraduate education, there are certain conflicts between the moral community of inquiry and the moral content of the major fields of learning—between, for example, what anthropology can teach about the human condition as over against how it goes about finding things out. Departments typically try to teach a little of both, the latter often under the rubric "methods." But while "methods" courses may tell students that there is a moral community of inquiry, it is likely that only the experience of seeking knowledge themselves through the discipline's own methods of inquiry will effectively bring students inside it.

All of this is not intended as a general attack on interdisciplinary studies, of which I am a warm if somewhat qualified admirer. But I want only to suggest that the price we pay for their breadth of perspective may lie in the moral education of our students, at least that part of their moral education that arises out of a sense of the importance of intellectual difficulties, and a personal commitment to confront them rather than evade them by dropping the question and shifting the perspective to another part of the intellectual forest. The policy implication may be that interdisciplinary studies are not inherently preferable to a program of coordinated studies within departments, but need to be examined in every case on their own merits. In addition, we might pay more attention to the methodology of interdisciplinary courses, and try to find ways of requiring ourselves to confront unwarranted assumptions and inadequate theories, and to ask at strategic moments for the evidence behind assertions in other people's disciplines.

IV

On "Change" versus Change

It may be useful to distinguish two quite different kinds of interdisciplinary studies: those that are introduced purposefully as an academic reform, and those that arise naturally out of intrinsic developments in the map of knowledge. The former reflect an ideological commitment to educational change for its own sake; they are often in part a response to vague but powerful pressures from the state or society that the university adapt itself to the new conditions of society, that it be more relevant to social problems and to the interests of a new mass student body. Such reforms are ordinarily well publicized, in keeping with their public relations function of persuading outsiders that the university really is progressive and responsive to social change. By contrast, the changes that arise out of the inner life of a discipline ordinarily go unnoticed beyond the boundaries of the department; they are not even perceived as change or reform in higher education. While the university is widely attacked as conservative, resistant to change, deeply committed to traditional forms and practices, at the same time we have seen an enormous explosion of knowledge in all areas of scholarly and scientific life over the past several decades. In every area and subject I know, there have been enormous changes in the map of knowledge since World War II, changes that have often been accompanied by equally large changes in the forms and contents of instruction. At the same time, new disciplines and sub-disciplines have emerged, sometimes, as with computer science and psycholinguistics, pressing for institutionalization as new academic departments. Here, in the private life of higher education, there is constant ferment and change but little publicity. It is the widely heralded, often short-lived academic innovations—instructional programs keyed to measures of competency or to contracts between students and teachers; the abolition of grading; academic credit for community participation; courses offered through videotape or remote computer consoles; and colleges oriented around relevant topics—that catch the eye of the public and politicians, and become the basis of the university's claim that it is not as conservative as charged.

As we observe the fashionable pursuit of educational innovations, innovations that are frequently accompanied by attacks on the narrow, ossified, specialized disciplines, we might reflect on the extent to which the disciplines, by providing us with external criteria and the machinery for forcing us to confront negative evidence, serve the moral growth of students and teachers as much as they do the growth of knowledge. We all are, for the most part, extremely indulgent to our own pieties. We need the help both of critical colleagues who are competent in our fields and of impersonal rules of inquiry to prevent us from acquiring followers rather than teaching students. Whatever their shortcomings, most discipline-based departments supply both; some other ways of organizing instruction do not. That fact, and not necessarily blind stubbornness, may at least partly account for the survival of the academic department under conditions of rapid change and in the face of widespread criticism.

Departments and Academic R&D

Departments, as we know, are often not hospitable to academic innovations generated outside their boundaries. They often take a jaundiced view of educational research and development, of experimentation, and reform. There are a number of reasons for this suspicion, and even hostility, on the part of academics toward academic R&D.

Disciplines, and the departments that represent them in the university, claim to possess a monopoly of expertise in a given area of scholarship or science. Research by outsiders on academic programs and on pedagogy in higher education, that is to say, on the form and content of instruction, is seen as a challenge to this expertise, a claim that others can know how knowledge in their field should be pursued and transmitted. This is not a trivial matter. The claim to expertise is the basis of the department's authority over everything that is important to it: the direction of its research; its selection, training, and certification of graduate students; its appointment and promotion of its own members. Indeed, the autonomy of the university is based to a very large extent on the aggregate claims to special expertise on the part of its departments. It is not surprising that externally generated academic innovations are more common where the claim to special expertise, and thus the autonomy, of academic departments is weakest—that is to say, in weaker departments and institutions.

This suspicion of outside intervention can be seen as merely a defense by the department of its power over its own affairs. It is more rarely mentioned that ultimately power rests on successful claims by the department to a special authority in its area of work. Where that claim is weakened—either by the weakness of the department, by changes in the map of learning, or by attacks on the legitimacy of academic authority based on political or social grounds—the department is less able to resist academic innovations. Thus, I am suggesting that innovations in the organization and forms of instruction are linked to successful attacks on academic authority. Political change and academic reform are indeed closely linked, as both political and academic reformers know.

It would seem that undergraduate teaching is more often the target of academic reform than is graduate education or the organization of research. This is partly because the department's claim to expertise in undergraduate education is not as clear as it is in graduate education and research. In addition, undergraduate teaching is often a prey to boredom, the result of the repetition of relatively elementary facts or principles by teachers whose interests lie elsewhere. Academic innovations, almost regardless of their character, promise to break the crust of boredom and routine and allow the teacher a fresh perspective on familiar materials and modes of presentation.

Graduate education and research are not inherently afflicted by boredom since they are linked to the incessant changes in knowledge arising out of scholarship and research. They thus do not need curricular innovations as an act of will, but can allow them to arise from changes in the subject itself.

Academics may also resist academic reforms in order to preserve an environment favorable to the pursuit of knowledge. Intellectual boldness and creativity require, I believe, a relatively stable and orderly institutional environment. The enormous efforts devoted to creating new forms of academic governance in French, German, and Dutch universities, for example, drain off the time and energies of teachers and students as well as destroy the delicate personal relationships that teaching and research of the highest quality require. It is an hypothesis worthy of test that research, scholarship, and teaching of the highest quality are likely to be carried on in a stable environment, or by people who have managed to insulate themselves from the noise and turmoil of university politics and academic reform.

Academic Division of Labor

My emphasis on the dominant norms and functions of university academic departments simplifies and distorts reality by implying that all the members of a department are oriented primarily to graduate teaching and to research and fill their departmental functions in similar ways. In fact, there is a very considerable division of academic labor, both within and between departments. But this arises *informally*, and not through a formal assignment of roles and functions to different departmental members. Thus, the formal characteristics (and the equality) of departments and their members is preserved, while a considerable variability in individual talent, preference, and disposition allows people to actually distribute their time and energy very differently among the various functions of the department: graduate and undergraduate teaching, research, university administration, consulting, and public service.

In every department some members are much more deeply interested and involved in the undergraduate program than the average departmental member. Such people must have done enough research to have gained a tenured appointment in the university (or if untenured they risk not gaining such an appointment), and they may continue to write and publish. But informally they come to be seen as especially interested in the undergraduates and over time come to play a disproportionate role in that part of the department functions. Some of these more teaching-oriented academics are senior professors (especially in the natural sciences) who are no longer working at the research frontier of their disciplines; others, younger men and women, may be temperamentally drawn to the undergraduates, and may accept the somewhat slower rates of promotion that accompany a lower level of research productivity.

Moreover, some departments in the university—for example, English and mathematics—play a larger role in undergraduate education than do others, and therefore place a somewhat higher value on teaching-oriented professors. It should, however, be emphasized that the division of labor within departments is not absolute, sharp, or formalized: almost no academics in American university departments do nothing but teach nor do any do nothing but research. Similarly, there is no sharp division of labor between departments in the university. This prevents the emergence of formal classes of academics, and avoids the dangers of a two-class system of teaching and research professors.

NOTES

....

1. A variety of public and private agencies carry on basic research outside the boundaries of universities: for example, the Museum of Natural History, the Library of Congress, the RAND Corporation, the National Bureau of Standards, and Bell Labs all support basic research in a variety of subjects. But the *disciplines* from

which they draw and to which they contribute are firmly rooted in universities and in their academic departments.

2. Professional schools other than law or medicine may place equal or greater weight on their master's degree, which is usually a more rigorous degree than offered in the academic departments, and is the basic academic qualification for practitioners in the field.

3. It is an empirical question how "normal" this is. How common it is for a department to be in substantial agreement about the nature of the field and about the graduate curriculum (the two are surely closely linked)? What are the sources of dissensus and what are its consequences for the academic careers and scholarly contributions of its graduate students? These are questions about which we need much more research. A further question calling for study is how departments arrive at such a concensus and how it is then institutionalized in the graduate curriculum.

4. It is hard enough to gain a concensus on an undergraduate curriculum *within* a department, almost impossible across departments.

REFERENCES

Ben-David, Joseph. *American Higher Education: Directions Old and New.* New York: McGraw-Hill, 1972.

Blau, Peter M. *The Organization of Academic Work.* New York: John Wiley and Sons, 1973.

Brubacher, John Selier, and Willis Rudy. *Higher Education in Transition: An American History, 1636–1968.* New York: Harper, 1968.

Corson, J. R. *The Governance of Colleges and Universities.* New York: McGraw-Hill, 1960.

Dressel, Paul L., F. C. Johnson, P. M. Marcer. *The Confidence Crisis: An Analysis of University Departments.* San Francisco: Jossey-Bass, 1970.

Dressel, Paul L., and Donald J. Reichard. "The University Department: Retrospect and Prospect." *Journal of Higher Education* 41, no. 5 (May 1970): 387–402.

Jencks, Christopher, and David Riesman. *The Academic Revolution.* Garden City, N.Y.: Doubleday, 1968.

Hawkins, Hugh. *A History of Johns Hopkins University (1874–1889).* Ithaca, N.Y.: Cornell University Press, 1960.

Hofstadter, Richard, and W. P. Metzger. *The Development of Academic Freedom in the Universities.* New York: Columbia University Press, 1955.

Rudolph, Frederick. *The American College and University.* New York: Knopf, 1962.

Stewart, Campbell. "The Place of Higher Education in a Changing Society." In *The American College*, edited by Nevitt Sanford. New York: Wiley, 1962.

Storr, Richard J. *Harper's University: The Beginnings: A History of the University of Chicago*. Chicago: University of Chicago Press, 1966.

Trow, Martin, ed. *Teachers and Students*. New York: McGraw-Hill, 1975.

Veysey, Laurence R. *The Emergence of the American University*. Chicago: University of Chicago Press, 1965.

10

MARTIN TROW AND HIS WIFE KATHERINE spent the academic year 1976–77 in Princeton. He was an academic visitor, one of some 150 invited each year, at the Institute for Advanced Study. They resided, along with the other visitors, in the Institute's residential area, known informally as "the compound." Like every year in life, this one had its ups and downs, but on the whole Trow's experience was not quite as rewarding, either intellectually or personally, as he had hoped. To come to terms sensibly with this reaction, he composed the essay "Guests without hosts."

He never published the essay, no doubt for reasons of diplomacy, because the essay is largely negative in tone. But I opted for its inclusion in this volume because it is a brilliant piece of social science analysis. In my remarks I will reflect on the essay. I suppose I am the right one to do this, because between 1994 and 2001 I directed a sister institute, the Center for Advanced Study in the Behavioral Sciences at Stanford. The officers of six such institutes— including mine and Princeton's—met annually. Accordingly, I possess some direct knowledge of the kind of setting that Trow was addressing.

His essay does not call for summarizing, because two of its virtues are clarity and organization. I only list the categories he invoked to account for what he experienced as a somewhat intellectually isolating and depersonalizing experience:

- Stratification. The Princeton Institute has a permanent faculty (and other categories) along with visitors. This contrasts with similar institutes, which have an administration and one class of visitors. Also, at Princeton the mathematicians and physicists regarded themselves as elites in relation to the "softer" social scientists and historians.

343

- Demography. Since there were very few "hosts"—that is, permanent faculty—in relation to many visitors, the former could not possibly invest time and attention to welcoming the latter.

- Cultural. The values of individualism and elitism, extreme at the Institute, made for little involvement with others and a fierce, largely negative culture in which scholars demonstrated their excellence and specialness by savaging others.

- Psychological. Affection for others was discouraged by the fact that visitors are transient and that emotional investment invites pain when they depart. He also mentioned the downplaying of feelings in general—except, perhaps, hostility—as part of the Institute's preferred psychological culture.

- Authority. He referred only briefly to authority, noting that it was weak and incapable of adjudicating conflicts. It might be added that the Institute was experiencing a leadership crisis at the time, and the director left his position the following year.

Trow had spent an earlier year at the Stanford Center. While noting that the two institutions had many similarities, such as little shared work, minimal formal collective life, and residential transience, he zeroed in on status differences as critical:

> the [Stanford] Center has no permanent members. This has a number of consequences, one of which can be captured in the phrase: no hosts, no guests . . . the existence of permanent members of the Institute makes them willy-nilly "hosts" while the visitors are the guests. At the Center the fellows are not guests, they *are* the Center and create whatever life it has anew every year.

This observation raises the most interesting analytic question in the essay. Evidently, the Princeton Institute's isolating culture is the result not of one factor but a combination of converging circumstances. At the same time the Institute shares some of these characteristics with other academic organizations, both sister institutes and academic departments and research units. Universities are noted for their stratified ranks and titles. As a rule collective life is minimal in academic life, despite official homage paid to the collegiality principle. Most academic units, especially at elite institutions, are populated by competitive people, and strike some balance between savagery and blandness in their respective cultures.

What, then, is the most decisive factor among all these? Taking the Stanford Center as comparison point, I would follow Trow's lead and mention several kinds of *hierarchy:*

- Only the Princeton Institute has such a deeply embedded distinction as that between permanent faculty and visitors. Early in its history the Center opted for one class of fellows, none with rank, status, or seniority.

- The Princeton Institute has a clear status system based on discipline; the Center, dominated by the social and behavioral sciences, minimizes such inequalities and comparisons.

- With respect to things that academics fight over—rank, promotion, curricula, appointments, and real and symbolic perquisites such as parking—the Center scrupulously arranges these in advance—thus minimizing competition on the scene during the residential year.

In my estimation, these are the main factors that make for the *communitas* and nostalgia that characterize most residential institutes and that Martin Trow missed at Princeton's.

—NEIL J. SMELSER

Guests without Hosts

Notes on the Institute for Advanced Study

Early in April of 1958, my wife and I arrived . . . in a Balinese village we intended, as anthropologists, to study. A small place . . . and relatively remote, it was its own world. We were intruders, professional ones, and the villagers dealt with us as Balinese seem always to deal with people not part of their life who yet press themselves upon them: as though we were not there. For them, and to a degree for ourselves, we were nonpersons, specters, invisible men.

We moved into an extended family compound . . . belonging to one of the four major factions in village life. But except for our landlord and the village chief . . . everyone ignored us in a way only a Balinese can do. As we wandered around, uncertain, wistful, eager to please, people seemed to look right through us with a gaze focused several yards behind us on some more actual stone or tree. Almost nobody greeted us; but nobody scowled or said anything unpleasant to us either, which would have been almost as satisfactory. If we ventured to approach someone (something one is powerfully inhibited from doing in such an atmosphere), he moved, negligently but definitively, away. If, seated or leaning against a wall, we had him trapped, he said nothing at all, or mumbled what for the Balinese is the ultimate nonword— "yes" . . . [The Balinese] acted as if we simply did not exist, which, in fact, as this behavior was designed to inform us, we did not, or anyway not yet.

—CLIFFORD GEERTZ, *Myth, Symbol, and Culture*

Size and the Ratio of Permanent Faculty to Visiting Members

The Institute for Advanced Study has twenty-four permanent members (faculty), divided into four schools, which range in size from two to eight, counting only the active faculty. Some 150 visiting members are invited to the Institute every year for one or both terms. In addition, there are professors emeriti, members with long-term appointments, visitors, and assistants. Each of these categories of membership in the Institute has a different claim on its resources. The Institute, for a small institution, is richly differentiated. Put differently, it is highly stratified. An important characteristic of the Institute is the ratio of permanent faculty to visiting members. Overall, at any given moment this is roughly 1:5, but it varies by school from 1:5 in the schools of natural science and history to 1:9 in the schools of social science and mathematics. The contrast with university academic departments is sharp; in any ordinary department in any given year the ratio of regular to visiting staff may be perhaps on the order of 10:1, with the regular members in the great majority.

Overload and Resistance by the Hosts

Implications of this for the relations between members and faculty at the Institute are very great. The permanent faculty are almost inevitably at least in part defined by their visitors as their hosts, and the visitors see themselves in some sense as guests. The visitors have in fact been invited by letter from some member of the faculty who may have described something of the planned program at the Institute in the scholar's field of work during his invitational year.[1] But given the ratio of visitors to faculty, the burdens of the host are very heavy—indeed, they are a potentially dangerous burden to the relatively few permanent faculty who may care to carry that burden at all. And that perhaps explains their considerable reluctance to be forced into that role. And yet, inevitably, visiting members do in fact expect some host-like behavior from the faculty members and from the Institute, both in the mechanics of their domestic arrangements and in their intellectual life. The danger to the faculty member who meets *any* of the expectations of the visitors is that those expectations will become almost unlimited. And, of course, as faculty members withdraw from this role, the burdens fall more heavily on those who show any inclination to meet the needs of the visitors. This leads clearly to the makings of frustration for visitors and of resentment and guilt of the faculty members.

The pressure on faculty members to perform as hosts is a function of (1) the simple objective problems that visitors run into, and (2) the kinds of expectations that visitors have about academic and scholarly settings like the Institute that they have experienced before. Under the first score are the simple problems of establishing routines with a secretary and finding how one can get research assistants and how one can be put in touch with people of similar interests. Under the second heading are the expectations that people develop in the course of their academic careers by virtue, for example, of having been visitors in academic departments, or at such other centers as the Center for Advanced Study at Palo Alto. All such experiences shape the expectations with which visitors come to the Institute. Of course, these may also be modified by discussions with others who have been visiting members at the Institute, or even with permanent members of the faculty before they arrive. Nevertheless, my impression is that, at least in the social science school, the expectations on the part of visiting members do not on the whole coincide with what the very few faculty members are prepared to do.

In addition to the burden on the time and energy of the relatively few permanent faculty, there is a reluctance to enter into personal relationships that are almost certain to be impermanent. This shows itself in a kind of psychological withdrawal on the part of the permanent members from the visitors, a resistance to developing affective ties that are likely to be short-lived. If the first problem arising out of the peculiar ratio of permanent faculty to visitors is a physical and temporal overload on the permanent faculty, the second can be seen as a sort of affective overload. Each year "old" friends leave and new candidates for "friendship" arrive, and this must be felt to be a great threat and a source of potential pain on the part of permanent faculty. I believe that this leads them to withdraw even further, and works in the same direction as the threat to their time and energy posed by the steady flow of relatively large numbers of visiting members, many of whom want something from them. One person put this last matter in a curious and interesting light. When he saw a new person in September emerging from an office held the previous year by someone he had come to know and like, he felt a sort of irrational anger and resentment—"What is that fellow doing in my friend's office?" was the form this feeling took. Put that way, of course, it is perfectly natural, but to the innocent chap coming out of that office on his first or second day at the Institute, and meeting the scarcely disguised resentment of the permanent faculty, matters are not so easy to understand or to accept.

I do not think I heard anyone at the Institute discuss any of the implications of the peculiar ratio of permanent faculty to visitors, so different from that in universities and colleges. Yet I believe this demographic fact, central to the idea of the Institute and to its relation to the world of scholarship, is a source of considerable strain to both permanent faculty and visiting members. We may note in addition here that these problems may be exacerbated by the selective recruitment to the permanent faculty at the Institute of scholars who may be a bit less sociable than the average, and who found at the Institute, or hoped to find, some refuge from frequent nonprofessional interaction with others. I cannot say, of course, how strong that special kind of selective recruitment is, but if it is in that direction it would further exacerbate the problems I am discussing.

The Paucity of Roles

Another important characteristic of the Institute, and central to its conception of its role and that of its permanent faculty, is the paucity of roles filled by its permanent faculty. The Institute exists, so I have been told, precisely to free a handful of outstanding scholars from all other competing and distracting obligations, thus allowing them to get on with their scholarly and scientific work. But a byproduct of that freedom from distraction is the paucity of roles and statuses filled by any individual permanent member. In a college or university an ordinary professor is a researcher, a teacher, a member of committees, and so forth. Further, each of these roles is certain to be further differentiated: a professor is very often connected to more than one research institute or center. He would be also a teacher in four or five different courses a year, sometimes collaboratively; he is a member of departmental, divisional, college, and university-wide committees, some of them standing committees, some ad hoc; he may have administrative responsibilities beyond his committee memberships. While a faculty member at the Institute is a member of the place as a whole and of the faculty of his school and has some role in the governance of each, these are very slight and symbolically subordinated as compared with his counterparts at the university.

This situation, which indeed is central to the idea of the Institute, means that unlike faculty members even in elite departments, where people can gain respect for other personal qualities and attributes as teachers of undergraduates or graduate students, as administrators, as good committee men, and so on, at the Institute there is an extraordinarily exclusive focus on an individual's scholarly performance and his scholarly distinction. And this enormous focus on one attribute of a scholar, I believe, is a very heavy burden on the permanent members. One form this focus takes is the weight placed on the maintenance of the highest standards of scholarly work as perhaps the sole criterion by which people assess themselves and one another. I think this extraordinary focus on scholarly distinction accounts for the relentless tone of *assessment* of the scholarly work of others—rather than its enjoyment or utility—and moreover an assessment that is largely negative and deprecatory. At the Institute I very rarely heard work praised but almost always deprecated. I think this arises also out of the fear of revealing that one's standards are lower by giving favorable notice where it is not warranted. The best evidence of one's own high standards is how few others can meet them, and from this perspective the safest stance to take to all work is that it is in some important respects lacking.

There must be an enormous psychological burden in sustaining the self-concept of a scholar or scientist of the very highest distinction. But how else can one justify the status of a permanent member of the Institute? And one must ask whether it is possible that this great burden may not contribute to a decline in scholarly creativity and productivity of some scholars and scientists after the person is appointed to the Institute; "I will write nothing if not the best." My guess is that the question of one's continued scholarly distinction is sufficiently problematic to cause difficulty both for the person's relations to himself and in his relation to the work of others. This is a large and serious question on which one would want to have a good deal more evidence.

The Lack of Shared Work

The third important characteristic of the Institute is the relative absence of shared work among the members. This is also an element of the Institute's philosophy—to provide a work setting for *individual* scholars of the highest distinction, and let them get on with their work without distraction. But shared work is almost always a distraction, and the circumstances of the Institute are designed to keep it to a minimum. The contrast with the life of a faculty member in a college or university is worth making: he is engaged with his fellows in innumerable ways—through the shaping of an undergraduate or graduate curriculum; the admission, assessment, and certification of students; the appointment and promotion of faculty members; the collective development of positions to take in relation to the college or university as a whole; the development of proposals for common research or student support; and so on. Indeed, the demands on faculty members for collective work, even apart from the possibilities of joint work in teaching and research, are so many that one can see them at some point as constituting an important institutionalized distraction. And yet that collective work, deprecated by most academics as a distraction from the really serious business of their lives, nonetheless has important secondary or latent functions for their lives as scholars and for the lives of their institutions. In a word, all that work can be seen as constituting a powerful centripetal force, pulling academic people closer together and serving as a counterforce to the powerful centrifugal tendencies of their own scientific and scholarly interests, which are almost always individual and private, pulling people away from their collective memberships and into their laboratories or studies. The interactions that are *required* by the collective work of academics generate affections and sentiments among them; it also requires them to evoke or create and reinforce norms to govern their collective activities. In a word it strengthens the forces of cohesion that make them an intellectual community, insofar as they are one. And those cohesive forces in turn have a variety of functions for sustaining the life of the institution in the face of potentially divisive forces—of scholarly competition, of the competition for resources, of academic politics, of interest and temperament and faction—of all the social, economic, cultural, political, and temperamental forces that drive poeple apart.

My impression is that the absence of very much collective work at the Institute makes for a community of very low cohesiveness—one bound together more by shared interests than by shared sentiments. And when those interests come, for whatever reason, not to be completely shared but to be divisive, then there are relatively few strong ties of sentiment and affection arising out of common work to mute the conflicts. I think that what we see at the Institute is a group of individuals devoted to their research where the centrifugal forces of very highly specialized theoretical scientific and scholarly work are very strong, while at the same time the absence of collective work greatly weakens the centripetal forces. And this, in turn, has effects on the cohesion of the Institution, on its forms of government, on its capacity to deal with internal conflict, and on such personal attributes as the civility of its members toward each other and toward the visiting members.

Shared work has the effect on the community that I have been describing through strengthening its social cohesion and the identification of its members with one another. But in addition it has a civilizing effect by requiring the participants to develop a set of norms and rules that govern the relations among them. In this regard the important aspect of shared work is that it forces participants to anticipate a future in which they will be continually involved with others; it forces them thus to take into account in their own life and action the fact that they will be living and working with others with whom they may have varying personal relations, and with some of whom they will almost certainly have differences of sentiment, value, and interest. When relations among persons are wholly voluntary, they need not make provision for the management of possible disagreement or conflict between them—they may continue the association only so long as it suits them. But when there is a body of shared work that is institutionalized and is not wholly an outcome of an agreement among the participants, then people must confront the difficult but familiar situation of having to live and work with people for an indefinite future whom one has not completely chosen to associate with.

It is precisely the involuntariness of the relations among persons that grow out of shared work that gives rise both to democratic governance and to the forms of civility. Let me suggest that the permanent members of the Institute govern the relations among themselves as if they were wholly voluntary, although there is in fact a certain involuntariness in their association arising out of their shared membership in an institution in whose fate each member has an interest. There is a certain very small amount of shared work that arises periodically—notably in connection with the appointment of new permanent members. But by design or preference, there is little routine shared work of a relatively low level of importance or personal significance, which is the stuff on which forms of governance and civility rest in other comparable institutions. Again, my impression is that the permanent faculty here do not take an interest in the administrative management of the Institute (which could in fact be shared work among them) except insofar as it affects their own personal work and the services available. In addition, my impression is that the appointment of the visiting members is not really shared work, in that by informal agreement each permanent member has each been given a certain number of visitors whom he may invite—and by this formula possible disagreements on the composition of the visiting membership has been largely obviated.[2] That is a familiar and workable way to avoid conflict, but one unintended consequence is that by avoiding conflict, the Institute has also avoided the necessity to develop good machinery, both formal and informal, for the resolution of conflict when it is unavoidable. Thus although conflict at the Institute is minimized in a variety of ways, when it does occur there are no good mechanisms for its containment or resolution, and it has the explosive and bitter quality that has been visible in past years.

Selective Recruitment

I have stressed the effect of the lack of shared work on the ethos of the Institute. But this is, of course, powerfully reinforced by the selective recruitment to the Institute of scholars and scientists who were attracted to it precisely for that reason—that is, men who especially disliked the non-scholarly aspects of university teaching, who were glad to get away from governance and administration (committee work) if not also from teaching. The Institute is almost by definition a refuge for the (distinguished) lone scholar from the noise and distraction of academic life. And yet, the Institute is not just an aggregate of individuals; it is also an institution. It *does* have collective work, whether it acknowledges that fact or not. How well it performs that shared work is partly a function of the kinds of people who are recruited to the Institute, their attitudes toward shared work, the way they define their collective responsibilities, and the organizational forms that they create or inherit for discharging those responsibilities. But unlike other larger institutions where the organizational forms have an independent influence on how the institution functions, at the Institute the forms are simple, easily modified, and rather directly a reflection of the sentiments and preferences of the faculty. Thus, it is their characteristics, and especially the selective recruitment to the faculty of scholars who are fleeing institutional responsibilities, that is decisive for the institutional (as opposed to the intellectual) life of the Institute.[3]

Weakness of Higher Authority

There is another problem of governance of the Institute, and that is the absence of a higher authority to which problems can be brought for adjudication when the governing structure itself can't deal with them. In universities there are occasions when within an academic department sharp differences arise between one group or another, or one sub-discipline or another about, say, the direction of development of the department or the precise nature of the next appointment or two. When the department itself cannot resolve that issue, it is possible to appeal to a dean or a provost or even the president to adjudicate the issue from the broader perspective of the university. A department, of course, knows that it pays a price for allowing such controversies to go outside the confines of the department—among other things, neither faction may get what it wants, and moreover the department may get a reputation for factionalism and litigiousness that may not serve it well in future university planning. Nevertheless, there are these higher levels to appeal to, and often it is possible to take advantage of those authorities without the department paying too high a price. My impression is that at the Institute the director has not been able to perform the role of an outside authority to whom appeals are made, but has rather been more like a department chairman who is centrally involved in the controversies themselves.

Civility

Self-governance and civility, as the Greeks well knew, are closely related— and indeed can be seen as different aspects of the same phenomenon. For the most part, I believe, civility in one's relations with others, like modes of governance, arises out of the expectation of having continuing interaction with them—the brute fact of having to take their existence and preferences into account since they will be consequential for one's own happiness. I want to distinguish civility sharply from friendship or personal warmth—I am speaking precisely of the patterns and norms that govern the relationships of people among whom there are not sentiments of personal warmth and affection. I cannot speak with any personal knowledge of the relations among the permanent members in this regard—whether they are governed by the norms of civility when personal sentiment and friendly feelings are absent. But I would suggest that with respect to visitors permanent members are not on the whole very civil nor do they feel themselves constrained to be. Indeed, their incivility is a way of asserting their complete freedom from the consequences of their personal relations with others—they are not pleasant because they do not have to be pleasant. This would be a harsh personal judgment—and it may of course be so read—except that I am suggesting that civility is to a very considerable extent the product of situational factors. I think it perfectly possible for a man to behave with great charm and warmth in his own private sphere and social life, and yet behave with coldness and indifference in a professional setting where the norms governing his relations with his colleagues and visiting colleagues are not operative. I am suggesting that in the Institute the permanent member does not apply to visiting members the standards of conduct that he takes as appropriate for his relations with his friends. And yet the Institute has not generated its own intrinsic forms of civility which, as I have suggested earlier, arise out of institutionalized shared work involving penalties for those who do not take into account the interests and sensibilities of others.

To a large extent permanent members of the Institute are shielded from the consequences of their actions, are able to act as if no one had any sanctions on them at all either now or in the future; that enables them to act as if they were European aristocrats—though without the elaborate forms of socialization that came to gentle and civilize conduct of that class around the concept of the "gentleman." The ordinary forms of civility between host and guest—the greeting and introduction, the expression of pleasure at one's presence, the expression of interest in one's welfare, the offer taking the form, "Is there some way in which I can help you get settled?", understood on both sides as an offer to give advice or to intervene with some administrative staff who could be of direct help, these ordinary civilities were for me and I think for many other visitors to the Institute wholly absent, nor did they emerge in the course of our stay. I was invited by one permanent member for tea in September and that was the first and only time I was in the home of a faculty member of the Institute. Until May, not a single permanent member apart from the two in my own school and the director ever spoke to me for any reason whatsoever. And not a single member ever asked about either my personal or professional welfare. Part of this behavior, I think, can be explained by my earlier reference to the dangers of becoming involved in the adjustment of visitors—the dangers of overload to the relatively few permanent members. But part, I think, can also be understood in the decline of civility in an institution that affirms the total freedom of each individual, which roots its philosophy as an institution on the weakness rather than the strength of social bonds, and that arranges the lives and experiences of its members so that in fact they do only very rarely have to take into account the sentiments and feelings of others. In this environment I think the solipsist in each of us would come to the fore. Our affections might not wither, but I suspect our concern for those with whom our affections are not engaged would decline, perhaps quite outside our notice.

To some visitors this absence of civility may be much less visible—if they have, in fact, been invited by a permanent member who has a specific interest in their work and who sees them as a colleague and a source of new ideas and stimulation to his own work. It is precisely where that personal interest and sentiment is absent that the Institute shows its profound indifference to the member who is really of no use to anyone at all.

The Institute and the Center for Advanced Study

My passing reference to the Center for Advanced Study in the Behavioral Sciences in Palo Alto suggests its potential usefulness as a comparative reference for a better understanding of the Institute. The similarities between the two institutions are fairly obvious: both exist primarily to give opportunities to scholars to do their work without the usual distractions and competitive obligations that the ordinary teaching scholar has to face in a college or university. The members in both institutions have no obligations except to carry on whatever work they themselves may choose for the period of their residence—in the case of the Institute either the lifetime residence of the permanent faculty, or the shorter periods of the visiting members, and at the Center the year of their appointment as fellows.

By contrast with the Institute, the Center for Advanced Study is wholly devoted to the social sciences, though this includes a very wide range of specialties, from law to social history to psychoanalysis, but including of course also the major social science academic subjects. Like the faculty and visitors at the Institute, the thirty-five or forty members of the Center at Palo Alto also do not have much shared work. They are all there (with a few exceptions) on a one-year appointment, and there are no permanent members apart from the director and a small administrative staff who play little or no role in the intellectual life of the Center. While in fact some members do engage in joint study or work during the time they are at the Center, that is wholly voluntary and thus it is not shared work of a kind that requires the creation of governance machinery. If differences between members arise, they all can anticipate returning to their own institutions after a year, and even during the period they are in residence there is no requirement that they make any collective decisions at all. Thus none of them has any interest in the future of the Center at Palo Alto beyond the mild interest they gain as its visiting members.

From this perspective we might suggest that the permanent faculty at the Institute indeed want the freedom from shared work that the short-term members of the Center for Advanced Study enjoy, and the privacy and freedom from distraction that goes with it. Nevertheless, they do in fact have some powerful interests of a long-term nature in the Institute and its composition and character, and those interests persist and generate occasional conflict despite the fact that its members are able to reduce the amount of routine shared work to the very minimum, indeed, to such a low level that it is not effective in sustaining a regular governing structure that will manage and contain conflict or allow it to be adjudicated elsewhere.

Perhaps the most important difference between the two think-tanks is that the Center has no permanent members. This has a number of consequences, one of which can be captured in the phrase: no hosts, no guests. As I have suggested above, the existence of permanent members at the Institute makes them willy-nilly hosts while the visitors are the guests. At the Center the fellows are not guests; they *are* the Center and create whatever life it has anew every year.

The "Craftown" Phenomenon

The implications of this are illuminated by an idea first suggested by Robert Merton in an unpublished study of housing projects that he wrote some thirty years ago. His insight was that in one of the projects where a whole community was being established de novo, without any township or village in place, the first residents were obliged to play a whole variety of roles in the management of the project and the creation of a government for the village. The level of involvement of all the participants was high since there was in effect a kind of forced participation in the communal life of the settlement. Involvement in this communal life led to a variety of other forms of association and patterns of relationship and sentiment, morale tended to be high, and the participants defined the community as a supportive and rewarding one. By contrast, where a housing project was established in an already existing community, the work of creating governing mechanisms and all the necessary public services had already been accomplished, the governing structure was in place, and the level of involvement of the newcomers in this structure was relatively low. This, in turn, had very many consequences for the experience of the participants in the two different communities. In a study of the Typographical Union in the mid-1950s, we used this insight to help us understand the peculiarly high level of political participation on the part of the union members in that particular union—the members themselves were drawn into the political life of the union in the absence of its monopoly by the paid administrative staff as in most other unions. Similarly, just about the same time Stanley Elkins heard Merton lecture on this idea and used it in an essay he wrote shortly thereafter to explain the very high level of participation by the first settlers of the frontier communities in the American West. The applications to the Center for Advanced Study and the Institute are fairly obvious. At the Institute there is already a governing or authoritative structure in place that is, so to speak, in charge of the intellectual life of the Institute. It is clear that the permanent members have their own ideas about the seminars— which constitute the shared intellectual life of the Institute at least in the social science and historical schools. It is not assumed that the visiting members, or guests, will play any very active role in that life. By contrast, at the Center for Advanced Study, where there is no permanent staff in residence, the whole intellectual life of the Center has to be created by the members and indeed it happens that way. Some fellows at the Center do not interest themselves in seminars and the like, but those who do have to create it themselves, and the act of doing so brings them into contact with one another, forces them to discuss their work with one another, to explore the extent to which their interests overlap or are complementary, and in general forces a degree of both sociability and intellectual communication that is not required where an authoritative leadership is already in place as at the Institute.

Status Anxiety and Standards

There is one other respect in which the Center differs from the Institute, and that is the absence at the Center of schools of science and mathematics. One has a sense at the Institute of a clear status hierarchy among the several schools, and of the consciousness on the part of the historians and social scientists of their distinctly subordinate status within the Institute, indeed, a status as schools not wholly accepted as legitimate by all of the scientists. The social scientists and at least some of the historians at the Institute working under the shadow of [Albert] Einstein and

[John] von Neumann suffer from a kind of "status insecurity." Their response to this often is to be more royalist than the king—a common response of marginal people in groups, an over-reaction toward the values and standards (or at least their conceptions of the values and standards) of high-status disciplines, not, in this case, in the direction of "scientism" but of "scholarship." There is a desperate concern to legitimate themselves by affirming and maintaining and, above all, demonstrating that the social scientists and historians reflect the highest standards in their disciplines. In this matter I felt too a marked sense of anxiety within these schools, this in turn leading to a certain joylessness and, for the most part, a negative evaluation of the work reported in the seminars. I had the sense that people were looking over their shoulders asking "what will the grown-ups say?" and very anxious that papers be "of very high quality." This, it seems to me, precluded irreverence and various kinds of speculative and innovative efforts, all of which run the risk of not appearing to be worthy and respectable intellectual efforts. At the seminars, for example, there were carefully crafted academic jokes reflecting a certain rather old-fashioned tradition of elegance, but very little spontaneous wit and humor; moreover, a rather sharp polemical tone and a relentless judgmental stance toward work. I cannot remember hearing a public expression of appreciation or approval of a paper, though what members may say to one another in private, of course, I do not know. But to revert to a point that I made earlier, when there is status insecurity, the best evidence that the highest standards are being upheld is the negative evaluation of almost everything that is done. Conversely, to praise something is to define your own standards; you then associate your standards with the offering under attack.

Thus the pervasive climate of judgment (1) of the social scientists by the historians and (2) of both historians and social scientists by the real scientists further heightens the exaggeration of standards and the evaluation against those standards that make every public performance a testing performance. This, as I have said, was associated with the absence of a sense of intellectual playfulness, or the trying out of new ideas and approaches for the sheer pleasure of intellectual life.

There was a general sense among participants that the social science/history seminar had not gone well—the papers were not very good—and so on. I did not agree, and found that relentless judgmentalism dreary and boring; many of the papers were lively and stimulating if one stopped giving gold stars or black marks. On the other hand, it may be illuminating to reflect on what seemed to work well by general consensus, and here I think the lectures in art history were thought to have been successful. These are highly formalized, elaborately prepared lectures in exquisitely refined and extremely specialized subjects. They are given within an intellectual community of mixed faculty and visiting members plus others from Princeton, and are sustained by a solid, clearly defined scholarly tradition well represented and legitimated at the Institute. This, at least, is the kind of scholarship that a scientist can appreciate, or at least accept as fully legitimate scholarship, and the sense of status anxiety was least evident here.

The Language of Feeling

One of my earliest impressions at the Institute was of the absence of expressions of feeling among the members when there was conversation— for example, in the cafeteria. I heard many different languages of scholarship at the Center at seminars and the like, but never a vocabulary by which feelings are expressed or discussed. My sense was that there is a kind of taboo on the expression of feeling or on the expression of concern for the feelings of others because such expressions of feeling are felt in a way to contaminate the process of continuous scholarly judgment, the setting or application of standards. There is a peculiar fear of non-cognitive factors, emotional factors, as subversive of scholarship of the highest standard. There is a sense in which the expression of such feeling is a confession of weakness—a realm in which one takes refuge from the severest criteria of scholarship. Feeling is in this perspective a mark of weakness; it is what people speak of to excuse the absence of scholarly distinction or brilliance. If you are really first-class you are tough and don't need to acknowledge fear, anxiety, and the like. I remember raising the question after a seminar of how a young scholar who had given a paper might have felt under a particularly brutal series of attacks, and how those attacks might have affected his performance. I was given the very clear feeling that this was not an appropriate subject for discussion.

On the Role of Expectations

I suspect that visiting members' morale and sense of satisfaction or dissatisfaction is conditioned to a considerable extent by the kinds of expectations of the Institute that they bring with them. I think those expectations are formed by a number of factors: (1) whether the member was invited or applied for membership; (2) whether he had a personal or close professional connection with one of the permanent faculty; (3) whether the visitor was rather junior or of fairly senior rank in his own institution; (4) whether the member had any experience as a visitor either at the Center for Advanced Study or in other academic departments or research centers here or abroad. In my own case I came with fairly high expectations about the year at the Institute and what it would be like. A number of factors disposed me to have rather stronger expectations of the Institute than was warranted, and therefore led me to be more deeply disappointed with what I found.

Nevertheless, I do not believe that the problems and difficulties I have been discussing were entirely a product of my own idiosyncratic characteristics and perspectives. There are structural characteristics of the Institute that cause problems for its visiting members. It may be that a more sustained attempt to illuminate these shared difficulties can shed light on the larger and more interesting question of whether and how the organizations in which scholarship and science are carried on—universities, departments, laboratories, and research centers—affect the lives and work of the scholars and scientists who work in those contexts. These notes represent an effort to turn my own experience at the Institute into an occasion for raising questions about the environments for intellectual work by looking at one such setting.

NOTES

....

The epigraph was drawn from Clifford Geertz, "Deep Play: Notes on the Balinese Cockfight," in *Myth, Symbol, and Culture* (New York: Norton, 1971), p. 1.

1. It would be interesting to see what these letters of invitation actually say,

since they heavily shape the expectations of the visitors, and thus their sense of accomplishment or frustration during their time in residence.

2. I am sure that the extent to which this is true varies among the several schools.

3. It is an interesting question whether and how the intellectual and the institutional lives of the Institute (what I have called in other connections the "private" and "public" lives of universities) affect one another. They surely do at the extremes: a severe crisis in the public life of the Institute must surely have some effects on the scholarly and scientific work of its members, though that might be hard to demonstrate. Nevertheless, if it is true, then that alone justifies some attention to the state of its public life.

11

FEW PEOPLE WHO CARE DEEPLY about universities and learning have ever had the opportunity to create an ideal organization to realize these values. Yet that was the opportunity presented to Martin Trow in 1977, when Vice Chancellor Michael Heyman asked if Trow would become director of a restructured higher education center, located on campus and connected with the university community. The result was the Center for Studies in Higher Education. The following document, the first annual report from the Center, expresses his convictions about the nature of such a unit and the principles on which it should operate. It is a remarkably idiosyncratic vision, and it resulted in a unique place of learning that still bears the stamp of its founder.

Trow grasped this unexpected opportunity and was given a free hand in shaping the nature of the reconstituted Center. He was quite explicit about what he did and did not want. He emphatically rejected the model of a Berkeley ORU (the local term for an organized research unit). Most ORUs received administrative support from the university, but funded research and other activities with external grants, usually from the federal government. Such research organizations generally required non-faculty staff. Large-scale social research of this sort had been the bread and butter of the preceding Center, but Trow felt that this kind of research "tends to dominate all other activities," producing "terrible pressures of deadlines, quarterly reports, proposal writing, and the contagious anxieties of a large staff on soft funds." Worst of all, such an organization "cannot also sustain an intellectual community."

This was precisely the aspiration of the new center, reiterated throughout this report: "to create and sustain a scholarly and intellectual community" at Berkeley. Trow envisioned a community drawn chiefly from regular faculty having interests in the "institutions and

364

processes of higher education." This was an idealistic notion—that the Center would justify its existence by nurturing this intellectual community, and that it would draw Berkeley scholars out of their disciplinary cocoons to ponder, discuss, and sometimes investigate broad issues affecting the campus. But Trow promised more. The Center would provide a service to the Berkeley administration, to the University of California, to higher education in the state of California, and to the worldwide community of scholars concerned with higher education. Thus, from the outset, the focus of the Center was "California and the world," and rather unmindful of higher education in the rest of the United States.

This plan was to be realized by having the Center serve as a meeting place for individuals from all of these diverse constituencies. For university administrators or state officials it would represent an academic safe haven, where their quotidian issues could be aired with theoretical detachment. Invited visitors would further enrich the mix with additional questions and fresh perspectives. Having recently written on the "public and the private lives" of higher education, Trow envisioned encompassing both, and examining both basic and applied issues as well. The intersection of these perspectives would create "mutual relevance" that might in turn illuminate learning or policy or administration or finance.

Realizing this vision for the Center required striking and maintaining a delicate balance. Students were at best an afterthought, and proved to be largely absent. The vision was not shared by the Berkeley College of Education (home to the original Center), and Trow had no wish to offer what he considered vocational graduate degrees in higher education. Instead, he devised a Center without students or research projects, to be supported by the university for the purpose of sustaining an intellectual community.

This gambit succeeded brilliantly internationally, as scholars from around the world found the Center to be, just as intended, a setting for interchanging serious ideas about myriad aspects of higher education. The stature of the Center also attracted practitioners from the UC administration, from community colleges, and from state government, for presentations and discussions about their particular institutions. Nurturing a higher education community among the Berkeley faculty was a greater challenge. The Center probably achieved this to a greater extent than any similar unit, but never to the degree envisioned by Trow. However, in the twelve years that he directed the Berkeley Center, it fulfilled to a remarkable extent the mission defined in this initial report.

As of this writing, the Center remains a living legacy to Martin Trow's intellectual vision and, importantly, to the spirit imbued through his stewardship. In the two decades since he stepped down as director, the Center has adapted to changing circumstances, adopted long-range projects, garnered external support, and incorporated a staff of non-faculty researchers. These adaptations reflect the solidity of its original foundation rather than any compromise of purpose. The Center remains a monument not only to his initial vision, but also to the personal values that Martin Trow instilled—uncompromising intellectual integrity in the analysis of higher education and implicit devotion to Berkeley, the University of California, and the best of international scholarship.

—ROGER L. GEIGER

New Directions for the Center for Studies in Higher Education

The 1977–78 Annual Report

The CSHE [Center for Studies in Higher Education] has just completed its first year under a new director and associate director, and with a quite sharply altered character and direction, certainly as compared with the Center for Research and Development of

Adapted from Martin Trow, "New Directions for the Center for Studies in Higher Education: The 1997–1978 Annual Report," Center for Studies in Higher Education, University of California, Berkeley, California (1978). Reprinted by permission of Center for Studies in Higher Education.

Higher Education that preceded it. In line with its new direction, the Center has changed its name, to the Center for Studies in Higher Education, and changed its location, from a suite of offices in the Great Western Building on Shattuck Avenue to South Hall Annex, next to the main library and almost exactly in the center of campus. Most important, it has changed its direction and program. In this report we will try to describe the new Center, summarize its first year's activities, and sketch our hopes and plans for its immediate future.

Conceptions of the Center: Its Aims and Directions

Under its first three directors, the Center for Higher Education at Berkeley emphasized research activity—initially the research interests of its director and associates, later an extensive program of research responsive to the office of education and to other funding agencies, public and private, which supplied the large budget of the Center during its R&D phase. But while this activity resulted in many useful books and reports, there emerged a growing feeling among Berkeley faculty members interested in the study of higher education that this campus needed a center that would be more directly a resource for the campus, for its faculty and students. This view, shared also by senior Berkeley administrative officers, led to the appointment of the present director and associate director in July 1977. Under its new leadership, the Center has taken on a different character and direction. And while this "new" Center is still developing its program and determining its range of activities and interests, the completion of one year of transition is an appropriate time to spell out a little more fully the idea the Center has of itself and its future.

The chief mission of the "new" Center for Higher Education at Berkeley is to create and sustain a scholarly and intellectual community, based on the Berkeley campus, of people who have a special interest in the institutions and processes of higher education. This "special interest" may be a scholarly or a policy-oriented one, or both. Indeed, one of the aims of the Center is to bring people with policy and scholarly interests in higher education into regular contact and communication with one another.

This community of scholars and administrators will be drawn first from the members of the Berkeley faculty and administration and students. Berkeley is fortunate—almost unique—in the number and variety of its faculty who have a major interest in higher education. These faculty members are scattered all over the campus—in the departments of history and political science, psychology and sociology, physics and chemistry, and in the professional schools of education, business administration, and public policy, to name just a few. The first mission of the Center is to create conditions and occasions for these people to come together to discuss issues of common interest, exchanging ideas, views, perspectives, and research findings.

But higher education at Berkeley is a part of three larger systems of special importance. One of these is the University of California, of which Berkeley is a part; another is the system of state-supported higher education in California; the third is the worldwide scholarly community devoted to the study of educational institutions and processes. Our aim is to enrich the local community by bringing into it representatives of these other communities that are vital to Berkeley's intellectual and institutional welfare. In addition to Berkeley campus people we are inviting to our seminars and colloquia members of the statewide university administration and faculty members from other UC campuses; members of the state legislative and administrative bodies that deal with the university; and scholars from other universities in the United States and overseas— members of the "invisible college" of scholars and practitioners around the world whose members study the institutions and processes of higher education.

Our guiding principle, we have said, is to create and sustain an intellectual community on the Berkeley campus, including but not confined to Berkeley people who work in this area. We are determined to include in that community the widest variety of interests in this area: it is precisely the interdisciplinary character of the community that justifies its being the central mission and purpose of the Center. We are convinced that each of the varied approaches to the study of higher education would be strengthened and made more fruitful and illuminating if it were informed by other ways of approaching the same issues and problems. Thus, to be interdisciplinary in this area is necessary because the object of study is a social institution that takes many forms and appears in every modern society, but whose characteristics and functions cut across disciplinary categories. We are interdisciplinary because an understanding of colleges and universities and the systems they comprise demands it.

We can summarize our intentions by capturing the major dimensions of research and scholarship on higher education in a fourfold typology (Table 11.1). Along one dimension we may distinguish between studies that address themselves to aspects of the public or the private lives of higher education. The public life includes all the problems and activities associated with the financing, administration, and governance of colleges and universities and systems of higher education. The private life of higher education is everything more directly related to teaching and learning—for example, the conduct of research, its effect on the development of disciplines, and the effect of those developments on the curriculum; new modes of instruction, the processes by which students are admitted and faculty members appointed and promoted. The line between the public and private lives of higher education is not sharp, but a great deal that we attend to can be usefully distinguished as part of one or the other system. The other dimension of this typology distinguishes between applied studies—those that are intended to affect educational programs, activities, or decisions—and basic studies that are aimed more generally at extending our knowledge or understanding of some aspect of higher education, without any intended application. The two dichotomized dimensions can be combined to form four types of research and scholarship in higher education.

TABLE 11.1   *A Typology of Research in Higher Education*

	Applied versus Basic	
Object of Study	Applied Research	Basic Research
The "public life" of higher education	I	II
The "private life" of higher education	III	IV

A Typology of Research in Higher Education

In Cell I we find a very large body of work on university finance, governance, and administration that is aimed at improving current practice. Much of the work of the Center for Research and Development in Higher Education came under this rubric—for example, their studies of the statewide coordination of higher education—as does much of the work of the Carnegie Council on Policy Studies in Higher Education and of the Carnegie Commission that preceded it.

Cell II includes broad historical and comparative studies of the creation, organization, finance, and administration of universities and university systems. An example would be Neil Smelser's study of the development of the University of California, or [Robert] Berdahl's studies of the British University Grants Committee.

Cell III can be illustrated by studies of new modes of instruction, research into the use of teaching assistants, or evaluations of campus-based Learning Centers or experimental colleges.

Cell IV would include studies of cognitive functioning; the social psychology of adult learning; or the physical or social organization of research centers as contexts for learning.

Of course, many studies would be located in more than one of these cells. Moreover, the line between these dimensions is not always clear: for example, much of the work of the SESAME group at Berkeley on the teaching and learning of science falls in both Cells III and IV. But it is not important to classify any given study or body of research; it is enough to suggest that nearly all work in higher education can be located in one or more of these cells. But the typology is immediately useful in allowing us to define some important aspects of the Center's purpose and program by reference to it.

First, we hope to have represented in the activities of the Center people with interests in each of the cells of this typology. Second, we believe that the Center can serve its most useful function by emphasizing the mutual relevance of work done in different cells of the typology: for example, the mutual relevance of basic comparative and historical studies on one hand, and policy-related studies of university administration or relevant state agencies, on the other. Similarly, we hope to stress the impact that activities in the public life of higher education have on its private life—for example, the ways in which new modes of governance or the introduction of collective bargaining affect the climate in which teaching and learning are carried on. Third, if we are asked to define the Center's interests, we can best answer by drawing a circle that includes all four cells of typology, and reply that our intention as a Center is to encourage and support discussion and study of problems that fall within these broad areas of inquiry in higher education and the relationships between them. But our special interest lies precisely at the boundaries, along the lines where applied and basic interests intersect, and at the intersection between learning, on one hand, and administration and finance, on the other.

The Role of Research at the Center

Our decision to emphasize the Center's community-building function has as a corollary a decision not to initiate or support large-scale research in higher education at the Center. This decision rises out of our belief that large-scale social research, and especially its administration, tends to dominate all other activities in any institution in which it is carried on. The research itself has an imperative quality: its need for resources, its timetables, are the first priority of any research institute. Staffs must be built and need continual support: research assistants, field interviewers, coders and programmers, administrative staff, bookkeepers, editors, and senior staff to analyze data and write the reports and proposals that keep the whole enterprise afloat. There is always a deadline to meet, studies are always running behind time or out of money, or both, and the office of education wants its quarterly reports. Staff members are always coming and going, and new ones must be recruited to carry out the new studies. The best energies—indeed, sometimes all energies—of such a center and its leadership goes into its research program, and properly so. But this same organization, so we believe, cannot also create and sustain an intellectual community centering on the varied interests of a membership that is drawn from different parts of a university. An intellectual community is not a research team, and cannot be made so.

The interests of such a community are not wholly predictable, nor are they likely to coincide with a Center's research program. And the occasional seminar or colloquium does not answer to the needs of such a community. The intellectual community defined by our typology requires that we bring people together regularly, over time, under conditions that facilitate the exchange of ideas between scholars and other interested people of quite dissimilar perspectives and orientations. That is a big task and worthy of our best efforts. We are quite sure that we could not give that task those efforts if we were also initiating our own or administering other people's large-scale research studies through the Center.

But having said that, it should not be thought that we are hostile to research on higher education. On the contrary, the staff of the Center are continuously engaged in research, as will be the majority of our visiting associates during their stay with us. This ongoing research as well as the results of completed studies are and will be reported and discussed in our seminars and meetings. The research and scholarship done by the members of the staff and visitors are at the heart of our activities. But for the reasons we have sketched above, we do not want to administer large-scale research projects through the Center.

That decision carries with it a set of organizational implications. It frees us in some ways, and restricts us in others. On one side, we can remain relatively small; we do not need a large research and administrative staff supported on soft money, to be reporting one set of studies, engaged in another, and planning, designing, writing proposals for yet another set with a view to the future. Our staff at the moment consists of three professionals and a secretary-receptionist. (We hope to add an additional part-time secretary to help with the work of our visitors, and two or three research assistants.) But our staff does not have to spend an inordinate amount of time in research administration. We can spend that time organizing and attending meetings, corresponding with prospective visitors and speakers, and thinking about the problems and areas on which the community or parts of it might wish to become engaged in our ongoing discussions and studies.

Our decision not to administer large-scale research through the Center will allow us to nurture and enrich an intellectual community at Berkeley. It also means that we will not be raising large sums of outside money. And that can be seen as a limitation, or even as a failure in itself. Large-scale research is one way—perhaps the only way—to bring large sums of money into a research unit. Insofar as an organized research unit in the University of California is defined as a machine for raising external funds, and its success is defined as the ratio of external to internally supplied funds, then the Center for Studies in Higher Education at Berkeley is likely to be a failure by definition as well as by deliberate policy.

We have no quarrel with research centers and institutes that do in fact raise large sums of money and engage in large-scale research activities. There are many areas of study—for example, much of what is called "big science"—in which major research efforts are best organized through interdisciplinary centers or institutes. And this is also the case in some areas of social science: for example, the Survey Research Center at Berkeley (as elsewhere) is far better able to design and administer large-scale sample surveys than is any single faculty member or group of faculty in a single department. This is not the case in the area of higher education. Other agencies and centers—for example, the Carnegie Council and the American Council on Education—are able to conduct large-scale studies, as well as are agencies of the government. What is (almost) lacking, and in our view needed, are places and conditions where people with varying perspectives but common interests in higher education meet over relatively long periods of time and come to know one another, one another's minds and ways of thought, by talking to one another about their common interests.

We hope that we can be assessed on our own terms and by our own goals, and not by the ratio of "soft" to "hard" money in our budget. And by remaining small we hope to avoid being the object of one of those grotesque exercises in the evaluation of educational institutions that make up so much of the contemporary evaluation industry, an industry that sprang full-grown from the ear of Congress some years ago. This industry evaluates complex institutions and processes for the most part by attending to proximate, visible, and easily measured outcomes of education, and succeeds in its mission by neglecting subtle, long-range, and difficult-to-measure effects on people and institutions, government and society, science and scholarship, which together comprise the real impact of colleges and universities. It should be clear that our aims are to achieve larger, more enduring effects, even though they may not be easily perceived in the short term. Relatively small budgets may make it easier for funding agencies, both public and private, to make the acts of faith that are embodied in a continued support of our Center.

But this is perhaps too severe. We can and will be engaged in activities of short-term usefulness to our colleagues, to the university, and to knowledge. The clearest of these perhaps will be our service to the university.

The Center and the University

Most organized research units see their function as providing services and resources to faculty members and graduate students in the area of their research, thereby serving the larger interests of science and scholarship. The Center for Studies in Higher Education also aims to serve the research interests of faculty and students, and through them the cause of knowledge. But by virtue of its substantive area of interest, the CSHE has an opportunity to serve the University of California more directly as an institution, not just indirectly by contributing to research on the life of the university. For the University of California, in all its enormous vitality and variety, is not only the locus of the Center, but is also a laboratory and a subject for study—the institution that all its members know best, and the obvious source of evidence and insight when any issue of higher education is being discussed. Its policies and practices are often the only "case material" that all participants in our discussions know in common and at first hand. And inevitably, its members have a more than academic interest in this university's welfare. This is not to say that CSHE will confine its attention to the University of California and its problems: the list of current and prospective visitors from other universities and from overseas would be enough to ensure that we will not be a victim of that kind of parochialism. In addition, our strong commitment to comparative and historical studies will lead us to examine higher education in other forms—for example, in community colleges—and in other times and places—for example, in eighteenth-century England, contemporary Sweden, Meiji Restoration Japan.

Nevertheless, the University of California will inevitably occupy a special place in our concerns and our activities: we know more about it and we care more about it than we do about any other single institution. And its character and internal diversity allows us to explore in it many problems, such as the impact on universities of new forms of government regulation, which take similar forms elsewhere.

We can illustrate one form our special interest in the University of California will take by reference to our seminar series. The first seminar we created is called "The University as Seen from Various Perspectives." Its membership includes people from Sacramento who deal with university affairs in the department of finance, the legislative analyst's office, the Postsecondary Education Commission, members of the UC statewide administration, members of the Berkeley campus administration, a faculty member from a state university campus, Berkeley faculty and visiting fellows and associates of the Center, as well as the Center's own staff. The "university" in the title of the seminar is intentionally ambiguous; at times it means the University of California, at other times it refers to the generic institution. Two of our first talks and discussions have centered on the preparation of the University of California budget, as seen from the office of the legislative analyst and the state department of finance; another talk focused on a UC statewide committee report on "university autonomy," a topic bearing directly on the relation between the university and the state.

The Center's seminars are, we believe, a significant service to the university; they not only add to the general stock of knowledge about the "public life of higher education," but also create a protected environment in which serious and difficult university issues can be discussed by people closely involved in them in an atmosphere of candor, rationality, and humor. These issues are ordinarily subjects not for discussion but for negotiation under circumstances in which the aim of all participants, quite properly, is to persuade or to find weakness in the arguments of others. The arenas of negotiation, decision, and action within the university, among its various units and levels of authority, and between the university and various state authorities, cannot allow the emergence of the free-wheeling and candid discussion that we try to create in our seminars. We must confess that before launching our seminar series we had some anxiety about the possible difficulties that might arise as we tried to bring into this "protected environment" issues directly bearing on current university policies and decisions. We feared—as it turned out needlessly—that the people who were engaged in decision making and negotiation would be wary about speaking on these matters, anticipating that their too candid words or inadvertent disclosures would come to haunt them when they left the seminar room and returned to the hurly-burly of state and university politics. And this was a serious concern, since our discussions, if they are to be of any value, depend precisely on the candor of the participants, their feeling that they are free to say what they think or know without its having consequences for the practical affairs and decisions about which they speak and for which they often carry a measure of responsibility. We have in fact not found our participants showing any special caution or reticence in what they say during our seminars. I suspect that we underestimated their capacity to change roles from actor to analytical observer. Perhaps we also underestimated the openness of our participants, and the climate of trust that still survives that allows people to step aside from their adversarial roles and postures and speak to (not merely at) one another in the service of mutual enlightenment. We did not underestimate the pleasures that lie in the discussion of significant issues without any concern that an impending decision may hinge on one's persuasiveness. About those pleasures we have no doubts; it simply is true, as we anticipated, that people find it rewarding to talk about their common interests in a protected environment sharply insulated from consequences outside the seminar room. It is especially rewarding, perhaps, to people who ordinarily only talk about these issues in decision-making arenas.

This, of course, emphasizes the subjective rewards of our seminars, especially those that deal with matters of public policy. Without those rewards there would be no seminars. But it may not be premature to suggest that the special conditions that our seminars create allow a growing and deepening understanding of the problems that face the university (again in its double meaning), and especially of public universities in their relation to state authorities. We are able, in these discussions, to range much more widely than can hard-pressed administrators, making the best case possible for presentation to a skeptical or hostile legislative committee. And in this freedom to deal with matters that cannot be brought into public debate—for example, the training and career aspirations of state and university administrators, or the changing patterns of negotiation between university and state over the past few decades, or the comparative problems faced by British and European universities—there is inevitably a deepening of understanding, a placing of current problems in wider perspective. And that is exactly what we intend.

What we have said of our seminar on "The University as Seen from Various Perspectives" applies also to the seminar we will be initiating this academic year to be called "The University as a Federal System." Here we will also stress the dual meaning of "the university"; at times we will focus on the University of California and its nine campuses; at other times we will be talking about other systems of higher education that involve a central authority charged with governing or coordinating a number of institutions. This description applies to many American state systems, as well as to the universities of the Federal Republic of Germany and to the British universities in relation to the University Grants Committee. It applies also to such federal universities as the University of Oxford or the University of London in relation to their component colleges. Here again we will be discussing sensitive questions currently or perennially at issue between center and "province"—issues such as equity, autonomy, authority, accountability, indeed the classic problems of democratic politics, but with the special character that these problems take when they arise in the context of a system of colleges or universities.

Another regular seminar to be initiated next year (there will be four altogether) will center on the community college in California and in the nation at large. We anticipate that Professor Dale Tillery, of the school of education at Berkeley, will play a leading role in the development of this seminar. Next year one of our visiting associates, Dr. William Strasser, president of Montgomery College, a large community college in Maryland, will be on hand to help initiate this seminar series.

The Center and University Governance

There is another danger in subjecting current university policy and programs to critical scrutiny in our seminars and colloquia. That danger is the tendency for us to become, quite inadvertently, a part of the university's political process, an illegitimate part of the machinery by which the university governs itself. This problem only arises when the subject of discussion is a policy or program currently under review; participants in the seminar, and not least the staff of the Center, will surely have their own views on these issues, and the very candor and openness that we need to illuminate issues will also tend to elicit arguments and not merely analyses on a prospective decision. This is a dilemma we must recognize, but if we do recognize it, we may be able to avoid the danger of destroying the insulation between our protected environment and the world of action and decision. We can, if we are thoughtful and aware, resist the temptation to substitute rhetoric for analysis, persuasion for illumination; we can, for example, ensure that at our seminars various points of view on an issue are presented in a fair-minded and sympathetic environment. This is not only a matter of conscience and of our desire to affirm and not undermine the legitimacy of the senate committees and administration structures by which the university is (under the regents) properly governed. It is also a matter of our own credibility. If the Center were seen to have an interest in the policy outcomes of discussions held within its walls, we would indeed come to be seen as a part, and an illegitimate part, of the governance machinery, a place where decisions can be influenced and not just analyzed. And that surely would be the end of the protected environment that is essential if our seminars and discussions are to have the character and to serve the intellectual functions that we intend for them to have.

The Center and Scholarship

We have perhaps said enough to make clear that we mean to deal with the problems of university administration and governance in full seriousness. The forms and processes of administration and decision making are a central part of the life of the university—any university—with large consequences for the private life of teaching and learning. But while we give administration the attention that we do, we are equally resolved not to be bounded in our interests or dominated in our perspectives by the public life of higher education. Nothing of any significance about higher education can be said without understanding and accepting the heavy weight of its organizational structures, its patterns of finance and admin-

istration, on every aspect of its life. Similarly, nothing of enduring significance can be said about higher education that confines itself to those issues and problems. We want both to address those issues and to transcend
them. This spirit will, we hope, infuse all our activities including, those
most sharply keyed to problems of policy. In our seminars and discussions we will resist the tendency for technical problems of administration—
for example, the development of information systems, or the patterns of
response to government regulations—to become divorced from their impact on the processes of teaching and learning, which are at the heart of
the university mission. Our interest and support for scholarship in this
area is embodied in the seminar on "Comparative and Historical Perspectives." This group includes university administrators and scholars
from many different departments on campus—physics, physiology, political science, history, English, education, law, city planning, public
policy. This spring the members of the seminar heard and discussed papers on "Models of the Educated Man in Western Civilization," a report
on ongoing research into nineteenth-century college life in the United
States as described in the letters and diaries of students, and a broad
discussion of current issues and problems in graduate education led by
the retiring graduate dean at Berkeley. This seminar, led by the Center's
associate director, himself a professor in the department of history at
Berkeley and a scholar who has done work on eighteenth- and nineteenth-
century British universities, is one of the several links we maintain with
humanistic scholarship, both among our own faculty and through visitors to the Center.

The Center and Its Visiting Fellows and Associates

As we noted earlier, the Center's major mission is the creation and encouragement of an intellectual community concerned with the study of
higher education in all its aspects. The heart of this community, as we
have noted, will consist of faculty members and students from the Berkeley campus. But our program aims to strengthen and enrich this local
community by inviting people who are not on the Berkeley campus to
join us for longer or shorter periods. Some of these, such as members of

the UC statewide administration, faculty members of nearby colleges and universities, and officials in the state government in Sacramento, have become part of our community on a long-term and continuing basis. Others, such as scholars from other parts of the United States and from universities and university systems overseas, will greatly enrich our discussions by bringing their own special interests in higher education, and their knowledge and experience in other comparable institutions, to our midst.

The Center's physical quarters, in South Hall Annex, have been designed expressly for visitors. At any given time, we have space for six or seven such visitors from outside the campus and beyond commuting distance. These visitors are carefully chosen and join us by invitation. The director and associate director of the Center know personally a large number of the people outside of Berkeley who are members of the "invisible college" of scholars and administrators concerned with the study of higher education. In addition, we solicit suggestions and recommendations from other associates of the Center, members of our seminars and the like, for the names of other potential visitors. We will invite people by reference to several criteria: first, their achievement and experience as scholars and administrators; second, the specific value of their experience and studies for the programs and seminars currently under way at the Center; and third, the possibility of arranging for their joint appointment with a professional school, academic department, or administrative unit in the university. We may also want to invite people who represent research or scholarly traditions not strongly represented at Berkeley. Apart from these criteria, we will be constrained first by our limited space, and second by our financial budget.

On this latter score, we are very grateful for two special grants for support of visitors to the Center, one from the chancellor's office and another from the graduate dean's office. This money allows us to invite a limited number of visitors who need support while here, Rather than providing the total support that our visitors may need, we will continue to arrange for our visitors to come on a joint appointment between the Center and a professional school, academic department, or administrative unit whenever possible. Such appointments will ordinarily be made for one quarter, but summer residence in Berkeley and at the Center may extend a visit for up to six months.

These joint appointments, we believe, have advantages for all concerned: they enable other units to bring distinguished visitors to teach a course and to be available to their graduate students for half their ordinary cost, making an appointment of a specialist in higher education practical for schools and departments such as business administration, sociology, political science, and the like, which might otherwise have difficulty in justifying a full stipend for what is for them a relatively esoteric field of study. For the visitor it provides a professional or disciplinary link that makes a visit to Berkeley even more attractive. Half a teaching load, ordinarily one course or seminar, is not a heavy burden and need not interfere unduly with a visitor's program of research or study. This program of research and study can be carried on at the Center where the visitor will be housed; there the Center can provide the visitor with an office and some administrative help, both of which also make such an appointment more attractive to the department in question. For the Center, such joint appointments enable us to stretch our limited resources and enable us to bring more, and more varied, visitors to campus. In addition, such joint appointments strengthen the Center's links to the professional schools and academic departments on campus in a most effective way. Finally, in support of our central purpose, such visitors enrich our seminars and meetings, give papers and talks, and are available through our Center to colleagues and graduate students from other parts of the campus. This has already proven to be an important and indeed vital part of our program.

Not all visitors to the Center require financial support from the Center. Some come on sabbatical leave, or with support from a foundation, their own institution, or government. Some of these also come as the guests of the Center and another academic department. But all visitors to the Center who are taken into the Center's ongoing life will be coming expressly by invitation. (This obviously does not apply to visitors who come for a day or two to learn more about the Center or to meet one of our colleagues.) Our resources are limited, and we must reserve them for those who we believe can make the largest contribution to the study of higher education at Berkeley. Having extended that invitation, we will not make any further distinction between those of our visitors who come with support from the Center and those who are supported in other ways. Much of our energies and resources will be addressed to making their visit to Berkeley rewarding to them as well as to the Center. Moreover, we hope that we can maintain scholarly and professional links with our visitors after they have returned to their home campuses: this, in a sense, will be our effort to strengthen the "invisible college" of students of higher education wherever their permanent post may be, and to make the Berkeley Center an important part of the network of personal and professional links that comprise such an "invisible college."

The Center and Its Links Abroad

Visitors, we anticipate, will over time come from all over the United States and from many different countries. However, our Center will have a "special relationship" with the academic communities of three other countries: Britain, Japan, and Sweden. The reasons are both substantive and fortuitous. Historically, the link between American and British universities has been close. The tie between the Center and British higher education developed because both the director and associate director of the Center have studied and written about British universities and know personally many of the academics, administrators, and politicians who are most closely concerned with scholarship and policy on British higher education. In this past year, we invited . . .[1]

Japan has the largest system of higher education after the United States (apart from the USSR), and one greatly influenced by American models. It has a lively community of scholars concerned with the study of higher education, both Japanese and Western, and many of these are members or associates of the Research Institute for Higher Education at Hiroshima University . . . [2] We hope that members or associates of the Hiroshima Institute will come to Berkeley as visiting associates in the future. We have much to learn from our Japanese colleagues, and it is not irrelevant that Berkeley is also a center for Japanese studies. Our connection with Sweden is no less welcome . . . [3] Sweden has planned its educational development with more care and direct research involvement in planning than is true of any other country. Their system is a product of comprehensive planning, a planning process that throws into bold relief many of the problems of university autonomy, social equality, and liberal versus vocational education that are seen, though more obscurely, elsewhere . . . [4]

Our special relationship with these countries will in no way preclude our having visitors from other countries. Indeed, we have already had long-term visits from academics from Australia and Spain, and during this coming year will have visiting associates and fellows from the United States, France, Canada, and Italy, as well as Britain. Our "special relationship" means only that we hope that our relations to these countries, and to the relevant scholarly communities in them, will be on a continuing and long-term basis.

Joint Appointments with Statewide Administration

The support from the chancellor's office and the dean of the graduate division allows the Center to make joint appointments with schools and departments on the Berkeley campus, as we have noted. But in addition, our interest in broad policy and administrative problems led us to propose to the president of the university that we make an annual joint appointment between our Center and his office of a distinguished visiting academic administrator. This proposal was warmly accepted by President Saxon. The first such appointment, Mr. Geoffrey Caston, registrar (i.e., chief administrative officer) of the University of Oxford, will be in residence at the Center between July and January 1978–79. Such appointments resemble those made between our Center and a school or department at Berkeley, in that the costs of the visitor's salary will be shared equally between statewide administration and the Center. But instead of the visitor teaching a course or seminar, this visitor will be asked to make a study (on a half-time basis) of some aspect of university administration, bringing to it his own experience and comparative perspective. The nature of the study will be arranged by agreement between the visitor and his host in the president's office. Mr. Caston, for example, will be making a broad study of the university's decision-making process, an investigation of particular interest to the vice president for academic affairs, Donald Swain. Mr. Caston's experience in Britain on the University Grants Committee, as well as his current post at Oxford, gives him special qualifications to make this study. And his appointment with the statewide administration gives him access to university documents and meetings that are critical to his study.

In the same letter in which we proposed the joint appointment of a distinguished visiting administrator, we also proposed to President Saxon that we establish an additional link between statewide administration and our Center. We proposed that each year he or his colleagues nominate a middle-level university civil servant to come to our Center in residence for a quarter. Such a person would be relieved of his day-to-day responsibilities, and come to the Center as a full member, occupying an office and taking part in our seminars and discussions. This administrative visitor to the Center would remain fully on the university payroll and might bring with him or her some longer-range assignment—for example, the preparation of a study or report—that he or she could appropriately do while in residence with us. This suggestion was also warmly accepted by President Saxon and the first such appointment is expected to be made later this academic year.

The impulse to make this proposal arose out of our recognition that, unlike the senior university administrators who ordinarily come up through the academic ranks before taking on administrative responsibilities, middle- and upper-middle-level university civil servants often have had little direct experience with academic life beyond their own experience as students. Moreover, they rarely have occasion to visit the campuses of the university, or if they do so, they even more rarely see faculty members or students who are not part of the campus administration. On the other hand, university civil servants play an enormously important role in the life of the university that most academics, including students of higher education, know little about. We cannot really understand university administration if we do not understand the work of university civil servants, and we cannot know that world unless we are able to know the men and women who staff those large and powerful administrative organizations. Thus, from the point of view of the Center and its interest in the study of higher education, such civil servants in residence at the Center will bring to its discussions the kind of detailed knowledge of university administration and a perspective that few academics can supply.

From the president's point of view, this arrangement with the Center can be seen as a part of his staff development program and a way to give able and promising younger members of his staff a chance to broaden their knowledge of the academic side of university life and exposure to the broader historical and comparative perspectives that are fostered by our Center. It also can be a way for the university to reward its ablest people, and indicate a special interest in their careers. These Center associates from University Hall will remain wholly on the university payroll while the Center will provide them with office space and the same conditions of support that we provide to our other visitors. We will include these people in our seminars and discussions; in exchange, we will expect them to tell us about their work in University Hall, and to discuss some aspect of university administration that they may be working on while with us. They will also be available for consultation by our Berkeley and visiting associates and by Berkeley students. Over time, we hope these visitors from University Hall will create a bridge of personal and professional ties across Oxford Street. Moreover, if this arrangement with statewide administration is successful, as we expect, we anticipate making a similar proposal to the Berkeley campus administration.

The Center and the Climate for Learning

Underlying and infusing all our activities at the Center is the climate for life and learning that we hope to create and sustain there. This climate is intangible, difficult to define or to describe, but of ultimate significance to our success. It is reflected in our attitudes toward ideas, toward learning and the university, and is rooted in our deepest values as well as in our styles of work and our relationships with one another. The kind of climate or atmosphere we hope to create for the Center can in part be defined by aspects of the academic life that we want to resist: the atmosphere of perpetual crisis and overload, the continual distraction from the central business of teaching and learning, the impersonality of large organizations and of the fleeting and tangential relationships that mark such organizations, the insulation between the public and private lives of the university, and, at this particular university, the low morale that arises in an institution that feels itself despised by governors and politicians not for its failures but for its achievements. Some of these forces and pressures are endemic to contemporary higher education, and are especially marked in multiversities that carry on both elite and mass forms of higher education side by side within the same institution. But we will do everything we can to resist those pressures that weigh on the academic spirit and dull the life of the mind. We have spoken of the Center as a protected environment, in the sense of its being a forum for discussion rather than an arena for negotiation and action. But the Center can also be a protected environment in a more general sense—that is, an environment that is protected against some of the pathologies of the multiversity.

For example, our decision to exclude large-scale contract research from the Center should reduce the terrible pressures of deadlines, quarterly reports, proposal writing, and the contagious anxieties of a large staff on soft funds. These pressures, and the work overloads that accompany them, are not, we believe, a good environment for broad and reflective discussion of problems or issues. If we are to seek wisdom as well as knowledge, we need some measure of serenity in our working lives and environment.

Our staff is and will continue to be very small. This greatly reduces the time spent on collective decision making and elaborate record keeping, and frees our energies for thinking about the Center, its mission, program, and climate. The small size of the staff also reduces the need for hierarchy, necessary in bureaucratic administrative staffs, but at odds with the collegial spirit of intellectual work and discussion.

We have spoken of our firm intention to bridge the gulf between policy studies and basic inquiry as between the public and private lives of higher education. We understand full well the severe pressures on senior administrators, struggling to maintain the autonomy and excellence of the university in a hostile environment. But we know how oppressive, how all-encompassing can be the climate of adversarial politics, with its harsh and often irrational demands for arguments, rhetoric, and budgetary formulas, and its remoteness from the worlds of art, science, and scholarship. We can serve, we believe, if we take that world seriously but not always on its own narrow terms, and bring to its practical and often brutal simplifications the richer and more modulated perspectives of history and comparative studies, and even, on occasion the insights of art and literature. The pressures on modern university administrators are very great. This Center may serve both action and understanding by creating an environment in which they can step aside from the arena and expand the narrow categories of its controversies by making them the object of scholarly discussion as well as negotiation and debate.

On a campus of 30,000 students and 1,500 faculty members, part of a university of more than 5,000 faculty with a central administrative staff of more than 600, we find that we need to know too many people to be able to know many of them very well. And the people whom we know at all will tend to be colleagues in our departments, or people in closely related administrative roles or offices. The implications of the scale of modern universities and university systems for what goes on inside them is an appropriate topic for one of our seminars, rather than an annual report. And yet it is appropriate here to explain why we are so determined to remain small in our seminars and in our staff. It is to create conditions under which people can come to know one another's minds, attitudes, and sensibilities through relationships that are not fleeting, tangential, or purely instrumental. The membership of our seminar will change from year to year, in part in response to the members' own changing interests and schedules, in part reflecting the fact that some members will be visitors to the Center. Moreover, the membership of the seminars will change on our initiative as we seek for new ideas and perspectives from new members. Nevertheless, we hope that at least a core of members of our seminars will continue to participate over long periods of time, giving the seminars the distinctive character of their own interests and qualities, as these subtly change over time in response to their interactions with one another.

One inherent virtue of interdisciplinary groups is that they make more difficult the arid pedantry and methodological ritualism that are the pathologies of high scholarship. They also make more difficult the technical jargons in which university administration as well as scholarship is often carried on—the pidgin English that links the several tribes of scholars and administrators who engage in verbal (and material) exchange at the frontiers. These languages may have some instrumental value in advancing knowledge within small communities of specialists or in certain kinds of technical negotiations across boundaries, but they exclude much that can illuminate their subjects—the questioning of assumptions, the examination of value implications, and above all the quality of feeling that is associated with learning and practice. We will listen with respect to professional reports of studies and action couched in the languages of scholarship and policy, but we will also try to remind ourselves that there are other ways of knowing and communicating, more personal, more direct, more informal—the languages by which people speak to one another when they most want to be understood.

We have spoken earlier of our dedication to a search for the links between knowledge and practice. But we are equally deeply committed to the search for the links between knowledge and practice on one side, and feeling on the other. This does not mean that our seminars will be encounter groups or T-groups. It does mean that we will stay alive to the quality of feeling lying behind what is said, for example, to the pleasures and pains of inquiry, and not merely to its results. We will also try to sustain a climate of discussion in which contributions and papers are a stimulus to thought and action rather than performances to be judged and graded.

In these and perhaps other ways still to be discovered we can resist the pressures that make the university more dispirited and dispiriting than it needs to be. If morale within the university is low, as it seems to be, it may be so because our proudest achievements are not recognized as achievements at all by powerful politicians who cannot find anything to praise in what is surely one of the great universities in the world. The politician's sour resentment, the contempt, not for the university's failures but for its achievements, takes the heart out of us, and its effects on life and learning are tangible; we feel them every day. In our small part of the world, we will reaffirm our commitment to those human and institutional qualities that make higher education, at Berkeley as elsewhere, a vital part of modern civilization, one of its few really successful institutions. Our Center is and hopes to be a protected environment in which controversial issues can be examined in a more leisurely and dispassionate way, and perhaps from broader perspectives than is ordinarily possible to the actors. But we are not neutral about everything. The Center is in the service of a more humane conception of the university, of what it may be as well as what it is. We will oppose the conception of the university as another branch or agency of state government, in favor of our sense of it as a unique cultural and intellectual resource of the whole society. But we are prepared to examine that bias too. What Kenneth Burke said ironically of sociology as a discipline is even more true of the study of higher education: "Everything is grist for the mill, including the mill."

The Center: Location and Space

Shortly after the Center for the Study of Higher Education was established in 1956 under the direction of T. R. McConnell, it was housed in an old redwood shingle residence at the corner of Gayley Road and Bancroft Way. When that house was torn down to make way for Boalt Hall, the Center moved to Tolman, and later, when it became the Center for Research and Development in Higher Education, with a large budget and staff, it occupied offices in the Educational Testing Services building on Center Street and later in the Great Western Building on Shattuck Avenue.

As part of the Berkeley administration's acceptance of a new character and direction for the Center for Studies in Higher Education, it agreed at the time of the appointment of new leadership in 1977 to provide space for the Center on campus. South Hall Annex became available, and was assigned to the Center in the spring of 1977. The Annex had been used as an office for student job placement and vocational guidance, and most recently as the home of a research project in library science. When the Center took it over in July 1977 it was really not useful—dingy, dirty, and unattractive. It clearly needed first aid to make it even temporarily useful to our Center staff, and more substantial modifications were needed if the space were to be suitable for our long-term program. On the positive side, the Annex is perfectly located for our purposes, lying squarely in the center of campus, on everyone's path to everywhere. We could not want a better location, and very much appreciate the administrative wisdom that made this valuable space available to us. Moreover, the building encloses about 1,900 square feet, which when properly divided and furnished, will give us the space we need for most of our activities. In response to our immediate need for working and planning space, Dean Elberg provided support for cleaning, painting, and repair of the existing facility. The newly spruced up space was available to us in April 1978, and we promptly moved in, with furniture and a library inherited from the Center for Research and Development in Higher Education. While the space provided a home for the staff, it had several major drawbacks for our permanent use. One was that the small offices that occupied half of the space were enclosed in glass partitions that only rose halfway to the ceiling; thus, they did not offer their occupants any visual or aural privacy. While this may have been compatible with former functions, it clearly will not do for offices for the Center's staff or visitors. In addition, the space available for seminars and meetings was not enclosed, and disturbed by every phone call or individual entering our front door.

We therefore initiated discussions with the chancellor's office about the need for a substantial modification and renovation of South Hall Annex. The needs of our program were clear, and the space in the Annex would meet them. We wanted our present offices enclosed from floor to ceiling, three new offices carved out of existing space, and a seminar room enclosed. Discussions with the office of facilities management were held, an architect was consulted, and again with help from Dean Elberg's office, preliminary sketches were prepared. One of these met our needs neatly, and we began the difficult process of getting funds and the various approvals necessary for such a work of renovation. We were very happy and gratified that the campus administration was able to supply the funds for the estimated cost of reconstruction at a time of financial stringency. We hoped that the actual construction could be completed by September 1978 so that the Center would be ready for its visitors and program for the fall quarter. Unfortunately, and perhaps inevitably, there were delays. It now seems likely that we will not be able to occupy the renovated space until the beginning of the winter quarter. This delay will cause some inconvenience for our program of seminars and meetings, and especially to our visitors, in the fall quarter.

Nevertheless, for all our impatience to settle into our permanent home, we do recognize that we are fortunate to have this beautifully located space and even more fortunate to have been given the resources necessary to make it useful to us. The renovated Center will have eleven small offices, of which six or seven will be available for visiting associates of the Center. The Center will also have a seminar room, seating perhaps twenty around a large table, and used at other times as a lounge and reading room. We have inherited a large stock of reports and periodicals, and, with our own subscriptions to journals and papers dealing with higher education, we will be able to provide an attractive reading room for faculty and students. We have no funds to maintain a research library in this building, but we are next door to the main library, Tolman with its educational/psychology library is nearby, and in addition we have established a working relationship with the excellent library of current books, reports, and journals maintained by the Carnegie Council on Policy Studies in Higher Education in its offices on Shattuck Avenue.

Together with its central location, our renovated quarters are very much in keeping with our conception of the Center . . . [5]

NOTES

1. The report went on to identify and introduce a number of them, as well as future visitors.

2. The report here introduced those who had visited or were to visit the Center.

3. An account of the director's own work in Sweden during the past year.

4. The report then gave details of five Swedish visitors who were due to visit the Center in the coming year.

5. The report concluded with a conventional account of all the academic activities of the director, the associate director, Sheldon Rothblatt, and the assistant director, Janet Ruyle, over the past year, their lectures, publications, meetings attended, and their research, along with a record of the seminars, colloquia, and meetings a held at the Center.

PART V

Governance and Reform
of the American University

12

THIS IS ONE OF MARTIN TROW'S BEST-KNOWN and most frequently quoted publications, which he followed up over the next two decades with essays on university leadership and presidents, two of which are reproduced in the chapters that follow. He continued to expand and rework this essay, adding valuable detail and updating developments at Berkeley, but I have selected the shorter, original one since it had more punch and clearer lines of argument.

In the early 1980s, major changes were under way within biology. There were some 250 biologists on the Berkeley campus, split among some 20 departments. Noticing various signs that the discipline as a whole was not keeping pace with its peers elsewhere, a provost commissioned an internal audit. This reported an irrelevant departmental structure, inadequate buildings and facilities, a failure to develop strong research groups in newer areas of biology, and a serious fall in Berkeley's reputation in the field. In August 1981 it recommended the creation of the Advisory Council on Biology, which became a powerful agent of change, as it consisted of some of Berkeley's most distinguished biologists and reported directly both to the deans and to the chancellor. All biology departments were placed temporarily under its guidance, and it recommended that new laboratory space be built for affinity research groups in different areas rather than for departments, which would require the renovation of existing life sciences facilities and the construction of two new buildings. Having accepted these recommendations, the chancellor, along with the president of the university, set out to raise the necessary funds, both in Sacramento and from private sources. By 1984, the funds had been raised, plans for reconstruction were in hand, and the reforms had been widely accepted by Berkeley's biologists. National rankings of its biology departments had also started to improve.

Trow's analysis of these events is prefaced by his explanation of why many observers thought that it was nearly impossible for university presidents or vice chancellors to accomplish anything of significance and therefore portrayed their role as largely symbolic. The first reason was the division of academic knowledge, which meant that much of the power and authority in academic institutions resides at the very bottom, in departments or chairs; second, the enormous complexity of modern universities made them seem almost unmanageable; and third, the movements in many countries toward greater central control left little room for institutional autonomy or therefore leadership.

In the light of his research, Trow decided that this literature, stressing the impotence of academic leaders and the apparently random and non-purposeful character of their responses to problems, had been misled by studying university leadership at a particular point in time, as if cutting a cross section of a thick cable, made up of many strands, each representing a program or activity. Instead, he suggested, they should examine it like a multi-stranded cable cut vertically along the dimension of time, so that one could see each strand extending backward and forward, moving along its own coherent, purposeful, even rational way, marked by its own set of actors with goals that are largely insulated from other strands, even though they intertwine.

Using this perspective, Trow suggested that it is "the multiplicity of . . . activities, governed by different norms and purposes and pursued in different ways that defines the comprehensive university." And the key to understanding academic leadership lies in the form of insulation of different activities governed by different values, and the ways in which they are brought together in the office of president. Trow pointed to the "unwritten treaty" between the university and the state, in which the state says to the university: "we will support your ambitions to be a world-class university if you will look after our bright children—white, black, or brown." So the chancellor's outreach programs to minority high schools, he argued, were part of the story of revitalization of biology at Berkeley. These two strands were not competitive but supportive, and the task of university leadership was to support both strands and weave them together.

He finally raised the question of under what conditions institutional leadership could be exercised effectively, and suggested that changes initiated by a university leader were more likely to succeed if they reflected the shared values of the academic community, and that successful leaders needed discretionary powers as well as discretionary resources to implement change.

This essay had a major impact on the literature on university leadership. Some observers have shared Trow's view that while the academic department may still be useful for administrative purposes, it has become increasingly irrelevant and even a hindrance in the creation of new knowledge. In the past decade or so, however, others such as Burton Clark, Frans van Vught, Sheila Slaughter, and Gary Rhoades on the entrepreneurial university have shown that, in some contexts, presidents can achieve substantial change.

—GRANT HARMAN

Leadership and Organization

The Case of Biology at Berkeley

I

My subject is leadership and organization in higher education. Leadership implies the ability to get something done. But if there is a consensual wisdom on this question currently, it is that leadership in higher education, especially leadership of universities, is hardly possible, since the nature of the institution and its relation to the larger society make it nearly impossible for presidents or vice chancellors or rectors or other university leaders to accomplish anything of significance.

The weakness of institutional leadership in higher education in all

Originally published as Martin Trow, "Leadership and Organization: The Case of Biology at Berkeley," chapter 7 in *Higher Education Organization: Conditions for Policy Implementation*, edited by Rune Premfors, pp. 148–78. Stockholm, Sweden: Almqvist & Wiksell International, 1984. Reprinted by permission of Almqvist & Wiksell Int.

advanced societies, it is argued, arises for at least three reasons, which vary in strength in different countries and under different circumstances. First, institutional leadership is weak because the extreme division of knowledge in academic society locates much of the effective authority and power in the institution at the bottom, in the departments or chairs. In universities, it is the fields of knowledge, the subjects of study, often highly specialized and esoteric, that are "the most important bases of organization" (Clark 1983b, p. 17). It follows that "a university-type organization is one in which there are many cells of specialization side by side and loosely connected at the operating level, together with only a small number of higher levels of coordination" (Clark, 1983b, p. 17). The bottom-heaviness of the university, arising out of the centrality of the lower-level units that manage teaching and learning, ensures a secondary or derivative role for institutional management. In such institutions, "made bottom heavy by the centrality and weight of the disciplines and professional fields, incremental adjustment is the pervasive and characteristic form of change. Since tasks and powers are extremely divided, global change is very difficult to effect . . . The leading false expectation in academic reform is that large results can be obtained by top-down manipulation. Instead, small results typically follow from efforts at the top, in the middle, or at the bottom, in the form of zig-and-zag adjustments, wrong experiments, and false starts, out of which precipitate some flows of change" (Clark, 1983a, p. 114).

Second, so the argument goes, the enormous complexity of colleges and universities, arising out of both the variety of activities that go on within them and the diversity of functions that they play in the larger society, make those institutions essentially unmanageable. The role of institutional leaders in those situations are in large part symbolic ones, to give a veneer of rationality to what is largely a non-rational process of uncoordinated responses to unanticipated events—in the pejorative sense, to rationalize as decisions what are the cumulative effects of many actions only a few of which are taken by the institutional leaders themselves. In this view, developed most fully by James March and his colleagues, colleges and universities are prototypical "organizational anarchies" characterized by problematic goals, unclear technology, and fluid participation—in which problems are more often evaded than solved through "garbage can decision processes" (Cohen and March, 1974, p. 2). Without clear purpose or leadership, it follows that "anything that requires a coordinated effort of the organization in order to start is unlikely to be started. Anything that requires a coordinated effort of the organization in order to be stopped, is unlikely to be stopped" (Cohen and March, 1974, p. 206).

And if the university cannot be led or moved, then consistently enough in their view

> the presidency is an illusion. Important aspects of the role seem to disappear on close examination. In particular, decision making in the university seems to result extensively from a process that decouples problems and choices and makes the president's role more commonly sporadic and symbolic than significant. (Cohen and March, 1974, p. 2)

Presidents of public universities are, they believe, especially weak:

> Public universities make weak budget presidents. The presidents of a public university must simultaneously negotiate the appropriations for his operating budget from the legislature or some intervening body and negotiate the allocation of that budget among his departments. The simultaneity and public character of those two negotiations restrict him seriously. (Cohen and March, 1974, p. 102)

And further, "for the most part, however, and particularly in the larger schools, presidents do not appear to have much to say about academic policy" (Cohen and March, 1974, p. 103).

Third, the broad movement in many countries toward greater central direction over broad educational systems in the name of democratization, broader access, predictability, administrative efficiency, and social utility, works against institutional autonomy, without which there is little room for institutional leadership. Indeed, in the discussions by Europeans of decision making within their own systems of higher education, there is little discussion of the role of institutional leadership, as opposed to management, perhaps for the simple reason that European institutions and those derived from European models do not give institutional leaders much power. Much of this writing addresses the capacity of central authority to make effective changes within institutions, and sees the central dialogue, so to speak, as between central planning agencies and the primary units, the disciplines and the departments, at the bottom. Maurice Kogan's term for the role of central leadership in the British university is *managerialism* and he sees it somewhat strengthened currently by the enormous pressures of budget cuts on the universities from above. But he certainly does not envision a particularly creative role for the university vice chancellors beyond the orderly management of decline. Similarly, Geoffrey Caston suggests that in British universities "leadership consists of effectively providing support, psychological, social and financial, for those who are teaching, learning and doing research." It is the maintenance of an environment in which these activities can be effectively carried on, and "an essential function of the university leader is therefore to coax and cajole those who command society's resources" (Caston, 1982).[1]

It may well be that these generalizations about the nature of academic institutions, and the difficulties of reforming them through purposeful leadership within the institution, are correct in a broad comparative perspective. But there are large and important categories of institutions, particularly in the United States, where they are not true.[2] In this essay I consider a deviant case, a case in which at least in one American university, substantial changes have been made and are continuing to be made through "a coordinated effort of the organization" that has required institutional leadership at the top, in the office of the university's president—called at Berkeley the "chancellor." The analysis of a deviant case need not have as its intention the overthrow of the truth of the relationship to which it is deviant. But deviant case analysis can help us to specify the conditions under which the main relationship obtains, and the conditions under which it does not (Lipset, Trow, and Coleman, 1956). And in so doing, it may enable us to see more clearly the mechanisms that link the elements in the broader relationship.

II

The case is drawn from recent and current events at the University of California, Berkeley, and has to do with how that particular university has responded to recent very rapid changes in the biological sciences, a problem faced by nearly every research university in the world that tries to stay at the forefront of knowledge.

It is a commonplace, though one with large consequences, that

the science of biology has undergone a revolution in the past twenty years which has transformed the ways in which living things are understood. It represents perhaps the most impressive example of human creativity since the revolutionary discoveries in the physical sciences in the early 1900's. In the broadest terms, this revolution is a consequence of unraveling those principles which apply to all life. Through molecular studies the underlying similarities in the chemistry of all living organisms have been demonstrated, broadening and transforming the sciences of biochemistry into an essential discipline for understanding the functions of all organisms. A second element has been the emergence of molecular genetics, the understanding of the genetic code, and the utilization of genetic engineering to open frontiers in research and industry. Thirdly, cell biology has emerged as a major discipline revealing insights into the similarities and differences of the substructures of all cells. Finally, the development of computers and new mathematical routines has been especially useful in this area, and has critical importance for many aspects of agriculture, as well as for such applied fields as epidemiology and toxicology.

In these ways the study of living things has matured into a quantitative science with a substructure of overlapping component disciplines which no longer have the precise disciplinary lines familiar in the past. (University of California, 1983)

This enormous revolution in the biological sciences, affecting every area and sub-discipline within it, has proceeded with accelerating speed, taking special impetus with the emergence of the ability to do genetic engineering—to clone and sequence genes—in 1973, and developing a whole variety of ramified and related discoveries since. As byproducts of these discoveries, new opportunities for applied research and development in many fields have opened up. In California, "new companies have been formed to take advantage of recent discoveries, and large industrial firms in the pharmaceutical, chemical, agricultural and energy areas are beginning to invest heavily in applications of biological technology" (University of California, 1983). Another spinoff of these rapid developments has been that a very large number of the brightest young people in the country are currently attracted into the biological sciences, further accelerating the advances of the science itself.

It is the great research universities, at least in the United States, which have been the locus of this revolution. But the revolution in biology did not just create an enormous ferment of excitement and seemingly endless flow of significant discoveries, each opening up yet another set of research possibilities. It did that, but it also generated a set of problems for mature research universities by the very success and rapidity of development of the science. By "mature" universities I mean those whose broad departmental organizations in biology, as in other fields, were already formed and in place when the revolution in biology began. In addition to the departmental organization of the science, the mature universities also had in place a large number of research labs, facilities, and equipment at the start of the biological revolution. What the rapid changes in biology over the past twenty years, and the even more rapid ones over the past decade, have done is to make the existing biological research facilities, and the departmental organization of biology, in many universities increasingly obsolescent, increasingly a hindrance rather than a help to the advance of the science.

I suspect that most mature research universities have experienced difficulties in responding to the rapid advance in biology, both organizationally and with respect to their research facilities. But these problems have been especially acute at Berkeley. First, the biological community at Berkeley is large, numbering some 250 ladder-rank biologists of one kind or another, not counting the many full-time researchers, postdoctoral fellows, visitors, and the like who are also part of the community. This biological community does not include a medical school; what might have been our medical school is, happily for us, a freestanding campus of the University of California in San Francisco.

At Berkeley, biology is currently organized in some nineteen or twenty different departments, ten of them in the large College of Letters and Science, which encompasses most of the academic disciplines on the campus. These 10 include about 120 biologists, with another 100 in the 4 large departments of the College of Natural Resources, and another 30 or so scattered in various professional schools, including chemistry, engineering, public health, and optometry.

The departments in which biology is done and taught at Berkeley reflect the history of the science over the past hundred years. The earliest of them center on the different types and development of organisms as revealed by the theory of evolution. *The Origin of Species* was published eight years before the university was founded. So we have departments of zoology (1870), botany (1890), bacteriology (1911), and the establishment of departments in the College of Agriculture with a more applied orientation such as entomology and parasitology (1891) and plant pathology (1903), for example. The rediscovery of genetics at the turn of the century was a unifying influence and left departmental residues (e.g., genetics, 1913). Somewhat later came biochemistry and virology (1948) and molecular biology (1964). So at Berkeley we see a kind of geological layering of departments reflecting different perspectives on the discipline. Altogether this makes for a marvelous, baroque structure that allows for all sorts of insights and connections that might not otherwise be made. But another result is that the field is cut departmentally in many ways that result in very odd combinations of research interests and activities in any one department. And the disadvantages of these arrangements have become increasingly apparent in recent years, at least to some biologists, as the rapid advances in molecular genetics cut across existing departmental structures and made them increasingly irrelevant, and indeed, a hindrance to their members. Scientists with similar interests, scattered over many departments and research facilities, have had trouble finding and stimulating each other. Moreover, new areas of research in biology, not formally organized into departments, are simply invisible outside the university. For example, in recent years Berkeley has not had the visibility that its distinguished faculty deserves in immunology, neurobiology, endocrinology, theoretical and applied ecology, plant cell and molecular biology, just to name some of the liveliest and most active areas in the field. As a distinguished committee of outside biologists[3] noted in their report,

> The general reputation of the biological sciences at UC Berkeley has declined over the years because of a failure to develop strong faculty groups in newer subject areas. For example, there is a substantial

number of neurobiologists on the campus, many with excellent reputations, but the area has not prospered as it might because of difficulties in achieving the proper degree of interaction between faculty members and the fullest development of the graduate program. (External Review, 1981, p. 10)

Berkeley has not been lacking in outstanding scientists, both young and old, in these areas, but scattered as they are throughout the different departments, they have not been able to work effectively within the university, or gain proper visibility outside it. Moreover, as this same External Review Committee noted,

Single departments have planned their recruitment of faculty members so that, over the years, each became a microcosm of biology. This has led to duplication and the physical separation of faculty members of like interests. In addition, this mode of recruitment can lead to the appointment of individuals whose interests are not highly relevant to the most urgent needs of the teaching and research programs when viewed as a whole. (External Review, 1981).

Nor was there assurance that the departments, which traditionally govern their own personnel policies, were going to reflect the new advances of biology in their new appointments; some would, and some would not.

III

But alongside the serious organizational problem stood another, even more pressing though closely linked to the organizational issue: the character and quality of research space and facilities at Berkeley. The largest single building on the Berkeley campus devoted to biological work was built more than fifty years ago; it is wholly inadequate for modern biological research. The External Review Committee observed in 1981 that

UC Berkeley is notable among major institutions in the United States in housing most of its biology programs in substandard buildings. They do not meet safety regulations and it is doubtful that even a complete renovation could bring them to the appropriate standard.

It is impossible to assess the impact that the grossly substandard physical facilities have had on teaching and research programs and on the professional development of the faculty . . . The future of biology at UC Berkeley depends upon the provision of proper laboratory facilities . . . The situation has been critical for years, to continue it invites disaster, physically and in terms of the health of the biological sciences as academic disciplines on the campus. (External Review, 1981, p. 11)

Some of the buildings that house biological laboratories are so dilapidated that they harbor insects and small mammals who are not employed by the university, and who interfere with its research activities.

The inadequacy of the biological space at Berkeley was visible in the early 1960s, when other universities were building or upgrading their lab facilities. But the effort then to get substantial improvement in facilities at Berkeley fell through, largely because the university at large was at that time placing higher priority on getting the newer campuses of the university built up. Moreover, a review of campus space had been made in 1956 that had established standards for the size of labs and offices, and by those standards Berkeley did not look bad in the early 1960s. Those standards themselves have come under sharp criticism in the biological community as having been short-sighted and inadequate even when drawn up. Certainly the 1956 formulas did not reflect the deterioration of the biological labs at Berkeley that had already occurred and the accelerated decline in their adequacy that would result from the explosion in the biological sciences just ahead.

In a way, the poor condition of Berkeley's labs is something of an advantage in the present efforts at reform and revitalization. Berkeley's lab facilities, are, with some exceptions, so clearly inadequate that their replacement or upgrading gains quick consensus from all parties—in the systemwide administration, where capital requests from all campuses are given priority, as well as in the state government, where at least part of the new space must be funded. And indeed, it is this concern about space that has been the driving force of the developing program for the revitalization of biological research and teaching at Berkeley.

Adequate laboratory facilities first became a problem for the university—that is, for its leadership—in 1978 or 1979, when the then vice chancellor, now the chancellor of the campus, began to hear complaints from biologists that they were having trouble attracting and retaining some of the ablest young people to whom they were offering appointments. This is indeed a serious symptom of a problem in a scientific or scholarly field, the kind of symptom that makes the patient even sicker. And on opening discussions with leading biologists, the vice chancellor, who was then carrying major responsibility for the academic side of the university, first learned that Berkeley's standing and reputation in some areas of biology was declining, and that the very high rankings earned by Berkeley's graduate biology departments in a national assessment in 1970 were no longer descriptive of its reputation in the community at large. There is nothing that so concentrates the mind of a senior academic administrator at Berkeley—and I dare say of their counterparts elsewhere—more than to hear that a department is slipping. And to hear that no one department but several important sub-disciplines within the biological sciences were in grave trouble and slipping fast concentrated the mind of the vice chancellor and his colleagues very firmly indeed. The decline was particularly precipitate in the new fields of biology where the most rapid progress was occuring. For example, in 1970 Berkeley ranked first in the national ratings of its two oldest biology departments, zoology and botany; by 1982 in a new set of national assessments of graduate departments,[4] Berkeley still ranked second and third in those traditional fields. But biochemistry had fallen in that decade from second to fourth in rank; cellular and molecular biology from second to eighth; and microbiology from second place to somewhere about thirtieth—it had nearly fallen off the scale. The conservatism of success of Berkeley biologists was destroyed by those salutary shocks; they were as useful to reform as losing a war.

IV

In the discussions between the vice chancellor and the leaders of the local biological community on campus, it became increasingly clear that an effort had to be made to provide new lab facilities if very able young faculty members were to be attracted and held. Emergency measures could be and were taken to provide special funds for upgrading lab facilities offered to new appointees, though these ad hoc arrangements made no sense in terms of the broader problems of the antiquated buildings themselves, and were enormously expensive. But if Berkeley were to make a serious effort to get a new building, it first had to learn what its biologists were actually doing, what projects and research interests were actually being pursued by the faculty on the campus, and that information had to be linked to the adequacy of existing space. The provost of the large College of Letters and Science—himself a former professor of botany—persuaded his counterpart in charge of the professional schools, where most of the rest of the biologists held their appointment, to jointly undertake a campuswide inventory of the biologists on campus, organized not by their departmental affiliation, but by their areas of research interest. The results of the inventory told the university administrators for the first time what the biologists on campus were actually doing, and, incidentally, identified research areas and sub-disciplines where Berkeley was weak as well as where it was strong. The inventory provided clear evidence for the need to reconsider the departmental organization of biology on campus, as well as providing the basis for the next step in what was already seen as a long-range planning process.

This inventory of faculty research interests began the planning process for biology at Berkeley, a process still unfolding. It had two qualities that characterize other planning documents in this program. First, the inventory generated new information and ideas for use in making decisions internally; but it is also served to justify the next step in the planning process, a broad assessment and evaluation of the state of the biological sciences at Berkeley. Second, while it was focused on the scientific and organizational questions of how faculty research interests were distributed, and the extent to which they did or did not coincide with departmental affiliations, the same information was already seen to have relevance for the nature and design of the laboratory facilities in the proposed new biology building. So the very first planning document linked knowledge and justification, as well as the organization of biology to research facilities. Those two linkages were to mark all the succeeding planning documents.

The next step, as I have suggested, was the development of a broad comprehensive review and assessment of the whole field of biology at Berkeley right across the campus. In the spring of 1980, the then vice chancellor, advised by his friend and colleague, the biologist then serving as dean of the College of Letters and Sciences, appointed a special Internal Biological Sciences Review Committee, with the charge, simply, "of evaluating the programs in the biological sciences on the Berkeley campus and analyzing the space needs of these sciences" (Internal Biology, 1981, p. 1). This committee was organized into four subcommittees, each chaired by a very distinguished Berkeley biologist, and each having six other highly respected and active research biologists on it. The four subcommittees reflected four broad areas of biology that had emerged as a kind of natural division of scientific labor in the field—groupings, incidentally, confirmed by the inventory. These groupings did not correspond to existing departmental lines, but were related to characteristics of the organisms that biologists study, and thus to the kinds of laboratories and facilities that they need in their research. One subcommittee addressed itself to problems and developments in biochemistry and molecular biology; a second, to cellular biology; a third, to organismal biology, that is, to the study of whole insects, plants, and animals; a fourth, to ecology and evolution, that is, to the study of populations rather than of single organisms. This division of intellectual labor thus links the organization of the science to the provision of new research labs and facilities in the current plan.

After this internal review committee was appointed, but before it started its work in July 1980, there was a major change in the administrative leadership of the Berkeley campus. The chancellor, who had served the previous eight years, retired and was replaced by the man who had served for some six years as his vice chancellor. The new chancellor had been, and indeed still is, a professor of law and city planning at Berkeley, but also by virtue of his long service on the Berkeley campus and as second in command during the previous administration, knew the Berkeley campus very well, and had, with his colleagues, started the planning process in biology. The new chancellor immediately appointed as his vice chancellor the biologist who had been serving under him as dean of the College of Letters and Science. It was important that the new vice chancellor knew and understood the nature of the revolution in biology, and was sympathetic with it. And indeed, as a botanist himself he was interested in the cellular structure and processes of the growth of plants, and was, in the words af a colleague, "a molecular kind of guy." This referred not to his own research but to his sympathy for the impact of the advances in molecular biology on all branches of the discipline.

For a knowledgeable biologist to be the second senior administrative officer on campus, and the only administrator besides the chancellor himself who had general authority across the whole campus, was of the greatest importance throughout these events. But of equal importance (though I do not want to minimize the significance of a genuine biologist so close to the chief campus officer), both he and the chancellor are active administrators who tend to initiate events and programs rather than wait for them to happen; they show that familiar drive toward achievement that we see in leading scholars and scientists and in some administrators, rather than the equally familiar tendency to lay low and try to avoid trouble.[5]

The report of the Internal Biology Review Committee, completed in August 1981, provided the major scientific underpinning for the subsequent efforts to strengthen the discipline at Berkeley. The report fulfilled certain functions:

1. First, it set forth in nontechnical language an overview of the changes underway in biology at large with a statement of their implications for teaching and research and for research facilities.

2. It reviewed the current status of the biological sciences on the Berkeley campus in detail, both organizationally and with respect to space.

3. It proposed the creation of a Chancellor's Advisory Council on Biology, a small group of outstanding Berkeley biologists, as the major instrument for reshaping and upgrading biology at Berkeley.

4. It proposed plans for the improvement of instruction in biology on campus.

5. It discussed and recommended specific areas of biology that should be given greater emphasis at Berkeley.

6. Finally, it developed a detailed assessment and recommendation of space needs across the whole range of the biological sciences, including an assessment of the adequacy and utilization of the existing laboratory space.

The report supplied the needed "campus plan for biology" that would explain and justify to the systemwide administration and to the state government why Berkeley needed new buildings for biology. But it did much more.

First, it reviewed the problems arising out of the departmental organization of biology at Berkeley, and considered and rejected the proposal to bring all the biological departments on campus into one College of Biology, with internal divisions and departmental membership rationalized to bring them in line with the actual inventory of research interests and activities. Instead, it recommended the creation of the Advisory Council on the Biological Sciences as the key instrument in reshaping and re-strengthening biology at Berkeley. Essentially, this Council, of some seven (now nine) members, each a very distinguished biologist drawn from different subfields, exercises an authority that rests on the collective scientific standing and reputation of its members, as well as on the power it derives from the chancellor.

The Council is essentially a mechanism for over-riding departmental authority on crucial issues. The deans of biology in the two large colleges, Letters and Science and Natural Resources, which include most of the biological departments, already had that authority, but had difficulty in exercising it in a large way against the scientific authority of each department. Moreover, the authority of each dean was restricted to the departments within his own college. The Advisory Council had two special virtues: it could look at the problems of biology—both organizational and material—across the university as a whole. In addition, it could put the great weight of its own scientific authority behind the advice it gave to the deans, helping them to counter the normally decisive expertise and scientific wisdom lodged in the department. It thus could provide needed credibility and faculty approval for the actions of the deans in implementing their plans and recommendations. It must be stressed that those plans and recommendations emerged in the course of ongoing consultations with the deans, who continued to have an input to them.

The Council exercises its advisory powers in a number of ways. First, it decides where and in what fields of biology Berkeley needs new strength. Then it explores with deans (who in turn discuss with departments) where new appointments in these areas will be located. A specific department may choose not to accept an appointment in a given sub-discipline, but in that event it may have to wait for places in biology to open up before it will get a new appointment. Finally, the Council recommends—

essentially names—the membership of the search committees for new appointments, thus ensuring that the quality of new appointments in biology will be both high and in the newly designated areas of emphasis. Needless to say, these search committees are not drawn at random from the roster of biologists on the faculty, but from a much narrower list, perhaps one-third of the total number, who are of course the biologists whom the Council members know to be active and successful researchers and who are therefore likely to make the right choice of junior colleagues. The Council does not itself make the appointment—that would indeed be an overload on a group of very active scientists—but it does not hesitate to comment on and question when an appointment is made by a department that does not look quite right to it, either in the quality of the person or in the nature of his subfield.[6]

Formally, as I have noted, the Council is advisory to the deans and provosts, and to the chancellor and vice chancellor, and meets regularly with the deans of the two colleges in which most of the biological departments are located. But its recommendations, at least for the present, are as good as decisions, and these are firmly in the service of its members' views of where the cutting edges of the biological sciences are.

On the organizational side then, the chancellor, on the recommendation of the university's leading biologists, has put all the biology departments at Berkeley into a kind of receivership under the authority of the Advisory Council—a condition in which the departments no longer have the ordinary degree of control over their own recruitment of academic staff or graduate students, their course offerings, or their assignment of laboratory space and facilities to their own members. Putting *all* the biology departments, strong and weak alike, under the guidance of the Advisory Council greatly reduced the difficulties that would arise from any explicit invidious distinctions among them, while allowing the Council complete freedom in the way it exercises its advisory functions (i.e., authority) in relation to the various departments.

But if the departments no longer have complete or nearly complete autonomy over their own faculty and graduate student recruitment, teaching, and research resources, then departmental membership becomes increasingly nominal. That is not accidental, but is the key to the proposed linkage of organizational structure to the nature and allocation of new research space.

The Internal Biology Review Committee, besides recommending the creation of the Council whose activities I have just sketched, made another important recommendation that linked the organizational changes in biology at Berkeley to proposed space additions. Responding to the marked discrepancy between the formal departmental affiliations of biologists and what they actually did in their research, the committee recommended that the new buildings it was proposing should include different kinds of laboratories and research space keyed, as I noted earlier, to the different kinds of organisms studied by biologists: molecules and genes, cells, whole organisms, and populations. These different kinds of study require different kinds of laboratory facilities, conditions of cleanliness and environmental control, different instruments, and so forth. In the new buildings biologists will be encouraged to locate their own laboratories in the spaces appropriate to what they actually do rather than according to their departmental affiliation, and in so doing, will create what the report calls "affinity groups"—temporary groups of scientists of whatever department, working on similar problems and needing similar kinds of laboratory facilities. While linked by common space needs, such affinity groups would also bring together people with similar or related interests, and thus respond to the criticism that research at the frontiers of biology is fragmented and invisible when done within the existing departmental organization at Berkeley. These affinity groups, since they represent research interests, can be less permanent than department affiliations, and can change as the interests of individual scientists change, or as the science itself leaves some sub-disciplines behind, its problem solved. Whether the existing departments should be abolished is therefore being left to time to determine; it may be that a more rational administrative structure will be needed in five or ten years, or it may appear then to be preferable to respond organizationally to rapid scientific change through these fluid and changing affinity groups centered around the labs. The decision not to undertake a general reorganization of the departmental structure of the biological sciences at Berkeley thus has to be seen as a positive and purposeful one, rather than an evasion or oversight. The case is made that the Advisory Council, by making the present departmental boundaries irrelevant to the development of the field, has given the campus time to allow a more appropriate organizational form to emerge out of experience; and certainly the postponement of that decision has greatly reduced the political problems that would face the chancellor and his colleagues if a major departmental reorganization were attempted at the beginning of the process rather than at its end.

On the broad issue of research facilities, the Internal Review Committee came up with a set of alternative plans for the program of building and renovation for biology on the campus. The first of these plans, which is strongly recommended by the committee, involved two new buildings and a substantial renovation to the existing Life Sciences Building. Each of the two new buildings would cost about $45 million. They would be designed for modern biological research, including what is called "high-tech biology." In addition, there would be a substantial renovation of the existing substandard biology buildings for use by those branches of biology not requiring high-tech lab facilities—libraries, museums, computer facilities, and the like. This renovation would cost perhaps an additional $40 million for the biology part alone. The total package would run, in current dollars, somewhere between $120 and $150 million.

The recommendations of the Internal Review Committee, both for a powerful Advisory Council to give guidance and direction to biology throughout the university, and for new and renovated space, were immediately and fully accepted by the chancellor. That, from a comparative perspective, is perhaps the most astonishing event in the whole story. The Advisory Council was appointed even before the Internal Review Committee could finish it work, and immediately began to sketch search committees for new faculty members in specific sub-disciplines. A firm of architectural consultants had been appointed in parallel with the Internal Review Committee and had begun to develop more detailed plans for the needed new space. Between the review committee and the architectural consultants, the plans for a new biology building had become a much larger plan for two new buildings and the major renovation of a third, over a decade. And the chancellor took on the commitment to raise the money for that whole enterprise.[7]

It is worth stressing that the chancellor, and only the chancellor, had the authority to accept these recommendations in the confidence that he could implement them. He had been careful to get the informal approval of the president of the university for the building program (he did not need it for the organizational changes on campus), and he had won the support of the vice president for financial and business management (systemwide) who had basic responsibility for presenting the capital request of the university to state government, and without whose support and advice Berkeley's efforts to get the approval of the legislature and the governor for the first phase of the building program would surely not be successful. But apart from the president and his staff, the chancellor did not need the formal approval of anyone else to begin serious work on the revitalization of biology at Berkeley. In a formal sense (and the formal structure of authority is important here as elsewhere) he did not need the consent of the academic senate, nor of any group of provosts or deans or department chairmen, nor of any student organization, nor initially of any state official. In fact, he did consult informally with the leadership of the academic senate, and formally with its Committee on Academic Planning, on such matters as the membership of the External Berkeley Review Committee, on the membership of the Advisory Council, and on other issues. Consultation with the biologists and their intellectual and administrative leaders on campus was broad and constant, and earned him the support of most of Berkeley's biological community, its scientific leadership, represented now on the powerful Advisory Council, and the relevant deans of the biological sciences.

The strongest opposition from within the biological community at Berkeley to the new arrangements came from evolutionary biologists and ecologists, who feared that the clear molecular bias of the new seven-person Council would hinder proper development of areas of biology concerned with populations rather than biochemical processes at the level of molecule, gene, and cell. Their protests were strong enough to lead the chancellor to add two members to the Council during its first year of operation, one an evolutionary biologist, the other an ecologist. While there are still a significant number of biologists who are critical of some aspect or other of the proposed reform, there appears to be broad satisfaction among biologists on campus with what has been done so far, and a general sense that the overall movement is in the right direction. It is difficult to describe very briefly the subtle and complex processes of shared governance in American research universities. It is true that American colleges and universities place large powers in the hands of their presidents and chancellors. But the leading research universities also have strong departments, and also often have strong academic senates. These govern with the president and his staff through a process of continuous consultation among academic and administrative leaders who see themselves in cooperative rather than adversarial roles. The relative importance of the several actors differs on different issues and in different circumstances, and it would require a careful analysis of many such issues to see the interplay of tradition, policy, and personal authority as these give rise to the myriad decisions that shape the life and fabric of great institutions.

At Berkeley, the academic senate includes all the regular academic members of the University, currently nearly two thousand. It does its work through a network of committees—on admissions, courses, academic policy and planning, research, graduate education, academic personnel, and academic freedom, among others. In some areas, for example, setting requirements for earning the several degrees, and the character and content of courses, the departments and senate committees together are almost wholly determining. In others, for example, the appointment and promotion of academic staff, the initiative lies with the departments and academic committees, but senior academic administrators have clear and defined if marginal influence. In the allocation of academic positions, and budget allocations more generally, the administration is preponderant, though again, depending on circumstances, it ordinarily consults with affected departments and relevant senate committees.

In the present case, the senate committees played a relatively small part in the course of events. The senate's major concern is the defense of Berkeley's high academic standards against other pressures and priorities, whether they come from the faculty or from administrators. But with respect to biology at Berkeley, the fears and motives of the leading administrators coincided almost exactly with those of the academic senate committees, and the two most relevant senate committees—the Committee of Courses, and the powerful Budget (i.e., academic personnel) Committee—have been glad to approve the recommendations of the equally tough Advisory Council and its related Committee on Instruction in Biology.

Having taken the scientific direction of biology at Berkeley in hand and given it immediately back to a group of elite scientists, all that remained for the chancellor was to raise the money for the building program. This has required, and continues to require:

1. Intensive work in Sacramento and throughout the state of California, marshaling support on key legislative committees, and among powerful alumni, to ensure favorable action in state government for funding the first new building.[8]

2. The strengthening of the campus development office, that is, the university's organization for raising funds from private sources, looking toward a broad capital fund campaign to build the second building and renovate the third.

3. Discussions with federal agencies and congressional committees, looking for federal help with the second and third buildings.

All this points to the importance for university leadership of the availability of *new* resources from both public and private sources, and the central role of a chief campus officer in an American university in raising new money.

The dynamic between the statement of a goal and its achievement as illustrated here is revealing. The chancellor surely could not guarantee to the biological community or to any other actors that all of the funds needed for the building program could in fact be raised. But he believed that by committing himself to a broader conception of the needs of the campus and the the larger sum that would be required to achieve it, he would make it more likely that the first stage can be achieved, and that in turn would increase the likelihood of achieving successive steps in the plan. There is, at least it is hoped, an element of a self-fulfilling prophecy in the large statement of plans and accompanying financial goals. The plan itself, its breadth and ambition, is a statement by the university of its determination to remain a leader in the country and the world in this area of science. It tells potential sources of funds—state government, federal agencies, private foundations, wealthy alumni, private corporations, and the rest—that their contributions will in fact be part of a bold and ambitious enterprise, one that will have large and visible effects on the university, on science, and on the economy of the state. Indeed, the large capital needs of the biological sciences may be part of an even larger program for the renewal of the physical plants across the whole campus. In the setting of these goals, and in his judgment of the right balance between audacity and foolhardiness, the chancellor can indeed exercise significant leadership. No one but the chancellor can set these symbolic goals, thereby reminding the university community of its own quality and distinction, and educating its funding sources about the levels of support required to maintain that distinction. But it is not enough for the chancellor to set these symbolic, institution-defining goals; the chancellor must himself lead the fundraising effort by direct and personal appeals to important sources of funds, both public and private. That link between fundraising (however backed by a strong and professional development office) and the statement of target goals is itself a way to discipline what otherwise might be empty rhetorical gestures. Where a university president (or chancellor) is strong, symbolic leadership is tied very closely to practical administrative activity, and the two necessarily discipline and reinforce one another in the person of the chancellor.

In addition to raising money the chancellor oversees a complex planning process requiring the development of numerous and lengthy reports. Public life in California is characterized by highly professional bureaucracies; this is true of both the university's own large systemwide administration and the various agencies of state government. And both university and state government agencies require very detailed professional planning documents that show where a campus wants to go and how it means to get there. The inventory of biological research at Berkeley began that process; the internal and external reviews extended it; and it continues, in such documents as:

1. Facilities Planning for the Biosciences (1981)
2. The Berkeley Campus Space Plan (1981)
3. Site Studies: Life Sciences Addition (1982)
4. The University of California Capital Improvement Program (1982)

These planning documents, needless to say, are costly to prepare. The earliest studies cost about $300,000 and were funded by the university itself from its own discretionary funds. But in 1982 the state committed a half million dollars for further study, thereby also committing itself, at least implicitly, to larger expenditures down the line. The next step is to gain another $1 million of state funds for preliminary architectural plans and sketches. As I have said, the direction and management of this planning process is squarely in the hands of the chancellor and his staff, and it is he who provides the links between fundraising and physical planning on the one hand, and the continued involvement of the biological community and their research needs, on the other.

V

The story that I have been telling describes a program for organizational change and reform that has been systematically developed over five years. It is not adequately described by "garbage can" models of decision making in an "organized anarchy" marked by "problematic goals, unclear technology, and fluid participation." On the contrary, it has been purposeful, coherent, and rational: the actors and elements of the program have been linked to one another in the service of the purposes of the whole enterprise. It has reflected the strong leadership of a chancellor and a vice chancellor who together identified a major problem facing the university, and then took sequential and coordinated actions aimed at meeting and solving the problem. Moreover, this is not a small and trivial problem, but involves a large number of people, both on and off campus, extending over a decade and involving the expenditure of many millions of dollars. It is likely to have the most profound consequences for teaching and research on the Berkeley campus, and for the university's contribution to science and industry more generally. Nor is this an isolated illustration of university leadership. It could be matched by the actions of the presidents of most of the leading research universities.

I have tried to say something about why I believe that Berkeley and big American research universities more generally are not adequately described by theories of university leadership that stress the impotence of institutional leaders, their largely illusory and symbolic role, and the somewhat random, non-purposeful character of their responses to the problems that they face. If we look at this question somewhat differently, we might ask why the writing on leadership in higher education generally is so gloomy about the prospects of leaders achieving very much under modern conditions. I would venture three reasons, without having any good sense of their relative importance.

First, much of the analysis of leadership and change in higher education by American and European scholars is focused on the reforms introduced by Western European governments into the organization of their national systems of higher education since World War II. These have been for the most part "global efforts," centrally initiated and applying to a whole set of institutions. And they have on the whole achieved rather less than was intended, for reasons that I think the studies of [Ladislav] Cerych and others have made clear. That experience, and the well-documented studies of those reform efforts, have helped to give a gloomy cast to the discussions of leadership in higher education generally.

Second, in the United States students of leadership have looked at American college and university presidents across a wide range of institutions, and have been more impressed with the constraints on them than with their discretion of resources for accomplishing very much.

It is true that in most American colleges and universities there is not a consensus around the values of competitive excellence, nor the discretionary resources of development programs in the service of those values. Instead, many interests, both on and off campus—departments and disciplines, faculty unions, student groups, trustees, intrusive legislative committees and state bureaucracies, political forces, and the like—push and pull the college presidents in ways that make difficult their initiation of sustained purposeful programs of any kind. The leading research universities, both public and private, remain an important exception to this generalization.

Third, I suspect that observers have been looking at the president's role as if it were a cross-section of a thick cable, made up of many differently colored strands or wires, each strand representing another program or activity, and all together in cross-section representing a heterogeneous collection of issues, solutions, and problems, showing little coherence or purpose, as described in March's "garbage can" model of decision making. But in the research university, I think this model is misleading. For if we cut this rope vertically along the dimension of time, we see that each strand extends backward and forward, moving along in its own coherent, purposeful, even rational way, each marked by its own set of actors and purposes that are largely insulated from other strands, even as they intertwine. So what appears as a random or haphazard set of problems, programs, evasions, and solutions in cross-section when viewed at a given moment, looks more like a set of purposeful programs, each being pursued in relative isolation within the boundaries of the same institution, when viewed along the dimension of time. And the variety of these purposeful programs, in values and participants, will be greater the more comprehensive and varied the role of the university in society at large.

It is the multiplicity of these activities, governed by different norms and purposes, and pursued in different ways, that defines the comprehensive university. And it is of some interest to consider how these activities, apparently governed by different and even incompatible values, can be pursued so intensively on the same campus, under the general authority of the same president or chancellor. The key, I think, lies in the forms of institutional insulation of activities governed by different values, and the ways in which they are brought together in the office of the president. For example, on the Berkeley campus itself, at the same time as this reform of biology was developing, a series of other initiatives and actions were being taken by the same chancellor that could also have illustrated the nature of leadership in a modern research university. For example, alongside this program for revitalization of biology, the chancellor initiated a change in the academic calendar from a quarter system to a semester system, requiring a review of every course and program on campus. At the same time, the chancellor ended a long-standing separation of student services and the academic program at Berkeley, and brought together those heretofore separated functions and activities under a single academic vice chancellor. One major activity of this new office is a set of outreach programs to secondary schools in the San Francisco Bay Area, particularly those that enroll large proportions of minority students. This effort is designed to increase the number of qualified minority students who come to Berkeley by strengthening their secondary school education and their preparation for higher education. At the same time, the campus was conducting a critical review of its school of education in which the chancellor took a leading role.

I mention these activities because they all came together in the office of the chancellor, although they were carried on quite separately and in some ways are highly insulated from one another. I doubt if any of the distinguished biologists involved in the renewal of their discipline at Berkeley knew very much about the outreach programs to the Bay Area inner-city high schools. There were of course some overlaps, but on the whole the constituencies for these activities were quite different.

But while the biology revitalization program and the outreach programs to minority high schools are insulated from one another within the university—they do not involve the same people or compete for the same resources—they are linked in the larger environment and therefore in the chancellor's office. Briefly put, a public university in the United States has to show concern for issues of equity and access, especially, as in California, when minority groups have a strong and growing influence in the state legislature and in state politics generally. The chancellor is personally committed to the intrinsic value of increasing the proportions of qualified minority students at Berkeley. But his programs are also politic: he and the university must be *seen* to be interested and active in this area. And that perception, and the relations between the university and the minority communities in California that it shapes, are absolutely crucial to the university's success in raising money for the rather elitist program in biology that I have described. If UC Berkeley were seen by state legislators as a cold, unfeeling elitist institution, with no interest in or programs aimed at their constituents, Berkeley would not have a chance of getting money for a biology building, either from the state or from private sources. This simply reflects the long-standing unwritten treaty between the university and the state of California, in which the state says to the university, "We will support your ambitions to be a world-class research university if you will look after our bright children—white, black, or brown." Any chancellor must attend to the *quid* as well as to the *quo* of that arrangement.

So the chancellor's outreach programs to minority high schools are part of the story of revitalization of biology at Berkeley. But these two strands, differently colored and serving different ends and values, are not competitive, but supportive, closely intertwined as they move along the dimension of time. It is true that the values of excellence and equity are often at odds in university planning and leadership, and the conflict helps defeat the plans of cabinet ministers and university presidents alike. But those values are not always at odds if, as in this case, the programs for equity are in the service of higher standards of performance and achievement, and the programs aimed at excellence in research are not seen to be at the expense of the teaching of the disadvantaged. My point here is that it is the task of university leadership to tend both these strands of university policy, and to weave them together. I need hardly say that it is more difficult to do if those activities are competing for the same resources.

VI

Finally, let me return to the issue I raised at the outset. Does the analysis of this deviant case, deviant at least from the broad proposition of the powerlessness of university leadership, allow us to specify a little more closely the conditions under which institutional leadership can be exercised effectively? Let me suggest two such conditions:

First, changes that a university president or chancellor initiates and coordinates are more likely to be achieved if they reflect shared values within the academic community. In the present case, we have seen a broadly shared and intense commitment among administrators and academic staff alike to the value of competitive excellence, to scientific achievement, and to the national and international standing that such achievement gains for individual scientists, departments, and the university as a whole.

Currently, two broad sets of values underpin institutional change in Western universities. One of these is academic "excellence," in research universities usually equated with recognized scientific or scholarly achievement. The other is "equity," the movement toward increased equality of access and educational achievement among previously disadvantaged social and ethnic groups in the population. Where these values are seen to be at odds, as is very often the case, the resulting lack of consensus in the academic community partly accounts for the weakness and indecisiveness of implementation of top-down reforms, and the resulting widely recognized failure of so many modern efforts to achieve intended changes and reforms in Western systems of higher education (Cerych, 1984). Many of the postwar efforts at reform initiated by governments, both in Europe and in the United States, have had equity as a major driving force or value, so many that we have come to assume that all reforms initiated or fostered by top leadership must embody equity values, and will most likely fail in the face of strong guild resistance and commitments to the maintenance of academic standards. But in the case of biology at Berkeley there was no reference by any actor to equity as a relevant issue at all; all the actors, including government agencies and politicians, have been single-mindedly committed to reversing the decline in the quality and standing of the biological sciences at Berkeley. And the arguments among the actors have been arguments not over ends but over means: for example, should we radically modify the departmental structure immediately, or create new laboratory space and affinity groups in new buildings, while postponing decisions about departmental organization? That kind of argument, and the compromises that it entails, involving certain immediate benefits to all actors while postponing other controversial issues, is a familiar organizational response to conflict over means, a response that is not so effective for reconciling fundamental conflicts over the ends of policy and the purposes of institutions.

The second condition for successful university leadership that emerges from this story is that leaders must have some discretion in order to be effective: they must have the authority to make decisions and the resources to implement them. By authority I mean that the president or chancellor must have the legal power to take important decisions, and that his exercise of those powers will ordinarily be accepted as legitimate by relevant audiences inside and outside the university, and particularly by the academic staff.

The chancellor at Berkeley, like his counterparts at other American research universities, but unlike most university presidents, rectors, and vice chancellors elsewhere, has large formal powers, over both budgets and appointments. He appoints not only the vice chancellors and their administrative staffs, but also the senior academic administrators—the provosts and deans. They, in turn, through authority delegated to them by the chancellor, appoint department chairmen and the academic review and promotion committees. As we have seen in the case of biology, the chancellor can intervene (in this case through his Advisory Council on Biology) to take the power to appoint search committees out of a department and place it in the hands of a committee advisory to him.

The chancellor also has great power over budgetary allocations on his campus, at least at the margins. A large part of the budget, of course, is committed to the salaries of tenured faculty, and to the support of existing programs and facilities and he has little discretion in those areas in the short run. But in the large and costly areas of support services that do not involve tenured faculty, the chancellor has broad discretion in appointing staff members and allocating funds and space.

Now it is true that when departments are functioning normally— and at Berkeley, as in other leading research universities, that means competing successfully for academic honors, research support, and distinguished faculty—they have considerable autonomy in the management of their own affairs. The stronger a department is, the more autonomy it has in making its own appointments, in determining the size and character of its own programs, and in naming its own chairmen. All of this is consistent with Burton Clark's proper stress on the "bottom-heaviness" of universities, rooted in the power of the operating units, which in turn flows from their command of a body of esoteric knowledge and the means of teaching and extending it (Clark, 1983b, p. 17). Ordinarily, Berkeley, like research universities everywhere, is governed through a process of continuous consultation among all the concerned and competent actors, with the issue of formal power and authority only one, and often not always even a major element in the outcomes, that is, in the decisions made and policies pursued. It is a mark of a weak or a second-rate university when its president intervenes often into the details of the routine operation of the departments.

But when things go wrong in a department—that is, when there is evidence that its scholarly qualities and national reputation are beginning to slip—another mark of a strong university is the readiness of its president to intervene firmly to put things right. He can do this in various ways, depending on the importance of the unit and the gravity of the problem. If the unit is small or the problem is not especially pressing, the remedy may be nothing more than the appointment (through a dean) of a new strong chairman from within the department or from within the same discipline in another university, who understands what needs to be done. But where the unit is large and important, and the decline in quality is sharp, both conditions met by biology at Berkeley, the chancellor may exercise his power to take the department(s) into receivership. This concept, borrowed from bankruptcy law, implies that the direction of a firm (or of a university department or group of departments) is taken out of the hands of its own management, and given over to others who are empowered to take such actions as are necessary to make the unit successful again, or to preside over its dissolution.

This power to put a department or a discipline into receivership is held by all American university presidents, and is not uncommonly used. In Berkeley, over the past decade, five schools or departments in addition to the biological sciences have been taken into receivership. The reasons for a department becoming a problem for central administration and the object of special attention leading to its being taken into receivership are varied. The department may have allowed the quality of its staff and their teaching and research to slip; it may have become highly factionalized for personal or academic or political reasons so that it cannot make decisions or govern itself; or it may be pursuing a direction of development in its intellectual commitments to teaching and research that is at odds with what central administrators or disciplinary leaders see as desirable for the standing and reputation of the university or its ability to attract able students or serve the larger society. But something in such departments has gone wrong, something that the department or group of departments cannot or will not remedy by themselves.

Academic receivership can take several forms. In some cases it involves the direct intervention and control by a senior university administrator—or a dean or a provost. In others it takes the form of the appointment of a new chairman from another discipline within the university, or from another discipline outside the university, with instructions to deal with the perceived problems. In still other cases an individual or group from within the troubled department may be appointed with special power and instructions to make changes in the direction or operation of the unit.

Central administrators in America colleges and universities ordinarily take an interest in the academic standards (and standing) of a department by playing a role in the appointment of new faculty members, and in the tenuring and promotion of existing staff. But ordinarily they do not intervene in shaping the direction of the intellectual life of a normal department. A department or school in a leading college or research university normally determines its own intellectual direction as reflected in the distribution of fields and sub-disciplines represented on its staff and the emphasis given to different areas of research. But a department is taken into receivership by the central administration in order to affect the direction of development and academic balance of that department or area; it may or may not also be concerned about the quality of appointments or promotions. In the case of biology at Berkeley, the general quality of the scientists on the faculty was high, and in many departments it was superlative. What was at issue was the broad direction of development of the biological sciences in the university, a direction that could not be planned or determined by any one department. The shaping of the direction of development of the science in the university was accomplished by giving powers, especially over the allocation of resources among sub-disciplines, to a small group of distinguished biologists charged with effecting agreed-upon changes of emphasis, and the coordination of the several units of the discipline in the university.[9]

The power of university presidents to put a department or a discipline into receivership, whether or not it is used, substantially affects the balance of power between departments and the central administration of the university. While it appears to be a major invasion of departmental autonomy—an autonomy rooted in [what Rune Premfors calls] "the extreme division of labor" leading "to a pronounced fragmentation of authority"—I think it can be shown that the exercising of this presidential power ordinarily engenders little opposition on the part of the academic staff outside the affected department(s). And this is for two reasons: first, the autonomy of the departments and schools insulates them from the action of central administration on any one of the others; its effects are not felt (and often are not even known) outside the affected department. Second, it is an unusual action taken against the department where things are not going well; and the action is taken in the name of academic excellence and the reputation of the university as a whole, values that gain widespread support in research universities.[10]

But it should be emphasized that the president's power to put one or more departments into receivership rests on an appeal to values shared throughout the institution. The chancellor at Berkeley had the power and authority to put the development of biology there into the hands of a small group of elite scientists in order to *raise* the quality of research and teaching in the discipline. He would have had a great deal more trouble with the academic staff and other constituencies if he had tried to weaken or abolish departmental prerogatives in order to *lower* standards—for example, in the service of greater access by less well-qualified students. So the authority exercised by a chief campus officer is attached as much to the intent and purposes of an act as it is to the substance of the act itself.

The chancellor at Berkeley also had to have discretionary resources, both money and staff, to carry out his plan. And finally, he had to have a supportive environment that shared with the university and its leadership a common conception of what the university is there for, what its role in the larger society is.

These conditions are today rarely found outside the great American research universities—for reasons embedded in the history and development of higher education in the United States and elsewhere (Trow, 1982). And that, briefly, is why it is broadly true that institutional leadership is not very effective in higher education around the world. But in some American colleges and universities there is a shared and passionate commitment to a single value, such as competitive excellence, which will override other values and interests when mobilized behind a program for reform. This is true of research universities particularly, but a concern for excellence in teaching in a small number of elite liberal arts colleges is another such overriding value (Clark, 1970), and the wish for institutional survival in some endangered American colleges is a third (Cheit, 1973).

Finally, in this essay I have been looking at developments in biology at Berkeley for what they can tell us about university leadership. But it may be useful, at the end of this exercise, to remind ourselves that university leadership exists to serve biology and its sister disciplines, not the other way around. So it may be appropriate to return to a question I raised at the outset, that is, how have research universities in different countries, with their different forms of organization and governance, responded to the very rapid growth of knowledge in biology over the past two decades, and to similar rapid advances in other areas of knowledge that strain their physical and organizational structures?

More specifically, how do universities with relatively weak institutional leadership—presidents, or vice chancellors, or rectors who are really chairmen of their academic senates, without internal staffs or discretionary funds or a tradition of activism—respond to problems arising out of the internal developments of the disciplines, and especially those that arise out of scientific revolutions such as we are experiencing currently in biology? I suspect that in Western Europe small groups of elite scientists in those fields respond to rapid scientific change by bypassing their university leaders and by dealing directly with central government funding agencies for new institutes, new buildings, and equipment.[11]

But however these countries, their governments, or university, or scientific communities, respond to rapid scientific advances, a further question arises: what difference does that make for the development of science or for the character of their universities? One hypothesis worthy of investigation would be that the major contributions to science are made by small elite sub-communities of scientists who in most modern societies make their own informal arrangements with public or private funding sources, and do not need the strong presidents and elaborate governance structures or American research universities. These latter may be necessary to hold together the diverse activities of big comprehensive universities in the United States, and especially to maintain the quality of elite research activities within what are institutions of mass higher education, housing academic work of quite varied standard within a single institution (Trow, 1976).

But while the American strong presidency may be neither possible nor necessary elsewhere, every advanced nation has to ask the question of where authority and resources are best located to respond to problems of rapid scientific advance (and decline) of the kind I have described. That authority must have certain characteristics to be effective. First, it must be able to see the movement of scientific progress as it is happening, and not just after the fact; therefore, it must have (or have access to) scientific expertise of a high order. It must be able to modify or create organizational arrangements for science across a whole university; that requires more authority and resources than a senior professor or departmental chairman ordinarily commands. It must have intimate knowledge of the academic scientists in a given institution, of their individual strengths and limitations, and of their willingness and capacity to contribute to new knowledge in a fast-moving discipline. It has to be close enough to the research frontier to know what is happening there, yet far enough away not to be inhibited by collegial friendships and departmental loyalties from taking drastic action (such as putting one or more departments into receivership) that some senior scientists will certainly oppose.

The presidents of American research universities and their senior academic administrators have that combination of qualities, however effectively they use them. What are the functional substitutes for a strong president in other countries with advanced research universities? Perhaps the partnerships between small groups of elite scientists who know where

a discipline is going and who is taking it there, and central science research funding bodies, together constitute the necessary combination of
deep knowledge, broad authority, and large resources. A research question well worth pursuing, with clear implications for public policy, is:
what form do such arrangements take in different countries, and how
effectively do they work?

NOTES

1. For an interesting report on the implementation of the budget cuts mandated
by the British government and the UGC [University Grants Committee] in 1981 at the
University of Manchester, which supports the observations of Kogan, Caston, and
others on the weakness of central authority in British universities, see Austin, 1982.

2. In one of the few case studies of major academic planning in an American
research university—New York University in the early 1960s—Baldridge (1971) observes that: "it is fascinating to note how deliberately and consciously the University
began to plan its future. The debate, factfinding, and committee work . . . went on
for more than a year. During this time the university's future was being debated on
one of those rare occasions when an organization really maps out its destiny. Rather
than responding impulsively to the pressure of the moment, the university was attempting to plot rationally its future course after a careful study of its needs. Of
course, this is just exactly what one might expect if textbook-style 'rational decision-
making' were really in control. However, such rationalistic schemes are rarely found
in real-life organizations, and NYU's deliberate attempt to chart its future is a remarkable exception to the "muddling-through" policy by which most organizations—
and universities in particular—live." I suggest that such a "deliberate attempt" to
chart the future of the university is not quite such a "remarkable exception" in American research universities, that most universities do not live by "muddling through,"
and that more close studies of actual cases of decision making in research universities
would uncover more such rational organizational behavior.

3. This committee of nine distinguished biologists from other universities, and
appointed by the chancellor, visited the Berkeley campus for a three-day period, read
the relevant documents, including a draft of the Internal Biology Review Committee
report, talked to senior and junior biologists and administrative officers, and visited
research facilities on campus. Its strong report supported the longer and more detailed report of the Interal Review Committee, especially in relation to the grave need
for new laboratory facilities at Berkeley, and it legitimated the "internal" analyses
and prescriptions of Berkeley's biologists to systemwide and state authorities.

4. For the 1970 ratings, see Roose-Anderson (1970); for the 1982 assessments, see Conference Board (1982).

5. By contrast, James March argues that since leadership in the university cannot accomplish much anyway, the individual characteristics of top administrators scarcely matter so long as they are competent managers (March, 1980).

6. The university makes six to eight new appointments in biology every year, reflecting a turnover of about 3 percent annually. In five years this means thirty to forty new appointments; if they are the right people they can have a significant impact on the discipline at Berkeley.

7. It may be noted that the chancellor's authority and actions are at variance with Corson's Dual Organization Model (Corson, 1960). The chancellor, like other university presidents, is responsible for both academic and support services; the reforms in biology at Berkeley tie them together especially closely.

8. In principle, the several chancellors of UC campuses communicate with state government only through the president and his administrative staff. But Berkeley, the oldest and most prestigious of UC campuses, has its own supporters in the state capital to whom the chancellor can appeal directly. However, he can only do that with the approval and cooperation of the president and his senior staff. The arguments that the chancellor uses to persuade legislators and alumni to support a new building for biology say much about the relations of the university to its social, economic, and political environments. There are three main arguments he uses:

1. State support for a new biology building is necessary to maintain the high standard of UC Berkeley as the leading publicly supported university in the United States. This is an appeal to the pride of Californians in their state university, and especially in Berkeley.

2. The new research facilities are needed to enable Berkeley to contribute to the emerging bio-tech industry, and in other ways to the economy of the state, as it has in the past.

3. New lab facilities are needed if Berkeley is to provide an effective education and training to students who look forward to biology-based centers in industry and agriculture. This is an appeal to the concerns of many Californians that the state university be able to provide a modern "relevant" education for its ablest youth that will prepare them for good jobs and successful careers.

9. Premfors's summary of Lane and Fredriksson (1982) is that whatever is done in terms of reforms or the introduction of planning systems will have little or no consequences, "because no real coordination of departmental interests is possible or feasible." That is, of course, a commentary on weak institutional leadership. The power of a president to put a department into receivership sharply, if temporarily,

tightens "the loose coupling" that ordinarily links the several parts and elements of universities (Weick, 1976), at least the coupling between the president's office and the specific units affected by the action.

10. On the role of "competitive excellence" as a value in American universities, and in the University of California in particular, see Smelser, 1974.

11. At Oxford a small group of university biologists, organized as The Enzyme Group, has indeed negotiated directly with the central Science Research Council for a new building and lab facilities, and other support, bypassing the University's vice chancellor and registrar. At Cambridge, the distinguished Medical Research Council Laboratory located nearby is wholly separate from the university, is supported by another central research council, and has few relations with the university or its biologists.

REFERENCES

Austin, D. "A Memoir." *Government and Opposition* 17, no. 4 (1882): 469–98.

Baldridge, J. V. *Power and Conflict in the University*. New York: Wiley, 1971.

Caston, G. "Leadership in Universities." Unpublished manuscript, 1982.

Cerych, L. "The Policy Perspective." In *Perspectives on Higher Education: Eight Disciplinary and Comparative Views*, edited by Burton R. Clark. Berkeley: University of California Press, 1984.

Cheit, E. *The New Depression in Higher Education—Two Years Later*. Berkeley: Carnegie Commission on Higher Education, 1973.

Clark, B. R. *The Distinctive College*. Chicago: Aldine, 1970.

———. "Governing the Higher Education System." In *Access to Higher Education*, edited by Oliver Fulton. Guilford: Society for Research into Higher Education, 1982.

———. "The Contradictions of Change in Academic Systems." *Higher Education* 12, no. 1 (1983a).

———. *The Higher Education System*. Berkeley: University of California Press, 1983b.

Cohen, M., and J. G. March. *Leadership and Ambiguity*. New York: McGraw-Hill, 1960.

Conference Board of Associated Research Councils. *An Assessment of Research-Doctorate Programs in the United States: Biological Sciences*. Washington, D.C.: National Academy Press, 1982.

Carson, J. *Governance of Colleges and Universities*. New York: McGraw-Hill, 1960.

External Review Committee. "The Biological Sciences." University of California, Berkeley, 1981.

Internal Biology Review Committee. "Final Report." University of California, Berkeley, 1981.

Lane, J. F., and B. Frederiksson. *Higher Education and Public Administration.* Stockholm: Almqvist & Wiksell International, 1983.

Lipset, S. M., M. A. Trow, and J. S. Coleman. *Union Democracy.* Glencoe, Ill.: The Free Press, 1956.

March, J. "How We Talk and How We Act." Seventh David E. Henry Lecture, University of Illinois, Urbana, Champaign, 1980.

March, J. G., and J. P. Olsen, eds. *Ambiguity and Choice in Organizations.* Bergen: Universitetsforlager, 1976.

Peck, R. D. "The Entrepreneurial College Presidency." *Educational Record* 63, no. 1 (1983).

Roose, K. D., and C. J. Anderson. *A Rating of Graduate Programs.* Washington, D.C.: American Council on Education, 1970.

Smelser, N. J. "Growth, Structural Change and Conflict in California Public Higher Education, 1950–1970." In *Public Higher Education in California.* Berkeley: University of California Press, 1974.

Trow, M. "Elite Higher Education: An Endangered Species?" *Minerva* 14, no. 3 (1976): 355–76. Reprinted as chapter 3 in this volume.

———. "Faculty and Planning in American Higher Education." Paper presented at a conference on "Faculty Planning and Opportunities," Centro de Ensenanza Technica y Superior (CETYL), Mexicali, Mexico.

University of California, Berkeley. "Revitalization of Biology Research and Instruction at the University of California, Berkeley." Unpublished document.

Weick, K. "Educational Organizations as Loosely Coupled Systems." *Administrative Science Quarterly* 21 (1976): 1–19.

13

TROW'S ESSAY ON LEADERSHIP and the presidency in America's research universities is most usefully read alongside the essay that follows, on the transformation of politics into administration of the University of California. They share a common and current set of governing and management principles and practices that characterize the workings of the nation's leading universities.

In this essay, Trow charts the forces of history as they shaped and have now come to typify the governance of our research universities (and much of American higher education as well). He distinguishes the governing arrangements in America from their UK and European counterparts, the latter having evolved from the guilds of doctors and masters in the Middle Ages and the former having been founded.

Most of this piece, however, deals with leadership in our "effort to get beyond the description by its critics of universities as 'organized anarchies' engaged in 'garbage-can' processes of decision making." Nevertheless, critics of the prevailing arrangements are accorded a fair hearing, for example, the presidency "is an illusion. Important aspects of its role seem to disappear on close examination. In particular, decision making . . . decouples problems and choices and makes the president's role more commonly sporadic and symbolic than significant."

In Trow's view, such criticisms misconstrue and/or misunderstand how research universities actually work. "Leadership in higher education in large part is in taking action to shape the character and direction of a college and university," he writes. He then discusses its four essential dimensions—the symbolic, political, managerial, and academic—and traces their impact on the evolution of the American university's governing structure: the development of shared governance as the preferred form of decision making and basis for the

433

allocation of authority; the multiplicity of funding sources and their link to enhanced institutional independence; the uniquely American role of lay governing boards; and the growing professionalism of the faculty and staff.

There is one point, however, that deserves somewhat more discussion than Trow provides, namely, the uniqueness of the president's role and its centrality to the workings of the university taken as a whole. The president holds the single office responsible for the totality of the university's endeavors and is the one solely accountable to the governing board for his or her performance. It is the president to whom the board turns for leadership of the entire university, not just a part of it; the coherent exercise of its executive powers; the preservation of its independence; the ceremonial and symbolic duties; the securing and prudent allocation of its resources; the selection and appointment of its officers; the advancement of its strategic purposes; and the protection of its character, values, standards, and culture, by way of example.

Thus, it troubled Trow that the presidency should now be judged by many critics to be nearly superfluous, even decorous, at worst and weak and ineffectual at best, and the university itself ungovernable. Those who see it this way regard the president as powerless, the faculties unrelentingly resistant to change, the unions single-minded in pursuit of their interests and lacking in institutional loyalty, the students viewing themselves as customers and finding fault with whatever the president does, and the governing board reducing the role of the president while enhancing its own.

Trow regards many of the critics as viewing university governance and management only in cross-sectional terms. He suggests taking a more disaggregated approach instead, which would help to discern and then to identify the connectedness of events when considered longitudinally rather than cross-sectionally, the latter presuming functional linkages to other discrete activities and events occurring simultaneously but elsewhere in the university when, in reality, no such linkages exist.

Trow judged universities more on outcomes than on process and their accomplishments and achievements were his marker. The contradictions between the perceived and often derided state of the structure and leadership of America's leading universities on the one hand, and their remarkable success and premier standing among the world's universities on the other, are not reconciled near the end of his essay, only stated: "These great research universities are among the most successful institutions in the world. They could not be if their presidents were unable to give them direction as well as the capacity for responding to what is almost always an unanticipated future. It is in the office of the president that the necessary resources and opportunities lie."

—DAVID PIERPONT GARDNER

Comparative Reflections on Leadership in Higher Education

I

In this essay I want, first, to explore in somewhat general terms what we mean by leadership in universities, what its major dimensions may be; second, to contrast the American university presidency with its counterparts in European countries; and, third, to sketch the historical sources of the unique role of the university president that we have developed in America. Finally, I will try to identify some of the structures and institutional mechanisms through which the American university president does in fact take his initiatives (here and elsewhere, the male pronoun is used conventionally to refer to both sexes), deploy his resources, and exercise leadership.

One caveat: many of my remarks about the presidency of American universities also apply to four-year colleges, and particularly to the best of them. But this essay will focus on the role of the presidency as it can

Originally published as Martin Trow, "Comparative Reflections on Leadership in Higher Education," *European Journal of Education*, 20, nos. 2–3 (1985): 143–59. It was revised from the Ninth David D. Henry Lecture given at the University of Illinois at Urbana, Champaign in October 1984. Reprinted by permission of Wiley-Blackwell.

be seen in the great American research universities, perhaps thirty or so in all, of which the University of Illinois is a leading example. Moreover, when I refer to university "presidents," I will be speaking mainly about chief campus officers, though both in the University of Illinois and in my own university, the chief campus officer is called "chancellor." The special problems of the heads of multi-campus systems deserve a lecture, or a library, of their own.[1]

Leadership in higher education in large part is the taking of effective action to shape the character and direction of a college or university, presumably for the better. That leadership shows itself chiefly along four dimensions: symbolic, political, managerial, and academic. Symbolic leadership is the ability to express, to project, indeed to seem to embody, the character of the institution, its central goals and values, in a powerful way. Internally, leadership of that kind serves to explain and justify the institution and its decisions to participants by linking its organization and processes to the larger purposes of teaching and learning in ways that strengthen their motivation and morale. Externally, a leader's ability to articulate the nature and purposes of the institution effectively helps to shape its image, affecting its capacity to gain support from its environment and to recruit able staff and students.[2] Political leadership refers to a leader's ability to resolve the conflicting demands and pressures of his many constituencies, internal and external, and to gain their support for the institution's goals and purposes, as he defines them. Managerial leadership is the familiar capacity to direct and coordinate the various support activities of the institution; this includes good judgment in the selection of staff, the ability to develop and manage a budget, plan for the future, and build and maintain a plant. Academic leadership shows itself, among other ways, as the ability to recognize excellence in teaching, learning, and research; in knowing where and how to intervene to strengthen academic structures; in the choice of able academic administrators, and in support for them in their efforts to recruit and advance talented teachers and scholars.

Any particular university president need not excel personally in all these dimensions of the presidency; leaders vary in how their talents and energies are distributed among these facets of academic life. Some are largely external presidents, presenting the image of the institution to its external constituencies and seeking their support, while giving to a provost or dean the main responsibility for academic affairs and to a vice president for administration the chief responsibility for internal management. Other presidents spend more of their time and attention on internal matters.

But however a leader fills the several dimensions of the role—in the definition of its character and purpose, in its quest for resources, in the management of its organization, or in the pursuit of ever higher levels of academic excellence—effective action in all areas requires that the president have the legal authority and resources to act, to choose among alternatives, even to create alternatives, in short, to exercise discretion. Without that discretion and the authority and resources behind it, a president or chancellor cannot exercise leadership, whatever his personal qualities.

So a discussion of leadership in American higher education must involve, first, a comparison of the potential for leadership—the power and opportunities for discretionary decisions and action—of American college and university presidents as compared with their counterparts abroad; second, some suggestions as to why those differences exist—an historical reference that allows us to see more clearly how and why our institutions and their presidents are as they are; and third, a somewhat closer examination of how American college and university presidents exercise power, and a look at some of the institutional characteristics and mechanisms that allow them to take initiatives.

II

The American university presidency in recent years has had a bad press. Some of the most influential theorists about the organization and governance of higher education argue that colleges and universities are really ungovernable, and that leadership in them is impossible. James March in his various writings, alone and with collaborators, has stressed the sheer chaos and unmanageability of organizations of higher education institutions characterized by "garbage-can decision processes," in which problems are more often evaded than solved. Colleges and universities, in his view, are prototypical "organized anarchies," characterized by ambiguous goals, unclear technology, and fluid participation.[3] Since their goals are ambiguous, nobody is sure where the organization is going or how it will get there. Decisions are often by-products of activity that is unintended and unplanned. They are not so much "made" as they "happen"— they are events in which problems, choices, and decision makers happen to coalesce to form temporary solutions. From this point of view, "an organization is a collection of choices looking for problems, issues and feelings looking for decision situations in which they might be aired, solutions looking for issues to which they might be the answer, and decision-makers looking for work."[4] Such inept, leaderless organizations must be unable to initiate anything or innovate. As Cohen and March put it somewhat epigrammatically, "anything that requires the coordinated effort of the organization to start is unlikely to be started. Anything that requires a coordinated effort of the organization in order to be stopped is unlikely to be stopped."[5] And if the university cannot be led or moved, then consistently enough in their view,

> the presidency is an illusion. Important aspects of the role seem to disappear on close examination. In particular, decision making in the university seems to result extensively from a process that decouples problems and choices and makes the president's role more commonly sporadic and symbolic than significant."[6]

Similarly, George Keller cites Cohen et al., approvingly when he says that "universities love to explore process and methodology but hate to make decisions . . . Decisions in a university often get made randomly—by deans, legislators, a financial officer, the president."[7]

But oddly enough, all of Keller's illustrative cases show just the contrary, whether he is talking about planning for cuts at the University of California, or the survival of a private college in Maryland, or responses to cuts at the University of Minnesota, Carnegie Mellon, or Teachers College, Columbia. These institutions are not exceptions. While each of course is unique, with its own configuration of problems and leaders, the capacity of American colleges and universities to adapt to new circumstances, whether demographic crisis, or budget cuts, or cultural and religious change, or technological explosions, is on the whole astonishing, and most of the gloomiest prophecies in recent decades have not been fulfilled. To take only one example: for at least a decade we have been told that starting in 1979 enrollments in American colleges and universities would begin to decline impelled inexorably by a decline in the size of the college age cohorts, a decline nationally of some 23 percent between 1979 and 1992 when these cohorts would be at their lowest levels. And according to these forecasts, the population of college-age youth would not start to grow again until perhaps 1995. It is true that the number of high school graduates peaked in 1979 as predicted; by 1984, the size of the graduating class had already fallen some 13 percent below the 1979 peak. But to almost everyone's surprise, enrollments in colleges and universities nationally did not fall; on the contrary, they actually grew by 8 percent between 1979 and 1984 overall during this time of shrinking college age cohorts.[8]

Of course, there are variations by region and by type of institution. But nevertheless, American colleges and universities have shown a remarkable capacity to respond both to recession and to declining age cohorts, and have continued to attract growing numbers. I would suggest that much of this capacity to respond creatively and successfully to difficult, and in some cases to life-threatening, circumstances must be attributed to the ability of institutional leaders to innovate, to motivate, above all to lead. Our task is to learn more about the nature of that effective and creative leadership and how it works, rather than to assert in the face of much contrary evidence that it is impossible.

The thoughtful 1984 report of the Commission on Strengthening Presidential Leadership,[9] is also rather gloomy about the state of the college and university presidency. In the course of giving sound advice to institutions, presidents, and governing boards, the report identifies and discusses some recent and current developments that the Commission believes have made the college and university presidency less attractive now to able people than it was formerly. Its authors are especially concerned with the growing constraints on the presidency ("more barbed wire around smaller corrals," as one of their informants put it). Oddly enough, though they reach the somber conclusion that "the American college and university presidency is in trouble," they note that "about one-fourth of all presidents [whom they interviewed] are quite satisfied with their situations (some are even euphoric); about half are clearly more satisfied than dissatisfied most of the time; and about one-fourth are dissatisfied—some even in despair."[10] But as one reads this report one is struck by the fact that many of the problems that university presidents face, including some of those that have grown in difficulty recently, arise out of the very strength and centrality of the role, a role that has no real counterpart outside the United States.

III

However constrained American college and university presidents may seem to American observers, however weak and ineffective they may appear to students of university organization, they look very strong by contrast with the power and influence of their "counterparts" abroad. The question may be raised of whether they *have* any true counterparts abroad. Certainly in any genuine sense they do not. The weakness of the "chief campus officer" (the rectors, vice chancellors, or presidents) of European institutions of higher education arises out of the history and development of those universities. They arose, as we know, initially as guilds of masters, in some places with important initiatives from students. European universities retained their character as corporate bodies of academics that in modern times came to be regulated, funded, and in varying degrees governed by agencies of the state. The basic power relationship in European higher education has been between the guild of academics and its chairman, the rector, on one side, and the relevant church authorities or governmental ministries on the other. Their discussions have centered on the issues of autonomy and support. The leading university academic officer, whether he is called rector, vice chancellor or president, was and still is largely a chairman of the corporate body, and on the Continent and in the British ancient universities was elected until recently by the guild from among its own members. On the Continent, he is still elected, though now from a wider and more politicized electorate.

There has been much talk in European academic circles since World War II about the desirability of strengthening the hand of the chief officer, making him more like his American counterparts, and indeed sometimes an effort to do that has been made merely by changing his name from "rector" to "president." But I do not think that European countries or institutions have actually gone very far in that direction, beyond the change of name. The broad reforms of higher education introduced since

1968 in almost all European countries have had the effect less of strengthening the president or rector than of weakening the professoriate, "democratizing" governance internally by giving more power and influence to the non-professorial staff and to students; and externally, by increasing the influence of politicians, civil servants, and organized economic interest groups on institutional and regional governing boards. The literature on these reforms and reorganizations is not about more powerful institutional leadership, but about more and more complex internal group politics, with central government trying to retain and extend its influence on the nature and direction of the institutions in the face of their claims to traditional autonomies and their newly expanded participatory democracy.

On the whole informed Europeans admire the American university and recognize the role of its strong presidency in defending its integrity while responding to the many needs of the society that supports it. But their history and academic traditions make it impossible for them to duplicate our arrangements; indeed, in some countries they seem to be moving in the opposite direction. For example, the current reform of French higher education has enormously complicated university government there; it has increased the number of central governmental councils that exercise direct control over aspects of university life, and it has increased the number of intermediate institutions standing between the university and central government. It has also further complicated and politicized the internal governance of each university.[11] The new Higher Education Guideline Law provides three elected committees to run the affairs of each university: a board of management, an academic council, and a council in charge of studies and university affairs. These councils vary in size from twenty to sixty people; members are elected every three years by a single electoral college composed of academic staff, technical personnel, students, and laymen through a system of proportional representation. The latter ensures that external political parties and factions are firmly represented on these councils; indeed, it is a matter of principle that each group having an interest in the affairs of the university be represented in its councils, and those representatives are expected to function directly in the interests of the group that they represent. Moreover, these councils appear to have overlapping functions.

In addition, the law provides for five national councils to develop national policies and guidelines on every aspect of university life, as well as permitting new regional and department (county) organizations to coordinate policies at their levels. This is, I may say, a structure worthy of Rube Goldberg; it is difficult to imagine this machinery being able to reach any decisions about anything. I gather that thus far French universities survive largely by not implementing many of the new rules; but that is a precarious way to survive.

Matters are not quite so bad with respect to institutional leadership in the United Kingdom, often cited as the system nearest to the United States in its forms of university organization among European countries. But even there, the University Grants Committee (UGC), long a conduit of advice from the universities and of funds from central government, has more recently become a conduit of advice to the universities from central government along with reduced funds, advice that in recent years has hardened into directives regarding the organization and priorities of individual universities. Moreover, British vice chancellors—the nearest equivalent to our own university presidents—have not on the whole been able to respond effectively to the political and economic challenges and stresses posed by the budget cuts of the 1980s.[12] Those cuts were distributed unevenly by the UGC among the several universities on criteria that have never been made clear or justified. They were then distributed within each institution, usually in the academically least defensible way, in part across the board, and in part by forced early retirement of senior staff, extremely expensive, and involving the loss of men and women who were often at the peak of their teaching and scholarly powers.

IV

So the comparative perspective on American higher education and its leadership is one of American exceptionalism, of a sharp contrast between the role of institutional leadership here as compared with that in almost every other modern society, as well as one of quite astonishing success. We can understand better the highly particularized character of the American college and university presidency if we look at it in historical perspective. The strength of the university presidency in this country as compared with its overseas counterparts arose out of the weakness of the academic profession in America throughout most of our history in conjunction with the tradition of noninvolvement by federal government in education generally, and in higher education particularly.

These two factors—the weak academic guild and weak central government—are also related to the strength of lay boards as the chief governing bodies of colleges and universities. The lay board originated at Harvard, the first American university. The founders of Harvard, community leaders most of whom had studied at the University of Cambridge, had intended to carry on the English tradition of resident faculty control. The senior academic members of the Oxford and Cambridge colleges, the "dons" constituted then, as now, a corporate body that governed each of the constituent colleges that make up those ancient universities. But in the colonial United States there simply were no scholars already in residence. Harvard had to be founded and not just developed. Without a body of scholars to be brought together who could govern themselves, the laymen who created the institution had to find someone to take responsibility for the operation of the infant university, and that person was the president. He was in fact the only professor to begin with, and he both governed and carried a major part of instruction himself, with some younger men to help him. And this pattern lasted for quite a long time in each new institution—long enough to set governing patterns throughout our history. Harvard was established for more than eighty-five years, Yale for some fifty, before either had another professor to stand alongside its president. For a very long time, both before and after the American Revolution, many colleges and universities relied wholly on the college president and a few tutors who would serve for a few years and then go on to another career.[13]

To this set of historical facts we may attribute the singular role of the college and university president in American higher education. He combined in himself the academic role with the administration of the institution. The members of the lay governing boards from the very beginning have had other things to do, and have delegated very large powers to the president whom they appointed, a president who did not until this century have to deal with a large or powerful body of academic peers. The American college and university president still holds his office wholly at the pleasure of the external board that appoints him. Most of the rest of the academic staff have tenure in their jobs. But the president of a college or university never has tenure, at least not as president (though he may return to a professorship if he has such an appointment in the institution). That lack of tenure in office partly accounts for the broad power the board delegates to him; they can always take it back, and often do.

So for a long time in American history there were very few who made academic life a career; as long as that was true there was no real challenge to the authority of the president so long as he had the support of the lay board that governed the institution. This, of course, is quite unlike arrangements in most other countries. European universities, as we know, arose out of guilds, the corporations of doctors and masters and other learned men in Paris, Bologna, and elsewhere. And where they arose differently, as in the modern universities, the academics in their faculties claimed the same powers as their counterparts in the ancient universities. In America, by contrast, colleges and universities were created by a lay board and a president. This has had an enormous impact on the development of our institutions.

The near absolute authority of the American college president has been lost in most of our universities over time, especially with the rise of the research university and the emergence of a genuine academic profession in the last decades of the nineteenth century. In this century, and especially in the stronger universities, a great deal of autonomy over academic affairs has been delegated to the faculty and its senates. But the American college or university president remains far more powerful than his counterparts in European institutions, whose formal authority and power is shared with the professoriate, junior staff, government ministries, advisory boards, student organizations, and trade unions, and where the rector or vice chancellor really is a political man, a power broker, a negotiator, a seeker for compromise without much power or authority of his own.

V

The role of the faculty in the governance of the leading colleges and universities in the United States is substantial and important, but it is as much a source of presidential power as a limitation on it. The two generations of presidential giants—[Andrew Dickson] White at Cornell, [Charles W.] Eliot at Harvard, [James B.] Angell at Michigan, [Daniel Coit] Gilman at Hopkins, [William Rainey] Harper at Chicago, [Charles R.] Van Hise at Wisconsin, [David Starr] Jordan at Stanford, [Benjamin Ide] Wheeler at California, among others—the men who governed the great American universities between the Civil War and World War I, essentially created the American academic profession, a development that coincided with the emergence and growth of the great research universities. Those creative presidents flourished, however, before their universities had large numbers of specialized scholars and scientists with high prestige in American society as well as national and international reputations in their disciplines. Those presidents recruited distinguished scholars and scientists, paid them decent salaries, rewarded their scholarship and research, and thus created the faculty of the modern research university, a body of men and women who could meet them, collectively at least, as equals. The American academic profession and its instruments—the senates on campus and the American Association of University Professors (AAUP) and the various disciplinary associations nationally—were the institutionalized expression or reflection of those scholars and scientists brought together in the new research universities by this generation of great university presidents. It was the growth of that body of academics, increasingly aware of their collective importance to the university and to its supporters and constituents outside the university, that gave rise to the modern university faculty, determined to be treated as members and not merely as employees of the university. They thus came to be included in the governance of the universities, in a role that stressed their right to be consulted on matters of importance to them.

In the leading universities, both public and private—though matters are quite different in the second- and third-tier universities—what has evolved is a system of shared governance, marked by a degree of cooperation and mutual trust that has survived the political stresses of the 1960s, the demands for greater accountability from state governments of the 1970s, the growth of federal law and regulation, the consequent elaboration and formalization of procedures, record keeping, and reporting, and the explosion of litigation against the university over the past two decades. Despite all of these forces and the internal stresses they have engendered, academic senates and committees in the leading universities still gain the willing and largely unrewarded participation of active and leading scholars and scientists in the process of governance by consultation. The nature of this shared governance by consultation is extremely complicated and subtle, never adequately captured in the description of the formal arrangements that differ on every campus. Moreover, the power of the faculty varies sharply, depending on the status of the university and of its faculty.

It is sometimes suggested that a strong academic senate reduces the power of the president or chancellor. I believe, on the contrary, that a strong senate enhances the power of the president. An academic senate is, above all, an instrument for the defense of academic and scholarly standards in the face of all the other pressures and demands on the university and on its president. Senates function on the whole through committees; committees are, or can be, excellent bodies for articulating and applying academic values to a variety of conditions and issues that arise. They are splendid at saying "no"; they are poor instruments for taking initiatives or implementing them. By being consulted routinely on a wide variety of initiatives emanating from the office of the president, the senate may in fact give wise and useful advice. But above all, it makes itself, and faculty sentiments, felt by giving or withholding its approval and legitimacy to presidential initiatives. Without that consultation and support, the relation of president and faculty would be largely adversarial—which is what we often see where the senate has been replaced by a faculty union, or where the faculty and president are deeply at odds. And there the power of the president is certainly diminished.

Of course, there are frictions between senate and president; the relationship at its best is marked, in Jacques Barzun's words, by "the good steady friction that shows the wheels are gripping." In such a happy relationship, faculty members recognize that just as the effectiveness of the president depends in large part on a strong senate, so also does the strength of the senate depend on a strong president. It is *not* a zero-sum game. For much of the senate's power is exercised through its advice to and influence on the president: where *he* has little power, *they* have little power. Effective power then lies outside the institution altogether, in the hands of politicians or ministries, as in European nations or some American states.

VI

I have suggested on historical and comparative grounds that the president of a leading American college or university can exercise leadership: symbolic, political, intellectual, and administrative. But what are his resources for the exercise of leadership, especially when looked at in a comparative perspective? What I will say here is familiar to all, and yet is often dismissed or discounted by commentators except when they are actually describing specific leaders and policies.

First, a president has substantial control over the budget of his institution and its allocation. Of course the president's discretion is constrained by the very large fraction of the budget committed to tenured faculty salaries, and to support services that must be funded if the institution is to continue to function. But looked at comparatively, the president of a leading American university has relatively large power over his budget and its allocation. In a public university, he usually works with a block grant; thus he can view the budget as a whole and make internal adjustments subject to the constraints that I have mentioned. By contrast, most European institutions are funded by central state authorities on what is closer to a line-item budget—sums are earmarked for particular chairs and the support staff around them, and to particular services, such as a library. The rector or president ordinarily has little power over these internal allocations of funds. Moreover, in the United States it is now widespread practice if not quite universal that faculty vacancies resulting from death or retirement revert to the president's office and are not the property of the departments where the vacancy occurred. This reversion of resources permits the president and his associates over time to modify the internal distribution of faculty places in response to changing student demand or market demand, to developments in the disciplines themselves, or to his own ideas about the right mix of fields and subjects.

Academic autonomy is related, if not perfectly, to the multiplicity of funding sources.[14] Here again, by contrast with their European counterparts, American universities are funded in a variety of ways, which in itself gives a president a certain power to bargain from strength in the face of demands from one or another of his funding sources. Even such public universities as the University of California are not state supported so much as "state aided." The University of California gets about two-fifths of its current operating budget from state sources; about 15 percent from federal grants and contracts; about 13 percent from fees, tuition, gifts, and endowments; and about one-third from various enterprises such as teaching hospitals, educational extension, and sales of educational services.[15]

But in addition to the sheer multiplicity of sources, some of them are more discretionary than others. The use of unearmarked private contributions, research overhead funds, some of the return on the endowment, is largely at the discretion of the president or chancellor, though over time, of course, those discretionary funds become encumbered by expectations if not by formal programmatic commitments. Programs and people supported by such discretionary funds come to expect that they will continue to be supported. But presidents and their staffs can vary the levels of those commitments, especially if they do so incrementally, and thus maintain a genuine degree of discretionary power over their allocations.

Even where discretion is not total, it may be large within a category. For example, a large sum comes to Berkeley and to our sister campuses through what are called "student registration fees," which are remarkably like what is called "tuition" elsewhere except that they are supposed to be spent on some kind of direct service to students, and not for the support of instruction or research. But "student services" is a very broad rubric indeed, and gives a chancellor at Berkeley equally broad discretion for shaping the mix of such services as between a learning center, medical services, counseling services, intramural athletics, recruitment and admissions, and various forms of remedial education and outreach to the secondary school system, among others.

The very size of student support services in American universities, as compared with those overseas, increases the power of presidents; where academic staff is largely tenured, and their programs and departments difficult to modify except slowly and incrementally, the president has far greater (though never total) freedom to restructure support services whose staff members are not tenured (though increasingly unionized). These large support staffs report to someone directly in the president's office, and they constitute a substantial body of resources and people whom the president can draw on in support of his own priorities, again within certain political, legal, and normative constraints. A large staff provides the resources to put behind the president's own ideas about a stronger development office, or larger affirmative action programs, or whatever it is he may think important.

But the discretionary resources built into student services are only part of the staff resources available to American university presidents. In the United States, the great authority of lay governing boards, much of it delegated to the president, together with the relatively smaller role of central government, ensured that as the public universities grew and needed larger administrative staffs, those staffs would be extensions of the president's office rather than civil servants responsible to a faculty body or to state authorities. As a result, the strong president, supported by his own large administrative staff, has been able to preserve much autonomy and power inside the university. Having his own internal staff allows the college or university president to deal with state authorities with equal skill and expertise, rather than as a scholarly amateur against a body of professional planners and managers. Several points about this large internal staff:

Many, and most of the top, staff people owe their appointments to the president they serve, and hold those appointments at his discretion. In some institutions there are "untouchables" on the staff, who have independent ties to the board or powerful alumni; these sometimes constitute a problem for new presidents. But on the whole, few members of the administrative staff have any formal or informal security of employment, and even they owe their advancement, and sometimes their jobs in periods of contraction, to the sitting president. They are for the most part his employees, in a part of the university that much more closely resembles the hierarchical structures of bureaucracies than the collegial structures of departments and research centers. Presidential leadership is often found in programs that rest largely on this administrative staff rather than on the reshaping of the academic programs directly; and that, I think, is because that is where so many of his discretionary resources lie.

These support staffs under the president's direction and leadership can also develop programs that further increase his discretion. For example, strengthening a development office, increasing the effectiveness of market research and student recruitment, writing better proposals for government or foundation grants, all increase the discretion of top administrators. These activities and funds can provide the staff support for new academic programs, new links to secondary schools, remedial courses, creative connections with local industry, and other colleges and universities. They give the president the needed resources to create priorities, to be an entrepreneur, and to take advantage of opportunities as they arise.

In the United States the president of a college or university is the link between "the administration" and its support services, on the one hand, and the faculty and its programs of teaching, learning, and research, on the other. And here again the American college and university differs fundamentally from its overseas counterparts. Almost everywhere else, alongside the rector or president stands a registrar, a "curator," an administrative officer who is not appointed by the president, and who is not really responsible to him but is appointed by the lay governing council or by a government ministry. In the United Kingdom, a vice chancellor plays a large part in the appointment of the registrar, but the appointment is rather like a senior civil service post, and ordinarily continues beyond the term of any sitting vice chancellor. And that sharp separation of the academic (and symbolic) leadership from the day-to-day management and administration of the institution enormously reduces the authority and discretion of the chief campus officer of European universities, as compared with his American counterparts.

In addition to the support staff I have spoken of, the American college or university president also appoints the chief academic officers; the vice president for academic affairs, the provost, the deans, and through them the department chairmen, who are both heads of their departments and administrative officers. The president appoints them, and can replace them. Of course, he cannot do so frivolously or too often without loss of respect and credibility. Nevertheless, the fact that the president appoints the senior academic administrators, unlike his counterparts overseas (and the British case is intermediate in this regard), gives him a degree of leverage over changes in the academic program: for example, the opportunity to influence the balance of subjects, the sub-disciplines represented, and above all the quality and character of new appointments.

Another consequence of the fact that the president appoints his senior administrative colleagues, his cabinet so to speak, is that he largely defines their areas of authority and responsibility; they are not inherent in the job or office, or in fixed regulations of the institution or ministry. University presidents in the United States (unlike their European counterparts) can and indeed often do change the administrative structures under them in the service of their own purposes and conceptions of the interests of the institution. And that restructuring—ordinarily at the beginning or early in the tenure of a president—may be one of his most creative acts. At Berkeley, for example, the current chancellor brought many student support services under the authority of a vice chancellor for undergraduate affairs, an academic officer, thus breaking down the previous insulation between student services and the academic program. Moreover, presidents can modify the charge and scope of responsibility of any given academic administrator in response to the interests, talents, and capacities of the individual whom they appoint to a post, as well as to new problems and opportunities that develop around it. In addition, leaders can create decision-making structures ad hoc, in response to different issues that arise.

If we ask what is the decision-making process at a college or university, we have to answer, "it depends on the issue." Different people and interests are brought together to solve or address different problems. But who is brought together to address what problems is determined chiefly by the president, and that indeed is an important area for the exercise of his discretion and the demonstration of his capacity for leadership. Should a senior academic officer be brought into a discussion of changes in admission procedures, which often conceal changes in academic standards? Should faculty members or academic senate committees be involved in decisions about the athletic program? Should a university financial officer be involved in discussions about a change in the requirements for graduation? What interests, what expertise, what individuals and perspectives should be brought together to deal with a particular problem; at what point will a greater diversity of perspectives not improve and inform a decision, but paralyze it? Those are among the most consequential judgments and decisions that a college or university president makes.

There is another mechanism of presidential power and initiative, one that lies directly at the heart of the academic enterprise, but that I think has not been adequately studied or discussed by students of American college and university life, and that is the power of a president to take a department or program into receivership. Various observers have emphasized that colleges and universities are organizationally bottom-heavy, in that expertise, with respect to both teaching and research, is located among the faculty members and in the departments. This is certainly true, and under ordinary conditions college and university presidents are wise not to interfere in the private life of departments, in what and how they teach, what they study, whom they appoint, and whom they promote. The autonomy of departments, rooted in their expertise, is an important constraint on the power of administrators, including presidents.

But in American colleges and universities that autonomy can be overridden and set aside when something goes wrong: when, for example, factional fights within a department make it ungovernable, or prevent new appointments from being made, or block all promotions; or other tendencies and events lead to a decline in the unit's standing in the periodic national ranking of departments, or a fall-off in its external research support, or a degree of politicization that affects the quality of instruction, or a loss in the department's ability to attract able students or junior staff. These are among the reasons that lead presidents to take departments into receivership. When they do, they take the government and management of the unit out of the hands of the department members themselves, and of their chairman, and put it in the hands of others, with a clear understanding on how to proceed and what to do. The caretaker may be a person from another related department, or from the same discipline in another university, or even a committee of leading scientists and scholars from within the same institution. In my own university, this has happened to five or six departments over the past decade, including most recently to all of the biological sciences in some twenty-five departments and schools.[16] And like all drastic sanctions, the power to put departments into receivership is a powerful threat as well as an act, and affects behavior even when it is not employed.

Control over the budget and especially over the discretionary resources in student services; the relatively large staff appointed by and responsible to the president; his power to set the institution's priorities, define problems, and specify who is to solve them; his power to take departments into receivership are some of the organizational resources and mechanisms for intervention and change by which leadership can be exercised in American research universities.

VII

To sum up, I think it would be useful to get beyond the descriptions of universities as "organized anarchies" engaged in "garbage-can processes of decision-making." I doubt whether these theories have any real influence over what college and university presidents actually do, but they stand in the way of a clearer description and understanding of what leadership in higher education consists of and how it functions.

Let me close with a query: if indeed the presidency of great research universities is as strong and effective as I claim, why has it had such a bad press in recent years, why it is seen as weak, as ineffective, and as unattractive as it is portrayed? Some speculations, if not explanations, may be helpful here.

First, much of the gloomiest writing about university leadership addresses the situation of weaker second- and third-rank institutions. In the American system, marked by a very high level of competitiveness among institutions for students, for faculty, for resources, for prestige and rank, the power of the leading universities as models, both as organizations and as normative communities, is very great. All universities judge themselves by the standards and criteria of the leading universities, and share their high expectations regarding research, graduate work, and institutional autonomy. But those second- and third-ranking institutions do not command the resources of the leading ones: their financial support, both public and private, their libraries and laboratories, their eminent faculties, all the traditions of autonomy that the leading institutions have gained over the years. It may be that the difficulties of university presidents in most institutions commonly arise out of the tension between their high aspirations and inadequate resources, and their resulting sense of relative failure when they compare themselves to Harvard, to Stanford, to Berkeley or Michigan or Illinois.

In addition to the costs of this kind of relative deprivation are the often frustrating experiences of university presidents even in the leading institutions. The corral does sometimes seem smaller, the barbed wire higher than it was, or at least as it is remembered.[17] It may be that the presidency of a research university is a more effective than attractive position. In one of the most poignant commentaries on the role, the report of the Commission on Presidential Leadership quotes one president as follows:

> On any issue I will enjoy an incredibly high 90 to 95 percent of faculty support. Even so, five percent are dissatisfied with my decision, and they remember. On the next issue, I'll again enjoy the same 90 to 95 percent support, but the five to ten percent of dissenters will be a different group, and they, too, will remember. Eventually one manages to make at least one decision against the convictions of virtually every member of the faculty. By recognizing and providing an outlet for such accumulated discontent, the formal evaluation process merely increases the speed by which courageous decision makers are turned over. This does nothing for attracting the best people into the jobs.[18]

This accumulation of discontent threatens to make the aggregate of many small successes into one big failure. And the inexorable erosion of support that this process describes casts its pall over both the role and the office.

Moreover, university presidents are most likely to underplay their power and effectiveness, and exaggerate the importance of the process of shared governance of which they are a part, than they are to claim undue credit for their achievements. In this democratic, indeed populist, age, the towering figures of the heroic age of the university presidency would surely find themselves under attack as authoritarian, power-driven, and without a sensitive concern for the interests of their varied constituencies in the university.

One example only: Clark Kerr, was, as we all know, a very strong chancellor of the University of California, Berkeley, from 1952 to 1958 and an equally strong president of the University of California system from 1958 to 1967. In both those roles he had an enormous impact on the institutions that he led—for example, he shaped the quite distinct characteristics of the new campuses of the university that were established during his tenure as president. And yet, in his seminal book, *The*

Uses of the University, perhaps the most illuminating essay on the modern research university, Kerr, after some nostalgic references to the giants of the past, observes that in his own time a university president is likely to be "the Captain of the Bureaucracy who is sometimes a galley slave on his own ship."[19] And he quotes Allan Nevins's observations that the type of president required by the new university, the "multiversity" as Kerr called it, "will be a coordinator rather than a creative leader . . . an expert executive, a tactful moderator." In Kerr's own words, "he is mostly a mediator."[20]

This, I suggest, is at odds with the realities of university leadership both as Clark Kerr employed it and as it now exists. Of course, leadership may be more visible and dramatic during periods of growth and expansion, and not all presidents carry to the role the talents that Kerr did. And of course, coordination and mediation was an important part of the job then as now. But boldness, the undertaking of initiatives, the acting by a president on and through the institution in the service of his own conception of its nature and future—in my view, all of that does not have the weight and emphasis in Kerr's analysis of university leadership that it did in his own exercise of leadership. Kerr's analysis reflects his concern (reflected again in the report of the Commission on Strengthening Presidential Leadership that he chaired) regarding the decline of institutional leadership as a result of the growth of countervailing forces and complex power centers within and around the university. I believe his analysis also reflects his sense that modern university leaders, if they are to be effective, must keep a low profile, must appear to be finding a "sense of the meeting," rather than imposing themselves on the institution and taking important initiatives within it. If we compare the modern university president to those of the heroic age, we find today more problems, more restraints, even more resources, more of everything except authority. The exercise of authority is today often "authoritarian" and successful presidents have learned the trick of exercising authority without appearing to do so, to lead while appearing to follow, or facilitate, or mediate, or coordinate.

Of course the interplay among the characteristics of the person who occupies the office, the role, and the university's institutional environment is tremendously complex, and successful leadership today requires high skills and careful attention to the process of governance. And finally, even when the presidency is successful, troubles multiply and opposition accumulates: it is perhaps inevitably a case of "doing better and feeling worse."

This may be why presidents tend to underplay their own effectiveness. But why do observers and analysts do likewise? I have already set forth some of the reasons, but there is one other, and that is the apparent anarchy of intertwined purposeful policies in universities. I suspect that observers have been looking at the university president's role as if it were a cross-section of a thick cable, made up of many differently colored strands or wires, each strand representing another program or activity, and all together in cross-section representing a heterogeneous collection of issues, solutions, and problems, showing little coherence or purpose. But in the research university this model is misleading. For if this rope is cut along the dimension of time, we see that each strand extends backward and forward, moving along in its own coherent, purposeful, even rational way, each marked by its own set of purposes that are largely insulated from other strands, even as they intertwine.[21] So what appears as a random or haphazard collection of events, problems, evasions, and solutions when viewed in cross section at a given moment, looks more like a set of purposeful programs, each being pursued in relative isolation within the boundaries of the same institution, when viewed along the dimension of time. And the variety of these programs in their purposes and participants will be greater the more comprehensive and varied the role of the university in society at large.

It is this multiplicity of activities, governed by different norms and purposes in different ways, that defines the comprehensive university. And it is of some interest to consider how these activities, apparently governed by different and even incompatible values, can be pursued on the same campus, under the general authority of the same president. The key lies in the institutional insulations of activities governed by different values, and the ways in which these activities are brought together in the office of the president. One common situation finds presidents serving what appear to be the mutually incompatible values of academic excellence and social equity, the latter taking the form of increased access to the institution of under-represented groups. In Berkeley currently, the commitment to excellence is represented by a major reform of the biological sciences very much keyed to strengthening modern currents in biology, in both research and teaching. This involved a major intervention by the chancellor with the advice and support of leading biologists on campus, an intervention that required the creation of new institutional forms and the temporary but substantial reduction of the power and autonomy of the existing biological departments to control their own faculty recruitment, graduate training, and the like. At the same time, other units of the chancellor's office were engaged in major efforts to upgrade the secondary education of minority groups in the cities surrounding Berkeley from which many of its undergraduates are drawn. These activities come together in the office of the chancellor, and only there, although they are carried on quite separately and in many ways are highly insulated from one another. It is doubtful if any of the distinguished biologists involved in the renewal of their discipline at Berkeley know very much about the outreach programs into the Oakland secondary schools, or the outreach staff know anything about developments in the biological sciences on campus. In the particular circumstances of Berkeley at the moment, and I suspect this is true much more widely, it is necessary for the university to be serving the values both of excellence and of equity, and to be seen to be doing so. How that is done depends very much on the sensitivity of a university leader both to his external political environment and to the internal groups and values with whom he must work, most notably the faculty.

There is of course an apparent contradiction in the values that govern these two kinds of programs. But these two strands of policy, differently colored and serving different ends and values, are not competitive but supportive, closely intertwined as they move along the dimension of time. It is, I suggest, the task of university leadership to tend both of these strands of university policy, and to weave them together. And if that is done effectively, it may not be visible to observers of the office of the president or chancellor, observers who may be more impressed by the illogic or inconsistency of the values served than by the skills and initiative that enter into their accommodation within the same institution. Of course, incoherence and the loss of institutional integrity always threaten the American research university that says "yes" to almost all claims on its energies, resources, and attention. But it is precisely the nature of leadership in American universities, the broad conceptions of its power and the resources at its disposal, that enable the university president or chancellor to give coherence, character, and direction to an institution so large in size and aspiration, so various in its functions and constituencies, so deeply implicated in the life of learning and of action, with links to so many parts of the surrounding society. These great research universities are among the most successful institutions in the world. They could not be if their presidents could not give them direction as well as the capacity for responding to what is almost always an unanticipated future. It is in the office of the president that the necessary resources and opportunities lie.

VIII

Problems that we have the resources to cope with can also be seen as opportunities. The great research universities currently face a series of such problems (or opportunities) that are uniquely the responsibility of their presidents, however useful their aides and staff members may be. Each of us will have his or her own short list of grave problems that face university presidents, and these lists will change over time, but my own list would include at least the following, though not necessarily in this order of importance:

1. There is the problem each president faces of accommodating to or reconciling demands for broadened access by students from historically underrepresented groups with the maintenance of the highest standards in teaching and research. This is the familiar tension in education between equity and excellence, both served in different ways within the same institution, and to differing degrees by different institutions.

2. There is the problem of the evolving relations between research universities and industry. The question presents itself as how to serve industry while using its funds, research facilities, and know-how for the university's own purposes, at the same time maintaining the unique qualities—the very integrity—of the university as a place committed to the pursuit of truth in an atmosphere of open inquiry and free communication.

3. There are the problems created for the university by the very rapid growth of scientific knowledge, and the impact of that growth on the organization of the schools and departments of science and technology, and on the physical facilities in which science is done within the university.

4. Closely linked to the third is the problem of maintaining a flow of new scientists and scholars into departments and research labs, without institutional growth and with a largely tenured and aging faculty that is not retiring in large numbers until the 1990s or later.

5. On the other side of the campus, there is the problem of sustaining the humanities and the performing arts—that is, of maintaining the crucial balance of subjects within the university—in face of the expansion of scientific and technological knowledge, and the growing attractiveness of professional training, especially at the undergraudate level.

6. And finally, the problem on which perhaps all others depend: the defense of freedom of speech and of academic freedom on campus in the face of intense pressure from vocal minorities of students and faculty who, unlike the rest of us, do not have to pursue the truth since they already possess it, and who are loathe to permit others with whom they disagree to express and propagate what they view to be error and pernicious doctrines. (The theological language here is intentional.)

What a list! Yet we expect presidents to cope with large problems, as no other national university system does, because in fact our society gives them the authority and the resources to cope. There are never enough resources, in their view, yet by and large they do cope. It is still in part a mystery how they cope so successfully, when so much of the theory of organizational leadership tells us they cannot and should not.

But I think that the office of the university president has not been properly appreciated; it has been the object more of compassion and criticism than of understanding. The university presidency deserves understanding, though I suspect that incumbents will continue to speak of it deprecatingly and, with good reason, as fraught with difficulties and constraints. And meanwhile, under their leadership in the extraordinary office, our research universities go on from strength to strength.

NOTES

....

1. On multi-campus systems, see Eugene Lee and Frank Bowen, *The Multi-campus University: A Study of Academic Governance* (New York: McGraw-Hill, 1971).

2. On the distinction between organizations and institutions, and the role of leadership in defining purpose and mission, see Philip Selznick, *Leadership in Administration* (Evanston, Ill.: Row, Peterson, 1957). Of special interest are pp. 5–28.

3. M. Cohen and J. G. March, *Leadership and Ambiguity* (New York: McGraw-Hill, 1974), p. 3.

4. Ibid., p. 81.

5. Ibid., p. 206.

6. Ibid., p. 2.

7. George Keller, *Academic Strategy* (Baltimore: Johns Hopkins University Press, 1983), p. 86.

8. For these figures and projections, see *Higher Education and National Affairs* 24 (February 1984), and *Chronicle of Higher Education,* April 4, 1984.

9. Commission on Strengthening Presidential Leadership, *Presidents Make a Difference* (Washington, D.C.: Association of Governing Boards, 1984).

10. Ibid., pp. xix and xviii.

11. See Guy Neave, "Strategic Planning, Reform and Governance in French Higher Education," *Studies in Higher Education* 10, no. 1, and Alain Bienayme, "The New Reforms in French Higher Education," *European Journal of Education* 19, no. 2.

12. See, for example, Maurice Kogan, "Implementing Expenditure Cuts in British Higher Education," in *Higher Education Organization,* ed. Rune Premfors (Stockholm: Alqvist & Wiksell, 1984).

13. See Frederick Rudolph, *The American College and University* (New York: Knopf, 1962), pp. 161–66.

14. See Martin Trow, "Defining the Issues in University-Government Relations," *Studies in Higher Education* 8, no. 2 (1983).

15. Private communication, University of California budget office.

16. See Martin Trow, "Leadership and Organization: The Case of Biology at Berkeley," in *Higher Education Organization,* ed. Rune Premfors (Stockholm: Almqvist & Wiksell, 1984). Reprinted as chapter 12 in this volume.

17. The phrase is drawn from Commission on Strengthening Presidential Leadership, *Presidents Make a Difference.*

18. Ibid., p. 54.

19. Clark Kerr, *The Uses of the University* (Cambridge, Mass.: Harvard University Press, 1963), p. 36.

20. Ibid., p. 36.

21. This image, and the next few paragraphs, are drawn from Trow, "Leadership and Organization," pp. 166–67.

14

THIS INCISIVE ESSAY AFFORDS a concise overview and interpretation of critical decision-making processes at the most acclaimed American public university. The system of shared governance that has evolved over the decades at the University of California (UC), Martin Trow argues, is distinctive, and the informal agreement, within the university and between UC and the state legislative and executive branches, on how best to conduct business via shared governance, accounts for much of the university's astonishing successes over the years.

The consensus around this distinctive brand of governance, he explains, is grounded on two "mutually reinforcing" principles that guide how "the university relates to the outside world and how it governs itself," namely, "the maximization of the university's autonomy," to which, of course, all universities aspire, and "the pursuit of preeminence." The resulting culture (my word, not his), reflecting those principles, yields an array of practices both uncommon and pivotal; these span, for example, such conventions as trust-based deference to senior administrators on administrative appointments, widespread administrative deference to faculty on academic decisions on appointment, promotion, and curriculum, with a vigorous but largely consultative and largely apolitical role for the faculty's systemwide academic senate, and its campus-based senate divisions.

Reinforcing the unwritten agreement between the university's internal constituencies and key state actors (executive and legislative) are two hugely significant provisions. First is the state's 1879 constitution itself, which recognizes the university as a "public trust"; Trow elaborates on the crucial importance of this charter document. Moreover, the duly famous California Master Plan for Higher Education (1960), the creative invention largely of Clark Kerr, delineated the scope and respective missions of California's three public seg-

462

ments. This "treaty" erected a largely impenetrable wall that, inter alia, protected the university against "mission creep" among public higher education segments. Thus, the university has enjoyed protections that tilt the policy arena in its favor in some basic ways.

Beyond these foundational public policy provisions, one explanation for the university's enviable degree of autonomy flows from the public goodwill UC has accrued via its many-faceted record of public service. Another, implicit in Trow's analysis, is UC's glowing achievements over the years. After all, three of its now ten campuses are indisputably world class, and another three (or maybe four, if we include health sciences specialized UC San Francisco) are powerhouse campuses by the norms of public research universities. This amazing array of campuses generates a huge dividend, namely, a heap of deference to the university, be it from the legislature, the public, or, indeed, from among the university's internal constituencies, including the faculty itself. After all, why quarrel with universally acclaimed success?

Some would wonder, myself included, whether this 1998 portrayal gave the university more insulation from the mean political fray than it actually had. Yes, the university unquestionably enjoyed special prerogatives, but the hard realities of UC's near-constant struggles with the state suggest that, drawing on the essay's subtitle, politics had not been superseded by administrative routinization to the degree that Trow suggests.

He concluded cautiously, saying it is difficult to anticipate the future of the vital governance principles to which the university and its allies have long clung. Now, a decade later, we can assess how durable those principles have proved to be, and test in some degree the author's thesis. Has the Trow analysis held up under a decade's fierce economic and political pressures? Has the UC genius embedded in the culture of shared governance held up?

I maintain that the ensuing decade has, alas, compromised the sanctity of university autonomy, frayed the unwritten agreement, weakened the treaty. Consider the occasional regental forays onto the political playing field; some damaging ethical issues (central office compensation; medical school practices) that undermine confidence in UC; and the loss of the university's monopoly in public doctoral education (at least at the edges). Moreover, the volatility of the academic labor market has pushed all research universities, including UC, into greater reliance on contingent faculty (in the UC context, read academic senate-ineligible faculty), eroding the principle of the UC faculty. Still further, the state's dizzying rollercoaster ride unleashed ferocious pressures upon all of California's public education due to budgetary shortfalls (severe at this writing), undercut UC's favored position, and challenged its strong apolitical culture.

None of these and other developments have struck lethal blows to the unwritten agreement that Trow depicted. UC lives on as a great university, not as pristine and majestic as its unrealized (and unrealizable) ideal version, but still, in the vernacular, awesome. Martin Trow never had illusions of nirvana; too much the realist, he. The organization he depicted may perhaps have been too good to be true, but only by a few degrees. Here as elsewhere, he reveals many truths, both descriptively and prescriptively, about the governing of these very odd organizations called universities.

—JACK SCHUSTER

Governance in the University of California

The Transformation of Politics into Administration

Introduction

The University of California (UC), on its nine campuses and its many properties and institutional connections all over the world, has an operating budget of more than $11 billion (1996–97),[1] more than 160,000 students, and almost that many employees. Within

Originally published as "Governance in the University of California: The Transformation of Politics into Administration," *Higher Education Policy* (March 1998): 1–15. It was revised from a paper prepared for a German-American conference "The University in Transition," March 17–21, 1997, Berkeley, California. Reprinted by permission of Palgrave Macmillan.

the state of California this university is one of 3 segments of public higher education, the other 2 being the California State University (CSU) on some 22 campuses with some 330,000 students, and the community colleges on some 100 sites around the state with more than a million students taking its courses. By law the University of California has a monopoly in the public sector on the awarding of the doctoral degree and a near monopoly on research; it also admits the most academically able of the graduates of California high schools. It is important that students in the other two public sectors are earning credits that would allow them to transfer at some point in their careers to the university, and many in fact do. Alongside the public sector are a large number of private universities and colleges, the best known being Stanford University and Cal Tech.

Any summary of the governance structures and processes of such an institution would take a long book, unfortunately one still to be written. To discuss how this system is governed, how myriad decisions are made about and within it, large and small, is not the work of an essay. So rather than work descriptively through the main elements in the governance of the university, I will try instead to explore what I see as the overriding aims and purposes behind the university's forms of governance and administration. I believe that we can understand a good deal if we see these as embodied in two broadly shared principles in the university, shared by regents, presidents, chancellors, and academics, principles of action shaping how the university relates to the outside world and how it governs itself. These two principles are, first, the maximization of the university's autonomy—its capacity to direct its own affairs; and second, the pursuit of preeminence—or how to become or remain the best university in the country in every possible department, service, and activity. This latter is the principle that Neil Smelser has called "competitive excellence"—a kind of excellence that is measured in comparisons with other leading research universities in this country and abroad.[2] In common language we want to be number one, and we want to be able to govern ourselves. These are not merely abstract principles or ideals; they are the criteria by which much of what is done in the university is directed and assessed.

These two values or principles are mutually reinforcing. University autonomy allows the university to remain largely meritocratic in its academic appointments and promotions, and, within limits, in student admissions and nonacademic staff appointments as well. And the vigorous pursuit of competitive excellence gives the university the worldwide reputation that is the major bulwark and support for its institutional autonomy.

These criteria together lead the university in a variety of ways to resist both political pressures from outside and the introduction of partisan political forces into the governance of the university. The first kind of resistance, against external political pressures, is the obvious defense of the university's autonomy; in the United States, a populist and politicized society, that is a continuing struggle, especially for public universities in California. The resistance to partisan political activity *within* the university is thought by most participants to be necessary to preserve it as a meritocracy guided by the principle of competitive excellence, and that only a severely meritocratic institution can maintain its academic quality and leadership.

Partisan politics—the politics of party and interest—is pursued with great passion in the United States, as we all know. And a central question throughout our history has been to what extent it is either desirable or possible to insulate any public institution from the influence of party politics. One device used by many European nations has been to create a civil service that in its own spheres of competence is to some degree independent of the political currents of the day. And the autonomy of universities in some European countries, with Germany as the model, is in part procured by treating academic scholars and scientists as members of the civil service, and thus protected from direct political influence in their intellectual work.

The United States did not go in that direction. But that has left the question of how American universities, and particularly public universities dependent on public funds, could be insulated from the direct play of party politics and political influence. Not all American universities have succeeded in that effort, or have been uniformly successful throughout their histories. This university has been remarkably (though not totally) successful in resisting political influence, which may partly account for its extraordinary success as an institution. Of course, the university has seen plenty of conflict with political overtones, and been exposed to a good deal of external political pressure over the years. But it is fair to say that despite these pressures, the university has preserved a very large measure of autonomy, certainly by comparison with other American public universities. These sweeping judgments would need a great deal of amplification to be persuasive. But rather than discuss these political disputes and pressures, I want to suggest that the central goal and function of our governance machinery is to resist those pressures, and to remove their causes as far as possible. I am talking about what governance in UC tries to do and, indeed, what it exists to do, and not the more complicated question of how successful it is or has been.

The Resistance to Politicization

The foundation of resistance by the university to political influence was first laid down in the constitution of the state in 1879, which declares that the university is a public trust and that its organization and government should be "entirely independent of all political or sectarian influence, and kept free therefrom in the appointment of the Regents and in the administration of its affairs."[3] This clause in the state constitution does not deflect all efforts by governors and legislators to influence the character and direction of the university, but it is a powerful if largely symbolic force asserting the autonomy of the university against the play of domestic politics.[4] Moreover, other elements in this clause in the constitution established the principle that the state's contribution to the support of the university come as a block grant, in ways that make it difficult for politicians of whatever stripe to intervene into the private life of the university—into its internal arrangements—through the vehicle of university's budget. The state does not support this or that chair or department or school or campus; it provides the money to the university as a whole, which then decides on its internal allocation. I need hardly say that legislators and governors are not shy about indicating their preferences respecting various aspects of the university's operations, and not infrequently try to link their support for the university's budget to the university's attention to or even compliance with their wishes. Senior university administrators spend a fair amount of time in discussions with various officials of the state government, in both the executive and legislative branches, and the university is sensitive to their concerns, as a public university ought to be. But in principle, a principle that is strongly defended, it remains finally the decision of the university what activities it pursues and how it spends its funds.[5]

The university's capacity to defend itself against partisan political interference in no way rests solely on the protection built into the California Constitution of 1879. Moreover, this resistance to political interference from outside has extended to a distaste for political activity inside the university as well, and a preference for administration over governance. Let's look briefly at some of the other ways the university tries to minimize the role of politics in the university.

UC Is Not a Democracy

One way of reducing the play of politics within the university is not to have many occasions for voting. And there are very few occasions for voting in the university's governance structure. Whatever else the University of California may be, it is not a democracy. And that is perhaps strange, located as it is in the most populist state of a broadly populist country, a state in which significant laws and revenue sources are commonly initiated and passed by the whole electorate, laws that override those made by the representative houses of the legislature. But starting with the regents, eighteen out of the total of twenty-five are appointed directly by the governor then in office when a place is vacant, and those are the regents who actually do the business of the board; there are seven *ex officio* members, four of whom are elected state officers who with some exceptions rarely attend meetings of the board; two are elected by the UC Alumni Association for one-year terms.[6] The seventh *ex officio* member is the president of the university. The appointed members of the board of regents serve for twelve years, ensuring that they will serve beyond the term of the governor who appointed them. A regent can be reappointed, but cannot be dismissed except for criminal behavior; in fact. none ever has been dismissed. All this is designed to make them independent of the governor who appointed them, at least over time.

The board of regents appoints the president of the university, with the advice of the academic senate; the board also appoints all chancellors on the advice of the president and a senate committee. Chancellors appoint all the senior academic and nonacademic administrators: they appoint the provosts and deans, and the latter appoint department chairmen, though usually on the advice and with the participation of the department in question, and sometimes of a committee of academics from other departments. Of course, a good deal of consultation goes on in connection with these appointments, but basically academic administrators are appointed by their superior officers, and can be and indeed occasionally are dismissed by their senior officers. The contrast here with European practice is very marked indeed, and largely accounts for the far greater power wielded by these academic officers as compared with their counterparts overseas. Incidentally, all these officers except for department chairmen serve without limit of term, another aspect of their office that strengthens their hands.

The Academic Senate and the Academic Community

If we are to find democracy anywhere in the university, it should be in the academic senate. But here too we see an aversion for democratic political processes in favor of appointive procedures and consensual decision making. The model is a guild rather than a bureaucracy, but guilds are no more formally democratic than bureaucracies.

But first a word about the academic community. In UC the academic senate consists of the whole body of academic personnel, from the newest assistant professor to emeriti professors. All have an equal standing in the senate, all have all its rights and privileges. Indeed, it is important to stress what American academics, and not just at UC, take for granted, that almost every assistant professor who gains tenure will, in the fullness of time, become a full professor. Merit and market together will affect how fast he or she makes that transition, but promotion is chiefly a matter of salary anyway. There is no *Mittlebau*, no body of academics who are not professors and not likely to become professors. So there is no significant conflict of interest between professorial ranks—and so no need for a separate representation of that class of academic personnel in the governance structure, or for the representative bodies in which, after appropriate campaigns and elections, such defined and distinct categories of academic personnel would be represented.

Moreover, like other leading American research universities, UC does not have an academic trade union. That is to say, the academics do not bargain collectively with any authorities about pay, working conditions, fringe benefits, or anything else. Thus, there is no organization at the heart of the university whose interest it is to cultivate and organize discontent, and to find allies for its positions in the larger political parties of the society. The academic senate, which I have already said consists of all the regular academics in the university, from assistant professor up, and some other senior academically linked administrators as well, manages its business through a variety of committees. But these committees are for the most part not elected. With some few exceptions, on each campus they are appointed by one committee that is elected—a committee on committees.[7] To become a member of that committee one cannot actively run for election—indeed, to be seen to want to be elected is almost certainly to fail to be elected. One is nominated by a group of friends and admirers, and other members of the senate vote for candidates on their judgment of the character of the nominee or of his or her nominators. But any connection with external political links is kept at some distance through the absence of campaigning. One result is that members who are elected or appointed to any senate committee have no obligations to any faction or group of constituents, and can speak in their own voices and as prompted by their own judgment and conscience. The absence of these external commitments eases the emergence of the compromise and consensus that are the basis of almost all actions by senate bodies. One might go so far as to suggest that the exclusion of factional and party organization within the governance structure of the university is precisely to allow for decisions to be made as the outcome of (sometime prolonged) discussion and the search for consensus, both in senate bodies and in their relations with administrative officers.

The academic senate in this university has rather more formal power and authority than is common in its counterparts in other American research universities. Roughly, and very briefly, senate bodies have primary responsibility for the academic programs on the several campuses, for the appointment and promotion of academic staff, and, more ambiguously, for the criteria for the admissions of students—though this latter has been at the heart of a real controversy within the university over the past two years. Beyond that, it is consulted and advises on everything else—but its weight in those consultations varies with the issue in question. Outside the realm of teaching, research, student admissions and assessment, and academic appointments and promotions, the role of the senate is to react to initiatives by administrative officers: to reject them when they seem at odds with academic values or procedures, to improve and refine them, and ultimately to legitimate administrative decisions and actions for the whole body of academics who can then believe that their interests and values are being protected. All this is known in the university as "shared governance." Above all, the academic senate works through consultation and advice, and in its quest for consensus, often very slowly. Wise administrators take that into account, and are patient. Problems arise when decisions have to be made quickly, or administrators claim that they do. But when the senate is working well with administrative officers, whether on a campus or in the president's office, the actions and decisions taken gain a measure of legitimacy and the willing acquiescence of the academic community that is required for anything in a university to be done well. The existence and work of the academic senate creates a climate on our campuses of what might be called "responsible inattention" to the many and remote activities of the university beyond the scholarly and scientific horizons of the academic staff. For ordinary academics, the existence of the senate and its committees lets them get on with their real work of teaching and research in all their manifold guises.

On Treaties and Bureaucratic Agreements between the University and State Government

The aversion to internal political dispute is linked to the university's resistance to external political pressures. Internally, as I have noted, we have no trade union, no politicized contest for office. But in addition, the university goes to some lengths to reduce the ordinary issues of dispute and controversy. For example, one issue that is commonly a source of controversy, in this country as well as abroad, between the academic community and the administrative officers, civil servants, or politicians who determine such things, is the level of academic pay—either for all academics, or for different ranks. But at least since World War II, UC has not experienced a significant controversy between the academic community and internal or external authorities over the issue of compensation. No one in the university comments on this peculiar fact because it is so taken for granted. How is this possible? Well, briefly it is because we do not negotiate our own broad salary schedules, but let other American universities do it for us. And that is through an agreement with the state legislature, and the appropriate civil servants in state government, that our salaries, rank by rank, will be roughly comparable to and competitive with the salaries of eight other named (and leading) American research universities, four public and four private. Their salaries are published, and are the guidelines for ours, the principle being that UC must be paid about as well as these other institutions if we are to be competitive with them for leading scholars and scientists. And while our salaries vary a bit from those averages, depending on the condition of California's economy, public authorities still accept in principle that we must be at or a little above the average of these other institutions, and if we fall behind in bad times we must catch up when times are better.[8] Of course, individual academics negotiate their own salaries in a somewhat different way, but that is within the broad guidelines that emerge from this treaty with the state that takes categorical salaries out of contention.

This example illustrates the link between external and internal politics at UC. The university enters into this treaty over how to set academic salaries with the state almost as an equal; the decision over academic salaries does not lie with politicians or civil servants, but has been absorbed into a formula and taken largely out of the political arena. As a consequence, there is one less big political issue within the university for political groups or factions to organize around. This transformation of politics into administration is precisely what [Vladimir] Lenin, who lived by the principle of the primacy of politics and conflict, warned against; but then that may be the best recommendation for what we do.

Indeed, it has been the habit and strategy of the University of California, almost from its beginning, to take its operations out of the political arena in every way possible, often by developing stable understandings and agreements with state officials regarding the formulas governing the funding of the university. These agreements cover such matters as the per capita state support for students and faculty, the extent and nature of state support for the maintenance of university buildings and facilities, as well as the agreement for setting academic salaries and increases. These agreements outlive governors and other elected officials, and provide an important insulation against the hostility or political gestures of governors (and we have had some in recent decades of both parties), a basis of stability that gives the university the ability to plan its future with some confidence. The officials in the president's office who look after these agreements will protest that they are not as stable as I suggest; that they are constantly under review and discussion, and need to be carefully tended by senior administrators and by the president of the university himself. Yes, of course, and that is an important part of the work of the office of the president; but those formulas and treaties are by and large still in place after the financial strains of the early 1990s and substantially reduce the direct influence of political considerations in the funding and operation of the university.

I said a moment ago that when our senior administrative officers negotiate an agreement with the state over some aspect of university life, and state funding for it, we meet with them almost as equals. The university has a considerable capacity to defend itself politically, though not primarily through the instruments of partisan politics. The University of California has 800,000 living alumni, including the current governor of the state, some 30 percent of the state's legislators, and one-quarter of California's congressional delegation in Washington, along with many leaders of business and industry. President Richard Atkinson has noted that among the many business leaders and entrepreneurs who are UC graduates are the chief executive officers of Intel Corp. and Sun Microsystems.[9] Moreover, the university makes very considerable efforts to bind its students and alumni to the university with ties of loyalty and affection, sentiments that are potential sources of support both material and political. But this kind of support does not rest on sentiment and loyalties alone. The university's longstanding commitment to public service of every kind has the effect of creating new friends and strengthening ties to groups and segments of the community who have never been to the university. Broad support in the society at large is always potential political support, and it helps to protect the university against the direct intervention of political interests in the life of the university. To a considerable degree it is the university's latent political power that insulates it from direct political interventions. And that latent political power, arising directly from the university's longstanding commitment to public service, is a major element in its ability to maintain its institutional autonomy.

Another treaty between the state and the university, perhaps the most important of all, is the Master Plan, fathered by Clark Kerr and embodied in state law in 1960. The Master Plan also serves to reduce the role of politics in the life of the university, in this case by defining in an authoritative way the relations between the university and the other segments of public higher education. Of course there are controversies between the University of California and the California State University, not least over the allocation of limited state funds available for higher education. But the Master Plan does in fact limit the nature and extent of such controversies: for example, it rules out the possibility of what is elsewhere called "institutional drift"—the tendency of non-university institutions to seek to gain full university status, complete with research resources and the right to award the doctoral degree. In many countries universities are continually struggling with what they see as the threat of the elevation of non-university institutions into the university sphere, with the consequent dilution of research resources and, as they fear, also the dilution of university academic standards. The Master Plan prevents that by assigning the three segments distinct spheres of work,[10] and by making clear that no CSU campus will be promoted to the status of a UC campus, however hard it might lobby in the state capital. That takes a big issue out of the political arena. Still, the California State Universities do offer master's degrees, and many of their graduates continue their education as graduate students in UC. And they have the name and standing of universities—though not research universities. European academics and civil servants can hardly imagine a university without a strong commitment to research, which makes this particular compromise there more difficult.

The university employs formulas to reduce controversy both internally and in its relations with the state. In 1996, in what he called "University of California's Budget Initiative," the president surrendered his power to allocate the state's block grant among the nine campuses, a power that of course entailed chronic controversy among the campuses and with the office of the president (OP) over that allocation. Instead, in agreement with the chancellors, the OP agreed to allocate the grant on a formula based on student enrollments on each campus. This reduces the OP to something like a conduit of state funding directly to the campuses. The OP thus loses a measure of influence over campus policy and practice, but effectively takes the allocation of the annual state allocation out of controversy.

And further, just now the university is exploring the possibility of writing yet another treaty with the state that would commit the state to "provide . . . UC with at least their current proportional share of the state's general fund budget, currently about 4 percent."[11] The formula would start with that level of current funding, but also commit the state to adjust future state support to both the growth in enrollments and also to growth in the California per capita personal income.[12] It also ties student fee increases to California's per capita income growth. Such an agreement would reduce the political influence of students on the legislature, allow fees to grow slowly and predictably, while stabilizing the portion of the university's income that comes from state sources. If the state government agrees, as currently seems likely, this would take yet another set of controversial issues out of the political arena.

There are of course downsides to the minimization of conflict within the university and the substitution of administration for governance. The principle behind this policy is to drive as many educational decisions as possible down from state government, and from the regents and the office of the president to the campuses, then to their schools and colleges and departments and on to the individual faculty members who are presumably most competent to make academic decisions. The policy necessarily weakens the office of the president and strengthens the chancellors; much of the power devolved to the campuses remains with the chancellors, who are not so anxious to devolve authority as is the president. The chancellors are also currently greatly strengthened by the rapid increase in private giving, almost all of it to the campuses rather than to the university as a whole, putting very large amounts of discretionary money in their hands.[13] All this is at the expense of the concept of "one university on nine campuses," of the power of the president to innovate and lead, and, incidentally, also of the power and influence of the academic senate, both systemwide and on the campuses.

But the right balance of power between the center (the office of the president) and the campuses is itself a controversial issue. My point here is that most of the formulas described above, many ironically developed on the initiative of the president, have weakened the role of university governance and decision making in relation to administration, and have shifted the center of gravity of the university to the campuses. The university today, for good or ill, is more a confederation of largely autonomous campuses than the federal university that it was even five years ago. But the office of the president still has important functions to perform. One of these is to buffer the campuses from the direct pressures of political forces as reflected in state government.

A Buffered University

The university, and all its campuses, deal with the state of California through the office of the president, and not through the chancellors. That means that the campuses, where the actual teaching and research goes on, are buffered by the office of the president, full of administrators who have a lot of experience dealing with the state government, both executive and legislative branches, and thwarting its interventions. Much time is spent by senior administrators dealing with elements of state government over issues of whose very existence the university's scholars and scientists are mercifully kept in ignorance. Not only does the office of the president buffer the campuses from direct involvement with state government, but the president and his staff, and all the chancellors are buffered in turn against intrusion by state government by the board of regents, who hold ultimate legal authority over all aspects of university life and effectively control all its assets. It is absolutely crucial for the autonomy of the university that the regents are inside the university, rather than an arm of government.

The regents have considerable freedom to avoid public discussion of controversial issues and to delay taking action on issues that are politically sensitive. Often, though not always, time drains the passion out of an issue, and allows it to be avoided altogether, or to be resolved quietly and administratively, rather than noisily and politically. A current example is the issue of providing university benefits to same-sex partners:

> An unlikely coalition that includes Regent Ward Connerly is pressuring the University of California to offer benefits to same-sex partners. But UC administrators—still recovering from the bitter affirmative action controversy—have been working hard to keep the issue out of

the public cross-fire. "We've known it's a looming issue and we won't escape it, but we have all the big issues we can deal with right now," said one regent, who requested anonymity.[14]

Markets as a Substitute for Politics

There are still other forces and circumstances that reduce the direct impact of politics on the university. One of these is the role of competition in various kinds of academic markets. I have mentioned that the overriding value of the university, around which consensus always crystallizes, is that of competitive excellence—the common wish to be, and to be seen to be, the best university in the country. The reputation of the university as a whole is an aggregate of the reputations of its nine campuses and of their academic departments and professional schools. Moreover, the university has been remarkably successful in persuading governors and legislators of the importance of this ideal, and even of the costs of achieving it. With this shared value always implicit in the university's decisions and actions, many of them become less controversial. To take an example close to home: in the late 1960s, a number of the leading research universities with whom Berkeley compares itself had established or were considering the establishment of a graduate school of public policy. Perhaps the best known of these was and is the John F. Kennedy school at Harvard. A distinguished political scientist at Berkeley successfully proposed the creation of such a school here. It has its own unique character, but it was created with less controversy than if the university as a whole were not committed to being in the vanguard of intellectual developments, both in the scholarly and scientific disciplines and in the education of professionals.

Or to take a much larger example: in the early and mid-1980s, there were signs that the quality of work coming out of some of Berkeley's departments of biology was falling behind those of its major competitors. This unwelcome discovery occasioned a quick and substantial reaction: working together, university leadership (the then chancellor and vice chancellor of the Berkeley campus) and the leading biologists on campus developed radical plans for revamping the biological sciences on campus, involving both fundamental restructuring of the departments of biology and the building of major new buildings for conducting advanced biological research and engineering.[15] This activity almost completely bypassed the academic senate in favor of specialist committees of biologists selected by top administrators and the leading scientists on campus—and there was little or no protest from the academic senate. In the service of competitive excellence, of the simple passion to be number one, the crucial decisions were too important to be left to the amateurs who happened to be leading the local senate at the moment. And the senate recognized and accepted that, as well as the leading administrators.[16]

Toward the end of his tenure in office, Chancellor [Chang Lin] Tien opened a meeting with German colleagues with a dramatic story about the recent recruitment of a highly prized biologist from another university. The cost of the new laboratories required to recruit the man ran to some $4 or $5 million, money provided by a call from the chancellor to a particularly generous donor. The story reflects the joint power of the market, the chancellor, and trust as alternatives to politics in university governance. The minimization of politics on and in the university has as its major goal the preservation of a chancellor's power to take this kind of dramatic action. It is no accident that the chancellor chose to illustrate what he can do with his freedom and the discretionary money he raises by pointing to the recruitment of one of those outstanding scholars and scientists who in the aggregate determine the quality of work done here, and thus the university's rank and reputation among the universities of the world. Harvard and Princeton may not trumpet their success in quite this way, but their presidents and provosts do exactly the same thing, which is why we call the principle that guides this behavior competitive excellence, or perhaps, the competitive pursuit of excellence.

Trust is another alternative to politics as a determinant of action. The recruitment of this scientist required an act of trust on the part of the donor, to whom there will be no real accountability for her gift beyond her knowledge of how it was spent, and perhaps a statement or demonstration of the university's gratitude for it. We might also observe in this story the measure of trust displayed by the academic senate, which would have been consulted on whether the scientist met Berkeley's standards for appointment, but probably not on the financial negotiations and commitments that brought him here. The senate could acquiesce in that appointment, I believe, largely because it was so clearly driven by the shared commitment to competitive excellence, and the shared pride in the university's national standing that is so powerful a force in this university. We might reflect a moment on the concentration of power and authority in the hands of a chancellor in this university so long as he can be seen as furthering the institution's reputation and academic standing among its peers. And that in turn is a function of the institution's autonomy. The University of California is in part a public institution, but in very large part a private corporate body. And much of what we call governance is designed to keep it that way.

On the Size of Administration, the Variety of Support Groups, and University Autonomy

I have been speaking of the minimization of organized political controversy both within the university and in its relations with its environment, and especially with state government. But if that is the case, what are all these administrators doing? The numbers are huge by European standards: roughly a thousand employees in the office of the president alone, and many more on each campus. There are several answers. One is that the governmental ministries (including the Treasury) that elsewhere are concerned with science and higher education are here largely inside our own structures, and the civil servants and managers who elsewhere would be public employees are here employees of the university.

The other reason is best suggested if I simply point to the groups and organizations in the larger society that have a genuine interest in the university and are part of its support system—who give it money or political support or both. And in reviewing these groups and organizations, keep in mind that the university employs people to attend to its relations with all of them. The list would include state and city governments; diverse and uncoordinated departments and agencies of the federal government; the university's large and important Alumni Association; the trade unions that represent substantial numbers of UC's support staff; foundations and other friends who contribute substantial funds to the university every year; many academic organizations, including those that grant the university its formal accreditation; business firms with whom we have important and growing connections—to name only a few. Nor should we forget the many individuals and groups who take us to court over real or imagined grievances, and for defense against whom the university employs a large staff of lawyers. The diversity of our interests, the many links between the university and the rest of civil society as well as governments, and above all the diversity of our sources of financial support are pillars of the university's autonomy, but also explain the size and diversity of the university's administrative staff.[17]

Failures of UC Governance

There have been at least four occasions since World War II when one felt the presence of external politics inside the university strongly. The first was in the late 1940s and early 1950s during a period of intense popular anticommunism, when the president and regents together imposed a special oath on the faculty requiring them to attest that they were not Communists. The faculty resisted, a number of leading scholars and scientists resigned rather than sign the oath, and other non-signers were dismissed.[18] The special oath was later withdrawn. In 1967, President Clark Kerr was dismissed by the regents under pressure from then Governor Ronald Reagan, reflecting his hostility toward Kerr arising out the events associated with the Free Speech Movement.[19] In the third event, during the 1980s and early 1990s a significant proportion of the faculty urged the regents, unsuccessfully, to end the university's administration of two national laboratories, at Livermore and Los Alamos, which were then active in designing nuclear and other weapons. The fourth event, in July 1995, involved the decision by the regents to end the practice of giving preference in admissions and academic appointments to members of particular racial and ethnic groups.[20]

All four cases involved strongly held political sentiments arising out of issues in the larger society that forced their way into the university. In the first case, the faculty faced pressures from the regents and senior administrators, and from outside forces, but were divided in their responses. In the second, Kerr's dismissal evoked a strong positive response from the faculty in his support. In the other two cases the faculty was split nearly down the middle. It is fair to say that in all four cases the governance process that I have described failed to insulate the university from the direct effects of external political sentiments and pressures. As for their lasting damage, the key question is what effect these events had on the level of trust within the university, between regents and president, and between administrators and the academic senate, a climate of trust without which these informal arrangements and consultations at the heart of shared governance could not work. My own judgment is that the oath controversy gave rise to deep resentments within the university toward the then president and regents, which dissipated only over time as that president and most of the regents involved left the university. But the net result may well have been the strengthening of UC's autonomy and also of academic freedom in the face of external political pressure. The firing of Kerr was clearly an arbitrary intervention from outside driven by the governor's personal hostility toward the president, was broadly unpopular within the university, and had little effect on the governance of the university subsequently. Indeed, like the oath controversy the reaction was so strong it may well have made a politically motivated dismissal of a UC president less likely thereafter. The unsuccessful movement by a group of engineers and scientists to force the surrender of the university's ties to the national labs was dealt with through the regular procedures of university governance, and in my view had little effect on the climate in the university, especially after the end of the cold war and the substantial shift of the work in both labs toward civilian projects.[21] Finally, the controversy over affirmative action in the university is still ongoing. It may have deeper consequences for the climate of trust within the university than any of the others. All parties are currently making efforts to repair the damage to the governance processes that resulted from the events surrounding the regents' actions of July 1995, but it will be some years before we can assess the full effects of the controversy on the university.

Conclusion

I have tried to suggest that the central function of governance in this university is to resist partisan pressures from outside the university, allowing it to respond only to those that it chooses, and so far as possible excluding partisan politics from its internal life. Those efforts in turn are aimed at the preservation of the autonomy of the university, of its capacity to make its own decisions, govern its own life, both intellectually and materially. Governance and administration in UC together aim to keep crucial academic decisions inside the university so far as possible, and once there, have them made on their merits, in the service of the value of competitive excellence through the processes of what we call "shared governance." We do not always succeed, in either the first aim or the second. It is even less certain what the future may hold for these jealously defended principles. But it is still fair to say that those are the aims and principles by which the university is governed, in every sense of that word, and by which it will continue to be governed in the immediate future.

NOTES

1. If the budgets of the three big national laboratories administered by the university are excluded, the operating budget of the university is (1996) about $8.5 billion. Of this, only about $2 billion comes from the state of California. The university is not precisely a state university, but a state-aided university. But those phrases do not adequately define the relationship of the University of California to the state's government.

2. Neil J. Smelser, "Growth, Structural Change, and Conflict in California Public Higher Education, 1950–1970," in *Public Higher Education in California,* ed. Neil Smelser and Gabriel Almond (Berkeley: University of California Press, 1974), pp. 9–143.

3. Verne A. Stadtman, *The University of California 1868–1968* (New York: McGraw Hill, 1970), p. 82.

4. Symbolic, because university lawyers are reluctant to actually test the constitutional protection in the courts for fear that it would not sustain the weight of institutional autonomy placed on it.

5. The legislature often attaches "budget language" to a budget it passes, indicating its interests in the way the budget is used by the university and pointing to particular activities or conditions it wants to see the university honoring. The university is sensitive to these indications of the legislature's wishes, and can anticipate having to explain how they were followed, or why they were not. But the university will not conform to such instructions if they seem to violate its sense of its own autonomy.

6. The regents themselves elect a student regent for a one-year term.

7. Each campus arranges its own senate rules. Currently, most campuses, but not Berkeley, also elect their divisional chair as well as their committee on committees.

8. "The governor's budget for UC also calls for . . . employee pay increases equivalent to an average 2 percent salary increase . . . and additional funding equivalent to a 3 percent parity increase for faculty. That funding would bring faculty salaries to within 1.6 percent of the average pay at UC's eight comparison institutions. This is a priority of Regents, who hope to close the faculty salary gap by 1998–99." "UC Begins Discussion of Long-term Fee Policy," *UC Focus* 11, no. 3 (February–March 1997): 7.

9. Annual Financial Report, University of California 1995–96, p. 5.

10. In addition to the three public segments—UC, CSU, and the community colleges—the Master Plan also recognizes and provides a place for California's many private colleges and universities.

11. "UC Begins Discussion of Long-term Fee Policy," p. 1.

12. The potential agreement is embodied in AB (Assembly Bill) 1415 (Bustamante), "The Higher Education Partnership Act of 1999," published by the University of California, July 8, 1997. My thanks to Associate Vice President Lawrence Hershman, director of the budget for UC, for a helpful conversation on these issues, though he is not responsible for my interpretations of its effects on governance.

13. For example, Berkeley received more than $182 million in 1996–97 from 66,000 contributors. "Direct state support now accounts for 38 percent of the campus's budget, compared with 52 per cent in 1985" ("Campus Gets More Gifts in 1996–97," *The Daily Californian*, August 8, 1997). Of course, many of those gifts are earmarked for particular uses by the donor, but that still leaves large sums at the discretion of the chancellor.

14. Pamela Burdman, "UC Pressed on Partner Benefits," *SF Chronicle*, April 5, 1997, p. 1.

15. Part of this story is told in Martin Trow, "Leadership and Organization: The Case of Biology at Berkeley," in *Higher Education Organization: Conditions for Policy Implementation,* ed. Rune Premfors (Stockholm: Almqvist and Wiksell, 1984), pp. 148–78. Reprinted as chapter 12 in this volume.

16. The current dean of the biological sciences has made reference to this reform as necessary "in order for us to maintain a high visibility [in biology] in the country."

17. Though there are legitimate questions about whether it has to be quite as big as it is.

18. David P. Gardner, *The California Oath Controversy* (Berkeley: University of California Press, 1967).

19. Stadtman, *The University of California 1868–1968*, pp. 487–93. The story is told in detail in Clark Kerr, *The Gold and the Blue: A Personal Memoir of the University of California 1949–1967* (Berkeley: University of California Press, 2003).

20. One perspective on these events can be found in Martin Trow, "A Divided UC Faculty Seeks a Path to Consensus on Affirmative Action, " *Public Affairs Report*, Institute of Governmental Studies, UC Berkeley, 37, no. 2, March 1996, pp. 9–13.

21. This controversy should perhaps not be labeled a failure of governance, but is included as an example of the intervention of national political issues directly into the life of the university.

15

MARTIN TROW DID NOT SET OUT to be a public intellectual. His writing, over the first two decades of his career, was published, with rare exceptions, in academic journals and books. We will never know what led him to decide to write and speak to a larger audience, and present negative evidence that disturbed the status quo and did not endear him to many of his colleagues. But given the major areas of his research—the university, its governance, faculty, and students— the arc of events, and the character of the man, it was, perhaps, inevitable that he would come to take difficult public positions on issues of great moral moment.

His evolution as a public intellectual began when UN Ambassador Jeanne Kirkpatrick was driven from a Berkeley stage in 1983 while attempting to deliver the Jefferson Lecture; the faculty senate deplored it as a violation of free speech. In a talk to a group of UC chancellors, later published in *Change* magazine, Trow argued it was, more especially, an issue of academic freedom, a rejection of negative evidence, which has "a special role in the moral impact of the academic disciplines."

Four years later, as a trustee of Carleton College, Trow stood against divesting stock in companies doing business in South Africa to protest apartheid. He warned his fellow trustees that "it is dangerous to transform political into moral judgments in order to take positions on them; to do so says something quite harsh, even unacceptable, to the other members of the community who do not agree with you. Such action says they are not just mistaken, but that they are morally insensitive, morally deficient." He later argued in the *Chronicle of Higher Education* that moralizing political issues creates pressures on other institutions to demonstrate their virtue by taking the "morally correct" position. The following year in "On a Board's Stance Toward Social and Political Issues," a paper written

485

for the Association of Governing Boards of Universities and Colleges National Conference, he returned to the issue of speech and academic freedom, focusing on the increasing exclusion of a segment of the political spectrum, almost anything right of center, from campus discussion.

Trow had expressed his concerns about affirmative action in 1978 following the *Bakke* decision: "Public policy should not be based on 'race' for any purpose. It is, in my view, a social category that is incompatible with a free and democratic society in which all are equal before the law." Throughout the 1990s, as academic administrators, if not their faculties, coalesced behind a drive for racial preferences in admissions, Trow found himself among those leading the counterattack at Berkeley and throughout the nation. In a 1993 letter to the Committee on Diversity of the Western Association of Schools and Colleges, he criticized their pro-preference recommendations as "nothing else than a political position that claims moral superiority to alternatives."

In 1995, partly at his urging, UC regents voted to abolish racial and ethnic preferences, and the following year California voters passed a proposition that prohibited public institutions from considering race, sex, or ethnicity in hiring or entry decisions. As lawsuits and pressures to restore racial preferences grew, Trow argued his case before the American Council of Education, UC regents, and, ultimately, in 1998, before the annual meeting of the American Association of Universities, which invited him to comment on *The Shape of the River.* Trow's courageous bearding of the academic lions in their den drew national press coverage and his talk, which had prompted Harvard President Neil Rudenstine to stomp angrily out of the meeting, was published the following spring in *The Public Interest.* It is the essay reprinted here.

To understand what drove Trow to speak out when he often had little to gain and much to lose, one might look to his 1980 paper entitled "Moral Problem in the Context of Higher Education." It concerns a young, talented, untenured researcher being pressured to reconsider research findings that colleagues worried might reflect badly on African Americans. "Whether or not it is present in this case," he wrote, "the role of political pressure and even coercion in academic life . . . is real and much more common than is ordinarily realized or talked about. Indeed, I believe it to be a most serious threat to the integrity of the academic enterprise at the present." He described Mr. B as "a person of considerable character. And he holds rather strongly to the norm that he is morally obligated to report the results of his analysis even when those results are inconvenient or awkward or inconsistent with his prior beliefs or value system. The data, he believes, have a life and reality of their own, and their analysis and interpretation must be consistent with the evidence." He might have been describing himself.

—JERRY LUBENOW

California after Racial Preferences

In his 1995 opinion in *Miller v. Johnson*, Supreme Court Justice Anthony Kennedy observed that "at the heart of the Constitution's guarantee of equal protection lies the simple command that the Government must treat citizens as individuals, not as simple components of a racial, religious, sexual or national class." William G. Bowen and Derek Bok place themselves squarely against that principle, as they try in their book, *The Shape of the River,* to justify admitting students to colleges and universities, both public and private, on the basis of their membership in a racial or national class.

The book, as I think the authors would agree, is as much a lawyer's brief aimed at future court decisions on affirmative action as it is a piece of social science research. That is a perfectly legitimate use of social science, especially since, as in the case of Bowen and Bok's book, the advocacy role is not hidden. But it does complicate the work of a critical reading, which certainly does not include a *New York Times* editorial that praised the book. Such a reading neither makes its assumptions clear nor

Originally published as Martin Trow, "California after Racial Preferences," *The Public Interest*, no. 135 (Spring 1999): 64–85. Reprinted by permission.

draws attention to negative evidence, as disinterested research must. Therefore, in this essay, I can do no more than draw attention to some of the unexamined assumptions on which Bowen and Bok form their analysis, and then consider some of the unintended, and often undesired, consequences of race preferences—especially in a large, racially and ethnically diverse public university such as the University of California (UC) system. In a sense, I will attempt to assess some of the (mostly non-money) costs of race preferences overlooked or neglected by Bowen and Bok in their defense of such policies.

The View from the Ivy Tower

My first impression on reading the book was how parochial it is, how clearly it reveals its origins east of the Hudson. Bowen and Bok do not address the problems with the academic preparation and performance of black Americans taken as a group, which affect their distribution among our 3,700 colleges and universities. They take, more or less as given, the number of motivated black high school graduates who are prepared for college at various levels and then argue that elite institutions should be able to take their color into account in their admissions policies.

But it slowly dawned on me that, apart from its far-reaching constitutional implications, this really is a tempest in a teapot. The book is inordinately concerned with a small number of able and talented black students who attend a small number of very selective colleges and universities—and by no means all of them. These students attend fairly prestigious colleges and universities and contribute to society in a variety of ways that will depend more on their own talents, energies, and unique qualities than on their alma mater. This may be heretical to presidents and former presidents of Ivy League universities, but perhaps not so heretical to those less concerned with the status attached to being a graduate of Yale or Princeton, and rather more concerned with what efforts and energies a student puts into his studies and with what success he discovers where his genius lies.

Indeed, I find it mildly embarrassing to see how intensely Bowen and Bok focus on a small number of elite universities to demonstrate that a small number of academically talented black students benefit from racial preferences. These students, they report, make friends with people of other races, do not resent having benefited from preferences, and go on to achieve professional and financial success. This may all be true, but it does not prove that these benefits, for a handful of very gifted students, are not offset by larger and costlier harms for higher education and society as a whole.

The authors have less concern for the stock of well-educated black people in our population, or the welfare of the society in which those people take their place, than for their own institutional pride, and the prestige attached in some circles to the numbers of trophy minority students they can enroll. Inevitably, whatever disclaimers they make, Bowen and Bok strongly suggest that black students who do not go to the most selective institutions, or would not be admitted under a race-neutral regime, would be greatly disadvantaged thereby.

They do not make that case, and I don't believe it for a second. Nowhere can they demonstrate, in their piles of survey data, that a black student who is admitted on his own merits to UC Riverside, or even to CSU San Diego, is significantly disadvantaged in relation to an affirmative action admit to Princeton or Harvard. More important, the book does not persuade me that blacks who do not attend a Harvard or a Yale are harmed as a result. The notion that you have to go to one of the most selective universities to fulfill your potential, or to become a leader in America, betrays an elitist conception of American life that ignores how widely dispersed power and influence are, how diverse the origins of our institutional leaders are. I accept that these selective institutions give their graduates advantages simply by virtue of their reputation as elite universities. That kind of advantage is built into the status system of our society, and minorities who are admitted to those institutions have as much right to that advantage as anybody else. But it is simply a fact that, now and in the future, the overwhelming majority of black leaders will come from other institutions—ones they enter without racial preferences. And the costs to blacks, and to American society as a whole, of the racial and ethnic preferences defended by Bowen and Bok, far outweigh the marginal advantage to the small number of highly qualified black students who are assured entry to any number of first-rate colleges and universities without racial preferences.

Cascading Choices

Moreover, the book simply finesses a whole set of questions that must be asked of race and ethnic preference policies when examined from beyond the Hudson and through the perspective of a wider range of colleges and universities. This bears on the especially contentious issue of "cascading"— what would happen if the most selective universities were to practice a race-neutral admissions policy. "Cascading" refers to the pattern of choices made by students who are refused entry to highly selective institutions, and are then admitted to somewhat less selective institutions. (In California, we are also seeing "cascading" upward from UC campuses without race preferences to more selective private colleges and universities that offer race and ethnic preferences.)

Bowen and Bok's discussion of this matter is confusing. Does anyone doubt that those students not admitted to the most selective Ivy League universities would certainly be admitted somewhere else—perhaps to a slightly less selective Ivy League school or even to another still less selective institution? Is there any question that they would go somewhere? And what evidence is there that they would not fare well in such places or make useful and important contributions to American life?

California, and especially the University of California system, can prove helpful in answering these questions. We have at UC a mini-laboratory of the "cascading" effect. In 1995, UC board of regents voted to abolish racial preferences in admissions; and, in 1996, California voters confirmed this decision by approving Proposition 209, which abolished all racial and ethnic preferences in state institutions. These changes were implemented on UC campuses in 1997 for graduate and professional schools, and in 1998 for undergraduate admissions.

If we compare the enrollments of California resident freshmen on all eight general campuses over those two transitional years,[1] we find that the total number of black registrants fell from 917 to 739, a decline of 178, or about 19 percent. Among Chicanos, the largest preferred group before Proposition 209, freshmen enrollments fell from 2,325 in 1997 to 2,211 in 1998—a decline of just under 5 percent. ("Chicano" is the University of California's category for Hispanics of Mexican origin. Other Hispanics are registered as "Latinos," regardless of origin.)

Indeed, the numbers more accurately describe not a dramatic decline among minority admissions but a redistribution of these students within UC system. The numbers of black and Chicano freshmen declined markedly at the most selective campuses, Berkeley and UCLA, but rose at the less selective campuses. The biggest drop in the numbers of Chicanos occurred at UC Berkeley, Los Angeles, and San Diego, which together showed a decline of 383 Chicano freshmen enrolled, most of whom clearly reacted by enrolling at UC Irvine, Davis, Riverside, and Santa Barbara, where their numbers grew by 269. Similarly, while black enrollments in 1998 at UC Berkeley and Los Angeles fell by 193 freshmen, these losses were partially offset by increases in black enrollments at the Irvine, Riverside, and Santa Cruz campuses.[2]

I do not believe that these students will receive an inferior undergraduate education because they have not been admitted to a more selective UC campus. And they will know that they owe their position solely to their own merits. They are not affirmative action admits, just new Cal students.

Fewer Minority Students?

But these figures showing a decline in black and Hispanic enrollments in UC between 1997 and 1998 are subject to one important qualification: total freshmen enrollments at all UC campuses rose by 1,195 between 1997 and 1998, but the number of new students in most racial and ethnic groups declined. In particular, the number of new students registering as white declined by 1,194. How can that be? The answer, largely neglected in discussions of Proposition 209's impact on UC, lies in the very large increase between those two years in the number of applicants who refused to provide information about their ethnicity—from 774 in 1997 to 3,441 students in 1998. That was the year when race would no longer help their chances for admission to their campus of choice.

The students who declined to identify themselves by race or ethnicity comprised 14 percent of all new freshmen, making them the third largest group in the university after whites (33 percent) and Asians (28 percent). No one knows the ethnic or racial distribution of these 3,441 students, many of whom said in effect, "Now that this information cannot legally be used in the admissions process, it is none of the university's business what my 'race' or 'ethnicity' is." But whatever that distribution, it does mean that the published figures on enrollments of the racial and ethnic minorities are almost certainly lower than the true figure. For example, the "declared" Chicanos comprise 9 percent of the total enrollment in the university. If only 3 percent of the "refused to answer" were Hispanics, that would add 103 to their total, almost making up for the apparent loss of 114 Chicanos between 1997 and 1998. Similarly, some "blacks" of mixed race might have taken this costless opportunity to refuse to make the painful choice between their racial or ethnic origins, as Tiger Woods has done. Whatever number that might be would reduce the apparent effect of Proposition 209 on the decline in the numbers of declared blacks between 1997 and 1998. (Another 377 enrolled students classified themselves as "Other," also of unknown ancestry.)

There is no doubt that the abolition of racial and ethnic preferences led to a decline in the number and proportion of blacks and Chicanos admitted to the most selective UC campuses, Berkeley and UCLA. However, three other UC campuses—Irvine, Santa Cruz, and Riverside—showed an increase in black enrollments in 1998 over 1997, with little change at UC Davis and San Diego. Blacks could hardly be said to have fled the university, despite fearful (or hopeful?) predictions to the contrary. Indeed, their "take rate"—the ratio of enrollments to admissions—is almost exactly the same as it was in 1996 throughout the university.

But here one would like to see further research on "cascading" in different universities and for different groups. For example, many of the blacks not admitted to Berkeley or UCLA undoubtedly had other options. They might have enrolled at other UC campuses, like many Hispanics who failed to get into Berkeley or UCLA. Alternatively, they may have accepted admissions offers from selective private universities and colleges, in California or elsewhere, which offered them attractive scholarship packages. I would also be curious whether some went to one of the twenty-two campuses of the California State University (CSU) system. That system is relatively selective, taking the top one-third of California's high school graduates, though most of the students who are rejected by Berkeley or UCLA could enter the CSU system almost automatically. If they did, they would profit from a CSU education and discover how easily a CSU graduate, who has been a serious student, can transfer to the University of California or another research university for graduate study, if so inclined.

In any event, UC provides a natural laboratory for the study of "cascading," and such a study might lead to more modest notions of its effects on life chances. Indeed, contrary to the physical image of "cascading," we might discover that some students, rejected by their UC campus of choice, "cascaded upward" to more—rather than less—selective institutions that are still applying race and ethnic preferences.

Race in Public and Private

Bowen and Bok also neglect to ask which groups should be preferred. They cite methodological concerns to justify confining their study to black students, but, by omitting other groups, they also distort our picture of racial preferences. Race in America, despite many who believe otherwise, is not a black-and-white problem; the huge number of racial and ethnic groups in our country greatly complicates any effort to deal with a particular group, as if it alone were the object of preference.

Race preference policies have broader implications, not least political ones, when the "people of color" admitted make up not 5 percent or 6 percent of the entering class but well over 50 percent of the university. This is true of the University of California, where nearly one-quarter of its student body consists of formerly preferred groups, now no longer preferred.[3] Proposition 209 expressly applies to public institutions and does not affect the practices of Stanford, USC, Caltech, or the many other private colleges and universities in California. Although leading public and private universities have come to resemble one another more in recent decades, private universities remain autonomous and are correspondingly less accountable to the public. By contrast, UC did not have the freedom to choose which groups in society it would prefer.

Bowen and Bok do not address this fundamental difference between private elite universities and selective public universities. Private universities have an extraordinary degree of autonomy to admit whom they please on whatever grounds they please. That is broadly accepted in this country, despite the inroads on their autonomy by OSHA [Occupational Safety and Health Administration] and other regulatory agencies. Public universities are in this respect quite different; state governments ordinarily have very strong views about the terms of access of their citizens to "their" universities. Even when, as in the case of UC, the government has granted a high measure of autonomy to the state university, it still requires that public universities make the criteria for admission clear and fair.

Notions of what is fair are contested and change over time, no doubt. But public universities, certainly in California, had taken the questionable step of selecting students on the basis of a racial formula. It is only now, after racial and ethnic preferences have been outlawed, that the university can move to selecting students through a consideration of their whole file. Factors other than test scores and high school grade point average can be considered, with the exception of race or ethnicity. And this is a clear improvement, welcomed by all sides of the Proposition 209 debate.

Moreover, even if some groups are to be preferred, how can a public university verify that a student is actually a member of that group? This may not be a problem at Princeton; however, it is a problem at Berkeley or at UC generally. It is not very difficult to imagine a way to identify "black" students at a small, private institution. For those students who claimed to be black, a small private university can simply apply the "one drop" criterion evidenced by skin color and the correlated features of hair, eyes, and physiognomy once used by the old racist society that we ought to have put behind us. However, that is not so easy at UC, and at many other large public universities, where applicants are not interviewed, and where the "one drop" criterion cannot be used to check a claim on an application form.

Furthermore, the policy of group preferences forces impossible choices on the rapidly growing number of Americans from multiracial backgrounds. Before racial preferences in public institutions were abolished in California, the university in effect said to applicants of mixed race: "You must choose between your father and your mother in marking the race/ethnicity box on UC's admissions form. If you choose the preferred race, you are more likely to be admitted to Berkeley and to get additional financial support. If you choose the other race or ethnicity, your chances of admission are simply poorer. If you choose to check the box labeled

'Other' or refuse to choose at all, we will treat you as if you were white, that is, negatively preferred." It cannot be right for any public institution to force a student whose parents are, say, Asian and Hispanic, to choose between his father and mother in asserting his own ethnic identity. Such students often resist those pressures, asserting with pride the dual or multiple nature of their ethnic roots. But group preferences reward one identity and punish the other. It is indefensible for public policy to force that choice.

The Nuremberg Dilemma

To reward a check in a box also invites fraud, especially when it appears to be a victimless crime (the person with the wrong skin color who will be excluded thereby is a very dim figure indeed). In addition, at UC, there is no way such fraud could be uncovered. When race preferences were being applied on UC campuses, no efforts were ever made to verify the truth of a claim to a preferred race or ethnicity. Indeed, when I asked about this, an official in an admissions office replied indignantly, "We are not in the business of enforcing Nuremberg laws." Precisely.

The Nazis employed the Nuremberg laws to define exactly what fraction of "impure" blood would deprive "non-Aryans" of citizenship and, eventually, of life. In California, however different the motives and consequences, any efforts to establish the truth of claims to some preferred category would require, first, that the university or some other agency set forth what fraction of a blood line would qualify, and then define the procedures for testing those claims. In some smaller universities the names of students claiming a preferred origin might be given to a student group on campus to investigate. But, at UC, students were and are ethnically anonymous if that is their choice. Moreover, on the slight chance that a fraudulent claim to a preference was uncovered, no penalties would have been imposed. Indeed, penalties would have required a formal statement of the conditions of blood and origin that would qualify for the preference, and that would return the university to the Nuremberg dilemma. Wisely, it chose not to do that.

But with neither procedures to confirm a claim to a preferred status nor penalties for fraud, it would be surprising if the amount of fraud did not grow, especially as teachers and guidance counselors realized the advantages a check in the right box would confer upon an applicant's chances of being admitted to Berkeley or another selective UC campus. The frequency of this kind of fraud cannot be known with any accuracy, but one incident will illustrate the form it takes. A university officer, visiting a local high school, observed a student checking the box labeled "Chicano" on his application form.

"Oh, you're Chicano," said the official by way of making friendly conversation.

"No," came the reply. "Actually I'm Iranian, but my teacher told me to check 'Chicano' if I wanted to get into Berkeley."

That was a rather straightforward claim to a fraudulent preference; the manipulation of Spanish surnames was more widespread. Here the confusion about what "Latino" means, whether it includes Portuguese and Brazilians and European Spaniards, invites a very broad interpretation, including the many part-Latinos who did not have Hispanic surnames. Who is a Latino, and how do you know? How much "blood" is required to qualify—both parents, one parent, one grandparent, or simple residence in a country that we call Hispanic? How about European Hispanics? How about the Portuguese, who have recently successfully argued their way onto a government preference list? Stories of questionable claims to a preferred status are known and retailed with a cynical chuckle in universities; before the change of policy in California, they fueled widespread cynicism about the fairness of all the admissions procedures. These are not "details" but insoluble issues in a country deeply reluctant to probe into ethnic and racial origins.

Finally, on the issue of how long the preferences should stay in place, the authors of *The Shape of the River* are more forthcoming: simply "for the foreseeable future." There may be goals for the application of preferences; there are no goals visible for the ending of preferences. The notion suggested is that one racial group, or more than one, must "for the foreseeable future" be exempt from the American ideal that individuals are judged, assessed, and rewarded for their own achievements. These are big issues of policy and implementation that the book simply avoids in the course of telling us about the mostly successful careers of black students who attended a few prestigious universities.

From "Jewish Peril" to "Yellow Peril"

One consequence of affirmative action, largely neglected in the literature justifying racial preferences, is the exclusion of certain other groups. In the East, where most private elite research universities are located, the excluded are generally white. As the symbolic representatives of the advantaged and repressive groups in American history—never mind who they actually are—they gain little sympathy. And the private universities may choose to prefer only blacks, and thus those who are excluded are not only white but apparently few in number. In California, we did not have that dubious privilege; before Proposition 209, we were required by federal law and regulations to prefer a variety of other racial and ethnic groups, chief among them, Chicanos.

Moreover, in California, those who are disadvantaged by their racial and national origins are more likely to be Asians, who outnumber whites on the most selective UC campuses, Berkeley and UCLA, and currently comprise 37 percent of the new Berkeley freshmen (as compared with about 28 percent white).[4] These "Asians" include a very wide variety of backgrounds—old and new Chinese, Japanese, Thai, Vietnamese of various kinds, Indonesians, Koreans, and more. (Filipinos and East Indian/Pakistanis are counted separately. They were also formerly preferred.)

Of course, many supporters of "diversity" never acknowledged the wide variety of backgrounds represented by "Asian" students at UC. On the contrary, the preference policies in California were a way of controlling the numbers of "Asians" at UC. No one actually said that, except occasional visitors like President [Bill] Clinton who warned Californians in 1995 of the dangers of abolishing racial preferences. Beware, he said, "there are universities in California that could fill their entire freshman classes with nothing but Asian Americans."

We are reminded of similar concerns about the "Jewish Peril" at elite Eastern private colleges and universities throughout the first half of this century. Quotas were employed to limit their numbers and were only dismantled after World War II, persisting into the 1950s at some universities. Then it was too many smart Jews; today, it's too many smart Asians and not enough room for everybody else.

Few leaders of leading private research universities today would defend their racist exclusionary policies of the past. But these same leaders have no difficulty in defending similar policies that exclude other people, with different "racial" characteristics. The difference presumably lies in the malign motives in the earlier racial exclusions and the benign ones today. But the consequences are remarkably similar. Students who are otherwise fully qualified for entry to a university are excluded because of their skin color or national origins. And a further irony is that some of the "Asians" who suffer this "benign" discrimination are the grandsons and granddaughters of people who were confined to relocation camps during World War II in another, and now widely regretted, expression of public racism in America.

For all these and other reasons the race and ethnic preference policy at UC was not only intrinsically unfair but was increasingly seen to be unfair by faculty and students alike, causing growing resentment over race and ethnicity among all groups and dividing the academic community. The more differentiated ethnic and racial groups have become, the more transparent are the injustices and inequities of policies based on group membership. Public policies based on race and ethnicity have a powerful and inherent tendency to reduce people in all their variety and complexity to their membership in a racial category. But higher education aims to further differentiate us, to encourage and educate our qualities of mind and character, to give more varied aspects to our individuality, and to teach us to nurture our unique qualities. Intelligence and creativity, if allowed, burst through the constraints of social origin; nurtured by our origins, we transcend them through the disciplines and freedoms of scholarship and science. People differ, and must be allowed to differ, in whether, and to what degree they choose to find their identities in their ethnic origins, but that is no business of public policy.

The End of Preferences at Boalt

Bowen and Bok also do not tell us how much preference they would defend, beyond defending whatever level was being applied in the institutions over the period they discussed. How much is enough? Here again some evidence from UC may be enlightening, this time from a professional school.

Before racial and ethnic preferences were abolished at the University of California in 1995, the relevant law was the Supreme Court's decision in the *Bakke* case of 1978, which outlawed racial quotas but permitted institutions to consider race as "one factor in admissions." But the Court declined to explain how much of a role in admissions race should play. Some institutions interpreted the decision as saying that "other things being equal," race could be a preference at the margin and acted on that principle. Others went much further, giving whatever weight to race and ethnicity in admissions that was necessary to achieve the particular racial mix they were seeking.

An example of this is the recent history of admissions to Berkeley's law school, Boalt Hall. After racial preferences were abolished, it was widely reported by the media in the summer of 1997 that, with the exception of one black student who had been accepted in the previous year but had delayed entry, no new minority students would enroll at Boalt. The figures for Boalt were reported before any other figures for other professional and graduate programs and were taken as representative of the effects of abolishing racial preferences on the graduate programs in the university.

They were not; when those figures were released many months later, it appeared that the proportions of blacks and Hispanics[5] entering Berkeley's graduate programs, apart from Boalt, had changed only slightly. Indeed, Proposition 209 has had little effect on new students in UC graduate schools (excluding the professional schools). Between 1996 and 1997—that is, when the new rules applied to UC's graduate schools—the office of the president reported that "the number of African Americans increased by 2 percent, while the 'other' and 'declined to state' categories increased by 25 percent." Those figures occasioned very little comment in the press.

One might have imagined that the university would want to spread the good news that the abolition of racial and ethnic preferences at the graduate level was having very little negative effect on the numbers of black and Hispanic students. But there were no press conferences or statements by senior administrative officers calling attention to these surprising figures, as they had in connection with the Boalt story. In this case, as in others in recent years, good news was treated by the university and its public relations offices as bad news, whereas what looked like bad news, especially the Boalt story, was trumpeted by university officials. Indeed, some within the university appeared to encourage even worse news to discredit the new race-blind policies. Bowen and Bok quote a director of a black recruitment program at Berkeley as saying, "We told [prospective students] that [Boalt] is a very hostile environment and that we're not welcome here . . . we weren't pushing them to come to Cal."

Boalt differed from most other graduate and professional programs in one important respect: it competed for the ablest minority applicants with other leading law schools—especially those at the top research universities—but unfortunately, it was almost always unsuccessful in that competition. Long before the regents' action or Proposition 209, Boalt was consistently losing all, or almost all, of its highly qualified minority candidates to more prestigious law schools that could offer more financial support, and perhaps more attractive positions upon graduation. The fact that Boalt could not hold its best applicants against the Ivy League law schools is no criticism of Boalt; other law schools are better endowed, even more prestigious, and even better launching pads for highly successful careers. But, in the fall of 1997, when no minority students enrolled in Boalt's entering class, administrators blamed the regents' abolition of racial preferences for the loss of "diversity" at Boalt.

Boalt was a story of the radical application of preferences, surely beyond what was envisioned in *Bakke*. The degree of preference in admissions to Boalt was not "race sensitive," but heavily "race determined."[6] We can see this now because, unlike most other graduate departments and professional schools, admissions to Boalt had been organized around a formula placing applicants into one of four "Ability Ranges," A through D, from the highest scores to the lowest, defined by a combination of the student's undergraduate grade point average and scores on the LSAT [Law School Admission Test].[7] In 1996, only 855 students were admitted to Boalt out of 4,684 who applied. But the proportions admitted were highly varied among the different ethnic and racial groups and in the different ranges.

For example, eighteen applicants from the preferred groups—chiefly blacks, Hispanics, and Native Americans—fell into the top two Ability

Ranges, and all but one of them were accepted. And that is true for the other two big groups, whites and Asians; almost all applicants from Range A were admitted. However, substantial differences in admission rates begin to appear among applicants from Range B (69 percent and 62 percent for Asians and whites, respectively, versus 94 percent for racially preferred groups), and are very large in the lower two Ability Ranges C and D. Of the 124 Asian applicants in Range C, only 24, or 19 percent, were admitted; and, of the 607 whites in that range, 101, or 17 percent, were admitted. But of the 35 members of the preferred groups in that range, 27, or fully 77 percent, were admitted. And, in Ability Range D, only 2 out of 492 Asian applicants were admitted (0.4 percent), as compared with 100 out of 696 (14 percent) preferred applicants. The proportion of whites admitted from that Ability Range, 19 out of 1,223, or 1.5 percent, was almost as low as among the Asians.

When we look at specific ethnic groups, the differences are even more striking. Of applicants in Ability Range C, 10 were students of Japanese origins; an equal number of black applicants were in that same Ability Range. All 10 black applicants in that Range were accepted, but not one of those of Japanese origins, of the 384 black applicants in Ability Range D, 62 were admitted. By contrast, of the 174 applicants of Chinese origins in that same Ability Range, not one was admitted to Boalt Hall.

When a university starts counting by eye shape or skin color, all notions of "how much" race preference is justifiable collapse; there are no criteria or numbers on which people can agree. And when merely being "race sensitive" is not sufficient to achieve a desired level of "diversity," as at Boalt, then officials are tempted to apply racial criteria as far as necessary to get the numbers right. The end of race preferences dramatically affected Boalt because of how much it had previously compensated for its weakness compared with prestigious Ivy League law schools for the most able minority applicants. When race preferences were abolished, Boalt could no longer admit large numbers of poorly qualified minority students in preference to white and Asian students with higher qualifications. And those less well qualified minority students admitted under the preference system could no longer mask Boalt's inability to compete successfully against Yale, Harvard, and Columbia for the most able minority students. By contrast, the graduate programs in arts and letters and the sciences did not experience declines in their minority enrollments because they did not have to change their admissions criteria and practice very much after preferences were abolished.

The Illusion of Consensus

Much is made by Bowen and Bok of the importance of diversity in a student body—of the value of exposing students to differing perspectives, values, and orientations for education. But, oddly enough, the American Association of Universities (AAU), along with its sister organizations on Dupont Circle, exhibits no diversity on the issue of race and ethnic preferences in higher education. I don't mean a near consensus, but rather, a perfect consensus, as reflected by the signatures of every AAU member, in a full-page advertisement in the *New York Times* in April 1997, expressing opposition to laws prohibiting race-blind policies.

The AAU, and academic leadership generally, are not typical in this respect; on the contrary, every other group in our society is divided on the wisdom of using race and ethnicity for such decisions, usually pretty evenly, from Congress and the courts, to business and the press, to professors and students, and above all, to the larger society and its voters. People debate these issues among themselves everywhere—except in the organizations of college and university leadership. No arguments there, at least none that anyone can hear. But two well-crafted surveys by the Roper Center of the University of Connecticut—one conducted on the nine UC campuses and another that questioned college and university professors nationwide—found that a majority of academics everywhere oppose preferences, and while different wordings get different distributions, everywhere there are substantial numbers on both sides.

What explains this curious combination of outward consensus and internal division? UC leaders have created a false illusion of a broad consensus within the university in favor of racial preferences. On these issues, administrators and their staffs presume to speak for the university. And they are the voice of the university. One would never guess from reading their newsletters, campus journals, and alumni magazines that there is substantial opposition to racial preferences within the academic community. In all our institutions, and most certainly in the University of California, the professional affirmative action community is large, broad, and strongly committed to the policies of group preference. This and the passion they bring to the issue help explain why the opposition, however well represented in the faculty, is nearly voiceless.

This peculiar consensus among university presidents arises out of a mixture of principle and a keen sense of who, on or around campus, can make trouble for them. People opposed to preferences do not make any significant trouble for senior university officers; groups that profit from and administer preference policies can and do. The officials who administer UC's large affirmative action bureaucracies have been appointed on the understanding that they support the preference system, or at least will not oppose it. I cannot think of a single senior administrator in the past two decades, either at Berkeley or in the office of the president, who has openly opposed preferences in admissions; if they had, they would not have been appointed to those jobs—and that includes appointments in the three years since race preferences have been abolished at UC. One result is a consensus on this issue among academic administrators that in no way reflects the diversity of views among the faculty or students.

Another result of this pattern of recruitment and retention of senior administrative staff is that university presidents do not commonly talk about admissions policies with people who oppose the preference system. The people they talk to—their own administrative staffs and senior academic administrators—share their views or keep quiet, as do most academics. One aspect of academic life that no one is inclined to discuss openly is the quiet intimidation of dissenters on this issue. Very few academics wish to offend both the senior administrators who govern their careers and budgets, and the well-organized affirmative action pressure groups that are not slow to stereotype faculty members as "racists" or, at the very least, "right-wingers."

Consensual Coercion

A second pillar of racial and ethnic preference policies is patronage—the jobs associated with the development and implementation of these policies. Jobs are a source of interests, linked in universities no differently than in other areas of life. The passion that lies behind the defense of race and ethnic preferences combines both material interest and feelings of moral superiority. As a result, opponents are demonized and dissent is silenced. While our colleges and universities proclaim their endorsement of diversity, many of them simply do not permit open dissent on the issue of affirmative action. A distinguished federal judge who knows academia well has observed that "groups holding considerable power in the university loathe speech with the wrong content about topics important to them, and . . . those who say the wrong things will have little peer or institutional protection . . . Many ideas may not be expressed, many subjects may not be discussed, and any discussion on matters of political salience has to avoid offending groups powerful in the university."

Indeed, although faculty members are sharply divided over racial preferences, such differences are expressed only under the security afforded by anonymity. Open meetings of campus senates on all nine UC campuses have passed resolutions by lopsided votes condemning the regents' decision to abolish racial preferences, but mail ballots at UC San Diego, Los Angeles, and Santa Barbara and the systemwide survey by the Roper Center showed UC faculty to be evenly divided on the issues.[8]

One reason for this dichotomy is that UC scholars and professors are not fearless Green Berets. The University of California, like other universities over the years, developed a strong climate and organizational structure in support of a policy of racial and ethnic preferences in admissions. From the president's office down, every campus and every college had administrative offices and academic senate committees to plan and enforce preferential policies; every department had and has an affirmative action officer to monitor its behavior. Every chancellor, provost, and dean on every UC campus, with varying degrees of enthusiasm, has supported preferences. Indeed, for many years no chancellor, provost, or dean was appointed in the University of California who shared the views of the current majority of regents on racial preferences. But there was and is no equivalent organization of people inside the university devoted to criticizing the preference policies or to reforming them. Even tenured professors do not like to run afoul of their deans and provosts, much less their chancellors, all of whom can be very clear about their own preferences, though not always on paper. I must confess that if I were still director of Berkeley's Center for Studies in Higher Education, I might not be writing in this way.

And, as I have already indicated, critics of racial and ethnic preferences always risk being tarred as racists. No matter how unwarranted and unfair, it is an awful epithet that can damage, even destroy, one's career. Can anyone be surprised if most University of California faculty members who did not share the official doctrines on admissions and appointments kept their views to themselves, at least until they had the protection of anonymity in a survey being conducted from Connecticut or a mail ballot?

The pattern of "consensual coercion" brands some viewpoints as illegitimate and deprives those who hold them of protection. Those who voice objectionable views are stereotyped and labeled as "highly partisan," "right-wingers," or even unwitting "racists." No longer do their arguments have to be read or heard; because their arguments are already known, they can be dismissed without benefit of the doubt. Already discredited, opponents of racial preferences are then demonized; they are not merely mistaken, but evil—and fair game for late-night calls and hate mail. This kind of coercion often does not need to go this far to be effective. That is what is meant when lawyers and others speak of the "chilling effect" of some practice or policy, and it is enough to stifle debate.

The regents' actions and Proposition 209 are slowly liberating UC campuses from these chilling effects. While I believe that the president, chancellors, and their senior staffs have not changed their views, it is now possible, indeed even necessary, for people to talk about how to admit students in ways that might preserve and enhance diversity without specific attention to their skin color or eye shape.

Proposition 209, together with the regents' actions, forced three important reforms at the University of California. First, it has forced the university to abandon its categorical formulas and to admit students by inspecting their folders rather than simply their scores and race. Some students have always been admitted on the basis of their individual qualities and promise—musicians, athletes, students from abroad—but now, this must be done more broadly. To make a decision about an individual on the basis of that person's own qualities, not of his group membership, is an important step forward.

To support race-blind or race-neutral policies does not mean that one does not take into account the actual nature of American society and its effects on academic performance and life chances. Our admissions officers will be able to take into account an individual's response to disadvantaged circumstances—for example, performing well and taking college preparatory courses in a school where few go on to college. We should reward that kind of initiative and motivation. Similarly, it seems to me sensible to take into account the handicaps on academic performance implicit in growing up in a household where English is the second language. But that is a characteristic of an individual and his situation, and not of an ethnic group, many of whose members come from homes in no way disadvantaged. These suggestions, which are the kinds of ideas that UC committees and admissions officers are currently struggling with, direct our attention to individual qualities rather than supposedly homogeneous racial qualities, and do not therefore negatively stereotype or put in question the student's own personal qualifications.

Another clear gain of Proposition 209 is that all students admitted to UC can now justifiably feel that they are here on their own individual merits, and are not affirmative action admits. Before Proposition 209, no member of a preferred group could be sure whether he was admitted on his own merits or in response to a university policy concerned with competitive numbers. Equally troubling, neither could their family or friends or classmates. Bowen and Bok assert, on the strength of their survey, that recipients of these preferences did not resent those privileges. I suspect that, had the authors investigated some other social issue, they would doubt any survey's capacity to assess adequately the deep and inevitable ambivalence felt by beneficiaries of racial preferences. Indeed, different research methods would be required; only long, intensive interviews might uncover the complex feelings that Bowen and Bok dismiss so cavalierly.

But Proposition 209's greatest contribution lies elsewhere. With racial preferences abolished, we will have to think more fundamentally about the problem of under-representation in higher education—that is, we will have to improve the quality of elementary and secondary education. The University of California has begun to do that in a serious way, with the help of a recent grant of $40 million from the California legislature. Each campus has a chance to develop a program for improving the quality of K–12 schooling in the state. That is exactly where our energies ought to be going—to improve the quality of education for all California youth, especially those who most need it. The aim is not to distribute a small number of qualified blacks among a very small number of elite universities; rather, it is to increase the whole number of qualified youth, among them many blacks and Hispanics, who are prepared and motivated to continue their education in colleges and universities that will accept them for their talents and aspirations—not for their skin color or national origins. Race and ethnic preferences mask the inadequacies of our schools and distract us from that overriding obligation.

NOTES

1. These figures are supplied by the University of California, office of the president.

2. California's Master Plan guarantees admission to the University of California to the top 12.5 percent of the graduates of California high schools, though not to any specific UC campus. Thus all of the minorities who were eligible for entry to the university in 1997 would also have been eligible in 1998. The effect of Proposition 209 was only on admission to those campuses that were admitting more selectively than required by the Master Plan as a result of the growth of UC-eligible applicants to those campuses beyond the number of places available. That led to a planned "cascading" within the university from more to less affected campuses, and to some unknown degree, from UC to other colleges and universities in California and elsewhere.

3. Not including the "refused to answer" category, Chicanos, blacks, American Indians, East Indian/Pakistanis, Latinos, and Filipino Americans add up to 24 percent of the newly enrolled freshmen in UC as a whole in 1998.

4. These, of course, do not include the unknown proportions of Asians who "refused to answer."

5. Graduate and professional schools at UC essentially set their own criteria for admission. While the University of California counted "Chicanos" and "Latinos" among its undergraduates, Boalt counted "Hispanics."

6. The data referred to here were obtained by Dan Guhr, a graduate student at Oxford University doing his dissertation on comparative patterns of access to higher education in several advanced societies.

7. For example, the chart for California residents defines Range A as including stepped combinations of GPAs from 4.00 to 3.80 and LSATs from 167 to 178. So a GPA of 4.00 and LSATs of 167 to 171 are included, as are a GPA of 3.80 and a LSAT score of 178.

8. The Roper Poll of UC faculty on all nine campuses was designed in consultation with members of UC faculty, including this writer, and had a response rate of

80 percent. It survived searching criticism on methodological grounds. The Roper Poll asked voting members of the academic senate whether they favored granting preferences to women and certain racial and ethnic groups, or whether they favored promoting equal opportunities in these areas without regard to an individual's race, sex, or ethnicity. A wide plurality (48 percent) favored the latter policy; only 31 percent favored the granting of race and ethnic preferences.

These findings are consistent with polls on this issue over the past twenty years, both among academics and in the general population. When the question was put differently in the form, "Do you favor or oppose using race, religion, sex, color, ethnicity, or national origin as a criterion for admission to the University of California?" the findings show a bare majority (52 percent) for retaining those as "criteria," and fell below 50 percent when asked about these preferences for appointments to the faculty. When asked in yet another question about their own understanding of the term *affirmative action,* given the choice between "granting preferences to women and certain racial and ethnic groups," or "promoting equal opportunities for all individuals without regard to their race, sex, or ethnicity," the faculty sample voted for the second definition over the first, by 43 percent to 37 percent. Another 15 percent accepted neither statement as their own meaning of the term. Indeed, one might note that over the years supporters of race and ethnic preferences have hijacked the term *affirmative action* to refer to their policies, contrary to the views of a plurality of UC faculty who still think it means "promoting equal opportunities."

The Roper Center also conducted a similar survey in October 1996 of academics in colleges and universities all over the country. This found even higher proportions of respondents opposed to racial and ethnic preferences in admissions and appointments than was found in UC survey.

PART VI

The Completion
of the Transformation

16

IN 1999 THROUGH THE SPRING OF 2000, Trow wrote several articles in which he considered the impact of Internet technologies on higher education, including continuing education and the third phase of his conceptual model, universal higher education. I selected this essay because it relates more closely to both to his original 1974 Organisation for Economic Co-operation and Development (OECD) essay and to his longtime interest in comparing America to Europe. He had begun this line of inquiry at least by 1994, when he, Diane Harley, and I held regular conversations at the Center for Studies in Higher Education about the looming impact of Internet technology on higher education.

In 1974, Trow's conception of universal higher education, here renamed "universal access," was understandably vague, almost a catch-all for the unknown future. However, it clearly contemplated the social need for helping those who had previously been excluded from higher education and for continued education beyond university. It also anticipated an expansion of learner motivations for education, an increased diversity of providers, a decrease in the boundaries between "life" and education, and a real-world orientation for education that would, at times, threaten or compete with formal higher education. Universal higher education was also the area in which experimentation could take place more easily, including experimentation with "use of videocassettes and TV's, and on computer and other technological aids to instruction." In our discussions twenty years later, however, it was clear to us that technology had become rather more than "an aid to instruction," and was now an "imperative," a driving force that would define anew the notion of universal higher education, adding the dimensions of ubiquity and constant availability.

Along with this reformulation of the concept of universal higher education came a set of issues and possibilities more sharply in focus than those Trow had described in 1974. First, the rapid pace of change and its profound impact on our lives and work practices meant that predicting the future was impossible and destabilizing in its own right. We had only to reflect on how quickly and profoundly email had overtaken our own interactions with the world to grasp this point. Second, Trow thought that a "lag in the political, legal, economic, and organizational structures that would allow some form of postsecondary education to be made available to the whole society through the use of new technologies" meant that Europeans were still not as ready as Americans to face the challenges brought on by universal higher education through the use of Internet technology.

Historically, there has been a strong link in the United States between higher education institutions and the provision of continuing education, which has been a proving ground for innovation with an organic connection to universal education. The new technology, however, was an equalizer, since it could provide Europe and European universities the increased ability to help graduates continue their education beyond formal degree-based schooling, a capacity that every modern society must provide its educated citizens in order to compete globally.

Trow concludes this essay by saying that "information technology now forces a revision of our conception of the conditions making for universal access: it allows, and becomes the vehicle for, universal access to higher education of a different order of magnitude, with courses of every kind and description available over the Internet in people's homes and workplaces. That involves profound changes in both institutional structures and attitudes regarding higher education."

Eight years later, this prescient statement, along with every major point in this article, remains consistent with our experience. For instance, the "available" in the statement above now increasingly includes the notion of "free" or "open" as more open courseware is available to everyone in the world. MIT has 1,800 of its courses available, and its example has inspired other higher education institutions around the world to join the open educational resources (OER) and open course ware (OCW) movement. One expression of this trend is the OpenCourseWare Consortium, whose members have posted more than six thousand open courses to the Web. And many public Internet-based service sites, including iTunes and You-Tube, now offer free video recordings of lectures from faculty at universities, including UC Berkeley, Cambridge, Carnegie Mellon, and Trinity College Dublin. The issues Trow describes in America and Europe have now expanded globally as huge and growing populations in the developing world strive toward mass higher education levels with a tiny fraction of the resources necessary to accomplish it. However, via the Internet, the shift from elite to mass is there blended with universal access, a possibility that Trow did not attempt to describe, or even anticipate, and about which much remains unknown and unpredictable. However, as we try to understand these unpredictable processes, his conceptual framework and vision provide the best starting point and guidance we have.

—GARY W. MATKIN

From Mass Higher Education to Universal Access

The American Advantage

Introduction

The history of higher education since World War II in both the United States and Europe has been a history of the expansion of access and its consequences. In Europe the growth was initially beyond the tiny numbers enrolled in the small numbers of European

Originally published as Martin Trow, "From Mass Higher Education to Universal Access: The American Advantage," *Minerva 37* (Spring 2000): 1–26. It was revised from a paper read at the North American and Western European Colloquium on Challenges Facing Higher Education, sponsored by the William and Flora Hewlett Foundation, Glion sur Montreux, May 14–16, 1998. With kind permission of Springer Science and Business Media.

universities before World War II to the 30 to 40 percent of the age grade currently enrolled in all forms of European postsecondary education. This large and rapid expansion of numbers has been taken in part through expansion of the elite universities, in part through the creation of non-university sectors and institutions. Both responses to the growth of demand for places reflected the growth in all modern societies of occupations demanding more than a secondary school education, and was marked, especially in recent decades, by a growth in the numbers of non-traditional students—mature, employed, studying part-time, and aiming at employment in the rapidly growing semi-professions and knowledge-based service industries. These students, defining by their origins and aspirations the emerging systems of mass higher education, have been oriented chiefly toward gaining useful skills and knowledge rather than to membership in a cultural elite marked by common bodies of arcane knowledge and cultivated ways of thinking and feeling.

The growth of mass higher education in Europe has been the subject of most of the commentary on higher education over the past half century. The growth of mass numbers has occasioned a host of related problems—of funding, organization, and governance, and of quite different conditions for teaching new kinds of students with diverse aspirations and academic talents. But the focus on the enormous problems of creating systems of mass higher education has not allowed much thought to the next stage of postsecondary higher education, that is, the extension of access beyond one-third or one-half of a population to a situation in which access to some form of postsecondary education is universally available throughout life and in people's homes and workplaces. The development of the new information technologies (IT) over the past few years creates new possibilities and new problems for European systems of higher education before they have fully solved those associated with the creation of mass higher education systems, a process still underway.[1]

In this essay I would like to reflect on some of the leading problems or issues facing research universities as they strive simultaneously to complete the creation of systems of mass higher education and also contemplate the development of Internet-based universal access. I will be viewing these problems inevitably from an American perspective, but in comparative context. I believe that universities on both sides of the Atlantic face these problems, but they take different forms and evoke different responses in our different societies. They are part of a larger crisis in higher education in Western societies, a crisis that is similar and yet different in America and Europe. That these problems flow from the partial success in creating and adapting systems of mass higher education over the past half century, both in the United States and in Europe, make them no less threatening to the institutions that achieved that success.

Among the major problems facing higher education at the turn of the millennium are the following:

1. The first is the developing impact of the new IT on traditional forms of higher education. I put this first, both because it is the most destabilizing or transforming development in higher education, and also because it is implicated in all the others. I am not alone in believing that one effect of developments in information technology is to put the survival of research universities at risk. Recently three American university presidents expressed that same view in almost identical words. "We cannot even be certain whether the university as we know it will survive at all, nor, if so, in what form . . . The existence of the university as it is now and as we know it is in doubt."[2] Leaders of European universities agree, though in less apocalyptic terms: "It is not an exaggeration to say that the issue of new information and communication technologies questions the basic functions of the university."[3]

2. Second I would place the escalating costs of higher education in the face of public fiscal stringency, and the resulting tendency toward significant underfunding of higher education almost everywhere, but most dramatically in European nations. Despite the large increase in numbers, European governments resist the imposition of student tuition charges. With some exceptions, the funding arrangements for mass institutions and systems still resemble the ways central governments supported universities fifty years ago—except that state support has not been able to keep pace with the growth in numbers. The result throughout Europe is a marked underfunding of higher education in which productivity gains are claimed (if not demonstrated) on the grounds that more students are being educated for the same or less money. To put further pressure on education budgets, in modern science every advance in knowledge in a given field is more expensive than the last, a serious problem for countries like the United Kingdom, where basic research is still largely carried out in universities.

3. The growth of numbers without parallel increase in support by the state threatens the maintenance of the quality of instruction and research. As enrollments grew staff-student ratios declined in most European systems of higher education. The response of governments has been to demand greater productivity from universities. The rationalization of university life and management, the pressures for efficiency in operation and outcome, the consequent loss of slack resources, the imposition of the criteria and language of business and industry all threaten the autonomy of the university and the capacity of its scholars and scientists to pursue long-term studies that do not promise short-term results. In some countries the growth of managerial control mechanisms by central government works in the same direction.

4. A variety of problems arise in creating or adapting structures of governance of elite research universities to institutions of mass higher education—a problem especially acute for European universities. A leading example, one of many, is the problem of creating strong institutional leadership able to act quickly and decisively in the face of rapidly developing problems and initiatives. Another is the question of what role if any research universities can or should play in the development of new institutions of universal access and lifelong learning through the new information technologies.

5. A problem for all advanced societies, but I believe especially severe in the United States, is the decline in cultural levels, shared knowledge, and literacy of students entering higher education. We are seeing a "new" post-linear generation, immersed from early childhood in video and audio cultures, and less able or inclined to read. This phenomenon may be especially pronounced in the United States, but is visible everywhere. In the United States this situation is made much worse by the weakness of our systems of elementary and secondary schools. It is a view widely held that the United States has the most successful system of higher education in the world, and the worst primary and secondary schools.[4] The two facts may well be related.

6. Over the past two decades, the globalization of our economies and research systems, the intensification of international industrial competition, and the rise of IT have all accelerated the commercialization of both research and teaching, and the movement of both increasingly outside the institutions of higher education.[5] The short-term problem posed

here is the maintenance of the integrity and autonomy of universities; the longer-term problem (and by long I mean decades and not centuries) is the survival of research universities. Some of the developments behind these trends—the closer relations between universities and private business in both Europe and the United States, and the decline of the distinction between pure and applied research—can be welcomed;[6] certainly the rapid movement of research findings into the market has many positive effects, for consumers as for national economies. Similarly, the emerging transformation of continuing education through IT enormously extends access to people in their homes and on their jobs throughout their lives, and gives new meaning to the notion of a "learning society." But both developments pose significant problems for existing structures of teaching and research.

7. We are seeing important and disquieting changes in the culture of the university. Some countries show a serious decline in morale among academics arising out of their growing work loads and a general deprofessionalization of the university teacher and lecturer—Britain offers the clearest example here.[7] Elsewhere, we see a decline in the university as a community,[8] marked by the weakening of the identification of academic scientists and scholars with their institutions, their growing reluctance to serve on academic senate or faculty committees and the like as they turn more and more to their scholarly communities and sub-disciplines, and in science, to research teams and industrial partners and consortia. This is accompanied by a loss of authority of the academic community and its committees to increasingly powerful university administrators and state authorities and to the market through the commercialization of research and teaching. This is not a matter of administrators seizing power away from academics; rather, the size and complexity of universities, the variety of specialized problems that confront them, and above all the speed of change all together work to increase the necessity for central administration to act decisively and rapidly. Academic committees have many virtues, among them the capacity to give legitimacy to decisions and policies, and sometimes even to increase the wisdom of decisions and the quality of policy. But decisiveness and speed are not among the qualities of academic committees, and they are increasingly required of academic administrators.

This is not intended as an exhaustive inventory of problems facing modern research universities; others will have their own lists. It is a way of beginning an exploration of the modern crisis of the university, in the United States as in other advanced societies.

The Emerging Crisis of Higher Education

The problems sketched above add up to a crisis, arising in Europe out of the incomplete transformation of systems of elite universities into systems of mass higher education, and in the United States out of emerging pressures on higher education to expand further to provide universal access to some form of postsecondary education.

These problems are related, and form a general crisis in the strict sense of a major turning point in the nature of our institutions of higher education. Crises of this order do not happen every day. The leading American universities experienced such a crisis after the Civil War, when over two or three decades they transformed themselves from elite liberal arts colleges into the research universities recognizable today. Similarly, European universities faced a crisis in the 1960s and 1970s of this century under the impact of growth and democratization, for which they were structurally unfitted. But, as I have noted, while the European universities are still trying to adapt to the growth in mass enrollments of the past three decades, they have been quite suddenly overtaken by pressures for universal access, and the transformation of the concept of a learning society from a rhetorical flourish into the beginnings of reality under the impact of the new technologies of information.[9]

The development of IT requires that we rethink the nature of universal access, the third of the major forms of development that higher education has undergone and continues to undergo in all advanced societies.[10] The distinctions among elite, mass, and universal access forms of higher education have become part of the ordinary discourse about education in rich societies, wherever they are found. I based my paper for the Organisation for Economic Co-operation and Development on my experience of the growth of higher education in the United States, on what I could see of the beginnings of movement beyond elite forms of higher education in the United Kingdom and Western European societies, and on my first experience of Japanese higher education at about that time.

But just as forces outside of higher education drove the expansion of elite universities into mass systems, so current developments are driving all national systems toward broader and broader access. The growing demand for lifelong learning is independent of the development of IT—information technology simply accelerates it. Rapid technological change (of which IT is a part) and the growth of international competition together increase the value and importance of a well-educated citizenry and workforce to every country. Advanced economies now live and die by their educated labor forces, and how they are employed.

The rapid development of IT makes possible what was once merely an educator's dream: that is, the possibility for all people in a society to have access to education all their lives, in subjects of their own choice and at times and places of their own convenience. It also requires a new and different conception of universal access to higher education—a change from my original conception of higher and higher levels of *enrollment* in colleges and universities by students of traditional college age, to a conception of access as *participation* in lifelong learning by people in their homes and workplaces. People of all ages and occupations can now be involved in more or less formal instruction, training, and education through computers and the Internet in varying subjects of use or interest to them, when and where they wish. The freeing of education and training from the constraints of time and place in ways hardly imaginable in the early 1970s enormously broadens the potential scope and range of lifelong learning. Of course, this has been possible on a limited scale for a very long time through correspondence courses, more latterly in several countries with the help of television. But IT changes the nature and potentialities of distance learning dramatically and qualitatively. The move toward universal participation in postsecondary education, already underway but not everywhere recognized, will surely have revolutionary consequences for our existing institutions and systems of higher education, as well as for the larger societies that sustain and depend on them.

Indeed, IT is involved in each of the major problems mentioned above. By liberating learning from constraints of time and space, it opens higher education to the same forces for commercialization of teaching that we have already seen in research as the distinction between pure and applied research has diminished.[11] Moreover, even before IT takes hold, the rapid expansion of enrollments, the diversification of student interests and talents, and the volatility of their academic preferences have led to an enormous expansion in the numbers of part-time non-tenured teachers on annual contract, a reserve army of workers that gives university administrators the measure of flexibility they need under the new conditions of constant uncertainty and change.[12] The expansion of enrollments, both on campus and at a distance, in people's homes and workplaces, strains traditional forms of quality control and diminishes confidence by governmental authorities in those institution-based quality control procedures, leading to increased demands for external assessments and control—a trend carried to its greatest lengths in the United Kingdom.[13] The constraints on state support for higher education drive student-staff ratios up, in the face of the broad consensus among teachers almost everywhere that students come to university more poorly prepared and less inclined to read than they used to—a natural consequence of the broadening of access, and of changes in secondary education and its graduation requirements that have made that broadening possible. Both of these tendencies make traditional academic standards more problematic—a problem more severe in European systems that still assume governmental responsibility for a uniform quality of university qualifications. And now education through the Internet poses special problems for quality control and for the accreditation of courses and programs.[14]

One could expand the links among these new problems. Behind them all lies the long secular trend that we see as the fundamental democratization of life in modern societies, a trend marked by the weakening of elite hierarchies, values, and prerogatives. Universities inherently are to some degree elite institutions: they admit students of higher than average talents to study difficult subjects taught by teachers who gain their academic qualifications through long and severe education and training. The growth of enrollments, and the extension of the name and status of university to what were formerly less prestigious institutions, have changed the relation of universities to governments, industry, and society. The spread of postsecondary education through IT, some of it awarding university-level qualifications and degrees, accelerates these democratizing tendencies and poses problems for all the arrangements, especially of governance and finance, which were traditionally associated with research universities.

The problems I have sketched above take very different forms in American and European universities. Universities in Europe and America share many features in common; that is not surprising, since American universities had their origins in England, Scotland, and Germany, and still show family resemblances. But behind these most visible, and in some respects substantial, similarities, lie quite fundamental differences, differences we have to keep in mind when we talk about our common problems. Because while we do have some problems in common, American responses to them are likely to reflect differences in our history, organizational structures, and public attitudes toward postsecondary education.

Let us first look at historical and structural features of American higher education that are specific to that system—not to make invidious comparisons, but to warn against the premature and misleading generalizations about problems facing higher education, and to highlight the potentially harmful effects of using American models uncritically for European practice and reform. While American higher education shows its origins in European models, it developed under quite different circumstances than did Europe's universities, in response to quite different historical social, cultural, and economic forces. There are lessons in our experience, but they are limited, and there is a danger of learning the wrong lessons, drawing inappropriate conclusions from the American experience.[15]

One example: the central principle of curricular organization in American colleges universities is the modular course, the accumulation of unit credits earned in these modular courses, and the banking and transferability of these credits among most of America's 3,700 colleges and universities. This arrangement, the dominant principle in all but a handful of American institutions, introduces an extraordinary degree of flexibility within the American system. Course credits, banked in each student's transcript, allow relatively easy transfer for students within an institution between major fields and between institutions. It allows students to "stop out" of formal education for a period of time for work or travel, and return to the same or a different institution, picking up his or her course of study without loss of time. Of course, the small number of highly selective institutions will not always accept a transfer from a less selective institution or a student with a poor academic record. But most American colleges and universities are not highly selective, or selective at all, and transfer of students among institutions with acceptance by the new institution of all or most of the credits earned in the old is very common. That very ease of "stop out" and transfer not only allows but encourages transfer between institutions. It also enormously facilitates lifelong learning, both within traditional institutions and at a distance. Students can combine credits earned in courses taken in traditional ways in traditional institutions with credits earned miles away and years later in other institutions through courses online.

Of course, this raises many problems: which distance courses will be awarded credit toward a degree by the institution offering the course; who will accredit the institutions offering distance course and assess the courses; what other institutions will accept credits earned in this way as credits toward their own degrees, are all questions currently under discussion in the United States, in a system in which there is no broad governmental authority to answer those questions. But these are fundamentally the same kinds of questions that attach to the transferability of credits earned in traditional institutions. While distance learning introduces certain special difficulties, there is little doubt they will be answered, with the answers varying to some extent among the relatively autonomous colleges and universities that make up the American system.

But while the modular course and unit credit system has many advantages for systems of mass higher education, and even more advantages for emerging systems of universal access, these advantages come at a price. The chief price is to the coherence of the course of study, and especially to the general education that comprises the bulk of the study for most students during the first half of their studies toward a degree. While most institutions have some general education requirements, they tend to be broad and easily fulfilled, little constraining on the preferences of students, who often choose courses for where they fit in a work and leisure schedule as much as for their content. A few American institutions require a few courses that comprise a small core of general studies; in other cases a major field, often in the sciences, imposes one or two introductory courses as preparation for being accepted to a major field of study. But on the whole the range of elective courses is large; the constraint on the wholly free choice of the student may be no more than that she choose a number from the tens or hundreds of courses labeled "humanities" or "the social sciences"—a widely employed device to discourage "premature specialization" known as "breadth requirements."

Moreover, even these mild constraints have been weakening rapidly. A recent study by the National Academic of Science of changes in the undergraduate curriculum in fifty leading American colleges and universities in this century finds that over this whole period there has been a steady de-emphasis of a common core of knowledge marked by a "precipitous drop in the number of basic courses that students are required to take."[16]

> The more an institution limits the choices among courses that students can make in fulfilling their general education requirement, the more that requirement can be said to have been structured. The extent to which an institution structures its general education programs demonstrates the extent to which it is willing to establish clear educational priorities, rather than leaving these to be determined by the students themselves.
>
> Overall, the NAS found that highly structured course requirements were the norm in 1914, 1939, and 1964, but that these had given way to a radically more latitudinarian approach by 1993. (Moreover, it also found that the average percentage of the overall graduation requirement composed by general education requirements dropped from 55 percent in 1914, to 46 percent in 1964, to 33 percent in 1993.) Specifically the findings include:
>> The de-emphasis of a common core of knowledge is illustrated by a precipitous drop in the number of basic courses that students were required to take. The average number of these mandatory courses fell from 9.9 in 1914, to 6.9 in 1964, to 2.5 in 1993.[17]

The result is that in the introductory general education part of their studies it is rare that any two American students will have taken the same array of courses, or that in any given course any two or more students will have read any book or books in common.[18] Teachers in American universities, especially in our mass institutions, cannot assume a common body of knowledge, or even of interest, among students in their introductory courses; every course before the specialized studies of the major starts from square one. Another consequence is that with no common academic culture, the only common culture among students, even in traditional institutions, is likely to be that of popular entertainment, or sports, or the fascination of the age grade in their search for friends and mates and identity. The enormous flexibility and responsiveness of American higher education to student preferences and market demand is bought at the price of this intellectual incoherence.

Distance learning reduces the distractions of campus life, but may exaggerate the anonymity of the big lecture hall in its virtual classroom. (It is still uncertain whether the radical voluntariness and self-selection to distance courses will in some measure overcome the thinness of the student cultures on the campuses of the mass institutions of American higher education; the answer will surely vary widely by the nature of the course and subject.) European educators may well be wary about paying this enormous price for moving toward American models. It is not just the inherent conservatism of academic institutions, or the insensitivity of state-funded European universities to market pressures. There are other good pedagogical reasons for Europeans to be skeptical about the apparent virtues of American higher education—so visible and attractive in its leading liberal arts colleges, research universities, and their graduate schools and departments.

Nevertheless, the flow of influence about forms and structures of higher education is today, as it has been since World War II, very much from the United States to Europe. Despite their deep-rooted distaste for American populism, and for what they see as the commercialization of science and culture and the threat to universities posed by the domination of markets and their interests, European academics and leaders are fascinated by American colleges and universities. (Americans are on the whole far less worried by the dangers of commercialization in intellectual life; in the United States the market preceded the society.) And many of their innovations are adaptations of American models—though in functional systems and under circumstances in which these elements come to serve quite different functions, or function quite differently. While European nations can borrow many of our institutional arrangements, such as the modular course and transferable academic credits, they have difficulty in overcoming or reproducing the cluster of structural and cultural features that add up to a distinct American advantage in the move first to mass higher education and then to universal access.

The American Advantage

American higher education today has quite different functions and structures from those elsewhere. In most countries in the world, higher education trains and educates the ruling strata, selects and recruits to government service and the "learned professions," confers status on those who earn degrees and qualifies them in various ways for the society's most challenging jobs and occupations. In the United States colleges and universities perform those functions, but also, and most important, they give substance to the idea that in America anything is possible to those with talent, energy, and motivation. This sense of American society with limitless possibilities for all, largely (though not exclusively) through higher education, is what is usually meant by the "American Dream." The end of the American Dream is continually proclaimed, usually by intellectuals who never believed in it to begin with, and wished no one else would. But this faith, fundamental to the American political system, survives beyond the hostility and cynicism of what the British call "the chattering classes," and underpins America's peculiar mixture of conservatism and radical populism. Through its role in fostering social mobility and the belief in a society open to talents, American higher education legitimates the social and political system, and thus is a central element in our society as it is nowhere else.[19]

The European models of higher education—the German, the French, the British, the Mediterranean—reflect their elite origins and functions in their structures. All characteristically are perched on top of an upper secondary system that both prepares and qualifies students for university entry. Students will have had their general education in secondary school, and in some systems, like the English, will already have begun to narrow their studies there, basically between the sciences and the "arts." Their university studies will not ordinarily include a period of general education, though there are some exceptions and will be more in the future. But broadly speaking, a university education in European systems has been a preparation for a professional career in the civil service, the learned professions, and in upper secondary and higher education. Only now is it expanding into the preparation of business managers and the semi-professions. The first degree in a European university, where it is offered

(BA, BPhil, Candidat., etc.) is ordinarily at a higher standard in their specialties than an American first degree (though all such generalizations are increasingly problematic). Postgraduate studies, particularly the doctorate, are ordinarily linked directly and immediately to the dissertation, without the postgraduate coursework that is required in our universities.

Much of what we do in our universities, especially but not only in the first two years, strikes Europeans as serving the function of their upper preparatory secondary schools. Indeed, historically our universities and colleges did a lot of secondary school work because we had no developed system of public secondary education until the end of the nineteenth century. And while the principle of "in loco parentis" is formally dead in most American colleges and universities, the spirit of responsibility for the physical and spiritual welfare of students is still strong in our institutions, in a way that is not present in European universities. English universities are a halfway house in this respect, but my sense is that they are also moving toward continental models both because of the influence of the European Union and its educational schemes, and also because the old nurturing relationship of teachers and students in British universities required a high teacher-student ratio that they have lost quite suddenly over the past decade. Elite American colleges and universities have relatively rich teacher-student ratios; others employ armies of para-educators—professional counselors, deans of student life, remedial specialists, and the like—whom the Europeans do not employ, certainly not in the same numbers. In the United States these para-academics preserve the pastoral function as the academics increasingly surrender that function in response to the increased emphasis on research and publication.

But the enormous diversity of American higher education, and the rapid growth and increasing diversity of European higher education systems, make all such generalizations less true (i.e., many more deviant cases) than they were even a decade ago. And that is because European systems are moving toward American models. That is not because we are rich and a superpower, nor does it reflect the power of American popular culture—elements in the Americanization of so many other institutions in other countries. It is because American higher education as a system is simply better adapted, normatively and structurally, to the requirements of a postindustrial age, an age that puts a great premium on the creation and wide distribution of knowledge and skill, one marked by such rapid social and technological change that decision makers in all countries begin to see (or at least believe in) the necessity for broader access to postsecondary education for their citizenry. So the new crisis of universal access arises, as I have suggested, while European universities are still trying to adapt their organizational, governance, and funding arrangements to their relatively new mass numbers. The United States, by contrast, had the structures for mass higher education in place long before they actually had mass higher education, which came with the GI Bill just after World War II and never went away.

The First System of Mass Higher Education

At this point we might ask three questions: (1) Why is it that the United States developed a system of mass higher education so much earlier than anyone else? (2) What have been the impediments to the transformation of elite European systems into systems of mass higher education? (3) How are the United States and other countries moving toward universal access, lifelong learning, the learning society? These phrases all point in the same direction, toward the breakdown of the boundaries between formal learning in the institutions of postsecondary education and the rest of life, the assimilation of postsecondary education into the ordinary life of the society.

The modern system of higher education in the United States was already in place a century ago; the emergence of modern European systems of higher education is still under way. By 1900, when only 4 percent of Americans of college age were attending college, we already had in place almost all of the central structural characteristics of American higher education: the lay board of trustees, the strong president and his administrative staff, the well-defined structure of faculty ranks, and in the selective institutions promotion through academic reputation linked to publication and a readiness to move from institution to institution in pursuit of a career. On the side of the curriculum, the elective system, the modular course, credit accumulation, and transfer based on the transcript of grades all were in place by 1900, as were the academic departments covering all known spheres of knowledge, and some not so well known. Underpinning all was the spirit of competition, institutional diversity, responsiveness to markets and especially to the market for students, and institutional autonomy marked by strong leadership and a diversity of sources of support. The United States already had the organizational and structural framework for a system of mass higher education long before it had mass enrollments. All that was needed was growth. That we have had in plenty, but with surprisingly little strain on a system that was already adapted to growth and change. Indeed, until this decade my own view is that the only major structural change in American higher education over the past century has been the invention and then the spread of the community colleges, linked easily and casually to four-year institutions through credit transfer, and in some places, through strong encouragement to strengthen those ties by state and local governments.[20] Of course American higher education is different in many ways from what it was in 1900, but our growth and development has not required changes in the basic structure of the system. It is those structural changes that are now taking place, with great difficulty, in Europe and the United Kingdom.

Europe Struggles toward Mass Higher Education

Let's look at some of the elements of mass higher education in the United States, and consider the extent to which European systems have created or introduced its chief elements:

- size and access beyond 15 percent of the age grade
- diversity of the forms of higher education beyond elite universities
- diversity of students in respect to social class, age, and ethnicity—including a large proportion of older, part-time, employed students
- a substantial component of vocational/professional education
- a high measure of institutional autonomy
- modular courses, credit accumulation, and transfer
- a strong chief executive and administrative staff

- multiple sources of support
- a relatively flat academic hierarchy rather than a powerful guild of full professors

On this list of elements of a system of mass higher education, European nations have in the past decade moved sharply toward mass numbers—in most countries upwards of 30 percent of the traditional college age cohorts are enrolled in some form of higher education. Many countries have a more diversified student population than they did just a decade ago, having seen marked increases in the enrollment of mature and part-time students. Some, like France, have a more diversified system of institutions; the United Kingdom (and Australia) have unified their systems, at least formally reducing the measure of diversity that was previously in place. Most European nations have tried to give their universities a larger measure of autonomy in the development of their curriculum and the appointment of their academic staff, but the limitations are still greater than most American research universities know. They move slowly toward modular courses and the accumulation of course credits, and even more slowly toward credit transfer. There are movements in several countries toward the rationalization of academic ranks, but that is resisted, in some countries successfully. Almost everywhere we see an increasing use of part-time, casual academic labor without job security as a way of dealing with declining resources and rapid unpredictable change, as in the United States.[21]

In Germany, for example, a former minister of science and culture in the state of Hesse writes about "governmental failures to support adequately the transformation of the German university into a system of mass higher education by failing to grant sufficient financial support or to contribute reform concepts."[22] Indeed, the resistance to basic reform has prevented Germany from creating a first degree, developing a mechanism for controlling access to its universities, or charging tuition, problems shared with other European countries—all substantial handicaps to developing a coherent system of mass higher education while preserving the elite sector. Moreover, many academics and administrators in Europe are aware that mass higher education and institutional autonomy require stronger institutional leadership, but the resistance by the academic guilds and governmental bureaucracies together is in most European nations very strong; most institutional leaders, with some exceptions, are still elected by the academic community, serve short terms, and have little real power to initiate reforms. What reforms have been introduced have come mainly from governmental ministries and have served their interests, especially in shifting responsibility for the increasingly apparent shortcomings of the institutions in the face of underfunding. For example, the then vice president of the German Conference of University Rectors noted recently that "the latest reforms in the German system of higher education have been introduced primarily for more effective management of scarce resources and with a view to shifting the onus for the functional shortcomings of the overcrowded and underfunded schools from the government onto the institutions of higher education."[23]

On the crucial issue (for Americans) of the diversity of sources of financial support, for Europeans, while there is a great deal of rhetoric about the desirability of wider support for higher education from the private sector (again with many glances in the direction of the United States), it is still the case that central governments provide most of the financial support for European higher education.[24] Mayer and many others complain about inadequate resources, and indeed, per capita support for university students has declined in almost every European country during the rapid expansion of enrollments over the past quarter century, in some cases dramatically. But her assumption, and those of most commentators in Europe, is that the key lies in additional support from central or regional government. While private industry in Europe has increased its support for university-based research in recent years, it is still a small fraction of governmental support. Moreover, there are still few private colleges or universities in Europe, and resistance to their creation remains strong.[25] Most important is the continuing refusal by European governments, supported by most academics, to allow universities to charge students tuition, and to retain tuition funds for their own development and use. "Free tuition" ("free" only in the sense that the cost of university education is paid for by taxpayers rather than the recipients) constitutes a significant entitlement for the mostly middle- and upper-middle-class families whose children go to university, and is fiercely defended by them and their children. The idea of setting aside a portion of tuition payments for student aid to poorer students is not on the table in Europe—indeed, in many countries the issue of tuition payments cannot even be raised, much less introduced. The resulting underfunding of higher education in most European nations greatly handicaps their capacity to respond creatively to growth, both of knowledge and of enrollments.

Of course, "underfunding" is a comparative concept. In 1993, the latest data available, the United States spent 2.5 percent of its GNP [gross national product] on higher education, more than twice the proportion spent by France (1.1 percent), Germany (1.0 percent), the United Kingdom and Italy (0.9 percent in both countries). (Only Canada at 2.6 percent was higher among the leading industrial nations reported.)[26] The GNP figures are also reported by proportions from public and private sources. With respect to the commitment of public resources, the United States at 1.3 percent of GNP is not far from the European countries named, all of which are at 0.9 percent of GNP except for Italy at 0.8 percent. Indeed, if we consider that the 1.3 percent from public sources in the United States includes support for a broad system of mostly public community colleges whose counterparts (where they exist) elsewhere are not counted as "higher education," we would probably find that public support in the United States is close to that in these other countries for similar kinds of institutions. The difference lies in the very great discrepancy between the United States and these other countries in the support for higher education from the private sector: student tuition, gifts, endowments, the sale of services of all kinds. In the United States the 1.3 percent of GNP provided by these private sources almost doubled the public commitment of 1.4 percent, as compared with the 0.2 percent of GNP in France, 0.1 percent in Germany, and 0 percent in the United Kingdom.[27] In 1999, I suspect that these figures from private sources would be slightly higher in all countries, including the United States; the large discrepancy would remain. Indeed, the Dearing Report (1997) observes that "none of the [European] countries considered were expecting to change significantly the proportion of GDP [Gross Domestic Product] which they devote to higher education."[28]

The advantages the United States has had in coping with the emergence of mass higher education are still there as universities on both sides of the Atlantic face the challenges of the new information technologies and their promise of universal access to postsecondary education.

Challenges Posed by the New Technologies: The Speed of Change as the Enemy of Policy

All of the problems that are emerging in our systems seem to call out for thoughtful and sweeping responses in higher educational policies. But ironically, the very forces that are generating our new problems hinder our capacity to develop broad, encompassing policies in response. In a very real sense, the rate of change of information technology outruns our capacity to develop sensible policies for its management. We have never seen anything quite like this before. All of our countries have had educational policies; some have even been successful, like the Land Grant Act of 1862 and the GI Bill after World War II in the United States. (Europeans can supply their own examples of successful policies for higher education.) But whether for good or ill, policies for higher education have not until now been undermined by the sudden irruption of new technologies. So I suggest that the very speed of technological development in this area is an independent force posing a severe challenge to policy makers.

One indicator of the speed of technological development can be seen in the decline in the costs of computer memory and in the speed with which information can be transmitted across the Web—the latter known as bandwidth. Both of these are crucial to the ease and flexibility of applications of IT, to education as to commercial activity. The fall in the price of memory is apparent to all who own personal computers. The intense competition in the communications industries that has led to a tremendous expansion of bandwidth in the past few years is less visible, but is at least as important as distance learning comes to more interactive and employ more audio and video elements alongside text. As a recent story in the *New York Times* reports:

> To grasp just how much bandwidth is being created, consider this:
> According to Telegeography Inc., a research firm in Washington,
> in 1997 the world's public telephone networks carried 81.8 billion
> minutes, or 155,632 years, worth of international phone calls. The
> newest optical systems can transmit the digital equivalent of all of
> those calls over a single fiber in about 11 days. "If anything, the

cost of communications is falling faster than the cost of computing, so assume unlimited bandwidth," said Howard Anderson, managing director of the Yankee Group, a technology consulting firm in Boston.[29]

Equally dramatic for its implications for higher education is the development of the capacity to print single copies of books through the Internet and fast printers, paste and bind them in board covers, and sell them for the same price as in their longer runs. This new development raises difficult problems for authors and publishers of books still under copyright, but few problems for the many books already in the public domain and long out of print—the kind that scholars commonly need and use.[30] Major publishers (Wiley, Macmillan, Cambridge University Press, Open University Press) already advertise on-demand titles, and these are only those whose copyrights they own. But the Library of Congress and other bodies are putting whole libraries on the Net, and these books will also be available for on-demand publication. Commercial bookstores are already selling books on-demand at their retail outlets; one of them advertises that you can get a book on demand in their store in about the time it takes a coffee shop (often inside the same bookstore) to make a cappuccino coffee—that is, about fifteen minutes—and charge the same price as if the book were printed and distributed in the traditional way. The Council of Europe claims that the print-on-demand technology is "now capable of producing perfect books at astonishing speeds and with minimum effort. Binding, long time a stumbling block, has been developed to acceptable standards and now either a soft or hard cover can be produced. A book of 600 pages, for example, can be printed in approximately 5 minutes."[31] The capital investment for the required computers and fast printers currently make on-demand publication impractical for the ordinary book-buyer, but not for a book store or university library. Consider the implications for the ways libraries currently purchase, store, handle, and loan books, and the costs of lending and retrieving them. It may soon be easier to print a book and give it to the user than to order, shelve store, retrieve, lend, retrieve again, and store again, as currently.

Since the beginning of the Western university the library has been the heart of the university—laboratories were late-comers. They have been a powerful centripetal force, bringing scholars and students together and keeping them in physical proximity, whether in cities or on rural campuses. But the storage of books, manuscripts, and other scholarly material, including sounds and pictures of all kinds, on the Net is transforming scholarly research, profoundly reducing the importance of the library as the repository of printed scholarly materials. (It reduces the significance of the museum for similar reasons.) A Stanford historian has reported that he spent ten years in his spare time in the archives of the Library of Congress writing a book on the first meetings of the American Congress that established many of the precedents that have governed its operations over the past two hundred years. He now can find all the documents he needed on the Net, available to him in his home or office. He remarks that the kind of research he did, requiring trips to the archives, will never be done again for studies using materials that are stored online. (And as we know from research on, for example, medieval manuscripts, such study can be more accurate and detailed since the manuscript on the Net allows high magnifications of difficult illuminations and blurred passages.)

A leading computer scientist recently observed as an aside in a talk at Berkeley, that "now that memory and bandwidth are essentially free, we can turn to the issues of what to do with our freedom." That does not mean that memory and bandwidth are literally free for ordinary teachers, scholars, and scientists, but that their costs are falling so rapidly that they will soon be felt to be free in the same way that we use electricity to light our houses without much regard for its cost. As for "what to do with our freedom," the applications are pouring out of our own laboratories and those of many commercial providers, and like print on demand many will have large consequences for both the public and the private lives of higher education—for its organization, structure, and finance as well as for the nature of teaching and learning. The speed of development of the software and applications is such that it defeats the efforts of scholars to report it, much less analyze it, in books. Instead, a recent special section of the *New York Times*[32] linked the special reports of seventeen *Times* reporters to capture the nature of developments in this area, at least at the moment of writing. While the articles in the section are about the use of the Web in various arenas of commercial life, it is useful to reflect that one important aspect of distance learning is a form of e-commerce, with the same concerns about start-up costs, the nature of the market, the labor force, the quality and attractiveness of the product to its consumers, its delivery, pricing, competition, and all the rest of the problems of commercial activity. The very terms of description of this aspect of higher education are offensive to many academics who entered the academic life to escape the ethos of buying and selling, the principle that governs so much of modern life that everything and everyone has a price. And while some tenured professors may well escape it, as least for a while, increasingly, for good or ill, these developments will transform the relations of teachers with students, of teachers with teachers, and of students with students. But how it will transform these relations is still unclear, still uncertain.

The speed of change captured in the *New York Times* report on e-commerce is the source of uncertainties; indeed, the central principle in thinking about the future impact of IT on higher education is uncertainty. It is inherent (1) in changes in the technologies and in their costs, (2) in the rate of expansion of their use, (3) in the nature of their use by students and teachers as the technology changes over time, and (4) in the policies of governments and universities toward their introduction and use.

1. Our capacity to plan rationally is reduced by the uncertainties of technological developments—a separate matter from the speed of development. I have suggested above that information technology even three to five years in the future will make the present technology look like Model T Fords on muddy dirt roads. But as we could not predict the enormous power of the Internet as the vehicle for so many computer applications even three years ago, so similarly we cannot today predict developments in this field very well even three years ahead.

The new technologies already in the works, already being tested, suggest capacities beyond anything we have seen or can barely imagine: the rapid delivery of massive amounts of information over ordinary telephone lines has already been achieved, as have similar speeds and volumes over cable installations. TVs already are a cheap and familiar vehicle for Internet communications. These modes all compete for primacy, and we do not know who will win. Most experts anticipate the convergence of technologies, blurring the lines between different appliances—phones, TVs, and computers—bringing costs down as they make distant interactive communications easier and cheaper.

But that merely extrapolates from existing technologies. More likely, over the next few years we will be seeing more fundamental developments in the organization and transfer of information. For example, Sun Microsystems has already announced "a product called Jini that uses Sun's Java programming language to harness the power of millions of computers, from mainframes to palm-sized devices. We now have all the ingredients to build a distributed computing fabric which approaches science fiction," [said one scientist]. "You will be able to sit with your laptop and it will be able to reach out across the network. And for the moments you need the power, it will become the largest supercomputer in the world."[33] Those and other technological developments carry powerful challenges for higher education, though few in the United States, and even fewer in Europe, have begun to think of their implications.

2. The technologies surely will develop and change, but we can't be sure how quickly or widely they will be adopted in our different societies. We can be reasonably sure that they will be adopted earlier by young people than by older generations whose work habits and modes of thought have already been shaped by earlier technologies. It may be that new technologies will require substantial time and effort to master, as earlier changes in the information technologies have, and that may slow their adoption, especially if older ones fill needs that are not easily expanded. On the other hand, it may be that more advanced technologies will be so much easier to use, as happened in other technologies, from telephones to automobiles to passenger aircraft, as to transform the population of users and the nature of use. The electric self-starter opened the automobile to use by women and older people. Ease of use and cost will surely have effects on how widely the new technologies are adopted. We cannot simply extrapolate either the extent or the nature of the use of new technologies from the existing technologies.

3. Apart from sheer acquisition and adoption of new information technologies is the question of what people and institutions are going to use them for. The Internet will be available, as it is now, for entertainment, for shopping and other commercial activities, for the acquisition of information, and also for more systematic forms of education. The key to IT use in the future will be the outcome of fierce competitions for people's time. For many people in our affluent societies how they choose to use their time will determine how they spend their money, and not the other way around.

4. But not all choices will be made by individuals making decisions about their use of leisure. Many consequential decisions will be made by large corporate bodies: by business and industry about the use of IT for training and continuing education of their workforce during working hours; by governments through the amount and kinds of regulation they impose on educational institutions that might want to provide some or all of that continuing education for the labor force; and by colleges and universities and other providers that will compete with one another for the opportunities to provide continuing education to the adult population on the job or in their homes. Colleges and universities will be making decisions about offering credit toward their degrees for courses taken online, as well as about the ownership of the intellectual property displayed online. We have as yet little idea about how those big institutions will be acting in these areas, except that they will probably differ among themselves.

We have some early clues. IT is developing most rapidly in the United States, where it is encouraged by America's economic, legal, political, and cultural openness to innovations that challenge elite structures and attitudes of all kinds. (See below.) But in all countries, the earliest adoption of IT for universal access through lifelong learning is by less prestigious or marginal institutions, and by those institutions, often the same ones, most strongly oriented to the market for students and other forms of external support. Outside the United States that is likely to be in the private sector of higher education, where a private sector exists. Since lifelong learning by IT threatens traditional structures of higher education with respect to such issues as funding and organization, quality assessment, examinations, and the criteria for earning degrees, it threatens the various forms of control and management that most governments have over their higher education systems. It remains to be seen whether European governments will encourage the development of lifelong learning through IT in all their universities and colleges, or try to restrict it to non-elite forms of higher education for whose quality and products government will take less and less responsibility, as, for example, the Open University in the United Kingdom and the weaker private colleges and cram schools in Japan.

These are all uncertainties. They confound our capacity to see very far ahead in this realm of social life, and that in turn affects our capacity to plan, and the kinds of planning that social institutions might make for a development of such enormous if uncertain importance to all our lives. And this poses two questions for researchers: how are governments and institutions currently designing policies for continuing education in the context of radical uncertainty, and how should they do so?

A researcher in this field today has to look at the emerging scene and at the same time try to do what I have suggested is impossible, that is, to peer into the future to the problems and conditions that may obtain five or ten years down the road. Some colleagues[34] and I have been trying to do that in California, trying first to find out what is going on in our institutions and their near neighbors, and then trying to see underlying patterns that might provide clues to at least the direction of development of these technologies in our colleges and universities, and in the new institutions that are growing up inside and around the familiar ones that we know.

Our early studies suggest two sets of observations, one having to do with the diversification of the new forms of instruction that reflects the enormous diversity of our students and subjects; the second bears on the implications of that diversity for governmental and institutional policy in this area.

1. We simply cannot talk sensibly about the role of IT in lifelong learning as so many commentators do, but must disaggregate the patterns of use of IT very finely along at least four crucial dimensions: by the nature of the subject taught; by the location of the student (whether inside a college or university, or at home or at the workplace); by the purpose of the instruction—whether to transmit skills and knowledge or to cultivate mind and sensibilities; and by the academic talents and motivations of the learner. There may well be other important dimensions, but this at least establishes the principle of disaggregation.[35]

2. A corollary of 1 is that our policies must reflect the enormous diversity of the educational effort, no longer an effort to educate a small segment of the population for the leading positions in all its institutions, but something close to the continuing education of the whole population for life in the rapidly changing and highly competitive economies and societies of the twenty-first century. If the provision of lifelong learning is to be as varied as its diverse student populations, then

policies must be responsive to the nature and goals of the educational effort, almost course by course, to the market for knowledge and information among consumers, and to the judgments of the academics who know better than anybody whom they are teaching and how those students learn.

A central policy issue for research universities is whether and how they will be involved in distance learning through the new technologies. European nations are showing a growing interest in continuing education, "not as a luxury but as a personal and national strategy for survival in a highly competitive global economy. Officials also see it as one way to combat Europe's persistently high unemployment rate." But "Universities are not the sole or even the primary provider of university-level continuing education in Europe. While statistics are hard to come by, experts say universities provide only a small part of professional or post-secondary-level adult education in most European countries. The rest is provided by private training schools, industrial associations, and training programs organized in-house by companies for their own employees. Educators say the challenge for universities is to stake out a bigger share of the market."[36] Their first answer, which is mostly to give continuing education over to other agencies, is not likely to be their last answer. A variety of pressures will surely lead at least some European universities more and more deeply into distance learning. Already, in Norway a decision has been made by the universities and colleges, and confirmed by the ministry in May 1999, to the effect "that responsibility for all lifelong learning at a higher-education level will stay with the higher-education institutions."[37]

How these conflicting requirements—of function, demand, and pedagogy—balance out cannot be the subject of general rules or state policy. On the contrary, it means that policies must allow—indeed, encourage—experimentation by those who introduce the use of these technologies into higher education, and especially into distance learning. If we must have national or regional policies, those policies might be of the form: "Give institutions and the people in them the freedom and resources to initiate from below, and to experiment in many different directions." And policy makers must accept that it is inherent in experiments that some may fail, in social and educational life as in the laboratory.

Policy as Experimentation

"Policy as experimentation" as a doctrine is very hard for modern governments to accept, seized as they are of the importance of this area of public life, prepared and willing to make large investments for the commonweal, and inherently unwilling to give it piecemeal to providers who are "experimenting." On this issue government ministers and civil servants might well reply, "Yes, experimentation is all very well in science, but we responsible authorities have to find out what works and what doesn't, determine which way we want to go, and then fund developments in that direction on a grand scale and hold its participants accountable. If extending access to lifelong learning through the new forms of information technology is important both for the domestic economy and international competitiveness, then surely it deserves substantial funding and leadership from central government."

That is a position that comes naturally to central government authorities. However reasonable, perhaps even inevitable it may be as a position for governmental bodies, I believe the expansion of access to lifelong learning through the new technologies, as far ahead as we can see, will take the form of a continuing series of experiments. The three elements defining experiments in higher education are: (1) the programs are not standardized, but vary sharply in character, funding, pedagogy, function, and the like; (2) they are transitory, on trial, not firmly institutionalized; and (3) they are under continual assessment for their costs and effectiveness.

The development of IT in higher education as in other spheres of life is such that we will not be able to standardize and freeze delivery systems or policies on the basis of what has proved over time to be successful. We do not have the luxury of allowing time to determine for us what is effective and what is less so. Technological developments alone will continually confound efforts to freeze or standardize educational forms. If that were not enough, other factors—for example, variations among academic subjects, the conditions of delivery, and student talents and motivations—will ensure that no standardization of forms and procedures is possible. If this sounds somewhat anarchic, that is in fact what we have been finding in California. And we have been trying to draw the implications of these findings or insights for the future.

Another American Advantage: The Idea of University Service

Most observers of American life and letters recognize the existence in America of a broad consensus around the notion that everyone should be involved in formal education for as long as possible; this is a central element of the nation's secular religion. This fundamental value underlies the inclusive sentiments and commitments to service and useful instruction that are the defining features of American higher education. It was captured a century and a half ago in Ezra Cornell's famous statement: "I would found an institution in which any person can find instruction in any study."[38] It found expression also in the guiding principles of the Federal Land Grant Act of 1862, which provided federal support for a college in every state "where the leading object shall be, without excluding other scientific or classical studies, to teach such branches of learning as are related to agriculture and the mechanic arts." It was also embodied in the Wisconsin idea of service by the university to the wider community.[39]

The Wisconsin idea, an aspect of the Progressive movement in American life and politics of the turn of the century, is of special importance in understanding American attitudes toward lifelong learning and useful studies of all kinds, and has been summarized in the University of Wisconsin's motto: "The boundaries of the University are the boundaries of the State." The idea incorporated two ideas keyed to service to the community: an elite notion of building more expertise into the affairs of state—a stream of thought that finds contemporary expression in the schools of public policy in many universities—and "the development of popular nontechnical lectures which carried the university to the people." This development, which took the name of "extension courses," later added technical courses of all kinds as the extension curriculum was expanded. Indeed, there was almost immediately "an acceleration of how-to courses which, if they did not show how to make American democracy more democratic, did show many an American who otherwise would have been beyond the effective range of the university how to make himself a more effective farmer or worker."[40] A century later that is a central motivation of the Western Governors' University (WGU), as also of its many competitors.[41] The WGU is a virtual university without a campus or classrooms, all of whose courses will be online, delivered electronically to students in their homes and workplaces.

The crucial difference with the European experience is that extension in the United States has been *university* extension; hardly a university in the country, and certainly no great public university, does not have an extension division, providing courses "for any person in [nearly] any study." From the perspective of the Western governors, their university is merely an adaptation of the idea of university extension to the potentialities of the new information technologies. In practical terms it will link together the online capacities of the extension divisions of the public (mostly land grant) universities in these Western states in a cooperative rather than competitive way. There will be plenty of competition for this new institution from other providers of online distance learning, both public and private. Meanwhile not only does the Western Governors' University promise to extend the reach of higher education further and longer into the working and leisure life of adults, but also—and here is the contemporary twist—it may do so not merely at no cost to the taxpayer, but as a source of income to the participating institutions. The Western governors see nothing incompatible between broadening and deepening access to forms of postsecondary education, and making money from it as well; indeed, many would say that the latter is a condition for the former. That is surely a perspective not widely shared among Europeans—but it greatly affects the ways that adult education through IT will develop, is developing, on different sides of the Atlantic.

These perspectives are very like those that introduce a multitude of books and papers on the information revolution. That literature, often enormously instructive though it is, is produced for the most part by those who are working in this area, who are excited by what they are doing and seeing, and by the potentialities for education, both inside and outside traditional institutions, that technological developments in this area hold. It is imbued with the excitement and fundamental optimism that C. P. Snow identified as the emotional climate of engineers and scientists, by contrast with the pervasive pessimism of humanistic writing in our time.[42]

The Search for Meaning: On the Survival of Elite Research Universities in an Age of Universal Access and Lifelong Learning

With the engineers and scientists, I also believe that we are in a revolution in higher and continuing education, although a revolution in its early stages. I see some of its enormous positive potentialities, but also that it may well have negative effects on central elements of the higher learning, and on traditional kinds of institutions and relationships that have long been associated with the pursuit of wisdom as well as of information and knowledge. Most of the new forms of distance learning thus far are found characteristically in elementary language instruction or introductory mathematics courses, or in various business-related subjects, and have been used to facilitate the transfer of specific skills and bodies of knowledge rather than to help students in "appreciating a poem, understanding an idea, finding significance in an historical event, following the logic of an argument, inquiring into ethical dilemmas, making rational and moral judgments—all of which require an exercise of mind that calls upon all the human faculties and which no technology, however sophisticated, can satisfy."[43] Research and reflection on the impact of these new technologies must be sensitive to their downsides as well as to their undeniable positive potentials, not least the potential to enable large parts of our populations to be involved, even if intermittently, in some kind of formal education all their lives.

A former president of Johns Hopkins, Steven Muller,[44] has speculated on what continuing functions elite universities will have in the future. He believes much library-based scholarship will no longer need to be based inside a university, and much of undergraduate education also can be carried effectively on the Internet. On the other hand, he believes that laboratory work and training cannot be divorced from direct personal interaction. Nor can the desire of students everywhere to be in each other's company, for the usual social and personal motives be satisfied in virtual classrooms. But a central and continuing function of the university is carried by the humanist scholar and teacher, concerned not primarily with the transfer of information or knowledge, but with the cultivation of critical and independent perspectives and the exploration of meaning. Two such teachers express their sense of the centrality of the direct relation of teacher and student, both with a text in hand.

> In the classroom, all any of us has to work with are a text . . . whatever background reading our often frantic schedules will allow, and—the crucial ingredient—the power of our own feeling-imagination at its most intense . . . to combine with the feeling-imagination of the writer in such a way as to kindle the feeling-imagination of those who come to us to learn. From such interactions, rather than from the passive transmission of information, come those moments of revelation, however rare, that change lives.[45]

And Gertrude Himmelfarb reflects on the technological revolution and its implications for humanistic studies:

> It takes a discriminating mind, a mind that is already stocked with knowledge and trained in critical discernment, to distinguish between . . . the trivial and the important, the ephemeral and the enduring, the true and the false. It is just this sense of discrimination that the humanities have traditionally cultivated, and that they must now cultivate even more strenuously, if the electronic revolution is to do more good than bad.

Himmelfarb continues with a warning of the loss of the capacity to read a book, "to study it, to think about it, to reflect upon it." To do that "we should have it in our hands, for that is the only way of letting it into our minds and our hearts." Great books "sustain our mind and inspire our imagination. It is there that we look for truth, for knowledge, for wisdom. And it is these ideals that we hope will survive our latest revolution."[46]

These of course are the classic concerns of the humanist scholar in the face of any technologies that come between learner and book, or teacher and learner. Those of us who grew up with reverence for those values and ideals of scholarship and learning will watch with concern whether they survive the revolutions in higher education already underway. But we need not assume that those values and the relationships that sustain them require that teacher, book, and student must share the same small physical space. The possibilities for elite forms of higher education through distance learning should not be foreclosed. We can already see the harbingers of elite forms on the Net in advanced scholarly seminars that bring together students and scholars around a manuscript on a screen across a continent. To deepen those relationships beyond scholarship to character forming may require another leap in the technology that will make prolonged audio/visual interactive connections cheap and easy. Beyond that, as always, it will be the motivation and intelligence of teachers and students who will make of those distant connections the vehicle for the shaping of the student's mind, character, and sensibility, and not the mere transmission of information and knowledge that we now associate with lifelong distance learning.

Conclusion

A knowledgeable European observer of European higher education observes that on the whole it is "about twenty or thirty years back on a continuum which has led the US into universal higher education." This essay takes that as a starting point for exploration. First, the same normative, cultural, and structural problems that account for the two- or three-decade lag of European higher education in the emergence of mass higher education is also making for a lag in the emergence in Europe of universal access. I make the point in this essay that the elite-mass-universal access model set forth in my OECD paper of the early 1970s assumed that universal access would come through larger and larger numbers in all countries having access through formal enrollments and attendance—part-time or at night—in non-elite institutions that might over time and for some fraction provide direct links through credit transfer to degree-granting institutions. That has been happening increasingly, though still on a modest scale. I now suggest a revision in our conception of the conditions making for universal access: that IT allows for universal access of a different order of magnitude, with courses of every kind and description available over the Net at times of their choosing in people's homes and workplaces, some for credit and some not, so that lifelong learning becomes the vehicle for universal access of a different kind than we are accustomed to.

While most European countries are still struggling to complete the structural reforms necessary to fully institutionalize mass higher education, few university-based academics or administrators have fully appreciated the implications of IT for universal access. Research universities in both the United States and Europe have been fully occupied exploiting the potentialities of the Internet for scientific research and scholarship, and increasingly for the enrichment of their taught courses and seminars. But the effects of the new technologies will have consequences far beyond those already visible in our institutions. IT will have, is having, a powerful corrosive effect on boundaries of all kinds—national, institutional, disciplinary. It is weakening the links of academics to their institutions, to their faculties, departments, and disciplines. Since so much research can be done outside of universities or colleges in the contexts of use it blurs the distinction between pure and applied research. It is drastically weakening the library as the central institution (along with labs) of the research university. Since research can be done anywhere it blurs the distinction between research universities and other kinds of institutions of higher education. Since it strengthens the market for education it strengthens students in relation to teachers, and blurs the distinction between learning and entertainment. And it is having a myriad of other consequences—for the relations of students and teachers, for accountability and assessment, for the ownership of intellectual property and publication and the use of publication for meritocratic assessment, and thus for the whole machinery of institutional controls that has been put in place in many European countries during their expansion. The most profound effects of IT will be to weaken the distinction between life and learning. As more and more postsecondary education goes online, the character of our familiar universities and colleges, in both Europe and America, will come into question.

One important difference between the United States and Europe is that few European elite research universities take responsibility for mass or universal access, while American research universities, especially the big public universities, ordinarily do. These leading American institutions command the necessary discretionary funds, and can recruit and retain the highly skilled engineers and scientists who command a premium in the private market for the new information technologies, and give them the freedom to experiment and initiate. That means that they can exploit IT and develop initiatives in this new sphere. Less distinguished institutions of mass higher education can't do that so well: they don't have the money or the people. The sharp divorce of most European elite research universities from lifelong learning must inhibit the development of the latter beyond the traditional evening and vacation courses.[47] On the whole and with some exceptions, European research universities don't want to do it, are not equipped to do it, don't see it as part of their mission or nature. And that may mean that these important developments in European higher education will not be given the kind of continuing and comparative study that they deserve. But universal access to higher education through the Internet will be no respecter of national boundaries, and will mirror the globalization of our economies, with similar consequences for national systems.

NOTES

1. M. Trow, "Problems in the Transition from Elite to Mass Higher Education," in *Policies for Higher Education*, from the General Report on the Conference on Future Structures of Post-Secondary Education (Paris: Organisation for Economic Co-operation and Development, 1974), pp. 55–101. Reprinted as chapter 2 in this volume.

2. Steven Muller, "The Management of the Modern University," in *University in Transition*, ed. Detlef Müller-Böling et al. (Gütersloh: Bertelsmann Foundation Publishers, 1998), pp. 222–30. The same view in almost the same words was echoed by Berkeley's Chancellor Robert Berdahl at his inauguration, April 1998, and by President Gerhard Casper of Stanford at a panel discussion at Berkeley on the same day.

3. Kenneth Edwards, *New Technologies for Teaching and Learning*, Association of European Universities, CRE Guide no. 1, April 1998, p. 25.

4. Among many expressions of that view: "I have [been] talking about the great success story of higher education in the United States. By contrast, the public K–12 system has been a disaster, a shocking deterioration of a once quite competent enterprise." Cornelius Pings, "The Ongoing Evolution of the American Research University," in Müller-Böling et al., eds., *University in Transition*, p. 69.

5. This process is explored in M. Gibbons, C. Limoges, H. Nowotny, S. Schwartz-

man, P. Scott, and M. Trow, *The New Production of Knowledge: The Dynamics of Science and Research in Contemporary Societies* (London: Sage, 1994).

6. For example, in 1997 the then chancellor of the University of California, Berkeley, observed that in his university "industrial funding is moving up the research stream," and described the process in the following way: "Companies want to collaborate. American business and foreign concerns know the university has an important role to play in basic engineering research. Some of the most creative experimentation now underway has to do with how the university and industry relate. As the hunt proceeds for the ultimate prototype, people are becoming convinced there may not be a single optimal paradigm—no one size fits all research models. At Berkeley most of our private funding comes through consortia. A group of faculty identify a group of companies that might be interested in that research. The companies pay from U.S. $5000 to U.S. $500,000 to join a consortium. They get demonstrations, work with faculty, and meet our graduate students. Their scientists and engineers spend time as visiting scholars, working in our labs. We have more than a dozen consortia operating on the Berkeley campus, and no two are alike. The sole similarity is that they all adhere to the basic academic model. There is little concern about secrecy. No limitations on publication. Everything our consortium members see and hear is in the public domain. This is a totally transparent process. What they want—and what we provide—is early access to research. In fast developing fields, six months is a lifetime. Some companies cut in-house research and buy into consortia to gain access to talent, facilities, and support that would be prohibitively expensive for all but the largest commercial concerns . . . At Berkeley private funding for research has grown from a very small portion 20 years ago to more than 20 percent of our current research budget." Chang-Lin Tien, "Research Funding and its Effect on the Research Agenda," in *University in Transition*, pp. 45–46.

7. On European academics, see Oliver Fulton, "Unity or Fragmentation, Convergence or Diversity," in *Universities and Their Leadership*, ed. William Bowen and Harold Shapiro (Princeton: Princeton University Press, 1998). For the United States, see B. R. Clark, "Small Worlds, Different Worlds: The Uniqueness and Troubles of American Academic Professions," *Daedalus* 126, no. 4 (Fall 1997): 21–42, esp. pp. 31–37.

8. Clark Kerr is only the most notable critic of these trends, on which most commentators agree. See Kerr, "Knowledge, Ethics and the New Academic Culture, "Part IV, *Higher Education Cannot Escape History: Issues for the Twenty-First Century* (Albany: State University of New York Press, 1994), pp. 131–56. The intense ambivalence of some senior administrators in American research universities regarding the pull of external research links and consulting on the faculty members is captured in the following: "A greater value placed on knowledge possessed by

professors and the resources to purchase research results is not all bad. Society benefits, and for those in universities it is heady stuff: more attention, more money, more glamour—more of everything except time or inclination to perform what might be called the professor's pastoral duties. The pull between 'inside' and 'outside' is not a zero-sum game. Outside activities open opportunities not only for teachers but also for students. They may well improve certain kinds of teaching by giving professors richer experiences and material. Nevertheless, the lure of the outside has to undermine institutional citizenship because a professor's marketability as a researcher or lecturer and commentator is largely personal—a function of disciplinary standing. In other words, there has been, in the postwar decades, a declining incentive to concentrate on the intramural community of students and teachers." Henry Rosovsky with Inge-Lise Amer, "A Neglected Topic: Professional Conduct of College and University Teachers," in *Universities and their Leadership*, ed. William G. Bowen and Harold T. Shapiro (Princeton: Princeton University Press, 1998), p. 123.

9. Note that universal access to postsecondary education leading to a "learning society" is not the same as open access to university for those who earn an *abitur* or *baccalaureate*.

10. Trow, "Problems in the Transition from Elite to Mass Higher Education." It is important to stress that while national systems can be broadly described in terms of these development phases, individual institutions may provide education across all these categories, though in different proportions.

11. See Gibbons et al., *The New Production of Knowledge*.

12. In the United States roughly 45 percent of all teachers in postsecondary institutions are in this category of part-time non-tenured staff, though the proportions are much smaller in research universities. These part-time instructors, whose numbers have grown in all countries with the expansion of enrollments, cannot develop any genuine mentoring relationships with students as they run from class to class and even institution to institution, and may therefore be the first to be replaced by teaching over the Net, especially since they have no security of employment. On the other hand, some of these part-timers prefer that status for personal reasons.

13. See M. Trow, "American Perspectives on British Higher Education under Thatcher and Major," *Oxford Review of Education* (Winter 1998): 111–29.

14. See, for example, Florence Olsen, "'Virtual' Institutions Challenge Accreditors to Devise New Ways of Measuring Quality," *Chronicle of Higher Education*, August 6, 1999. http://chronicle.com/free/v45/i48/48a02901.htm.

15. On the origins of the American system, see M. Trow, "Federalism in American Higher Education," in *Higher Learning in America: 1980–2000*, ed. Arthur Levine (Baltimore: Johns Hopkins University Press, 1993), pp. 39–67. Reprinted as chapter 4 in this volume.

16. National Association of Scholars, *The Dissolution of General Education: 1914–1993*, Princeton, N.J., 1999, ISBN 0-9653143-0-8 and http://www.nas.org/study.html.

17. Ibid.

18. The enormous diversity of American higher education makes some qualification always necessary. The smaller the institution, of course, the more likely students will have had courses in common; also, on the whole elite institutions impose more course requirements on their students; they have greater confidence in their own academic authority and are less responsive to student preferences. But all that is relative.

19. See M. Trow, "Class, Race and Higher Education in the United States," in *Democracy in Comparative Perspective*, ed. Larry Diamond and Gary Marks (Newbury Park: Sage, 1992), pp. 275–93. Reprinted as chapter 5 in this volume.

20. Others might suggest that the massive growth in federal support for university-based research, starting really during World War II, would also qualify as a major structural change, at least in the realm of support for the system. But the principle of federal support for research was in place much earlier; here we can debate when quantitative becomes qualitative change.

21. A German university leader observed at an international conference that Germany still had to create a first degree, find a way to control entry to its universities, and begin to charge tuition. On structural and funding problems in European universities, see "The Decline of German Universities," *Science* 271 (July 12, 1996): 172–74, and the articles on higher education in Europe in *Science* 271 (February 2, 1996), including "European Union," and also "U.S.-Style Universities for Germany?" *Science* 280 (June 19, 1998): 1826–27. France, like every other European country, struggles to transform its traditional elite system into a system of mass higher education. And they are doing better than most—they have diversified more successfully, and have moved toward greater institutional autonomy while broadening their resource base. They speak of a revolution in the culture of the universities, which seems to refer to the changes associated with diversification, autonomy, and a greater involvement of the teaching staff in the development of institutional mission and identity. But when we look at what they have achieved, it seems clear that while moving toward American models they still have a long way to go. For example, France suffers a degree of overcrowding in many of their universities that is almost unknown in the United States; they have less student-teacher contact than is common in the United States, even in our first two years; they have not solved the problem of credit transfer, even between French universities, much less among EU countries; they do not allow for the easy movement between major fields that is common in the United States. Nor do most French universities provide extension courses and continuing education as many American universities do. Moreover,

they are just beginning to make the connections between universities and local government, business, and industry that are common in the United States. And they still show the traditional marked separation between teaching in the university and research elsewhere. France is trying to overcome this last separation by appointment of university and *grandes écoles* teachers to research groups in the CNRS [Centre National de la Recherche Scientifique], though my impression is that the students see little of this until the small minority that pursue research enter doctoral programs. See "France: An Elite System Struggles with Mass Education," *Science* 271 (February 2, 1996).

22. Evelies Mayer, "Whom Do German Universities Now Serve?" in *German Universities Past and Future*, ed. Mitchell G. Ash (Oxford: Berghahn, 1997), p. 192. On these and other problems, see other essays in this volume, many of which stress the continuing power of the Humboldtian ethos to block the reforms needed for the transition from elite to mass higher education.

23. Rainer Künzel, "Political Control and Funding," in ibid., p. 173. Much the same could be said about the motivations of the massive interventions by British central governments into the universities over the past two decades.

24. For important exceptions, and perhaps precursors of the future, see B. R. Clark, *Creating Entrepreneurial Universities: Organizational Pathways of Transformation* (Oxford: Pergamon/IAU Press, 1998).

25. See "U.S.-Style Universities for Germany?" The Japanese have an advantage over European systems in having a large and varied private sector, enrolling about three-quarters of all students in four-year colleges and universities, and 90 percent in two-year colleges. They share with European countries a preeminent set of state universities wholly funded by central government, and therefore not highly responsive to the market. But the private sector defeated efforts by central government to restrict the growth of higher education in the late 1980s and early 1990s. For a critical analysis of Japanese policy and practice in higher education, see Ikuo Amano, "Education in a More Affluent Japan," *Assessment in Education* 4, no. 1 (1997): 51–66, and his 'Structural Changes in Japan's Higher Education System—from a Planning to a Market Model," *Higher Education* 34 (1997): 125–39. See also Akiro Arimoto, "Massification of Higher Education and Academic Reforms in Japan," in *Academic Reforms in the World*, Research Institute for Higher Education, International Seminar Reports no. 10, Hiroshima University, Japan, July 1997, pp. 21–55; Kazuyuki Kitamura, "Policy Issue in Japanese Higher Education," *Higher Education* 34 (1997): 141–50; and Ulrich Teichler, "Higher Education in Japan," in *Goals and Purposes of Higher Education in the 21st Century*, ed. Arnold Burgen (London: Jessica Kingsley, 1996), pp. 192–209.

26. Canada is exceptional in its very high commitment to higher education from public sources—2.2 percent of its 2.6 percent total. Japan only commits about

1.0 percent of its GNP to higher education, but over half of that, 0.6 percent, comes from private sources—the only country among this group similar to the United States in this respect.

27. Organisation for Economic Co-operation and Development, Center for Educational Research and Innovation, *Education At A Glance: OECD Indicators*, 1996. Of course, private support for British universities is not 0 percent; some British universities, for example, Warwick, Oxbridge, LSE [London School of Economics], gain substantial support from the sale of services, college endowments, tuition payments by overseas students, and the like. But all in all, it is unlikely that they add up to more than the 0.1 percent or 0.2 percent from private sources for German and French universities.

28. *National Committee of Inquiry into Higher Education* (The Dearing Report), 1997, Appendix 5, Section 10, "The role and background to higher education in Europe," para. 10.32.

29. Seth Schiesel, "Jumping Off the Bandwidth Wagon," *The New York Times*, July 11, 1999.

30. See *Freedom to publish (on demand) our cultural diversity*, Council of Europe, n.d. (1999). See also Andrew Malcolm, "A Very Short Run: The Arrival of "Print on Demand" and "The Future of the Publisher-Author Relationship," *Times Literary Supplement*, June 18, 1999, pp. 14–15.

31. "Freedom to Publish," p. 11.

32. E-Commerce, *The New York Times*, September 22, 1999, pp. D-1–69.

33. "Science Fiction Power for the PC," *International Herald-Tribune*, July 16, 1998, pp. 1, 10.

34. My colleagues on this project are Dr. Diane Harley, of the Center for Studies in Higher Education at Berkeley, and Dr. Gary Matkin, associate director of UC Berkeley Extension. The first fruits of our work can be found in Martin Trow, "The Development of Information Technology in American Higher Education," *Daedalus* 120, no. 4 (Fall 1997): 293–314, and "Lifelong Learning through the New Information Technologies," *Higher Education Policy* 12 (1999): 201–17.

35. The bearing of the diversity of higher education on the nature of distance learning is a large subject that deserves separate treatment. A beginning can be found in Trow, "The Development of Information Technology," especially pp. 294–298. See also B. R. Clark, "Small Worlds, Different Worlds: The Uniqueness and Troubles of American Academic Professions," *Daedalus* 120, no. 4 (Fall 1997): 21–42.

36. Burton Bollag, "In Europe, Workers and Professionals Head Back to the Classroom," *Chronicle of Higher Education*, September 3, 1999, p. A87.

37. Ibid. On the American pattern, see below, note 41 and ff.

38. Quoted in Richard Hofstadter and Wilson Smith, eds., *American Higher*

Education: A Documentary History (Chicago: University of Chicago Press, 1961), p. 555.

39. On the involvement of state and land-grant universities in distance learning, see Kellog Commission on the Future of State and Land-Grant Universities, *Returning to our Roots: A Learning Society*, September 1999.

40. Frederick Rudolph, *The American College and University* (New York: Alfred A. Knopf, 1962), pp. 363–65.

41. These themes are more fully developed in my "Lifelong Learning through the New Information Technologies."

42. C. P. Snow, *The Two Cultures: And a Second Look* (Cambridge: Cambridge University Press, 1964).

43. Gertrude Himmelfarb, "Revolution in the Library," *The American Scholar*, Spring 1997, p. 204.

44. Muller, "The Management of the Modern University."

45. Maynard Mack, quoted in *The American Scholar*, Spring, 1998, p. 176. Whether those moments of revelation can be achieved over the Internet seems to me one of the most important questions for the future of higher education.

46. Himmelfarb, "Revolution in the Library." It may be that the spread of "books on demand" over the Web will in some measure reconcile the concerns of humanists with the new technologies.

47. Britain's Open University has much experience as an open access institution, and has the resources to experiment and initiate in technology-based distance learning, but it is exceptional among non-research universities in this respect.

17

THE CONCEPTUAL FRAMEWORK for the analysis of expanding higher education systems that Trow outlined in 1974, and is reprinted as chapter 2 of this volume, has stood the test of time. Reread through European eyes, it is remarkable how relevant it remains to contemporary debates and issues. In these reflections, written some thirty years later, he elaborates and updates it, both theoretically and empirically, especially with reference to developments in Europe and the United States.

While they have been widely adopted, the "elite," "mass," and "universal" descriptors have generally been seen as stages of development (with relatively little attention given to the final stage—perhaps because it was long perceived as having limited applicability beyond the United States). However, as with a lot of the popularization of social science concepts, many later commentators got it wrong by limiting their application to sequential stages of system development. This was not the intention either of Trow's original paper or of this essay, which discusses how modern higher education systems have simultaneously to confront the differing functions of elite, mass, and universal higher education. Consideration of how this might be done provides its central theme.

In this task, Trow is able to draw on a vast knowledge of the traditions and circumstances of higher education systems and institutions on different continents and examines it through the lens of some classic sociological concepts. It is indeed a joy to read a contemporary piece on higher education that refers to Max Weber! Much of his discussion employs a Weberian ideal type form of analysis, and is large in scope and comparative reach, but it also contains many fascinating and illuminating examples and insights, for example, in explaining why student dropout is regarded so differently in Sweden and the United Kingdom. The essay takes a comparative look at the changing relationship between higher education and society while, at the same time, has interesting things to say about the private lives of higher education institutions: the forms of instruction they offer, their curricula, their access arrangements, and their forms of management and decision making. It combines a considerable knowledge of the detailed workings of the higher education systems in several countries with the insights from a "sociological imagination" of the highest order. And to these it adds a strong awareness of practical matters—how much does it all cost and who is going to pay? The final ingredient of this rich brew are the author's own values and concerns which, though never overstated so as to disfigure the overall analysis, are there for all to see, and to accept or reject.

The European reader cannot help but note that in Trow's terminology, Europe has "problems" whereas the United States has a "model" and there is perhaps an underlying assumption that the United States has on the whole got most things "about right." European eyes might be a bit more skeptical, and find, for example, some U.S. developments in the areas of managerialism and academic capitalism possibly threatening to some of the essential functions of higher education. Trow also perhaps takes a rather rosy view of how meritocracies tend to work in practice. It is by no means evident that elite universities always recruit only the ablest students. All sorts of social processes and conditions affect who walks through the doors of elite universities and colleges. The elite reproduction view of higher education does not get much of a hearing in this essay.

On the whole, Trow tends to express most concern about the elite parts of higher education and the factors that will determine their well-being. Like others, he tends to elide the notion of elite functions of higher education into a focus on elite institutions of higher education. This may be empirically typical but it is not empirically universal. The steepness of the status hierarchy of institutions varies considerably between countries. In some places, system differentiation takes more of a horizontal than a vertical form. This does not mean that elite, mass, and universal functions cannot be identified but they may sit alongside each other in the same institutions and academic departments. Trow recognizes this possibility but does not really address its merits and demerits, other than finding that it usually means less money for the elite.

Trow had his views and preferences and so too will his readers. They will find in this essay an enormous breadth of knowledge, powerful analysis, and much wisdom and humanity. In 1974, he gave us an analysis of what was happening in higher education that served us well for more than thirty years. In this essay, he provided us with a further analysis that will continue to inform debate and understanding about higher education's place and role in the world for the next thirty years.

—JOHN BRENNAN

Reflections on the Transition from Elite to Mass to Universal Access

Forms and Phases of Higher Education in Modern Societies since World War II

Introduction

This essay seeks to reflect and update a set of concepts, first introduced more than thirty years ago, regarding the transformation of higher education (Trow, 1973).[1]

The ideas of this original essay, as nicely summed up recently by British author John Brennan (2004), illustrate three forms of higher education: (1) elite—shaping the mind and character of a ruling class; preparation for elite roles; (2) mass—transmission of skills and preparation for a broader range of technical and economic elite roles; and (3) universal—adaptation of the "whole population" to rapid social and technological

Originally published as Martin Trow, "Reflections on the Transition from Elite to Mass to Universal Access: Forms and Phases of Higher Education in Modern Societies since WWII," in *International Handbook on Higher Education*, edited by J. F. Forest and Philip G. Altbach, 243–80. New York: Springer, 2006. With kind permission of Springer Science and Business Media.

change. Table 17.1 provides a useful summary of these stages of higher education development. Brennan observes that "while these may not capture all of the nuances of current higher education debates, they nevertheless appear to be remarkably prescient of some of the key issues that we face as we embark in the UK on the move, in Trow's terms, from mass to universal higher education. It should also be emphasized that Trow never saw these distinctions as empirical descriptions of real higher education systems, rather as models or 'ideal types' to aid our comprehension of such systems. And a further point to remember is that although he saw these forms as sequential stages, he did not regard it as inevitable that the later stages would completely replace the earlier ones. In particular, he saw definite possibilities of examples of elite forms surviving in the mass and universal stages."[2]

Three decades later, this essay revisits some of these concepts and models, exploring the question of their continuing usefulness in understanding modern systems of higher education, so much larger, more diverse and complex than the systems the earlier essay addressed. And it raises the question of whether and where those concepts would need to be modified to illuminate contemporary conditions—and even whether that is possible—and highlight these themes within the context of recent developments in Europe.

Aspects of Growth

World War II was the watershed event for higher education in modern democratic societies. Those societies came out of the war with levels of enrollment that had been roughly constant at 3 to 5 percent of the relevant age groups during the decades before the war. But after the war, great social and political changes arising out of the successful war against fascism created a growing demand in European and American economies for increasing numbers of graduates with more than a secondary school education. And the demand that rose in those societies for entry to higher education extended to groups and strata that had not thought of going to university before the war. These demands resulted in a very rapid expansion of the systems of higher education, beginning in the 1960s and developing very rapidly though unevenly in the 1970s and 1980s.

TABLE 17.1 *Trow's Conceptions of Elite, Mass, and Universal Higher Education*

	Elite	Mass	Universal
Attitudes to access	A *privilege* of birth or talent or both	A *right* for those with certain qualifications	An *obligation* for the middle and upper classes
Functions of higher education	Shaping mind and character of ruling class; preparation for elite roles	Transmission of skills; preparation for broader range of technical and economic elite roles	Adaptation of "whole population" to rapid social and technological change
Curriculum and forms of instruction	Highly structured in terms of academic or professional conceptions of knowledge	Modular, flexible, and semistructured sequence of courses	Boundaries and sequences break down; distinctions between learning and life break down
The student "career"	"Sponsored" after secondary school; works uninterruptedly until gains degree	Increasing numbers delay entry; more drop out	Much postponement of entry, softening of boundaries between formal education and other aspects of life; term-time working
Institutional characteristics	–Homogenous with high and common standards; –Small residential communities –Clear and impermeable boundaries	–Comprehensive with more diverse standards; "Cities of intellect"—mixed residential/commuting –Boundaries fuzzy and permeable	–Great diversity with no common standards –Aggregates of people enrolled some of whom are rarely or never on campus –Boundaries weak or nonexistent
Locus of power and decision making	"The Athenaeum"—small elite group, shared values and assumptions	Ordinary political processes of interest groups and party programs	"Mass publics" question special privileges and immunities of academe
Academic standards	Broadly shared and relatively high (in meritocratic phase)	Variable; system/institutions "become holding companies for quite different kinds of academic enterprises"	Criterion shifts from "standards" to "value added"

Access and selection	Meritocratic achievement based on school performance	Meritocratic plus "compensatory Programs" to achieve equality of opportunity	"Open," emphasis on "equality of group achievement" (class, ethnic)
Forms of academic administration	Part-time academics who are "amateurs at administration"	Selected/appointed for limited periods. Former academics now full-time administrators plus large and growing bureaucracy	More specialist full-time professionals. Managerial techniques imported from outside academe
Internal governance	Senior professors	Professors and junior staff with increasing influence from students	Breakdown of consensus-making institutional governance insoluble; decision-making flows into hands of political authority

Source: From John Brennan, "The Social Role of the Contemporary University: Contradictions, Boundaries and Change," in *Ten Years On: Changing Education in a Changing World,* Center for Higher Education Research and Information (Milton Keynes: The Open University, 2004), p. 24. The first full statement of these ideas was published in M. Trow, "Problems in the Transition from Elite to Mass Higher Education, in *Policies for Higher Education,* from the General Report on the Conference on Future Structures of Post-Secondary Education (Paris: OECD, 1974), were developed in later papers, cited in the notes.

Note: Elite, 0–15 percent; mass, 16–50 percent; universal, more than 50 percent.

The growth of higher education manifests itself in at least three quite different ways, and these in turn have given rise to different sets of problems. There was first the rate of growth: in many countries of Western Europe the numbers of students in higher education doubled within five-year periods during the decade of the 1960s and doubled again in seven, eight, or ten years by the middle of the 1970s. Second, growth obviously affected the absolute size of both systems and individual institutions. And third, growth was reflected in changes in the proportion of the relevant age group enrolled in institutions of higher education.

Each of these manifestations of growth carried its own peculiar problems in its wake. For example, a high growth rate placed great strains on the existing structures of governance, of administration, and above all of socialization. When a very large proportion of all the members of an institution are new recruits, they threaten to overwhelm the processes whereby recruits to a more slowly growing system are inducted into its value system and learn its norms and forms. When a faculty or department grows from, say, five to twenty members within three or four years, and when the new staff are predominantly young men and women fresh from postgraduate study, then they largely define the norms of academic life in that faculty and its standards. And if the postgraduate student population also grows rapidly and there is loss of a close apprenticeship relationship between faculty members and students, then the student culture becomes the chief socializing force for new postgraduate students, with consequences for the intellectual and academic life of the institution—this was seen in America as well as in France, Italy, West Germany, and Japan. High growth rates increased the chances for academic innovation; they also weakened the forms and processes by which teachers and students are inducted into a community of scholars during periods of stability or slow growth. In the 1960s and 1970s of the last century, European universities saw marked changes in their governance arrangements, with the empowerment of junior faculty and to some degree of students as well. They also saw higher levels of student discontent, reflecting the weakening of traditional forms of academic communities.

Growth also manifested itself in the growing proportions of the relevant age groups enrolled in institutions of higher education. In many European countries, that proportion, just after World War II, was about 4 or 5 percent; only 25 years later it reached between 10 and 20 percent. By 2000, the figures in most European countries were up around 30 percent, and going higher.

The expansion of European higher education after World War II was both large and rapid. For example, Sweden had 14,000 university students in 1947. By 1960, the number had more than doubled to 35,000; by 1965, it had doubled again to about 70,000, with another doubling by 1971, when university students comprised about 24 percent of the relevant age group. France saw an equally dramatic growth in its university population, from 200,000 in 1960 to more than 400,000 in 1965, with another doubling by the mid-1970s (reaching an enrollment of about 17 percent of the relevant age group). Denmark doubled its university student population between 1960 and 1966, from 19,000 to 34,000; by the mid-1970s, it had doubled again to 70,000, about 13 percent of the age group. In the United Kingdom, the Robbins Report anticipated university enrollments growing from about 130,000 in 1962 to 220,000 by 1973 and to nearly 350,000 by 1980. In reality, nearly 400,000 (about 13 percent of the relevant age group) were enrolled in all forms of full-time higher education by 1973, and somewhere between 800,000 and 1,000,000 by 1981 (with roughly half in universities). By the year 2000, following the merger of the polytechnics and the universities, enrollments in all forms of higher education in the United Kingdom had reached more than 2.1 million.[3]

Growth in the proportions of the population that have access to higher education raises a number of questions central to the issue of the nature and functions of higher education. For example, the proportions entering higher education in every country vary sharply in different regional groups, religious and ethnic groups, and socioeconomic classes. Everywhere the proportions from the upper and middle classes are still significantly higher than from the working classes or farmers, despite a generation of efforts to close that gap. When the proportions of an age group going into higher education were very small, the political issue of equality in educational opportunity was centered much more on higher primary and secondary education. But the higher the proportion of the age group going on to higher education, the more the democratic and egalitarian concerns for equality of opportunity come to center on the increasingly important sector of tertiary education. These differences in access to higher education, which were not reduced but rather increased during the early stages of expansion, become a sharp political issue within the context of the democratic and egalitarian values that are increasingly strong in Western European countries, and these values created strong pressures for reducing these differences in group rates of enrollment. In many countries governments introduced policies of affirmative action designed to increase the proportions of students from lower income strata. The more important access to higher education becomes for the life chances of large number of students, the stronger these pressures become. The persistent tendency of intellectually elite institutions such as the universities to be both the home and the source of the social and economic elite is a major source of tension between the institutions of higher education, still in principle meritocratic, and the increasingly strong egalitarian values of Western society.

The irony of course is that while universities in Western democracies became increasingly meritocratic during the twentieth century, especially after World War II, the societies around them became increasingly egalitarian.

The rising rate of enrollment of a particular age group has another important significance, one not so directly political. As more students from an age cohort go to college or university each year, the meaning of college attendance changes—first from being a privilege to being a right, and then, as was true first in the United States and now in the EU [European Union], to being something close to an obligation for students in some class and ethnic groups. This shift in the meaning and significance of attendance in the tertiary sector has enormous consequences for student motivation, and thus also for the curriculum and for the intellectual climate of these institutions.

Phases in the Development of Higher Education

What the numbers (reflecting the rapid growth of higher education after World War II in all advanced industrial societies) conceal are two fundamentally different processes. One of these was the expansion of the elite universities—the growth of traditional university functions in the traditional, if somewhat modified, forms of universities. The other was the transformation of elite university systems into systems of mass higher education, performing a great variety of new functions (at least new to universities) for a much larger proportion of the university age group. As enrollments in the higher education institutions of every rich democracy grew in the postwar years, from 5 percent just before and after the war to 30 to 50 percent of the relevant age groups at the turn of the millennium, they passed through several phases. We can refer to these as the phases of elite and then mass higher education, phases that currently are opening up even further to become systems of universal access. Since this model of phases and phase transitions in higher education was first developed in the early 1970s,[4] the proportions enrolled in higher education become more and more difficult to define with any precision, for several reasons. First, the diversification of higher education—of students, studies, and institutions—makes it more difficult to identify institutions as centering primarily on elite, mass, or universal access forms of higher education; many institutions provide recognizable forms of all three side by side in the same institution. Moreover, the possibility of enrolling for studies in higher education throughout life makes it impossible in principle, and increasingly difficult in practice, to ever determine what proportion of an age cohort has ever been exposed to some kind of postsecondary education or taken a degree, until all the members of the age cohort have died.

Differences in the structure and traditions of different national systems make generalization across national lines suspect. For example, the universities of the United Kingdom and of Sweden would seem to resemble one another closely, in their attention to teaching and research, as well as in their concern for the welfare of the students in their institutions. Yet the tradition of British universities (with some exceptions) has been to encourage students to complete their studies toward a degree within three years. Those who leave before taking their degrees are treated as if they had never attended the university, and are referred to collectively as "wastage." By contrast, in Sweden studies in colleges and universities are built around professional "programs" that may or may not have their roots in a single academic discipline, and that aim not so much toward earning a degree as for gaining a qualification in a specific profession or occupation.

So it is not unusual, nor is it much decried, when students leave a Swedish university for a job upon completion of the professional course of study in a program, without gaining the academic degree provided for by the same institution.

Nevertheless, it still remains useful, especially in looking back over the past half century, to refer to a model of growth—along with its sources and consequences for three different forms of higher education—of sufficient generality to apply to different national systems over this time period. But it is fair to question whether that model will be as useful in predicting developments over the next half century as it has been over the past half century.

In Britain, as on the European Continent, growth in the early years of expansion was achieved mainly by expanding the elite university system. But the old institutions could not expand indefinitely; they were limited by their traditions, organizations, functions, and finance.

In European countries, an increased enrollment in higher education beyond about 15 percent of the relevant age group required not merely the further expansion of the elite university systems, but the rapid development of mass higher education through the growth of popular non-elite institutions. Systems of mass higher education differed from systems composed predominantly of elite higher education not just quantitatively but also qualitatively. They differed obviously in the proportions of the relevant age group that they enrolled, but also in the ways in which students and teachers viewed attendance in university or college; in the functions of gaining entry for the student; in the functions of the system for the society; in their curricula; in the typical student's career; in the degree of student homogeneity; in the character of academic standards; in the size of institutions; in the forms of instruction; in the relationships between students and faculty; in the nature of institutional boundaries; in the patterns of institutional administration and governance; and in the principles and procedures for selecting both students and staff. In other words, the differences between these phases are quite fundamental and relate to every aspect of higher education. Let us look at each of these aspects of higher education in its several phases a little more closely.

On the Changing Nature of Elite Higher Education

To reflect on the changes over this past half century, it will be useful to consider the nature of elite higher education in traditional universities, before the great expansions of the 1960s and 1970s. American and British universities differed in certain important respects from those on the European Continent. They were similar in certain respects, such as in their function of training and educating a relatively small group of future leaders of the society—on the Continent, largely for the civil service, politics, and the learned professions, while in the United Kingdom, for the academic staffs of the universities and upper secondary schools, and for the church, but not (by and large) for the learned professions, to which access was gained more commonly through apprenticeship. But both in the United Kingdom and on the Continent, the higher education of the elite in universities was defined both by its cultural content and by the character of the relationships through which it was carried on. In much of traditional elite higher education, as at Oxford and Cambridge, the two were very closely linked: a certain kind of relation between teacher and student within a community of scholars was designed to teach gentlemen how to live a certain way of life; it was not meant to train young persons for specific occupations. Indeed, it rather looked down on that.

Elite higher education as the education of a gentleman for a style of life appropriate to a certain status in society was contrasted sharply with the training of experts for specific occupations. The education of a gentleman (United Kingdom) or of a broadly cultivated man (Continent) was intended to prepare for a variety of leadership roles, the technical aspects of which could be learned on the job. Max Weber regarded this distinction between the education of the cultivated man and that of the expert as the source of the main conflict emerging in European higher education after World War I. The rise of mass higher education since World War II has been widely viewed as the ascendancy of technical and vocational education over liberal and general education.

The rise of science within the university challenged this conception of elite higher education, but there was no way of excluding it, since it was clearly linked to national economic and military power, even if indirectly.

And science could be finally accepted as a somewhat subordinate member of the academic community, acceptable so long as it pursued "pure" or "basic" rather than "applied" knowledge. And science borrowed also from the long and established place of mathematics from classical and medieval times in the curriculum of the university.

But the growth of mass higher education since World War II has led to changes in the character of both liberal and vocational studies, and not merely to the expansion of the latter. The pronounced distinction between them—with elite higher education always taken to mean a form of liberal education, and mass higher education a form of vocational education—no longer obtains. There are many schools and programs, both undergraduate and graduate, which are very much oriented toward specialized training for careers in government or industry, and yet are carried on through a pattern of relations between students and teachers that is not much different from that which characterized the collegiate arrangements at Oxford or Cambridge. The emphasis on the transmission of a general culture and a style of life was a characteristic feature of the traditional forms of elite higher education. However, this may mislead us in our search for its descendants today. I think that we will still find forms of elite higher education in the grandes écoles, in the advanced research seminars of the German universities, in the graduate departments and some of the professional schools of American universities, in the undergraduate courses of study at the Massachusetts Institute of Technology as well as in the undergraduate colleges of Harvard and Chicago universities, in the leading American liberal arts colleges, and some of the undergraduate studies at British universities. In these schools and graduate departments, relationships are broad rather than narrow; the teachers are concerned with the values and character of the students; teachers and students often meet outside the setting of formal instruction; their concerns when they meet are not confined to what is contained in syllabus and lectures. They are places for socialization—for the shaping of mind and character, and not merely the transmission of information, skills, and knowledge. Elite higher education today has more to do with the forms of teaching and learning, with the settings in which it is carried on, and with the relations of teacher and student, than it does with the content of the curriculum.

What do these quite varied kinds of elite higher education have in common today? Surely not a commitment to the cultivation of the particular qualities of mind and bearing that marked the traditional collegiate ideal at Oxford and Cambridge. The higher education of elites over the hundred years between 1850 and 1950 rested on a broad consensus among educated persons about what knowledge was of most worth, and what qualities of mind and character should be possessed by the educated person. Before World War II, notions in Europe and America about what characterized an educated person changed over time, and differed to some extent from one society to another, and even to some extent between parts of the same society. Nevertheless, there was some agreement on the question. Today, there is no agreement on what is the irreducible and essential content of higher education for an elite, and we are required to describe it more by reference to its forms than to its content.

Under present-day circumstances, then, elite forms of higher education are no longer uniformly marked by attempts to infuse a general moral and cultural outlook, by efforts to shape qualities of mind and feeling, attitudes and character. It may also try to transmit skills and knowledge, but that is not what makes it "elite higher education" in the sense that we have been using the term to characterize both a kind of education and a kind of institution in which it was most commonly experienced. This kind of education is still carried on through a relatively close and prolonged relationship between student and teacher, and depends on the creation and maintenance of settings within which such a relationship can exist. Whatever the specific content of the course of study and syllabus—and that indeed varies very widely—this form of higher education conveys (and intends to convey) to students that they can accomplish large and important things in the world, that they can make important discoveries, lead great institutions, influence their country's laws and government, and add substantially to knowledge. In this sense, institutions of elite higher education are arrangements for raising ambition and for providing social support and intellectual resources for the achievement of ambition. By contrast, mass higher education is centered on the transmission of skills and knowledge through relations between teachers and students that are briefer and more impersonal, and is designed to prepare students for relatively more modest roles in society, even in such occupations of high status as the learned professions, the civil service, and business management. (Of course, these two types of higher education often overlap or merge imperceptibly into one another.)

Elite higher education makes large demands on students, demands that are implicit in its intention to infuse a moral and cultural outlook, in contrast with the provision of training. It is in severe competition with other formations and institutions in society which also make large demands on the young person—for example, the family, careers, groups of peers, and radical political movements. Elite higher education thus has placed students at odds with other kinds of obligations, and generated forms of tension in ways which mass higher education does not. It also tries to provide greater social and psychological support for students who are exposed to these normative demands and emotional strains. Thus, to perform its tasks, elite higher education has been more likely to be residential than is mass higher education, or at least to be lived within a close and supportive academic community. For the same reasons, it was an activity to which the student was formerly expected to give all his time, at least during the school term. The financial burdens of university life, and the greater presence of students from modest homes in the university, has made paid work during the university study year much more widely necessary and accepted. Similarly, as elite higher education was thought to be incompatible with paid work, it was also thought to be incompatible with student marriage (and in the United Kingdom, for much of the nineteenth century, for marriage by teachers). Work and family present conflicting commitments and obligations, and interfere with the socialization most effectively accomplished in near totally encompassing social institutions.

In contemporary elite institutions we can see the survival of the forms and structures of the traditional university, though now much diluted and with less authority in the students' lives. Ironically, it is most closely approximated in the graduate schools and advanced seminars of American, British, and continental universities, which are now the centers of intensive socialization to the norms of scholarly and scientific life as well as to the highly specialized skills that now together comprise the professional training of the modern academic doctorate.

Meanwhile, with some exceptions, undergraduate education (even in universities) comes more closely to resemble the education provided in parallel departments and subjects in institutions of mass higher education. And the growing demand for easing transfer between institutions and across national boundaries increases the significance and value of a standardized training in subjects, providing students with a basic knowledge and skills in the subject that can be recognized in similar institutions elsewhere.

But if the traditional forms and functions of elite higher education are increasingly attenuated, some special characteristics still attach to the institutions of highest status in every country. One of those is the encouragement of ambition and the creation of personal ties and links that will help in the pursuit of ambition after leaving the university.

The encouragement of ambition is a central distinguishing characteristic of elite higher education. The institutions that offer this kind of education recruit students who are ambitious; they then nurture and focus that ambition, and their graduates are disproportionately successful in the competition for positions of leadership in the larger society. In the United States, this is the feature that distinguishes forms of elite higher education from the myriad small, often denominational, liberal arts colleges—institutions that also try to shape character through personal relations between students and teachers. In Britain, the new (formerly polytechnic) universities are now exemplars of the now common multifunctional institutions of higher education. In some are found undergraduate and graduate courses and programs of studies that can hardly be distinguished from their counterparts in Oxbridge, while nearby one can find programs for mature students in one or another of the new semi-professions. In this respect, these former polytechnics closely resemble the many public colleges and universities in the United States, which offer a first degree and a variety of vocationally linked master's degrees, often to mature students, in an atmosphere of serious study and learning but of limited genuine research. And just a little bit further away from some of the old and new British universities are their franchised programs in former further education colleges, largely open to nearly all upper secondary school graduates, and resembling two-year community colleges (America's chief institutions of universal access). While these non-research universities (itself an unimaginable idea in 1974) have many strengths and virtues, it is fair to say that they do not encourage high ambition, nor leave students with the sense that they have been prepared to gain the highest levels of leadership in the various institutions of society.

Ambition and its encouragement are only one of the cluster of features that links elite higher education to the status and function of elites in society. We see here how, in academic life as elsewhere, advantage engenders advantage, and through which elite institutions tend to become centers of academic distinction. In the United States, the relatively small numbers of scholars and scientists who later make significant contributions to their disciplines are disproportionately the graduates of a small number of graduate schools and departments of elite universities. The elements involved are very many, and very hard to disentangle. In general, certain departments of leading universities are known and favored by able and ambitious students, and departments can be highly selective in their policies of admission. In part by virtue of their attractiveness to leading scholars and scientists, these departments are able to give their students a superior education in their respective disciplines. They are then able to place their better graduates on the teaching staffs of their own and other leading departments in their disciplines, and this in turn gives those graduates access to better students, more stimulating colleagues, better resources (such as libraries and laboratories), and more congenial arrangements for learning. The prestige of a degree from a leading department, and of teaching in another such department, gives an individual scientist or scholar access to opportunities for research, which in turn help him or her to make important contributions to the discipline. A young person gains a heightened self-confidence from association with (and approval by) leading figures in the field, and this self-confidence is important in forming the individual's level of intellectual aspiration and heightening his capacity.

While there is surely a relationship between elite higher education, intellectual distinction, and the achievement of leading positions in society's institutions, it must be stressed that they are not identical. Higher education for an elite is not necessarily (or always) intellectually distinguished, nor its graduates uniformly highly successful, nor is academic excellence found only in the institutions that provide an education of the type described here.

Phases in the Development of Higher Education: Aspects of Transition

The transitions between phases in the development of modern higher education systems require changes in all aspects of their structures and functions. As reflected in Brennan's (2004) analysis (see Table 17.1), important dimensions of change include the size of the system, institutional diversity, access and selection policies, governance and administration, the curriculum and forms of instruction, and academic standards.

Size of the System

Countries that develop a system of elite higher education in modern times seem able to expand it without changing its character in fundamental ways until it is providing places for about 15 percent of the relevant age group. At that point (or thereabouts) the system begins to change its character; if the transition is made successfully, the system is then able to develop institutions that can grow without being transformed, until they start to admit more than 30 percent of the relevant age group. Beyond that—and in this respect, also led by the United States—large sections of the population are sending nearly all their sons and daughters to some kind of higher education, and the system must again create new forms of higher education as it begins to move rapidly toward universal access. In our increasingly meritocratic societies, personal qualities of talent and initiative come to play a larger role in adult achievement than before. This, perhaps a welcome development, is further (and maybe the most significant) evidence of the decline of the importance of elite higher education in modern life.

Attitudes toward Access

The ease of access to higher education is closely linked to conceptions that people—students and their parents, and increasingly college and university teachers and administrators—have of college and university attendance. When access is highly limited, it is generally seen as a privilege, either of birth or talent, or both. When more than about 15 percent of the relevant age group have access, people increasingly begin to see entry to higher education as a right for those who have certain formal qualifications. And when the proportion of the country's population entering some form of postsecondary education approaches 50 percent (and in some sectors of the society, it is then of course much higher), attendance in higher education becomes increasingly seen as an obligation: for children from the middle and upper middle classes—in European countries as well as in the United States—failure to go on to higher education from secondary school is increasingly considered a mark of some defect of mind or character that has to be explained, justified, or apologized for. Moreover, as greater numbers of people go on to higher education, the best jobs and opportunities (and, generally, the economic rewards in life) come to be reserved for people who have completed a university degree, and this greatly contributes to the sense of obligation that is felt by many students upon entry to a higher education institution.

Functions of Higher Education

The different phases are also associated with different functions of higher education, both for students and for society at large. Elite higher education has been concerned primarily with shaping the mind and character of the ruling class, as it prepares students for broad elite roles in government and the learned professions. In mass higher education, the institutions are still preparing elites, but a much broader range of elites that includes the leading strata of all the technical and economic organizations of the society. And the emphasis shifts from the shaping of character to the transmission of skills for more specific technical elite roles. In institutions marked by universal access, there is concern with the preparation of large numbers for life in an advanced industrial society; they are training not primarily elites (either broadly or narrowly defined), but the whole population, and their chief concern is to maximize the adaptability of that population to a society whose chief characteristic is rapid social and technological change.

The Curriculum and Forms of Instruction

The curriculum and forms of instruction naturally reflect changes in the definition of the meaning of being a student, and of the functions that higher education plays for students and for the society at large. The curriculum in elite institutions has tended to be highly structured, reflecting academic conceptions of the degree course or professional conceptions of professional requirements. The courses of study, shaped largely by the character of the final examination, were on the whole highly specialized, and governed by the professors' notions of what constituted an educated man or a qualified professional. In institutions of mass higher education, the curriculum becomes more modular, marked by semi-structured sequences of courses, with the focus on earning unit credits (the unit of exchange in modular courses), allowing more flexible combinations of courses and easier access and movement between major fields, and indeed among institutions. Unit credits and a modular curriculum are still more common in higher technical colleges than in European universities. Decades of discussion have had little influence on modularization in the universities; the Bologna initiative addresses that issue directly, with what success remains to be seen.

In universal higher education (as it emerges), there is a survival of the modular course, but increasingly instruction is relatively unstructured; the boundaries of the course itself begin to break down, as do required sequences of courses. It is very difficult to justify course requirements where no single conception of higher education obtains, and the rejection of academic forms, structures, and standards also extends to examinations and assessment, as distinctions between learning and life become attenuated. This is emphasized for the growing number of students who are studying at a distance, often online and directly or indirectly linked to their jobs. Attendance at the emerging institutions of higher education designed for universal access is merely another kind of experience not qualitatively different from any other experiences in modern society that give one resources for coping with the problems of contemporary life. And, in universal access, since coursework does not clearly qualify people for specific jobs, it is less clear why assessment of performance is necessary.

There are parallel differences in the typical forms of instruction, and thus, in the relationships between student and teacher. In elite systems, the characteristic form of instruction is the tutorial or seminar, marked (on the whole) by a personal relationship between student and teacher. While the distance between the senior professor and the ordinary undergraduate may be very great, his research students are likely to be working with him in a close apprentice relationship. This is compatible with the central function of the shaping of character and the preparation of a broad or general elite, whose specific adult roles and activities would vary widely so that one could hardly train for them in the course of the university career. And the defense of these forms of instruction in the grandes écoles of France, during the period of rapid expansion that filled the lecture rooms of the universities to overflowing, made it clear where the elite functions in France are meant to survive.

Under the conditions of mass higher education the emphasis is on the transmission of skills and knowledge, with formal instruction carried on through large lectures often taught by teaching assistants or the growing number of part-time instructors without strong or long-term connections to the institution. In universal higher education, the direct personal relationship of the student and teacher is subordinated to a broad exposure of the student to new or more sophisticated perspectives.

There is heavier reliance on distance learning and on other technological aids to instruction. As mass higher education becomes more focused on preparation for jobs and careers, it begins to resemble open access institutions. Open access institutions and teaching in turn come to resemble mass higher education, with even more focus on the vocational training of mature and part-time students by migratory instructors, often at a distance.

The Student Career

The academic careers of the students in different forms of higher education differ also. In elite institutions, the student ordinarily enters directly after completion of secondary schooling; the student is in residence and continues his work uninterruptedly (except for holidays) until he gains a degree. He is in this sense sponsored and in competition only for academic honors. In the mass institution, some students attend immediately after finishing secondary school, although increasing numbers delay entry until after a period of work or travel, and even more return as mature adults. Easier access and a more heterogeneous student population lead to higher "wastage" rates. But the students are now a mixed residential-commuting population, as vocational training becomes a larger component of their higher education. In institutions of universal access there is much postponement of entry, "stopping out" of enrollment in any college, and large numbers of students with experience in adult occupations. The emphasis on lifelong learning is compatible with the softening of the boundaries between formal education and other forms of life experience.

Moreover, in all the forms of higher education, but especially in the mass and universal forms, as student numbers from poor homes increase, a growing proportion are also working for pay at nonacademic jobs— first during vacations and then during term time. This trend has implications for the meaning of being a student, for the curriculum (less outside reading and study can be assigned or assumed), for student motivations, and for the relationships of students with their teachers. And it is hard to discourage this practice, especially when it is done out of necessity by needy students. It can be ignored when it is the occasional "poor but able" student who has to work for his fees and maintenance. But it is a different institution when the proportion of working students is 30, 40, or 50 percent, or higher.

Institutional Characteristics and Boundaries

Systems at different phases of their development differ also in their diversity. Elite systems tend to be highly homogeneous, with the component institutions in a single country very much like one another. They tend to be universities with high and common standards, though they also include highly specialized technical schools with special access to parts of the civil service. Mass systems began to be more comprehensive, with more diverse standards, though with some linkages among the several segments of the system that allow mobility of students and staff. In systems of universal access, there is great diversity in the character of component institutions, with no common standards among them. Indeed, the very notion of standards is itself challenged and problematical.

Over time, as the number of institutions grew during the transition to a mass system, they became more diverse. The high and common standards that European systems claimed and tried to sustain broke down, despite heroic efforts (as in the United Kingdom) to maintain those characteristics of the old elite system of universities. But the effort under Anthony Crosland (1965–66) to achieve diversity of cost as well as of function through prescriptive planning (the binary system) ran against the political forces of equality, the bureaucratic preferences for standardization, and the academic tendency of institutions to model themselves on the most prestigious. Under these pressures the binary policy in Britain broke down in 1992 with the merger of universities and polytechnics.

The inclusion in the university world of institutions created and designed for mass functions (as in the merger of universities and polytechnics in the United Kingdom) made the old assertions of equal or common standards, even within the same subjects, no longer credible. And when the subjects themselves diversified, recruiting different kinds of students on different criteria and teaching them different curricula, the efforts to claim common standards of excellence or quality in a mass system became derisory.

The typical institutions in the three systems differ in size and character as well. Elite institutions were commonly "communities" that ranged up to two or three thousand students in residence. As they grew, they were likely to be sub-structured so that their component units, like the Oxford and Cambridge colleges, remained relatively small. The lower-division colleges in big American research universities are examples of this tendency. The real size of units in those institutions differed from their nominal size as a result of the sub-structuring in small teaching/learning units; many of these had no formal existence, but were created spontaneously by students and teachers. In the European continental universities, the communities were defined by membership in a department or program, or in the research lab, or in the advanced seminars led by a particular professor.

The comprehensive institutions that characterize mass higher education are less "communities" than they are "cities of intellect" with up to thirty or forty thousand students (or more) and staff making up a mixed residential and commuting population. Institutions of universal access are unlimited in size; they may be simply aggregates of people enrolled for instruction, most of whom are rarely or never on the central campus except to attend a specific class; they may share little in common and do not in any sense comprise a community rooted in frequent association, shared norms and values, and a sense of common identification.

Today, we find "virtual communities" brought together online for a single course or a degree program. We have not yet found the limit to the size of institutions providing distance learning, if there is such a limit.

As we might guess from these trends, elite institutions were (and still tend to be) marked off from the surrounding society by clear and relatively impermeable boundaries, in the extreme case by physical walls. In mass institutions there are still boundaries, but they are more fuzzy and more permeable; there is relatively easy movement in and out of mass institutions, and a much less clear concept of membership, though there are still formal definitions of membership that are relevant for a variety of academic and nonacademic purposes. In institutions of universal access, boundaries are very weak, shading off to none at all. At some point anyone who may sign on to an online course, or (as the case in most open universities) switch on a televised broadcast of a lecture, may be thought of for that moment as being part of an extended university, and the question of whether he is submitting work regularly or has matriculated is of only marginal significance, except for purposes of credentialing.

The Locus of Power and Decision Making

The three types of systems differ in their source of ultimate authority; in the nature of their academic standards; and in their principles of recruitment and selection. With respect to both ultimate power and effective decisions, elite institutions have been governed by relatively small elite groups: leaders in significant institutions—political, economic, and academic—who know one another, share basic values and assumptions, and make decisions through informal face-to-face contact. An example of this would be the small number of leading civil servants, government ministers, university vice chancellors, and members of the University Grants Commission who shaped the face of the British university system for many years, through meetings in small committee rooms or around tables at the Athenaeum Club. The boards of trustees or regents of elite American colleges and universities are another example. In Europe the powerful groups would be senior professors, senior ministers, and civil servants, sometimes members of parliaments who took a special interest in the universities, and maybe (as in Italy) professors themselves. Democratic tendencies, more so in Europe than in the United States, brought lower-level administrative staff and students into the governing boards, but with more symbolic than real significance.

Mass higher education continues to be influenced by these elite groups, but is increasingly shaped by more democratic political processes and influenced by attentive audiences. These are parts of the general public who have special interests and qualifications, and develop a common view about higher education in general or some special aspect, such as the forms and content of technical education. Higher education policies for these kinds of institutions increasingly become subject to the ordinary political processes of interest groups and party programs, reflected among deliberations in state and governmental legislatures. One kind of attentive audience is the employers of the graduates of mass higher education systems, who are interested in the nature of their skills and qualifications. Another attentive audience is the body of old graduates who retain an interest in the character and fortunes of their old college or university. These groups often develop political instrumentalities of their own, such as associations with an elected leadership, and develop lines of communication to the smaller groups in government, legislatures, and in the universities themselves who make the actual decisions, both day-to-day and over the long range.

When the system moves toward universal access, increasingly large portions of the population begin to be affected by it, either through their own past or present attendance, or that of some friend or relative. In addition, the universities and colleges—what is taught there and the activities of their staff and students—come to be of general interest, not just in the pages of the serious press and magazines, but also reported in the popular journals and on television. They thus attract the interest of mass publics, who increasingly come to see themselves as having a legitimate interest in what goes on in the institutions of higher education, if for no other reason than their enormous public cost and obvious impact on society. And these mass publics begin to make their sentiments known, either through letters to public officials or through their votes in special or general elections.

The change in the size and character of the publics who have an interest in higher education and exert an influence on higher education policy greatly influences the nature and content of the discussions about higher education, particularly, who takes part in them and the decisions that flow out of them. The claims of academic men to a special expertise, and of their institutions to special privileges and immunities, are increasingly questioned; much of what academic men understand by academic freedom, and the significance of the security of academic tenure for the protection of their pursuit of truth regardless of political interests or popular sentiment, are all challenged by the growing intervention of popular sentiments into these formerly elite arenas. The weakness of tenure or job security for the teaching staff of open access institutions is a reflection of the weakness of the autonomy of those institutions, which come increasingly to be seen as at the service of other institutions in the society.

Academic Standards

The implications of these transitions for academic standards are equally clear: in elite systems and institutions, at least in their meritocratic phase, these were likely to be broadly shared and relatively high. Currently, as some fields and subjects are increasingly politicized, they vary a good deal between institutions and subjects. In the systems and institutions of mass higher education, standards become variable, differing in severity and character in different parts of the system or institution, appropriately so since both system and institution have become holding companies for quite different kinds of academic enterprises. Again, this illustrates the convergence of elite and mass forms of higher education in modern societies.

In institutions of universal access, there tends to be a different criterion of achievement: not so much the achievement of some academic standard, but whether there has been any "value added" by virtue of the educational experience. That is the justification of universal higher education, as it is of the nonacademic forms of primary and secondary schools; obviously, this changes in a fundamental way the basis for judging individual or institutional activities. For example, if the criterion of success is "value added," it may be better to admit students who are academically very weak, rather than those with a strong record, since presumably it will be easier to raise the performance of those who start low than of those who are already performing well.

That argument is in fact made for the principle of open access. Whatever substance it has, it does suggest how fundamental is the shift to universal access.

Access and Selection

The principles of student selection also differ in the different phases. In elite systems, the criterion of ascribed status gave way in most Western societies (more or less rapidly over the past century and a half) to meritocratic achievement measured by secondary school performance or grades on special examinations. Meritocratic criteria are now modified by giving special advantage to what are seen to be disadvantaged sectors: minority ethnic groups, or new immigrants, or poor whites. But so much of the status and achievement of elite universities rests on their recruitment of the ablest students in the society that these marginal departures from the application of universalistic criteria have not yet had much effect on the character of instruction in those institutions, except in specific and especially vulnerable subjects.

In institutions of mass higher education, there is a general acceptance of meritocratic criteria, where access is limited, though the criteria are ordinarily not as severe as in the elite colleges and universities. But this is heavily qualified by a commitment to equality of educational opportunity, leading to compensatory programs and the introduction of additional nonacademic criteria designed to reduce inequities in the opportunities for admission of deprived social groups and categories. Here, again, we see a narrowing of the differences between elite and mass institutions.

In the institutions of universal higher education, which by definition are wholly open either to anyone who wishes to enroll or to those who have certain minimal educational qualifications, the criterion is whether an individual has chosen to associate himself with the institution voluntarily. The aim of universal access is toward the equality of group achievement rather than an equality of individual opportunity, and efforts are made to achieve a social, class, ethnic, and racial distribution in higher education reflecting that of the population at large. And of course the more closely the system enrolls the entirety of an age group, the better it reflects the distribution of subgroups in the population at large. At the limiting case, of course, it is democratic in the same sense that compulsory forms of primary and secondary education are, with surviving variations in the character and quality of the education offered in different places and different kinds of institutions. We can already see hints of this philosophy of admissions, and of these criteria for access, even in the present transitional period between mass and universal access higher education in European countries. Further education is where education meets social justice. Again, in the provision of universal access to its community colleges, the United States has led the way.

Forms of Academic Administration

The characteristic institutions in the three systems differ also in their forms of institutional administration. The typical elite university is governed by academics who are essentially amateurs at administration, whether they serve on committees, on boards, or in legislatures. In some countries, they may have the help of a full-time civil servant or registrar and a staff of experts to deal with matters of finance. But in elite institutions, the head of the administrative staff is commonly an academic elected or appointed to the office for a limited period of time. As institutions become larger and their functions more varied during the transition phase to mass higher education, their administrative staff becomes larger; there is now more commonly a top leadership of men who were formerly academics but who now are clearly full-time university administrators. And below them there is a large and growing bureaucratic staff of non-academics. As the system grows even further toward universal access, the enormous costs of education generate pressures for greater financial accountability and more sophisticated forms of program management. Universities employ increasingly large numbers of full-time professionals, such as systems analysts and economists knowledgeable about program budgeting, specialists in financing capital growth, and so forth. In that phase, the centralization and rationalization of university administration generates problems. The functions of the institution itself become increasingly more diverse, and its outputs more difficult to quantify, just as the management procedures have become more dependent on quantified data for the assessment of costs and benefits. But the data for assessment have to be supplied by those being assessed, which raises questions common to every command economy about the reliability of information coming up from below.

The rationalization of university administration—based on the systematic collection and analysis of quantitative data on the costs of discrete activities, and on measures of the outputs or benefits of these activities—is a response to the growth in the size and cost of higher education and to growing demands for public accountability regarding its efficiency. In their heavy reliance on quantified data, however, these managerial techniques become a powerful independent force working against the survival of elite institutions, and of those functions and activities that cannot be easily justified by reference to quantitative measures, of either their costs or benefits. There is a certain danger in the argument that the development of these managerial techniques, as also of the increasing centralization of control, are inevitable, given the growth in the size and cost of higher education. An emphasis on the inevitability of these trends and forces may preclude our asking the critical questions: how are these new techniques of administration being applied, what are their consequences, and what are the limits of centralization in relation to institutional autonomy? We should at least be aware of how these techniques may undermine those activities and functions of higher education that cannot be justified by reference to visible and easily measurable outputs.

But the development of mass higher education does not necessarily involve the destruction of elite institutions or parts of institutions, or their transformation into mass institutions. Indeed, elite forms of higher education continue to perform functions that cannot be performed as well by mass higher education—among them, the education, training, and socialization of very highly selected students for intellectual work at the highest levels of performance and creativity. And as we observe the system of mass higher education in the United States, and the patterns of growth toward mass higher education elsewhere, we see that they involve the creation and extension of functions and activities and institutions rather than the disappearance of the old.

But while elite institutions and centers tend to survive and defend their unique characteristics in the face of the growth and transformation of the system around them, they are not always successful. Their special characteristics and integrity are threatened by those egalitarian values that define all differences as inequities, by the standardizing force of central governmental control, and by the powerful leveling influence of the new forms of rationalized management and administration. The rationalization of academic administration is a reflection and a product of the movement toward mass higher education, but it is not neutral toward other forms of higher education. In this respect it works against the diversity of the system that is also a characteristic—indeed, a central defining characteristic—of mass higher education. And this creates a dilemma for policy makers.

Internal Governance

The forms and processes of internal governance of institutions of higher education vary enormously, from country to country and between institutions. But on the whole, elite institutions almost everywhere (except in the United States and the United Kingdom) were formerly governed by their senior professors who elected a weak part-time rector to chair their meetings; those who did not hold chairs ordinarily played little or no part in major institutional decisions. As institutions grew, non-chair-holding academics and non-professorial staff increasingly challenged the monopolistic power of what came to be seen as the professorial oligarchy. And, as seen in institutions of mass higher education as well, internal power in some countries and universities came to be shared to varying degrees with junior staff. Moreover, for a while, during periods of student activism, student leaders claimed a right to influence institutional decisions, and the forms and extent of student participation became a major issue in some places during the transition from elite to mass higher education. But the heavy focus of mass higher education—and of open access institutions—on vocational training and credentialing has muted the demands of activist students to be represented on the decision-making bodies. Students are commonly not enrolled in the same institution long enough to make their voices heard. The ones who do are likely to be deeply immersed in their research studies and dissertations. So the weakness of the academic community in the governance of institutions of mass higher education is filled less by students or junior staff than by agencies of government.

Matters are a bit different in elite universities where the academics are still a force. But there, problems of institutional governance are greatly sharpened by the breakdown of the academic consensus that occurs with growth and the transition from elite to mass higher education. Elite universities, with their narrow traditional range of functions and homogeneous bodies of students and teachers, could formerly assume the broad acceptance by their participants of the basic character and values of the institution. But for elite institutions the move toward mass higher education, with its wider range of functions, means the recruitment of new kinds of students and teachers, from more diverse backgrounds and with more varied views and conceptions of what higher education and their own institutions ought to be. At the same time, junior staff, whose interests and attitudes often differ sharply from those of the senior professors, may gain in power and influence. And student leaders, drawn from more diverse backgrounds and affected by radical political currents, sometimes challenge many of the traditional values and assumptions of the university. In many institutions, the old consensus upon which elite universities were based has broken down, both within the faculty and among the students. Relations among colleagues and between teachers and students no longer can be built on a broad set of shared assumptions, but instead are increasingly uncertain and a source of continual strain and conflict. The move toward participatory forms of governance in universities often presupposes the survival of the old consensus, or the possibility of its re-creation. But more commonly, participatory forms of democracy may introduce into the institutions of mass higher education the conflicts of interest and ideology that are more familiar (and more effectively managed) in the political institutions of society. [This reference to student participation illustrates a general principle that emerges from this analysis: that the "same" phenomenon may have very different meaning and consequences in different phases of higher education. Thus "student participation" in the governance of a small elite institution marked by high value consensus, may in fact be merely the participation of the most junior members of a genuine academic community, held together by shared values regarding academic life. By contrast, "student participation" in a large mass institution marked by value dissensus may heighten the kind of interest and ideological conflicts that academic institutions, whatever their size or character, have great difficulty in containing or resolving. This is not always recognized; and the arguments for student participation drawn from experience in small elite liberal arts colleges are often applied indiscriminately to mass institutions. (This is true of other aspects of governance and forms of administration as well.)]

The growth of numbers, in itself, begins to change the conception that students have of their attendance in college or university. When enrollment rates are 4 or 5 percent of the relevant age group, students naturally see themselves as part of a highly privileged minority. Though this does not mean that they are necessarily passive or deferential, it does make them feel—along with their professors and lecturers—that they are part of a small privileged institution with a very clear set of common interests embodied in common values, symbols and ceremonies, modes of speech, and lifestyle. All that affirmed the communal identity of the academic institution against the rest of society.

The growth of higher education toward and beyond 15 percent of the relevant age group—and, in the larger European countries, toward student numbers of a million or more rather than fifty thousand—inevitably changed that. Students have come to see their entry into a university as a right earned by fulfilling certain requirements. And for an increasing proportion, attendance is in part obligatory: larger numbers in all countries attend a university at least partly because people in their parents' social strata send their children to university "as a matter of course." Such students feel less like members of a chosen elite upon arrival, and they enter universities that are larger (and in some cases very much larger) than their counterparts of thirty years ago. There is little question that the communal aspects of universities that have grown without being able or willing to create smaller units internally, have declined, along with the sense on the part of the students and teachers of their being members of a special estate.

The growth of numbers and the shift in the conception of attendance from privilege to right are accompanied by changes in the principles and processes of selection. As the gates to higher education gradually open, the older, close links between a handful of elite preparatory schools, public schools, lycées, gymnasiums (whether private or state-supported), and the elite universities become attenuated, and new avenues of access to higher education begin to open up.

Logically, if the move toward mass higher education were the result of state policy and careful planning, the development of a broad system of comprehensive secondary schools—carrying larger and larger numbers from every social strata to the point of university entry—would precede the growth of mass higher education itself. In practice, however, the explosive expansion of higher education over the past two decades has almost everywhere preceded the move toward broad comprehensive secondary education aimed at preparing larger numbers for entry to higher education.

Caveats

The three phases of higher education transformation discussed in this chapter—elite, mass, and universal or open access education—are, in Max Weber's sense, ideal types. They are abstracted from empirical reality and emphasize the functional relationships among the several components of an institutional system common to all advanced industrial societies rather than the unique characteristics of any one. Therefore, the description of any phase cannot be taken as a full or adequate description of any single national system.

These ideal types are designed to define and illuminate the problems of higher education common to a number of countries. These problems are of three broad kinds: (1) The functional relationships among the various components or aspects of given systems—for example, the degree of compatibility or strain between a given pattern of student admissions and the dominant forms of university curriculum. In many European countries, university education is predicated on the assumption that a broad liberal education has been gained in the preparatory secondary schools: the gymnasium, the lycée, the sixth form of British secondary schools. As the selectivity and rigor of education in those schools has declined with massification, students increasingly arrive at the university without the underpinning of broad cultural knowledge formerly assumed. (2) The problems arising during the transition from one phase to the next when existing (more or less functional) relationships are progressively disrupted by uneven and differently timed changes in the patterns and characteristics of the system. An example might be the survival of the professorial oligarchy as a mode of institutional, faculty, or departmental governance as the growth in the numbers and functions of junior staff increases their responsibilities, importance, and self-confidence. (3) The problems arising in the relations between institutions of higher education and the larger society and its economic and political institutions, as higher education moves from one phase to another. An example here might be the greater emphasis on the public accountability for funds spent on higher education, and the growing encroachment on the autonomy of higher education institutions in the allocation and use of these funds, as costs rise and the higher education system becomes more consequential and more significant to a wider range of social, political, and economic activities.

It must be emphasized that the movement of a system from elite to mass higher education or from mass to universal higher education does not necessarily mean that the forms and patterns of the prior phase or phases disappear or are transformed. On the contrary, the evidence suggests that each phase survives in some institutions and in parts of others, while the system as a whole evolves to carry the larger numbers of students and the broader, more diverse functions of the next phase. Its newest—and gradually, its most important—institutions have the characteristics of the next phase. So, in a mass system, elite institutions may not only survive but flourish, while elite functions continue to be performed within mass institutions. Similarly, both elite and mass institutions survive as, beginning in the United States, nations move toward universal access to higher education.

But this observation points to a characteristic problem of all mixed-phase systems: the problem arising from the strains inherent in the continuing existence of forms of higher education based on fundamentally different principles and oriented to quite different kinds of functions. The question follows: how successfully, and through what institutions and mechanisms, does a system continue to perform elite functions, when the emphasis of the system has shifted to the forms and functions of mass higher education? How successfully can a system perform diverse functions that require quite different structures, values, and relationships—especially when central governing agencies are pressed, by both bureaucratic rules and egalitarian politics, to treat institutions and individuals equally and in standard ways?

The analysis of the phases of development of higher education should not be taken to imply that the elements and components of a system of higher education change at equal rates, and that a system moves evenly toward the characteristic forms of the next phase. In fact, development is very uneven: numerical expansion may produce a more diversified student body before the curriculum has been similarly diversified; the curriculum may become more diversified before the recruitment and training of staff has changed to meet the new requirements of the changed curriculum; the staff may have become more diverse before the forms of institutional governance reflect the changes in the character of the teachers, and begin to distribute institutional authority to reflect academic responsibility more closely. A close analysis of developments in any given system must attend to (1) the sequence of change of its several parts and patterns; (2) the strains and problems arising therefrom; and (3) the extent to which the changes in different countries show common sequential patterns among the various parts and elements of their systems.

The model is not intended to be a simplified snapshot or overview of modern systems of higher education at different times and places. The stress is on the analysis of the strains created at the phase transitions. The model argues that these phase transitions create tensions and problems for the institutions undergoing change, for the systems of which they are part and, in European countries especially, for the governments whose ministries and governments make the fundamental policies regarding the size and shape of their systems of higher education.

Much of the history of higher education in rich societies over the past half century has been driven by responses of the institutions and systems to the transitions from elite higher education to the much larger systems and their broader access that emerged in the second half of the twentieth century.

The analysis of the phases of higher education in advanced industrial societies, of the developments of parts of the system during these phases, and of the problems that arise at the transition points between phases and among elements changing at different rates within a phase is designed to illuminate problems and patterns common to different societies and systems.

Quality, Equality, and Expansion, and the Dilemmas They Generate

Higher education in the countries under review is linked to their national societies in three ways: by governmental policies, support, and management; by the market for its products; and by a measure of societal trust in the integrity and competence of the institutions. These three forms of links vary in strength in different countries, at different times, and with respect to different kinds of institutions. The model discussed in this essay is a way of looking at the tensions generated among these forms of links over time, as the systems and institutions grew in modern democracies after World War II, and at the way governments and societies responded to those tensions. In its predictions, the model assumed a certain range of weights among the three major links between higher education and their environing societies. One assumption was that growth, particularly in Europe, would create severe problems for societies in which, at the time of writing, the predominantly small elite institutions were wholly or almost wholly supported by governmental agencies. These tensions took many forms, but a central one was between the quality of higher education provided by the institutions and the pressures for greater equality of provision under conditions of expansion. Those tensions took many forms (addressed in this essay), not least of which were those tensions linking quality to funding and governmental support.

At the beginning of the rapid growth era, the steady expansion of higher education appeared to some observers, especially in the United Kingdom, to constitute a serious threat to academic standards. The question of standards is nominally a question of the quality of an academic program, how rigorous and demanding on the one hand, how rich and stimulating on the other.

At one extreme we think of a group of learned and imaginative scholars and scientists teaching highly selected and motivated students in a situation of large intellectual resources—cultural, scientific, and academic. At the other extreme are institutions staffed by less well-educated and less accomplished teachers, teaching less able and less well-motivated students under less favorable conditions marked by lower salaries, a poorer staff-student ratio, a smaller library, fewer laboratory places, and all in a less stimulating and lively intellectual environment. Many countries, responding to the democratic spirit emerging from World War II, were at the beginning of the expansion period committed, at least in principle, to a growth of their systems of higher education in ways that did not lower the quality and standards of the higher education already offered. This would involve the achievement of education at a high and common standard of quality throughout the system, whatever the varied functions of the different institutions might be. And this dual commitment—to continued growth and also to high quality in all parts of the system—posed a dilemma.

The dilemma had, and still has, three components. First, there is the strong egalitarian sentiment that all provision in higher education ought to be substantially of equal quality (and thus of cost). In the absence of good or reliable measures of the effects of higher education on the adult careers of graduates, people tended then to assess the quality of education by reference to its internal processes, and this leads to equating quality with cost. Governmental efforts at the evaluation of programs and departments of higher education in recent decades have tried to break this identification of quality with cost, but broadly unsuccessfully.[5] The second is that the criteria against which new forms of mass higher education are assessed are typically those of the older, costlier forms of elite higher education. And third, a rapid and potentially almost unlimited growth of higher education, at the per capita cost levels of the former small elite systems, placed intolerable burdens on national and state budgets that were also having to cope with growing demands from other public agencies, such as social welfare, preschool education and child care, primary and secondary school systems, housing, transportation, and defense.

When applied to higher education, the egalitarian position—which cuts across class lines and party preferences—was and is highly critical of any tendency to institutionalize differences between one sector and another of higher education. Egalitarians in many countries were committed to closing the gulf between the several parts of their higher education systems and to reducing the differentials in the status, quality, costs, and amenities of its different segments and institutions. People with those sentiments, who might be called "unitarians" in their commitment to a single system of institutions, governed by common standards of education throughout, were often also committed to reforming universities and making them serve more of the functions of the non-elite forms of higher education, while at the same time raising the quality of the non-elite forms of higher education (especially of higher technical education) to that of the university standard. This position—liberal, humane, and generous—argued that the formal differentiations between the several forms and sectors of higher education almost always led to invidious distinctions between them, and ultimately to very marked differences in the quality of their staff and students, and in other respects as well. People holding these views also observed that the weaker or low-status segments of the system are those characteristically associated with (and used by) students from working- and lower-middle-class origins, so that the status differentiation in higher education is closely linked to that of the class structure as a whole. They argued that any sectors of education outside the system that included the universities must necessarily be made up of second-class institutions for second-class (and most commonly working-class) citizens, as historically they have been. Essentially, their slogan is "nothing if not the best"—especially for youngsters from those strata of the society that have often gotten less or, if anything, second best.

But while this position is humane and generous in its concern for the equality of educational opportunities for working-class people, it is—in its insistence on a "leveling upward," in cost as well as quality—inevitably in conflict with a continued and rapid expansion of access to higher education. No society, no matter how rich, can afford a system of higher education for 20 percent or 30 percent or 40 percent of the relevant age group at the cost levels of the elite higher education that it formerly provided for 5 percent of the population. Insofar as egalitarians insist that there be no major differentials in per capita costs among various sectors of the system of higher education, and yet also insist on expansion, then they force a "leveling downward" in costs, and perhaps in quality as well. The best example of this position has been the funding of higher education in the United Kingdom, where expansion coupled with strong egalitarian sentiments have led to a decline in the per capita student support by government for institutions (what was called the "unit of resource") of something between two-thirds and three-quarters between 1979 and 2004. Insofar as they are committed to a high and common support for universities throughout the system, governments were forced to face the necessity of imposing a restraint on expansion, or else lowering support levels for the institutions. The crucial question in this unitarian position is whether it is a commitment only to a common set of standards throughout the system, or to a common high set of standards as well.

This unitarian or egalitarian position is basically incompatible with the very marked differences between institutions in their staff-student ratios, research activity, need for support staff, libraries and laboratories, and other aspects of cost and quality. While it is possible in principle to argue that some institutions would be more expensive because they carry a larger research responsibility, it is very difficult in practice to argue for a genuine unitarian system while forbidding certain parts of that system or institutions within it to engage in research. And research is inherently highly expensive. Moreover, there is a tendency everywhere to identify research with the highest standards of higher education, an identification that has a strong component of reality in it. It is research that attracts the most able and creative academic minds, and it is the institutions that recruit those people that gain higher status in any system of higher education. Therefore, a genuinely egalitarian policy must allow every institution to attract people who are innovative intellectually, and that means supporting their research and giving them the high degree of autonomy they need to create new knowledge, new fields of study, and new combinations of disciplines. These activities are very hard to rationalize and program closely, despite the new forms of academic management being introduced everywhere. For this and other reasons, a unitarian position that wants to raise standards in all institutions to that of the leading universities tends to constrain the growth of the system; if every new place, every new institution is potentially as expensive as the most costly of the old, then growth must be very carefully planned and sharply restricted, or alternatively, that state support per student (i.e., the unit of resource) be allowed to decline sharply. However, where the egalitarian spirit overrides that of a commitment to high standards across institutions and sectors, as in much of the United States, the slogan is not "nothing if not the best" but rather the expansionist slogan "something is better than nothing." Under those circumstances there tends to be a "leveling downward" coupled with expansion, rather than a "leveling upward" with its inherent tendencies toward a constraint on growth. The major exception to this rule is where there are alternative sources of support for institutions other than the state. And that is, so far, almost exclusively in the United States, and for a relatively small number of elite colleges and universities, both public and private.

The key question in this dilemma is whether new forms of higher education can fulfill their functions at a standard that earns high status and satisfies egalitarians, while reducing per capita costs in ways that will allow genuine expansion toward mass higher education. The Open University in Great Britain is certainly one effort in that direction. But the Open University, despite its name, is not a typical institution of universal access. On the contrary, it is a characteristically ingenious way of increasing access to an elite institution by substituting motivation for formal qualifications, and by allowing people to combine university work with full-time employment. Some of the characteristics of an elite university have been discarded, but the university maintains the high standards of elite British universities and its very clear boundaries. The Open University is an interesting transitional institution between the elite and mass phases of British higher education.

Alternatively, a society may reject the arguments of the unitarians and egalitarians and develop a system that sustains internal diversity in costs and quality as well as in forms and functions, as per the American model. (As suggested later in this chapter, such an approach is much more difficult in systems that are financed, and thus ultimately governed, from a central government agency.) But in either case, the more ambitious and energetic the new institutions are, the more they will demand the libraries and research facilities, the salary schedules, and other amenities of the old institutions, and the more likely they are to drive their per capita costs up. It may be worth exploring how the forms of this dilemma differ in different societies.

The effect of expansion on standards and quality is a complex and uncertain issue. In the early stages of the current phase of growth, beginning in the 1950s, there was widespread concern among academics and others, captured in the slogan "more means worse," that the pool of talented youth able to profit from higher education was small and limited, and that expansion beyond the numbers provided by this pool would necessarily mean a decline in student quality.

However, in the early years of expansion the abilities of those segments of the student population that had not previously entered universities put those fears to rest. Nevertheless, some observers suggested that the new students were, if not less able, then less highly motivated, or less well prepared by their secondary schools, for serious academic work. This feeling was widespread, even if there was no good evidence to support the hypothesis, and some reason to suspect that real students in the (then) present were being compared with idealized students in some mythical Golden Age located variously in the past, depending on the age of the speaker.

Concerns about the academic quality or promise of the "new" students coming to universities were also damped down by the emergence of alternative non-university forms of higher education—the polytechnics and colleges of further education—which admitted students on lower (or at least different) criteria than did the traditional universities.

There was a somewhat more persistent and plausible concern held by many that the rapid expansion of higher education lowered the average quality or the adequacy of the preparation of college and university teachers. Still others feared that growth was affecting the relations between teachers and students adversely, making them more remote and impersonal (where they were not so already). And others suggested that mass higher education must affect the intellectual climate of colleges and universities, introducing into them the vulgarities of the marketplace, of vocational training, of mass politics and popular culture.

Whatever the validity of those fears—and they were not wholly without substance—no society could make the political and financial decision to radically restrain expansion in order to maintain an equality of cost and provision at high standards across the board. That would have precluded the emergence of mass higher education, and that was unstoppable for a variety of social, political, and economic reasons. The solution everywhere was a combination of the creation of cheaper alternatives to the elite universities, plus a reduction in per capita support for higher education institutions of all kinds by central governments. But in all European countries the problems were made more acute by the commitments of governments (in varying degree) to resist the creation of private forms of higher education,[6] to resist also the imposition of levels of student tuition at anywhere near the economic costs of tuition, and their parallel failure to introduce adequate programs of student loans and grants for poorer students. And only a handful of European institutions have found ways to gain substantial support through services to (and joint projects with) the private sector, or have gained the support of their graduates in any way comparable to American colleges and universities.

American Higher Education as a Model

Despite all the difficulties, and with some reservations chiefly arising from a reluctance to surrender ultimate governmental control and finance, European systems of higher education move toward American models. The Bologna agreements make this manifest: the commitment to a fixed term first degree, the transferability of credits, and common criteria for access are only the most visible of the tendencies toward convergence on American models. European systems move in that direction not because the United States is rich and a superpower, or because of the power of American popular culture—elements in the Americanization of so many other institutions in other countries. It is because American higher education as a system is simply better adapted, normatively and structurally, to the requirements of a postindustrial age, which puts a great premium on the creation and wide distribution of knowledge and skill, and is marked by such rapid social and technological change that decision makers in all countries begin to see (or at least believe in) the necessity for broader access to postsecondary education.

But even while European universities are still trying to adapt their organizational, governance, and funding arrangements to their relatively new mass numbers, the United States, by contrast, had the structures for mass higher education in place long before they actually had mass higher education, which came with the GI Bill just after World War II. And the structures for universal access, in the form of open access community colleges, were already in place in the first decades of the twentieth century, even before the enrollment numbers signifying mass education had arrived.

Why is it, then, that the United States developed a system of mass higher education so much earlier than anyone else? What have been the impediments to the transformation of elite European systems into systems of mass higher education now? And how are the United States and other countries moving toward universal access, lifelong learning, "the learning society"? These phrases all point in the same direction, toward the breakdown of the boundaries between formal learning in the institutions of postsecondary education and the rest of life, the assimilation of postsecondary education into the ordinary life of the society.

The modern system of higher education in the United States was already in place more than a century ago; in contrast, the emergence of modern European systems of higher education is still under way. By 1900, when only 4 percent of Americans of college age were attending college, almost all of the central structural characteristics of American higher education were already evident: the research university alongside liberals arts colleges and various forms of vocational institutions, each of them governed by a lay board of trustees, led by a strong president and his administrative staff, with a well-defined structure of faculty ranks; and in the selective institutions, promotion through academic reputation linked to publication and a readiness to move from institution to institution in pursuit of a career. In terms of the curriculum, the elective system, the modular course, and credit accumulation and transfer based on the transcript of grades were all in place by 1900, as were the academic departments covering the known spheres of knowledge, as well as some not so well known.[7]

Indeed, if World War II was the watershed in the history of modern European higher education in its move toward mass provision, then the American Civil War was the watershed for American higher education. For it was during that war that the Congress passed the Morrill Act, which provided federal funds for the creation of universities, or of additions to existing universities. The creation of what were called "land grant colleges"[8] (referring to the sources of the money allocated to the new institutions) greatly increased institutional diversity in American higher education, combining (in the same institutions) technical and higher vocational subjects with the liberal arts. The land grant colleges also brought with them the spirit of public service, the obligation of the university to serve the larger society and not just government, the church, and the learned professions. That commitment to service served American universities well when, over time, the costs of higher education exceeded the state or federal government's capacity to support them; it gave legitimacy to the universities to turn for help and support to the groups and institutions in the larger society whom they have been serving. Today, European higher education suffers from the inability of central governments to adequately fund their growing needs. It is rarely noticed in national comparisons of funding that in the United States the substantial support from governmental sources is matched by private giving to colleges and universities, public and private.

In addition to the political and organizational innovations that gave the United States an advantage in responding to the growth of enrollments that followed World War II, underpinning all was the spirit of competition, institutional diversity, responsiveness to markets (and especially to the market for students), and institutional autonomy marked by strong leadership and a diversity of sources of support. The United States had the organizational and structural framework for a system of mass higher education long before it had mass enrollments. And it had the framework for universal access long before those numbers appeared in the system. Only growth was needed. That happened in plenty, and with surprisingly little strain on a system already adapted to growth and change. Indeed, the only major structural change in American higher education over the past century was the invention and spread of the community colleges, linked easily and casually to four-year institutions through credit transfer, and in some places, through strong encouragement to strengthen those ties by state and local governments. The current expansion of distance learning, much of it provided by for-profit institutions, is another major addition to the American diversity of provision, and of special significance for universal access.

Of course, American higher education differs in many ways from what it was in 1865 or 1900, but growth and development have not required changes in the basic structure of the system. It is those structural changes that are now taking place, with great difficulty, in Europe and the United Kingdom.

Current (2005) Problems for European Higher Education

All European systems are currently struggling with adaptations of their own, often very old, organizational and curricular arrangements to the requirements of mass higher education. And the central response of the European Union to these demands has been the agreements embodied in the Bologna Process, as they were enunciated in that city in June 1999. Bologna is very much a part of broader EU policy, and aims at constructing a European Higher Education Area.

Central to the reforms embodied in those agreements are a movement toward the English/American degree pattern of three years to an undergraduate degree, whatever its title (in the United Kingdom and the United States it is the bachelor's degree) and two further years to a master's degree, the now familiar 3/2 plan. Other reforms are also part of the agreement, but basically what is aimed at is a degree of rationalization—or as the Process puts it, a "harmonization"—of the disparate curricular and academic time arrangements of different countries, in part to allow a greater degree of movement of students among them, and in part to reduce the prolonged periods of study (or at least of formal enrollment) that students undergo in some countries before a degree is earned.[9] What the policy did not have was much input, if any, from the European academic community, whose members were presumably going to implement the new arrangements. Bologna until now has been very much a top-down politically driven process, and in noted scholar Guy Neave's view, likely to lead to resistance at the institutional level in many countries. Neave (2004) points to the distance between the planners of Bologna and the academics who are being asked to "embed"—that is, actually implement—it in their own institutions:

> Policy implementation is a reiterative process. It is re-negotiated, and very often sadly mangled as The Word from On High works its way down through successive levels in the great chain of decision-making. Institutions and beneath them Faculties, Schools and Departments, reinterpret the Divine Message, according to their particular theology and sectarianism. Each interprets the directive—or the policy—

to its own advantage, emphasizing its strengths and shoveling whatever weaknesses it is prepared to admit to itself, beneath the rug.

Viewed by those who sit in authority—whether in Rectorate or Ministry—what emerges as "policy response" bears only a distant relationship to what Authority had originally in mind. It is greatly frustrating. Naturally, such frustration has its very own scholarly terminology—"resistance to change," "Ivory Tower-ism" or even, as I have seen from time to time, "Humboldtian" attitudes. What is perceived as obduracy by reformers reflects that basic feature students of higher education have long noted and dissected—namely, that higher education may, depending on national administrative culture, be top driven. It is also "bottom heavy." Thus, the assumption of linearity that underpins the Bologna Process, viewed from within the Pays politique is questionable indeed when viewed from what we know about institutional behavior seen from the standpoint of [the academic world]. It is precisely the "bottom heavy" nature of higher education that Bologna has chosen to leave aside. Or, to discount it, at least. It is, I think, a very grievous error.[10]

Whatever the state or fate of the Bologna Process, the actual condition of European university systems (with some exceptions) does not seem to hold great promise for early or successful reform. Perhaps the most intense interest has focused on developments in British higher education, in part because it is England (not the United States) that provides the template for the academic timetable at the heart of the Bologna Process— the 3/2 model toward which other countries are to be "harmonized."[11]

The multiple problems of higher education in the United Kingdom have been more visible than those on the European Continent for the past two decades because the British have traditionally linked the quality of the education provided in their universities to the "unit of resource"— the state support for the universities as measured on a student per capita basis. This also defines the student-staff ratio, whose steady deterioration has been a matter of concern to the English, if less so for continental universities. The unit of resource links growth to funding to quality in a visible way, and while it did not prevent a very deep decline in British support for their colleges and universities over the past several decades, the evidence of under-funding has finally persuaded the British government to permit the universities to charge a tuition of up to £3,000 per student.[12] And the ability of universities to charge that sum depends on whether their students are prepared to pay it. Thus, it is bound to be imposed differentially between selecting and recruiting universities. Still, even where it can be put in place, that figure is still quite inadequate, and most observers assume it will have to go higher. By contrast, continental nations during their period of rapid growth simply added institutions and allowed enrollments to grow without demonstrating great concern for declining staff-student ratios.

To take Germany as an example, the vice president for academic affairs at International University Bremen illustrates Neave's point from the perspective of an administrator of an institution who would have to "embed"—that is, implement—the Bologna reforms: "The main but unstated purpose of the German bachelor's degree is to reduce the overcrowding in the universities and thereby to save money in the federal higher education budget. A second purpose is to conform to the new Europeanwide standardized-degree structure budget that will allow greater mobility among students internationally. Yet there is no coherent pedagogical or intellectual basis for the initiative. Not once in the debate in Europe about the introduction of the bachelor's degree have I heard an argument about how it improves what or how students learn, how it strengthens the students' ability to cope in the rapidly expanding marketplace of ideas and information, or how it provides a more solid basis for the student's further education, either in the professions or in research. It's all about saving money and getting students out of the classroom and, it is hoped, into the workforce."[13]

But behind and beyond the problems posed by the Bologna Process lies the chronic under-funding of almost all the European systems, rooted partly in their deep reluctance or refusal to charge realistic fees to students. "The reluctance of the German people to pay fees to their universities— which, with very few exceptions are all public institutions and therefore supported almost exclusively by tax revenues—reflect deeply held beliefs about the state's responsibility to educate the citizenry. Germans pay tax rates that by American standards are exorbitantly high, and in return, they expect things in the public domain—including university education—to be free, or at least very inexpensive."[14] And this is not merely a strongly held belief, but is written into the nation's Federal Constitution.

Add to the European commitment to free university education the near absence of endowments for institutions. "The tax laws are such that it is highly unlikely that a tradition of giving endowed funds will ever take root."[15] Under-funding is likely to remain a chronic problem for most European nations, not least the newest (and poorest) members of the EU that have just joined the club.

The defenses by higher education systems and institutions against most reforms are multiple and overlapping. For example, Germany has been notorious for the difficulties it creates for gaining a chair in a university. According to one observer, "The process of becoming a professor in Germany has traditionally involved completing what amounts to a second dissertation after obtaining the doctorate. The so-called Habilitation, which all applicants for professorships must finish requires post-doctoral candidates to pursue research for several years under the supervision of an established professor and to write another thesis. As a result, most German academics are in their early 40s by the time they become full professors [if they ever do so]. [A new law] would have phased out the Habilitation by 2010 and made junior professorships—available to candidates who had completed their Ph.D.'s within the previous six years—the sole path to full professorships . . . [But] an eight-judge panel of the Federal Constitutional Court ruled 5 to 3 against the government last month, invalidating a 2002 statute that create new junior-professors positions at German universities."[16]

The conservatism of the German system, marked by the diversity of arrangements among the Länder, the requirement that they all agree on many issues, conservative and powerful educational bureaucracies and courts, and equally powerful ordinarius (chaired) professors who substantially govern their universities, is perhaps extreme. But while other European countries have somewhat greater flexibility, none of them has created the funding base plus the level of institutional autonomy plus the strong institutional leadership with extended tenure that is required to create and sustain universities of great quality under conditions of mass higher education.[17]

The issue of institutional diversity, and of the emergence of a group of elite universities that can challenge the leading American research universities, was involved in the closely contested political decision in the United Kingdom to allow the differential imposition of student tuition fees.[18] Such a policy comes up squarely against strong national and ideological commitments to equality among the institutions of higher education in a nation-state. As if the universities didn't have enough problems getting a measure of common reforms of the degree structures within the EU, they have also run into problems in getting agreement from American universities for the new arrangements. "Europe's grand plan to harmonize the Continent's disparate systems of higher education is coming up against an unexpected obstacle: Many American graduate schools say they won't accept Europe's new three-year undergraduate degree."[19] While American universities make an exception in favor of the English three-year degree, on the grounds that they know the quality of that degree and have had long experience with its holders, American elite research universities are not prepared to be as tolerant of the new three-year degree on the European Continent. But a major motivation of the reform of the degree structure was to encourage and make possible mobility among universities, both within the EU and with American universities.

Of course, the actual progress toward the reforms of national systems differs widely among the members of the European Union. And despite the deep conservatism of European academics and university systems, there is a growing recognition of the necessity to introduce a pattern for change of the systems and their constituent institutions that would increase the probabilities of a successful transition from elite to mass higher education, while preserving (or creating) a group of world-class universities.

Necessary reforms include the further diversification of the types of institutions of higher education in both form and function, mirroring the growing diversity in the origins and destinations of students as the systems have grown. Some of the emerging mass systems have provided, under different names and arrangements in different societies: (1) a sector of research universities, awarding degrees up through the doctorate; (2) a sector of colleges, devoted primarily to teaching and the awarding of first professional degrees; (3) a system of open door institutions, giving access to working and mature students, awarding certificates and, for a very small minority, enabling transfer to a college or university; and

(4) an open university, allowing studies at various levels of proficiency to study at a distance for a variety of awards.

Additional reforms associated with the transition to mass higher education require granting the institutions greater freedom from governmental regulation. This involves enabling or permitting the institutions to supplement support from the public purse by raising funds through tuition and through services provided to the private sector, as well as through the more traditional sources of support for research and private gifts. Among other necessary reforms are the strengthening of the role of the institutional president, under whatever name; the creation of strong, regular, and recurrent procedures for quality control within the institution; and the creation of procedures for the external monitoring of the adequacy of the internal quality control procedures in each institution and department, through regular and periodic audit of those procedures.

Every society with a growing system of higher education shows some of these changes; few show them all. The absence of some or most of them have created severe problems for countries whose systems are making the transition to mass higher education, or moving toward universal access.[20]

A Look Ahead

The fact that the Western university has survived in recognizable form for 800 years, and the modern research university for 150, is no guarantee that it will survive in much the same form for the next 2. Some trends in higher education can be predicted with some measure of confidence, rooted in deep-seated forces in Western society that are not likely to be reversed in any foreseeable future. Chief among these are what Max Weber saw more than eighty years ago as the master secular trends of our time—democratization and rationalization, processes that in higher education take the special forms of massification and universal access.

What does that mean, and how might those trends play out over the next quarter century? Some guesses, based on the foregoing analysis of trends in the higher education systems of modern societies, are as follows:

- In higher education in 2030, there will be more of everything: more institutions, more kinds of institutions, more students and teachers, and more diversity among both institutions and participants.

- The development of the economy in advanced societies will continue to increase the demand for a labor force with more than a secondary school education, and reduce the size and numbers of the occupations that do not. But the demand for higher education will increase what is required by the occupational structure. Higher education's chief characteristic is that it gives its recipients a capacity to adapt to change; it will continue to be one of the few advantages parents can give to their children in a rapidly changing world, and more and more people will become aware of that.

- The technical upgrading of jobs, and the link between the success of a business and the training and skill of its labor force will accelerate the interest of industry in supporting and continuing the education of their employees. A good deal of advanced education already takes place in the private sector; this will grow rapidly, as will the creation and development of "learning centers" inside and outside of industry, serving a growing demand for the continuing education of the labor force.

- Private business and industry, as well as individuals, will increasingly pay for what they want and need by way of further and adult education. Government at every level will be contributing a smaller proportion of the total costs of higher education; there are too many other demands on public money to support the continually growing demands of education of all kinds. As a result, colleges and universities will become even more successful at selling their services, and the knowledge their research generates, to individuals and business interests. But governments will continue to be significant, even where inadequate, to the support of certain kinds of higher education, particularly that which continues to be provided in universities insulated from market forces.

We are moving toward a situation that might be described as a "learning society," with very large parts of the population more or less continually engaged in formal education of one kind or another. Under those circumstances, education becomes more highly distributed, taking many different forms in different locations, offering a variety of certificates and degrees. The growing distribution of continuing and distance education will increasingly blur the distinction between education and the rest of society. Distinctions that we make today among "higher" or "continuing" or "adult" or "remedial" or "further" education will be increasingly difficult to make as these activities are carried on, without being so identified or distinguished, as part of the ordinary activities of economic, political, military, and leisure institutions. Moreover, the success of such education will be attested not through examinations and certificates, but through an individual's performance on a job, or of a unit performing a function or service. And that will make increasingly irrelevant government-sponsored external assessments and evaluations, which will come increasingly to be confined to subjects not responsive to market forces.

More generally, the broad movement from elite to open access systems of higher education is associated with, and in part defined by, the increasing permeability of boundaries of all kinds—between institutions and the surrounding societies, between departments and disciplines as both teaching and research become more interdisciplinary, between universities and private business and industry, and between formal education and the informal learning that goes on in a learning society that depends on the constant accretion of new knowledge.

The uncertainty factor in this scenario is technology, especially the technology of communications. Education in recent decades has seen many announcements of abortive "technological revolutions" to be properly skeptical of new announcements of yet another. Yet it seems likely that in the near future much of what is done today among people working in physical proximity may be possible to approximate through electronic links among people who are physically separated. And that will be an educational revolution.

But teachers and students will continue to come together in places called colleges and universities, for longer or shorter periods, to study and learn together even when the same learning might be carried on at a distance. The wish of people to be in each other's presence, and the spontaneity of interaction and relationship that allows, cannot be duplicated through technology, or at least any that we are likely to see in place in the next quarter century.

Some kinds of education, perhaps the most important kinds, involve the shaping of mind and character, not only the way we think but also the way we feel and see the world. That kind of education, we have learned, requires that people care about one another beyond their usefulness to one another as carriers or recipients of bodies of information and skill. It is uncertain whether that kind of relationship can develop properly through electronic links. Moreover, some of the most important kinds of knowledge are tacit, not fully articulated or rationalized, gained through apprenticeship and direct association with those who possess it. If that is true, then institutions much like the colleges and universities we are familiar with, will survive at the center of educative webs, surrounded by all the other kinds of advanced learning and education that will characterize the learning society of the future.

The institutions, structural conditions, and attitudes that define a learning society are already in place in the United States, just as the institutions of mass higher education were already in place in America a century ago, waiting for the mass expansion of enrollments into them. But a learning society developing spontaneously, in response to the demands of their societies and economies, will be hard for European governments and institutions to accept. In all of them, higher education has been a provision of government, largely central government, and it is (and will continue to be) hard for them to give more of the power over these systems to the market.

The broad effect of direct governmental authority over higher education is a tendency toward the further democratization of their systems, and that means in effect efforts to level the institutions in their claims on resources. That, together with strong resistance in European nations to introducing tuition charges or private institutions, leads to the chronic under-funding of European elite institutions and programs. We already see that higher education is being asked to provide advanced and continuing education for everyone without the intellectual resources of elite higher education to draw on. Elite universities and their functions are vulnerable, both politically and financially; under enough pressure, their research activities can move to industry and research laboratories, their humanistic scholarship to think-tanks, museums, and foundations.

One scenario is that the great European research universities will survive, but with poorer staff-student ratios, more external accountability and management, becoming more and more the servants of other institutions, public and private, and less able to define their own roles and missions. They would thus come increasingly to look like other institutions of mass higher education, different only in their historical and cultural pretensions. Alternative scenarios require European universities to raise more money and exercise more autonomy.

Democratization has as one of its major characteristics cultural and institutional leveling, powered by the passions and forces behind the concept of equality. This is much more the case in the public than in the private realms, thus more visible in Europe than in the United States, and within the United States, more in the public than in the private universities. If this process of leveling proceeds apace in the realm of higher education, it will tend to reduce the difference between elite and mass higher education, at the same time that mass higher education tends to become more diverse and increasingly open to universal access. Studies of the high culture—humanistic scholarship, the liberal arts—are to some degree insulated from the market, and will be most resistant to these developments. But apart from some exceptional subjects and places, higher education may over time come to reflect the simultaneous standardization and marginal differentiation of commodities in the global market. All this might happen just slowly enough, masked by the traditional forms, titles, and ceremonies of university life on the one hand, and the revolution in communications on the other, so that our children and grandchildren may not even notice.

NOTES

1. "Problems in the Transition from Elite to Mass Higher Education," in Policies for Higher Education, from the General Report on the Conference on Future Structures of Post-Secondary Education, 55–101 (Paris: OECD, 1974). Reprinted by the Carnegie Commission on Higher Education in Berkeley, California, 1973. Reprinted as chapter 2 in this volume. The essay also draws on other of my papers

published subsequently. Among these are: "Elite Higher Education: An Endangered Species?" Minerva (London) 14, no. 3 (Autumn 1976): 355–76 (reprinted as chapter 3 in this volume); "Elite and Mass Higher Education: American Models and European Realities," in Research into Higher Education: Processes and Structures (Stockholm: National Board of Universities and Colleges, 197); and "Comparative Perspectives on Access," in Access to Higher Education, ed. Oliver Fulton (Guildford, England: Society for Research into Higher Education, 1981), 89–121.

2. John Brennan, "The Social Role of the Contemporary University: Contradictions, Boundaries and Change," in Ten Years On: Changing Education in a Changing World, Center for Higher Education Research and Information, Milton Keynes, The Open University, p. 24.

3. Gareth Parry, "British Higher Education in the Prism of Devolution," in Understanding Mass Higher Education: Comparative Perspectives on Access, ed. Ted Tapper and David Palfreyman (London: RoutledgeFalmer, 2005). The age participation rate had climbed to 33 percent (though it varied from 45 percent in Scotland to 28 percent in Wales), having doubled in a decade. But the age participation rate loses analytical value everywhere as the numbers of mature and foreign students grow.

4. See Table 17.1.

5. External evaluation in all countries has mostly found academic excellence to be present in the old elite universities that did research. The requirements of research—big libraries and laboratories, and low academic teaching loads—are what drives the cost of universities up, as compared with non-research institutions of higher education. Evaluation doesn't change that.

6. The church-related universities in various European countries have a measure of autonomy, but are dependent on state support to almost the same degree as the secular institutions.

7. On the emergence of the American system from its colonial roots, see Trow, "In Praise of Weakness: Chartering, the University of the United States, and Dartmouth College," Higher Education Policy 16 (2003): 9–26, and "From Mass Higher Education to Universal Access: The American Advantage," Minerva 37 (Spring 2000): 1–26 (reprinted as chapter 16 in this volume).

8. The terms university and college have been more loosely and promiscuously applied in the United States than is customary in Europe. Most of the land grant colleges were or shortly became research universities, some were and remained four-year colleges. The language of the Morrill Act referred to "colleges."

9. For an informed, critical, and skeptical view of the Bologna Process, see Guy Neave, presidential address to the 26th Annual Meeting of the European Association for Institutional Research, Barcelona, September 5, 2004.

10. Ibid.

11. Recent moves toward devolution in the United Kingdom permit the Scottish

university system to deviate from the English model. Scottish universities start with a four-year degree to the bachelor's, and will resist a move to a three-year degree. It currently can refuse to follow the English move toward tuition payments, making up the difference in revenue from its own power to raise taxes. See Parry, "British Higher Education."

12. See M. Trow, "The Decline of Diversity, Autonomy and Trust in Post-war Britain," Perspectives 8, no. 4 (October 2004): 7–11. Summary of a paper prepared for a conference on the White Paper of 2003, sponsored by The Center for Studies of Higher Education, UC Berkeley, and New College, Oxford, September 28–30, 2004.

13. Thomas John Hochstettler, "Aspiring to Steeples of Excellence at German Universities," The Chronicle Review, July 30, 2004.

14. Ibid.

15. Ibid.

16. Aisha Labi, "German Court Overturns Law Designed to Streamline Path to Professorship," The Chronicle of Higher Education International, August 13, 2004.

17. Europe's difficulties in competing with American universities arise in part from the weight of European egalitarianism, "which strives to provide a solid education to as many students as possible while refraining from rewarding exceptional talent." Martin Enserink, "Reinventing Europe's Universities," Science 304, no. 5673 (May 14, 2004): 951–53. On the poor international standing of French universities, see Gilbert Bereziat, "Université Pierre et Marie Curie: France's Number One University in the Top 500 Higher Education Institutions in the World." Bereziat, president of the Universitaire Pierre and Marie Curie University, notes that his university is "the leading higher education institution in France," though it ranks only sixty-fifth among world universities.

18. For a brief overview of Europe's difficulties in competing with American universities, which emphasizes the weight of European egalitarianism, "which strives to provide a solid education to as many students as possible while refraining from rewarding exceptional talent," see Enserink, "Reinventing Europe's Universities." On the current unhappiness in French universities, see Michael Balter, "Reform Plan Seen as Halting Step," Science 292 (May 4, 2004).

19. Burton Bollag, "Many American Graduate Schools are Cool to Europe's New 3-year Diplomas," The Chronicle of Higher Education International, October 15, 2004.

20. This chapter does not discuss two large and important systems of higher education, one growing rapidly, the other contracting. Japanese society is experiencing a very large demographic decline, felt strongly among this generation of college age youth. During its period of growth after World War II, Japanese educators showed great interest in the ideas sketched in this essay, an interest reflected in the Japanese translation of two collections of previously authored works on higher edu-

cation transformation (Trow, 1976, 2000; see Introduction, p. 45, n. 1). Currently, more salient issues have to do with the relations between the universities and the Ministry of Education than with the management of growth. The impact of the demographic decline in Japan is felt by the very large number of private institutions, and especially by the less prestigious ones, some of which have already closed their doors.

Matters could not be more different in China, whose higher education system is growing rapidly from a very small base, trying to keep up with the rapid growth of the economy, and with the full support of a government that can focus resources where it wishes without much concern for public sentiment or the views of the academic community. Chinese academics have also shown a keen interest in the ideas sketched in this essay, as reflected in the translation into Chinese of some of the papers cited in this essay on the growth and transformation of higher education systems in their move toward mass higher education (Trow, 2001; see Introduction, p. 45, n. 7).

REFERENCES

Balter, M. "Reform Plan Seen as Halting Step." Science 292 (May 4, 2004)
Brennan, J. "The Social Role of the Contemporary University: Contradictions, Boundaries and Change." In Ten Years On: Changing Education in a Changing World, edited by the Center for Higher Education Research and Information (CHERI). Buckingham: The Open University Press, 2004.
Enserink, M. "Reinventing Europe's Universities, Science 304, no. 5673 (May 14, 2004): 951–53.
Neave, G. Presidential address to the 26th Annual Meeting of the European Association for Institutional Research, Barcelona, September 5, 2004.
Parry, G. "British Higher Education in the Prism of Devolution." In Understanding Mass Higher Education: Comparative Perspectives on Access, edited by T. Tapper and D. Palfreyman. London: RoutledgeFalmer, 2005.
Trow, M. The University in the Highly Educated Society: From Elite to Mass Higher Education. Tokyo: Tokyo University Press, 1976, 2000. [in Japanese]
Trow, M. Essays on the Transformation of Higher Education in Advanced Industrial Societies. Tokyo: Tamagawa University Press, 2000. [in Japanese]
Trow, M. Selected Essays on Martin Trow's Educational Thinking. Xiamen, Fujian: Xiamen University Press, PRC, 2001. [in Chinese]

Contributors

....

JOHN BRENNAN is professor of higher education research at the UK Open University, where he is also director of the Centre for Higher Education Research and Information. A sociologist by training, his research interests lie in the area of higher education and social change and he has undertaken many national and international research projects on themes such as higher education and employment, the student experience, quality assurance, widening participation, and the role of universities in social transformation. He has published several books and many articles on these topics.

MICHAEL BURRAGE's academic career crossed that of Martin Trow at the Swedish Collegium for Advanced Study, Uppsala, 1988–89; at the University of Hokkaido, 1991; at the London School of Economics, 1993–94; and at the Center for the Study of Higher Education and the Institute of Governmental Studies at UC Berkeley on several occasions in 1990s. He is the author most recently of *Revolution and the Making of the Contemporary Legal Profession: England, France, and the United States* (Oxford University Press, 2006) and *Class Formation, Civil Society and the State: A Comparative Analysis of Russia, France, the US and England* (Palgrave, 2008).

JOHN AUBREY DOUGLASS is senior research fellow in public policy and higher education at the Center for Studies in Higher Education at the University of California, Berkeley. He has served as the chief policy analyst for the University of California's systemwide academic senate and held teaching and research positions at the UC Santa Barbara, Sciences Po (Paris), and the Oxford Center for Higher Education Policy Studies. His articles have appeared in numerous academic journals and he is the author of *The Condi-*

611

tions for Admissions (Stanford University Press, 2007) and *The California Idea and American Higher Education* (Stanford University Press, 2000).

OLIVER FULTON first collaborated with Martin Trow as a graduate research assistant at UC Berkeley when Trow was working with A. H. Halsey on their study of British academics published in 1971. Trow then took him on as a full-time researcher on two successive waves of Carnegie surveys of the American academic profession between 1969 and 1976: they coauthored a number of publications at that time, and continued to discuss and debate higher education, and read each other's drafts, until shortly before Trow's death. Fulton has been a research fellow in Edinburgh, and briefly in Beijing and Vienna, as well as UC Berkeley, and has written widely on the academic profession and on university governance and management, often in a comparative perspective. He is now emeritus professor of higher education in the Centre for the Study of Education and Training at Lancaster University, where he was employed for almost thirty years.

DAVID PIERPONT GARDNER served as the tenth president of the University of Utah from 1973 to 1983 before becoming the University of California's fifteenth president in August 1983, serving in that capacity until October 1992. Dr. Gardner chaired the National Commission on Excellence in Education, whose 1983 report, *A Nation at Risk,* helped spark the national effort to improve and reform schooling in the United States. He is a member of the National Academy of Education and the American Philosophical Society and is a fellow of the American Academy of Arts and Sciences and the National Academy of Public Administration. He is also an honorary fellow of Clare Hall, Cambridge University, England.

ROGER L. GEIGER is Distinguished Professor of Higher Education at Pennsylvania State University, and editor since 1993 of *Perspectives on the History of Higher Education.* His four volumes on American research universities in the twentieth century, benefited from a stay at the Center for Studies in Higher Education, UC Berkeley. In 2004, his study *Knowledge and Money: Research Universities and the Paradox of the Marketplace* was published by Stanford University Press and his most recent work, coauthored with Creso Sá, *Tapping the Riches of Science: Universities and the Promise of Economic Growth,* was published by Harvard University Press in 2008.

NATHAN GLAZER, professor of sociology at Harvard University since 1969, now emeritus, was a colleague of Martin Trow at UC Berkeley, 1957–58, and again in 1963–69. He was an editor of *Commentary* in the 1940s, at Doubleday Anchor and Random House in the 1950s, and of the public policy journal *The Public Interest* from 1973 to 2003. His books have dealt with American ethnicity and social policy, and include *Beyond the Melting Pot* (1963 and 1970), *We Are All Multiculturalists Now* (1997), and most recently, *From a Cause to a Style: Modernist Architecture's Encounter with the American City* (2007).

A. H. HALSEY was born into the English cockney working-class family, grew up on a council estate, and went to a grammar school and on to the London School of Economics. He met Martin Trow when a fellow at the Center for Advanced Study in the Behavioral Sciences, Stanford, and they began their lifelong friendship and partnership in the sociology of education on both sides of the Atlantic. He has published numerous works in what he calls the "political arithmetic" tradition, documenting the state of society and addressing social and political issues through the field testing of social policy in advance of national implementation. He is now emeritus professorial fellow at Nuffield College in Oxford University.

GRANT HARMAN is an emeritus professor of educational management and director of the Centre for Higher Education Management and Policy at the University of New England, Armidale, Australia. His main research interests are in higher education management and policy and in recent years he has published on various topic areas, including university-industry research links, university research commercialisation, quality assurance, and adjustment of the academic profession to a more commercial environment. Since 1996, he has been editor in chief of the journal *Higher Education*, published by Springer in the Netherlands. He was a visiting scholar at UC Berkeley's Center for Studies in Higher Education in 1982–83.

After twenty-five years as an editor and bureau chief in San Francisco and London with *Newsweek,* JERRY LUBENOW became director of publications at the Institute of Governmental Studies, UC Berkeley. He founded the Berkeley Public Policy Press, a general publisher of social science research on government, politics, and public policy, and continues to serve as its editor as well as being a senior consultant to the UC Washington Center.

As dean of continuing education at UC Irvine, GARY W. MATKIN oversees University Extension, which offers 2,400 courses a year to approximately 35,000 students, the Summer Session, and the UCI Distance Learning Center. He serves as principal investigator of several Foundation grants, including those from the William and Flora Hewlett Foundation's Open Educational Resources initiative. He regularly consults with U.S. universities and international organizations such as the OECD (Paris) about continuing, distance, and online education, writes about it frequently, and is the author of *Technology Transfer and the University* (1990) and *Using Financial Information in Continuing Education* (1997).

GUY NEAVE retired from Twente University (Netherlands) as professor of comparative higher education policy in 2006. He is currently scientific director of the Centro de Investiçaçao de Politicas do Ensino Superior (CIPES) Porto, Portugal. An historian by training, he is foreign associate of the U.S. National Academy of Education. He has written extensively on higher education policy in Western Europe. With Burton R. Clark he served as editor in chief of the *Encyclopedia of Higher Education* (1992) and with Thorsten Nybom and Kjell Bluckert, edited *The European Research University in Historical Parentheses* (2006) He lives in the Far West of the Paris basin.

GARETH PARRY is professor of education at the University of Sheffield in the United Kingdom. Previously he held academic positions at Surrey, Warwick, and City Universities and the University of London Institute of Education. The early part of his career was spent teaching in further education colleges in London. He has been a consultant to the Dearing Committee of Inquiry into Higher Education (1996–97) and the Foster review of further education colleges (2004–5). His research is focused on policy reform and system change in tertiary education. In 2001, he was elected a fellow of the Society for Research into Higher Education.

JACK SCHUSTER was a congressional aide and an assistant to the chancellor at UC Berkeley before joining the faculty of Claremont Graduate University's faculty in 1977, where he is now professor emeritus of education and public policy. He has been a visiting professor or fellow at Michigan, Oxford, Melbourne, Haifa, Harvard, and the Brookings Institution. He is the author or coauthor of six books on various aspects of higher education and the American faculty, among them *American Professors* (1986) with Howard R. Bowen (which received the Ness Award) and most recently *The American Faculty* (2006) with Martin J. Finkelstein.

NEIL J. SMELSER was born in Kahoka, Missouri, and reared in Phoenix, Arizona. He received BA degrees from Harvard and Oxford and a PhD from Harvard in 1958. He served two institutions—as faculty member at the University of California at Berkeley (1958–94) and as director of the Center for Advanced Study in the Behavioral Sciences, Stanford (1994–2001). His research has been in the areas of social theory, social change, social movements, economic sociology, sociology of education, psychoanalysis, and contemporary terrorism. He met Martin Trow as a colleague in sociology at Berkeley in the late 1950s, and at that institution they maintained almost a half century of mutual intellectual respect and deep personal friendship.

ULRICH TEICHLER has been professor at the International Centre for Higher Education Research, University of Kassel, since 1978 and its director since 1992. He has been researcher at the Max Planck Institute for Educational Research, Berlin, for extended periods in Japan, the Netherlands, and the United States, and a visiting professor at Northwestern University, the College of Europe, Hiroshima University, and Open University, United Kingdom. He is a winner of the Research Prize of CIEE (Council on International Educational Exchange) and of the UNESCO Comenius Prize, and his widely published works on comparing education systems include *Higher Education Systems: Conceptual Frameworks, Comparative Perspectives, Empirical Findings* (Sense, Rotterdam, 2007).

SIM VAN DER RYN is professor emeritus of architecture at the University of California, where he taught from 1961 to 1995. He began the field of post-occupancy evaluation of buildings to see how actual use and performance coincided with clients' and architects' assumptions, and got to know Martin Trow through this research. He served as California state architect in the 1970s, initiating major initiatives in energy efficiency and renewable energy in state facilities. Considered the "father of green architecture," he has authored seven books, lives in northern California, and is president of the Ecological Design Institute.

About the Author

....

Martin Trow was born in New York City in 1926, and was a graduate of schools in that city. His undergraduate studies were interrupted by three years of service in the United States Navy (1943–46), which he left with the rank of lieutenant (j.g.). In 1947, he took a degree in mechanical engineering at the Stevens Institute of Technology in New Jersey. After graduation from Stevens, he worked briefly as an engineer, while taking courses at night at the New School for Social Research in New York. In 1948, he began his graduate studies in sociology at Columbia University, completing his doctoral degree in 1956. Between 1953 and 1957, he taught and did research at Bennington College in Vermont. In that year he joined the sociology department at the University of California, Berkeley. In 1969, he moved to the Graduate (now the Goldman) School of Public Policy at Berkeley, where he held a professorship until his death. From 1976 to 1988, he also served as director of the Center for Studies in Higher Education at Berkeley.

Among the many books and articles that Professor Trow wrote or edited, alone and with others, on issues in political sociology and comparative education are *Union Democracy* (with S. M. Lipset and James Coleman, 1956); *Right-Wing Radicalism and Political Intolerance* (1957, 1980); *The British Academics* (with A. H. Halsey, 1971); *Students and Colleges* (with B. R. Clark et al., 1972); "Problems in the Transition from Elite to Mass Higher Education" (1974); *Teachers and Students* (ed., 1975); *University and Society* (with Thorsten Nybom, ed., 1991); *The New Production of Knowledge* (with Michael Gibbons et al., 1994); *Accountability of Colleges and Universities* (with Patricia Graham and Richard Lyman, 1995); and more than 170 published essays and papers in books and professional journals worldwide. His papers have been translated into Japanese, Greek, Spanish, German, Hebrew, French, Polish, Russian, Italian, Chinese, Czech, Danish, and Swedish. A collection of his essays, *The University in the Highly Educated Society*: *From Elite to Mass Higher Education*, 1976), translated and published in Japan by Tokyo University Press, is in its fifth printing; another collection in Japanese, *Essays on the Transformation of Higher Education in Advanced Industrial Societies* (Tokyo: Tamagawa University Press), was published in 2000. In 2001, a collection of his papers was published in China, translated into Chinese, under the title *Selected Essays on Martin Trow's Educational Thinking* (Xiamen, Fujian: Xiamen University Press, PRC, 2001). Another larger collection of his papers in Chinese translation is currently (2009) under preparation.

Professor Trow was a fellow of the Center for Advanced Study in the Behavioral Sciences in Palo Alto (1964–65), a visiting member of the Institute for Advanced Study in Princeton (1976–77), and a fellow of the Swedish Center for Advanced Study in the Social Sciences in Uppsala (1988). In 1993, he was Distinguished Visiting Scholar at the Suntory-Toyota International Centre of Economics and Related Disciplines at the London School of Economics. During the spring semester 2002, Professor Trow was the Benedict Distinguished Visiting Professor at Carleton College in Minnesota.

Among the honorary degrees awarded to Professor Trow were those from Carleton College, Minnesota (1978), the University of Sussex (United Kingdom, 1988), the University of Stockholm (1990), the University of Northumbria at Newcastle (United Kingdom, 1996), the University of Warwick (United Kingdom, 1997), and the University of Lancaster (United Kingdom, 1999). In 1991, he was elected a foreign member of the Royal Swedish Academy of Sciences. He was also a fellow of the American Academy of Arts and Sciences, a fellow and vice president of the National Academy of Education, a fellow of the American Association for the Advancement of Science, and a fellow (and vice president) of the Society for Research in Higher Education in Great Britain. He was a trustee of Carleton College in Minnesota for more than two decades (1980–2001).

Professor Trow directed two large National Surveys of Higher Education of faculty, graduate students, and undergraduate students (1969 and 1976) for the Carnegie Commission on Higher Education, then directed by Clark Kerr, and served on his advisory committee during his terms as director of the commission and of its successor, the Carnegie Council on Higher Education.

Martin Trow held many offices and served on many of the committees of the Academic Senate of the University of California, including a term as chairman of the Berkeley Division. In 1969–70, he chaired the Commission on Isla

Vista, appointed by then President Charles J. Hitch after the disturbances on the Santa Barbara Campus of the University; the report of the commission was published in 1970. Between 1990 and 1992, he served first as vice chair and then as chairman of the universitywide Academic Council of the academic senate of the University of California, and was one of its two representatives to the board of regents of the University. In 1997, he was awarded the Berkeley Citation for Distinguished Achievement and Notable Service to the university, the university's highest award.

Professor Trow's public service included a term as chairman of the National Advisory Committee on Accreditation and Institutional Eligibility to the Secretary of the U.S. Department of Education, Washington (1991–92), as well as service on committees of the National Research Council, advisory boards of the National Institute of Education, and the College Entrance Examination Board. For many years he was a member of the governing board of the International Council for Educational Development. He also served on the editorial boards of a number of professional journals.

In 1993, Professor Trow became emeritus professor at the University of California, and was then recalled as professor in the graduate school. He served as consultant to the chancellor of the Swedish universities and colleges, and was a member of international advisory committees to the universities of Uppsala, Linköping, and Umeå in Sweden.

During 1995, Professor Trow was a member (with Patricia Graham and Richard Lyman) of a national commission supported by the Mellon Foundation and Columbia University, addressing issues of accreditation and accountability in American higher education; the commission issued its report, *Accountability of Colleges and Universities,* in October 1995. In 1996, he gave testimony to the Dearing Committee of Inquiry on Higher Education in Great Britain, and read papers at meetings of the Committee of Vice Chancellors and Principals and the Society for Research in Higher Education in Britain, and at meetings and conferences in the Netherlands, Germany, and Sweden as well as in the United States.

In 1998, Professor Trow was Distinguished Visiting Scholar at the Institute for Studies in Higher Education at Hokkaido University, Sapporo, Japan, and lectured widely in that country. In 1999, he gave lectures and led seminars at University College London and the University of Lancaster, as well as the University of British Columbia. In January 2000, he chaired a panel and read a paper at the second Glion Conference on Higher Education at the University of

California, San Diego. In March 2000, he chaired a panel and gave a paper on aspects of information technology at the Peter Sather International Symposium on New Technologies and the Future of Higher Education at Berkeley. In 2000, he was a consultant to the chancellor of the Swedish universities on problems associated with their implementation of a new national law on colleges and universities, and in addition led seminars at the University of Stockholm, the University of Uppsala, and the University of Newcastle in the United Kingdom. In 2003–5, he presented lectures at Oxford, the British Open University, the University of Tel Aviv, and the Technion in Haifa, among others.

From 2001 to 2005, Professor Trow was chairman of the International Advisory Board to the Swedish National Agency for Higher Education. In 2006, he served on the S. Neaman Working Group on The Future Research University of Israel. In addition, he was a research associate at the Research Institute for Independent Higher Education at the Association of Japanese Private Universities. In 2004, Professor Trow was elected chairman of the board of the California Association of Scholars, a chapter of the National Association of Scholars.

A select bibliography of important works of Martin Trow is available at http://igs.berkeley.edu/oldsitearchive/announcements/trow_memorial.html, with links to some that are available on line. A full bibliography of his 173 works is available at http://gspp.berkeley.edu/academics/emeritus/docs/Trow_Publica tions_and_Lectures_2006.pdf.

American exceptionalism, 107, 442
American influence on European higher education, 521, 524–26, 595–97
American popular sentiments toward education, 59, 64, 66–68, 71, 108, 124, 211–33
American Revolution, 56, 185, 191–93, 214
American values, 108. *See also* American popular sentiments toward education
"Asians," 497–98
assessment: in elite institutions, 160; external assessment vs. internal motivations, 281–88; of graduate students, 325; at Princeton, 350–51; of teaching, 281–96; in the U.K., of research, 271–81; under universal access, 96, 573; and University of California, Berkeley, 406–9, 414, 417
Athenaeum Club, 99
autonomy of higher education institutions, 91, 104–5, 123, 139, 447; colonial, 189–91; delegation of, 444; in Europe, 529, 601, 607; Germany, 466; in Great Britain, 265, 277, 283, 285, 294; private vs. public universities, 493–94; in the U.S. 179–80, 185, 597. *See also* departments: autonomy of; higher education; University of California: autonomy of, principles of

Bailyn, Bernard, 191
Barzun, Jacques, 446
Berkeley. *See* University of California, Berkeley
Boalt Hall. *See under* University of California, Berkeley
Bok, Derek, 487–507
Bologna agreements, 595; process, 598–99
Bowen, William G., 487–507
Brennan, John, 556–57
Britain. *See* Great Britain

California, state of: constitution of, 1879, 467–68; Master Plan 1960, 474; Proposition 209 (1996), 480–81, 490–94, 497, 504–6; unwritten treaty with University of, 421

California State University, 180, 465, 474, 492
Canada, 382, 531; funding of higher education, 177
Caston, Geoffrey, 400
Clark, Burton, 398, 423
class: European guilt about, 224, 232, 254; and higher education, 110–11, 212–26, 232, 260, 285; and the U.S.
Clinton, President Bill, 497
college attendance, meanings of, 558–62. *See* students: self-perceptions of
colonial experience and charters, 186–91
community colleges, 262–64, 581, 597
Conant, James, 61, 76
Connerly, Ward (regent of the University of California), 476
consensual coercion, 505
Constitution of the U.S., 177, 214
Cremin, Lawrence, 61
Crosland, Anthony, 252
curriculum, 95–96; in American secondary schools, 70–72; in universities, modularization of, 295, 521–24; vocational vs. liberal studies, 149, 243–44, 572–74

Dartmouth College, case of, 1819, 197–98
Debs, Eugene, 212
democratization and higher education, 73, 92, 130–31, 261, 519, 561–62, 607–8; U.S. vs. Europe, 73, 521–24, 607–8
departments: assessment of, in the U.K., 281–85; autonomy of, 164, 170, 179–80, 185, 325, 330–31, 338, 452; growth of, 90, 164; and presidents, 447, 452; in receivership, 411, 424–26, 452–53
deprofessionalization, in the U.K., 287. *See also* academic guilds
disciplines, as moral communities, 334–35
distance learning, 524, 534, 539, 543. *See also* lifelong learning
diversity of institutions: absence of, in U.K., 247, 250–54; and academic

standards, 125; enemies of, 103; forces against, 158; in U.S., 98, 131–32, 137–39, 179–82, 601–8

egalitarian values, 92, 137, 140, 154–59, 561–62. *See also* democratization and higher education

elite higher education: apprenticeship within, 130, 164; changes in, 565–70; conservatism of, 156–57; convergence with, 579; costs of, 250; enemies of, 152–53, 242–44; expansion of, 93; functions of, 151; institutions, 162–63; and mass higher education, 93–98; within mass higher education, 106, 165–68, 244; meanings of, 146–47, 149–51, 558–59; survival of, 102, 147–49, 582–83, 606–8; threats to, 242–44

enrollments: dilemmas of, 121; in Europe, 93; in higher education, 62–64, 88–90, 126–27, 221; in secondary schools, 62–64. *See also* growth of higher education

equality: and egalitarian values, 589–94; of individual vs. group achievement, 110–11, 580; of opportunity vs. achievement, 226

ethnic groups, 225–33

European Union, harmonization of higher education, 598–602

extension courses, 448, 520 541–44, 555. *See also* service ideal

federal government: Higher Education Amendments 1972, 194, 200–201; increased role of, 201–4; limited role of, 184–86, 188; self-denying ordinance of, 201–3

federalism in the U.S., 177–78. *See also* state governments in the U.S.

France: elite institutions in, 161–71; higher education in, 96, 244; Vincennes, 110–11

freedom: at Institute for Advanced Studies, Princeton, 349–57; of Internet, 534, 539, 547; at University of California, Berkeley, 376, 411, 415, 481; of University of California,

Berkeley, chancellor, 478; of University of California regents, 476; of university presidents, 448. *See also* academic freedom

funding of higher education: public vs. private (U.S. vs. Europe), 530–31, 600–601, 606; underfunding in Europe, 600–608

Geertz, Clifford, 346

German universities: elite and mass, 244, 529–30; government and funding of, 157, 339, 466, 530, 600–601; model of, 323–24, 330, 525; professors in, 601; reform, of, 599–601; research seminars in, 149, 163, 566; and secondary schools, 159; student culture of, 90, 560

G.I. Bill (Servicemen's Readjustment Act 1944), 200–201, 527

governance, 103; changes in, 577–79, 581–86; in Europe, 529–30; role of University of California faculty, 444–46; shared governance at University of California, 414, 445–46; unwritten treaty and state, 426. *See* France; German universities; Great Britain

graduate education, functions of, 325–28

Great Britain: "A" levels, 109, 246, 254–55; binary line, 242–45, 264–65, 575–76; Colleges of Advanced Technology, 169, 243, 275; Colleges of Further Education, 262–63, 266; Committee of Vice Chancellors and Principals, 245; Council of National Academic Awards, 247–48, 252, 266, 285; dissenting academies, 188–90; elitism in, 162, 169–70; external examiners, 245; "gold standard" of, 248–49, 258; Higher Education Funding Council, 277–78; higher education in, 97, 99; honors degrees, 245; mechanics Institutes, 215; polytechnics, 137, 242–43, 247, 252–53, 264, 285; student grants in, 97, 246, 260; tuition fees, 599–602; unit of resource, 245–46, 599–600; University Grants

Morrill Act of 1862, 184, 194, 199–200, 596
Muller, Steven (former president of Johns Hopkins), 543–44
multiversity, 163–65, 455; pathologies of, 386

National Academy of Sciences, 523
Neave, Guy, 242–43, 598–99
New York Times, 487, 502, 532, 534–35
Nuremberg laws, 495

occupational structure, transformation of, 56–58, 64, 72, 128–32, 604
Open University, Great Britain, 124, 133, 254–59, 266, 593
Oxford and Cambridge (Oxbridge), 98, 148–50, 190, 243, 247, 255, 275, 442, 565–67, 569, 576

planning: in education, 125–33; pathologies of, 305–6; prescriptive vs. systems, 135–40
politics: exclusion of, 466, 470; transformation of, 472–73
Powell, Colin, General, 228
presidents of American universities; absence of tenure, 443–44; administrations of, 449–51; consensus among, 503; erosion of support for, 454; vs. European, 444, 447; giants, 445, 454–55; origins, 443; problems of, 458–59; resources of, 447–49. *See also* academic leadership
Princeton University, 478, 489; Institute for Advanced Study, 346–65
private education: colonial blurring of differences, 187; in Great Britain, 169–71; in lifelong learning, 605–8; in the U.S. 169, 181–83
private lives of higher education institutions, 369, 385–86, 534; typology of, 369
profession: weakness of, vs. Europe, 188–89, 443. *See* academic guilds
public and private colleges, compared, 181, 493, 603. *See also* colonial experience and charters

race and ethnicity in American higher education, 224–33
racial preferences: abolition of University of California, 490–91; in admissions, 489; consensus on, 502–3; faculty opinion, 502; patronage and, 503. *See also* affirmative action; California, state of: Proposition 209; University of California: regents of
research in higher education, typology of, 369
Roper Center, University of Connecticut, 502, 504
Rothblatt, Sheldon, 243–44

"sandwich courses," 97, 147
San Francisco State College, 314
Saxon, David S. (president of the University of California), 383–84
secondary education: in California, 506–7; debates about, in U.S., 55–57; elite institutions of, 58–59; failure of, 73–74; mass enrollments in, 62–64
service ideal: at Cornell University, 541; at University of California, 473; at University of Wisconsin, 541
shared governance, 445–56, 471. *See also* University of California
slavery, guilt about, 225–32
Snow, C. P., 542–43
socialism, American attitudes toward, 212–19
social mobility and higher education, 127, 211–27, 525. *See also* class
space: in academic institutions, 168, 303–14; of biological sciences, 404–5, 409; Center for Studies in Higher Education, 389–91; expropriation of, 312–14; old vs. new, 315–17; spontaneous use of, 304; at Swarthmore College, 315; at University of California, Berkeley, School of Architecture, 314; waste of, 315
Stanford University, 260, 263, 291, 445, 453, 465, 493, 534; Center for Advanced Study in the Behavioral Sciences, Palo Alto, 357–62; scandals at, 203
state governments in the U.S., 177–98

University of Michigan, 179, 445, 453

University of Oxford, 376–77, 383. *See also* Oxford and Cambridge

University of the United States, defeat of proposal for, 194–96

University of Wisconsin, 164, 444, 540–41

values, changes in, 134–35

"wastage," 147, 163, 255

Weber, Max, 217, 334, 563, 586, 604; cultivated man vs. expert, 148; ideal types, 105

Western Governors University, 542

Williams, Shirley, 254, 258

Yale College. *See* Yale University

Yale University, 189–91, 199, 260, 264, 323, 443, 488–89, 501